THE
FOOTBALL
ABSTRACT

THE
FOOTBALL
ABSTRACT

Bob Carroll, Pete Palmer, John Thorn

A FOOTBALL INK BOOK

WARNER BOOKS

A Warner Communications Company

A Warner Communications Company

Printed in the United States of America
First Printing: August 1989
10 9 8 7 6 5 4 3 2 1

Library of Congress Cataloging-in-Publication Data

Carroll, Bob
      The football abstract / Bob Carroll, Pete Palmer, John Thorn.
          p.   cm.
      ISBN 0-446-38731-2
      1. Football—United States—Records.   I. Palmer, Pete.
II. Thorn, John. 1947-   .   III. Title.
GV955.C25   1989
796.332'64'0973021—dc19   89-9180
                                                CIP

CONTENTS

Introduction vii

TEAM REVIEWS, 1988 SEASON

The National Football Conference

The American Football Conference

PLAYER AND COACH RATINGS

ESSAYS

INTRODUCTION

Remember the 1988 pro football season? When the NFL used real players for all sixteen regular-season games? When Bill Walsh was hot and the game's other anointed geniuses (Noll, Shula, Gibbs, and Landry) were not? When Boomer and the Bengal lancers shuffled from last place to the last minute of the last game before being vanquished? When the Eagles were the parity poopers of the NFC East and nary a word was heard about the Giants' "dynasty"?

There were hundreds of other stories and odd bits worth reflecting upon just for their own sake, and we will, but the real reason we wrote this book was to figure out where the game was headed in 1989. Not exactly a novel proposition, granted—there are plenty of pigskin prognosticators out there. And yes, we offer the usual mix of reviews and previews, predictions and prescriptions, stats and stories, and of course we've got lots and lots of ratings. But this book is different from what has come before—it examines the pro football season just passed with the aid of actual play-by-play data and drive charts for the key games, plus new statistics that reveal who the stars and stiffs really were. We're dishing out more than opinion here (though Lord knows there's plenty of that, too); we've let the numbers speak.

Those of you who like baseball nearly as well as football will recognize in the title of this book a tribute to Bill James and his approach to baseball analysis—develop some tools, do the digging, display the results, and discuss what they mean. If the numbers reveal that Al Toon is only the sixteenth-best wide receiver in the NFL, Jets' fans may dispute the result, but they at least will have to argue with our standard of evaluation rather than our opinion. Were the Falcons right to put all their eggs in John Settle's basket by trading Gerald Riggs to Washington? Did the Skins do what they needed to do to return to the playoffs? Read the team reviews of the Redskins and Falcons, and let the numbers reveal the future.

If the numbers show that the Patriots would do better to start Doug Flutie than either Steve Grogan or Tony Eason, again, it's not just us shooting from the lip. Will the Cowboys perk up under Jimmy Johnson? (Yes, they're bound to, just as they would have under Tom Landry.) And would you believe a 1994 NFC Pro Bowl quarterback tandem of Vinny Testaverde and Chris Miller? Remember who told you that first.

The bottom line here is that we're going to have us some fun in these pages. We'll equip you to win some arguments with your buddies and maybe even to win a friendly bet or two (no, our talk about standard deviations is not a sleaze-ball attempt to inject sex into this book). We'll offer some fashion tips to Oilers' Coach Glanville (Jerry, *sweetheart*! Basic black adds twenty *pounds*!). And we'll tell you who really belongs in the Hall of Fame and who got in on a pass.

Finally, we'll tell you what we'd do if we were named as triumvirs to run the NFL, stuff like how to reduce the number of yellow flags and, in a separate step, knee injuries. We'll even get rid of the ludicrous situational substitution that has made the pro game resemble nothing so much as an ant farm—and at the same time eliminate steroid use.

You're going to know so much about how pro football stacks up for 1989 that watching the games will be a drag, only confirming what we told you. Second lie: We're going to get a lot of folks upset, but not you.

We'd like to thank Rick Horgan, our editor at Warner, who has volunteered to take the heat for any mistakes we have made. And our praise goes to G&H Soho, who designed and produced this beast of a book; to Pica Graphics and Terry Brykczynski, who set it into type; Scott Kurtz, David Sassian, and Nina Bernard, for editorial and production aid; and to David Reuther, for his singular grab bag of editorial and production tricks.

TEAM REVIEWS
1988 SEASON

THE NATIONAL FOOTBALL CONFERENCE

THE AMERICAN FOOTBALL CONFERENCE

A glossary of statistical terms and list of abbreviations used in this book can be found on pages 293–295.

NATIONAL FOOTBALL CONFERENCE

ATLANTA FALCONS

The Last 5 Seasons

	1984	1985	1986	1987	1988
Won-Lost	4-12	4-12	7-8-1	3-12	5-11
Percentage	.250	.250	.469	.200	.313
Division Finish	4	4	3	4	4
Games Behind	11	7	3	10	5
Total Points	281	282	280	205	244
Per Game	17.6	17.6	17.5	13.7	15.3
Opponent Points	382	452	280	436	315
Per Game	23.9	28.3	17.5	29.1	19.7
Net Points	-101	-170	0	-231	-71
Predicted Net Wins	-2.5	-4.3	0.0	-5.8	-1.8
Delta Net Wins	-1.5	0.3	-0.5	1.3	-1.2
Total Yards on Offense	5044	4960	5106	4066	4582
Per Game	315.3	310.0	319.1	271.1	286.4
Total Yards Allowed on Defense	5279	5850	4908	5907	5692
Per Game	329.9	365.6	306.8	393.8	355.8
Net Difference	-235	-890	198	-1841	-1110
Offensive Turnovers	41	30	33	49	37
Defensive Takeaways	32	34	36	27	38
Net Turnovers	-9	4	3	-22	1
Predicted Net Points	-56	-58	29	-241	-89
Delta Net Points	-45	-112	-29	10	18
Net Rushing Yards	1994	2466	2524	1298	2016
Per Game	124.6	154.1	157.8	86.5	126.0
Average Gain	4.1	4.4	4.4	3.9	4.2
Opponent Net Rushing Yards	2153	2052	1916	2734	2319
Per Game	134.6	128.3	119.8	182.3	144.9
Average Gain	4.0	4.7	4.0	4.6	4.5
Net Passing Yards	3050	2494	2582	2768	2566
Per Game	190.6	155.9	161.4	184.5	160.4
Times Sacked	67	69	56	46	43
Passer Rating in Yards	4.2	3.2	3.9	2.7	3.5
Opponent Net Passing Yards	3126	3798	2992	3173	3373
Per Game	195.4	237.4	187.0	211.5	210.8
Times Sacked	38	42	26	17	30
Passer Rating Defense	5.9	5.4	4.6	5.9	4.6
Passer Rating Net	-1.7	-2.2	-0.7	-3.1	-1.1
Yards per Drive Offense	27.1	24.8	26.2	21.6	23.1
Yards per Drive Defense	28.2	29.8	25.2	31.3	27.4
Average Time of Possession	30:14	33:11	32:35	26:01	28:07

THE 1988 SEASON

DATE	AT	OPPONENT	SCORE	R	SPREAD	Tu	Net YDS	Rush YDS	Pass YDS	TURN
09/04	A	Detroit	17-31	L	+4	a	359-230	172-142	187- 88	4-1
09/11	H	New Orleans	21-29	L	+8.5	g	307-434	161-212	146-222	4-4
09/18	A	S. Francisco	34-17	W	+14	g	367-426	196-104	171-322	2-4
09/25	A	Dallas	20-26	L	+6.5	a	305-323	107-113	198-210	2-1
10/02	H	Seattle	20-31	L	+4	g	385-317	140-168	245-149	3-1
10/09	H	L.A. Rams	0-33	L	+6.5	g	150-501	73-252	77-249	2-1
10/16	A	Denver	14-30	L	+13	g	311-406	174-104	137-302	3-1
10/23	H	N.Y. Giants	16-23	L	+7.5	g	368-346	152-121	216-225	2-3
10/30	A	Philadelphia	27-24	W	+10.5	a	294-424	92-155	202-269	1-3
11/06	H	Green Bay	20- 0	W	-3	g	341-284	164-101	177-183	3-7
11/13	H	San Diego	7-10	L	-5.5	g	245-355	57-185	188-170	3-2
11/20	A	L.A. Raiders	12- 6	W	+7.5	g	280-212	130- 65	150-147	2-3
11/27	H	Tampa Bay	17-10	W	-4	g	289-313	181-127	108-186	2-4
12/04	A	S. Francisco	3-13	L	+7	g	177-378	43-140	134-238	1-0
12/11	A	L.A. Rams	7-22	L	+7.5	g	193-418	65-127	128-291	2-2
12/18	A	New Orleans	9-10	L	+8.5	a	202-325	109-203	93-122	0-2
						Avg.	286-356	126-145	160-211	2-2

			WINS	LOSSES
Season Record:	5-11-0	POINTS:	22- 11	12- 23
Vs. Spread:	9- 7-0	Net YDS: 5-11-0	314-332	273-367
Home:	2- 6-0	Rush YDS: 7- 9-0	153-110	114-161
On Artificial Turf:	1- 3-0	Pass YDS: 4-12-0	162-221	159-206
Art. Turf vs. Spread:	3- 1-0	TURN: 7- 7-2	2- 4	2- 2

GETTING SERIOUS

They appear, at last, to be getting serious in Atlanta.

Sometimes a franchise piddles around for years, losing games, losing fans, losing respect, and seeming to have no inclination to change its ways. After a while, you forget they're even around, except for the one time each year they come to town to hand your team a victory. They have a few good players who would be all-stars on other teams, but season after season their efforts go for naught, until even their abilities become obscured in the pervading miasma of failure. Then suddenly, because of new ownership, or a new coach, or sometimes just a rededication of the old hands, the franchise rolls up its sleeves, gets to work, and builds a winner. In extreme cases, the new order may last for a decade. The Steelers of the 1970s are the prototype. The Broncos did it in the middle of the same decade. The Saints and Bills are the newest examples, and the Falcons may be next.

The Birds probably won't make it to .500 in 1989—1990 seems a more realistic target—but they are laying a strong foundation. The trick for them now is to fight the temptation to go for a free-agent quick fix, to put up a Quonset hut that will house a few wins and then crumble to dust. If they and their fans can only be patient a little longer, the result may be an edifice to rival Tara.

Patience, however, may be hard to come by in '89. With three 10-6 teams above them in the tough Western Division of the NFC, the Falcons have little chance for the playoffs. Atlanta plays a schedule in which half their opponents won at least ten games last season (facing San Francisco, the Rams, and New Orleans, twice each; and Buffalo and Minnesota, once each). Another, the Indianapolis Colts, won nine. The question is whether, when the inevitable defeats come, the front office will gut it up and hang on to the youngsters that are the Falcons' future. The answer will show whether they're serious in Atlanta.

SETTLING IN

The Falcons' surprise star in '88 was running back John Settle, one of those underdog-makes-good stories that gets us misty. As an undrafted free agent from tiny Appalachian State (North Carolina), he saw little action as a rookie in '87, rushing only 19 times. But he started strong last season, gaining 102 yards on only 10 carries against the Saints in Atlanta's second outing. When three-time Pro Bowler Gerald Riggs was knocked out for half the season with a knee injury, the squat 207-pounder settled in to become the Birds' running game. He finished with 1,024 yards. To find another free agent who topped the thousand-yard barrier, you have to go back to the early days of the American Football League with Paul Lowe of the Chargers in 1963 and Clem Daniels of the Raiders in 1965, the year Settle was born. Settle is anything but a picture runner—his rolling-fireplug look is accented by the Falcons' red uniform—but he chugs with good power, cutting ability, and speed.

The youngster also led the Falcons in pass catching, a mixed blessing in that it reflects problems at wide receiver. In nine of his games, his combined yards topped 100, and his

SETTLE'S RUSHING AND RECEIVING IN 1988

| OPPONENT | SCORE | R | RUSHING | | | | RECEIVING | | | | TOT |
			ATT	YDS	AVG	TD	NO	YDS	AVG	TD	YDS
Detroit	17-31	L	7	23	3.3	1	2	16	8.0	0	39
New Orleans	21-29	L	10	102	10.2	1	4	34	8.5	0	136
S. Francisco	34-17	W	6	15	2.5	0	0	0	0.0	0	15
Dallas	20-26	L	9	51	5.7	0	2	16	8.0	0	67
Seattle	20-31	L	21	115	5.5	0	6	71	11.8	0	186
L.A. Rams	0-33	L	13	69	5.3	0	6	57	9.5	0	126
Denver	14-30	L	25	125	5.0	1	7	46	6.6	1	171
N.Y. Giants	16-23	L	19	85	4.5	1	7	50	7.1	0	135
Philadelphia	27-24	W	15	51	3.4	0	1	16	16.0	0	67
Green Bay	20- 0	W	23	93	4.0	1	4	30	7.5	0	123
San Diego	7-10	L	14	25	1.8	0	10	106	10.6	0	131
L.A. Raiders	12- 6	W	19	76	4.0	1	4	39	9.8	0	115
Tampa Bay	17-10	W	12	83	6.9	1	3	22	7.3	0	105
S. Francisco	3-13	L	8	16	2.0	0	6	40	6.7	0	56
L.A. Rams	7-22	L	10	29	2.9	0	5	15	3.0	0	44
New Orleans	9-10	L	21	66	3.1	0	1	12	12.0	0	78
			232	1024	4.4	7	68	570	8.4	1	1594

season total of 1,594 ranked fourth in the NFL, behind only Eric Dickerson, Roger Craig, and Herschel Walker.

Riggs returned at the end of the season and showed his leg was okay. He now ranks twenty-second all-time in NFL rushing with 6,631 yards. Kenny Flowers, the former Clemson star, missed the entire season with a knee injury, but is expected back in 1989.

THE FRANCHISE QB

The Falcons have struggled at quarterback since Steve Bartkowski was in his prime. As a result their basic attack has been to run the ball down the opposition's throat until it gagged. Most of the time it was the Falcons who upchucked losses. Although Riggs piled up excellent yardage, the offense was one-dimensional and lacked the sure passing touch that opens the field. And whenever the Falcons fell behind, you could head for the exits.

That should change as Chris Miller continues to develop. The Falcons are convinced he is the "franchise quarterback" who can lead them to Valhalla. Of course, with a nickel for every potential franchise QB who's come into the NFL in the last twenty years, you could buy a franchise that already has one. Bartkowski was a franchiser and the Falcons still lost. Miller, a former Oregon whiz, held out until halfway through the '87 season, then threw nine interceptions in three late games when he was force-fed into the lineup. Last year he began to come on. Although he lost all of his receivers to injuries at one time or another and missed seventeen quarters himself with a sprained ankle, Miller passed for 2,133 yards. Equally important, he cut his interceptions to 12 in 351 attempts. Only twenty-four, he's shown excellent leadership ability. Well, hell, he's three years older than Alexander the Great was when he conquered the world,

and putting the Falcons in a Super Bowl is only marginally harder.

SMURFS

More than half the Atlanta pass completions last season were to running backs. Too many. Three of their top four receivers were backs. Far too many.

The team favors small, speedy WRs. The incumbent crew has more quick than Nestlés, but their size also makes them vulnerable. Veteran Stacey Bailey (157 pounds) played in only ten games. Second-year man Floyd Dixon (170 pounds) missed two starts with a fractured cheek and played the rest of the season wearing a protective mask. Rookie Michael Haynes (180 pounds) missed one game.

Adding to the problem, tight end Alex Higdon caught three passes. The first two were for touchdowns and the third ended his season with a knee injury. Higdon, at least, isn't undersized at 247 pounds.

UP FRONT

Every team has injuries, of course. The Falcons may have had a few more than their share in 1988, but it's not the number that is significant. A team with wall-to-wall talent such as Cincinnati can lose a key player like Joe Walter, send in Brian Blados, and keep rolling. And Atlanta simply can't replace someone like All-Pro guard Bill Fralic, who was kayoed for the two final games. At this point the Falcons can have fewer injuries than any team in their division and still be hurt more.

Last season the Falcons' only offensive lineman to start all sixteen games was offensive tackle Mike Kenn.

BURYIN' MARION

One of the ironies of Atlanta football is that Coach Marion Campbell, the old Swamp Fox, built his reputation as a defensive coach. Then, when he became head Falcon in '87, the defense got swamped. The crew that had allowed a highly respectable 280 points for Dan Henning in '86 fell all over itself in giving up 436—an average of 29.1—in Campbell's first year. To be burned for that kind of average, the opposition practically has to score in the locker room. You couldn't even blame it on the strike: The replacement team was only tagged for 73 points in three games, a 24.3 average.

Once again there were injuries, a new system, and Campbell couldn't decide between a 3-4 or 4-3 alignment. But mostly it was not enough hitters.

Last season Campbell got things together and the D dropped its average points allowed to under twenty. If they could lose four or five more points per game this year, they'd really have something. That biggest little word in the English language, IF!

IF California floats away into the Pacific, the Falcons will only have to beat New Orleans. . . .

Anyway, there was improvement in 1988. Rookie linebacker Aundray Bruce, with six sacks, looked like he might almost be worth what the Falcons are paying him—a sum that would cover the national debt of several Third World countries. Another rookie LB, Marcus Cotton, started five games and had five sacks. The front three (the number Campbell finally opted for when the league wouldn't let him use a 10-10 defense) could have helped out more. The Birds held only one opponent to under 100 yards rushing.

CB Scott Case led the NFL with ten interceptions and made the Pro Bowl. The rap on Case is that he's slow, which in a CB is worse than diabetes in a honeybee. A lot of intercepts at the corner usually tells you who is getting picked on.

Campbell is going to need all his experience, guile, smarts, and luck to get any more out of the defense than he got last year.

WHAT ARE THEY DOING TO OUR CHILDREN?

The NFL worries all the time about its image. The league wants it all—to be wealthy, respected, and loved. Don't you think they should do something about the terrible trick they're playing on our kids?

Here, the little nippers come out of geography class with one set of ideas about the way this country is laid out. And then they look at the NFL standings and discover that Atlanta and New Orleans are in the West and Phoenix is in the East. Are we raising a Lost Generation?

Don't stand at the top of Arrowhead Stadium and look for an ocean, but maybe—just maybe—Kansas City is "West." And, if you want to call Tampa Bay and Houston "Central," it's okay. Us oldtimers still think "Central" is a telephone exchange.

But Atlanta out west? Come on!

We have a theory . . . that the Falcons (and, until recently, the Saints) have been so forlorn for so many years because they look at that "NFC West" above their division and *know* they're not supposed to win it.

You scoff, but we are a nation that follows directions on labels. Did your mother put Mr. Yuk in your lunch box? Do your pillows still have those little tags? Have the Falcons won a Super Bowl?

Atlanta in the West! They'd like to do a little when-in-Rome-ing, but they don't speak the language. Put a Falcon in a string tie and cowboy boots and he looks as silly as the Bengals' uniforms or Jerry Glanville in plaid. Does the phrase "fish out of water" ring a bell? "Atlanta Wins the West"—no self-respecting newspaper would ever run that headline. It would be as preposterous as "Buddy Ryan Has No Comment" or "Dexter Manley Voted Mr. Congeniality." So, knowing that the league and the world expect them to suffer in silence while quietly filling the last line in the standings, the Falcons have done the honorable thing for years.

Had they not been laboring under the wrong label, the Falcons might have been the "Team of the Decade" instead of the "Team of the Decayed."

ATLANTA FALCONS STATISTICS

1988 TEAM STATISTICS	AF	OPP
TOTAL FIRST DOWNS	257	312
Rushing	106	124
Passing	136	168
Penalty	15	20
3rd Down Made/Att.	89/239	86/214
Pct.	37.2%	40.2%
4th Down Made/Att.	6/8	5/10
Pct.	75.0%	50.0%
TOTAL NET YARDS	4582	5692
Avg. per Game	286.4	355.8
Total Plays	1002	1052
Avg. per Play	4.6	5.4

(Continued)

1988 TEAM STATISTICS	AF	OPP
NET YARDS RUSHING	2016	2319
Avg. per Game	126.0	144.9
Total Rushes	478	518
NET YARDS PASSING	2566	3373
Avg. per Game	160.4	210.8
Tackled/Yards Lost	43/348	20/211
Gross Yards	2914	3584
Attempts/Completions	481/250	504/281
Pct. of Completions	52.0%	55.8%
Had Intercepted	19	24
PUNTS/AVERAGE	98/40.0	73/39.6
NET PUNTING AVG.	35.7	32.7

(Continued)

1988 TEAM STATISTICS	AF	OPP
PENALTIES/YARDS	67/542	92/761
FUMBLES/BALL LOST	29/18	29/14
TOUCHDOWNS	27	34
Rushing	11	14
Passing	13	17
Returns	3	3
TIME OF POSSESSION	450:01	509:59

SCORE/PERIODS	1	2	3	4	OT	TOTAL
Falcons	33	82	45	84	0	244
Opponents	50	89	75	101	0	315

SCORING	TDR	TDP	TDRt	PAT	FG	S	TP
Davis				25/27	29/30		82
Settle	7	1					48
Haynes		4					24
Bailey		2					12
Dixon		2					12
Higdon		2					12
Dils	1						6
Gann			1				6
Lang		1					6
C. Miller	1						6
Moore			1				6
Primus	1						6
Riggs	1						6
Tuggle			1				6
Whisenhunt		1					6
Falcons	11	13	3	25/27	19/30	0	244
Opponents	14	17	3	31/34	26/36	1	315

RUSHING	NO	YDS	AVG	LG	TD
Settle	232	1024	4.4	62	7
Riggs	113	488	4.3	34	1
Lang	53	191	3.6	19	0
Miller	31	138	4.5	29	1
Primus	35	95	2.7	29t	1
Dixon	7	69	9.9	24	0
Millen	1	7	7.0	7	0
Hester	1	3	3.0	3	0
Dils	2	1	0.5	1t	1
Stamps	3	0	0.0	3	0
Falcons	478	2016	4.2	62	11
Opponents	518	2319	4.5	44	14

RECEIVING	NO	YDS	AVG	LG	TD
Settle	68	570	8.4	27	1
Lang	37	398	10.8	50	1
Dixon	28	368	13.1	36	2
Riggs	22	171	7.8	30	0
Bailey	17	437	25.7	68t	2
Whisenhunt	16	174	10.9	25	1
Haynes	13	232	17.8	49t	4
Hester	12	176	14.7	41	0
Wilkins	11	134	12.2	33	0

(Continued)

RECEIVING	NO	YDS	AVG	LG	TD
Primus	8	42	5.3	8	0
Milling	5	66	13.2	34	0
Matthews	5	64	12.8	21	0
Stamps	5	22	4.4	7	0
Higdon	3	60	20.0	34t	2
Falcons	250	2914	11.7	68t	13
Opponents	281	3584	12.8	68t	17

INTERCEPTIONS	NO	YDS	AVG	LG	TD
Case	10	47	4.7	12	0
Moore	5	56	11.2	47t	1
Clark	4	40	10.0	21	0
Bruce	2	10	5.0	10	0
Gordon	2	10	5.0	10	0
Butler	1	22	22.0	22	0
Falcons	24	185	7.7	47t	1
Opponents	19	214	11.3	58	2

PUNTING	NO	YDS	AVG	TB	In 20	LG	Blk
Donnelly	98	3920	40.0	6	27	61	0
Falcons	98	3920	40.0	6	27	61	0
Opponents	73	2893	39.6	8	21	56	0

PUNT RETURNS	NO	FC	YDS	AVG	LG	TD
Barnes	34	8	307	9.0	68	0
Cooper	2	1	10	5.0	10	0
Matthews	6	0	26	4.3	10	0
Falcons	42	9	343	8.2	68	0
Opponents	51	23	297	5.8	31	0

KICKOFF RETURNS	NO	YDS	AVG	LG	TD
Barnes	6	142	23.7	36	0
Cooper	16	331	20.7	28	0
Haynes	6	113	18.8	25	0
Stamps	12	219	18.3	27	0
Gordon	14	209	14.9	32	0
Dukes	1	13	13.0	13	0
Primus	1	13	13.0	13	0
Lang	1	12	12.0	12	0
Shelley	2	5	2.5	5	0
Falcons	59	1057	17.9	36	0
Opponents	48	982	20.5	41	0

FIELD GOALS	1-19	20-29	30-39	40-49	50+	TOTAL
Davis	1-1	3-4	6-9	8-12	1-4	19-30
Falcons	1-1	3-4	6-9	8-12	1-4	19-30
Opponents	0-0	10-11	8-11	7-12	1-2	26-36

FIELD GOALS BY Davis: 19 of 30
(19G)(41N)(47G,41G)(43G,24G)(32G,52N,30G)
( )( )(32G,37G,31G)(23N)(54N,52G,39N,43G)
(40N,41N)(46G,41G,51N)(40G,32N)(42N,21G)
(34N)(27G,43G,39G)

PASSING	ATT	COM	YARD	PCT.	Avg G	TD	%TD	IN	%IN	LG	SAKS/YDS	RATE
Miller	351	184	2133	52.4	6.08	11	3.1	12	3.4	68t	24/207	67.3
Dils	99	49	566	49.5	5.72	2	2.0	5	5.1	50	15/112	52.8
Millen	31	17	215	54.8	6.94	0	0.0	2	6.5	38	6/29	49.8
Falcons	481	250	2914	52.0	6.06	13	2.7	19	4.0	68t	43/348	63.2
Opponents	504	281	3584	55.8	7.11	17	3.4	24	4.8	68t	30/211	69.6

CHICAGO BEARS

The Last 5 Seasons

	1984	1985	1986	1987	1988
Won-Lost	10-6	15-1	14-2	11-4	12-4
Percentage	.625	.938	.875	.733	.750
Division Finish	1	1	1	1	1
Games Behind	0	0	0	0	0
Total Points	325	456	352	356	312
Per Game	20.3	28.5	22.0	23.7	19.5
Opponent Points	248	198	187	282	215
Per Game	15.5	12.4	11.7	18.8	13.4
Net Points	77	258	165	74	97
Predicted Net Wins	1.9	6.4	4.1	1.9	2.4
Delta Net Wins	0.1	0.6	1.9	1.6	1.6
Total Yards on Offense	5437	5837	5459	5044	5317
Per Game	339.8	364.8	341.2	336.3	332.3
Total Yards Allowed on Defense	3863	4135	4130	4215	4360
Per Game	241.4	258.4	258.1	281.0	272.5
Net Difference	1574	1702	1329	829	957
Offensive Turnovers	31	31	47	44	34
Defensive Takeaways	34	54	47	24	35
Net Turnovers	3	23	0	-20	1
Predicted Net Points	143	234	111	-11	84
Delta Net Points	-66	24	54	85	13
Net Rushing Yards	2974	2761	2700	1954	2319
Per Game	185.9	172.6	168.8	130.3	144.9
Average Gain	4.4	4.5	4.5	4.0	4.2
Opponent Net Rushing Yards	1377	1319	1463	1413	1326
Per Game	86.1	82.4	91.4	94.2	82.9
Average Gain	3.6	3.7	3.4	3.4	3.4
Net Passing Yards	2463	3076	2759	3090	2998
Per Game	153.9	192.3	172.4	206.0	187.4
Times Sacked	36	43	24	48	24
Passer Rating in Yards	4.5	5.3	4.0	4.1	5.1
Opponent Net Passing Yards	2486	2816	2667	2802	3034
Per Game	155.4	176.0	166.7	186.8	189.6
Times Sacked	72	64	62	70	43
Passer Rating Defense	3.3	2.5	2.4	4.3	3.5
Passer Rating Net	1.2	2.9	1.6	-0.1	1.6
Yards per Drive Offense	27.0	28.8	26.6	26.7	28.0
Yards per Drive Defense	19.5	20.0	19.3	21.6	23.3
Average Time of Possession	35:08	34:33	32:21	31:58	33:02

8

1984 PLAYOFFS
Won Divisional Playoff from Washington, 23-19
Lost NFC Championship Game to San Francisco, 0-23

1985 PLAYOFFS
Won Divisional Playoff from N.Y. Giants, 21-0
Won NFC Championship Game from L.A. Rams, 24-0
Won Super Bowl XX from New England, 46-10

1986 PLAYOFFS
Lost Divisional Playoff to Washington, 13-27

1987 PLAYOFFS
Lost Divisional Playoff to Washington, 17-21

1988 PLAYOFFS
Won Divisional Playoff from Philadelphia, 20-12
Lost NFC Championship Game to San Francisco, 3-28

THE 1988 SEASON

DATE	AT	OPPONENT	SCORE	R	SPREAD	Tu	Net YDS	Rush YDS	Pass YDS	TURN
09/04	H	Miami	34- 7	W	-3.5	g	427-163	262- 45	165-118	0-2
09/11	A	Indianapolis	17-13	W	-2	a	332-173	154-108	178- 65	1-3
09/18	H	Minnesota	7-31	L	-3	g	235-376	70-127	165-249	5-1
09/25	A	Green Bay	24- 6	W	-6	g	358-233	242- 34	116-199	3-3
10/02	H	Buffalo	24- 3	W	-4	g	417-218	157- 0	260-218	2-1
10/09	A	Detroit	24- 7	W	-6.5	a	323-262	101- 42	222-220	1-2
10/16	H	Dallas	17- 7	W	-7	g	385-291	124- 96	261-195	1-2
10/24	H*	S. Francisco	10- 9	W	-2.5	g	237-213	122- 78	115-135	1-1
10/30	A	New England	7-30	L	-5	a	208-350	134-185	74-165	3-1
11/06	H	Tampa Bay	28-10	W	-9.5	g	338-357	69- 84	269-273	3-2
11/13	A	Washington	34-14	W	+3.5	g	418-323	145- 28	273-295	1-5
11/20	A	Tampa Bay	27-15	W	-7	g	339-321	139-168	200-153	4-3
11/27	H	Green Bay	16- 0	W	-13	g	372-189	213- 22	159-167	2-2
12/05	A*	L.A. Rams	3-23	L	+3	g	213-364	114-132	99-232	3-3
12/11	H	Detroit	13-12	W	-10	g	250-310	82-115	168-195	1-2
12/19	A*	Minnesota	27-28	L	+6	a	465-218	185- 62	280-156	3-2
						Avg.	332-273	145- 83	188-190	2-2

				WINS		LOSSES	
Season Record:	12- 4-0		POINTS:	22- 9		11- 28	
Vs. Spread:	11- 5-0		Net YDS:	11- 5-0	350-254	280-327	
Home:	7- 1-0		Rush YDS:	10- 6-0	151- 68	126-127	
On Artificial Turf:	2- 2-0		Pass YDS:	7- 9-0	199-186	155-201	
Art. Turf vs. Spread:	3- 1-0		TURN:	6- 6-4	2- 2	4- 2	

* Monday Night

TWILIGHT OF THE GODS

In the year 2085 they'll be celebrating the hundredth anniversary of the Bears Defense in the 1985 playoffs. Some purists will keep carping that Super Bowl XX actually took place in the following year and the apologists will say things like, "Well, back in those pioneer days, teams only played two platoons and offensive linemen couldn't carry laser pistols"—or whatever rules they have in 2085. It won't matter. The football world will still be standing in awe of the achievement. Maybe even kneeling in awe. Holding three playoff opponents to a total of ten points! Unbelievable!

"But all of those opponents were from Earth."

"Shut up."

We bring this up because here in 1989 we have to consider the possibility that we may not have that Bears Defense with us much longer. We saw the beginnings of the breakup last year. In another season or two—perhaps even this season—the Bears Defense will slip to the level of "good."

And if "good" comes, can "mediocre" be far behind? So we must treasure them while they are here. Cheer them. Honor them. Tender unto them peeled grapes and ripe pomegranates. For when they are gone, we will never see their like again.

The vintage years were 1985–88. True, the pieces were in place in 1984, when the Bruins won their first of five straight division titles. And certainly the '84 defense did a fine job, but The Defense really burst on the public consciousness during its magnificent triumph in the 1985 playoffs. That was when we first began measuring every other defense in the league against the mighty Midway Monsters, as in phrases like "almost as good as the Bears," or "may someday rival the Bears," or "will try to match the Bears."

At first a lot of the credit was given to the "46" defense, a tactic designed by then defensive coordinator Buddy Ryan. The publicity helped win Ryan the job as head coach at Philadelphia. But in the years that have followed, other teams tried the "46," and none of them matched the Bears' defensive record. It remains a quality alignment, but you get the idea that the Bears' personnel could have done pretty well lining up single-file.

For two more years that personnel remained stable: Dan Hampton, Steve McMichael, William Perry, and Richard Dent up front; Otis Wilson, Mike Singletary, and Wilbur Marshall backing the line; Mike Richardson, Dave Duerson, and Gary Fencik in the secondary. Hampton, McMichael, Dent, Singletary, Marshall, Wilson, and Duerson were all named to one or more Pro Bowls, and "The Refrigerator" Perry became a national cult figure. Only Vestee Jackson, who replaced Leslie Frazier at cornerback in '86, was a new face. On the sideline Vince Tobin replaced Ryan as def-co in '86 and The Defense continued to roll, despite Buddy's dire predictions of what would happen without him.

But after the 1987 season Fencik retired and Wilbur Marshall signed with Washington as a free agent. Otis Wilson moved from left linebacker to right linebacker to replace Marshall, but his season ended when he tore up his knee in an exhibition game, and The Defense was out two Pro Bowl linebackers. Against Minnesota in the third regular season game, Perry broke his arm and missed the rest of the year. The RLB spot continued as a jinx, felling Wilson's replacement, Jim Morrissey, and three rookies until Morrissey returned. Shaun Gayle, Fencik's replacement, went out for the season with a neck injury on October 9. And in Week 13, Dent suffered a broken fibula where the bone meets the ankle. With five of the old crew gone for all or a significant part of the season and even the subs needing subs, the Bears did a remarkable job in keeping their defensive stats within hailing distance of those of the previous three years:

Per Game	1985	1986	1987	1988
Points (vs. Defense Only)	11.88	9.93	16.93	12.31
Total Plays	59.06	62.63	65.93	61.06
Total Yards Allowed	258.44	258.13	281.00	272.50
Average Gain	4.38	4.12	4.26	4.46
Third-Down Efficiency	29.61	32.46	35.40	31.34
Fumbles Recovered	1.25	1.00	0.73	0.56
Rushing Attempts	22.44	26.69	27.47	24.31
Net Rushing Yards	82.44	91.44	94.20	82.88
Average Gain	3.67	3.43	3.43	3.41
Rushing TDs	0.38	0.25	0.33	0.44
Pass Attempts	32.63	32.06	33.80	34.06
Pass Completions	15.56	15.19	17.00	15.31
Percentage	47.70	47.37	50.30	44.95
Total Yards	206.19	198.13	219.07	212.44
Average Gain	6.32	6.18	6.48	6.24
Sacks	4.00	3.88	4.67	2.69
Yards Lost / Tackled	30.19	31.44	32.27	22.81
Net Passing Yards	176.00	166.69	186.80	189.63
TD Passing	1.00	0.75	1.60	1.13
Interceptions	2.13	1.94	0.87	1.63
NFL Passer Rating	51.20	49.90	76.10	69.60
NEWS Rating	3.69	3.69	5.80	4.42

Perry, Gayle, and Dent are expected back in '89—Wilson signed as a free agent with the Raiders—but it remains to be seen if their injuries have left any permanent effects. Another problem is age. Al Harris, who replaced Perry in the line, is thirty-three. McMichael and Hampton are thirty-two. And Singletary is thirty-one. It's not being an alarmist to expect one or more of them to begin slipping. The key to The Defense is the play of Singletary, perhaps the best all-around defensive player in football, and of McMichael and Hampton, two of the best down linemen. Those three close the middle so completely a virus would have trouble gaining a yard. And that allows the others freedom to range. Cornerback Richardson and strong safety Duerson are twenty-eight and twenty-nine respectively, about the age when many defensive backs lose a step.

The clock is ticking.

CHARISMA

Last season the *Houston Post*, tired of printing news, decided to manufacture some. They sent out a survey to rank the twenty-eight teams in terms of charisma. No doubt they rejected sillier survey ideas like "estimate the number of UFOs that landed in Arkansas last year" or "rank the first twenty-eight cornflakes in the bowl in order of crispness, excitement, and effect on saving the whales."

Inquiring minds want to know, so the first thing we wondered was who-in-hell the *Post* sent the survey to? They didn't send it to us, which was sorely disappointing. Then we began wondering who-in-hell *replied* to the thing? Who in this weird world would have the temerity, the gall, the audacity, the unmitigated *chutzpah* to presume to speak for the American pro football fan on a matter that can't even be defined?

The eleven broadcasters and newsmen who replied chose the Bears by a wide margin as the team most dripping with charisma. If they'd let it go at that, there wouldn't be any argument. How can you argue about an opinion based on personal feelings? We think Kirstie Alley is sexy as the devil; but one of our closest friends prefers Ted Danson, and we can't change her mind.

But they didn't let it go at that. The eleven oracles ranked each team in nine categories to come up with their total ranking. For example, the number one coach in charisma was Mike Ditka, followed by Jerry Glanville and Buddy Ryan. Somehow Glanville never struck us as charismatic, but then neither did Leo Gorcey. We figured we knew which way this was heading until we saw Don Shula ranked fifth. Charisma? We watched part of his halftime commentary on TV during the playoffs and slept through a second half touchdown. In the accompanying *Post* story there was an admission that Ditka got the top rating because of his heart attack. Apparently there had been some confusion on the part of the respondees between charisma and concern.

The Bears' uniforms finished second behind Dallas. Did anyone know that the Bears' orange-and-blue was originally used because those were the colors of the Staley Starch Co. of Decatur, Illinois? Does that rate as charisma? The Bengals finished seventeenth in uniforms. The respondees must have heard a rumor that eleven NFL teams had joined a nudist colony.

In "playing style" the Bears came in second. Okay, if you love defense. But the Dolphins came in first! What? There's something charismatic about having no defense, too?

Tied for first in "pattern of success" were the 49ers, Redskins, and Bears. This makes perfect sense if none of the respondees are over the age of fourteen. The Cowboys, who had twenty consecutive winning seasons, finished sixth.

Apparently unrelated to "pattern of success" was "tradition." The Packers came in first, we're guessing because they've only had tradition to brag about for the last twenty years. The Steelers, who had a tradition of losing for forty years, came in second. The Bears, who have won championships in five different decades and division crowns in six, were third.

As we all know, charisma—like pornography—is in the glands of the beholder.

GONE TODAY AND HERE TOMORROW?

Each season has two McMahon Watches. The first is to see when he'll be hurt and sidelined. The second is to determine when or if he'll come back before the Bears are knocked out of the playoffs. It only *seems* like we've been doing this annually since Ike was President.

You've got to hand it to McMahon. He's found a way to keep his name and face and sneer in the public consciousness while playing less football than Dan Quayle played soldier. There's no telling how many motorcycles or tacos (or whatever else he's selling this season) the yearly McMahon Watches have been worth in sales. You could make a case that McMahon is good for the economy. You could do that a lot easier than you could prove he's good for the Bears.

Don't misunderstand. Just because his act has become boring is no reason to give him the hook. Don Shula is boring. Winning is boring (or so those in Atlanta hear). The Bears' defense is boring to the people who play against them; there's not much variety to stomp, stomp, stomp. And we've seen Ditka's soup commercial so many times that anything floating in broth makes us queasy. Keep the D. Keep Ditka. McMahon must go.

There's nothing personal in this. Sure, some people find McMahon an arrogant, obnoxious, smart-ass. Some people think his headband is on too tight. Some people insist they publish his I.Q. instead of his completion percentage. Bosh! You can be a wisenheimer and maybe a little crazy and still play quarterback in the NFL. And anybody who thinks McMahon is dumb probably thinks they named the Loop after him. Nevertheless he must be bade a fond farewell.

We don't mind that he sometimes says unflattering things about his teammates and coaches. He even got the trainer last year. Let them plot their own revenge. Leeches in the whirlpool, anyone?

And we're not suggesting that there's anything fake about McMahon's injuries. To those who look for a psychosomatic reason in his head, we say there's nothing to that. We just don't care anymore whether he has a shoulder separation, a busted rib, or a paper cut. Enough is enough!

He's a pretty good quarterback on those rare occasions when he's available. If you look at his career record, it won't knock your socks off, but the averages aren't bad. (Although, if you want a good laugh, pick up the old copy of *Sport* magazine where they named him the best QB in the NFL.)

The problem isn't the averages. It's the totals. They are too low. That's because in seven years as the Bears' "starter," McMahon has played less than four seasons. In those seven years, he's only thrown 52.2 percent of the Bears' passes. What kind of starter is that? Better starters you'll find in any auto graveyard. During the past three seasons, he's started twenty-one of the Bears' forty-seven regular season games. This is a "regular"? Here is his career record:

YEAR	ATT	COM	PCT	YARD	Avg G	TD	%TD	IN	%IN	RATE	NEWS*
1982	210	120	57.1	1501	7.15	9	4.3	7	3.3	80.1	6.08
1983	295	175	59.3	2184	7.40	12	4.1	13	4.4	77.6	5.83
1984	143	85	59.4	1146	8.01	8	5.6	2	1.4	97.8	7.94
1985	313	178	56.9	2392	7.64	15	4.8	11	3.5	82.6	6.54
1986	150	77	51.3	995	6.63	5	3.3	8	5.3	61.4	4.57
1987	210	125	59.5	1639	7.80	12	5.7	8	3.8	87.4	6.66
1988	192	114	59.4	1346	7.01	6	3.1	7	3.6	76.0	5.68
	1513	874	57.8	11203	7.40	67	4.4	56	3.7	80.4	6.18

* NEWS Rate = YDS + (10 X TD) - (45 X IN) / Att

Last season, with all those quarterback injuries, a few guys played straight through. We can use them to judge what a real starter does. Jim Kelly threw 99.6 percent of the Bills' passes, Jim Everett and Boomer Esiason did 99 percent of their teams' passing. Marino, 97.5, Cunningham 96.3, Hebert 95.9. McMahon did 41.6 percent, the year before 42.6, and in 1986, 36.1. Do you see a pattern there? McMahon's highest percentage was his 80.2 as a rookie!

If McMahon were any other quarterback on any other team, he'd just be a guy on IR so often people'd think those were his initials. But a couple years ago some sort of mystique got started that he was the Answer Man to the Eternal Question, "Can the Bears win this week?" You heard that the Bears were better with him in there (which was true) and that they couldn't win without him (which wasn't).

The sorry state of affairs with the Bears is that even after it's been proved time and again that they can win with another quarterback, there are team members who still don't feel whole going out on the field with Mike Tomczak or Jim Harbaugh under center. In their heart-of-hearts they're waiting for the Answer Man.

Neither Tomczak nor Harbaugh is now the QB that McMahon was in his healthy days. But you can expect them to show up ready to throw most of the time. And the only thing you can take to the bank is that, as long as McMahon is the one everyone awaits with bated breath, neither Tomczak nor Harbaugh will develop into the leader the team needs for sixteen games instead of just now and then.

As this is being written, there are reports of a possible trade involving McMahon.

CHICAGO BEARS STATISTICS

1988 TEAM STATISTICS	CB	OPP
TOTAL FIRST DOWNS	303	264
Rushing	137	76
Passing	134	158
Penalty	32	30
3rd Down Made/Att.	91/217	68/216
Pct.	41.9%	31.5%
4th Down Made/Att.	7/17	8/18
Pct.	41.2%	44.4%
TOTAL NET YARDS	5317	4360
Avg. per Game	332.3	272.5
Total Plays	1040	977
Avg. per Play	5.1	4.5
NET YARDS RUSHING	2319	1326
Avg. per Game	144.9	82.9
Total Rushes	555	389
NET YARDS PASSING	2998	3034
Avg. per Game	187.4	189.6
Tackled/Yards Lost	24/175	43/365
Gross Yards	3173	3399
Attempts/Completions	461/248	545/245
Pct. of Completions	53.8%	45.0%
Had Intercepted	15	26
PUNTS/AVERAGE	79/41.5	90/40.2
NET PUNTING AVG.	33.4	34.8
PENALTIES/YARDS	88/644	102/804
FUMBLES/BALL LOST	37/19	17/9
TOUCHDOWNS	38	25
Rushing	25	5
Passing	13	18
Returns	0	2
TIME OF POSSESSION	—	—

SCORE/PERIODS	1	2	3	4	OT	TOTAL
Bears	77	131	42	62	0	312
Opponents	49	56	50	60	0	215

SCORING	TDR	TDP	TDRt	PAT	FG	S	TP
Butler				37/38	15/19		82
Anderson	12						72
Gentry	1	3					24
McKinnon	1	3					24
McMahon	4						24
Morris		4					24
Sanders	3						18
Moorehead		2					12
Suhey	2						12
Harbaugh	1						6
Muster		1					6
Tomczak	1						6
McMichael						1	2
Bears	25	13	0	37/38	15/19	1	312
Opponents	5	18	2	22/25	13/22	2	215

RUSHING	NO	YDS	AVG	LG	TD
Anderson	249	1106	4.4	30t	12
Sanders	95	332	3.5	20t	3
Suhey	87	253	2.9	19	2
Muster	44	197	4.5	15	0
Harbaugh	19	110	5.8	19	1
McMahon	26	104	4.0	16	4
Gentry	7	86	12.3	58t	1

(Continued)

RUSHING	NO	YDS	AVG	LG	TD
Morris	3	40	13.3	21	0
Tomczak	13	40	3.1	17	1
McKinnon	3	25	8.3	12	1
Thomas	5	20	4.0	8	0
Davis	1	3	3.0	3	0
Kozlowski	1	3	3.0	3	0
Wagner	2	0	0.0	0	0
Bears	555	2319	4.2	80t	25
Opponents	389	1326	3.4	32	5

RECEIVING	NO	YDS	AVG	LG	TD
McKinnon	45	704	15.6	76t	3
Anderson	39	371	9.5	36	0
Gentry	33	486	14.7	45	3
Morris	28	498	17.8	63t	4
Muster	21	236	11.2	40t	1
Suhey	20	154	7.7	29	0
Davis	15	220	14.7	36	0
Thorton	15	135	9.0	19	0
Moorehead	14	133	9.5	28	2
Sanders	9	94	10.4	39	0
Boso	6	50	8.3	15	0
Kozlowski	3	92	30.7	50	0
Bears	248	3173	12.8	76t	13
Opponents	245	3399	13.9	80t	18

INTERCEPTIONS	NO	YDS	AVG	LG	TD
Jackson	8	94	11.8	46	0
Tate	4	35	8.8	17	0
Morrissey	3	13	4.3	13	0
Duerson	2	18	9.0	18	0
Richardson	2	15	7.5	15	0
Krumm	2	14	7.0	14	0
Rivera	2	0	0.0	0	0
Douglass	1	35	35.0	35	0

(Continued)

INTERCEPTIONS	NO	YDS	AVG	LG	TD
Singletary	1	13	13.0	13	0
Gayle	1	0	0.0	0	0
Bears	26	237	9.1	46	0
Opponents	15	175	11.7	94t	1

PUNTING	NO	YDS	AVG	TB	In 20	LG	Blk
Wagner	79	3282	41.5	10	18	70	0
Bears	79	3282	41.5	10	18	70	1
Opponents	90	3622	40.2	10	29	62	0

PUNT RETURNS	NO	FC	YDS	AVG	LG	TD
McKinnon	34	8	277	8.1	23	0
Davis	3	1	17	5.7	13	0
Kozlowski	1	0	0	0.0	0	0
Bears	38	9	294	7.7	23	0
Opponents	40	9	447	11.2	64	0

KICKOFF RETURNS	NO	YDS	AVG	LG	TD
Gentry	27	578	21.4	51	0
Sanders	13	248	19.1	38	0
Muster	3	33	11.0	15	0
Kozlowski	2	37	18.5	24	0
Duerson	0	0	—	0	0
Bears	45	896	19.9	51	0
Opponents	56	1130	20.2	51	0

FIELD GOALS	1-19	20-29	30-39	40-49	50+	TOTAL
Butler	1-1	4-4	7-8	3-6	0-0	15-19
Bears	1-1	4-4	7-8	3-6	0-0	15-19
Opponents	0-0	7-7	3-5	2-8	1-2	13-22

FIELD GOALS BY Butler: 15 of 19
(40N,44N)(40G,37N)( )(35G)(22G)(37G)(21G,42N)
(18G)( )( )(32G,24G)(36G,43G)( )(39G)(35G,32G)(20G,45G)

PASSING	ATT	COM	YARD	PCT.	Avg G	TD	%TD	IN	%IN	LG	SAKS/YDS	RATE
McMahon	192	114	1346	59.4	7.01	6	3.1	7	3.6	63t	13/79	76.0
Tomczak	170	86	1310	50.6	7.71	7	4.1	6	3.5	76t	5/47	75.4
Harbaugh	97	47	514	48.5	5.30	0	0.0	2	2.1	56	6/49	55.9
Anderson	1	0	0	0.0	0.00	0	0.0	0	0.0	0	0/0	39.6
Wagner	1	1	3	100.0	3.00	0	0.0	0	0.0	3	0/0	79.2
Bears	461	248	3173	53.8	6.88	13	2.8	15	3.3	76t	24/175	71.4
Opponents	545	245	3399	45.0	6.24	18	3.3	26	4.8	80t	43/365	56.7

DALLAS COWBOYS

The Last 5 Seasons

	1984	1985	1986	1987	1988
Won-Lost	9-7	10-6	7-9	7-8	3-13
Percentage	.563	.625	.438	.467	.188
Division Finish	2-t	1-t	3	2-t	5
Games Behind	2	0	7	4	7
Total Points	308	357	346	340	265
Per Game	19.3	22.3	21.6	22.7	16.6
Opponent Points	308	333	337	348	381
Per Game	19.3	20.8	21.1	23.2	23.8
Net Points	0	24	9	-8	-116
Predicted Net Wins	0.0	0.6	0.2	-0.2	-2.9
Delta Net Wins	1.0	1.4	-1.2	-0.3	-2.1
Total Yards on Offense	5320	5602	5474	5056	5483
Per Game	332.5	350.1	342.1	337.1	342.7
Total Yards Allowed on Defense	5036	5608	4985	5061	5414
Per Game	314.8	350.5	311.6	337.4	338.4
Net Difference	284	-6	489	-5	69
Offensive Turnovers	43	41	41	40	40
Defensive Takeaways	44	48	35	43	19
Net Turnovers	1	7	-6	3	-21
Predicted Net Points	28	28	17	12	-78
Delta Net Points	-28	-4	-8	-20	-38
Net Rushing Yards	1714	1741	1969	1865	1995
Per Game	107.1	108.8	123.1	124.3	124.7
Average Gain	3.7	3.8	4.4	4.0	4.3
Opponent Net Rushing Yards	2226	1853	2200	1617	1858
Per Game	139.1	115.8	137.5	107.8	116.1
Average Gain	4.4	4.0	4.4	3.5	4.1
Net Passing Yards	3606	3861	3505	3191	3488
Per Game	225.4	241.3	219.1	212.7	218.0
Times Sacked	48	44	60	52	35
Passer Rating in Yards	4.0	4.8	4.3	4.5	4.2
Opponent Net Passing Yards	2810	3755	2785	3444	3556
Per Game	175.6	234.7	174.1	229.6	222.3
Times Sacked	57	62	53	51	46
Passer Rating Defense	3.0	4.0	4.3	4.7	6.0
Passer Rating Net	1.0	0.7	0.0	-0.2	-1.8
Yards per Drive Offense	23.9	26.7	25.9	24.9	28.0
Yards per Drive Defense	21.8	26.6	24.0	24.7	27.9
Average Time of Possession	29:00	30:34	31:14	30:41	30:41

14

1985 PLAYOFFS
Lost Divisional Playoff to L.A. Rams, 0-20

THE 1988 SEASON

DATE	AT	OPPONENT	SCORE	R	SPREAD	Tu	Net YDS	Rush YDS	Pass YDS	TURN
09/12	A*	Phoenix	17-14	W	+3.5	g	352-367	190-130	162-237	1-1
09/18	H	N.Y. Giants	10-12	L	+2.5	a	366-278	91-128	275-150	2-2
09/25	H	Atlanta	26-20	W	+3	a	323-305	113-107	210-198	1-2
10/03	A*	New Orleans	17-20	L	-6.5	a	457-333	187- 65	270-268	3-1
10/09	H	Washington	17-35	L	+6.5	a	361-350	60-180	301-170	5-1
10/16	A	Chicago♦	7-17	L	+2	g	291-385	96-124	195-261	2-1
10/23	A	Philadelphia	23-24	L	+7	a	437-339	109- 65	328-274	1-2
10/30	H	Phoenix	10-16	L	+5.5	a	228-295	125-160	103-135	2-0
11/06	A	N.Y. Giants	21-29	L	-3	a	365-262	103-111	262-151	3-2
11/13	H	Minnesota	3-43	L	+5.5	a	160-325	102-103	58-222	7-1
11/20	H	Cincinnati	24-38	L	+3.5	a	355-410	179-214	176-196	2-1
11/24	H	Houston	17-25	L	+4.5	a	282-355	79-145	203-210	2-0
12/04	A	Cleveland	21-24	L	+5.5	g	410-302	163- 27	247-275	1-1
12/11	A	Washington	24-17	W	+10.5	g	444-372	124- 24	320-348	2-5
12/18	H	Philadelphia	7-23	L	+6.5	a	239-371	137-133	102-238	3-0
						Avg.	338-337	124-114	214-222	2-1

				WINS	LOSSES
Season Record:	3-12-0	POINTS:		22- 17	15- 26
Vs. Spread:	6- 9-0	Net YDS:	8- 7-0	373-348	329-334
Home:	1- 7-0	RushYDS:	7- 8-0	142- 87	119-121
On Artificial Turf:	1-10-0	PassYDS:	6- 9-0	231-261	210-213
Art. Turf vs. Spread:	3- 8-0	TURN:	3- 9-3	1- 3	3- 1

* Monday Night

RUSH TO JUDGMENT

It got ugly in Dallas last season.

Only a few years ago, when Dallas was "America's Team," they really weren't. Across the country fans rooted for their own team first—the Giants, Packers, Broncos, Bills, and so forth. Only second would they give a cheer for the Cowboys. Oh, sure, there was always a Quisling or two. If you looked hard enough, you'd find somebody in Cincinnati who said he thirsted for Cowboy wins and Bengal losses. Those kind always jump aboard a winner because it makes them feel less inferior. They should go with their feelings. They *are* inferior.

But *real* football fans in Minnesota loved the Vikings. In New England the Patriots came first. Only after the geographical favorite lost would any real fan tune in CBS for the second game to watch the Cowboys. Since they were always on, it might be more accurate to call them "CBS's Team." Familiarity doesn't breed contempt; it breeds children and acceptance. You couldn't quite love the Cowboys, but you could accept them. And because you always knew the names of more of their players than the other team's, you found yourself saying it would be okay if they won. Maybe even a good thing.

And they usually did. For twenty seasons the Cowboys won more often than they lost. So by the end of a long

Sunday of TV football, you usually got a little lift. That helped you like Dallas a little more. Another thing that helped was that they really were fun to watch. They didn't look like every other NFL team when they set up their offense. They had shotguns and flankers and splits and all sorts of stuff before anyone else. And speed! They always seemed to be the fastest guys on the field. No doubt about it, they were "America's Second Choice."

Still, in little pockets all over the country, you could find a cadre of Cowboy-haters—fans who thought those smart-ass Cowpokes played lace-curtain football. At the Monday coffee break they'd sit around and tell each other that Roger was a prig, Too-Tall was a freak, Tony didn't run hard, and Tom was a robot. They fed on their jealousy and waited. The Cowboy-haters knew their day would come. They laid in a stock of Gloat for the celebration.

The bottles were almost uncorked in 1986 when the Cowboys were 7-9. Still, it might not be anything more than a bad bounce. Better wait. Then '87 was a strike year and you couldn't be certain of anything. That 7–8 mark could be an illusion; 1988 would tell the tale.

Yet when *Götterdämmerung* came, it was so utter, so *ugly* that even the most virulent Cowboy-hater had to shed a tear—3–13! My God, it was worse than Detroit!

For a while it was amusing to watch the Cowboys pile up losses. But then you began hearing how the fans and media had turned vicious in Dallas. The backbiting of the hired hands who fed civic pride and empty typewriters for so long took all the fun out of it.

Landry, the sixty-four-year-old emotionless clone the Cowboy-haters had always sneered at, took most of the local goring. Strangely, it was like watching the final reel when the humanoid is destroyed by hysterical humans. All along you figured he was just a pile of machinery. But now you know he's hurting.

Football's always been a what-have-you-done-for-me-lately game—as witness the treatment of *l'ancien régime* in the wake of the sale to Daddy Warbucks of **Arkansas**—but it's hard to ignore Landry's Dallas legacy.

PRO COACHES WITH OVER 100 WINS (entering 1989)

	YR	REG.SEASON W	L	T	PLAYOFFS W	L	T	TOTAL W	L	T
George Halas	40	319	148	31	6	3	0	325	151	31
*Don Shula	26	261	111	6	16	13	0	277	124	6
*Tom Landry	29	250	162	6	20	16	0	270	179	6
Curly Lambeau	33	226	132	22	3	2	0	229	134	22
Paul Brown	25	215	104	9	9	8	0	224	112	9
*Chuck Noll	20	168	125	1	15	7	0	183	132	1
Bud Grant	18	158	96	5	10	12	0	168	108	5
*Chuck Knox	16	148	89	1	7	11	0	155	100	1
Steve Owen	23	151	100	17	2	8	0	153	108	17
Hank Stram	17	131	97	10	5	3	0	136	100	10
Weeb Ewbank	20	130	129	7	4	1	0	134	130	7
Sid Gillman	18	122	99	7	1	5	0	123	104	7
George Allen	12	116	47	5	2	7	0	118	54	5
Don Coryell	14	111	83	1	3	6	0	114	89	1
John Madden	10	103	32	7	9	7	0	112	39	7
Buddy Parker	15	104	75	9	3	1	0	107	76	9
Vince Lombardi	10	96	34	6	9	1	0	105	35	6
*Bill Walsh	10	92	59	1	10	4	0	100	63	1

* Active in 1988

The interesting thing isn't that only two coaches stand ahead of Landry. Look at the names of those lined up behind him!

Anyone who can read has to respect the man. That probably explains why the *Dallas Times Herald* held a poll by telephone: "Is it time for Tom Landry to give up coaching?" Naturally, they left any possible successor unnamed so they could be certain to get the result they wanted. When Landry misread a yard line and called a play resulting in a loss, one Dallas newswriter headlined, SENILITY STRIKES AGAIN. We've heard people say newsmen should be muzzled; those in Dallas also need distemper shots.

The tip-off that Landry was still doing a good job was that he lost games but never lost the team. You've seen it happen before: A team loses a couple of close ones, then it gets blown out once or twice, and by the end of the season, you could beat them with the girls from Sister Mary's. The 'Pokes lost three games by a total of six points early, then faltered against Chicago and Washington—certainly no disgrace. Landry got them back on track to play tough against the next three opponents. Then Minnesota and Cincinnati ripped them up real good. That could have been the end, but Landry rallied them again. In the last four games, they gave Houston and Cleveland a battle and beat Washington, the previous year's Super Bowl champs.

The fact that the Cowboys were competitive most of the time in a season when they played seven games against playoff teams (and ten against teams with winning records) went over the heads of the short and short-sighted. The Cowboys aren't *that* bad, and Jimmy Johnson will probably do just fine.

WHAT HAPPENED: THE FIRST EXCUSE

The 1988 season was so un-Cowboyish that the natural question is "What happened?" Assuming for the moment that Landry still has all his faculties, why did his team lose so many games? A simple answer is that they scored only 16.6 points per game and gave up 23.8. Bad as that is, a team with such a point difference should win at least five games. *The Cowboys won three.*

Even more mystifying, Dallas outgained its opponents in total yards, 5,483–5,414. There wasn't any great disparity between rushing and passing, either. The Cowboys out-rushed the opposition, 124.7 yards per game to 116.1, and were outpassed by 218.0 to 222.3. Those are the figures of an 8–8 team. *The Cowboys won three games.*

One stat jumps right out at you. Turnovers! The Cowboys turned the ball over to the opposition 40 times. Was that the problem? Not exactly. Dallas has had around 40 turnovers a season for years. That's the price of a high-tech offense. But in a normal Dallas season, the 'Pokes take the ball back about the same number of times, evening things out. That didn't happen in '88, when they managed only 19 takeaways—a minus 21.

Yet even the horrible giveaway-takeaway ratio isn't the whole answer. Even with the −21 ratio, they still should have scored around 280 points and given up around 365.

That's roughly the same ratio as Tampa Bay had. *The Buccaneers won five games.*

Okay, let's see what we have. A team is about equal to the opposition in offense and defense. It could break even, but it loses three extra games by a poor takeaway ratio. It should win five games but only wins three, losing two because of God-knows-what.

What kind of team is that? You don't even have to check the roster: you know that's a young team. A team in its prime plays nearer to what the numbers say. An old team will usually sneak in an extra win or two.

All right. You want us to prove it? Take a look at the Cowboys' depth chart with years of NFL experience listed instead of the names:

OFFENSE			DEFENSE		SPECIALISTS
STARTERS	SUBSTITUTES		STARTERS	SUBSTUTES	
WR- 2,	WR- 1,	WR- 3	LE-14,	DE-14	P- 4
LT- 1,	T- 2		LT- 4,	DT- 2	PK- 2
LG- 3,	G- 7		RT- 2		
C-13,	C- 2		RE- 6		
RG- 4			LLB- 2,	LB- 3	
RT- 2,	T- 3		MLB- 5,	LB- 5	
TE- 3,	TE- 4		OLB-10		
WR- 1,	WR- 2,	WR- 2	LCB- 8,	CB- 3	
QB- 5,	QB- 2,	QB- 1	RCB- 2,	CB- 2	
RB- 3,	RB- 3,	RB- 1	SS- 6,	SS- 5,	SS-1
FB- 9,	FB- 5		FS- 8,	FS- 5	

```
Average Experience of Roster       4.2

Average Experience of Offensive Starters     4.2
   Starting Wide Receivers      1.5
   Starting Tight End      3.0
   Starting Offensive Line      3.8
   Starting Quarterback      5.0
   Starting Runners      6.0
Average Experience of All Offensive Players     3.4

Average Experience of Defensive Starters     6.1
   Starting Front Four     6.5
   Starting Linebackers     5.7
   Starting Secondary     6.0
Average Experience of All Defensive Players     4.4

Average Experience of Specialists     3.0
```

Even with two fourteen-year vets (Too-Tall Jones and Randy White) and a thirteen-year vet (Tom Rafferty), the 1988 roster averaged only 4.2 seasons in the NFL. The worst part was that the inexperience was where you don't want it—up front on the offense. The team had no veteran wide receivers, and when Bob White replaced Rafferty at center, as he often did, the Cowboys averaged 2.4 years from tackle to tackle.

Younger teams than the Cowboys have won, of course. It can be done. Just not very often.

WHAT HAPPENED: THE SECOND EXCUSE

Once upon a time the Cowboys drafted better than anybody. Then they stopped doing that and began drafting worse than anybody. Some said it was because they always drafted high. Don't believe it. Even if a team wins the Super Bowl year after year, it should be able to draft from one to two long-term starters each season. Maybe not Pro Bowlers, but reliable guys who'll stick around and help for nine or ten years. The first three rounds are where the ripe pickings are.

For years the 'Pokes would take some wild flyer early. If the guy came through, as Calvin Hill of Yale did, they looked like geniuses. If he flopped, they had so much talent on the roster that no one noticed. But as the talent thinned, those off-the-wall picks became unaffordable luxuries.

Look at the Cowboys for the first five drafts of this decade.

YEAR	ROUND 1	ROUND 2	ROUND 3
1980	None	None	Bill Roe-LB & James Jones-RB
	Also *TIMMY NEWSOME-FB (R-6)		
1981	Howard Richards-OT	Doug Donley-WR	GLEN TITENSOR-OG
1982	Rod Hill-CB	Jeff Rohrer-LB	Jim Eliopulos-LB
1983	*JIM JEFFCOAT-DRE	Mike Walter-LB	Bryan Caldwell-DE
1984	Billy Cannon-LB	VICTOR SCOTT-DB	Fred Cornwell-TE
	Also *EUGENE LOCKHART-MLB (R-6) & STEVE DeOSSIE-LB (R-4)		

Here and in table following, name in caps indicates on '88 active roster at end of November 1988; * indicates starter.

Only six players from those drafts are still on the Cowboys' roster, and only three are starters. To be fair, Rohrer was on Injured Reserve in 1988 and may come back. The worst part is that only one starter and two subs came on the first three rounds. Did the computer have a five-year virus?

YEAR	ROUND 1	ROUND 2	ROUND 3
1985	*KEVIN BROOKS-DLT	Jesse Penn-LB	*CRAWFORD KER-RG
	Also *HERSCHEL WALKER-RB (R-5)		
1986	Mike Sherrard-WR	DARRYL CLACK-RB	MARK WALEN-DT
	Also *THORNTON CHANDLER-TE (R-6) & GARTH JAX-LB (R-11)		
1987	*DANNY NOONAN-DLT	RON FRANCIS-CB	Jeff Zimmerman-OG
	Also *KEVIN GOGAN-ORT (R-8), KELVIN MARTIN-WR (R-4), EVERETT GAY-WR (R-5), & KEVIN SWEENEY-QB (R-7)		
1988	*MICHAEL IRVIN-WR	Ken Norton-LB	Mark Hutson-OG
	Also *DAVE WIDELL-OLT (R-4), SCOTT SECULES-QB (R-6), & MARK HIGGS-RB (R-8)		

The good news is that things picked up in 1985 and have been going much better since. Irvin and Widell started as rookies. Zimmerman, Norton, and Hutson were on IR and Sherrard was listed as Physically Unable to Perform in '88, so there's still hope for them.

WHAT HAPPENED: THE THIRD EXCUSE

Whenever a team loses, the quarterback gets the blame. Steve Pelluer had been around since 1984 but he had started only thirteen games. He showed his inexperience early with some key miscues. When we tracked him at the end of the season, we were surprised to see that he actually passed well most of the time. With all the stuff about "The Troy Aikman Derby," we'd sort of given Pelluer up as a lost cause. He threw well enough to win six times (he was in the upper 25 percent of NEWS ratings in those games). One of those, however, was against Cincinnati, when he relieved Kevin Sweeney in a game already lost. He had five poor outings (lower 25 percent NEWS), but only two of those were truly dreadful. In one of his middling appearances, in Week 10, he couldn't move the team and was relieved by Sweeney.

WK	OPPONENT	SCORE	ATT	COM	YDS	TD	IN	RATE	
1	Pittsburgh	24-21	37	24	289	2	2	5.64	T
2	Phoenix	17-14	24	12	162	0	1	4.88	L
3	N.Y. Giants	10-12	36	20	275	1	2	5.42	T
4	Atlanta	26-20	26	17	216	2	1	7.35	W
5	New Orleans	17-20	35	23	271	2	1	7.03	W
6	Washington	17-35	33	14	269	1	3	4.36	L
7	Chicago	7-17	(Injured in 1st Quarter)						
8	Philadelphia	23-24	46	32	342	1	1	6.67	W
9	Phoenix	10-16	31	9	132	1	2	1.68	L
10	N.Y. Giants	21-29	18	10	96	0	0	5.33	T
11	Minnesota	3-43	(Did not play)						
12	Cincinnati	24-38	23	16	185	2	1	6.52	W
13	Houston	17-25	32	17	203	0	1	4.94	L
14	Cleveland	21-24	32	20	247	2	0	8.34	W
15	Washington	24-17	36	21	333	3	1	8.83	W
16	Philadelphia	7-23	26	10	119	0	3	-0.61	L
			435	245	3139	17	19	5.64	(6-5-2)

Tell you what we think of Pelluer. He may be the Craig Morton of the nineties. Morton, if you recall, could never satisfy them in Dallas. When he went to Denver, he turned out to be a pretty fair quarterback. Maybe what Steve needs is a new team.

DALLAS COWBOYS STATISTICS

1988 TEAM STATISTICS	DC	OPP
TOTAL FIRST DOWNS	311	279
Rushing	112	93
Passing	175	180
Penalty	24	24
3rd Down Made/Att.	80/213	89/222
Pct.	37.6%	40.1%
4th Down Made/Att.	7/15	4/10
Pct.	46.7%	40.0%
TOTAL NET YARDS	5483	5414
Avg. per Game	342.7	338.4
Total Plays	1059	1020
Avg. per Play	5.2	5.3
NET YARDS RUSHING	1995	1858
Avg. per Game	124.7	116.1
Total Rushes	469	454
NET YARDS PASSING	3488	3556
Avg. per Game	218.0	222.3
Tackled/Yards Lost	35/239	46/327
Gross Yards	3727	3883
Attempts/Completions	555/307	520/263
Pct. of Completions	55.3%	50.6%
Had Intercepted	27	10
PUNTS/AVERAGE	80/40.7	86/41.6
NET PUNTING AVG.	34.1	35.9
PENALTIES/YARDS	141/1148	93/764
FUMBLES/BALL LOST	22/13	25/9
TOUCHDOWNS	32	44
Rushing	10	13
Passing	21	30
Returns	1	1
TIME OF POSSESSION	—	—

SCORE/PERIODS	1	2	3	4	OT	TOTAL
Cowboys	71	47	64	83	0	265
Opponents	80	125	74	102	0	381

SCORING	TDR	TDP	TDRt	PAT	FG	S	TP
Ruzek				12/22	27/27		63
Walker	5	2					42
Alexander		6					36
Irvin		5					30
Martin		3					18
Newsome	3						18
Folsom		2					12
Pelluer	2						12
Noonan			1			1	8
Zendejas				1/3	5/5		8
Chandler		1					6
Clack		1					6
Gay		1					6
Cowboys	10	21	1	13/25	32/32	1	265
Opponents	13	28	1	24/29	41/44	2	381

RUSHING	NO	YDS	AVG	LG	TD
Walker	361	1514	4.2	38	5
Pelluer	51	319	6.3	27	2
Newsome	32	75	2.3	8	3
Clack	10	46	4.6	17	0
Sweeney	7	34	4.9	10	0
Fowler	3	6	2.0	4	0
Irvin	1	2	2.0	2	0
Martin	4	-4	-1.0	11	0
Cowboys	469	1995	4.3	38	10
Opponents	454	1858	4.1	51t	13

RECEIVING	NO	YDS	AVG	LG	TD
Alexander	54	788	14.6	50t	6
Walker	53	505	9.5	50	2
Martin	49	622	12.7	35t	3
Irvin	32	654	20.4	61t	5
Newsome	30	236	7.9	32	0
Chandler	18	186	10.3	29	1

(Continued)

(Continued)

RECEIVING	NO	YDS	AVG	LG	TD
Clack	17	126	7.4	18	1
Gay	15	205	13.7	25	1
Cosbie	12	112	9.3	21	0
Fowler	10	64	6.4	13	0
Folsom	9	84	9.3	20	2
Edwards	5	93	18.6	27	0
Burbage	2	50	25.0	41	0
Newton	1	2	2.0	2	0
Cowboys	307	3727	12.1	61t	21
Opponents	263	3874	14.7	73t	30

INTERCEPTIONS	NO	YDS	AVG	LG	TD
Williams	2	18	9.0	12	0
Downs	2	3	1.5	3	0
Walls	2	0	0.0	0	0
Francis	1	29	29.0	29	0
Noonan	1	17	17.0	17t	1
Bates	1	0	0.0	0	0
Hendrix	1	0	0.0	0	0
Cowboys	10	67	6.7	29	1
Opponents	27	314	11.6	66	0

PUNTING	NO	YDS	AVG	TB	In 20	LG	Blk
Saxon	80	3271	40.7	15	24	55	0
Cowboys	80	3271	40.7	15	24	55	0
Opponents	86	3574	41.6	5	18	40	0

PUNT RETURNS	NO	FC	YDS	AVG	LG	TD
Martin	44	16	360	8.0	21	0
Walls	1	0	0	0.0	0	0
Cowboys	45	16	360	8.4	21	0
Opponents	37	15	239	6.5	18	0

KICKOFF RETURNS	NO	YDS	AVG	LG	TD
Burbage	20	448	22.4	53	0
Clack	32	690	21.6	40	0
Martin	12	210	17.5	31	0
Higgs	2	31	15.5	17	0
Smith	2	24	12.0	13	0
B. White	1	7	7.0	7	0
Cowboys	69	1410	20.4	53	0
Opponents	56	1060	18.9	44	0

FIELD GOALS	1-19	20-29	30-39	40-49	50+	TOTAL
Zendejas	0-0	0-0	0-0	1-3	0-0	1-3
Ruzek	0-0	4-5	4-7	4-7	2-3	14-22
Cowboys	0-0	4-5	4-7	4-10	1-3	13-25
Opponents	0-0	9-9	8-9	6-10	1-1	24-29

FIELD GOALS BY Zendejas: 1 of 3
(49N)(47G,49N)
Ruzek: 14 of 22
( )( )(41G,28N)(43N,24G)(39N,39G)
(45G,53N)(42N,35N)(26G,34G,30G)(39G)
( )(50G)(44G)(29G)(48B,50N)(22G,47N,37N)( )

PASSING	ATT	COM	YARD	PCT.	Avg G	TD	%TD	IN	%IN	LG	SAKS/YDS	RATE
Pelluer	435	245	3139	56.3	7.22	17	3.9	19	4.4	61t	21/112	73.9
D. White	42	29	274	69.1	6.52	1	2.4	3	7.1	24	4/47	65.0
Sweeney	78	33	314	42.3	4.03	3	3.9	5	6.4	28	9/80	40.1
Cowboys	555	307	3727	55.3	6.71	21	3.8	27	4.9	61t	35/239	68.5
Opponents	520	263	3874	50.6	7.45	30	5.8	10	1.9	73t	46/327	86.5

DETROIT LIONS

The Last 5 Seasons

	1984	1985	1986	1987	1988
Won-Lost	4-11-1	7-9	5-11	4-11	4-12
Percentage	.281	.438	.313	.267	.250
Division Finish	4	3-t	3	4-t	4-t
Games Behind	5.5	8	9	7	8
Total Points	283	307	277	269	220
Per Game	17.7	19.2	17.3	17.9	13.8
Opponent Points	408	366	326	384	313
Per Game	25.5	22.9	20.4	25.6	19.6
Net Points	-125	-59	-49	-115	-93
Predicted Net Wins	-3.1	-1.5	-1.2	-2.9	-2.3
Delta Net Wins	-0.4	0.5	-1.8	-0.6	-1.7
Total Yards on Offense	5318	4476	4555	4391	3405
Per Game	332.4	279.8	284.7	292.7	212.8
Total Yards Allowed on Defense	5319	5591	5149	5273	5316
Per Game	332.4	349.4	321.8	351.5	332.3
Net Difference	-1	-1115	-594	-882	-1911
Offensive Turnovers	36	41	37	37	33
Defensive Takeaways	25	36	41	32	36
Net Turnovers	-11	-5	4	-5	3
Predicted Net Points	-44	-113	-34	-94	-147
Delta Net Points	-81	54	-15	-21	54
Net Rushing Yards	2017	1538	1771	1435	1243
Per Game	126.1	96.1	110.7	95.7	77.7
Average Gain	4.5	3.4	3.8	3.6	3.2
Opponent Net Rushing Yards	1808	2685	2349	2070	2037
Per Game	113.0	167.8	146.8	138.0	127.3
Average Gain	3.5	4.8	4.5	4.1	4.0
Net Passing Yards	3301	2938	2784	2956	2162
Per Game	206.3	183.6	174.0	197.1	135.1
Times Sacked	61	53	39	26	52
Passer Rating in Yards	4.2	4.2	3.8	3.6	2.8
Opponent Net Passing Yards	3511	2906	2800	3203	3279
Per Game	219.4	181.6	175.0	213.5	204.9
Times Sacked	37	45	41	42	47
Passer Rating Defense	6.3	4.3	3.8	5.1	5.0
Passer Rating Net	-2.0	-0.1	-0.0	-1.5	-2.2
Yards per Drive Offense	27.8	23.2	23.1	23.2	17.9
Yards per Drive Defense	28.6	28.8	26.4	27.9	28.0
Average Time of Possession	29:43	27:30	29:42	28:19	27:27

THE 1988 SEASON

DATE	AT	OPPONENT	SCORE	R	SPREAD	Tu	Net YDS	Rush YDS	Pass YDS	TURN
09/04	H	Atlanta	31-17	W	-4	a	230-359	142-172	88-187	1-4
09/11	A	L.A. Rams	10-17	L	+10	g	198-315	76-191	122-124	3-2
09/18	H	New Orleans	14-22	L	+5.5	a	272-401	40-119	232-282	2-2
09/25	H	N.Y. Jets	10-17	L	+2	a	183-316	86- 86	97-230	1-1
10/02	A	S. Francisco	13-20	L	+13.5	g	297-339	49-176	248-163	2-1
10/09	H	Chicago	7-24	L	+6.5	a	262-323	42-101	220-222	2-1
10/16	A	N.Y. Giants	10-30	L	+11	a	113-402	48-122	65-280	2-2
10/23	A	Kansas City	7- 6	W	+6.5	a	215-171	127- 61	88-110	3-2
10/30	H	N.Y. Giants	10-13	L	+7	a	146-279	48- 83	98-196	2-2
11/06	A	Minnesota	17-44	L	+11	a	89-553	68-198	21-355	2-1
11/13	H	Tampa Bay	20-23	L	-2	a	278-304	75-225	203- 79	3-4
11/20	A	Green Bay	19- 9	W	+4	g	270-356	156- 52	114-304	1-3
11/24	H	Minnesota	0-23	L	+6.5	a	60-353	18-181	42-172	2-0
12/04	H	Green Bay	30-14	W	-3	a	220-360	94- 92	126-268	1-6
12/11	A	Chicago	12-13	L	+10	g	310-250	115- 82	195-168	2-1
12/18	A	Tampa Bay	10-21	L	+3	g	250-242	59-103	191-139	4-4
						Avg.	212-333	78-128	134-205	2-2

			WINS	LOSSES
Season Record:	4-12-0	POINTS:	22- 12	11- 22
Vs. Spread:	8- 8-0	Net YDS: 3-13-0	234-312	205-340
Home:	2- 6-0	Rush YDS: 4-11-1	130- 94	60-139
On Artificial Turf:	3- 8-0	Pass YDS: 4-12-0	104-217	145-201
Art. Turf vs. Spread:	4- 7-0	TURN: 4- 7-5	2- 4	2- 2

WHERE'S JOE SCHMIDT WHEN YOU REALLY NEED HIM?

In 1972 Lions coach Joe Schmidt, the former great linebacker, resigned under fire after taking several years of abuse for his team's play. His sin? He'd finished second in his division four years in a row.

Ah, the good old days! During the 1960s and '70s, the Lions disappointed their partisans with close-but-no-cigar seasons. From 1958, when they last won an NFL championship, through 1981, Detroit finished in second place twelve times. Had Motor City fans of that period foreseen what would happen in the mid and late eighties, they'd have held victory parades for the second-placers.

The Lions haven't simply lost football games with the frequency that Donald Duck loses his temper. Worse, they've become dreary. They lose ugly. The offense managed as many as three touchdowns in only one 1988 game, the season opener. In an era of spectacular offenses, Detroit has the leastest.

Eleven games into the '88 season, with the toothless Lions at 2–9, Coach Darryl Rogers was fired and replaced by defensive coordinator Wayne Fontes. When the team responded to the change by winning two of its last five games, Fontes was promoted from interim head coach to permanent head in an impermanent profession.

We had the impression that when a coach is canned in mid-year, teams usually win a few games for the new boss before the season rings down. Almost any change is enough to spark a win or two. But, we thought, that new enthusiasm usually petered out. So we looked at mid-season coaching changes in the '80s, starting with situations such as that of Fontes, in which the replacement coach returned as head coach the next year.

NEW COACH CONTINUED INTO FOLLOWING SEASON

YEAR	TEAM	COACH	RECORD	NEXT YR
1984	New England	Ron Meyer	5- 3-0	
		Raymond Berry	4- 4-0	9- 7-0
1984	Cleveland	Sam Rutigliano	1- 7-0	
		M. Schottenheimer	4- 4-0	8- 8-0
1985	Buffalo	Kay Stephenson	0- 4-0	
		Hank Bullough	2-10-0	4-12-0
1985	Houston	Hugh Campbell	5- 9-0	
		Jerry Glanville	0- 2-0	9- 6-0
1986	San Diego	Don Coryell	1- 7-0	
		Al Saunders	3- 5-0	8- 7-0

(Continued)

YEAR	TEAM	COACH	RECORD	NEXT YR	
1986	Buffalo	Hank Bullough	2- 7-0		
		Marv Levy	2- 5-0	7- 8-0	
1986	Indianapolis	Rod Dowhower	0-13-0		
		Ron Meyer	3- 0-0	9- 6-0	
1988	Detroit	Darryl Rogers	2- 9-0		
		Wayne Fontes	2- 3-0	?	

REMAINDER OF SEASON

Great improvement	2	(Schottenheimer, Meyer)
Slight improvement	4	(Bullough, Saunders, Levy, Fontes)
No improvement	2	(Berry, Glanville)

FOLLOWING SEASON

Great improvement	6	(Berry*, Schottenheimer, Glanville, Saunders, Levy, Meyer)
No improvement	1	(Bullough)

* Regular-season record the same, but Patriots reached Super Bowl

Our impression would appear to be wrong. But on second thought, the only replacement coaches in this group we remembered as being out-and-out designated as "interim" were Fontes and Glanville, and we're not so sure about Glanville. Maybe we just think of him as an interim kind of guy, like the comedy act that fills in while the stars change costumes.

When we looked at the replacement coaches who were themselves replaced before the following season, we got a different picture.

NEW COACH HIRED FOR FOLLOWING SEASON

YEAR	TEAM	COACH	RECORD	NEXT YR	
1980	New Orleans	Dick Nolan	0-12-0		
		Dick Stanfel	1- 3-0	4-12-0	Bum Phillips
1982	Seattle	Jack Patera	0- 2-0		
		Mike McCormack	4- 3-0	9- 7-0	Chuck Knox
1983	Houston	Ed Biles	0- 6-0		
		Chuck Studley	2- 8-0	3-13-0	Hugh Campbell
1984	Indianapolis	Frank Kush	4-11-0		
		Hal Hunter	0- 1-0	5-11-0	Rod Dowhower
1985	New Orleans	Bum Phillips	4- 8-0		
		Wade Phillips	1- 3-0	7- 9-0	Jim Mora
1985	Philadelphia	Marion Campbell	6- 9-0		
		Fred Bruney	1- 0-0	5-10-1	Buddy Ryan

REMAINDER OF SEASON (INTERIM COACH)

Significant improvement	1	(McCormack)
No significant change	5	

FOLLOWING SEASON (NEW COACH)

Significant improvement	1	(Knox)
Slight improvement	4	(Phillips, Campbell, Dowhower, Mora)
Decrease	1	(Ryan)

The only "interim" coach with a significantly improved record for more than one game was Mike McCormack, who simply came down from his spot as Director of Football Operations for the Seahawks to finish the shortened '82 season.

There's not enough evidence to prove anything. Our surmise is that the old coach is often replaced because the team is not playing up to its ability. An interim coach almost always comes from the staff, so he doesn't change the system. The players respond with some short-term enthusiasm and win a few games, but the record is still bad. The following season, you might expect some improvement because the team is healthier, wealthier, or wiser. And it probably doesn't matter who is the coach, as long as he's not a complete incompetent. A brand new coach from the outside may actually get poorer immediate results than a carryover because he changes the system the players are used to. But after a season or so, whether the coach is a genius or a dud, it comes back to the talent on hand.

GOOD LUCK, WAYNE

With only five games under his belt, there's no telling if Wayne Fontes is a genius or a dud or somewhere in between. He has some points in his favor. He's been assisting in the NFL for thirteen years, so he's paid his dues. He was the Lions' defensive coordinator, and the defense was the best part of the team. Upon being named head coach, he didn't suddenly decide he knew all about the offensive side; instead he brought in two good men, Lynn Dickey to coach the quarterbacks and Mouse Davis as an offensive assistant. And he did get the juices flowing among his troops for those five games.

It would be nice to see the Lions do well enough to stoke a little enthusiasm among Detroit fandom. At the beginning of the decade, the Lions were one of the best-supported franchises in the NFL.

YEAR	GM	ATTENDANCE	AVERAGE	RECORD
1979	8	520,589*	65,074	2-14-0
1980	8	621,353*	77,669	9 -7-0
1981	8	603,679	75,460	8 -8-0
1982	5	352,481	70,496	4- 5-0
1983	8	553,595	69,199	9 -7-0
1984	8	457,238	57,155	4-11-1
1985	8	504,613	63,077	7- 9-0
1986	8	432,429	54,054	5-11-0
1987	8	190,758	23,845	4-11-0
1988	8	296,607	37,076	4-12-0

* New Lions record

Eight short years ago this franchise drew over 600,000 with a .500 team. But five straight losing seasons, four with double-digit loss columns, have turned the fans off. The '87 figures are a little misleading because they include two strike games that were held *in camera*. But there's nothing misleading about the 1988 numbers—less than 50 percent capacity in the 80,638 seats at the Silver Dome.

They say it was confusing calling signals because the "huts" echoed back. The Dome was the only arena in the NFL where receivers could literally hear "footsteps."

Fontes can still win them back. No one expects a Super Bowl or even a division championship in '89. An 8-8 season would look like manna. But if all else fails, at least the Lions might try to be *interesting* losers.

Early last season, Darryl Rogers said, "If we were in a free-wheeling offense, it seems to me we'd make a lot of mistakes." But as it turned out, his biggest mistake was not being in a free-wheeling offense.

Owner William Clay Ford said it best: "We're boring and we're losing. I can't think of two worse adjectives to apply to the way we're playing."

THE TOOTHLESS LIONS

As things stand, only Androcles could love this team. But it's not truly hopeless. Fontes starts with a set of linebackers who can play with anyone. ROLB Mike Cofer had 12 sacks, and LOLB George Jamison is okay. ILB's Dennis Gibson and Chris Spielman are strong. Spielman got a lot of votes for Rookie of the Year. Another rookie, SS Bennie Blades, may develop into an outstanding defensive back. The defense desperately needs a horse up front, but it won't be Reggie Rogers. The number one draft pick in 1987 missed thirty days as a rookie for "personal and emotional counseling," then was charged with homicide last year for a drunk driving accident. On the wish list are a couple of defensive backs who can cover man-for-man. Still, a team could go 8–8 with the Lions' '88 defenders.

The kicking game is in good—uh—feet. Punter Jim Arnold made several All-Pro teams, and not just because he worked overtime. PK Ed Murray only missed one field goal try and one PAT all season. Ironically the PAT miss cost Fontes a chance for a third win.

It's when you look at the offense that the thought of a .500 season evaporates. It's hard to tell where to begin. Maybe by hoping that some of the '88 ineptitude was the fallout of Coach Rogers' conservative offense. That would hold more appeal if the Lions weren't generally considered the slowest team in football.

The line was supposed to be the one saving grace, but it became part of the problem. OTs Lomas Brown and Harvey Salem are still respected in spite of the chinks in the wall last season.

WR Pete Mandley would make a fine second receiver for some team. With the Lions he's number one. None of the receivers had an average gain worth reporting, and no tight end caught as many as twenty passes.

All that's bad enough, but it's when he turns to the backfield that Fontes may want to sit down and cry.

Garry James, the Lions' busiest runner, looked like a find as a rookie in 1986, when he ran for 688 yards. His average dropped a full yard to 3.3 per rush in '87. Last season it fell to 3.0, an amazing figure for someone who carried 182 times. One way to judge a runner's effectiveness is to count the games in which he ran at least eight times (twice a quarter) and finished with a rushing average over 4.1 (the league average). James had twelve games with eight or more attempts and was over the average only once. Veteran fullback James Jones wasn't much better, topping 4.1 once in six games of over eight carries. His season average was 3.3. Tony Paige had a 4.0 average, but carried only 52 times.

The team average for all runners was a horrid 3.2. Three-point-two is weak beer; the Lions' running game was far less intoxicating. Were the runners really that bad, or can the line be blamed for leaving holes unopened? At present the verdict seems to be it was a mutual accomplishment. James and Jones are reliable, if unspectacular, pass catchers.

A running game with some oomph would take some of the pressure off quarterback Chuck Long. The former Iowa All-America tore up a knee in the sixth game and made only a token appearance after that. But even before his injury he'd shown few signs of being the franchise quarterback the Lions thought they'd drafted in 1986. He came up lacking in leadership, passing, and ball handling. His tap-dancing was okay.

Nevertheless Chuck's chucking is the best shot for Detroit's improvement in '89. He's played only one full season as the Lions' starter and may thrive under a more open offense.

If Long continues to falter or hobble, Detroit may have to go to Rusty Hilger again. The Raiders reject was signed after the fifth game, when backup Eric Hipple went down. He'd barely learned the names of the coaches when Long was also hurt, and Rusty was thrust into the regular's role. He lived up to his nickname. Although he has a strong arm, he never solved his battle with accuracy. In his eleven games, he completed only about two of every five tosses.

If somehow Fontes can make a silk-purse-offense out of this porcine crew, he could lure some Detroiters back to those empty seats at the Silver Dome. Nobody likes to lose, but a worse sin is to be boring.

DETROIT LIONS STATISTICS

1988 TEAM STATISTICS	DL	OPP
TOTAL FIRST DOWNS	227	334
Rushing	64	128
Passing	141	179
Penalty	22	27
3rd Down Made/Att.	72/216	98/217
Pct.	33.3%	45.2%
4th Down Made/Att.	7/12	4/10
Pct.	58.3%	40.0%
TOTAL NET YARDS	3405	5316
Avg. per Game	212.8	332.3
Total Plays	920	1071
Avg. per Play	3.7	5.0
NET YARDS RUSHING	1243	2037
Avg. per Game	77.7	127.3
Total Rushes	391	511
NET YARDS PASSING	2162	3279
Avg. per Game	135.1	204.9
Tackled/Yards Lost	42/410	47/393
Gross Yards	2572	3672
Attempts/Completions	477/213	513/337
Pct. of Completions	44.7%	65.7%
Had Intercepted	18	15
PUNTS/AVERAGE	97/42.4	74/39.4
NET PUNTING AVG.	35.9	31.7
PENALTIES/YARDS	94/804	106/869
FUMBLES/BALL LOST	31/15	35/21
TOUCHDOWNS	23	34
Rushing	7	16
Passing	13	17
Returns	3	1
TIME OF POSSESSION	439:52	521:21

SCORE/PERIODS	1	2	3	4	OT	TOTAL
Lions	36	87	51	46	0	220
Opponents	34	93	78	105	3	313

SCORING	TDR	TDP	TDRt	PAT	FG	S	TP
Murray				22/23	20/21		82
James	5	2					42
Mandley	1	4					30
Chadwick		3					18
Jamison			2				12
Bland		2					12
Lewis		1					6

SCORING	TDR	TDP	TDRt	PAT	FG	S	TP
Lee		1					6
S. Williams	1						6
Mitchell							
Lions	7	13	3	2 2/23	20/21		220
Opp.	17	18	1	3 2/34	25/29	1	313

RUSHING	NO	YDS	AVG	LG	TD
James	182	552	3.0	35	5
Jones	96	314	3.3	13	0
Paige	52	207	4.0	20	0
Mandley	6	44	7.3	21t	1
Painter	17	42	2.5	13	0
Hilger	18	27	1.5	11	0
Long	7	22	3.1	11	0
S. Williams	9	22	2.4	5	1
Hipple	1	5	5.0	5	0
Woolfolk	1	4	4.0	4	0
Bland	1	4	4.0	4	0
Witkowski	1	0	0.0	0	0
Lions	391	1243	3.2	35	7
Opponents	511	2037	4.0	37	16

RECEIVING	NO	YDS	AVG	LG	TD
Mandley	44	617	14.0	56	4
James	39	382	9.8	39t	2
Jones	29	259	8.9	40	0
Lee	22	261	11.9	18	1
Bland	21	307	14.6	35	2
Chadwick	20	304	15.2	32	3
Carter	13	145	11.2	31	0
Paige	11	100	9.1	15	0
Starring	5	89	17.8	40	0
S. Williams	3	46	15.3	32	0
Lewis	3	32	10.7	23	1
Craig	2	29	14.5	18	0
Painter	1	1	1.0	1	0
Lions	213	2572	12.1	56	13
Opponents	337	3672	10.9	51t	17

INTERCEPTIONS	NO	YDS	AVG	LG	TD
Mitchell	3	107	35.7	90t	1
Jamison	3	56	18.7	52t	1

(Continued)

(Continued)

INTERCEPTIONS	NO	YDS	AVG	LG	TD
Griffin	2	31	15.5	31	0
Blades	2	12	6.0	7	0
Cherry	2	0	0.0	0	0
Holmes	1	32	32.0	32	0
Williams	1	5	5.0	5	0
McNorton	1	4	4.0	4	0
Lions	15	247	16.5	90t	2
Opponents	18	159	8.8	34	0

PUNTING	NO	YDS	AVG	TB	In 20	LG	Blk
Arnold	97	4110	42.4	4	22	69	0
Lions	97	4110	42.4	4	22	69	0
Opponents	74	2915	39.4	11	19	67	0

PUNT RETURNS	NO	FC	YDS	AVG	LG	TD
Mandley	37	7	287	7.8	25	0
Bland	5	1	59	11.8	24	0
Lions	42	8	346	8.2	25	0
Opponents	57	19	483	8.5	77t	1

KICKOFF RETURNS	NO	YDS	AVG	LG	TD
Lee	18	355	19.7	39	0
Painter	17	347	20.4	32	0
Bland	8	179	22.4	29	0
Starring	8	130	16.3	22	0
Woolfolk	4	99	24.8	46	0
Morris	2	41	20.5	25	0
Andolsek	1	3	3.0	3	0
Saleaumua	1	0	0.0	0	0
Lions	59	1154	19.6	46	0
Opponents	56	1076	19.2	41	0

FIELD GOALS	1-19	20-29	30-39	40-49	50+	TOTAL
Murray	1-1	8-8	9-9	2-2	0-1	20-21
Lions	1-1	8-8	9-9	2-2	0-1	20-21
Opponents	3-3	7-7	10-12	4-4	1-3	25-29

FIELD GOALS BY Murray: 20 of 21
(37G)(30G)( )(39G)(24G,34G)( )(32G)( )
(37G)(48G)(39G,52N,38G)(22G,37G,19G,
26G)( )(26G,23G,23G)(25G,44G)(27G)

PASSING	ATT	COM	YARD	PCT.	Avg G	TD	%TD	IN	%IN	LG	SAKS/YDS	RATE
Hilger	306	126	1558	41.2	5.09	7	2.3	12	3.9	56	31/251	49.1
Long	141	75	856	53.2	6.07	6	4.3	6	4.3	40	18/134	68.1
Hipple	27	12	158	44.4	5.85	0	0.0	0	0.0	31	3/25	63.5
Arnold	1	0	0	0.0	0.00	0	0.0	0	0.0	00	0/0	39.6
Witkowski	1	0	0	0.0	0.00	0	0.0	0	0.0	00	0/0	39.6
Jones	1	0	0	0.0	0.00	0	0.0	0	0.0	00	0/0	39.6
Lions	477	213	2572	44.7	5.39	13	2.7	18	3.8	56	52/410	55.0
Opponents	513	337	3672	65.7	7.16	17	3.3	15	2.9	51t	47/393	85.6

GREEN BAY PACKERS

The Last 5 Seasons

	1984	1985	1986	1987	1988
Won-Lost	8-8	8-8	4-12	5-9-1	4-12
Percentage	.500	.500	.250	.367	.250
Division Finish	2	2	4	3	4-t
Games Behind	2	7	10	5.5	8
Total Points	390	337	254	255	240
Per Game	24.4	21.1	15.9	17.0	15.0
Opponent Points	309	355	418	300	315
Per Game	19.3	22.2	26.1	20.0	19.7
Net Points	81	-18	-164	-45	-75
Predicted Net Wins	2.0	-0.4	-4.1	-1.1	-1.9
Delta Net Wins	-2.0	0.4	0.1	-0.9	-2.1
Total Yards on Offense	5449	5371	5061	4482	4664
Per Game	340.6	335.7	316.3	298.8	291.5
Total Yards Allowed on Defense	5291	5173	5015	4923	4843
Per Game	330.7	323.3	313.4	328.2	302.7
Net Difference	158	198	46	-441	-179
Offensive Turnovers	37	45	45	35	50
Defensive Takeaways	42	40	32	42	41
Net Turnovers	5	-5	-13	7	-9
Predicted Net Points	33	-4	-48	-9	-51
Delta Net Points	48	-14	-116	-36	-24
Net Rushing Yards	2019	2208	1614	1801	1379
Per Game	126.2	138.0	100.9	120.1	86.2
Average Gain	4.4	4.7	3.8	3.9	3.6
Opponent Net Rushing Yards	2145	2047	2095	1920	2110
Per Game	134.1	127.9	130.9	128.0	131.9
Average Gain	3.9	4.1	3.7	3.7	4.1
Net Passing Yards	3430	3163	3447	2681	3285
Per Game	214.4	197.7	215.4	178.7	205.3
Times Sacked	42	50	37	45	51
Passer Rating in Yards	4.3	3.8	4.0	4.1	3.7
Opponent Net Passing Yards	3146	3126	2920	3003	2733
Per Game	196.6	195.4	182.5	200.2	170.8
Times Sacked	44	48	28	34	30
Passer Rating Defense	3.5	4.8	4.9	4.6	3.9
Passer Rating Net	0.8	-1.0	-0.9	-0.5	-0.2
Yards per Drive Offense	25.7	25.5	25.7	22.1	23.0
Yards per Drive Defense	25.2	24.6	26.1	24.7	23.3
Average Time of Possession	26:48	28:59	28:11	29:02	29:16

THE 1988 SEASON

DATE	AT	OPPONENT	SCORE	R	SPREAD	Tu	Net YDS	Rush YDS	Pass YDS	TURN
09/04	H	L.A. Rams	7-34	L	+4	g	209-290	78-114	131-176	7-1
09/11	H	Tampa Bay	10-13	L	-6	g	240-266	59-148	181-118	2-2
09/18	A	Miami	17-24	L	+10	g	338-354	78- 98	260-256	0-3
09/25	H	Chicago	6-24	L	+6	g	233-358	34-242	199-116	3-3
10/02	A	Tampa Bay	24-27	L	+2.5	g	426-368	72- 85	354-283	3-5
10/09	H	New England	45- 3	W	+2.5	g	399-269	207- 76	192-193	0-5
10/16	A	Minnesota	34-14	W	+10	a	355-324	125- 67	230-257	2-5
10/23	H	Washington	17-20	L	+5	g	205-385	82-160	123-225	0-3
10/30	A	Buffalo	0-28	L	+7	a	131-261	77-195	54- 66	4-3
11/06	A	Atlanta	0-20	L	+3	g	284-341	101-164	183-177	7-3
11/13	H	Indianapolis	13-20	L	+4.5	g	297-247	98-136	199-111	4-1
11/20	H	Detroit	9-19	L	-4	g	356-270	52-156	304-114	3-1
11/27	H	Chicago	0-16	L	+13	g	189-372	22-213	167-159	2-2
12/04	A	Detroit	14-30	L	+3	a	360-220	92- 94	268-126	6-1
12/11	H	Minnesota	18- 6	W	+10.5	g	298-255	97- 44	201-211	4-2
12/18	A	Phoenix	26-17	W	+6	g	344-265	105-118	239-147	3-1
						Avg.	292-303	86-132	205-171	3-3

				WINS	LOSSES
Season Record:	4-12-0		POINTS:	31- 10	10- 23
Vs. Spread:	6-10-0		Net YDS:	8- 8-0 349-278	272-311
Home:	2- 6-0		Rush YDS:	3-13-0 134- 76	70-150
On Artificial Turf:	1- 2-0		Pass YDS:	10- 6-0 216-202	202-161
Art. Turf vs. Spread:	1- 2-0		TURN:	5- 8-3 2- 3	3- 2

THE GHOST OF GREEN BAY

The worst thing that ever happened to football in Green Bay was Vince Lombardi.

In 1958 the Packers were a hopeless 1–10–1 and hadn't had a winning season since Truman beat Dewey. The Pack was so bad that both sides were underdogs in intrasquad games. Had the publicly owned team followed its usual routine and hired another Good Joe as coach, it could have continued losing games as regularly as kindergarteners lose their mittens. After another five years of that, the only people in the stands at Lambeau Field would have been three pinochle players, a claustrophobe avoiding crowds, and a hermit. Then the good people of Green Bay could have sold their tattered franchise to Altoona or Des Moines and pocketed a nice profit. Maybe they could have used the money to build a swimming pool or put up a statue. By now, twenty-five years later, hardly anyone in Wisconsin would remember they once had a team in the NFL. (Do you remember the Staten Island Stapletons or the Pottsville Maroons? Yes, they were once NFL teams.)

But instead of hiring a Good Joe, Green Bay hired a Great Vince, who made all the right moves and had the Packers playing in the NFL Championship Game two years after he got there. When he stepped down after the '67 season, he'd given Green Bay five NFL crowns, two Super Bowls, and the nickname "Titletown, U.S.A."

He also condemned Packer fans to feeling like kids on December 26 forever after. And he made it hell for every Packer coach who came after him, for though they can be *successive*, they can never be *successful*. Not as long as the Ghost of Vince Lombardi haunts Lambeau Field rattling his Super Bowl trophies.

To put it bluntly, they haven't come close to matching Lombardi.

- *Phil Bengtson*, 1968–1970, 20–21–1, one winning season.
- *Dan Devine*, 1971–1974, 25–28–4, one winning season, Central Division Champion 1972, lost only playoff game.
- *Bart Starr*, 1975–1983, 53–77–3, two winning seasons, 1–1 in 1982 Super Bowl Tournament.
- *Forrest Gregg*, 1984–1987, 25–37–1, no winning seasons.
- *Lindy Infante*, 1988, 4–12–0 in first season.

How much trying to live up to the Ghost of Lombardi has hurt each of these is hard to say. Bengtson, a former Lombardi assistant and his hand-picked successor, could never get out of his shadow. Devine couldn't wait to get out of Green Bay after some of the locals expressed their comparisons with Lombardi in various vicious ways. Starr and Gregg were former Lombardi players, and so they were always compared with the master. Perhaps Infante, with no direct Lombardi connections in his past, may someday be judged on his own merits.

WHY THE GHOST WILL ALWAYS BE FIRST

No future Green Bay team—no *NFL* team—will ever again be as dominant as Lombardi's Packers were over an eight-year stretch. The Steelers of the seventies came closest but fell one championship and a few percentage points short. No team of the eighties will do it. And unless they

THE BEST EIGHT-YEAR PERIODS SINCE LOMBARDI'S

GREEN BAY

1960	8-5-0
1961	12-3-0*
1962	14-1-0*
1963	11-2-1
1964	8-5-1
1965	12-3-1*
1966	14-2-0*
1967	12-4-1*

91-25-4
.784

MIAMI		PITTSBURGH		RAIDERS		DALLAS	
1971	12-4-1	1972	12-4-0	1973	10-5-1	1976	11-4-0
1972	17-0-0*	1973	10-5-0	1974	13-3-0	1977	15-2-0*
1973	15-2-0*	1974	13-3-0*	1975	12-4-0	1978	14-5-0
1974	11-4-0	1975	15-2-0*	1976	16-1-0*	1979	11-6-0
1975	10-4-0	1976	11-5-0	1977	12-4-0	1980	14-5-0
1976	6-8-0	1977	9-6-0	1978	9-7-0	1981	13-5-0
1977	10-4-0	1978	17-2-0*	1979	9-7-0	1982	8-4-0
1978	11-6-0	1979	15-4-0*	1980	15-5-0*	1983	12-5-0

92-32-1	102-31-0	96-36-1	98-36-0
.742	.778	.727	.731

CHICAGO		WASHINGTON		SAN FRANCISCO	
1981	6-10-0	1981	8-8-0	1981	16-3-0*
1982	3-6-0	1982	12-1-0*	1982	3-6-0
1983	8-8-0	1983	16-3-0	1983	11-7-0
1984	11-7-0	1984	11-6-0	1984	18-1-0*
1985	18-1-0*	1985	10-6-0	1985	10-7-0
1986	14-3-0	1986	14-5-0	1986	10-6-0
1987	11-5-0	1987	14-4-0*	1987	13-3-0
1988	13-5-0	1988	7-9-0	1988	13-6-0*

84-45-0	92-42-0	94-39-0
.651	.687	.707

* Won league championship

change the rules you can bet against it happening right through the next century.

The problem isn't parity in and of itself. It's the number of games that must be played and the number of teams in the league.

Until the Super Bowl, Lombardi's Packers played fourteen-game schedules in 1961–62, then won NFL Championships with a single playoff each season. (There was an American Football League championship, but no one believed it was as important as the NFL's.) In '65 the Pack had to win a division playoff with Baltimore to get to the NFL title game, but still had only two games in which they were at risk of sudden elimination. In '66 with the Super Bowl, they still had only two playoff games, counting the Big I. In 1967 the NFL was split into four divisions, and the Packers won two playoff games to get to the Big II. Today's teams must get through sixteen games (with more chance for injury to key players) and then stay alive through three sudden-risk games. In other words, to match Lombardi's five championships in eight seasons, a team would have to win at least fifteen postseason games, whereas Vince's Pack did it in nine.

The other factor is that the modern twenty-eight-team NFL dilutes the draft. Lombardi inherited some high draft picks when there were only twelve teams in the NFL. With twelve teams each draft brought 3 of the top 36 college seniors in the first three rounds. Even by the twelfth round, they were in the top 144. Through most of his seasons, Lombardi was in a fourteen-team league. His first three picks came out of those believed to be the best 42 college seniors. If he drafted last on the twelfth round, he got the college senior ranked number 168 in the country. Of course the AFL was drafting at the same time, but if an NFL team really wanted a kid, they could outbid the other league.

Now there are twenty-eight teams. If you draft last on the third round, you get the player rated 84th. By the last round, the 336th. It makes it harder for a team to move to the top but even harder to stay there for long. A couple of poor drafts and a team loses its replacement continuity. In three or four years it falls apart. Drafting wasn't Lombardi's strongest point, but in the seasons *after* he played for his first NFL championship, he was able to draft TE Marv Fleming, OG Gale Gillingham, OC Ken Bowman, RB Donny Anderson, RB Jim Grabowski, RB Elijah Pitts, RB Travis Williams, DE Lionel Aldridge, DT Ron Kostelnik, LB Dave Robinson, DB Tom Brown, and DB Herb Adderley. Of these only Adderley is in the Hall of Fame, but they all became useful members of championship teams. It would take an unbelievable run of good luck for a modern team to draft the same amount of talent in only a few years.

We're not trying to make Lombardi's accomplishment seem any less wonderful. We're only trying to show why even he couldn't do it today.

UNLUCKY LINDY

Lindy Infante, the newest hopeful to try climbing Lombardi Mountain, earned his reputation as an offensive genius. He was quarterback-receivers coach for Forrest Gregg at Cincinnati, an indirect Lombardi connection. In 1981 he was given much of the credit for the powerful offense that took the Bengals to the Super Bowl. At Cleveland in 1986–87, as Marty Schottenheimer's offensive coordinator, he helped the Browns score 391 and 390 points.

Infante's forte has always been the passing game. His Browns teams were less than intimidating on the ground. His Packers were even less than that. RB Brent Fullwood had his second straight disappointing season since the Packers drafted him number one in '87. Bo Jackson's successor at Auburn, Fullwood hasn't rushed for as much in either of his seasons with Green Bay as Jackson has in his two half-seasons with the Raiders. In a postseason interview Infante blamed Fullwood's problems on injuries and his unfamiliarity with the new offensive system. "An octagonal peg in a round hole," Infante called him. Rookie Keith Woodside finished the season as the starter but gained only 195 yards on 83 carries for a miserable 2.3 average gain.

Ironically the Packers' strength in Infante's first year was the defense. Hank Bullough, the defensive coordinator, parlayed a terrific linebacker (Tim Harris), three other good linebackers, and a slow but effective secondary into a group that kept the Pack in most of its games.

With a little scoring Green Bay could have won two or three more times, which would have made Lindy's first year a roaring success. But Infante's new offensive scheme could muster only 15 points a game. Lindy described his way as a "multiple approach," a "reaction-type offense" and one that will "take . . . what the defense gives up. It's not one that tries to cram a square peg in a round hole." Hoping for more variety in his pass patterns than his imagery, Infante started the season with Randy Wright at QB and concluded with Don Majkowski. Only Wright had anything in common with former Infante protégé Bernie Kosar: they both finished the season injured.

WK	OPPONENT	SCORE	ATT	CO	YDS	TD	IN	RATE*	QB
1	L.A. Rams	7-34	24	11	130	0	1	3.54	Wright
			10	5	49	1	1	1.40	Majkowski relieved
2	Tampa B.	10-13	27	22	181	1	0	7.07	Wright
3	Miami	17-24	23	18	184	0	0	8.00	Wright
			19	11	105	0	0	5.53	Majkowski relieved
4	Chicago	6-24	41	19	242	0	2	3.71	Wright
5	Tampa B.	24-27	51	28	321	1	2	4.53	Wright
			1	1	56	0	0	—	Majkowski relieved
6	New Eng.	45- 3	26	18	210	1	0	8.46	Majkowski
7	Minn.	34-14	32	19	243	0	1	6.19	Majkowski
8	Wash.	17-20	25	8	134	2	0	6.16	Majkowski
9	Buffalo	0-28	29	11	93	0	1	1.66	Majkowski
10	Atlanta	0-20	32	14	162	0	2	2.25	Majkowski
			6	3	24	0	2	—	Wright relieved
11	Ind.	13-20	41	24	216	1	0	5.51	Majkowski
12	Detroit	9-19	44	30	327	1	0	7.66	Majkowski
13	Chicago	0-16	30	14	184	0	2	3.13	Majkowski
14	Detroit	14-30	52	29	284	2	3	3.25	Wright
15	Minn.	18- 6	20	11	124	0	2	1.70	Wright
			10	5	85	1	1	5.00	Majkowski relieved
16	Phoenix	26-17	36	18	255	2	2	5.14	Majkowski
Majkowski			336	178	2119	9	11	5.10	2-5-5†
Wright			244	141	1490	4	13	3.87	2-5-0†

* NEWS Rate = YDS + (10 X TD) - (45 X IN) / Att
† W-L-T indicates superior, inferior, and average performances
(W = NEWS of 6.48 or more, L = NEWS of 5.10 or less, T = NEWS from 5.11 to 6.47)

If Lindy can settle on one quarterback (and keep him healthy), it might answer a lot of questions both for and about Infante and his offense. One nagging question from his first year is how could a team—any team—beat the Vikings twice yet lose a pair each to the Lions and Buccaneers?

GREEN BAY PACKERS STATISTICS

1988 TEAM STATISTICS	GB	OPP
TOTAL FIRST DOWNS	280	281
Rushing	77	130
Passing	176	136
Penalty	27	15
3rd Down Made/Att.	77/215	76/215
Pct.	35.8%	35.3%
4th Down Made/Att.	7/14	8/16
Pct.	50.0%	50.0%
TOTAL NET YARDS	4664	4843
Avg. per Game	291.5	302.7
Total Plays	1018	1018
Avg. per Play	4.6	4.8
NET YARDS RUSHING	1379	2110
Avg. per Game	86.2	131.9
Total Rushes	385	514
NET YARDS PASSING	3285	2733
Avg. per Game	205.3	170.8
Tackled/Yards Lost	51/324	30/216
Gross Yards	3609	2949
Attempts/Completions	582/319	474/256
Pct. of Completions	54.8%	54.0%
Had Intercepted	24	20
PUNTS/AVERAGE	86/38.2	76/37.6
NET PUNTING AVG.	31.8	33.6
PENALTIES/YARDS	94/785	112/903
FUMBLES/BALL LOST	44/26	33/21
TOUCHDOWNS	29	34
Rushing	14	17
Passing	13	12
Returns	2	5
TIME OF POSSESSION	—	—

SCORE/PERIODS	1	2	3	4	OT	TOTAL
Packers	58	58	47	77	0	240
Opponents	78	131	38	68	0	315

SCORING	TDR	TDP	TDRt	PAT	FG	S	TP
Fullwood	7	1					48
Zendejas				17/19	9/6		44
Woodside	3	2					30
West		3					18
Matthews		2					12
Wright	2						12
Harris			1			2	10
Dawson				1/2	3/5		10
D.Dorsey				3/4	1/3		6
Davis	1						6
Didier		1					6
Hackett		1					6
Scott		1					6
Majkowski	1						6
Mason		1					6
Pitts			1				6
Sharpe		1					6
Burrow				2/4	0/1		2
Packers	14	13	2	23/29	13/25	2	240
Opponents	17	12	5	34/34	25/35	1	315

RUSHING	NO	YDS	AVG	LG	TD
Fullwood	101	483	4.8	33t	7
Majkowski	47	225	4.8	24	1
Woodside	83	195	2.3	10	3
Mason	48	194	4.0	17	0
Davis	39	121	3.1	27	1
Carruth	49	114	2.3	14	0
Wright	8	43	5.4	19	2
Matthews	3	3	1.0	4	0
Collins	2	2	1.0	2	0
Stanley	1	1	1.0	1	0
Sharpe	4	-2	-0.5	5	0
Packers	385	1379	3.6	33t	14
Opponents	514	2110	4.1	80t	17

RECEIVING	NO	YDS	AVG	LG	TD
Sharpe	55	791	14.4	51	1
Kemp	48	620	12.9	36	0
Woodside	39	352	9.0	49t	2
West	30	276	9.2	35	3
Stanley	28	436	15.6	56	0
Carruth	24	211	8.8	31	0
Scott	20	275	13.8	41	1
Fullwood	20	128	6.4	30t	1
Matthews	15	167	11.1	25	2
Epps	11	99	9.0	25	0
Davis	11	81	7.4	11	0
Mason	8	84	10.5	39	1
Didier	5	37	7.4	15	1
Bolton	2	33	16.5	18	0
Collins	2	17	8.5	9	0
Hackett	1	2	2.0	2t	1
Packers	319	3609	11.3	56	13
Opponents	256	2949	11.5	46t	12

INTERCEPTIONS	NO	YDS	AVG	LG	TD
Murphy	5	19	3.8	9	0
Cecil	4	56	14.0	33	0
Lee	3	37	12.3	27	0
Stills	3	29	9.7	17	0
D. Brown	3	27	9.0	15	0
Pitts	2	56	28.0	31	0
Packers	20	224	11.2	33	0
Opponents	24	386	16.1	90t	4

PUNTING	NO	YDS	AVG	TB	In 20	LG	Blk
Bracken	85	3287	38.7	12	20	62	1
Packers	86	2387	38.2	12	20	62	1
Opponents	76	2859	37.6	5	22	69	1

PUNT RETURNS	NO	FC	YDS	AVG	LG	TD
Pitts	9	6	93	10.3	63t	1
Sharpe	9	7	48	5.3	14	0
Stanley	12	3	52	4.3	15	0
Jefferson	5	2	15	3.0	9	0
Packers	35	18	208	5.9	63t	1
Opponents	39	14	314	8.1	46	0

KICKOFF RETURNS	NO	YDS	AVG	LG	TD
Jefferson	4	116	29.0	46	0
Fullwood	21	421	20.0	31	0
Stanley	2	39	19.5	22	0
Woodside	19	343	18.1	29	0
Scott	12	207	17.3	27	0
Pitts	1	17	17.0	17	0
Sharpe	1	17	17.0	17	0
Hackett	1	9	9.0	9	0
Winter	1	7	7.0	7	0
Stills	1	4	4.0	4	0
Hill	1	1	1.0	1	0
Packers	64	1181	18.5	46	0
Opponents	49	966	19.7	37	0

FIELD GOALS	1-19	20-29	30-39	40-49	50+	TOTAL
Zendejas	0-0	2-3	4-5	2-6	1-2	9-16
D.Dorsey P	0-0	4-4	1-2	0-4	0-0	5-10
Dawson GB	0-0	2-2	1-2	0-1	0-0	3-5
Dawson Ph	0-0	2-3	1-2	0-1	0-0	3-6
D.Dorsey GB	0-0	1-1	0-0	0-2	0-0	1-3
Burrow	0-0	0-0	0-0	0-1	0-0	0-1
Packers	0-0	5-6	5-7	2-10	1-2	13-25
Opponents	tk	tk	tk	tk	tk	tk

FIELD GOALS BY:
Zendejas: ( )(50G,48N,52N)(36G)( )
(44G,32N,43N)(25G,43N)(37G,22G,36G,45G)
(34G,46N,24N)
Dawson: ( )(45N)(22G,20G)(32G,36N)
D.Dorsey: (48N,43N)( )(20G)
Burrow: (49N)

PASSING	ATT	COM	YARD	PCT.	Avg G	TD	%TD	IN	%IN	LG	SAKS/YDS	RATE
Wright	244	141	1490	57.8	6.11	4	1.6	13	5.3	51	20/148	58.9
Majkowski	336	178	2119	53.0	6.31	9	2.7	11	3.3	56	31/176	67.8
Packers	582	319	3609	54.8	6.20	13	2.2	24	4.1	56	51/324	63.9
Opponents	474	256	2949	54.0	6.22	12	2.5	20	4.2	46t	30/216	63.9

LOS ANGELES RAMS

The Last 5 Seasons

	1984	1985	1986	1987	1988
Won-Lost	10-6	11-5	10-6	6-9	10-6
Percentage	.625	.688	.625	.400	.625
Division Finish	2	1	2	3	1-t
Games Behind	5	0	0.5	7	0
Total Points	346	340	309	317	407
Per Game	21.6	21.3	19.3	21.1	25.4
Opponent Points	316	277	267	361	293
Per Game	19.8	17.3	16.7	24.1	18.3
Net Points	30	63	42	-44	114
Predicted Net Wins	0.8	1.6	1.0	-1.1	2.8
Delta Net Wins	1.3	1.4	1.0	-0.4	-0.8
Total Yards on Offense	5006	4520	4653	4651	5808
Per Game	312.9	282.5	290.8	310.1	363.0
Total Yards Allowed on Defense	5266	4648	4871	5121	4986
Per Game	329.1	290.5	304.4	341.4	311.6
Net Difference	-260	-128	-218	-470	822
Offensive Turnovers	35	35	37	33	34
Defensive Takeaways	39	46	43	27	37
Net Turnovers	4	11	6	-6	3
Predicted Net Points	-6	33	6	-63	81
Delta Net Points	36	30	36	19	33
Net Rushing Yards	2864	2057	2457	2097	2003
Per Game	179.0	128.6	153.6	139.8	125.2
Average Gain	5.3	4.1	4.3	4.1	4.0
Opponent Net Rushing Yards	1600	1586	1681	1732	1686
Per Game	100.0	99.1	105.1	115.5	105.4
Average Gain	3.6	3.6	3.7	4.1	4.1
Net Passing Yards	2142	2463	2196	2554	3805
Per Game	133.9	153.9	137.3	170.3	237.8
Times Sacked	32	57	27	25	28
Passer Rating in Yards	3.9	4.3	3.9	4.3	6.0
Opponent Net Passing Yards	3666	3062	3190	3389	3300
Per Game	229.1	191.4	199.4	225.9	206.3
Times Sacked	43	56	39	38	56
Passer Rating Defense	5.1	3.2	3.6	5.5	4.0
Passer Rating Net	-1.1	1.1	0.3	-1.2	2.1
Yards per Drive Offense	25.8	21.5	21.8	24.2	28.5
Yards per Drive Defense	26.5	22.3	23.0	27.7	24.1
Average Time of Possession	28:22	29:51	29:41	29:59	31:08

1984 PLAYOFFS
Lost Wild Card Game to N.Y. Giants, 13-16

1985 PLAYOFFS
Won Divisional Playoff from Dallas, 20-0
Lost NFC Championship Game to Chicago, 0-24

1986 PLAYOFFS
Lost Wild Card Game to Washington, 7-19

1988 PLAYOFFS
Lost Wild Card Game to Minnesota, 17-28

THE 1988 SEASON

DATE	AT	OPPONENT	SCORE	R	SPREAD	Tu	Net YDS	Rush YDS	Pass YDS	TURN
09/04	A	Green Bay	34- 7	W	-4	g	290-209	114- 78	176-131	1-7
09/11	H	Detroit	17-10	W	-10	g	315-198	191- 76	124-122	2-3
09/18	A	L.A. Raiders	22-17	W	-1	g	313-408	140-103	173-305	1-1
09/25	A	N.Y. Giants	45-31	W	+3.5	a	369-363	137- 79	232-284	1-3
10/02	H	Phoenix	27-41	L	-7.5	g	353-519	85-187	268-332	3-1
10/09	A	Atlanta	33- 0	W	-6.5	g	501-150	252- 73	249- 77	1-2
10/16	H	S. Francisco	21-24	L	+0	g	237-429	42-245	195-184	4-2
10/23	H	Seattle	31-10	W	-4.5	g	465-296	154-153	311-143	3-5
10/30	A	New Orleans	12-10	W	+2	g	332-242	96- 33	236-209	0-2
11/06	A	Philadelphia	24-30	L	-1.5	a	427-436	69-123	358-313	5-0
11/13	H	New Orleans	10-14	L	-3.5	g	256-337	60- 88	196-249	2-3
11/20	H	San Diego	24-38	L	-11	g	363-297	151-101	212-196	2-1
11/27	A	Denver	24-35	L	+0	g	484-368	132- 98	352-270	3-1
12/05	H*	Chicago	23- 3	W	-3	g	364-213	132-114	232- 99	3-3
12/11	H	Atlanta	22- 7	W	-7.5	g	418-193	127- 65	291-128	2-2
12/18	A	S. Francisco	38-16	W	+6	g	322-316	121- 70	201-246	1-1
						Avg.	363-311	125-105	238-206	2-2

			WINS	LOSSES
Season Record:	10- 6-0	POINTS:	28- 11	22- 30
Vs. Spread:	9- 7-0	Net YDS: 11- 5-0	369-259	353-398
Home:	4- 4-0	Rush YDS: 12- 4-0	146- 84	90-140
On Artificial Turf:	2- 1-0	Pass YDS: 11- 5-0	223-174	264-257
Art. Turf vs. Spread:	2- 1-0	TURN: 7- 5-4	2- 3	3- 1

* Monday Night

THE TRADE

The best part of the three-way Halloween trade the Rams pulled off in 1987 was that they got rid of Eric Dickerson.

Now whoa there, hoss, you say. Granted L.A. got enough first- and second-round draft choices to stock an expansion team—three firsts and three seconds in '88 and '89—but what about a bird in the hand? Draft choices, no matter how high, are gambles. Even if all six become productive players—a very iffy proposition—it's unlikely that any of them will match the accomplishments past, present, and future of Dickerson. Eric the Dread is a certain Hall of Famer, a perennial rushing leader, and one of only a handful of impact running backs in the NFL. How can losing him be the *best* part of the deal for the team with whirlpools on their helmets?

Okay, hear us out. We are second only to Dickerson him-

self in our admiration for the erstwhile Ram rusher. We certainly don't mean to imply that his presence on the Colts detracts in the slightest from Indianapolis' ability to win football games. He has thus far proved a worthwhile investment for the Irsays and is likely to continue to be so. It's not Eric's talent that the Rams are better off without. It's Eric.

Dickerson and Coach John Robinson both arrived at Ramsville in 1983. They made a beautiful couple. Here was the coach who'd cranked out All-American tailbacks at USC like Oscar Mayer cranks out wieners, and the rangy runner, who produced 100-yard games like French's produces mustard. Hot dog! The rushing game was delicious. But the Rams' quarterbacks were mostly onions, and Robinson's crew passed like gallstones. Although the Rams won more often than they lost, they regularly finished behind San Francisco and couldn't get past the playoffs. They needed a signal caller they could relish.

YEAR	RECORD	FIN	PLAYOFF	P/Gm RUSH	P/Gm PASS	REGULAR QUARTERBACK
1983	9-7	2	1-1	140.8	201.3	Vince Ferragamo
1984	10-6	2	0-1	179.0	133.9	Jeff Kemp
1985	11-5	1	1-1	128.6	153.9	Dieter Brock
1986	10-6	2	0-1	153.6	137.3	Steve Bartkowski-Steve Dils-Jim Everett

At the top of the 1987 season, Robinson and the Rams decided that their hope for the future lay in the strong right arm of Jim Everett, the 6'5" slinger L.A. had obtained from Houston for two players, two first-round draft choices, and a fifth-rounder midway through the '86 season. Everett hadn't wowed the critics in his rookie half-year but considering the price paid, the Rams had made their bed. The signal that Everett was to be the featured performer in the entourage came when L.A. imported quarterback guru Ernie Zampese as offensive coordinator. Zampese came from San Diego, where he'd coordinated Air Coryell.

That left the Rams with two minds. Pulling in one direction was the tried-and-true—Dickerson and tons of ground yards. In the other direction was the untried-and-who-knew? Everett and the air. The strike in '87 muddied the evidence, but in the three nonstrike games before Dickerson was traded, the Rams gave every indication that they were a team moving in two directions at once and getting nowhere.

RECORD	RUSH Per/Game				PASS Per/Game				P/Gm
	ATT	YARDS	AVG	TD	ATT	YARDS	AVG	TD	TURN
0-3	29.6	123.3	4.2	1.0	33.6	137.3	4.1	0.0	3.3

Everett was at sea. His three-game passing marks didn't pass: 45 of 101 for 412 yards, no touchdowns, and 6 interceptions. His NFL rating was 33.3 and his NEWS 1.41. Dickerson had 277 of the Rams' rushing yards, even though he carried only seven times in L.A.'s first game back from the strike. But the Rams had to consider that Eric might have only a few more top rushing years. The best guesstimate said upright runners like Dickerson tended to slip at year eight. Upright Eric was in season five. On the other hand, Everett—with luck—could be the Rams' QB for the next decade. Robinson and Zampese had faith that he'd develop.

Also in the Rams' thinking were the draft choices they'd passed on to Houston. The Rams were aging. Replacements were a prime consideration. Cinching the decision was Dickerson's demand to be traded if the Rams refused to renegotiate his $682,000 contract. (*Demand* doesn't quite do justice to "Hey, let me go. Release me. Waive me. Please, release me. . . . If I had a dog that I couldn't stand or bit me, I'd shoot him. I'd kill him or I'd just get rid of him. I mean, get rid of me. I'd gladly leave.")

So L.A. had a talented, expensive disruption who no longer fit into their future. Unless they ushered him out of town or paid him more than he was worth to them, he'd continue to plead his case to the media. Worse, the offensive philosophy would remain split. How could the players accept a pass-oriented attack with a faltering quarterback and the best runner in football sharing the same backfield? As long as Dickerson was around, Everett was unlikely to develop the confidence or leadership Robinson and Zampese swore he had in him somewhere. The 1987 season looked lost anyway. The Rams were 1–5, counting the strike games. But the Dickerson-Everett dichotomy would affect the team as long as they were both in Rams' blue-and-gold.

And *that's* why we say the best part of the deal for the Rams was getting rid of Dickerson.

Under the circumstances L.A. should have considered themselves lucky to trade Dickerson for a 1962 Sam Huff bubble gum card. Indianapolis and Buffalo had needs too. Whether they realized just how much the Rams needed to shed Dickerson mattered little. The deal was swung.

Once out of the shadow of Dickerson, Everett came on strong. The improvement in the Rams' offense was matched by the improvement in their won-lost record.

RECORD	RUSH Per/Game				PASS Per/Game				P/Gm
	ATT	YARDS	AVG	TD	ATT	YARDS	AVG	TD	TURN
5-4	36.3	144.1	4.0	1.2	26.8	189.1	7.1	1.2	1.7

But Everett's marks showed an even greater jump. His rating in the NFL system for the remainder of the season was 104.6. He finished at an ordinary-looking 68.4, but that was 35 points better than his rate before Dickerson was dealt. Everett's NEWS rate showed a similar gain: 8.21 for the season, but 11.40 post-Dickerson.

The only sour note for the Rams in the post-trade games of 1987 was that Everett suffered a broken leg in the next-to-last game. Aha! Eric never broke his leg, you say. There's no pleasing some people.

Okay, Everett was arguably the best passer in the NFC in 1988, and unarguably the best who started all his team's games. So there!

OTHER HUMONGOUS TRADES

It was not the biggest trade in NFL history, nor even the biggest involving the Rams. Officially it ranks fifth in league history.

The largest trade *not* involving the Rams was a fifteen-player swap between Cleveland and Baltimore in 1953. That one is chiefly remembered for sending the Browns future Hall of Fame OT Mike McCormack and All-Pro DT Don Colo. The Colts received ten players, including a couple of eventual All-Pros in DB Bert Rechichar and OG Art Spinney. Their best-known acquisition was another DB named Don Shula.

No draft choices were involved, though both teams were essentially dealing young players. McCormack and Colo were important members of two Browns championship teams, and Rechichar and Spinney were important to two later Colts' champs. In effect both teams came out winners.

Washington and the Rams made a fifteen-player deal in 1971. The Redskins received aging LBs Jack Pardee and Myron Pottios, DT Diron Talbert, and OG John Wilber. A year later Washington's "Over-the-Hill-Gang" reached the Super Bowl. The Rams got only one player but gained seven draft choices and won seven straight division titles, from 1973 through 1979. Washington was the short-term winner, and Los Angeles the winner in the long run.

The Rams' first huge deal was in 1952, when they gave the Dallas Texans ten players—none of whom stayed around long—for the rights to University of California LB Les Richter, who became one of the top defensive players of the 1950s.

Perhaps encouraged by their one-sided win in the Richter trade, the Rams made a similar deal in 1959 to get Hall of Fame RB Ollie Matson from the then-Chicago Cardinals. L.A. sent the Cards nine players, including a draft choice. The Cards, perennial losers, upgraded their offensive and defensive lines for several seasons. Matson had one good year for the Rams, but was no longer the great player that L.A. had bargained for.

If there was a lesson in all this, it was: Only trade a lot of players (or draft choices) for a lot of players or one untested great player. Avoid giving up *beaucoup* players (or draft choices) for one great star with mileage on him.

So, in 1987, the Colts got one great star with mileage on him. The Bills received an untested great player in LB Cornelius Bennett, whom the Colts had been unable to sign. And the Rams got RB Greg Bell from the Bills, along with their first-round draft choice in 1988 and their first- and second-round choices in 1989, *and* RB Owen Gill from the Colts, along with their first- and second-round '88 choices and their first-round choice in '89.

Instant analysis at the time said the Colts won the battle, the Rams won the war, and the Bills were a casualty. The nice thing about instant analysis is that everyone's so excited about what's happening at the time that they almost never remember what was said about it.

WHO WON?

With a season-and-a-half in the till, it's too soon to ring out the register.

Up till now, the Colts got nearly what they wanted—into the playoffs in '87 and a near-miss for a Wild Card in '88. A playoff berth in '89 would be nice. A Super Bowl berth even better. What they lost won't show up—figuratively and literally—until a couple of seasons hence. If Dickerson is still going strong in 1992, they'll have no reason to complain.

Bennett was expected to be good, but he turned out even better. Only Lawrence Taylor ranks ahead of him as an outside linebacker. The three draft choices they gave up would have to go some to match his impact. Right now, the Bills are getting votes as the biggest winner in The Trade, if only because their '88 team went farther than either the Colts or Rams.

What the evaluaters are not figuring into the equation is that the Rams were ahead as soon as Dickerson left town, for great as he is, he was hurting the team. Anything after his farewell party was gravy.

Owen Gill disappeared from the Ram roster after one game. Greg Bell was a pleasant—nay, smashing—surprise. He had a history of injuries with the Bills and was supposedly infected with apathy. He rushed only 8 times for 26 yards after coming to the Rams in '87. Last year he suddenly found himself and gained only 407 fewer yards than did Dickerson with the Colts, which placed him third in the NFC. Although he gained three-quarters of the yardage, we still think of him as only half the back that Dickerson is (which is still mighty good). If he avoids the problems he had in Buffalo, he might get up to two-thirds.

The Rams' real profit will come from the draft choices. The progress report on the 1988 picks:

RB Gaston Green, the first-rounder from Buffalo, didn't see much action, running third behind Bell and Charles White. He was pretty ordinary on kickoff returns. Still considered a potential game breaker, he was oft-injured at UCLA. The rumor mill grinds him as trade bait.

WR Aaron Cox, the first-round choice from Indianapolis, ended the season as a starter. Although he finished fifth on the Rams in catches, he had an exciting 21.1 yards-per-catch average and 5 touchdowns. He's about the same size as Henry Ellard, and the Rams hope lightning will strike twice.

LB Fred Strickland, the second-round pick from Indianapolis, was a semiregular by season's end. He seems like a natural, strong against the run and sufficiently quick against the pass. He was named to several all-rookie teams.

Advantage: Los Angeles.

LINER NOTES

The Rams were sixth in preventing sacks in 1988 and first in getting them, which would seem to speak well for their offensive and defensive lines. Don't believe everything you hear.

On the offense, LT Irv Pankey is thirty-one, with bad knees and a weight problem. C Doug Smith is thirty-three. He's good, but probably overrated as a Pro Bowl alternate. RT Jackie Slater has been a great tackle for years. And years. And years. He's thirty-five. Replacements are much needed for the '90s.

As for the defense, most of the sacks came from the linebacking corps. Kevin Greene had 16.5 to lead the team. Gary Jeter, essentially a sub in passing situations, had 11.5, but he's thirty-four. The starting front threesome is determined but light (in the NFL sense, where "light" is a guy you wouldn't let sit on a good chair). To learn what happens to a light defensive line when it goes up against a good, big offensive line, the Rams could send a query to Denver. Or they could look at game films of their playoff game with the Vikings.

LOS ANGELES RAMS STATISTICS

1988 TEAM STATISTICS	LAR	OPP
TOTAL FIRST DOWNS	333	289
Rushing	114	100
Passing	203	166
Penalty	16	23
3rd Down Made/Att.	83/209	77/226
Pct.	39.8%	34.1%
4th Down Made/Att.	4/8	11/16
Pct.	50.0%	68.8%
TOTAL NET YARDS	5808	4986
Avg. per Game	363.0	311.6
Total Plays	1057	1041
Avg. per Play	5.5	4.8
NET YARDS RUSHING	2003	1686
Avg. per Game	125.2	105.4
Total Rushes	507	414
NET YARDS PASSING	3805	3300
Avg. per Game	237.8	206.3
Tackled/Yards Lost	28/197	56/394
Gross Yards	4002	3694
Attempts/Completions	522/312	571/307
Pct. of Completions	59.8%	53.8%
Had Intercepted	18	22
PUNTS/AVERAGE	76/39.5	93/39.9
NET PUNTING AVG.	34.2	33.9
PENALTIES/YARDS	78/587	111/937
FUMBLES/BALL LOST	28/16	36/15
TOUCHDOWNS	48	35
Rushing	16	12
Passing	31	17
Returns	1	6
TIME OF POSSESSION	31:09	28:51

SCORE/PERIODS	1	2	3	4	OT	TOTAL
Rams	81	146	92	88	0	407
Opponents	37	94	76	86	0	293

SCORING	TDR	TDP	TDRt	PAT	FG	S	TP
Lansford				45/48	24/32		117
Bell	16						108
Ellard		10					60
D. Johnson		6					36
A. Cox		5					30
Holohan		3					18
McGee		3					18
Delpino		2					12
Gray			1				6
Greene						1	2

(Continued)

SCORING	TDR	TDP	TDRt	PAT	FG	S	TP
Rams	16	31	1	45/48	24/32	1	407
Opponents	12	17	6	35/35	16/23	0	293

RUSHING	NO	YDS	AVG	LG	TD
Bell	288	1212	4.2	44	16
White	88	323	3.7	13	0
Delpino	34	147	4.3	13	0
Green	35	117	3.3	13	0
Everett	34	105	3.1	19	0
McGee	22	69	3.1	12	0
Brown	3	24	8.0	13	0
Ellard	1	7	7.0	7	0
Guman	1	1	1.0	1	0
Herrmann	1	-1	-1.0	-1	0
Rams	507	2003	3.9	44	16
Opponents	414	1686	4.1	46t	12

RECEIVING	NO	YDS	AVG	LG	TD
Ellard	86	1414	16.4	68	10
Holohan	59	656	11.1	29	3
D. Johnson	42	350	8.3	23	6
Delpino	30	312	10.4	38	2
Cox	28	590	21.1	69t	5
Bell	24	124	5.2	20	2
McGee	16	117	7.3	16	3
Anderson	11	319	29.0	56	0
Green	6	57	9.5	19	0
White	6	36	6.0	18	0
Young	2	27	13.5	18	0
Brown	2	16	8.0	10	0
Rams	312	4002	12.8	69t	31
Opponents	307	3694	12.0	59	17

INTERCEPTIONS	NO	YDS	AVG	LG	TD
J. Johnson	4	18	4.5	11	0
Gray	3	83	27.7	47t	1
Irvin	3	25	8.3	22	0
Stewart	2	61	30.5	43	0
Newman	2	27	13.5	27	0
Kelm	2	15	7.5	9	0
Meisner	1	20	20.0	20	0
Owens	1	11	11.0	11	0
Greene	1	10	10.0	10	0
J. Washington	1	7	7.0	7	0
Sutton	1	1	1.0	1	0
Jerue	1	0	0.0	0	0

(Continued)

(Continued)

INTERCEPTIONS	NO	YDS	AVG	LG	TD
Newsome	0	3	—	3	0
Rams	22	281	12.8	47t	1
Opponents	18	138	7.7	34	1

PUNTING	NO	YDS	AVG	TB	In 20	LG	Blk
Hatcher	36	1424	39.6	1	13	54	0
Camarillo	40	1579	39.5	2	11	57	0
Rams	76	3003	39.5	3	24	57	0
Opponents	93	3714	39.9	12	21	61	1

PUNT RETURNS	NO	FC	YDS	AVG	LG	TD
Hicks	25	0	144	5.8	13	0
Ellard	17	3	119	7.0	34	0
Sutton	3	6	52	17.3	46	0
Irvin	1	1	2	2.0	2	0
J. Johnson	2	1	4	2.0	4	0
Gray	1	0	1	1.0	1	0
Rams	49	11	322	6.6	46	0
Opponents	43	21	347	8.1	30	0

KICKOFF RETURNS	NO	YDS	AVG	LG	TD
Delpino	14	333	23.8	38	0
Brown	19	401	21.1	73	0
Green	17	345	20.3	44	0
Sutton	2	41	20.5	25	0
White	2	38	18.5	23	0
McDonald	3	34	11.3	22	0
McGee	1	0	0.0	0	0
Stewart	1	1	0.0	0	0
Rams	59	1191	20.2	73	0
Opponents	81	1563	19.3	93t	0

FIELD GOALS	1-19	20-29	30-39	40-49	50+	TOTAL
Lansford	1-1	9-12	8-10	6-8	0-1	24-32
Rams	1-1	9-12	8-10	6-8	0-1	24-32
Opponents	0-0	3-3	7-10	4-7	2-3	16-23

FIELD GOALS BY Lansford: 24 of 32
(52N,33G,29G)(46G)(37G,46G)(31N,41G)
(25N)(40G,25G)( )(39G,43N)(37G,27N,18G,
47G,30G)(22G,44N)(23G)(20G)(25G,27G,22G)
(35G,36G,32G)(49G)

PASSING	ATT	COM	YARD	PCT.	Avg G	TD	%TD	IN	%IN	LG	SAKS/YDS	RATE
Everett	517	308	3964	59.6	7.66	31	6.0	18	3.5	69t	28/197	89.2
Herrmann	5	4	38	80.0	7.60	0	0.0	0	0.0	15	0/0	98.4
Rams	522	312	4002	59.8	7.66	31	5.9	18	3.4	69t	28/197	89.3
Opponents	571	307	3694	53.8	6.47	17	3.0	22	3.9	59	56/394	67.7

MINNESOTA VIKINGS

The Last 5 Seasons

	1984	1985	1986	1987	1988
Won-Lost	3-13	7-9	9-7	8-7	11-5
Percentage	.188	.438	.563	.533	.688
Division Finish	5	3-t	2	2	2
Games Behind	7	8	5	3	1
Total Points	276	346	398	336	406
Per Game	17.3	21.6	24.9	22.4	25.4
Opponent Points	484	359	273	335	233
Per Game	30.3	22.4	17.1	22.3	14.6
Net Points	-208	-13	125	1	173
Predicted Net Wins	-5.2	-0.3	3.1	0.0	4.3
Delta Net Wins	0.2	-0.7	-2.1	0.5	-1.3
Total Yards on Offense	4716	5151	5651	4809	5595
Per Game	294.8	321.9	353.2	320.6	349.7
Total Yards Allowed on Defense	6352	5464	5012	4824	4091
Per Game	397.0	341.5	313.3	321.6	255.7
Net Difference	1636	-313	639	-15	1504
Offensive Turnovers	41	47	29	33	30
Defensive Takeaways	29	44	42	37	53
Net Turnovers	-12	-3	13	4	23
Predicted Net Points	-184	-38	105	15	217
Delta Net Points	-24	25	20	-14	-44
Net Rushing Yards	1844	1516	1738	1983	1806
Per Game	115.3	94.8	108.6	132.2	112.9
Average Gain	4.2	3.7	3.8	4.1	3.6
Opponent Net Rushing Yards	2573	2223	1796	1724	1602
Per Game	160.8	138.9	112.3	114.9	100.1
Average Gain	4.7	4.1	3.7	3.9	3.7
Net Passing Yards	2872	3635	3913	2826	3789
Per Game	179.5	227.2	244.6	188.4	236.8
Times Sacked	64	45	44	52	47
Passer Rating in Yards	3.2	4.1	6.3	4.0	5.6
Opponent Net Passing Yards	3779	3241	3216	3100	2489
Per Game	236.2	202.6	201.0	206.7	155.6
Times Sacked	25	33	38	41	37
Passer Rating Defense	7.1	4.7	4.3	4.0	1.9
Passer Rating Net	-3.8	-0.6	2.0	-0.0	3.7
Yards per Drive Offense	23.6	25.6	29.3	24.7	25.9
Yards per Drive Defense	32.9	27.3	25.8	24.4	19.7
Average Time of Possession	28:14	28:07	30:15	29:20	31:05

1987 PLAYOFFS	1988 PLAYOFFS
Won Wild Card Game from New Orleans, 44-10	Won Wild Card Game from L.A. Rams, 28-17
Won Divisional Playoff from San Francisco, 36-24	Lost Divisional Playoff to San Francisco, 9-34
Lost NFC Championship Game to Washington, 10-17	

THE 1988 SEASON

DATE	AT	OPPONENT	SCORE	R	SPREAD	Tu	Net YDS	Rush YDS	Pass YDS	TURN
09/04	A	Buffalo	10-13	L	-3	a	300-300	130-114	170-186	2-1
09/11	H	New England	36- 6	W	-6.5	a	415-214	150-103	265-111	2-5
09/18	A	Chicago	31- 7	W	+3	g	376-235	127- 70	249-165	1-5
09/25	H	Philadelphia	23-21	W	-6	a	392-205	105- 70	287-135	3-2
10/02	A	Miami	7-24	L	-3	g	353-342	58- 78	295-264	4-3
10/09	H	Tampa Bay	14-13	W	-13	a	276-331	69-177	207-154	2-3
10/16	H	Green Bay	14-34	L	-10	a	324-355	67-125	257-230	5-2
10/23	A	Tampa Bay	49-20	W	-3.5	g	443-243	138- 28	305-215	1-7
10/30	A	S. Francisco	21-24	L	+4	g	321-339	92-130	229-209	3-2
11/06	H	Detroit	44-17	W	-11	a	553- 89	198- 68	355- 21	1-2
11/13	A	Dallas	43- 3	W	-3.5	a	325-160	103-102	222- 58	1-7
11/20	H	Indianapolis	12- 3	W	-4.5	a	274-213	82-103	192-110	0-2
11/24	A	Detroit	23- 0	W	-6.5	a	353- 60	181- 18	172- 42	0-2
12/04	H	New Orleans	45- 3	W	-4	a	426-233	209-126	217-107	1-3
12/11	A	Green Bay	6-18	L	-10.5	g	255-298	44- 97	211-201	2-4
12/19	H*	Chicago	28-27	W	-6	a	218-465	62-185	156-280	2-3
						Avg.	350-255	113-100	237-156	2-3

				WINS	LOSSES
Season Record:	11- 5-0	POINTS:		32- 11	12- 23
Vs. Spread:	9- 7-0	Net YDS:	10- 5-1	368-223	311-327
Home:	7- 1-0	Rush YDS:	9- 7-0	129- 95	78-109
On Artificial Turf:	9- 2-0	Pass YDS:	14- 2-0	239-127	232-218
Art. Turf vs. Spread:	6- 5-0	TURN:	11- 5-0	1- 4	3- 2

* Monday Night

WHY THE VIKINGS NEVER HAD A CHANCE

We told you last November that the Vikings weren't going to win the Super Bowl. Remember? Well, maybe it was somebody else we told. We know we told *somebody*.

At the time all the prognosticators were ooohing and ahhhing over the Minnesota defense. And with good reason. The Vikings were in the middle of the streak that saw them go four games without allowing a touchdown, something unheard of in this day and age. It was too early to pick the winner of XXIII, but folks were saying the Vikes had a great shot at it. We didn't think so.

Whoever it was we told about the Vikings asked if we thought the Minnesota offense was poor. Heavens, no, we said. That was silly. The Vikes had already scored more than forty points in three different games, and they did it a fourth time before the season was over. They could score points, all right.

"I know!" said Whoever. "You believe in the hot-team theory, and you think Minnesota's peaking too early." No, we said, the idea that a team should peak at playoff time has merit, but most of the time you can't tell who's peaked until

the Super Bowl is over. Then it's safe to say the winner peaked.

No, our decision about the Vikings *was* based on some misgivings about their offense, but not its ability to explode in any given game. We just didn't think they ran well enough to win three or maybe four games in a row against the best NFL teams. We'd just happened to check the past five Super Bowl winners and noticed . . .

No, wait, that's not true. We didn't just "happen" to check; we were looking for a pattern so we could know before anybody else who was going to win. Call it ego. And we found one, a pattern. Here, let us show you 1987 as an example.

What we did was put down the rushing average per game and passing average per game for all the 1987 playoff teams and compare them with the league averages. Then we did the same thing for the defenses against rushing and passing. For example, San Francisco rushed for an average of 149.1 yards per game; which was 25.2 yards better than the league's 123.9 average. When we'd done it for all the teams, we added the pluses and minuses together and got a total. Frankly we were hoping that the actual Super Bowl winner would end with the highest total. Or second highest.

1987

	OFFENSE				DEFENSE				
	RUSH		PASS		RUSH		PASS		TOTAL
NFL	123.9		203.9		123.9		203.9		
SF	149.1	+25.2	250.0	+46.1	107.4	+16.5	165.6	+38.3	+126.1
Chi	130.3	+ 6.4	206.0	+ 2.1	94.2	+29.7	186.8	+17.1	+55.3
Den	131.3	+ 7.4	243.6	+39.7	134.5	-10.6	186.4	+17.5	+54.0
NO*	146.0	+22.1	184.9	-19.0	103.3	+20.6	186.7	+17.2	+40.9
Wash	140.1	+16.2	233.0	+29.1	111.9	+12.0	222.9	-19.0	+38.3
Cle	116.3	- 7.6	230.3	+26.4	95.5	+28.4	188.7	+15.2	+32.0
Ind	142.9	+19.0	190.1	-13.8	119.3	+ 4.6	184.0	+19.9	+29.7
Hou*	128.2	+ 4.3	220.0	+16.1	123.2	+ .7	209.7	- 5.8	+15.3
Min*	132.2	+ 8.3	188.4	-15.5	114.9	+ 9.0	206.7	- 2.8	- 1.0
Sea*	134.9	+11.0	180.8	-23.1	146.7	-22.8	197.2	+ 6.7	-28.2

* Wild Card team

As you can see, Washington ended up fifth. Clunk! There went our idea. Nevertheless we ran the same procedure for the four Super Bowls before, in case 1987 was a goofy year because of the strike. We stopped at 1983 because '82 was another strike year. By 1986 we knew we were on the wrong track. The 49ers had this fabulous +104.6, and the Giants were a mere +38.7, trailing the +83.1 Bears.

Maybe, we theorized, a team with an extremely high mark was doomed to fail. But in 1985 the Bears had a mark of +106.5 and won Super Bowl XX. Back to the drawing board.

It went on that way, but the time wasn't wasted. We did discover that all of the last five winners had two things in common.

First, their total rating was at least a +35. That seemed to be the cutoff point for proper balance. The teams below that were either generally lackluster in all four areas—rushing, passing, rushing defense, and passing defense—or they had some glaring weakness that negated their other numbers. It wasn't necessary that a winner have all positive marks: Washington had a suspect pass defense in '87; the Giants were slightly subpar in both passing and pass defense in '86; Chicago's passing was 12.2 under the league average in 1985; and San Francisco's pass defense yardage was 5.4 yards worse than an average team in '84. Only the Raiders in '83 had pluses all the way across.

After we thought about that, it made sense. The Bears of '85 ran so well and defensed so well they didn't pass as often as most teams. The '84 49ers led most of the time late, so teams were passing to try to catch up. A negative in passing or pass defense didn't necessarily mean a team was poor at something.

However, every Super Bowl winner from the 1984 through the 1987 seasons had two things in common besides an overall rating above 35. For one thing, they stopped the other guys from running.

Here are the rushing defense records (remember a plus means fewer yards given up than average).

1987 Washington	+12.0
1986 N.Y. Giants	+38.4
1985 Chicago	+42.5
1984 San Francisco	+11.7
1983 Raiders	+30.6

"Say, the Vikings ended the '88 season at +21.3, so how come they can't win the . . ."

Hush! We said two things in common. Each team that won also ran for at least a +10 yards over the league average.

1987 Washington	+16.2
1986 N.Y. Giants	+21.6
1985 Chicago	+47.7
1984 San Francisco	+30.1
1983 Raiders	+10.3

Minnesota was a -8.5 in rushing. Ergo: no Super Bowl win.

Here are the marks for the 1988 playoff teams. According to our theory, only the 49ers, the Bears, the Bengals, and the Bills had the proper mix at the start of the playoffs.

1988

	OFFENSE				DEFENSE				
	RUSH		PASS		RUSH		PASS		TOTAL
NFL	121.4		202.2		121.4		202.2		
SF	157.7	+36.3	211.1	+ 8.9	99.3	+22.1	186.7	+15.5	+82.8
Chi	144.9	+23.5	187.4	-14.8	82.9	+38.5	189.6	+12.6	+57.2
Cin	169.4	+48.0	209.2	+ 7.0	128.0	- 6.6	195.8	+ 6.4	+54.8
Buf	133.3	+11.9	198.9	- 3.3	115.9	+ 5.5	170.3	+31.9	+46.0

(Continued)

(Continued)

	OFFENSE				DEFENSE				
	RUSH		PASS		RUSH		PASS		TOTAL
NFL	121.4		202.2		121.4		202.2		
Min*	112.9	- 8.5	236.8	+34.6	100.1	+21.3	155.6	+46.6	+94.0
Rams*	125.2	+ 3.8	237.8	+35.6	105.4	+16.0	206.3	- 4.1	+51.3
Hou*	140.6	+19.2	184.8	-17.4	99.5	+21.9	204.1	- 1.9	+21.8
Cle*	98.4	-23.0	214.8	+11.8	120.0	+ 1.4	177.9	+24.3	+14.5
Phi	121.6	+ .2	217.8	+15.6	103.3	+18.1	259.2	-57.0	-23.1
Sea	130.4	+ 9.0	172.3	-29.9	142.8	-21.4	209.6	- 7.4	-49.7

* Wild Card team

It's interesting, but not significant, that those four ended up in the conference championship games. Any one or two of them could have been knocked off earlier by a team that rated lower than 35 overall, or, like Minnesota, that had a glaring rushing weakness. A weakness doesn't mean a weak team. We're not talking about Detroit here. Minnesota was extremely strong in everything but rushing. Such a team might win one or even two playoff games, but not three—except in the unlikely situation where every team with championship potential got knocked off earlier. Denver got all the way to the Super Bowl two years in a row with a running attack below +10.

WHY IT WORKS . . .
AND MAY NOT TOMORROW

Before you rush out and bet the mortgage against some playoff team this year, a quick caution. What we think we have here is a trend—what makes a winning playoff team in the late 1980s. We're not certain that everything we said was true fifteen years ago or will be true forever. Things change.

We think—and we emphasize *think*—that what we're seeing is related to the rules changes a dozen years ago that made it easier to pass. If you recall, it was just about then that people stopped saying you had to have a great quarterback to win the Super Bowl and started saying you had to have a *good* quarterback. Prior to the rules changes, only great passers could sustain peak performance through the playoffs to the end. After the rules were liberalized, good quarterbacks could play at a winning level for the three (or four) crucial playoff games.

For a couple of years the balance shifted so that you needed a "great" defense to win. In effect, a great defense was one that could shut down the opposition's "good" passer. We think the '83 Raiders, with Lester Hayes and Mike Haynes as cornerbacks, represented the end of this trend. Everybody rushed out to get fast little CBs who could cover. And when several teams had shut-down pass defenses, what was left? Run the ball.

Defenses like the Vikings' and the Bears' can stop the other guy from running or passing. The difference is that the Vikings can't run themselves. So we *think* what's happening now is that a team—even a terrific team—that depends preponderantly on its passing attack will, in the course of the playoffs, meet a defense that can stop it (or its passer will just have a bad day). When that happens, they have to reach back for the run. And it isn't there.

The trouble with trends is that sooner or later somebody figures out what to do about them and adjusts. And then we're off in a new direction.

THE VIKINGS RUNNERS(?)

The first thing you have to see is how the Minnesota rushing was split up last year.

	Darrin Nelson			Allen Rice			Alfred Anderson			Rick Fenney			D.J. Dozier			Darryl Harris		
WK	AT	YDS	T	AT	YDS	T	AT	YDS	T	AT	YDS	T	AT	YDS	T	AT	YDS	T
1	10	50	0	4	-1	1	4	18	0	8	28	0	IR					
2	13	68	1	9	15	0	3	20	0	7	20	0	IR			5	14	1
3	inj.			16	64	0	7	14	0	4	19	0	IR			6	25	0
4	inj.			25	56	0	8	32	1	3	11	0	IR					
5	4	15	0	4	20	0	4	6	0	1	4	0	IR			1	1	0
6	13	52	0	4	11	1	2	6	0				IR					
7	7	36	0	1	3	1	3	15	0	4	13	0	IR					
8	8	10	0	7	15	1	4	10	0	7	37	1	10	34	1			
9	8	23	0	4	1	0	3	2	0	6	35	1	5	21	0			
10				5	14	2	6	34	1	6	48	1	10	32	0	9	39	0
11	7	11	0				3	15	0	5	19	0	4	36	1	4	2	0

(Continued)

	Darrin Nelson			Allen Rice			Alfred Anderson			Rick Fenney			D.J. Dozier			Darryl Harris		
WK	AT	YDS	T	AT	YDS	T	AT	YDS	T	AT	YDS	T	AT	YDS	T	AT	YDS	T
12	11	16	0	5	8	0	6	25	0	4	37	0						
13	10	23	0	13	59	0	19	53	2	inact.			2	7	0	4	21	0
14	14	60	0	5	33	0	6	15	1	inact.			7	36	0	4	46	0
15	5	13	0	3	6	0	4	13	0	?			3	2	0			
16	2	3	0	5	18	0	5	22	1	?			1	-1	0	1	3	0

It looks like rushing by committee. No back rushed for as much as 70 yards in any game. Darrin Nelson twice got over 60, but he's only 184 pounds. Ten to fifteen rushes a game is about his limit. You can see that after Allen Rice, a hefty 204-pounder, gained 64 yards in Week 3, they tried him as a heavy-duty type the next week, with very poor results. From then on, he was mostly used in short-yardage situations.

Alfred Anderson, at 223 pounds, was the only back who ran in every game, but only once did he get more than eight carries. His 3.4 average explains why. Rick Fenney had a better average, but ran less. Darryl Harris is smaller than Nelson and less talented.

D. J. Dozier seems to be in Coach Jerry Burns' doghouse. At least the word was that he was kept on IR after he was ready to play. The biggest problem is he can't block, so he and Nelson make a poor combination. So far alternating them hasn't worked well either. Both could use a big, tough fullback like Tom Rathman, but so far neither Anderson nor Fenney has done the job.

To really appreciate how poorly committee-rushing worked in 1988, you have to look at the next chart. We set it up with each opponent's per game rushing defense—the number of yards that an average rushing attack could reasonably expect to gain—and then put down the number of yards gained by the Vikings' running backs (exclusive of reverses and QB scrambles).

WK	OPPONENT	SCORE	R	OPP AVG	RB YDS	DIFF
1	Buffalo	10-13	L	115	95	-20
2	New England	36- 6	W	131	137	+ 6
3	Chicago	31- 7	W	83	122	+39
4	Philadelphia	23-21	W	103	99	- 4
5	Miami	7-24	L	157	46	-111
6	Tampa Bay	14-13	W	97	69	-28
7	Green Bay	14-34	L	132	67	-65
8	Tampa Bay	49-20	W	97	106	+ 9
9	S. Francisco	21-24	L	99	82	-17
10	Detroit	44-17	W	127	167	+40
11	Dallas	43- 3	W	116	83	-33
12	Indianapolis	12- 3	W	106	86	-20
13	Detroit	23- 0	W	127	163	+36
14	New Orleans	45- 3	W	111	154	+43
15	Green Bay	6-18	L	132	34	-98
16	Chicago	28-27	W	83	45	-38
				1816	1591	-225

As bad as the numbers are, they are even worse than you think. The six times Minnesota's runners gained more than their opponent's rushing average were all blowouts, where the Vikes would have run more than usual in the fourth quarter.

Peee-ew!

THAT QB CONTROVERSY

Considering that (1) Wade Wilson ended up as the NFC's top-rated passer, according to the league's rating system, and (2) the Vikings lived by the pass, you may have wondered (3) why-in-hell there was so much flipping of QBs last season.

First, game by game (we'll use the NEWS rates to evaluate the performances; 5.11+ is average, 6.48+ is good):

				WADE WILSON						TOMMY KRAMER					
WK	OPPONENT	SCORE	R	AT	CO	YDS	T	I	NEWS	AT	CO	YDS	T	I	NEWS
1	Buffalo	10-13	L	33	19	204	0	1	4.82						
2	New Eng.	36- 6	W	5	5	73	0	0	—	27	12	209	1	1	6.44
3	Chicago	31- 7	W	2	0	0	0	0	—	25	15	258	3	1	9.72
4	Phila.	23-21	W	3	2	22	0	0	—	34	17	299	0	1	7.47
5	Miami	7-24	L							33	13	220	0	4	1.21
6	Tampa B.	14-13	W							30	19	209	1	1	5.80
7	Green B.	14-34	L	26	17	248	1	1	8.19	12	3	37	0	0	3.08
8	Tampa B.	49-20	W	30	22	335	3	0	12.17						
9	S.Fran.	21-24	L	30	18	243	1	2	5.43						
10	Detroit	44-17	W	35	28	391	2	1	10.46						

(Continued)

(Continued)

WK	OPPONENT	SCORE	R	WADE WILSON						TOMMY KRAMER					
				AT	CO	YDS	T	I	NEWS	AT	CO	YDS	T	I	NEWS
11	Dallas	43- 3	W	27	12	240	3	1	8.33	3	1	11	0	0	—
12	Ind.	12- 3	W	29	17	192	0	0	6.62						
13	Detroit	23- 0	W	21	16	186	0	0	8.86						
14	New Orl.	45- 3	W	22	13	215	3	1	9.09	2	2	8	0	0	—
15	Green B.	6-18	L	41	20	233	0	1	4.58						
16	Chicago	28-27	W	28	15	164	2	1	4.96	7	1	13	0	0	—

Wilson yelled like a real Viking when Burns put Kramer in the final game against the Bears just as it was getting close. But really we weren't that impressed with Wilson all season.

He started the first games and was ineffective. He had a shoulder separation the second time out, and Kramer came in and beat three tough teams in a row. When Tommy faltered, Wilson came back just in time for the cake part of the schedule. Through Week 12, Wilson had great numbers, but had lost his only try against a winning team, San Francisco. The Viking defense beat Indianapolis (in Week 12) and put the Saints game (Week 14) out of reach so early that Wilson still hadn't shown he could win a tough game by the third quarter against the Bears.

So when the Bears showed signs of life in a game Minnesota had to win, Burns went to his twelve-year veteran, the QB who'd beaten Chicago earlier in the season. As it turned out, Tommy didn't do anything to win the game. But he didn't lose it either, which was all that really mattered.

Kramer is thirty-four and has had injury problems. He also has streaks where he can't hit his targets. Wilson is thirty, healthy, and coming off great numbers. But as far as we're concerned, he still hasn't proved he's a first-rate QB.

MINNESOTA VIKINGS STATISTICS

1988 TEAM STATISTICS	MV	OPP
TOTAL FIRST DOWNS	318	243
Rushing	112	85
Passing	187	132
Penalty	19	26
3rd Down Made/Att.	83/222	59/203
Pct.	37.4%	29.1%
4th Down Made/Att.	8/17	3/7
Pct.	47.1%	42.9%
TOTAL NET YARDS	5595	4091
Avg. per Game	349.7	255.7
Total Plays	1068	952
Avg. per Play	5.2	4.3
NET YARDS RUSHING	1806	1602
Avg. per Game	112.9	100.1
Total Rushes	501	435
NET YARDS PASSING	3789	2489
Avg. per Game	236.8	155.6
Tackled/Yards Lost	46/311	37/274
Gross Yards	4100	2763
Attempts/Completions	520/294	480/219
Pct. of Completions	56.5%	45.6%
Had Intercepted	18	36
PUNTS/AVERAGE	86/39.4	96/42.3
NET PUNTING AVG.	32.6	35.1
PENALTIES/YARDS	118/998	91/753
FUMBLES/BALL LOST	22/12	36/17
TOUCHDOWNS	49	24
Rushing	22	10
Passing	20	12
Returns	7	2
TIME OF POSSESSION	—	—

SCORE/PERIODS	1	2	3	4	OT	TOTAL
Vikings	82	132	91	101	0	406
Opponents	46	73	62	52	0	233

SCORING	TDR	TDP	TDRt	PAT	FG	S	TP
C. Nelson				48/49	20/25		108
Anderson	7	1					48
Carter		6					36
Rice	6						36
Jones		5					30
Jordan		5					30
Fenney	3						18
Dozier	2						12
Lee		2					12
Wilson	2						12
Ashley		1					6
Edwards		1					6
Gustafson	1						6
D.Harris	1						6
Hilton	1						6
Lewis	1						6
C. Martin		1					6
D. Nelson	1						6
Solomon		1					6
Thomas		1					6
Holt						1	2
Doleman/Baker						1	2
Vikings	22	20	7	48/49	20/25	2	406
Opponents	10	12	2	22/24	21/25	2	233

RUSHING	NO	YDS	AVG	LG	TD
D. Nelson	112	380	3.4	27	1
Rice	110	322	2.9	24	6
Anderson	87	300	3.4	18	7
Fenney	55	271	4.9	28	3
Dozier	42	167	4.0	19t	2
D. Harris	34	151	4.4	34	1
Wilson	36	136	3.8	15	2
Carter	4	42	10.3	21	0
Gannon	4	29	7.3	15	0

(Continued)

RUSHING	NO	YDS	AVG	LG	TD
Kramer	14	8	0.6	5	0
Jones	1	7	7.0	7	0
Scribner	1	0	0.0	0	0
Mularkey	1	-6	-6.0	-6	0
Vikings	501	1806	3.6	34	22
Opponents	435	1602	3.7	51t	10

RECEIVING	NO	YDS	AVG	LG	TD
Carter	72	1225	17.0	67t	6
Jordan	57	756	13.3	38	5
Jones	40	778	19.5	68t	5
Rice	30	279	9.3	38	0
Anderson	23	242	10.5	19	1
D. Nelson	16	105	6.6	27	0
Gustafson	15	231	15.4	47	1
Fenney	15	224	14.9	42	0
Lewis	11	141	12.8	46t	1
D. Harris	6	30	5.0	7	0
Dozier	5	49	9.8	20	0
Mularkey	3	39	13.0	19	0
Hilton	1	1	1.0	1t	1
Vikings	294	4100	13.9	68t	20
Opponents	219	2763	12.6	76t	12

INTERCEPTIONS	NO	YDS	AVG	LG	TD
Lee	8	118	14.8	58t	2
Browner	5	29	5.8	18	0
Solomon	4	84	21.0	78t	1
Rutland	3	63	21.0	36	0
Fullington	3	57	19.0	40	0
Harris	3	46	15.3	27	0
Howard	3	16	5.3	10	0
Edwards	2	47	23.5	37t	1
Holt	2	15	7.5	15	0
Ashley	1	94	94.0	94t	1
Henderson	1	13	13.0	13	0

(Continued)

INTERCEPTIONS	NO	YDS	AVG	LG	TD
Thomas	1	7	7.0	7	0
Vikings	36	589	16.4	94t	5
Opponents	18	212	11.8	52t	1

PUNTING	NO	YDS	AVG	TB	In 20	LG	Blk
Scribnert	84	3387	40.3	9	23	55	2
Vikings	86	3387	39.4	9	23	55	2
Opponents	96	4059	42.3	7	15	62	1

PUNT RETURNS	NO	FC	YDS	AVG	LG	TD
Lewis	58	19	550	9.5	64	0
Carter	1	1	3	3.0	3	0
Vikings	59	20	553	9.4	64	0
Opponents	39	13	405	10.4	40	0

KICKOFF RETURNS	NO	YDS	AVG	LG	TD
D. Harris	39	833	21.4	30	0
D. Nelson	9	210	23.3	30	0
Dozier	5	105	21.0	27	0
Carter	1	9	0.0	0	0
Lewis	1	12	12.0	12	0
Rice	1	0	0.0	0	0
Vikings	56	1160	20.7	30	0
Opponents	81	1622	20.0	44	0

FIELD GOALS	1-19	20-29	30-39	40-49	50+	TOTAL
C. Nelson	2-3	7-7	10-10	1-5	0-0	20-25
Vikings	2-3	7-7	10-10	1-5	0-0	20-25
Opponents	1-1	6-7	8-8	4-7	2-2	21-25

FIELD GOALS BY C.Nelson: 20 of 25
(42N,30G)(39G,24G)(37G)(21G,27G,45N,32G)
(40N)( )(49N)( )( )(18G)(39G,27G)(25G,26G,30G,
49G)(21G,33G,18G)(37G)(18N,38G,37G)( )

PASSING	ATT	COM	YARD	PCT.	Avg G	TD	%TD	IN	%IN	LG	SAKS/YDS	RATE
Wilson	332	204	2746	61.4	8.27	15	4.5	9	2.7	68t	33/227	91.5
Kramer	173	83	1264	48.0	7.31	5	2.9	9	5.2	47	11/62	60.5
Gannon	15	7	90	46.7	6.00	0	0.0	0	0.0	19	3/22	66.0
Vikings	520	294	4100	56.5	7.88	12	2.5	36	7.5	76t	37/274	41.2
Opponents	480	219	2763	45.6	5.76	20	3.8	18	3.5	68t	47/311	80.4

NEW ORLEANS SAINTS

The Last 5 Seasons

	1984	1985	1986	1987	1988
Won-Lost	7-9	5-11	7-9	12-3	10-6
Percentage	.438	.313	.438	.800	.625
Division Finish	3	3	4	2	1-t
Games Behind	8	6	3.5	1	0
Total Points	298	294	288	422	312
Per Game	18.6	18.4	18.0	28.1	19.5
Opponent Points	361	401	287	283	283
Per Game	22.6	25.1	17.9	18.9	17.7
Net Points	-63	-107	1	139	29
Predicted Net Wins	-1.6	-2.7	0.0	3.5	0.7
Delta Net Wins	0.6	-0.3	-1.0	1.0	1.3
Total Yards on Offense	5008	4479	4742	4964	5131
Per Game	313.0	279.9	296.4	330.9	320.7
Total Yards Allowed on Defense	4914	5815	5102	4350	5106
Per Game	307.1	363.4	318.9	290.0	319.1
Net Difference	94	- 1336	-360	614	25
Offensive Turnovers	41	36	43	28	32
Defensive Takeaways	23	37	43	48	32
Net Turnovers	-18	1	0	20	0
Predicted Net Points	-64	-107	-30	131	2
Delta Net Points	1	0	31	8	27
Net Rushing Yards	2171	1683	2074	2190	2046
Per Game	135.7	105.2	129.6	146.0	127.9
Average Gain	4.2	3.9	4.1	3.8	4.0
Opponent Net Rushing Yards	2461	2162	1559	1550	1779
Per Game	153.8	135.1	97.4	103.3	111.2
Average Gain	4.5	4.3	3.2	4.0	4.0
Net Passing Yards	2837	2796	2668	2774	3085
Per Game	177.3	174.8	166.8	184.9	192.8
Times Sacked	45	58	27	29	24
Passer Rating in Yards	3.4	3.5	3.7	5.6	4.9
Opponent Net Passing Yards	2453	3653	3543	2800	3327
Per Game	153.3	228.3	221.4	186.7	207.9
Times Sacked	55	46	47	47	31
Passer Rating Defense	4.4	5.2	4.1	3.2	5.1
Passer Rating Net	-1.0	-1.7	-0.4	2.4	-0.2
Yards per Drive Offense	25.3	21.2	23.9	26.1	28.3
Yards per Drive Defense	26.1	28.4	25.4	22.2	26.6
Average Time of Possession	30:13	28:33	27:59	34:01	32:37

1987 PLAYOFFS
Lost Wild Card Playoff to Minnesota, 10-44

THE 1988 SEASON

DATE	AT	OPPONENT	SCORE	R	SPREAD	Tu	Net YDS	Rush YDS	Pass YDS	TURN
09/04	H	S. Francisco	33-34	L	+0	a	344-289	147-124	197-165	3-2
09/11	A	Atlanta	29-21	W	-8.5	g	434-307	212-161	222-146	4-4
09/18	A	Detroit	22-14	W	-5.5	a	401-272	119- 40	282-232	2-2
09/25	H	Tampa Bay	13- 9	W	-13.5	a	268-296	117- 92	151-204	1-1
10/03	H*	Dallas	20-17	W	-6.5	a	333-457	65-187	268-270	1-3
10/09	A	San Diego	23-17	W	-4.5	g	365-206	134- 93	231-113	1-2
10/16	A	Seattle	20-19	W	+2.5	a	318-434	141- 93	177-341	3-2
10/23	H	L.A. Raiders	20- 6	W	-4.5	a	317-367	190-185	127-182	0-3
10/30	H	L.A. Rams	10-12	L	-2	a	242-332	33- 96	209-236	2-0
11/06	A	Washington	24-27	L	+3.5	g	322-412	50-113	272-299	0-1
11/13	A	L.A. Rams	14-10	W	+3.5	g	337-256	88- 60	249-196	3-2
11/20	H	Denver	42- 0	W	-4.5	a	385-258	196- 52	189-206	0-1
11/27	H	N.Y. Giants	12-13	L	-5.5	a	255-219	155- 14	100-205	5-5
12/04	A	Minnesota	3-45	L	+4	a	233-426	126-209	107-217	3-1
12/11	A	S. Francisco	17-30	L	+6.5	g	252-373	70-152	182-221	2-2
12/18	H	Atlanta	10- 9	W	-8.5	a	325-202	203-109	122- 93	2-0
						Avg.	321-319	128-111	193-208	2-2

			WINS	LOSSES
Season Record:	10- 6-0	POINTS:	21- 12	17- 27
Vs. Spread:	7- 9-0	Net YDS: 8- 8-0	348-306	275-342
Home:	5- 3-0	Rush YDS: 11- 5-0	147-107	97-118
On Artificial Turf:	7- 4-0	Pass YDS: 6-10-0	202-198	178-224
Art. Turf vs. Spread:	4- 7-0	TURN: 5- 6-5	2- 2	3- 2

* Monday Night

WAY DOWN SOUTH IN THE LAND OF RAZZ

It's hard to believe the reports that some of you good folks in the Super Dome were booing at the end of last season. Even in the bad old days, when the Saints were the Ain'ts and New Orleans was the Party Town Without Parity, the fans didn't boo a whole lot. Of course those of 'em what showed up had bags over their heads, so maybe the sound was muffled. But that was a long time ago. The 1988 Saints were 10–6, numbers that must look awfully good in Detroit. There must be some mistake; there's booze in the Big Easy, not boos. Or maybe the wire service got the dateline wrong and it really happened in Philadelphia. Never in good-hearted, fun-loving, all-forgiving New Orleans where, Mark Russell says, mortal sin is only a misdemeanor.

If it's true that a few of you Saints fans registered your displeasure by using the B word, you must be new arrivals in the city, probably from Pittsburgh or Dallas or some other place where you honed your elocution. You are obviously unaware of the Saints' unique history. Allow us to enlighten you.

New Orleans joined the NFL in 1967, one year after Atlanta and Miami and one year before Cincinnati. In the intervening years, the Dolphins have had thirteen winning seasons, including nine division championships, four con-ference titles, and two Super Bowl apearances. The Bengals have had eight winning seasons, finished on top in their division four times, and have two conference titles. The Falcons—one of the NFL's least successful franchises—have nevertheless enjoyed five winning seasons and won a division crown in 1980. Meanwhile, dear newcomer, what has happened to the football team of your city?

In twenty-two seasons, the Saints have never won a Super Bowl, conference championship, or a division title. Never! Not once! And until Mr. Jim Mora arrived to coach them, it's been a matter of sad fact that the sad sack Saints have found their way to the same number of winning seasons as Napoleon found in Russia. Zero. They were more accustomed to dwelling on the bottom than a Mississippi catfish. Twice they got to 8–8, in 1979 and 1983. Each time, becoming light-headed in the rarefied air of .500 ball, they plummeted back to the depths the following season.

Compare the Saints' regular-season totals with all the other so-called expansion teams since 1966:

Miami Dolphins	204-128-4	.614
Cincinnati Bengals	154-153-1	.502
Seattle Seahawks	96-100-0	.489
Atlanta Falcons	126-205-5	.381
New Orleans Saints	112-205-5	.353
Tampa Bay Buccaneers	57-138-1	.292

But wait, you say, aren't things even worse in Tampa Bay? Not really: the Bucs have only existed since 1976 and they've twice won their division title. No, for extended and continuous futility, the Saints are in a class by themselves. If they'd been in a *league* by themselves, they'd have still somehow managed to finish second. At least the Saints B.M. (Before Mora) would have.

And now, you newcomers to New Orleans, let us explain about Mr. Mora. Since that gentleman came on the scene in 1986, the Saints have been 29–19, with two straight winning seasons. They even reached the playoffs in 1987. Okay, they lost, but they got there. Do you realize that Mora is already the franchise's winningest coach after only three seasons? Would you believe that he has one-fourth of all the Saints' victories in their entire history? And you booed his team? Kicked any dogs lately?

Now, don't you feel ashamed of yourselves?

A TALE OF TWO SEASONS

Having put the lives of the Saints in perspective and a few rowdies in their place, we will admit that real fans in New Orleans did have a right to be a tad disappointed with the way things turned out in 1988. The 10–6 record may have been the second best in the team's history, but the folks in New Orleans were really hoping for a Super Bowl.

Oh sure, pie in the sky, you say. Well, wait a minute, the Saints had more than the law of averages working for them. They reached the midpoint of the '88 season with a 7–1 record. That wasn't just good for the lead in their division, it was the best in the NFC. Why, with just an ordinary second half, they figured to get home-field advantage all the way through the playoffs. Then on to Miami and after that we can think about running Mora for President and Bobby Hebert for Secretary of State.

In anticipation of the celebration—no city knows better how to celebrate than New Orleans—fans flocked to the Super Dome in record numbers. The 521,156 attendees at eight home games represented 94.4 percent of the Dome's capacity.

However, when the second-half chickens hatched, they turned out to be less than ordinary. The Saints staggered to a 3–5 finish. Their 10–6 was the same mark as the 49ers and Rams posted, but both finished ahead of the Saints in the division, according to the NFL's byzantine tie-breaking system. In one legalistic swoop, New Orleans lost its second playoff appearance and first division championship.

The offense caught much of the blame.

	TOTAL OFFENSE				RUSHING			PASSING				TOT
	ATT	YARD	AVG	TRN	ATT	YARD	AVG	ATT	SK	YARD	AVG	PTS
1st Half	532	2780	5.2	15	283	1125	4.0	238	11	1655	6.7	180
2nd Half	502	2351	4.7	17	229	921	4.0	260	13	1430	5.2	132

An even more revealing stat: after eight games the Saints had converted 60 of 118 third-down attempts, a fantastic 50.8 rate. On most third-and-three-or-more situations, QB Hebert set up in a shotgun with four WRs split two on each side. A quick throw usually brought a first down. In the final eight games, 44 of 110 third downs were converted, a respectable 40 percent, but a sharp drop from the clip that had New Orleans marching through opponents like Sherman marched through—oops! Like Lee marched through Bull Run.

While the falloff in offensive productivity is obvious—22.5 points per game to 16.5—it's not so clear from the numbers exactly which Saints should be taken out and shot at dawn. Was QB Hebert the chief culprit? His stats show he slipped during the second half of the season but still threw the ball at a highly respectable rate.

	ATT	COM	PCT	YARD	TD	%TD	IN	%IN	Avg G	RATE
1st Half	237	148	62.4	1737	12	5.1	6	2.5	7.33	91.0
2nd Half	241	132	54.8	1419	8	3.3	9	3.7	5.89	72.3

The running game also fell off in productivity, as evidenced by the table below.

	Dalton Hilliard				Ironhead Heyward				Rueben Mayes			
	ATT	YDS	AVG	TD	ATT	YDS	AVG	TD	ATT	YDS	AVG	TD
1st Half	121	443	3.7	3	75	336	4.5	1	75	312	4.2	1
2nd Half	83	380	4.6	2	9	19	2.1	0	95	316	3.3	2

Mayes, a 1,000-yard rusher in 1986, was returning from knee surgery. By the end of the season, he'd regained his starting job from reliable Dalton Hilliard, but that's not to say he was running as effectively as he had two years before. The chief loss was rookie Ironhead Heyward, the huge breakaway back. Until he tore up a knee cartilage, Ironhead had provided a remarkable combination of speed and power. The chief worry about Heyward for 1989 isn't his knee. At

250 pounds, he's a blockbuster runner, but his weight has been known to rise to the level of a sumo-wrestling tag team.

WR Eric Martin was one of the few Saints to improve his numbers over the second half. He set New Orleans records for receptions and yards in a season and was elected to the Pro Bowl. But even though Martin became only the third Saints receiver to top 1,000 yards—the others being Dan Abramowicz in 1969 and Wes Chandler in 1979—his 12.7 yards per catch underlines the team's lack of a long-distance pass threat. Lonzell Hill, on the other side, is no burner either. With regular Hoby Brenner laid up much of the 1988 season, John Tice did most of the TE receiving.

	Eric Martin				Lonzell Hill				John Tice			
	PC	YDS	AVG	TD	PC	YDS	AVG	TD	PC	YDS	AVG	TD
1st Half	40	479	12.0	4	31	333	10.7	5	15	197	13.1	0
2nd Half	45	604	13.4	3	35	370	10.6	2	11	100	9.1	1

Possibly the season's major loss was RT Stan Brock, who went on IR after the seventh game. The Saints aren't any deeper than a bayou, and Brock's blocking was never really replaced.

Just what happened to Morten Andersen is a Great Unsolved Mystery of the NFL. The most accurate field goaler who ever laid foot to ball was uncharacteristically off in the second half of the season.

> 1st Half: 17 of 20 attempts—85.0%
> 2nd Half: 9 of 16 attempts—56.3%

His three misses in the first half were from 53, 39, and 45 yards out. Starting in Game 10 he had three straight failures at 53, 49, and 52 yards, certainly nothing to worry about, it would seem. But maybe he did. In subsequent games Morten proved mortal from distances of 29, 40, 32, and 34 yards, all chip shots for the old Andersen. The 29-yarder could have provided the winning points against the Giants, and the 40- and 32-yarders came at key moments in the eventual loss to the 49ers in Week 15, a game the Saints had to win.

Andersen made the Pro Bowl again, and no one has suggested that GM Jim Finks should go looking for another kicker, but 1988 wasn't one of Morten's best years.

Meanwhile on the other side of the football . . .

	TOTAL OFFENSE				RUSHING			PASSING				TOT
	ATT	YARD	AVG	TAK	ATT	YARD	AVG	ATT	SK	YARD	AVG	PTS
1st Half	489	2628	5.4	19	212	974	4.6	257	20	1654	6.0	137
2nd Half	489	2478	5.1	12	230	805	3.4	248	11	1673	6.5	146

. . . the defense held its own for the most part, although drive-ending sacks and takeaways decreased sharply. The Saints' offense showed the significant sag in the second half. But was its dip the cause or merely a symptom?

Coach Mora: "I don't think it was either offense or defense. The teams we played in the second half of our season record-wise were better than the teams we played in the first half."

Can it be that simple? In the first half, our'n were better than their'n; in the second half their'n were better than our'n.

A look at the team records supports Mora's view.

FIRST EIGHT GAMES: 7-1

	AT	SCORE	OPP. SEASON RECORD*	OPP. PRE-GM RECORD	OPP. POST-GM RECORD
San Francisco	H	33-34	8- 6	—	9- 6
Atlanta	A	29-21	5- 9	0- 1	5- 9
Detroit	A	22-14	4-11	1- 1	3-10
Tampa Bay	H	13- 9	5-10	1- 2	4- 8
Dallas	H	20-17	3-12	2- 2	1-10
San Diego	A	23-17	6- 9	2- 3	4- 6
Seattle	A	20-19	9- 6	4- 2	5- 4
Raiders	H	20- 6	7- 8	3- 4	4- 4
H:3-1 A:4-0		180-137	47-71	13-15	35-57

* Games against New Orleans subtracted

Only two opponents—San Francisco and Seattle—among the first eight had winning records for the season (with the games against New Orleans subtracted from their records). But the weakness of the slate wasn't so evident at the time.

Atlanta had lost only once when they faced the Saints. Tampa Bay, San Diego, and the Raiders were each one game under .500. Detroit and Dallas were at break-even. Who knew they'd win only three more games between them?

LAST EIGHT GAMES: 3-5

	AT	SCORE	OPP. SEASON RECORD*	OPP. PRE-GM RECORD	OPP. POST-GM RECORD
Rams	H	10-12	9- 5	6- 2	3- 4
Washington	A	24-27	6- 9	5- 4	1- 5
Rams	A	14-10	9- 5	7- 3	2- 2
Denver	H	42- 0	8- 7	6- 5	2- 2
Giants	H	12-13	9- 6	8- 4	1- 2
Minnesota	A	3-45	10- 5	9- 4	1- 1
San Francisco	A	17-30	8- 6	9- 5	0- 1
Atlanta	H	10- 9	5- 9	5-10	—
H:2-2 A:1-3		132-146	64-52	55-34	10-17

* Games against New Orleans subtracted

In the second half of the season, New Orleans took on six teams that finished with winning records. Their own record reflects that fact.

It reflects something else, too. The Saints have come a long way since the baggie days. But they still have a way to go to rank with the league's best.

NEW ORLEANS SAINTS STATISTICS

1988 TEAM STATISTICS	NO	OPP
TOTAL FIRST DOWNS	306	286
Rushing	108	97
Passing	179	167
Penalty	19	22
3rd Down Made/Att.	104/227	73/203
Pct.	45.8%	36.0%
4th Down Made/Att.	4/6	7/14
Pct.	66.7%	50.0%
TOTAL NET YARDS	5131	5106
Avg. per Game	320.7	319.1
Total Plays	1034	978
Avg. per Play	5.0	5.2
NET YARDS RUSHING	2046	1779
Avg. per Game	127.9	111.2
Total Rushes	512	442
NET YARDS PASSING	3085	3327
Avg. per Game	192.8	207.9
Tackled/Yards Lost	24/171	31/252
Gross Yards	3256	3579
Attempts/Completions	498/286	505/277
Pct. of Completions	57.4%	54.9%
Had Intercepted	16	17
PUNTS/AVERAGE	73/39.9	70/40.2
NET PUNTING AVG.	34.3	32.6
PENALTIES/YARDS	101/821	77/628
FUMBLES/BALL LOST	29/16	27/15
TOUCHDOWNS	33	29
Rushing	9	7
Passing	21	19
Returns	3	3
TIME OF POSSESSION	—	—

SCORE/PERIODS	1	2	3	4	OT	TOTAL
Saints	64	93	101	54	0	312
Opponents	51	111	70	51	0	283

SCORING	TDR	TDP	TDRt	PAT	FG	S	TP
Anderson				32/33	26/36		110
Hill		7					42
Martin		7					42
Hilliard	5	1					36
Mayes	3						18
Clark		2					12
Perriman		2					12
Gray			1				6
Heyward	1						6
Jordan			1				6
Scales		1					6
Tice		1					6
Waymer			1				6
Jackson						1	2
Saints	9	21	3	32/33	26/36	2	312
Opponents	7	19	3	28/29	27/34	0	283

RUSHING	NO	YDS	AVG	LG	TD
Hilliard	204	823	4.0	36	5
Mayes	170	628	3.7	21	3
Heyward	74	355	7.8	73t	1
Jordan	19	115	6.1	44	0
Hebert	37	79	2.1	16	0
Perriman	3	17	5.7	17	0
Martin	2	12	6.0	9	0
Hansen	1	10	10.0	10	0

(Continued)

RUSHING	NO	YDS	AVG	LG	TD
Hill	2	7	3.5	5	0
Saints	512	2046	4.0	73t	9
Opponents	442	1779	4.0	62	7

RECEIVING	NO	YDS	AVG	LG	TD
Martin	85	1083	12.7	40t	7
Hill	66	703	10.7	35	7
Hilliard	34	335	9.9	26	1
Tice	26	297	11.4	40	1
Clark	19	245	12.9	21t	2
Perriman	16	215	13.4	33	2
Heyward	13	105	8.1	18	0
Mayes	11	103	9.4	25	0
Jordan	5	70	14.0	25	0
Brenner	5	67	13.4	24	0
Scales	2	20	10.0	14	1
Hebert	2	0	0.0	2	0
Pattison	1	8	8.0	8	0
Benson	1	5	5.0	5	0
Saints	286	3256	11.4	40t	21
Opponents	277	3579	12.9	85t	19

INTERCEPTIONS	NO	YDS	AVG	LG	TD
Atkins	4	42	10.5	40	0
Waymer	3	91	30.3	44	0
Jakes	3	61	20.3	39	0
Sutton	3	32	10.7	34	0
Johnson	1	34	34.0	34	0
Mack	1	19	19.0	19	0
Jackson	1	16	16.0	16	0
Cook	1	0	0.0	0	0
Saints	17	295	17.4	44	0
Opponents	16	226	14.1	78t	2

PUNTING	NO	YDS	AVG	TB	In 20	LG	Blk
Hansen	72	2913	40.5	8	19	64	1
Saints	72	2913	40.5	8	19	64	1
Opponents	70	2815	40.2	6	15	56	1

PUNT RETURNS	NO	FC	YDS	AVG	LG	TD
Gray	25	8	305	12.2	66t	1
Hill	10	4	108	10.8	31	0
Saints	35	12	413	11.8	66t	1
Opponents	39	16	248	6.4	17	0

KICKOFF RETURNS	NO	YDS	AVG	LG	TD
Atkins	20	424	21.2	57	0
Gray	32	670	20.9	39	0
Mayes	7	132	18.9	33	0
Hilliard	6	111	18.5	30	0
Martin	3	32	10.7	18	0
Waymer	2	39	19.5	29	0
Saints	70	1408	20.1	57	0
Opponents	43	823	19.1	40	0

FIELD GOALS	1-19	20-29	30-39	40-49	50+	TOTAL
Anderson	1-1	11-12	8-11	5-8	1-4	26-36
Saints	1-1	11-12	8-11	5-8	1-4	26-36
Opponents	2-2	6-8	10-13	9-10	0-1	27-34

FIELD GOALS BY Anderson: 26 of 36
(20G)(41G,29G,28G)(53N,37G,29G)(28G,
41G,39N)(27G,49G)(27G,35G,45N,34G)
(23G,31G)(51G,25G)(33G)(19G,53N,49N)
(52N)( )(27G,41G,26G,29N,45G)(36G)(38G,
40N,32N)(34N,30G)

PASSING	ATT	COM	YARD	PCT.	Avg G	TD	%TD	IN	%IN	LG	SAKS/YDS	RATE
Hebert	478	280	3156	58.6	6.60	20	4.2	15	3.1	40t	24/171	79.3
Wilson	16	5	73	31.3	4.56	0	0.0	1	6.3	25	0/0	21.1
Hilliard	2	1	27	50.0	13.5	1	50.0	0	0.0	27t	0/0	135.4
Fourcade	1	0	0	0.0	0.00	0	0.0	0	0.0	0	0/0	39.6
Hill	1	0	0	0.0	0.00	0	0.0	0	0.0	0	0/0	39.6
Saints	498	286	3256	57.4	6.54	21	4.2	16	3.2	40t	24/171	77.9
Opponents	505	277	3579	54.9	7.09	19	3.8	17	3.4	85t	31/252	75.8

NEW YORK GIANTS

The Last 5 Seasons

	1984	1985	1986	1987	1988
Won-Lost	9-7	10-6	14-2	6-9	10-6
Percentage	.563	.625	.875	.400	.625
Division Finish	2-t	1-t	1	5	1-t
Games Behind	2	0	0	5	0
Total Points	299	399	371	280	359
Per Game	18.7	24.9	23.2	18.7	22.4
Opponent Points	301	283	236	312	304
Per Game	18.8	17.7	14.8	20.8	19.0
Net Points	-2	116	135	-32	55
Predicted Net Wins	-0.1	2.9	3.4	-0.8	1.4
Delta Net Wins	1.0	-0.9	2.6	-0.7	0.6
Total Yards on Offense	5292	5884	5378	4659	4955
Per Game	330.8	367.8	336.1	310.6	309.7
Total Yards Allowed on Defense	5193	4320	4757	4658	5086
Per Game	324.6	270.0	297.3	310.5	317.9
Net Difference	99	1564	621	1	-131
Offensive Turnovers	27	38	32	42	27
Defensive Takeaways	35	37	43	34	33
Net Turnovers	8	-1	11	-8	6
Predicted Net Points	40	126	96	-32	13
Delta Net Points	-42	-10	39	0	42
Net Rushing Yards	1660	2451	2245	1457	1689
Per Game	103.8	153.2	140.3	97.1	105.6
Average Gain	3.4	4.2	4.0	3.3	3.4
Opponent Net Rushing Yards	1818	1482	1284	1768	1759
Per Game	113.6	92.6	80.3	117.9	109.9
Average Gain	3.8	3.5	3.7	3.6	3.9
Net Passing Yards	3632	3433	3133	3202	3266
Per Game	227.0	214.6	195.8	213.5	204.1
Times Sacked	55	52	46	61	60
Passer Rating in Yards	5.2	5.0	4.6	4.4	4.9
Opponent Net Passing Yards	3375	2838	3473	2890	3327
Per Game	210.9	177.4	217.1	192.7	207.9
Times Sacked	48	68	59	55	52
Passer Rating Defense	4.7	3.2	3.9	3.8	4.7
Passer Rating Net	0.4	1.8	0.6	0.6	0.2
Yards per Drive Offense	25.6	27.5	27.0	21.8	23.9
Yards per Drive Defense	25.2	20.1	23.1	22.0	25.9
Average Time of Possession	30:44	31:49	31:50	28:20	29:23

1984 PLAYOFFS
Won Wild Card Game from L.A. Rams, 16-13
Lost Divisional Playoff to San Francisco, 10-21

1985 PLAYOFFS
Won Wild Card Game from San Francisco, 17-3
Lost Divisional Playoff to Chicago, 0-21

1986 PLAYOFFS
Won Divisional Playoff from San Francisco, 49-3
Won NFC Championship from Washington, 17-0
Won Super Bowl XXI from Denver, 39-20

THE 1988 SEASON

DATE	AT	OPPONENT	SCORE	R	SPREAD	Tu	Net YDS	Rush YDS	Pass YDS	TURN
09/05	H*	Washington	27-20	W	-2	a	218-386	56-117	162-269	1-2
09/11	H	S. Francisco	17-20	L	-2.5	a	309-430	112-181	197-249	0-2
09/18	A	Dallas	12-10	W	-3	a	278-366	128- 91	150-275	2-2
09/25	H	L.A. Rams	31-45	L	-3.5	a	363-369	79-137	284-232	3-1
10/02	A	Washington	24-23	W	+3.5	g	264-344	74- 93	190-251	1-3
10/10	A*	Philadelphia	13-24	L	+2	a	436-452	100-109	336-343	1-0
10/16	H	Detroit	30-10	W	-11	a	402-113	122- 48	280- 65	2-2
10/23	A	Atlanta	23-16	W	-7.5	g	346-368	121-152	225-216	3-2
10/30	A	Detroit	13-10	W	-7	a	279-146	83- 48	196- 98	2-2
11/06	H	Dallas	29-21	W	-5.5	a	262-365	111-103	151-262	2-3
11/13	A	Phoenix	17-24	L	+1.5	g	280-485	92-142	188-343	0-2
11/20	H	Philadelphia	17-23	L	-3.5	a	394-283	77-108	317-175	3-1
11/27	A	New Orleans	13-12	W	+5.5	a	219-255	14-155	205-100	5-5
12/04	H	Phoenix	44- 7	W	-4	a	301-158	170- 66	131- 92	1-5
12/11	H	Kansas City	28-12	W	-9.5	a	244-258	159-107	85-151	1-1
12/18	A	N.Y. Jets	21-27	L	-6.5	a	367-298	197-100	170-198	1-0
						Avg.	310-317	106-110	204-207	2-2

				WINS	LOSSES
Season Record:	10- 6-0	POINTS:		24- 14	19- 27
Vs. Spread:	7- 9-0	Net YDS	5-11-0	281-276	358-386
Home:	5- 3-0	Rush YDS:	7- 9-0	104- 98	110-130
On Artificial Turf:	8- 5-0	Pass YDS:	7- 9-0	178-178	249-257
Art. Turf vs. Spread:	6- 7-0	TURN:	6- 5-5	2- 3	1- 1

* Monday Night

BREAKING TIES IS SOOOOO HARD TO DO

The Giants had the Eastern Division title and a playoff berth in their grasp last year. In fact they had it grasped by the throat right down to the final thirty-seven seconds of the regular season. Then the Jets' Ken O'Brien hit Al Toon in the corner of the endzone for a five-yard touchdown to turn a 21–20 Giants lead into a 27–21 Giants defeat. Make that the *coroner* of the endzone because the TD killed the Giants' season. The game was officially a Jets' home game at Giants Stadium, the field both teams share, but the majority in the stands cheered for the Giants throughout, anticipating a division crown and a step toward the Super Bowl. The Jets didn't feel that way about it.

The loss left the Giants with a 10–6 record, not good enough to top the Eagles' identical 10–6 record. A few cynical New Yorkers grumbled about a sinister plot by the NFL. Hadn't Pete Rozelle once been the Rams' PR man? And didn't the Rams bump our Giants out of even a Wild Card spot? Shouldn't that be looked into? Other non-paranoid New Yorkers, if that's not an oxymoron, longed for the good old days when teams finishing with duplicate records played off the difference. It seems almost like adding insult to injury to mention that the Giants lost two out of three playoffs in those good old days.

The NFL dropped playing off for division titles and wild cards years ago in the interest of fairness, competition, excitement, and the fact that it would play hell with television schedules. To avoid having miniplayoffs that might detract from the scheduled playoffs, the NFL chooses to deny that two identical records are really identical.

The Giants' recent experience in mistaken identicals would seem to make this a good time to examine the NFL's fabled tie-breaking procedure, the secret agenda that, as each season winds down, causes sportscasters to fall all over themselves explaining the possibilities if Team A wins or Team B loses or the bachelor is behind Door Number Two. Stop making that face! This will be educational.

Take a deep breath . . . here we go.

The first tie-breaker: head-to-head. Remember, division

teams play each other twice each season. If two teams end with, say, 10–6 records, but one team won both games between the two, it will be the division champ. It will also get the crown if it wins one game and ties the other. If the two 10–6 teams split their meetings, this tie-breaker is no longer in force. It matters not if Team A's win was 45–0 and Team B's win was 14–13. The league doesn't recognize identical records, but one win is as good as another.

As far as the '88 Giants went, this tie-breaker knocked them out of the championship. In their two meetings the Giants lost to the Eagles 13–24 on a great Monday Night effort by Randall Cunningham in October and 17–23 in November. The second game went into overtime, and the Eagles set up for a field goal at the Giants' twenty-one. Lawrence Taylor blew in and blocked the kick. The ball bounced crazily into the arms of Eagles DE Clyde Simmons, who ran for the winning touchdown. "It's a game of inches," Simmons said later, showing less originality than he had on the field. Suppose the ball had bounced to a Giant who'd run the other way. If the teams had still finished 10–6, after splitting their games, we'd move on merrily to . . .

The second tie-breaker: the best won-lost-tied percentage in games played within the *division*. Here's the whole Eastern Division record for 1988, in games against division rivals:

TEAM	VS.DIV	PCT.
Philadelphia	6-2-0	.750
N.Y. Giants	5-3-0	.625
Washington	4-4-0	.500
Phoenix	3-5-0	.375
Dallas	2-6-0	.250

You can see that the Giants lost this tie-breaker on the two Philadelphia losses and a loss to Phoenix the week before the blocked-field-goal game. That Cardinal sin was kind of typical of what usually beat the Giants. Neil Lomax passed for 353 yards against a secondary that was not very effective all season in spite of a pretty decent pass rush (52 sacks). Eleven other NFC teams allowed fewer total yards passing. Lomax's 44-yard bomb to Roy Green early in the fourth quarter put the Cards in front to stay. But just for a second, imagine that Green had dropped the ball and the Giants had won. If they were still tied with the Eagles after the division percentage was figured, we'd hop happily to . . .

Tie-breaker three: the best won-lost-tied percentage in games within the conference. Again, the record of the Eastern Division, this time against all NFC rivals:

TEAM	VS.NFC	PCT.
Philadelphia	8-4-0	.667
New York	9-5-0	.643
Washington	6-6-0	.500
Phoenix	6-6-0	.500
Dallas	3-9-0	.250

Doggone, if those Eagles don't win this one, too! On percentage. The Giants won more conference games but also lost more. However, in the whole season, New York humbled only one team that closed with a winning record, and it was a conference game. In Week 13, they edged the Saints in the Super Dome by 13–12, when PK Paul McFadden cashed a 35-yard field goal with twenty-one seconds left. Despite the close score, the Giants could take pride in winning a toughie with a banged-up Phil Simms on the sideline. The running game, which had been a joke, became a laugh riot here, gaining 14 yards on 17 attempts.

The fourth tie-breaker is the best won-lost-tied percentage in games the teams have in common. Outside the Eastern Division, the only teams the Giants and Eagles played in common were the Rams and the Falcons. Somehow the Eagles contrived to beat L.A. and lose to the Falcons. The Giants did it the right way, knocking off Atlanta and losing to the Rams. The loss to L.A. is what deprived the Giants of a Wild Card berth. (As we said earlier, the tie-breaker countdown starts with head-to-head.)

The fifth tie-breaker is best net points in the division, which probably explains the cruelty perpetrated on the Cardinals the week after the New Orleans game. Simms came back. More amazingly, so did the running game—170 yards—as New York had its largest offensive output since the Super Bowl year in crushing the Cards 44–7. The why may have been the net-points tie-breaker but if you want to look for a how, try an offensive line shuffle that had rookies John Elliott and Eric Moore at LT and RG and second-year Doug Riesenberg at RT. Elliott had flunked an early season trial but apparently learned a lot while watching.

Tie-breaker number six is the best net points in all games. This is sort of interesting because the Giants and Eagles had some things in common. Both depended on passes to get from here to there because neither one could run a lick. Well, the Giants could in their final three games, but up until then, they were worse than the Eagles. Both teams had shaky defenses that depended on a strong pass rush to offset a suspect secondary. When Lawrence Taylor missed the first four games on a drug suspension, the Giants were really hurting against the pass. They had only seven sacks and had given up over a thousand net yards through the air. Those of you who figure L.T.'s suspension was a slap on the wrist might add to the penalty the two losses while he was out. Had either been a win, the Giants would have won the East and tie-breakers be damned!

Speaking of tie-breakers, the seventh one is strength of schedule. Neither team was exactly stretched to the breaking point on this one. The Giants had two games with Detroit, which was like having two Christmases. They also played soft touches like the Falcons, Chiefs, and Jets—oops!

Anyway, if you take out the games against the Eagles, Philadelphia opponents were 114–118–0 for a .491 percentage. The Giants, with their games taken out, played a 100–128–2 schedule for a .439 percentage.

The eighth tie-breaker is best net touchdowns in all games. Of course, by the time you get down this far, you might as well flip a coin.

For the ninth tie-breaker, they flip a coin. If the coin landed on its edge, they'd probably go alphabetically, a way that New Yorkers would have preferred as the first tie-breaker in '88.

L.T.

One can hardly mention the Giants without saying something about Lawrence Taylor. The season closed with him on the All-Pro teams again, instead of in the playoffs.

There doesn't seem to be anyone around anymore who doesn't want to declare him the greatest outside linebacker ever. It seems a little niggling to mention that the three-man line has changed the position in the last decade. An outside linebacker is more like what the defensive end used to be on four- and five-man lines. It makes more sense to compare L.T. with Deacon Jones or Gino Marchetti than with Jack Ham or Chuck Howley—although, in truth, that doesn't quite do it either. Maybe what we really need is a special name for a position that didn't exist a short while back. How about wide defender, the way ends became wide receivers? There aren't any ends anymore, unless they're tight. Of course, who wants loose ends?

We thought you might like to look at Taylor's regular season sack record below and compare it with Reggie White's (for more on White, see the essay on the Eagles).

```
                TAYLOR
  YEAR   GM    SACKS    AVG/PG
  1981   16 (Sacks unofficial
                until 1982)
  1982    9    7.5      0.83
  1983   16    9.0      0.56
  1984   16   11.5      0.72
  1985   16   13.0      0.81
  1986   16   20.5*     1.28
  1987   12   12.0      1.00
  1988   12   15.5      1.29
        ───────────────────
  7 yr   97   89.0      0.92

  * Led NFL
```

```
                WHITE
  YEAR   GM    SACK    AVG/PG
  USFL   34   23.5      0.69
  1985   13   13.0      1.00
  1986   16   18.0      1.13
  1987   12   21.0*     1.75
  1988   16   18.0*     1.13
        ───────────────────
  NFL    57   70.0      1.23
```

The first thought that comes to mind is that L.T. had his best sack season (on a per game basis) in 1988. Yet because of his drug suspension, last year can't be considered vintage. The second thought, or perhaps the reflex thought, is to bemoan the fact that one of the game's greatest players seems to be well on his way to destroying his life and career by his use of drugs.

But then you have to ask yourself, is it really any more tragic that someone with talent, success, and wealth throws it all away for a noseful of white crap, than when someone you never heard of loses everything to what we blasphemously call an "act of God"? Some poor shmoe who never had a chance for much more than a boring job, a nagging wife, and a couple of wiseass kids? And maybe rooting for the Giants on a Sunday afternoon?

THE GREATEST?

Speaking of Phil Simms, everybody knows he's only been in one Pro Bowl, which says he's almost never been the best or even the second-best quarterback in the NFC, much less the NFL. Whether you agree with that assessment or not, somebody should mention that he's been a good quarterback for a number of seasons. Maybe he doesn't blaze, but there's something to be said for steady heat.

Now that he's moving up to the top in most of the Giants' career stats for passing, maybe we should begin to consider whether he's the all-time greatest QB the Giants have had. Below are the things you need to know in making the determination for Simms (1979–81, 1983–88) and the other likely candidates: Charlie Conerly (1948–61), Y.A. Tittle (1961–64), and Fran Tarkenton (1967–71).

PASSING PER GAME AVERAGES WITH GIANTS

PER GAME	ATT	COM	YARD	TD	IN
Simms	29.84	16.07	212.61	1.30	1.13
Tarkenton	27.51	15.23	201.52	1.52	1.22
Tittle	24.22	13.54	193.31	1.78	1.26
Conerly	17.60	8.81	121.04	1.07	1.04

PASSING: CAREER TOTALS WITH GIANTS

GAMES	NO	PASS ATTEMPTS		COMPLETIONS		COMP. PCT.	
Conerly	161	SIMMS	3253	SIMMS	1752	Tittle	55.9
SIMMS	109	Conerly	2833	Conerly	1418	Tarkenton	55.4
Tarkenton	69	Tarkenton	1898	Tarkenton	1051	SIMMS	53.9
Tittle	54	Tittle	1308	Tittle	731	Conerly	50.1

YARDS GAINED		AVERAGE GAIN		TOUCHDOWNS		TD PCT.	
SIMMS	23174	Tittle	7.98	Conerly	173	Tittle	7.3
Conerly	19488	Tarkenton	7.33	SIMMS	142	Conerly	6.1
Tarkenton	13905	SIMMS	7.12	Tarkenton	105	Tarkenton	5.5
Tittle	10439	Conerly	6.88	Tittle	96	SIMMS	4.4

INTERCEPTIONS		INT. PCT.		NFL RATE		NEWS RATE	
Conerly	167	SIMMS	3.78	Tittle	84.7	Tittle	6.38
SIMMS	123	Tarkenton	3.79	Tarkenton	81.4	Tarkenton	6.17
Tarkenton	72	Tittle	5.2	SIMMS	75.4	SIMMS	5.80
Tittle	68	Conerly	5.9	Conerly	68.3	Conerly	4.84

CAREER HIGHLIGHTS WITH GIANTS

- *Conerly*: World Championship 1956, NFL East Titles 1958–59. Chosen for Pro Bowl following 1950 and 1956 seasons.
- *Tittle*: NFL East Titles 1961–63. United Press MVP 1962. Chosen for Pro Bowl following 1961 and 1962 seasons.
- *Tarkenton*: Chosen for Pro Bowl following 1967, 1968, 1969, and 1970 seasons.
- *Simms*: 1–1 Playoffs 1981; 1–1 Playoffs 1984; 1–1 Playoffs 1985; NFC East Title, 3–0 Playoffs, including Super Bowl XXI. Pro Bowl after 1985 season.

As you can see, the greatest quarterback the Giants ever had was—but why belabor the obvious?

THAT LAST-MINUTE RUSH

The sudden resurfacing of the Giants' running game for the first time since 1986 allowed Joe Morris to have his third 1,000-yard season, something no Giants runner had ever done. The only other Giant to have even 2,000-yarders was Ron Johnson, way back in 1970 and '72. While we rejoice for little Joe, we'd feel more comfortable about his 1988 achievement if we didn't know that a third of it came in those last three games. Up until then, he'd been having a pretty punk year.

Joe Morris	ATT	YDS	AVG	TD	ATT-YDS/PG
GAMES 1-13	224	724	3.2	4	17.2 / 55.7
14 Phoenix	32	122	3.8	1	
15 Kansas City	31	140	4.5	0	
16 N.Y. Jets	20	97	4.9	0	
3 GAME TOTAL	83	359	4.3	1	27.6 / 119.7
SEASON TOTAL	307	1083	3.5	5	19.2 / 67.7

Well, being basically of a suspicious nature, we wondered if there might be something at work in New York's rushing revival other than putting some kids who wanted to block into the line. We figured the Giants are going to come out in 1989 expecting to pick up where they left off. So before that balloon floats skyward, we'd better subject it to a prick.

A closer look at those last three games indicates the Giants weren't running against anything that might even vaguely resemble the Chicago Bears.

Week 14: The opponents were the Phoenix Cardinals, who had a per-game season average against rushing (excluding Week 14) of 27.6 attempts for 117.0 yards. That's not bad, but it's not how the Cardinals were at the end of the season, when they were collapsing like a rubber boat on a cactus sea. Notice what they did against rushing in Weeks 13 through 15.

WK	Opponent	ATT	YARDS
13	Philadelphia	21	94
14	GIANTS	53	170
15	Philadelphia	34	141

You practically had to visit the Hopewell Home for the Aged to find anyone who ran worse than the Eagles, so holding them to 94 in Week 13 didn't rank with putting a man on the moon as an accomplishment. But letting the Eagles rush for 141 yards, as the Cardinals did in Week 15, was darn near as rare. So did the Giants' 170 yards in Week 14 signal New York rising from the ashes or Phoenix falling into the ashcan?

Week 15: This should hardly count. Everybody ran on the Chiefs. Believe it or not, Kansas City held the Giants to 3.2 yards *less* than K.C.'s other opponents averaged in the other fifteen games. Look!

WK	Opponent	ATT	YARDS
14	N.Y. Jets	35	179
15	GIANTS	39	159
16	San Diego	45	246

The rest of Kansas City's opponents in 1988 averaged 38.0 attempts and 162.2 yards per game. What was wrong with the Giants?

Week 16: Okay, here's one they earned. The Jets averaged 32.3 attempts and a decent 128.5 yards per game in rushing defense for the other fifteen games. They were not in the midst of an *el foldo,* a situation that in itself was unusual for the Jets at this time of year. The Giants ripped through them for 197 yards on 33 carries. Yay, Giants!

Oh yes, the Jets won.

Which is where we began this piece.

NEW YORK GIANTS STATISTICS

1988 TEAM STATISTICS	NYG	OPP
TOTAL FIRST DOWNS	317	291
Rushing	123	95
Passing	168	177
Penalty	26	19
3rd Down Made/Att.	80/219	96/247
Pct.	36.5%	38.9%
4th Down Made/Att.	8/18	9/14
Pct.	44.4%	64.3%
TOTAL NET YARDS	4955	5086
Avg. per Game	309.7	317.9
Total Plays	1078	1072
Avg. per Play	4.6	4.7
NET YARDS RUSHING	1689	1759
Avg. per Game	105.6	109.9
Total Rushes	493	454
NET YARDS PASSING	3266	3327
Avg. per Game	204.1	207.9
Tackled/Yards Lost	60/450	52/428
Gross Yards	3716	3755
Attempts/Completions	525/290	566/294
Pct. of Completions	55.2%	51.9%
Had Intercepted	14	15
PUNTS/AVERAGE	81/39.9	93/39.8
NET PUNTING AVG.	33.7	34.2
PENALTIES/YARDS	88/660	116/902
FUMBLES/BALL LOST	32/13	36/18
TOUCHDOWNS	41	33
Rushing	15	8
Passing	22	23
Returns	4	2
TIME OF POSSESSION	—	—

SCORE/PERIODS	1	2	3	4	OT	TOTAL
Giants	59	83	95	119	3	359
Opponents	59	101	53	85	6	304

SCORING	TDR	TDP	TDRt	PAT	FG	S	TP
McFadden				25/27	14/19		67
Anderson	8						48
Allegre				14/14	10/11		44
Baker		7					42
Morris	5						30
Bavaro		4					24
Manuel		4					24
Carthon	2	1					18
Robinson		3					18
Banks			1				6
Burt			1				6
Flynn			1				6
Ingram		1					6
P. Johnson			1				6
Mowatt		1					6
Turner		1					6
Collins						1	2

(Continued)

SCORING	TDR	TDP	TDRt	PAT	FG	S	TP
Giants	15	22	4	39/41	24/30	1	359
Opponents	8	23	2	31/32	25/33	0	304

RUSHING	NO	YDS	AVG	LG	TD
Morris	307	1083	3.5	27	5
Anderson	65	208	3.2	11	8
Simms	33	152	4.6	17	0
Carthon	46	146	3.2	8	2
Adams	29	76	2.6	15	0
Manuel	4	27	6.8	14	0
Rouson	1	1	1.0	1	0
Rutledge	3	-1	-0.3	0	0
Hostetler	5	-3	-0.6	0	0
Giants	493	1689	3.4	27	15
Opponents	454	1759	3.9	38	8

RECEIVING	NO	YDS	AVG	LG	TD
Manuel	65	1029	15.8	46	4
Bavaro	53	672	12.7	36	4
Baker	40	656	16.4	85t	7
Adams	27	174	6.4	19	0
Morris	22	166	7.5	24	0
Carthon	19	194	10.2	24	1
Mowatt	15	196	13.1	38t	1
Ingram	13	158	12.2	32	1
Turner	10	128	12.8	28t	1
Anderson	9	57	6.3	13	0
Robinson	7	143	20.4	62t	3
McConkey	5	72	14.4	28	0
Rouson	4	61	15.3	31	0
Hostetler	1	10	10.0	10	0
Giants	290	3716	12.8	85t	22
Opponents	294	3755	12.8	80t	23

INTERCEPTIONS	NO	YDS	AVG	LG	TD
S.White	4	70	17.5	39	0
Kinard	3	46	15.3	39	0
Carson	2	66	33.0	66	0
P. Johnson	1	33	33.0	33t	1
A. White	1	29	29.0	29	0
Reasons	1	20	20.0	20	0
Banks	1	15	15.0	15t	1
Collins	1	13	13.0	13	0
Williams	1	0	0.0	0	0
Giants	15	292	19.5	66	2
Opponents	14	116	8.3	30	0

PUNTING	NO	YDS	AVG	TB	In 20	LG	Blk
Buford	73	3012	41.3	10	13	66	2
Landeta	6	222	37.0	0	1	53	0
Giants	81	3234	39.9	10	14	66	2
Opponents	93	3697	39.8	8	26	66	1

PUNT RETURNS	NO	FC	YDS	AVG	LG	TD
McConkey	40	25	313	7.8	35	0
Baker	5	0	34	6.8	11	0
Flynn	1	0	4	4.0	4	0
Kinard	1	0	8	8.0	8	0
Giants	47	25	359	7.6	35	0
Opponents	38	11	303	8.0	32	0

KICKOFF RETURNS	NO	YDS	AVG	LG	TD
Guggemos	17	344	20.2	40	0
Hill	13	262	20.2	30	0
Ingram	8	129	16.1	27	0
Rouson	8	130	16.3	21	0
Haddix	6	123	20.5	24	0
Collins	4	67	16.8	26	0
S. White	3	62	20.7	26	0
McConkey	2	30	15.0	17	0
Beckman	1	7	7.0	7	0

(Continued)

KICKOFF RETURNS	NO	YDS	AVG	LG	TD
Giants	62	1154	18.6	40	0
Opponents	73	1269	17.4	44	0

FIELD GOALS	1-19	20-29	30-39	40-49	50+	TOTAL
McFadden	0-0	4-4	4-6	5-6	1-3	14-19
Allegre	0-0	3-3	5-6	2-2	0-0	10-11
Giants	0-0	7-7	9-12	7-8	1-3	24-30
Opponents	0-0	7-10	10-14	7-7	1-2	25-33

FIELD GOALS BY McFadden 14 of 19
( )( )( )( )(32G)( )( )(21G,27G,45G)(42G,
57N,33G)(37G,50G,47G)(39N,40G)(21G)
(46G,35G)(21G)(62N)(31N,49N)
Allegre: (23G,32G)(36G,39N)(32G)
(34G)( )(47G,22G)(33G,48G,25G)

PASSING	ATT	COM	YARD	PCT.	Avg G	TD	%TD	IN	%IN	LG	SAKS/YDS	RATE
Simms	479	263	3359	54.9	7.01	21	4.4	11	2.3	62t	53/405	82.1
Hostetler	29	16	244	55.2	8.41	1	3.4	2	6.9	85t	5/31	65.9
Rutledge	17	11	113	64.7	6.65	0	0.0	1	5.9	33	2/14	59.2
Giants	525	290	3716	55.2	7.08	22	4.2	14	2.7	85t	60/450	80.5
Opponents	566	294	3755	51.9	6.63	23	4.1	15	2.7	80t	52/428	75.5

PHILADELPHIA EAGLES

The Last 5 Seasons

	1984	1985	1986	1987	1988
Won-Lost	6-9-1	7-9	5-10-1	7-8	10-6
Percentage	.406	.438	.344	.467	.625
Division Finish	5	4	4	2-t	1-t
Games Behind	4.5	3	8.5	4	0
Total Points	278	286	256	337	379
Per Game	17.4	17.9	16.0	22.5	23.7
Opponent Points	320	310	312	380	319
Per Game	20.0	19.4	19.5	25.3	19.9
Net Points	-42	-24	-56	-43	60
Predicted Net Wins	-1.0	-0.6	-1.4	-1.1	1.5
Delta Net Wins	-0.5	-0.4	-1.1	0.6	0.5
Total Yards on Offense	4698	5216	4542	5077	5430
Per Game	293.6	326.0	283.9	338.5	339.4
Total Yards Allowed on Defense	5239	5135	5224	5249	5799
Per Game	327.4	320.9	326.5	349.9	362.4
Net Difference	-541	81	-682	-172	-369
Offensive Turnovers	33	40	27	35	26
Defensive Takeaways	31	32	36	48	44
Net Turnovers	-2	-8	9	13	18
Predicted Net Points	-53	-25	-21	38	41
Delta Net Points	11	1	-35	-81	19
Net Rushing Yards	1338	1630	2002	2027	1945
Per Game	83.6	101.9	125.1	135.1	121.6
Average Gain	3.5	3.8	4.0	4.0	4.2
Opponent Net Rushing Yards	2189	2205	1989	1643	1652
Per Game	136.8	137.8	124.3	109.5	103.3
Average Gain	3.9	4.2	4.3	3.8	3.5
Net Passing Yards	3360	3586	2540	3050	3485
Per Game	210.0	224.1	158.8	203.3	217.8
Times Sacked	60	55	104	72	57
Passer Rating in Yards	4.2	4.0	3.2	4.4	4.7
Opponent Net Passing Yards	3050	2930	3235	3606	4147
Per Game	190.6	183.1	202.2	240.4	259.2
Times Sacked	60	53	53	57	42
Passer Rating Defense	4.3	4.3	4.1	4.8	4.7
Passer Rating Net	-0.1	-0.3	-0.9	-0.4	-0.1
Yards per Drive Offense	22.6	25.2	21.1	22.5	25.6
Yards per Drive Defense	25.6	24.8	24.5	23.4	26.0
Average Time of Possession	29:30	29:13	31:57	31:41	31:08

1988 PLAYOFFS
Lost Divisional Playoff Game to Chicago, 12-20

THE 1988 SEASON

DATE	AT	OPPONENT	SCORE	R	SPREAD	Tu	Net YDS	Rush YDS	Pass YDS	TURN
09/04	A	Tampa Bay	41-14	W	-6	g	389-362	141- 43	248-319	2-5
09/11	H	Cincinnati	24-28	L	-5	a	415-431	190- 78	225-353	1-3
09/18	A	Washington	10-17	L	+4.5	g	299-285	90-150	209-135	0-2
09/25	A	Minnesota	21-23	L	+6	a	205-392	70-105	135-287	2-3
10/02	H	Houston	32-23	W	-4	a	455-194	190- 55	265-139	1-3
10/10	H*	N.Y. Giants	24-13	W	-2	a	452-436	109-100	343-336	0-1
10/16	A	Cleveland	3-19	L	+0	g	119-361	71-182	48-179	2-1
10/23	H	Dallas	24-23	W	-5.5	a	339-437	65-109	274-328	2-1
10/30	H	Atlanta	24-27	L	-10.5	a	424-294	155- 92	269-202	3-1
11/06	H	L.A. Rams	30-24	W	+1.5	a	436-427	123- 69	313-358	0-5
11/13	A	Pittsburgh	27-26	W	-3	a	358-361	106-164	252-197	3-1
11/20	A	N.Y. Giants	23-17	W	+3.5	a	283-394	108- 77	175-317	1-3
11/27	H	Phoenix	31-21	W	-5.5	a	292-369	94-167	198-202	4-5
12/04	H	Washington	19-20	L	-3.5	a	310-410	163- 81	147-329	3-4
12/10	A	Phoenix	23-17	W	+2	g	283-399	141- 46	142-353	2-4
12/18	A	Dallas	23- 7	W	-2	a	371-239	133-137	238-102	0-3
						Avg.	339-362	122-103	218-259	2-3

					WINS		LOSSES	
Season Record:	10- 6-0		POINTS:		28- 19		17- 22	
Vs. Spread:	9- 7-0		Net YDS:	7- 9-0	366-362		295-362	
Home:	5- 3-0		Rush YDS:	9- 7-0	121- 97		123-115	
On Artificial Turf:	8- 4-0		Pass YDS:	6-10-0	245-265		172-248	
Art. Turf vs. Spread:	7- 5-0		TURN:	12- 4-0	2- 3		2- 2	

* Monday Night

mOST vALUABLE pLAYER

We probably shouldn't admit this. A couple of years ago we watched the Eagles play a preseason game. They had this big kid at quarterback who always seemed to be either running for a first down, running for his life, or getting sacked. Lot of guts, we said, but his passing didn't impress us. Of course we didn't see that much of it. When he wasn't getting buried, he was racing around end. After the game we made our judgment: "He might make a good linebacker, but he'll never be a quarterback."

Well, we still think Randall Cunningham would make a good linebacker, but we were a little off about the other position. All right, we were *way* off. Dead wrong. Satisfied?

Cunningham is a very good quarterback. As a matter of fact, we are convinced he was the most valuable player in the NFL last season. You'll notice we didn't capitalize the phrase. There's a reason. Most of the MVP awards we saw went to Cincinnati's Boomer Esiason, and we don't exactly disagree. Normally MVPs are offensive players, and not just because they are more glamorous then defenders. It's a team game, but an offensive player can usually make a bigger impact on the outcome than a defender. There have been some exceptions, but we said "usually." If you're going to pick an offensive player, you'll pick a quarterback nine out of ten times. Call him the most important player on the offense or just the most visible. And once you've settled on a quarterback, you look at his team's record and his passing record and you make your choice.

	TEAM	ATT	COM	PCT.	YARD	Avg G	TD	%TD	IN	%IN	RATE	NEWS*
Esiason	12-4	388	223	57.5	3572	9.21	28	7.2	14	3.6	97.4	8.30
Cunningham	10-6	560	301	53.8	3808	6.80	24	4.3	16	2.9	77.6	5.89

* NEWS Rate = YDS + (10 X TD) - (45 X IN) / Att

There's no comparison, really. Boomer's Bengals had a better season than Randall's Eagles. And Boomer was a better (or more efficient) passer, according to the NFL's rating system or our NEWS system (which we believe is a tad more accurate). Some fans would want to add in Cunningham's rushing. Okay.

	AT	YDS	AVG	TD
Esiason	43	248	5.8	1
Cunningham	93	624	6.7	6

Certainly a big edge to Cunningham, but not enough to offset Esiason's lead in passing.

We're not about to get into intangibles like "leadership," and "clutch ability," or any of those other unmeasurables some folks prate about so learnedly. At best those things are like beauty—in the eye of the beholder. We're just simple folk, looking at plain numbers, and handing Esiason an MVP Award. Wear it in good health, Boomer.

However, we still think Cunningham was the most valuable player (lowercase all the way) last season. To his team.

The Bengals would have still been a fair team with an average quarterback. With an average guy at QB for the Eagles, they would have been Sparrows.

Again, look at the numbers. Esiason, rushing and passing, accounted for 3,820 of the Bengals' 6,057 yards—63.1 percent. If we subtract the yards he lost when he was sacked—no more unfair than crediting him for every yard gained passing—we find that he accounted for 59 percent of the yards. That's terrific, but Cunningham got 81.6 percent of the Eagles' net yards. Holy Toledo! Subtract his sack yardage—and Cunningham gets sacked a lot—and it's still 73.5 percent.

The numbers are even more impressive if you look at them game by game.

CUNNINGHAM IN 1988

WK	OPP.	SCORE	AT	CO	YDS	TD	IN	NEWS*	R†	NO/YD	AT	YDS	TD	YARD	-SAK
1	TB	41-14	12	7	156	2	1	10.92	W	0/ 0	5	21	1	45.5	45.5
2	Cin	24-28	36	25	261	1	1	6.28	W	4/36	9	85	0	83.4	74.7
3	Was	10-17	35	15	236	1	0	7.03	W	6/45	6	40	0	92.3	77.3
4	Min	21-23	23	13	187	2	1	7.04	W	8/52	4	18	0	100.0	74.6
5	Hou	32-23	38	24	289	2	0	8.13	W	3/24	3	59	1	76.5	71.2
6	NYG	24-13	41	31	369	3	0	9.73	W	4/26	2	8	0	83.4	77.7
7	Cle	3-19	27	15	114	0	2	0.89	L	9/66	3	22	0	114.3	58.8
8	Dal	24-23	53	26	298	2	1	5.15	T	5/24	5	35	0	98.2	91.2
9	Atl	24-27	48	21	289	2	2	4.56	L	3/20	6	54	0	80.9	76.2
10	Rams	30-24	39	22	323	3	0	9.05	W	1/10	8	53	0	88.5	86.2
11	Pit	27-26	41	25	276	0	2	4.54	L	2/24	8	48	2	90.5	83.8
12	NYG	23-17	36	14	224	0	1	4.97	L	5/49	8	65	1	102.1	84.8
13	Pho	31-21	35	17	214	2	2	4.11	L	3/25	3	1	0	73.6	65.1
14	Was	19-20	32	16	165	1	2	2.66	L	3/18	7	49	0	69.0	63.2
15	Pho	23-17	26	10	169	1	1	5.15	T	3/27	9	21	1	67.1	57.6
16	Dal	23- 7	38	20	238	2	0	6.79	W	0/ 0	5	50	0	77.6	77.6
W-L-T†: 8-6-2			560	301	3808	24	16	5.89		57/442	93	624	6	81.6	73.5

* NEWS Rate = YDS + (10 X TD) - (45 X IN) / Att

† W-L-T indicates superior, inferior, and average performances
  (W = NEWS of 6.48 or more, L = NEWS of 5.10 or less, T = NEWS from 5.11 to 6.47)

You want to hear something else? Cunningham was directly responsible for—that is, he either threw for or ran for—30 of the Eagles' 42 offensive touchdowns (71.4 percent). Esiason was directly responsible for 29 of the Bengals' 55 touchdowns (52.7 percent), about the same ratio as we had on yards.

Let's take a look at the way the season went.

The Eagles marched to the playoffs kind of like James Fenimore Cooper's Indians marched to Fort William Henry. They were out there somewhere, sometimes you heard drums or a broken twig, but you never knew for sure if they

were skulking about until they stood atop the parapet with reeking scalps from New York, Phoenix, Washington, and Dallas dangling from their belts. Only then did someone shout, "Hey, where in hell did them varmints come from?"

It turns out they'd been hiding behind a 3-4 record in their first seven games. The Giants, Cards, and Redskins were only 4-3 at that time, but they were the favorites. Two weeks later the Giants had pulled out to 6-3 and the Eagles lagged in fourth place at 4-5. You had to figure the Cardinals might drop away, but the Giants had a soft schedule and the Redskins were the defending Super Bowl champs. So about that time, unless you were from Philadelphia, you took your eye off the Eagles and they disappeared into the underbrush.

In the meantime the Bengals won their first six games. Again, unless you were from Philadelphia, which team would you track?

So while Cincinnati was winning blowouts by 45–21, 36–19, 44–21, and 42–7, you may not have noticed that the Eagles won seven of their last nine games. And you surely never savvied the margins in those games. Two of the wins were by a single point—over Dallas and Pittsburgh. Three were by six points—over the Rams, the Giants, and the Cards. Only Philadelphia's first win over Phoenix (by 10 points) and the season-ending win over Dallas (by 16 points) had comfortable margins.

Cincinnati probably would have won a 42–7 game with Turk Schonert at QB. Maybe the score would have been only 28–14, but a win is a win. The Eagles could have been 5–11 with Matt Cavanaugh under center.

Esiason was MVP, but Randall Cunningham was the mvp.

THE TROUBLE
WITH RANDALL . . .

Cunningham may have been the most important player to his team of anyone in the NFL, but he wasn't the best quarterback. We're not even certain we'd rather have him than any other QB in the NFC's Eastern Division. Let's see, Pelluer hasn't proved himself at Dallas; neither has Rypien at Washington, and Williams is getting older; Lomax might be our druther except for his arthritic hip. That leaves the Giants' Phil Simms. Hmmm. Would we rather have Simms than Cunningham?

Simms is thirty-three and Cunningham is twenty-six. With Phil you get experience; with Randall you get youth. Well, Randall will have plenty of experience in five years and Phil will just be old.

Simms used to get hurt all the time, but he's been durable lately. Cunningham must be made of iron. Take Randall.

Simms is a better passer.

	ATT	COM	PCT.	YARD	Avg G	TD	%TD	IN	%IN	RATE	NEWS
Simms	479	263	54.9	3359	7.01	21	4.4	11	2.3	82.1	6.41

But not by that much. And he can't run with Randall.

So, okay, we'd take Cunningham on our team. We'd even feel comfortable with our choice if it wasn't for two things.

First of all, he runs too much. Granted none of the Eagles' running backs had much luck last season. But when a quarterback leads his team in rushing (for the second consecutive year), we don't see the glass as half full. To us it's half empty. We think of a running quarterback as an IR waiting to happen. If a running back gets hurt running the ball, well, running the ball is his job. That's why most of them don't last much more than a half dozen years. When a quarterback runs on purpose, he's risking his team's whole attack for the sake of a few yards. Norm Van Brocklin said a quarterback should run only out of sheer terror. Van Brocklin played quarterback in the NFL for twelve years and quit with both his knees intact.

We know Cunningham isn't Bobby Douglass, the Bears' QB in the early seventies. Douglass was a terrific runner and lousy passer. When he ran, the Bears sometimes scored; when he passed, the opponents often did. Cunningham can

pass, and quite well, too. That's why we hate to see him afoot so much. His arm is more valuable than his feet.

Understand, maneuverability, agility, and a little speed are desirable in a quarterback. They help him avoid a pass rush. And we're not against one or two surprise bootlegs, a quarterback sneak, and a scramble a game. But any QB who runs more than three times a game on purpose had better have a good backup. Randall averaged nearly twice that many per game last season.

It is true that Cunningham's running helps his receivers get open by pulling defenders up from the secondary to cover him when he starts to dash. From a yardage standpoint he comes out ahead. Maybe he could find some compromise that wouldn't bring him into such constant violent contact with large persons who wish to do him harm.

Because he runs so well, it's surprising that he's so often sacked—our second misgiving. Sure, he plays behind a tissue paper line. But the numbers are still too high. He's getting better, but he averaged three to four sacks a game last season. Esiason averaged under two.

	GAMES	PASSES	SACKS	TOT. ATT	PERCENT	PER GAME
1985	6/ 4	81	20	101	19.8	3.3
1986	15/ 5	209	72	281	25.6	4.8
1987	12/12	406	54	460	11.7	4.5
1988	16/16	560	57	617	9.2	3.6
	49/37	1256	203	1459	13.9	4.1

Aside from the obvious disruption of drives all those sacks make for, we're back to that injury worry again. Just why Cunningham gets sacked so often is hard to figure. Supposedly he reads defenses well, and he certainly has the running ability to escape a rush. There's something to be said for waiting till the last second for a receiver to break open, but that usually gets a quarterback creamed after he's thrown the ball. Our best guess is that he has too much faith in his running ability. He starts to run instead of throwing the ball away and is sometimes sacked. When he gets away with it, he's credited with a rushing attempt.

Between the running and the sacking, Cunningham takes more hits in a season than a blackjack table. But if he stays healthy—and we think of it as a big "if"—he will get even better. And with his combination of brains, courage, and talent, he could end up as one of the best quarterbacks who ever played the game. Not bad for a linebacker.

OUR BUDDY

It would be interesting if fifty years from now the only thing Buddy Ryan was remembered for was that he coached Randall Cunningham. It would also be a little surprising. Say what you will, Ryan—who always seems to say what he wills—has gotten impressive results. Going from 5-10-1 to 7-8 in his first two seasons looked good, but actually it was better than that. Ryan made no secret of his contempt for the replacement players he had for the strike games in '87 and lost all three games if not by design, at least by disdain. His stance endeared him to his union players, and when they came back, they played like hell for him. He figures his '87 record as 7-5, and he's probably right. It might not even be too much to say that the 1988 Eastern Division title was won by Buddy's handling of the '87 strike. On paper the Eagles don't match up as a playoff team, but Ryan gets his men to play as well as they can. And sometimes better. What more can you ask of a coach?

Apparently that he keep his mouth shut once in a while. Buddy's criticism of the replacement players procured by the front office did not endear him to those charged with that responsibility. His ego (he gave himself an A-double-plus for his first year as the Eagles' coach), his cutting remarks about players he's cut ("Trade him for a six-pack, and it doesn't have to be cold!"), and his feud with Mike Ditka set him up for a fall. His praise of his own players was probably what led owner Norman Braman to announce that he expected to be in the playoffs in '88. Many took that as meaning Buddy had to win or else. Now that he's won, can he do it again?

While there are many who would savor seeing Ryan take a tumble, few of them are likely to be journalists. Ol' Buddy is always good for a controversial quote, and that certainly makes life easier for the chroniclers of the *Daily Fish Wrapper*. Ryan fired would make a good story for a week, but

Ryan working is a whole season's worth of articles. He's the best combination of coaching and copy in the NFL.

It was probably Ryan's mouth that kept him from becoming a head coach a long time ago. He was on the staff of the Jets' Super Bowl team in 1968, and some of Bud Grant's strong Viking teams in the seventies. He finally hit public awareness as defensive coordinator for the Bears' championship team in 1985, when his "46" defense was on every fan's lips and every coach's blackboard. Just who should get the credit for Chicago's Super Bowl victory that year is the source of his Ditka phobia.

As a certified defensive genius (Buddy wouldn't limit "genius" with a modifier), Ryan gets more out of his Eagle defenders than might at first be apparent. They give up a boatload of yards—362.4 per game in 1988—but Ryan doesn't count yards. He points out that his team shuts down the run very well—103.3 yards per game—forcing the opposition to pass. And once the ball's in the air, his troops go after it. They've been on the plus side in turnovers in each of his three seasons. Last year they were 18 to the good, better than one per game ahead of the other guys. The result was that they were outgained by 369 yards but still outscored their opponents by 60 points.

SACK KING

While Ryan doesn't have the defensive stalwarts in Philadelphia that he had in Chicago, the Eagles possess one absolutely great defender. Reggie White, at 6'5" and 285 pounds, is every quarterback's nightmare. Since entering the Eagles' nest in 1985, after two years fooling around in the USFL, White has established himself as the world's premier sack artist. Interestingly enough, he improved his marks once he came to play with the grownups.

YEAR	GM	SACK	P/GM
USFL	34	23.5	0.69
1985	13	13.0	1.00
1986	16	18.0	1.13
1987	12	21.0*	1.75
1988	16	18.0*	1.13
NFL	57	70.0	1.23

* Led NFL

At least part of the reason for his many sacks is the way Ryan moves him around in the "46" defense. He's likely to be anywhere along the line, thus disrupting blocking schemes. The technical name for it is "creating havoc."

White is a Baptist minister when he's not crunching quarterbacks. We loved the irony when Ryan said, "Every time we win, he credits the Lord, but whenever we lose, everybody blames me." Gosh, Buddy, from what you said we thought they were the same.

PHILADELPHIA EAGLES STATISTICS

1988 TEAM STATISTICS	PE	OPP
TOTAL FIRST DOWNS	318	311
Rushing	105	85
Passing	179	199
Penalty	34	27
3rd Down Made/Att.	92/246	74/225
Pct.	37.4%	32.9%
4th Down Made/Att.	8/12	10/19
Pct.	66.7%	52.6%
TOTAL NET YARDS	5430	5799
Avg. per Game	339.4	362.4
Total Plays	1102	1086
Avg. per Play	4.9	5.3
NET YARDS RUSHING	1945	1652
Avg. per Game	121.6	103.3
Total Rushes	464	466
NET YARDS PASSING	3485	4147
Avg. per Game	217.8	259.2
Tackled/Yards Lost	57/442	42/296
Gross Yards	3927	4443
Attempts/Completions	581/309	578/309
Pct. of Completions	53.2%	45.5%
Had Intercepted	17	32
PUNTS/AVERAGE	104/39.7	85/37.8
NET PUNTING AVG.	34.3	32.4
PENALTIES/YARDS	115/907	115/897
FUMBLES/BALL LOST	29/9	28/12
TOUCHDOWNS	44	37
Rushing	17	11
Passing	25	23
Returns	2	3
TIME OF POSSESSION	—	—

SCORE/PERIODS	1	2	3	4	OT	TOTAL
Eagles	76	131	65	101	6	379
Opponents	111	47	73	88	0	319

SCORING	TDR	TDP	TDRt	PAT	FG	S	TP
Zendejas,	D-P			35/36	20/27		95
Zendejas,	P			30/31	19/24		87
Byars	6	4					60
Carter		6	1				42
Cunningham	6						36
K. Jackson		6					36
Toney	4	1					30
Quick		4					24
Dorsey				9/9	4/7		21
Johnson		2					12
Simmons			1			1	8
Garrity		1					6
Giles		1					6
Hoage	1						6
Dawson				3/3		1	3
Jenkins						1	2
Eagles	17	25	2	42/43	23/32	2	379
Opponents	11	23	3	35/37	20/29	1	312

RUSHING	NO	YDS	AVG	LG	TD
Cunningham	93	624	6.7	33t	6
Byars	152	517	3.4	52	6
Toney	139	502	3.6	20	4
Haddix	57	185	3.2	15	0

(Continued)

RUSHING	NO	YDS	AVG	LG	TD
Hoage	1	38	38.0	38t	1
Teltschik	2	36	18.0	23	0
Tautalatasi	14	28	2.0	9	0
Abercrombie	5	14	2.8	5	0
Carter	1	1	1.0	1	0
Eagles	464	1945	4.2	52	17
Opponents	466	1652	3.5	65	11

RECEIVING	NO	YDS	AVG	LG	TD
K. Jackson	81	869	10.7	41	6
Byars	72	705	9.8	37t	4
Carter	39	761	19.5	80t	6
Toney	34	256	7.5	24	1
Quick	22	508	23.1	55t	4
Johnson	19	417	21.9	54	2
Garrity	17	208	12.2	20	1
Haddix	12	82	6.8	14	0
Giles	6	57	9.5	17	1
Tautalatasi	5	48	9.6	21	0
Konecny	1	18	18.0	18	0
Abercrombie	1	-2	-2.0	-2	0
Eagles	309	3927	12.7	80t	25
Opponents	309	4443	14.4	93t	23

INTERCEPTIONS	NO	YDS	AVG	LG	TD
Hoage	8	116	14.5	38	0
Allen	5	76	15.2	21	0
Hopkins	5	21	4.2	11	0
Joyner	4	96	24.0	30	0
Frizzell	3	19	6.3	13	0
Waters	3	19	6.3	14	0
Young	2	5	2.5	5	0
Everett	1	0	0.0	0	0
Brown	1	-5	-5.0	-5	0
Bell	0	24	—	24	9
Eagles	32	371	11.6	38	0
Opponents	17	98	5.8	29	0

PUNTING	NO	YDS	AVG	TB	In 20	LG	Blk
Cunningham	3	167	55.7	0	0	58	0
Teltschik	98	3958	40.4	8	28	70	3
Eagles	104	4125	39.7	8	28	70	3
Opponents	85	3209	37.8	11	17	56	3

PUNT RETURNS	NO	FC	YDS	AVG	LG	TD
Konecny	33	25	233	7.1	24	0
Eagles	33	25	233	7.1	24	0
Opponents	47	27	393	8.4	68	0

KICKOFF RETURNS	NO	YDS	AVG	LG	TD
Beals	34	625	18.4	32	0
Konecny	17	276	16.2	25	0
Abercrombie	5	87	17.4	31	0
Byars	2	20	10.0	14	0
Jenkins	1	20	20.0	20	0
Bartlett	0	0	—	0	0
Eagles	59	1028	17.4	32	0
Opponents	63	1266	20.1	73	0

FIELD GOALS	1-19	20-29	30-39	40-49	50+	TOTAL
Zendejas, DP	2-2	6-6	7-9	4-7	1-3	20-27
Zendejas, P	2-2	6-6	7-9	3-4	1-3	19-24
Dorsey	0-0	3-3	1-2	0-2	0-0	4-7
Dawson	0-0	0-1	0-0	0-0	0-0	0-1
Eagles	2-2	9-10	8-11	3-6	1-3	23-32
Opponents	0-0	9-12	6-7	4-8	1-2	20-29

FIELD GOALS BY Zendejas: 20 of 27
(49N)(47G,49N)( )( )(22G,39G,41G)(37G)
(39G)(28G,51N)(23G,50G,40G)(56N,34G,
18G)(37G,31N)(28G)(40G,45N,19G)( )(37G,
35N,27G,27G)
Dorsey: (23G,26G)(42N,34G)(23G,35N,47N)
Dawson: ( )( )( )(22N)
Eagles: (23G,26G)(42N,34G)(23G,35N,47N)(22N)
(22G,39G,41G)(37G)(39G)(28G,51N)(23G,50G,40G)
(56N,34G,18G)(37G,31N)(28G)(40G,45N,19G)( )(37G,
35N,27G,27G)

PASSING	ATT	COM	YARD	PCT.	Avg G	TD	%TD	IN	%IN	LG	SAKS/YDS	RATE
Cunningham	560	301	3808	53.8	6.80	24	4.3	16	2.9	80t	57/442	77.6
Cavanaugh	16	7	101	43.8	6.31	1	6.3	1	6.3	42	0/0	59.6
Teltschik	3	1	18	33.3	6.00	0	0.0	0	0.0	18	0/0	54.9
Byars	2	0	0	0.0	0.00	0	0.0	0	0.0	0	0/0	39.6
Eagles	581	309	3927	53.2	6.76	25	4.3	17	2.9	80t	57/442	76.7
Opponents	578	309	4443	53.5	7.69	23	4.0	32	5.5	93t	42/296	68.9

PHOENIX CARDINALS

The Last 5 Seasons

	1984	1985	1986	1987	1988
Won-Lost	9-7	5-11	4-11-1	7-8	7-9
Percentage	.563	.313	.281	.467	.438
Division Finish	2-t	5	5	2-t	3-t
Games Behind	2	5	9.5	4	3
Total Points	423	278	218	362	344
Per Game	26.4	17.4	13.6	24.1	21.5
Opponent Points	345	414	351	368	398
Per Game	21.6	25.9	21.9	24.5	24.9
Net Points	78	-136	-133	-6	-54
Predicted Net Wins	2.0	-3.4	-3.3	-0.2	-1.4
Delta Net Wins	-1.0	0.4	-0.2	-0.3	0.4
Total Yards on Offense	6345	5086	4503	5326	5807
Per Game	396.6	317.9	281.4	355.1	362.9
Total Yards Allowed on Defense	5094	5381	4864	5384	5159
Per Game	318.4	336.3	304.0	358.9	322.4
Net Difference	1251	-295	-361	-58	648
Offensive Turnovers	36	34	29	27	35
Defensive Takeaways	33	27	22	33	29
Net Turnovers	-3	-7	-7	6	-6
Predicted Net Points	92	-53	-58	19	30
Delta Net Points	-14	-83	-75	-25	-84
Net Rushing Yards	2088	1974	1787	1873	2027
Per Game	130.5	123.4	111.7	124.9	126.7
Average Gain	4.3	4.7	4.3	4.1	4.2
Opponent Net Rushing Yards	1923	2378	2227	2001	1925
Per Game	120.2	148.6	139.2	133.4	120.3
Average Gain	4.4	4.3	4.0	4.1	4.1
Net Passing Yards	4257	3112	2716	3453	3780
Per Game	266.1	194.5	169.8	230.2	236.3
Times Sacked	49	65	59	54	60
Passer Rating in Yards	6.2	4.2	3.5	5.2	5.1
Opponent Net Passing Yards	3171	3003	2637	3383	3234
Per Game	198.2	187.7	164.8	225.5	202.1
Times Sacked	55	32	41	41	39
Passer Rating Defense	4.5	5.6	5.0	5.7	5.1
Passer Rating Net	1.7	-1.4	-1.5	-0.6	-0.0
Yards per Drive Offense	30.7	24.9	23.2	28.2	28.5
Yards per Drive Defense	24.7	26.9	25.9	29.1	26.2
Average Time of Possession	32:43	29:22	29:18	30:33	31:27

THE 1988 SEASON

DATE	AT	OPPONENT	SCORE	R	SPREAD	Tu	Net YDS	Rush YDS	Pass YDS	TURN
09/04	A	Cincinnati	14-21	L	+5.5	a	374-403	167-152	207-251	2-1
09/12	H*	Dallas	14-17	L	-2.5	g	367-352	130-190	237-162	1-1
09/18	A	Tampa Bay	30-24	W	-3	g	475-298	181-114	294-184	0-3
09/25	H	Washington	30-21	W	+3	g	323-335	185- 53	138-282	1-2
10/02	A	L.A. Rams	41-27	W	+7.5	g	519-353	187- 85	332-268	1-3
10/09	H	Pittsburgh	31-14	W	-6	g	388-203	103- 78	285-125	3-2
10/16	A	Washington	17-33	L	+6	g	381-386	76- 97	305-289	2-1
10/23	H	Cleveland	21-29	L	+1	g	330-369	169- 68	161-301	4-4
10/30	A	Dallas	16-10	W	+3	a	295-228	160-125	135-103	0-2
11/06	H	S. Francisco	24-23	W	+3.5	g	355-357	67-240	288-117	3-0
11/13	H	N.Y. Giants	24-17	W	-1.5	g	485-280	142- 92	343-188	2-0
11/20	A	Houston	20-38	L	+6.5	a	314-385	60-124	254-261	2-0
11/27	A	Philadelphia	21-31	L	+5.5	a	369-292	167- 94	202-198	5-4
12/04	A	N.Y. Giants	7-44	L	+4	a	158-301	66-170	92-131	5-1
12/10	H	Philadelphia	17-23	L	-2	g	399-283	46-141	353-142	4-2
12/18	H	Green Bay	17-26	L	-6	g	265-344	118-105	147-239	1-3
						Avg.	362-323	127-121	236-203	2-2

			WINS	LOSSES
Season Record:	7- 9-0	POINTS:	28- 19	16- 29
Vs. Spread:	7- 9-0	Net YDS: 8- 8-0	406-293	329-346
Home:	4- 4-0	Rush YDS: 10- 6-0	146-112	111-127
On Artificial Turf:	1- 4-0	Pass YDS: 10- 6-0	259-181	218-219
Art. Turf vs. Spread:	1- 4-0	TURN: 5- 9-2	1- 2	3- 2

* Monday Night

SWAN DIVE INTO THE CACTUS

You can count on the birds. Swallows always return to Capistrano; buzzards forever come back to Hinckley; Hitchcock's movie eternally appears on The Late Show; and the NFL's Cardinals are ever among the league's disappointments. On Tuesday, November 15, 1988, the Phoenix Cardinals and their new fans could look at these standings in the NFC's Eastern Division:

NFC EAST	W	L	T	PCT.	PF	PA	Streak	Division			Conf.		
Phoenix	7	4	0	.636	262	236	W-3	3	2	0	6	2	0
N.Y. Giants	7	4	0	.636	236	223	L-2	4	2	0	7	4	0
Philadelphia	6	5	0	.545	260	237	W-2	2	1	0	4	3	0
Washington	6	5	0	.545	257	270	L-1	3	3	0	5	4	0
Dallas	2	9	0	.182	172	254	L-7	1	5	0	2	8	0

The scramble for the division title was just that—a scramble. But the Cardinals had to like their chances. Two days before, they'd extended their winning streak to three games and moved into a tie for the division lead by defeating the Giants. A win over New York, with whom they now shared first place, could be doubly important should the race end in a tie because head-to-head competition was the first tie-breaker. A division title and playoff berth would make a triumphant beginning to the team's residence in Phoenix.

Life was good.

Time passed. So did Neil Lomax.

At a little after five P.M. on Sunday, December 18, the Cardinals completed their first season in Phoenix on a sour note by losing to the Green Bay Packers, 17–26. By then the Cards were used to losing. They dropped their last five. In a row. Consecutively.

Had standings been published for those five weeks alone, they would have looked like this:

NFC EAST	W	L	T	PCT.	PF	PA	Streak	Division			Conf.		
Philadelphia	4	1	0	.800	119	82	W-2	4	1	0	4	1	0
N.Y. Giants	3	2	0	.600	123	81	L-1	1	1	0	2	1	0
Washington	1	4	0	.200	88	117	L-2	1	1	?	1	2	0
Dallas	1	4	0	.200	93	127	L-1	1	1	0	1	1	0
Phoenix	0	5	0	.000	82	162	L-5	0	3	0	0	4	0

Life was still good. But the Cardinals sucked.

WHY NOT
ST. LOUIS?

In St. Louis several ironic chuckles were heard, along with a smattering of horse laughs and an occasional "I-knew-it-all-along." But some St. Louisans didn't note the Cardinals' latest fall from grace and most didn't care. They'd given up on the football Cards years ago. In 1985, to be exact.

The people of St. Louis have gotten a bad rap by the NFL. Most fans around the country think St. Louis lost its football team because the city's population refused to flock in multitudes to Busch Stadium to cheer lustily for the latest 5–11 edition of the football team. You hear things like, "St. Louis is a baseball city and will never support a pro football team." The first part is undoubtedly true. St. Louisans do indeed favor their baseball Cardinals. And why shouldn't they? Over the years, the baseballers have brought numerous world and league championships to the city. The footballers, on the other hand, managed only two division crowns (1974–75)—followed by immediate elimination from the playoffs—in twenty-eight seasons.

However, a check of the attendance figures for the football Cardinals' last ten seasons shows that fans supported the team ably from 1978 through 1981, setting new total attendance records in three of those four years. The team responded with a 23–41 won-lost record.

YEAR	CARDS' RECORD	HOME GM	HOME ATTEND.	AVERAGE ATTEND.	LARGEST CROWD	SMALLEST CROWD	NFL RANK
1978	6-10-0	8	361,720*	45,215	49,282	39,200	25
1979	5-11-0	8	376,771*	47,096	50,855*	39,802	24
1980	5-11-0	8	373,573	46,696	50,701	35,942	24
1981	7- 9-0	8	384,375*	48,046	50,351	46,214	24
1982	5- 4-0	4	163,901	40,975	50,705	35,308	na[†]
1983	8- 7-1	8	309,612	38,701	48,532	21,902	27
1984	9- 7-0	8	372,154	46,519	51,010*	35,785	23
1985	5-11-0	8	325,353	40,669	49,347	28,090	25
1986	4-11-1	8	284,380	35,547	49,077	23,957	28
1987	7- 8-0	7	194,748	27,821	47,241	22,449[‡]	26

* New Cardinals record

[†] Not applicable; strike year: teams did not play the same number of home games.

[‡] Lowest for nonstrike game; the only strike game drew 11.

The strike in 1982 hurt all teams, but the Cardinals recovered to their old level in 1984, when a rare winning team and a "save-the-Cardinals" move helped sell tickets. But by 1985 it was obvious to everyone that the football team was a lame duck. Bidwill would move them somewhere that bid well. Only then did the people of St. Louis desert the team, abandoning it to the desert.

The problem that owner Bill Bidwill had with the city was the ballpark. Busch Stadium is fine for baseball, but its capacity of 51,392 meant that the team—no matter how enthusiastically embraced by the fans—could never rise out of the bottom quarter of teams in league attendance. While fans and media urged Bidwill to hire better players and suggested he was what chicks say, he could argue that his situation made it impossible for him to spend as lavishly as teams that could count on at least 100,000 more attendees per season.

His solution—that the city should build him a new stadium at public expense—was rejected by the city. Certainly the timing was not propitious, considering the economy of the early eighties. Besides, his flirtations with Jacksonville, Phoenix, and other cities seeking an NFL franchise eventually killed what fan support he had. By 1987 the Cardinals had to move.

Phoenix was anxious to oblige. The first seven crowds at Sun Devil Stadium (capacity 74,000) would have broken the old St. Louis single game attendance mark, despite the highest ticket prices in the NFL.

DATE	OPPONENT	PRE-GM RECORD	ATT.
September 12*	Dallas	0-1	67,139
September 25	Washington	1-2	61,973
October 9	Pittsburgh	3-2	53,278
October 23	Cleveland	4-3	61,261
November 6	San Francisco	5-4	64,544
November 13	N.Y. Giants	6-4	65,324
December 10[†]	Philadelphia	7-7	54,832
December 18	Green Bay	7-8	44,586
			472,937

* Monday Night

[†] Saturday afternoon

The average ducat goes for $38. If you want to see more than players' backs, add $40–50. And, if you want one of those 228 seats in the loge section, you'd better already own an oil well.

It remains to be seen how the folks of Phoenix will react to this first disappointment by their new team. If the past is prologue to the future, they'll see many more for this star-crossed franchise.

Curiously the Cardinals are the oldest continuing operation in the NFL, having begun in 1899 as the Morgan Athletic Club on Chicago's South Side, twenty-one years before the league was formed. A couple of seasons into their existence, the Morgans purchased some used, faded, red jerseys from the University of Chicago. Somehow, pinkish-gray became "cardinal red," and the team had a name. What it never had was good luck.

The Cardinals have always been jinxed. In forty NFL seasons in Chicago, they managed only two championships, and the 1925 title is disputed to this day. Bill Bidwill's father, Charles, built the second title team in 1947 but died that year before he ever got to see them play. They lost their championship the next year in the worst blizzard ever to hit Philadelphia. Always Chicago's "second" pro football team, the Cards decided to quit competing with the Bears and took their frustrations to St. Louis in 1960.

ANATOMY OF A COLLAPSE

Though the Cards' 1988 collapse came as no surprise in St. Louis, it was a new happenstance in Phoenix. Rather than simply chalk it up to the inevitable Cardinals' way of doing things, we thought it might be interesting to see if we could pinpoint what went wrong by looking at the stats.

The first step is about as surprising as learning that a cactus makes a lousy whoopee cushion:

Games	1-11	12-16
Record	7-4	0-5
Points Scored per Game	23.8	16.4
Points Allowed per Game	21.5	32.4

Aha! we say. The offense slipped a little and the defense went to pieces. Blame the defense. This theory is lent credence by an unfortunate incident that occurred at Houston in the first game of the five-loss dive. The Cards' starting free safety, Lonnie Young, was knocked out for the season with an elbow injury on the first play of the game. A few plays later his sub, Travis Curtis, went out with an ankle. Both were placed on IR. When Curtis healed faster than expected, the Cards tried to re-activate him early, necessitating running him through waivers. Washington grabbed him, exacerbating an already simmering feud between Cards Coach Gene Stallings and the Redskins' Joe Gibbs. Meanwhile, Phoenix was left with journeyman Lester Lyles at FS.

According to our hypothesis, the loss of Young opened the Cards' defense to deep passes. Then, when they tried to compensate by blitzing, they became vulnerable to the run and the whole defense collapsed.

A pretty theory. But look at this:

Games	OFFENSE		DEFENSE	
	1-11	12-16	1-11	12-16
Net Yards per Game	388.8	306.0	322.5	321.0
Off. Plays per Game	70.1	66.2	60.6	69.4
Average Gain	5.5	4.6	5.3	4.6

That doesn't look like a *defensive* collapse to us. The defense, never a record-setter, played pretty much at the same average speed right through to the end. If anything, it improved. Yet the scoring figures show the Cardinals gave up many more points per game in the collapse. Maybe a closer look will help explain:

Games	OFFENSE		DEFENSE	
	1-11	12-16	1-11	12-16
Rushing Yards per Game	142.7	91.4	117.4	126.8
Rushing Att. per Game	32.5	24.4	25.6	37.0
Average Gain	4.4	3.7	4.6	3.4
Pass Att. per Game	33.8	38.0	32.5	30.0
Completions per Game	19.2	22.2	17.3	14.8
Percentage	56.7	58.4	53.1	49.3
Net Yards per Game	248.4	209.6	206.6	194.2
Gross Yards per Game	272.4	238.8	225.2	212.4
Average Gain	8.1	6.3	6.9	7.1
Interceptions per Game	0.9	1.8	1.0	1.0
Sacked per Game	3.7	3.8	2.5	2.4
Yards Lost per Game	24.1	29.2	18.5	18.2

The rushing game dropped more than 50 yards a game, only partly explained by the fewer attempts. The passing game fell by 40 yards, despite averaging 3 more completions per contest.

An immediate new theory comes to mind. The offense kept putting the defense in a short field position. Opponents could score more by gaining less. This would be even more likely if turnovers by the Cardinals increased. Sure enough, when we checked, Phoenix went from a zero ratio in Game 11 (as many takeaways as giveaways) to a −9 at season's end.

We think we have it now. The onus for the Cardinals' collapse is mainly on the offense.

NAMING NAMES

Let's see if we can zoom in a little more. Let's round up the usual suspects.

Quarterback Neil Lomax's arthritic hip was well publicized in 1988, but through the Giants game in Week 11, he was having a great season. He was injured near the end of that game and missed the next two, with backup Cliff Stoudt taking over. Then Lomax returned for the last three losses.

Per game passing records:

	Games	ATT	COM	PCT.	YARD	Avg G	TD	IN	NEWS*
Lomax	1-11	30.5	18.4	60.3	248.7	8.17	1.7	0.7	7.66
Stoudt	12-13	36.0	21.5	59.7	238.5	6.65	2.0	2.0	3.46
Lomax	14-16	36.0	17.6	49.1	219.7	6.10	0.3	1.0	4.94

* NEWS Rate = YDS + (10 X TD) - (45 X IN) / Att

With Stoudt in there, interceptions more than doubled and the average gain per pass decreased by a yard and a half. Once Lomax returned, the average gain dropped another half yard and TD passes all but disappeared.

A check of the Cards' major receivers indicates that the major drop-off in production was at tight end.

RECEIVERS	GAMES 1-11				GAMES 12-16			
	PC	YDS	AVG	TD	PC	YDS	AVG	TD
J.T. Smith, WR	4.8	59.9	12.4	0.3	5.0	65.4	10.9	0.4
Roy Green, WR	4.3	78.6	18.4	0.6	4.2	46.4	11.0	0.0
Robert Awalt, TE	2.5	28.3	11.5	0.3	2.2	28.6	13.0	0.2
Jay Novacek, TE	2.7	44.8	16.4	0.4	1.6	15.2	9.5	0.0
Earl Ferrell, FB	2.5	21.0	8.3	0.2	2.0	16.8	8.4	0.0
Stump Mitchell, RB	1.5	14.8	10.2	0.1	1.8	10.2	5.7	0.0
Ernie Jones, WR	1.2	20.9	17.7	0.1	2.0	53.2	26.6	0.4
WIDE RECEIVERS	10.3	159.4	15.5	1.0	11.2	165.0	14.7	0.8
TIGHT ENDS	5.2	73.1	14.1	0.6	3.8	43.8	11.5	0.2
BACKS	4.0	35.8	8.9	0.3	3.8	27.0	7.1	0.0
Totals	19.5	268.3	13.8	1.9	18.8	235.8	12.5	1.0

Jay Novacek was so productive early in the year that *Pro Football Weekly* named him to its Mid-Season All-NFL Team. He tailed off badly in the second half, and Robert Awalt didn't pick up the slack. The evidence is that the Cards kept their long passing game but lost the short tosses that keep drives going. That's symptomatic of a team playing desperation catch-up. The number of rushing attempts dropped off, presumably because the Cardinals trailed and passed to try to catch up. However, that doesn't explain the dip in Earl Ferrell's productivity. The Cardinals insist it had nothing to do with his failing his drug test at the end of the season.

RUNNERS	GAMES 1-11				GAMES 12-16			
Per Game	ATT	YDS	AVG	TD	ATT	YDS	AVG	TD
Earl Ferrell, FB	13.5	66.3	4.9	0.4	10.8	39.4	3.6	0.6
Stump Mitchell, RB	10.7	47.1	4.4	0.2	9.2	41.6	4.5	0.4
Tony Jordan, FB	5.5	14.5	2.6	0.3	-	-	-	-
Totals	29.7	127.9	4.3	0.8	22.0	81.0	3.7	1.0

Fullback Tony Jordan went on IR at midyear.

THE MISTAKES

The lethal combination of offensive lassitude and mistakes and some slovenly special teams play doomed the Cardinals in their last five games. Had the offense performed at the same level as in the first eleven games, Phoenix might have overcome some of the errors. Let's have a look at those five season-ending defeats.

Loss Number One: The Oilers held the Cards without a first down through twenty-five minutes of the first half and built up a 24-7 halftime lead en route to a 38-20 win.

Although it gave up 38 points, the defense was killed by an ineffective offense.

Loss Number Two: The Cards outgained the Eagles, but Stoudt threw four interceptions and Ferrell fumbled on a first-and-goal situation. Another Phoenix TD was called back on a penalty. 31-21, Eagles. Here we blame the offensive errors in what was otherwise a good performance.

Loss Number Three: Val Sikahema fumbled the opening kickoff to hand the Giants a field goal. A three-downs-and-out series by the Cards on their first possession gave New York good field position, and Phoenix was down 10-0 within the first six minutes. When they tried to play catch-up, Lomax threw two interceptions and the runners coughed up two fumbles. The Giants took it from there, 44-7.

Loss Number Four: The Cardinals turned the ball over twice in the first quarter, leading to two Eagle touchdowns. After getting down 21–0, the Cardinals put on their best offensive performance of the losing streak, gaining 399 yards. It wasn't quite enough, as Philadelphia won 23–17.

Loss Number Five: The Cardinals held onto the ball, but Lomax wasn't effective, going 15-for-33 and being sacked 3 times for a net of only 147 yards. Green Bay was more productive: 244 passing yards. The Cards' punting team allowed Green Bay a 63-yard touchdown return. It was 26–17, Green Bay, and a sad end to the Cardinals' first season in their new home.

PHOENIX CARDINALS STATISTICS

1988 TEAM STATISTICS	PC	OPP
TOTAL FIRST DOWNS	336	301
Rushing	122	110
Passing	195	171
Penalty	19	20
3rd Down Made/Att.	92/230	75/210
Pct.	40.0%	35.7%
4th Down Made/Att.	12/20	5/10
Pct.	60.0%	50.0%
TOTAL NET YARDS	5807	5169
Avg. per Game	362.9	323.1
Total Plays	1102	1014
Avg. per Play	5.3	5.1
NET YARDS RUSHING	2027	1925
Avg. per Game	126.7	120.3
Total Rushes	480	467
NET YARDS PASSING	3780	3244
Avg. per Game	236.3	202.8
Tackled/Yards Lost	60/411	39/295
Gross Yards	4191	3539
Attempts/Completions	562/322	508/264
Pct. of Completions	57.3%	52.0%
Had Intercepted	19	16
PUNTS/AVERAGE	80/40.3	83/41.1
NET PUNTING AVG.	32.9	33.1
PENALTIES/YARDS	99/790	103/770
FUMBLES/BALL LOST	34/16	27/13
TOUCHDOWNS	44	51
Rushing	15	19
Passing	26	30
Returns	3	2
TIME OF POSSESSION	—	—

SCORE/PERIODS	1	2	3	4	OT	TOTAL
Cardinals	67	114	51	112	0	344
Opponents	101	106	84	107	0	398

SCORING	TDR	TDP	TDRt	PAT	FG	S	TP
Del Greco				42/44	12/21		78
Ferrell	7	2					54
Green		7					42
S. Mitchell	4	1					30
J. Smith		5					30
Awalt		4					24
Novacek		4					24
Jones		3					18
Jordan	3						18
Junior			1				6
Lomax	1						6
Mack			1				6
Saddler			1				6
Harvey						1	2
Cardinals	15	26	3	42/44	12/21	1	344
Opponents	19	30	2	47/51	13/22	3	398

RUSHING	NO	YDS	AVG	LG	TD
Ferrell	202	924	4.6	47	7
S. Mitchell	164	726	4.4	47	4
Jordan	61	160	2.6	12	3
Stoudt	14	57	4.1	14	0
Lomax	17	55	3.2	13	1
Wolfley	9	43	4.8	20	0
Horne	3	20	6.7	20	0
J. Smith	1	15	15.0	15	0
Novacek	1	10	10.0	10	0
Del Greco	1	8	8.0	8	0
Jeffery	3	8	2.7	9	0
Green	4	1	0.3	18	0
Cardinals	480	2027	4.2	47	15
Opponents	467	1925	4.1	52	19

RECEIVING	NO	YDS	AVG	LG	TD
J. Smith	83	986	11.9	29	5
Green	68	1097	16.1	52	7
Awalt	39	454	11.6	52t	4
Novacek	38	569	15.0	42t	4
Ferrell	38	315	8.3	30	2
S. Mitchell	25	214	8.6	28	1
Jones	23	496	21.6	93t	3
Jordan	4	24	6.0	12	0
Wolfley	2	11	5.5	8	0
Moore	1	15	15.0	15	0
Holmes	1	10	10.0	10	0
Cardinals	322	4191	13.0	93t	26
Opponents	264	3539	13.4	61t	30

INTERCEPTIONS	NO	YDS	AVG	LG	TD
Mack	3	33	11.0	12	0
Carter	3	0	0.9	0	0
McDonald	2	11	5.5	11	0
Lyles	2	0	9.0	0	0
Curtis	1	18	18.0	18	0
Le. Smith	1	15	15.0	15	0
Clasby	1	7	7.0	7	0
Junior	1	2	2.0	2	0
Young	1	2	2.0	2	0
R. Mitchell	1	0	0.0	0	0
Cardinals	16	88	5.5	18	0
Opponents	19	264	13.9	39	0

PUNTING	NO	YDS	AVG	TB	In 20	LG	Blk
Horne	79	3228	40.9	9	16	66	1
Cardinals	80	3228	40.3	9	16	66	1
Opponents	83	3414	41.1	10	18	62	0

PUNT RETURNS	NO	FC	YDS	AVG	LG	TD
Sikahema	33	8	341	10.3	28	0
J. Smith	17	2	119	7.0	15	0

(Continued)

(Continued)

PUNT RETURNS	NO	FC	YDS	AVG	LG	TD
Hunley	1	0	3	3.0	3	0
McAdoo	1	0	0	0.0	0	0
McDonald	0	1	0	—	0	0
Cardinals	52	11	463	8.9	28	0
Opponents	41	11	416	10.1	63t	1

KICKOFF RETURNS	NO	YDS	AVG	LG	TD
Sikahema	23	475	20.7	39	0
McAdoo, TB-Phoe	13	311	23.9	32	0
McAdoo, Phoe	9	203	22.6	32	0
Jones	11	147	13.4	22	0
S. Mitchell	10	221	22.1	41	0
Clark	2	10	5.0	7	0
Ferrell	2	25	12.5	14	0
Jeffery	1	11	11.0	11	0

(Continued)

KICKOFF RETURNS	NO	YDS	AVG	LG	TD
Phillips	1	4	4.0	4	0
Schillinger	1	10	10.0	10	0
Cardinals	60	1106	18.4	41	0
Opponents	65	1379	21.2	92t	1

FIELD GOALS	1-19	20-29	30-39	40-49	50+	TOTAL
Del Greco	1-1	4-6	3-3	3-9	1-2	12-21
Cardinals	1-1	4-6	3-3	3-9	1-2	12-21
Opponents	0-0	5-6	4-5	4-11	0-0	13-22

FIELD GOALS BY Del Greco: 12 of 21
(58N)(40N)(47G,37G,47N,23G)( )(43G,51G)
(19G)(38G,47N,47N)( )(32G)(24G)(28G)( )
(44N,28N)( )(40G,48N)(20G,20N)

PASSING	ATT	COM	YARD	PCT.	Avg G	TD	%TD	IN	%IN	LG	SAKS/YDS	RATE
Lomax	443	255	3395	57.6	7.66	20	4.5	11	2.5	93t	46/315	86.7
Stoudt	113	63	747	55.8	6.61	6	5.3	8	7.1	52t	13/85	64.3
Tupa	6	4	49	66.7	8.17	0	0.0	0	0.0	22	1/11	91.7
Cardinals	562	322	4191	57.3	7.46	26	4.6	19	3.4	93t	60/411	82.2
Opponents	508	264	3539	52.0	6.97	30	5.9	16	3.1	61t	39/295	81.0

SAN FRANCISCO 49ERS

The Last 5 Seasons

	1984	1985	1986	1987	1988
Won-Lost	15-1	10-6	10-5-1	13-2	10-6
Percentage	.938	.625	.656	.867	.625
Division Finish	1	2	1	1	1-t
Games Behind	0	1	0	0	0
Total Points	475	411	374	459	369
Per Game	29.7	25.7	23.4	30.6	23.1
Opponent Points	227	263	247	253	294
Per Game	14.2	16.4	15.4	16.9	18.4
Net Points	248	148	127	206	75
Predicted Net Wins	6.2	3.7	3.2	5.2	1.9
Delta Net Wins	0.8	-1.7	-0.7	0.3	0.1
Total Yards on Offense	6366	5920	6082	5987	5900
Per Game	397.9	370.0	380.1	399.1	368.8
Total Yards Allowed on Defense	5176	5191	4880	4095	4575
Per Game	323.5	324.4	305.0	273.0	285.9
Net Difference	1190	729	1202	1892	1325
Offensive Turnovers	22	34	29	26	26
Defensive Takeaways	38	35	49	38	38
Net Turnovers	16	1	20	12	12
Predicted Net Points	163	65	180	206	158
Delta Net Points	85	83	-53	0	-83
Net Rushing Yards	2465	2232	1986	2237	2523
Per Game	154.1	139.5	124.1	149.1	157.7
Average Gain	4.6	4.7	3.9	4.3	4.8
Opponent Net Rushing Yards	1795	1683	1555	1611	1588
Per Game	112.2	105.2	97.2	107.4	99.3
Average Gain	4.2	3.9	3.8	3.8	3.6
Net Passing Yards	3901	3688	4096	3750	3377
Per Game	243.8	230.5	256.0	250.0	211.1
Times Sacked	27	42	26	29	47
Passer Rating in Yards	7.2	5.6	5.6	6.7	5.4
Opponent Net Passing Yards	3381	3508	3325	2484	2987
Per Game	211.3	219.3	207.8	165.6	186.7
Times Sacked	51	60	51	37	42
Passer Rating Defense	4.0	4.1	2.7	3.0	3.9
Passer Rating Net	3.2	1.5	2.9	3.8	1.5
Yards per Drive Offense	34.6	28.9	29.0	32.2	29.6
Yards per Drive Defense	26.8	24.5	23.5	21.3	22.6
Average Time of Possession	30:26	28:45	30:28	31:43	30:31

1984 PLAYOFFS
Won Divisional Playoff from N.Y. Giants, 21-10
Won NFC Championship from Chicago, 23-0
Won Super Bowl XIX from Miami, 38-16

1985 PLAYOFFS
Lost Wild Card Playoff to N.Y. Giants, 3-17

1986 PLAYOFFS
Lost Divisional Playoff to N.Y. Giants, 3-49

1987 PLAYOFFS
Lost Divisional Playoff to Minnesota, 24-36

1988 PLAYOFFS
Won Divisional Playoff from Minnesota, 34-9
Won NFC Championship Game from Chicago, 28-3
Won Super Bowl XXIII from Cincinnati, 20-16

THE 1988 SEASON

DATE	AT	OPPONENT	SCORE	R	SPREAD	Tu	Net YDS	Rush YDS	Pass YDS	TURN
09/04	A	New Orleans	34-33	W	+0	a	289-344	124-147	165-197	2-3
09/11	A	N.Y. Giants	20-17	W	+2.5	a	430-309	181-112	249-197	2-0
09/18	H	Atlanta	17-34	L	-14	g	426-367	104-196	322-171	4-2
09/25	A	Seattle	38- 7	W	-2	a	580-154	239- 29	341-125	1-5
10/02	H	Detroit	20-13	W	-13.5	g	339-297	176- 49	163-248	1-2
10/09	H	Denver	13-16	L	-6.5	g	417-314	246-147	171-167	4-3
10/16	A	L.A. Rams	24-21	W	+0	g	429-237	245- 42	184-195	2-4
10/24	A*	Chicago	9-10	L	+2.5	g	213-237	78-122	135-115	1-1
10/30	H	Minnesota	24-21	W	-4	g	339-321	130- 92	209-229	2-3
11/06	A	Phoenix	23-24	L	-3.5	g	357-355	240- 67	117-288	0-3
11/13	H	L.A. Raiders	3- 9	L	-7	g	219-251	83-159	136- 92	2-1
11/21	H*	Washington	37-21	W	-3.5	g	320-327	112- 56	208-271	2-4
11/27	A	San Diego	48-10	W	-7	g	475-312	203-136	272-176	0-3
12/04	A	Atlanta	13- 3	W	-7	g	378-177	140- 43	238-134	0-1
12/11	H	New Orleans	30-17	W	-6.5	g	373-252	152- 70	221-182	2-2
12/18	H	L.A. Rams	16-38	L	-6	g	316-322	70-121	246-201	1-1
						Avg.	369-286	158- 99	211-187	2-2

				WINS	LOSSES
Season Record:	10- 6-0	POINTS:		29- 16	14- 22
Vs. Spread:	9- 7-0	Net YDS:	11- 5-0	395-273	325-308
Home:	4- 4-0	Rush YDS:	11- 5-0	170- 78	137-135
On Artificial Turf:	3- 0-0	Pass YDS:	10- 6-0	225-195	188-172
Art. Turf vs. Spread:	3- 0-0	TURN:	9- 4-3	1- 3	2- 2

* Monday Night

OLD MAN WALSH

For several years there's been a rumor making the rounds that Bill Walsh is a genius. A second rumor has it that Walsh started the first rumor.

"Genius" always seems a little highfalutin for somebody who spends his time putting little X's and O's in a playbook, but it takes all kinds. The only certified MENSA member we ever knew was smart as hell and made his living cleaning people's houses. Most geniuses don't get their names in the paper, so maybe lots of people we've met are in the genius range. Except for that guy down the street who revs his motorcycle every day at dawn.

When we were in school they gave us a test and told us they figured IQs by dividing the chronological age into the mental age and moving the decimal point. Like, if you were ten in birthdays but eleven in smarts, 11 divided by 10 meant your IQ was 1.10 which became 110. They said the genius cutoff was 140. We never saw the test scores, but we heard they later used ours in arithmetic class when they showed how to divide big numbers into little ones. Anyway, if our teachers were telling the truth, Bill Walsh is 58 from the neck down and 81 from the neck up. No wonder he retired from coaching after the Super Bowl, handing the reins over to George Seifert. But you know they'll be crying to have him back on the field as soon as the 49ers lose two in a row.

You can't really blame them. Until Walsh took over as head coach, the closest the 49ers ever came to a Super Bowl was losing the NFC Championship Games in 1970 and '71. The year before he arrived, the team was 2–14.

Okay, the year *after* he arrived the team was 2–14, too, and the word "genius" wasn't heard. But since then it's been mostly beer and skittles. The impressive thing to our thinking was that he got to three Super Bowls with three essentially different teams, reloading on the run, so that the 49ers didn't crash in between. Here are the lineups for the Super Bowl peaks.

	1981		1984		1988
	OFFENSE		**OFFENSE**		**OFFENSE**
WR	Dwight Clark	WR	Dwight Clark	WR	John Taylor
LT	Dan Audick	LT	Bubba Paris	LT	Steve Wallace
LG	John Ayers	LG	John Ayers	LG	Jesse Sapolu
C	Fred Quillan	C	Fred Quillan	C	Randy Cross
RG	Randy Cross	RG	Randy Cross	RG	Guy McIntyre
RT	Keith Fahnhorst	RT	Keith Fahnhorst	RT	Harris Barton
TE	Charle Young	TE	Russ Francis	TE	John Frank
WR	Freddie Solomon	WR	Freddie Solomon	WR	Jerry Rice
QB	Joe Montana	QB	Joe Montana	QB	Joe Montana
RB	Ricky Patton	RB	Wendell Tyler	RB	Roger Craig
RB	Earl Cooper	RB	Roger Craig	FB	Tom Rathman
	DEFENSE		**DEFENSE**		**DEFENSE**
LE	Jim Stuckey	LE	Lawrence Pillers	LE	Larry Roberts
NT	Archie Reese	NT	Manu Tuiasosopo	NT	Michael Carter
RE	Fred Dean	RE	Dwaine Board	RE	Kevin Fagan
E-LB	Dwaine Board	LOB	Dan Bunz	LOB	Charles Haley
LLB	Jack Reynolds	LIB	Riki Ellison	LIB	Jim Fahnhorst
RLB	Bobby Leopold	RIB	Jack Reynolds	RIB	Michael Walter
RLB	Keena Turner	ROB	Keena Turner	ROB	Keena Turner
LCB	Ronnie Lott	LCB	Ronnie Lott	LCB	Tim McKyer
RCB	Eric Wright	RCB	Eric Wright	RCB	Don Griffin
SS	Carlton Williamson	SS	Carlton Williamson	SS	Jeff Fuller
FS	Dwight Hicks	FS	Dwight Hicks	FS	Ronnie Lott
	SPECIALISTS		**SPECIALISTS**		**SPECIALISTS**
PK	Ray Wersching	PK	Ray Wersching	PK	Mike Cofer
P	Jim Miller	P	Max Runager	P	Barry Helton

But between 1981 and 1984, he was 3–6 in the strike-shortened '82 season, which shouldn't count, and then 10–6 in 1983. After the '84 win, he went 10–6, 10–5–1, and 13–2. In other words, he wasn't getting the highest draft choices to rebuild with.

We wondered how he did it.

washed-up free agents "Hacksaw" Reynolds and Fred Dean were outstanding. Board and Turner also helped in closing down the enemy running attack and rushing the passer. Three rookies started in the secondary. Lott and Williamson made the All-Rookie team and Lott was unanimous All-NFL.

1981 (Regulars only)

- Inherited from earlier administrations, *7*: Ayers, Cross, K.Fahnhorst, Quillan, Reese, Solomon, Wersching.
- Drafted by Walsh (numbers in parentheses indicate draft round), *10*: '79 Montana (3), Clark (10); '80 Cooper (1a), Stuckey (1b), Turner (2), Miller (3), Leopold (8); '81 Lott (1), Wright (2), Williamson (3).
- Free Agents, Waivers, and Trades, *7*: '79 Board, Hicks; '80 Patton, Young; '81 Audick, Dean, Reynolds.

This was Montana's first year as the unchallenged starter, and his passes to Clark, Solomon, Cooper, and Young provided most of the attack. The running game was by committee and averaged only 3.5 per attempt. Patton led with 543 yards. Four of the five regular linemen were inherited, and the fifth was a free agent. The key to victory was the defense, which allowed only 250 points. Supposedly

1984 (Regulars only)

- From '81 Regulars, *15*: Ayers, Board, Clark, Cross, K.Fahnhorst, Hicks, Lott, Montana, Reynolds, Quillan, Solomon, Turner, Wersching, Williamson, Wright. (Bunz was a sub in '81, inherited.)
- Drafted by Walsh (numbers in parentheses indicate draft round), *3*: '82 Paris (2); '83 Craig (2), Ellison (5).
- Free Agents, Waivers, and Trades, *5*: '80 Pillers; '82 Francis; '83 Tyler; '84 Runager, Tuiasosopo.

Although this team had fifteen holdovers from '81, it had a different personality, a high-scoring, veteran team at its peak. Tyler, acquired from the Rams in '83, rushed for 1,262 yards and Craig had 649 rushing yards and caught 71 passes. Montana's NFL Passer Rating was 102.9. The offense, which scored 475 points, blew away the opposition. While the attack drew raves, the defense quietly throttled foes, allowing only 227 points. Ironically, the team's only All-NFL was OT Fahnhorst.

1988 (Regulars only)

- From '84 Regulars, *5*: Craig, Cross, Montana, Turner, Lott.
- Drafted by Walsh (numbers in parentheses indicate draft round), *16*: '83 Sapolu (11); '84 Frank (2), McIntyre (3), Carter (5a), Fuller (5b); '85 Rice (1); '86 Roberts (2), Rathman (3a), McKyer (3b), Taylor (3c), Haley (4a), Wallace (4b), Fagan (4c), Griffin (6); '87 Barton (1); '88 Helton (4).
- Free Agents, Waivers, and Trades, *3*: '84 Walter; '87 J. Fahnhorst; '88 Cofer.

This team doesn't have the punch of the '84 group or the defense of either '81 or '84, but it's very young and should be a power for years. *Can you believe that eight starters came from the '86 draft when the first-round pick had been traded to Dallas?* The only "aging" vets are Cross (thirty-five), who announced his retirement after the Super Bowl, and Montana (thirty-three). One tip-off to the team's future is that it got stronger through the season. The 'Niners were 6–5 at midseason, two games behind the Saints and one behind the Rams.

So if you put all three teams together, you can see what Walsh's strong points are. He's very good with veterans ('84), youngsters ('88), or players just coming to maturity ('81). He can win with a strong running game ('84, '88) or a weak one ('81). He always has a strong passing attack and defense (pick a year). He can draft brilliantly (as in '81 and '86), but he's not afraid of trades, waivers, or free agents (Reynolds, Dean, Tyler, and Francis).

We must have missed something. Anybody who could do all that would be some kind of genius.

THE QUARTERBACK CONTROVERSY

Last season was a poor year for quarterback controversies. So many quarterbacks got poleaxed that most teams were thankful if they could just put a healthy body under center. There was a minicontroversy in Indianapolis with Gary Hogeboom, but no one seemed to care about that. The annual Will-McMahon-Return-in-Time charade in Chicago ran out of steam through repetition. The Let's-Launch-Pelluer-into-Orbit Movement fell apart in Dallas when Kevin Sweeney couldn't cut it. Williams-Rypien had the makings in Washington until the Redskins dropped out of contention. And the Schroeder-Beuerlein duel on the Raiders got bogged down in mutual inadequacy.

The best of the lot could have been Kramer-versus-Wilson in Vikingland, but that was over almost before it started.

The strangest quarterback controversy had to be in San Francisco. In the '87 playoff loss to Minnesota, Walsh sent Steve Young in to replace Montana when Joe was ineffective. Considering it was do-or-die at the time, the only controversy should have been whether Walsh waited too long to make the switch.

A week after the loss Walsh announced that the battle for the 49er quarterback post would be open once training camp started. Young had been an expensive and talented benchwarmer throughout '87, and Montana, then going into his tenth season, has a back problem that required surgery in 1986. Most observers took Walsh's announcement as a sop to keep Young content while he waits around to become Montana's successor. Amazingly, some people took him seriously.

The camp battle was about as open as an election in Leningrad. Montana had a so-so exhibition season but opened at QB in Week 1. Joe was effective against the Saints but hurt his elbow in a fall and had trouble throwing some passes.

WK	AT	OPPONENT	SCORE	R	QB	AT	CO	YDS	T	I	NEWS
1	A	New Orleans	34-33	W	Montana	23	13	161	3	1	6.34
					Young	3	1	4	0	0	—

Young practiced all week, so Walsh started him against the Giants, even though Montana announced on Thursday that his elbow was okay. Young is a scrambler. He led the Giants' rush a merry chase during the first half and wore them down. With the score tied 10-10, Montana came in fresh in the second half and played the hero with a 78-yard pass to Rice for the winning score. But the next week Montana had what some observers called his "worst game as a 49er," throwing three interceptions in a loss to Atlanta. Walsh left him in all the way.

WK	AT	OPPONENT	SCORE	R	QB	AT	CO	YDS	T	I	NEWS
2	A	N.Y. Giants	20-17	W	Young	18	11	115	0	0	6.38
					Montana	18	10	148	1	0	8.78
3	H	Atlanta	17-34	L	Montana	48	32	343	2	3	4.75

Nevertheless Montana told reporters during the following week that he was "tentative" on some throws because of the thought of Young looking over his shoulder. That was news to Walsh. He and Joe sat down and talked. The next week Joe was back on the beam.

WK	AT	OPPONENT	SCORE	R	QB	AT	CO	YDS	T	I	NEWS
4	A	Seattle	38- 7	W	Montana	29	20	302	4	1	10.24
					Young	6	4	49	1	0	—
5	H	Detroit	20-13	W	Montana	30	19	182	0	0	6.07
6	H	Denver	13-16	L	Montana	24	12	191	0	1	6.08
					Young	3	0	0	0	2	—
7	A	L.A. Rams	24-21	W	Montana	31	21	203	0	1	5.10
					Young	2	0	0	0	0	—
8	A*	Chicago	9-10	L	Montana	29	13	168	1	1	4.59
					Young	1	1	1	0	0	—

* Monday Night

Win or lose, Montana was the quarterback through Week 8, with Young serving as mop-up. The Bears roughed Joe up, but he was penciled in as the starter for Week 9 until he tripped in practice and wrenched his back. Young started and won an important game over the Vikings, and word spread that Montana was out as number one. Walsh went with Young again in Week 10. He didn't do a bad job, but the 49ers lost.

WK	AT	OPPONENT	SCORE	R	QB	AT	CO	YDS	T	I	NEWS
9	H	Minnesota	24-21	W	Young	25	14	232	1	0	9.68
10	A	Phoenix	23-24	L	Young	27	14	145	1	0	5.74

With Montana's back okay again, he went all the way against the Raiders, even though the 49ers couldn't score a touchdown. But from then on, Joe was at the top of his game. The 49ers reeled off four straight victories to win another division crown. With the title in the till, both quarterbacks tuned up for the playoffs in the Week 16 loss to the Rams, a game that was meaningless to the 49ers.

WK	AT	OPPONENT	SCORE	R	QB	AT	CO	YDS	T	I	NEWS
11	H	L.A. Raiders	3- 9	L	Montana	31	16	160	0	0	5.16
12	H*	Washington	37-21	W	Montana	23	15	218	2	1	8.39
					Young	2	0	0	0	0	—
13	A	San Diego	48-10	W	Montana	22	14	271	3	0	13.68
					Young	3	2	14	0	0	—
14	A	Atlanta	13- 3	W	Montana	34	20	230	1	0	7.06
15	H	New Orleans	30-17	W	Montana	29	18	233	1	1	6.83
16	H	L.A. Rams	16-38	L	Montana	26	15	171	0	0	6.58
					Young	11	7	120	0	0	10.90

* Monday Night

Looking back, Walsh's moves make so much sense that we wonder what the fuss was about. He placated Young to some extent and kept him involved. That was important because of Montana's shaky health. Joe was never benched unless he was hurt. That Walsh held him out both times an extra week after he said he could go comes under the "better safe than sorry" heading. Walsh could afford the luxury of protecting Montana an extra week because he had Young behind him, rather than the typical "emergency" backup.

An additional factor may have been the development of the 49ers' offensive line. At the beginning it was iffy. A scrambler such as Young had a better chance of surviving than Montana, who is now primarily a pocket passer. By the end of the season, when the 49ers made their rush to the title, the line had become one of the better NFL fronts.

Walsh caught some criticism over his handling of the QBs. But thinking it over, we'd have made exactly the same moves—if anybody'd asked us.

SAN FRANCISCO 49ERS STATISTICS

1988 TEAM STATISTICS	SF	OPP
TOTAL FIRST DOWNS	326	277
Rushing	141	90
Passing	167	160
Penalty	18	27
3rd Down Made/Att.	94/225	88/225
Pct.	41.8%	39.1%
4th Down Made/Att.	5/10	6/16
Pct.	50.0%	37.5%

(Continued) 1988 TEAM STATISTICS	SF	OPP
TOTAL NET YARDS	5900	4575
Avg. per Game	368.8	285.9
Total Plays	1076	1013
Avg. per Play	5.5	4.5
NET YARDS RUSHING	2523	1588
Avg. per Game	157.7	99.3
Total Rushes	527	441

(Continued)

(Continued)

1988 TEAM STATISTICS	SF	OPP
NET YARDS PASSING	3377	2987
Avg. per Game	211.1	186.7
Tackled/Yards Lost	47/298	42/297
Gross Yards	3675	3284
Attempts/Completions	502/293	530/292
Pct. of Completions	58.4%	55.1%
Had Intercepted	14	22
PUNTS/AVERAGE	80/38.7	86/41.0
NET PUNTING AVG.	32.1	32.7
PENALTIES/YARDS	115/986	76/603
FUMBLES/BALL LOST	27/12	30/16
TOUCHDOWNS	41	34
Rushing	18	8
Passing	21	25
Returns	2	1
TIME OF POSSESSION	—	—

SCORE/PERIODS	1	2	3	4	OT	TOTAL
49ers	54	140	95	80	0	369
Opponents	31	92	77	91	3	294

SCORING	TDR	TDP	TDRt	PAT	FG	S	TP
Cofer				40/41	27/38		121
Craig	9	1					60
Rice	1	9					60
Taylor		2	2				24
Frank		3					18
Montana	3						18
Wilson		3					18
DuBose	2						12
Jones		2					12
Rathman	2						12
McIntyre		1					6
Young	1						6
Haley						1	2
49ers	18	21	2	40/41	27/38	1	369
Opponents	8	25	1	34/34	18/24	1	294

RUSHING	NO	YDS	AVG	LG	TD
Craig	310	1502	4.8	46t	9
Rathman	102	427	4.2	26	2
Young	27	184	6.8	49t	1
Montana	38	132	3.5	15	3
DuBose	24	116	4.8	37t	2
Rice	13	107	8.2	29	1
Sydney	9	50	5.6	13	0
Flagler	3	5	1.7	4	0
Helton	1	0	0.0	0	0
49ers	527	2523	4.8	49t	18
Opponents	441	1588	3.6	36t	8

RECEIVING	NO	YDS	AVG	LG	TD
Craig	76	534	7.0	22	1
Rice	64	1306	20.4	96t	9
Rathman	42	382	9.1	24	0
Wilson	33	405	12.3	31	3
Frank	16	195	12.2	38	3
Taylor	14	325	23.2	73t	2

(Continued)

RECEIVING	NO	YDS	AVG	LG	TD
Heller	14	140	10.0	22	0
Greer	8	120	15.0	31	0
Jones	8	57	7.1	18t	2
DuBose	6	57	9.5	13	0
Flagler	4	72	18.0	57	0
Chandler	4	33	8.3	9	0
Sydney	2	18	9.0	9	0
McIntyre	1	17	17.0	17t	1
Nicholas	1	14	14.0	14	0
49ers	293	3675	12.5	96t	21
Opponents	292	3284	11.2	67t	25

INTERCEPTIONS	NO	YDS	AVG	LG	TD
McKyer	7	11	1.6	7	0
Lott	5	59	11.8	44	0
Fuller	4	18	4.5	10	0
Holmoe	2	0	0.0	0	0
Wright	2	02	-1.0	0	0
Turner	1	2	2.0	2	0
Carter	1	0	0.0	0	0
49ers	22	88	5.0	44	0
Opponents	14	185	13.2	47t	1

PUNTING	NO	YDS	AVG	TB	In 20	LG	Blk
Helton	78	3069	39.3	5	22	53	1
Runager	1	24	24.0	0	0	24	0
49ers	80	3093	38.7	5	22	53	1
Opponents	86	3522	41.0	5	21	57	0

PUNT RETURNS	NO	FC	YDS	AVG	LG	TD
Taylor	44	7	556	12.6	95t	2
Chandler	6	5	28	4.7	13	0
Griffin	4	3	28	7.0	10	0
49ers	54	15	612	11.3	95t	2
Opponents	47	10	426	9.1	41	0

KICKOFF RETURNS	NO	YDS	AVG	LG	TD
DuBose	32	608	19.0	44	0
Taylor	12	225	18.8	29	0
Rodgers	6	98	16.3	24	0
Craig	2	32	16.0	17	0
Sydney	1	8	8.0	8	0
Thomas	1	5	5.0	5	0
Wilson	1	2	2.0	2	0
49ers	55	978	17.8	44	0
Opponents	73	1362	18.7	40	0

FIELD GOALS	1-19	20-29	30-39	40-49	50+	TOTAL
Cofer	1-1	9-10	9-11	7-11	1-5	27-38
49ers	1-1	9-10	9-11	7-11	1-5	27-38
Opponents	2-2	8-8	3-6	4-7	1-1	18-24

FIELD GOALS BY Cofer: 27 of 38
(25G,32G)(35G,62N,26G,35N)(38G)(31N,52N,21G,55N)
(29G,29G)(37G,47N,27G)(40G,47N)(51N)(45N,30G)(42G,
27G,30G)(44G)(52G)(45G,32G)(23N,40N,31G,23G)(40G,47G,
19G)(23G,46G,36G)

PASSING	ATT	COM	YARD	PCT.	Avg G	TD	%TD	IN	%IN	LG	SAKS/YDS	RATE
Montana	397	238	2981	59.9	7.51	18	4.5	10	2.5	96t	34/223	87.9
Young	101	54	680	53.5	6.73	3	3.0	3	3.0	73t	13/75	72.2
Rice	3	1	14	33.3	4.67	0	0.0	1	33.3	14	0/0	9.7
Sydney	1	0	0	00	0.00	0	0.0	0	0.0	0	0/0	39.6
49ers	502	293	3675	58.4	7.32	21	4.2	14	2.8	96t	47/298	83.5
Opponents	530	292	3284	55.1	6.20	25	4.7	22	4.2	67t	42/297	72.2

TAMPA BAY BUCCANEERS

The Last 5 Seasons

	1984	1985	1986	1987	1988
Won-Lost	6-10	2-14	2-14	4-11	5-11
Percentage	.375	.125	.125	.267	.313
Division Finish	3	5	5	4-t	3
Games Behind	4	13	12	7	7
Total Points	335	294	239	286	261
Per Game	20.9	18.4	14.9	19.1	16.3
Opponent Points	380	448	473	360	350
Per Game	23.8	28.0	29.6	24.0	21.9
Net Points	-45	-154	-234	-74	-89
Predicted Net Wins	-1.1	-3.8	-5.8	-1.9	-2.2
Delta Net Wins	-0.9	-2.2	-0.2	-1.6	-0.8
Total Yards on Offense	5321	4766	4361	4381	5061
Per Game	332.6	297.9	272.6	292.1	316.3
Total Yards Allowed on Defense	5474	6108	6333	4987	5155
Per Game	342.1	381.8	395.8	332.5	322.2
Net Difference	-153	-1342	-1972	-606	-94
Offensive Turnovers	43	48	42	31	52
Defensive Takeaways	32	40	32	36	33
Net Turnovers	-11	-8	-10	5	-19
Predicted Net Points	-57	-144	-204	-31	-84
Delta Net Points	12	-10	-30	-43	-5
Net Rushing Yards	1776	1644	1863	1365	1753
Per Game	111.0	102.8	116.4	91.0	109.6
Average Gain	3.7	3.8	4.1	3.5	3.9
Opponent Net Rushing Yards	2233	2430	2648	2038	1551
Per Game	139.6	151.9	165.5	135.9	96.9
Average Gain	4.4	4.4	4.7	4.1	3.2
Net Passing Yards	3545	3122	2498	3016	3308
Per Game	221.6	195.1	156.1	201.1	206.8
Times Sacked	45	40	56	43	34
Passer Rating in Yards	4.5	4.0	2.9	4.4	3.4
Opponent Net Passing Yards	3241	3678	3685	2949	3604
Per Game	202.6	229.9	230.3	196.6	225.3
Times Sacked	32	35	19	39	20
Passer Rating Defense	5.0	5.6	6.6	5.0	5.2
Passer Rating Net	-0.6	-1.7	-3.7	-0.5	-1.8
Yards per Drive Offense	28.2	22.8	22.4	23.2	25.4
Yards per Drive Defense	28.4	29.4	33.9	26.1	26.4
Average Time of Possession	31:17	27:55	28:40	28:37	29:00

THE 1988 SEASON

DATE	AT	OPPONENT	SCORE	R	SPREAD	Tu	Net YDS	Rush YDS	Pass YDS	TURN
09/04	H	Philadelphia	14-41	L	+6	g	362-389	43-141	319-248	5-2
09/11	A	Green Bay	13-10	W	+6	g	266-240	148- 59	118-181	2-2
09/18	H	Phoenix	24-30	L	+3	g	298-475	114-181	184-294	3-0
09/25	A	New Orleans	9-13	L	+13.5	a	296-268	92-117	204-151	1-1
10/02	H	Green Bay	27-24	W	-2.5	g	368-426	85- 72	283-354	5-3
10/09	A	Minnesota	13-14	L	+13	a	331-276	177- 69	154-207	3-2
10/16	A	Indianapolis	31-35	L	+5.5	a	483-343	39-103	444-240	2-2
10/23	H	Minnesota	20-49	L	+3.5	g	243-443	28-138	215-305	7-1
10/30	H	Miami	14-17	L	+4	g	362-309	79- 43	283-266	5-0
11/06	A	Chicago	10-28	L	+9.5	g	357-338	84- 69	273-269	2-3
11/13	A	Detroit	23-20	W	+2	a	304-278	225- 75	79-203	4-3
11/20	H	Chicago	15-27	L	+7	g	321-339	168-139	153-200	3-4
11/27	A	Atlanta	10-17	L	+4	g	313-289	127-181	186-108	4-2
12/04	H	Buffalo	10- 5	W	+8.5	g	253-273	110- 39	143-234	0-2
12/11	A	New England	7-10	L	+9	a	262-223	131- 76	131-147	2-2
12/18	H	Detroit	21-10	W	-3	g	242-250	103- 59	139-191	4-4
						Avg.	316-322	110- 98	207-225	3-2

		WINS	LOSSES
Season Record:	5-11-0		
Vs. Spread:	10- 6-0		
Home:	3- 5-0		
On Artificial Turf:	1- 4-0		
Art. Turf vs. Spread:	5- 0-0		

		WINS	LOSSES
POINTS:		19- 14	15- 26
Net YDS:	9- 7-0	287-293	330-336
Rush YDS:	10- 6-0	134- 61	98-114
Pass YDS:	6-10-0	152-233	231-221
TURN:	3- 8-5	3- 3	3- 2

WHO?

Everybody thinks Tampa Bay drafted Vinny Testaverde in 1987 so they could get a "franchise" quarterback and eventually build up to a winning team. As sensible as that seems, it's not the real reason. What they got with Vinny was visibility. Of all the teams in the NFL, the Buccaneers have always been the least remembered. Ask most fans to name the twenty-eight NFL teams and if they're really good they'll get through twenty-seven. After that, they go "uh" a couple of times and come up with the Memphis Showboats.

You think that's an exaggeration? Okay, some fans in Chicago, Minneapolis, Green Bay, and Detroit might remember Tampa Bay, but only because their teams play the Bucs twice in a season. Fans of teams that play the Bucs only once assume that spot on the schedule is an open date. Come to think of it, there are a lot of fans in Detroit who think the whole Lions' schedule is an open date. But that's another story. Let's return to—wait a minute—we had it a minute ago . . .

Tampa Bay!

The Buccaneers' obscurity is indirectly their own fault. They lose and so they're ignored. They've only been on Monday Night TV three times, the last time in 1982. Seattle came into the league in 1976, the same year as TB, and the Seahawks have been on thirteen times. The Bucs haven't burned up the tube with playoff appearances either: three games in thirteen years and none since 1981. And because they're perceived as such confirmed losers, and boring losers at that, our local station opts out when the Bucs are in the second game of a Sunday doubleheader. Maybe it's that way where you live. Did you enjoy seeing *It's a Wonderful Life* in colorization? Again?

In a national test, the answer to the question "Name three things about the Tampa Bay Buccaneers" was (1) Vinny Testaverde is their quarterback, (2) they lost their first twenty-six NFL games, and (3) who?

We think that will change.

We won't go out on a skinny limb and predict the Bucs will be the Team of the Nineties, but they seem to be improving each year. When they get to the right side of .500—something they haven't done since the strike season of '82—you'll begin to see them on TV again. And then you'll be able to name some of their players besides Vinny.

IF WE CAN PUT A MAN ON THE MOON, WHY CAN'T THE BUCS WIN?

The Bucs' improvement in 1988 over 1987 wasn't immediately apparent in their won-lost record; 5-11 isn't much different from the 4-11 of the previous season. However, two of the '87 wins were in the replacement games; the regulars were 2-10. Worse, they were 0-4 at the end of the season when Vinny became the starter. In 1988 Testaverde was 5-10 as a starter, and that's a significant improvement.

Statistically the Bucs' improvement shows up in defense against the run, which was pretty good. The pass defense slipped, partly because Tampa Bay didn't have a pass rush, but at least teams had to go to the pass to beat them. It's symptomatic of young teams to learn to stop the run before they learn pass defense. And the Bucs are a very young team.

Another symptom of young football teams is that they

	ATT	COM	PCT.	YARD	AvgG	TD	%TD	IN	%IN
1987	165	71	43.0	1081	6.55	5	3.0	6	3.6
1988	466	222	47.6	3240	6.95	13	2.8	35	7.5

That he increased his attempts, completions, yards, and touchdowns is to be expected. He played in only six games in '87. His completion percentage went up in '88, but not dramatically—likewise his average gain per pass. His percentage of touchdowns changed negligibly.

But, oh! the interceptions!

If that 35 looks high to you, you're right. Only George Blanda with 42 in 1962 ever threw more in a season. It seemed like every news report of a Tampa Bay game started with, "Vinny Testaverde threw X interceptions today as . . ." In Week 14 the Bucs beat the Bills in one of the biggest upsets of the season. Our TV-caster led off: "Vinny Testaverde didn't throw any interceptions today as . . ."

Various explanations were given, none of them completely satisfactory:

Testaverde forces the ball. True, but so do many strong-armed, young quarterbacks and some weak-armed, old ones. Marino forces a lot of passes; he's intercepted, but not like Vinny.

His receivers are inexperienced. True, and they're just learning to knock down what they can't catch, but the Bucs' receivers aren't any younger than those of some other teams.

He's dumb. Well, he doesn't sound like he's dumb. And, since you hear that about every young QB having problems—remember Terry Bradshaw?—it's not very credible.

He's color-blind. It turns out he is, but so what? You can tell the teams apart in black-and-white.

He's not mobile. Have you ever seen Marino run?

He tries to do too much. Probably true, but the Bucs need him to do a lot.

He's still learning. What? After a year and a half in the NFL, he doesn't know all the answers?

All those interceptions produced a 48.8 in the NFL's passer rating system, last among twenty-eight qualifiers. We think the NFL's system is weighted wrong; in effect it awards a 20-yard bonus for every completion, an 80-yard bonus for a touchdown pass, and a 100-yard penalty for each interception. We prefer NEWS (for New System), which starts with a passer's yards gained, skips the completion bonus, and limits the TD bonus to 10 yards and the intercep-

tion penalty to 45 (the average yards lost to a team by a turnover). Total that up and divide by the number of attempts and you'll get a figure that's readable as yards. Vinny's 3.85 was twenty-seventh in the league, ahead of Detroit's Rusty Hilger.

Here are both ratings for the last two years.

	RATE	NEWS
1987	60.2	5.49
1988	48.8	3.85

After we checked out all the qualifiers' NEWS ratings and put them in order from highest to lowest, we saw that the top seven (25 percent) were at 6.48 or better and the bottom seven were at 5.11 or less, with 14 passers (50 percent) in between. Well, we said, we certainly can't miss this opportunity.

When you look at a passer's stats at the end of a game, don't you feel a little tinge of frustration? So many yards, so many completions, touchdowns, interceptions. But did the guy have a good day or not? How many interceptions will offset a high yardage total? If he didn't throw a TD pass, was it a worthwhile performance? How can you tell?

It made sense to us that a passer had a good day if his record would put him in the top quarter of the regulars in the league. If he could have a 6.48 day, he'd beat 75 percent of the other quarterbacks in the league—assuming that they performed at their normal seasonal rate and everyone else on his team performed equally to everyone else on the other side. Of course, those are ridiculous assumptions, but that doesn't matter. All we're doing is measuring the passer's day. We decided to credit a QB whose stats were 6.48 or better with a WIN (a better-than-average performance) even if his team lost. And even if the rival QB had a better day. And, using the same logic, we gave him a LOSS (a performance less than 75 percent of the league's starters' averages) if his NEWS was 5.11 or under for the game. Anything between 5.11 and 6.48 was an ordinary performance and we called it a TIE.

Then we looked at Testaverde's '88 season, game by game.

WK	OPP	SCORE	R	ATT	COM	YARD	TD	IN	RATE	W-L-T
1	Philadelphia	14-41	L	45	21	324	2	5	2.86	L
2	Green Bay	13-10	W	24	11	135	0	0	5.63	T
3	Phoenix	24-30	L	28	16	211	1	2	4.68	L
4	New Orleans	9-13	L	33	14	230	0	1	5.61	T

(Continued)

WK	OPP	SCORE	R	ATT	COM	YARD	TD	IN	RATE	W-L-T
5	Green Bay	27-24	W	37	20	300	1	4	3.51	L
6	Minnesota	13-14	L	25	12	170	1	2	3.60	L
7	Indianapolis	31-35	L	42	25	469	2	2	9.50	W
8	Minnesota	20-49	L	45	19	223	1	6	-0.82	L
9	Miami	14-17	L	DNP						
10	Chicago	10-28	L	52	22	305	1	2	4.33	L
11	Detroit	23-20	W	13	9	107	0	2	1.31	L
12	Chicago	15-27	L	22	7	86	0	2	-0.18	L
13	Atlanta	10-17	L	29	12	190	0	3	1.90	L
14	Buffalo	10- 5	W	29	12	156	0	0	5.37	T
15	New England	7-10	L	19	10	145	1	1	5.79	T
16	Detroit	21-10	W	23	12	189	3	3	4.09	L
		(5-11)		466	222	3240	13	35	3.85	1-10-4

One superior performance out of fifteen wasn't very good. Even four okay jobs didn't help a whole lot. Figure that in an ideal world, he'd end up with a 3–12 record as a starter by splitting the four okays. We know his real-life record was 5–10. It happens that way sometimes. In real life, Tampa Bay lost his one really outstanding game, the 469-yard job he pulled on Indianapolis. But remember, the won-lost-tied stuff is just shorthand for good job, average job, and poor job. Vinny was all right about a third of the time. Even the top QBs are lucky to reach that level in two-thirds of their starts. But that's what he needs to shoot for.

Incidentally that 469-yard job was the tenth-highest single game total in NFL history. Notice the "was." One week later Marino threw for 521 against the Jets, the second-highest ever, and bumped Vinny out of the Top Ten. The public perception of Testaverde suffers quite a bit because he plays in the same state as the Dolphins' QB, which invites constant comparison. Vinny would look a lot better if he did his throwing for the Boise Bucs.

PERKINS' FOLLY

We can't leave Tampa Bay without a look at Coach Ray Perkins' decision to kick off in the overtime period of the Bucs' game with New England on December 11. He came off looking pretty dumb when the Patriots marched right down the field and kicked a field goal to win. You always receive in overtime, right?

Not quite. Going into the '88 season, there had been 139 overtime games in the NFL and the old American Football League. In 134 of them, the team winning the coin toss chose to receive. But on only 44 occasions, 31.7 percent, did the receiving team drive straight down and score. In 95 games, 68.3 percent, the receiving team gave up the ball and let the team that had kicked off have a shot. Now it is true that the receiving team won 72 of the 139, or 51.8 percent, but only 28 after they'd once given up the ball. And 56 times the team that kicked off won the game. In other words, stop

'em once and it's two-to-one you'll win. Eleven games ended tied.

Of the five pre-'88 games when a team chose to kick off in overtime, the kicking team won. One of those was a mistake. In the 1962 AFL Championship Game, Butch Haynes of the Dallas Texans (now Kansas City) got confused and called the wrong thing after he'd won the coin toss. Dallas had to kick off. They held Houston a couple of times to finally win in 17:54 on a field goal after an interception of a George Blanda pass.

Okay, if you're following this, it means that in a very general sense, you stand a slightly better chance of winning by receiving. But only in a general sense. There were three factors that made Perkins kick in this particular case.

First, neither team was tearing up the pea patch on offense. After sixty minutes, the score was tied 7–7. Tampa Bay had 262 yards, split evenly between rushing and passing. The Pats had about 90 yards less, with a little more passing than rushing. Logically the Bucs would stop the Pats and get the ball in fair field position. Remember: two-to-one if you stop them once.

Second, there was a stiff wind blowing down the field. One account put it at twenty-five m.p.h. By throwing that wind in New England's face, Perkins would hamper the Pats' passing and force them to run. Tampa was far better against rushing than passing. Moreover, if the Pats ever got the ball downfield for a field goal try, kicker Jason Staurovsky had limited range and was none too steady even with no wind.

And third, if TB received, they figured to start at their own 20. Testaverde was being ragged by the media for his interceptions, but he'd got through this game with only a single miscue. An interception at the Tampa 20 would hand the game to New England and certainly wouldn't help Vinny's psyche. Of course, Perkins would never admit that this was part of his thinking.

Given these three factors, the most incredibly stupid thing Perkins could have done was to choose to receive. So far as we know, Perkins has never been incredibly stupid. He made the smart move.

So then the gods of football, who have used Tampa Bay as their personal plaything since 1976, decreed that Tony Eason would complete three straight passes and Staurovsky would kick like Morten Andersen. So much for brains!

Oh, by the way, on October 9 Denver chose to kick off in overtime against the Raiders. The Broncos won, but then the gods have always liked Denver better. Perhaps because it's closer to heaven.

TAMPA BAY BUCCANEERS STATISTICS

1988 TEAM STATISTICS	TB	OPP
TOTAL FIRST DOWNS	295	293
Rushing	91	104
Passing	173	169
Penalty	31	20
3rd Down Made/Att.	72/202	101/227
Pct.	35.6%	44.5%
4th Down Made/Att.	2/11	6/9
Pct.	18.2%	66.7%
TOTAL NET YARDS	5061	5155
Avg. per Game	316.3	322.2
Total Plays	998	1025
Avg. per Play	5.1	5.0
NET YARDS RUSHING	1753	1551
Avg. per Game	109.6	96.9
Total Rushes	452	478
NET YARDS PASSING	3308	3604
Avg. per Game	206.8	225.3
Tackled/Yards Lost	34/300	20/140
Gross Yards	3608	3744
Attempts/Completions	512/253	527/304
Pct. of Completions	49.4%	57.7%
Had Intercepted	36	21
PUNTS/AVERAGE	68/36.4	77/39.0
NET PUNTING AVG.	32.4	33.2
PENALTIES/YARDS	102/816	105/872
FUMBLES/BALL LOST	27/16	29/12
TOUCHDOWNS	28	42
Rushing	11	21
Passing	16	19
Returns	1	2
TIME OF POSSESSION	470:23	493:45

SCORE/PERIODS	1	2	3	4	OT	TOTAL
Buccaneers	27	75	41	118	0	261
Opponents	105	93	95	54	3	350

SCORING	TDR	TDP	TDRt	PAT	FG	S	TP
Igwebuike				21/21	19/25		78
Hill		9					54
Tate	7	1					48
Carrier		5					30
Carney				6/6	2/5		12
Howard	1						6
Murphy			1				6
Pillow		1					6
D. Smith	1						6
Testaverde	1						6
Wilder	1						6
Goode						1	2
Criswell				1/1			1
Buccaneers	11	16	1	28/28	21/30	1	261
Opponents	21	19	2	42/42	18/30	1	350

RUSHING	NO	YDS	AVG	LG	TD
Tate	122	467	3.8	47t	7
Howard	115	452	3.9	29t	1

(Continued)

RUSHING	NO	YDS	AVG	LG	TD
Wilder	86	343	4.0	19	1
Goode	63	231	3.7	22	0
Testaverde	28	138	4.9	24	1
J. Smith	20	87	4.4	23	0
D. Smith	13	46	3.5	15	1
Criswell	2	0	0.0	0	0
Ferguson	1	0	0.0	0	0
Hill	2	-11	5.5	3	0
Buccaneers	452	1753	3.9	47t	11
Opponents	478	1551	3.2	48	21

RECEIVING	NO	YDS	AVG	LG	TD
Hill	58	1040	17.9	42t	9
Carrier	57	970	17.0	59t	5
Hall	39	555	14.2	37	0
J. Smith	16	134	8.4	22	0
Pillow	15	206	13.7	34	1
Wilder	15	124	8.3	24	0
D. Smith	12	138	11.5	25	0
Howard	11	97	8.8	16	0
Magee	9	103	11.4	25	0
Goode	7	68	9.7	22	0
G. Taylor	5	53	10.6	14	0
Tate	5	23	4.6	9	1
Starring	3	75	25.0	53	0
Parks	1	22	22.0	22	0
Buccaneers	253	3608	14.3	59t	16
Opponents	304	3744	12.3	56	19

INTERCEPTIONS	NO	YDS	AVG	LG	TD
Hamilton	6	123	20.5	58	0
Reynolds	4	7	2.3	7	0
Elder	3	9	3.0	9	0
Robinson	2	28	14.0	28	0
Harris	2	26	13.0	24	0
Murphy	1	35	35.0	35t	1
Marve	1	29	29.0	29	0
Futrell	1	26	26.0	26	0
R. Jones	1	0	0.0	0	0
Buccaneers	21	283	13.5	58	1
Opponents	36	486	13.5	46	2

PUNTING	NO	YDS	AVG	TB	In 20	LG	Blk
Criswell	68	2477	36.4	0	20	62	0
Buccaneers	68	2477	36.4	0	20	62	0
Opponents	77	3004	39.0	6	24	66	0

PUNT RETURNS	NO	FC	YDS	AVG	LG	TD
Futrell	27	10	283	10.5	40	0
J. Smith	8	3	45	5.6	20	0
Elder	1	0	0	0.0	0	0
Buccaneers	36	13	328	9.1	40	0
Opponents	38	13	273	7.2	25	0

KICKOFF RETURNS	NO	YDS	AVG	LG	TD
Elder	34	772	22.7	51	0
J. Smith	10	180	18.0	26	0
D. Smith	9	188	20.9	30	0
McAdoo	4	108	27.0	31	0
Pillow	3	38	12.7	17	0
Futrell	2	38	19.0	20	0
Howard	2	21	9.0	9	0
Buccaneers	64	1345	21.0	51	0
Opponents	52	1129	21.7	57	0

FIELD GOALS	1-19	20-29	30-39	40-49	50+	TOTAL
Igwebuike	1-1	6-6	7-8	3-6	2-4	19-25
Carney	0-0	2-3	0-1	0-1	0-0	2-5
Buccaneers	1-1	8-9	7-9	3-7	2-4	21-30
Opponents	0-0	6-6	6-11	5-9	1-4	18-30

FIELD GOALS BY Igwebuike: 19 of 25
( )(53G,58N,28G)(34G,47N)(25G,35G,35G)
(45G,54N,44G)(31G,36G)(39G)(18G,32G)( )
(44N,45G,40N)(23G,22G,52G)(27G,37N,23G)
Carney: 2 of 5
(35N,24G)(29G,29N)(40N)

PASSING	ATT	COM	YARD	PCT.	Avg G	TD	%TD	IN	%IN	LG	SAKS/YDS	RATE
Testaverde	466	222	3240	47.6	6.95	13	2.8	35	7.5	59t	33/292	48.8
Ferguson	46	31	368	67.4	8.00	3	6.5	1	2.2	34	1/8	104.3
Buccaneers	512	253	3608	49.4	7.05	16	3.1	36	7.0	59t	34/300	53.7
Opponents	527	304	3744	57.7	7.10	19	3.6	21	4.0	56	20/140	75.2

WASHINGTON REDSKINS

The Last 5 Seasons

	1984	1985	1986	1987	1988
Won-Lost	11-5	10-6	12-4	11-4	7-9
Percentage	.688	.625	.750	.733	.438
Division Finish	1	1-t	2	1	3-t
Games Behind	0	0	2	0	3
Total Points	426	297	368	379	345
Per Game	26.6	18.6	23.0	25.3	21.6
Opponent Points	310	312	296	285	387
Per Game	19.4	19.5	18.5	19.0	24.2
Net Points	116	-15	72	94	-42
Predicted Net Wins	2.9	-0.4	1.8	2.3	-1.0
Delta Net Wins	0.1	2.4	2.2	1.2	0.0
Total Yards on Offense	5350	5338	5601	5597	5679
Per Game	334.4	333.6	350.1	373.1	354.9
Total Yards Allowed on Defense	5361	4480	5297	5022	5194
Per Game	335.1	280.0	331.1	334.8	324.6
Net Difference	-11	858	304	575	485
Offensive Turnovers	28	40	32	37	46
Defensive Takeaways	43	34	28	34	22
Net Turnovers	15	-6	-4	-3	-24
Predicted Net Points	59	48	9	36	-56
Delta Net Points	57	-63	63	58	14
Net Rushing Yards	2274	2523	1732	2102	1543
Per Game	142.1	157.7	108.3	140.1	96.4
Average Gain	3.9	4.4	3.7	4.2	3.5
Opponent Net Rushing Yards	1589	1734	1805	1679	1745
Per Game	99.3	108.4	112.8	111.9	109.1
Average Gain	4.1	4.1	3.9	3.8	3.9
Net Passing Yards	3076	2815	3869	3495	4136
Per Game	192.3	175.9	241.8	233.0	258.5
Times Sacked	48	52	28	27	24
Passer Rating in Yards	5.1	3.5	5.4	5.9	5.4
Opponent Net Passing Yards	3772	2746	3492	3343	3449
Per Game	235.8	171.6	218.3	222.9	215.6
Times Sacked	66	52	55	53	43
Passer Rating Defense	4.8	3.7	4.9	4.3	5.7
Passer Rating Net	0.3	-0.1	0.6	1.5	-0.2
Yards per Drive Offense	27.3	26.8	28.3	27.8	28.4
Yards per Drive Defense	26.9	22.6	26.5	24.4	26.4
Average Time of Possession	32:49	33:17	29:56	30:30	30:57

1984 PLAYOFFS
Lost Divisional Playoff to Chicago, 19-23

1986 PLAYOFFS
Won Wild Card Game from L.A. Rams, 19-7
Won Divisional Playoff from Chicago, 27-13
Lost AFC Championship to N.Y. Giants, 0-17

1987 PLAYOFFS
Won Divisional Playoff from Chicago, 21-17
Won NFC Championship from Minnesota, 17-10
Won Super Bowl XXII from Denver, 42-10

THE 1988 SEASON

DATE	AT	OPPONENT	SCORE	R	SPREAD	Tu	Net YDS	Rush YDS	Pass YDS	TURN
09/05	A*	N.Y. Giants	20-27	L	+2	a	386-218	117- 56	269-162	2-1
09/11	H	Pittsburgh	30-29	W	-8	g	515-341	93- 83	422-258	3-1
09/18	H	Philadelphia	17-10	W	-4.5	g	285-299	150- 90	135-209	2-0
09/25	A	Phoenix	21-30	L	-3	g	335-323	53-185	282-138	2-1
10/02	H	N.Y. Giants	23-24	L	-3.5	g	344-264	93- 74	251-190	3-1
10/09	A	Dallas	35-17	W	-2	a	350-361	180- 60	170-301	1-5
10/16	H	Phoenix	33-17	W	-6	g	386-381	97- 76	289-305	1-2
10/23	A	Green Bay	20-17	W	-5	g	385-205	160- 82	225-123	3-0
10/30	A	Houston	17-41	L	-1	a	250-336	29-152	221-184	6-2
11/06	H	New Orleans	27-24	W	-3.5	g	412-322	113- 50	299-272	1-0
11/13	H	Chicago	14-34	L	-3.5	g	323-418	28-145	295-273	5-1
11/21	A*	S. Francisco	21-37	L	+3.5	g	327-320	56-112	271-208	4-2
11/27	H	Cleveland	13-17	L	-1	g	227-324	103-158	124-166	2-1
12/04	A	Philadelphia	20-19	W	+3.5	a	410-310	81-163	329-147	4-3
12/11	H	Dallas	17-24	L	-6.5	g	372-444	24-124	348-320	5-2
12/17	A	Cincinnati	17-20	L	+7	a	372-318	166-135	206-183	2-0
						Avg.	355-324	96-109	259-215	3-1

				WINS	LOSSES
Season Record:	7- 9-0	POINTS:		26- 19	18- 28
Vs. Spread:	5-11-0	Net YDS:	10- 6-0	392-317	326-329
Home:	4- 4-0	Rush YDS:	9- 7-0	125- 86	74-127
On Artificial Turf:	2- 3-0	Pass YDS:	12- 4-0	267-231	252-203
Art. Turf vs. Spread:	3- 2-0	TURN:	2-14-0	2- 2	3- 1

* Monday Night

CHANGES

When a team wins a Super Bowl, and wins it big at that, you don't expect a lot of changes the next time around. Who would have thought that changes would be the major theme of the '88 Redskins? By the end of the season, Coach Joe Gibbs was speculating that owner Jack Kent Cooke and GM Bobby Beathard might want to make a big change—in the head coaching position.*

Neither Cooke nor Beathard has lost a sense of perspective. Gibbs is paranoid, but he's still regarded as an exceptional coach. One publication named him the greatest of all time in a burst of post-Super Bowl XXII enthusiasm. Gibbs was smart enough to point out he hadn't been around long enough to justify that ranking, but few would argue that he belongs in the top two or three active coaches who weren't in the NFL before 1970.

One of his strengths is his willingness to make changes when he thinks they'll help. Just ask Jay Schroeder. Despite some second-guessing by, among others, Gibbs himself, most of the Redskins' changes in '88 were thrust upon him by circumstances beyond his control.

His biggest pain in the neck was the number of times the ball changed hands *away* from his Redskins. Usually one of the leaders in takeaways-giveaways, the '88 'Skins were a woeful −9 in that department, the worst in the NFL. They had at least one more turnover than their opponents in fourteen games.

THE LINEBACKER

The most heralded change from the Super Bowl lineup was the signing of LB Wilbur Marshall, the former Bears All-Pro. Marshall's $1.4 million in '88 was supposed to make him the world's highest-priced defensive footballer (excluding certain southwestern universities), but rookies Neal Smith of Kansas City and Aundray Bruce of Atlanta made about $70,000 and $500,000 more, respectively. Considering that Marshall brought his new employers five more years of NFL craftiness than did Smith and Bruce combined, he was probably a bargain.

Funny thing. Fans get upset when they hear that some player gets a seven-figure salary for going out sixteen times

*Surprise—as this book went to press, it was Beathard who stepped down, but only after securing Gerald Riggs from Atlanta.

a year and getting his jock knocked off by the likes of Lawrence Taylor or Anthony Munoz. Yet it bothers those fans not a whit that an owner might make eight or nine figures for sitting in his private box sixteen times a year and bitching. *We* think the only people underpaid in pro football are the guys who write books about it.

Anyhow, Marshall did his job okay in 1988. He showed up for all the games, made 133 tackles, 3 interceptions, batted down 4 passes, hurried the quarterback 10 times, and sacked him 4. He didn't make the Pro Bowl, but that was mostly a combination of his Redskins mates being generally less dominating on D than his Bears and, perhaps, a certain amount of backlash. His teammate Charles Mann made the '88 Hawaii squad on the strength of his '87 season, while Dexter Manley was excluded because he has a big mouth. Manley also felt he lost some votes when he was fined for spitting on Saints OT Jim Dombrowski. "To hell with the NFL and the players," Manley decided with his usual diplomacy.

THE WEEKLY LINE

Last season the Redskins probably had more good-to-great and formerly-great linemen than any team has a right to have, with fourteen Pro Bowl trips scattered among seven wide-bodies. On the other hand, Washington needed them all in 1988 when Gibbs shuffled them around like they were a hand of seven-card stud, looking for the best combination. The starters were changed seven times, and no less than six different combos made up the Washington front wall. Mark May, the only one of the crew to start all sixteen games, was selected for the Pro Bowl for the first time. He missed only four offensive plays all season and, according to 'Skins stats, allowed only one sack.

A. Games 1-2

LT	LG	C	RG	RT
Joe Jacoby	Raleigh McKenzie	Jeff Bostic	R.C. Thielemann	Mark May

B. Games 3-5

LT	LG	C	RG	RT
Jacoby	Thielmann	McKenzie	May	Jim Lachey

C. Games 6-9

LT	LG	C	RG	RT
Jacoby	McKenzie	Bostic	May	Lachey

D. Games 10-12

LT	LG	C	RG	RT
Lachey	McKenzie	Bostic	Thielmann	May

E. Game 13

LT	LG	C	RG	RT
Lachey	Russ Grimm	Bostic	May	Jacoby

F. Games 14-15

LT	LG	C	RG	RT
Lachey	Grimm	McKenzie	May	Jacoby

G. Game 16

LT	LG	C	RG	RT
Lachey	Grimm	Bostic	May	Jacoby

Part of the movement was caused by injuries, but some of it came about because of disappointing performances. Center Jeff Bostic was eaten alive by the Giants in the opener. LT Joe Jacoby started the first nine games but was blamed for six QB fumbles on blind-side tackles. He wound up the season a RT. Russ Grimm started the season on injured reserve and was available for only six games. Jim Lachey wasn't acquired until after the first game.

Naturally all that switching around disrupted the whole attack, but it's axiomatic that run blocking takes better timing than pass blocking, so we weren't surprised that the Redskins had trouble running the ball all season (though the line changes weren't the only problem there). Just for fun, we decided to check which combination had the best record. In the table below, the E and G lines are shown simply as E because the personnel was the same.

	A	B	C	D	E†	F
Won-Lost	1-1	1-2	3-1	1-2	0-2	1-1
Rush Yards	105.0	148.0	116.5	65.7	134.5	52.5
Avg. Gain	3.9	3.6	3.9	2.6	3.8	3.0
Pass Yards	345.5	222.7	226.3	298.7	165.0	338.5
Avg. Gain*	6.5	6.7	6.4	7.1	6.9	7.1
Sacks	2.0	2.7	1.8	1.0	1.0	0.0

* Net Yards / (Attempts + Sacks)
† Lineup for Games 13 and 16 (E and G) the same.

After the season, R.C. Thielemann, who'll be thirty-four in '89, asked to be traded or released.

ONE DIVIDED BY THREE

Under Gibbs the 'Skins have thrived on a one-back offense. One might even say they perfected it. But after '88, Gibbs admitted he was thinking about using two backs.

For a one-back offense to work, you need not one back but *the* back. Washington had John Riggins once and later George Rogers. They were big, heavy-duty guys who could run between the tackles all day until the defensive line became applesauce in the fourth quarter. If a sweep was called for, they had just enough speed to make it credible.

When we measure running backs, we usually look at their yards gained, average gain, and touchdowns scored. The "attempts" column isn't a big bragging point. Yet just about everybody—the good, the bad, and the ugly—averages between 3.7 and 4.3 per rush over a season. And if you project that to, say, 275 carries, you might think they're all capable of gaining over a thousand yards in a season, if they only had the chance. Some might, but most would find that average slipping further and further the more they ran. Many others would never get to the 275-attempts plateau because they couldn't take the heavy pounding. The trick is to be able to carry the football 18 to 25 times a game for sixteen weeks and still maintain a decent average. That's what really separates the all-timer from the part-timer. That's what Riggins and Rogers did for the Redskins.

In Timmy Smith, the 'Skins thought they had the heir-apparent to Rogers' spot. When he ran for 204 yards in 22 carries to help destroy Denver in Super Bowl XXII, they were sure. Gibbs even answered some of his admirers by asking if he was so smart, why did he have Smith on the bench most of the season?

Smith opened '88 as the regular and had a good day against the Giants. But in each succeeding game his average gain per attempt fell off. By the fifth game he shared time with Kelvin Bryant. And in the sixth game Bryant became the starter.

Kelvin is an extremely elusive runner and a better receiver than Smith. He helped balance the offense, and the Redskins won four of five. But Bryant is tall and so thin he looks like a handful of soda straws running the ball. He'd barely become a regular when folks began questioning if he'd last the season. That was answered in the tenth game, when he went out for the year with a knee injury. Gibbs admitted after the season that it had been a mistake to run Bryant 20 to 25 times a game. He's scheduled for spot duty, mostly as a receiver, in '89.

When Bryant was sidelined, Smith returned as the starter but couldn't do much of anything right. A two-fumble performance against San Francisco in Week 12, when he could gain only six yards in a dozen carries, ended his usefulness as far as Gibbs was concerned.

Rookie Jamie Morris, the younger brother of the Giants' Joe, finished the season. He set a league record with 45 carries in the final game against Cincinnati, 7 more attempts than Riggins ever made in a Redskins game. But Jamie is only 185 pounds, 10 pounds less than his big brother. He enters 1989 as the incumbent, but only a full sixteen-game schedule will show whether he's a real flash or just one in the pan.

		SMITH (1-5, 11-12)					BRYANT (6-10)					MORRIS (13-16)				
WK	OPP	AT	YDS	AVG	LG	TD	AT	YDS	AVG	LG	TD	AT	YDS	AVG	LG	TD
1	Giants	20	100	5.0	21	0	2	5	2.5	3	0					
2	Pitts.	15	58	3.9	16	0	5	24	4.8	14	0	9	11	1.2	9	1
3	Phila.	31	107	3.5	22	1	4	15	3.8	10	0	2	29	14.5	27	1
4	Phoenix	18	54	3.0	29	0										
5	Giants	11	12	1.1	6	0	11	78	7.1	16	0					
6	Dallas	8	26	3.3	6	0	23	118	5.1	17	1					
7	Phoenix	3	7	2.3	4	0	22	73	3.3	9	0					
8	Gr.Bay	6	22	3.6	7	0	27	140	5.2	25	0					
9	Houston	2	1	0.5	1	1	7	20	2.8	8	0					
10	N.Or.	25	71	2.8	9	0	6	25	4.2	9	0	1	3	3.0	3	0
11	Chicago	4	6	1.5	3	0						5	21	4.2	10	0
12	S.F.	12	6	0.5	4	0						8	19	2.4	4	0

(Continued)

WK	OPP	SMITH (1-5, 11-12)					BRYANT (6-10)					MORRIS (13-16)				
		AT	YDS	AVG	LG	TD	AT	YDS	AVG	LG	TD	AT	YDS	AVG	LG	TD
13	Cleve.											19	74	3.9	13	0
14	Phila.											19	84	4.4	25	0
15	Dallas											13	25	1.9	6	0
16	Cin.											45	152	3.4	12	0

THE QUARTERBACK (?)

Changes at quarterback weren't unexpected in Washington. After all, Gibbs had replaced starter Jay Schroeder with Doug Williams at the tail of the Super Bowl season. In pre-'88 estimates, either was penciled in as the possible regular. However, Schroeder complained so loud he was being shafted he had to be shifted. When the 'Skins dealt him to the Raiders for Lachey, it seemed they'd dodged the QB-controversy bullet.

After three games Williams underwent an emergency appendectomy. Replacement Mark Rypien hadn't fired an NFL pass in anger in three years, but he replaced him so well that he led the NFC in passing by the time Williams was ready to return. From there on, no matter which one started, some segment of Redskinville knew it was the wrong choice.

Each played well in both starting and relieving roles. So well, in fact, that the team set season records for passing in attempts, completions, yards, touchdowns, and first downs. Not bad for a club that numbers Sammy Baugh, Sonny Jurgensen, and Joe Theismann among its distinguished alumni.

As of this moment Williams has the starting job. Rypien has not yet shown any sign of falling victim to the foot-in-mouth disease that claimed Schroeder. At twenty-seven, he's seven years younger than Williams.

		WILLIAMS (W-L: 4-6) (1-3, 8-12, 15-16)						RYPIEN (W-L: 3-3) (5-7, 13-14)					
WK	OPP	ATT	COM	YDS	LG	TD	IN	ATT	COM	YDS	LG	TD	IN
1	Giants	50	24	288	28	2	0						
2	Pitts.	52	30	430	58	2	1						
3	Phila.	23	12	142	33	0	1						
4	Phoenix							41	26	303	26	3	1
5	Giants							27	16	282	49	2	1
6	Dallas							21	13	187	34	3	0
7	Phoenix							27	15	303	60	4	0
8	Gr.Bay	43	25	225	22	2	1						
9	Houston	31	15	188	30	0	1	12	8	66	15	1	0
10	N.Or.	28	29	299	46	2	1						
11	Chicago	19	6	69	19	0	1	33	14	257	46	2	4
12	S.F.	41	27	271	22	3	2						
13	Cleve.							24	11	135	25	1	2
14	Phila.	32	20	206	28	1	0	17	8	123	28	1	3
15	Dallas	40	17	274	41	1	2	6	3	74	55	1	0
16	Cin.	22	17	217	45	2	1						

THE VERDICT OF HISTORY

The Redskins went into 1988 with the lead in the NFL Team of the Decade race. In case that's a contest you haven't heard of, we'll explain. Every sport marks its eras by the most dominant team of its time, like they used to do with countries. Remember the Age of Greece, the Age of Rome, and so on? Well, national eras last a lot longer than sports-team eras, possibly because Rome drafted well. It's a convenient shorthand that helps us avoid cluttering our minds with dates. In sports, with a shorter time span, the eras are divided into decades, like the way we think of recent American history in convenient ten-year gulps: the Depression, World War Two, the Cold War, the Vietnam War, the—

enough! This is getting morbid. Back to sports. For instance, in baseball you could call the 1950s, when the Yankees won eight pennants and six World Series, the Decade of the Yankees. And you could flip the idea and call the Yankees the Team of the Decade. Complex stuff, but you see how it works.

Now in the NFL, the Steelers were the Team of the Seventies (in a close race with the Dolphins), the Packers the Team of the Sixties. If you wanted to go back farther and really show how old you are, you might pick the Browns as the Team of the Fifties, the Bears of the Forties, the Packers the Thirties, and the Canton Bulldogs the Team of the Twenties. But as the Reagan Era (see what we mean?) came to a close, some people were getting a little antsy about naming a Team of the Eighties. They probably figured if they didn't hurry up and tag the decade with a team they'd forget the whole ten years.

Well, as we said, the 'Skins had the lead going into last season, but it wasn't even by a nose, more like a nostril. They were tied for second with the 49ers in 1980s regular-season wins. The Dolphins led that but hadn't won a Super Bowl since the seventies. The Redskins had two Big-Saucer wins, as did the 49ers and Raiders. Washington's paper-thin edge came from appearing in one more Large-Dish, albeit they lost.

After the 49ers' third Super Bowl win, nearly everyone was happy to name them the Team of the Decade. But there's still one year left. The Redskins can still be the Team of the Eighties if they can win the first Super Bowl to be played in the nineties.

WASHINGTON REDSKINS STATISTICS

1988 TEAM STATISTICS	WR	OPP
TOTAL FIRST DOWNS	306	293
Rushing	87	112
Passing	202	153
Penalty	17	28
3rd Down Made/Att.	97/223	76/202
Pct.	43.5%	37.6%
4th Down Made/Att.	10/16	4/10
Pct.	62.5%	40.0%
TOTAL NET YARDS	5679	5184
Avg. per Game	354.9	324.0
Total Plays	1053	982
Avg. per Play	5.4	5.3
NET YARDS RUSHING	1543	1745
Avg. per Game	96.4	109.1
Total Rushes	437	442
NET YARDS PASSING	4136	3439
Avg. per Game	258.5	214.9
Tackled/Yards Lost	24/203	43/305
Gross Yards	4339	3744
Attempts/Completions	592/327	497/261
Pct. of Completions	55.2%	52.5%
Had Intercepted	25	14
PUNTS/AVERAGE	67/38.2	79/39.4
NET PUNTING AVG.	29.8	34.2
PENALTIES/YARDS	96/817	91/711
FUMBLES/BALL LOST	34/21	23/8
TOUCHDOWNS	41	46
Rushing	8	17
Passing	33	24
Returns	0	5
TIME OF POSSESSION	—	—

SCORE/PERIODS	1	2	3	4	OT	TOTAL
Redskins	86	79	89	91	0	345
Opponents	70	125	64	125	3	387

SCORING	TDR	TDP	TDRt	PAT	FG	S	TP
Lohmiller				40/41	19/26		97
Sanders		12					72
Clark		7					42
Bryant	1	5					36
Monk	5						30
Smith	3						18
Morris	2						12
Orr		2					12
Allen		1					6
Griffin		1					6
Rypien	1						6
D. Williams	1						6
Caldwell						1	2
Redskins	8	33	0	40/41	19/26	1	345
Opponents	17	24	5	43/46	22/36	1	387

RUSHING	NO	YDS	AVG	LG	TD
Bryant	108	498	4.6	25	1
Smith	155	470	3.0	29	3
Morris	126	437	3.5	27t	2
Monk	7	46	6.6	23	0
Rypien	9	31	3.4	19t	1
Oliphant	8	30	3.8	20	0
Griffin	6	23	3.8	9	0
Sanders	2	14	7.0	7	0
Clark	2	6	3.0	4	0
Archer	3	1	0.3	4	0
D. Williams	9	0	0.0	4	1
G. Coleman	2	-13	-6.5	0	0
Redskins	437	1543	3.5	29	8
Opponents	442	1745	3.9	50t	17

RECEIVING	NO	YDS	AVG	LG	TD
Sanders	73	1148	15.7	55t	12
Monk	72	946	13.1	46t	5
Clark	59	892	15.1	60t	7
Bryant	42	447	10.6	47	5
McEwen	23	323	14.0	46	0
Oliphant	15	111	7.4	16	0
Warren	12	112	9.3	32	0
Orr	11	222	20.2	58	2
Smith	8	53	6.6	16	0
Allen	5	48	9.6	18	1
Caravello	2	15	7.5	8	0
Jones	2	10	5.0	9	0
Griffin	2	9	4.5	5	1
Morris	1	3	3.0	3	0
Redskins	327	4339	13.3	60t	33
Opponents	261	3744	14.3	80t	24

INTERCEPTIONS	NO	YDS	AVG	LG	TD
Wilburn	4	24	6.0	14	0
Marshall	3	61	20.3	43	0
Walton	3	54	18.0	29	0
Bowles	1	20	20.0	20	0
Curtis, P-W	1	18	18.0	18	0
Green	1	12	12.0	12	0
Davis	1	11	11.0	11	0
M. Coleman	1	11	11.0	11	0
Redskins	14	193	13.8	43	0
Opponents	25	271	10.8	40	0

PUNTING	NO	YDS	AVG	TB	In 20	LG	Blk
Barnhardt	15	628	41.9	2	1	55	0
G. Coleman	39	1505	38.6	3	8	52	0
Cox	6	221	36.8	1	0	55	1
Lohmiller	6	208	34.7	0	1	42	0
Redskins	67	2562	38.2	6	10	55	1
Opponents	79	3116	39.4	2	21	54	1

PUNT RETURNS	NO	FC	YDS	AVG	LG	TD
Shepard	12	2	104	8.7	23	0
Allen	10	2	62	6.2	14	0
Green	9	0	103	11.4	32	0
Clark	8	3	48	6.0	34	0
Oliphant	7	0	24	3.4	11	0
Johnson	3	1	26	8.7	15	0
Orr	2	0	10	5.0	10	0
Caldwell	1	0	0	0.0	0	0
Gage	0	1	0	—	0	0
Redskins	52	9	377	7.3	34	0
Opponents	39	7	448	11.5	95t	1

KICKOFF RETURNS	NO	YDS	AVG	LG	TD
Morris	21	413	19.7	35	0
Sanders	19	362	19.1	31	0
Shepard	16	329	20.6	44	0
Oliphant	7	127	18.1	26	0
Gage	5	60	12.0	17	0

(Continued)

KICKOFF RETURNS	NO	YDS	AVG	LG	TD
Griffin	3	45	15.0	24	0
Hamilton	1	7	7.0	7	0
Harbour	1	6	6.0	6	0
Orr	1	6	6.0	6	0
Redskins	74	1355	18.3	44	0
Opponents	61	1111	18.2	32	0

FIELD GOALS	1-19	20-29	30-39	40-49	50+	TOTAL
Lohmiller	1-1	6-8	5-7	7-10	0-0	19-26
Redskins	1-1	6-8	5-7	7-10	0-0	19-26
Opponents	2-2	6-7	8-11	4-12	2-4	22-36

FIELD GOALS BY Lohmiller: 19 of 26
(26G,25G)(37G,35N,46G,19G)(27N,34G)(44N)(30G,36N)
(40N)(20G)(33G,46N,20G)(46G)(42G,23G)( )( )(21G,40G)
(37G,44G)(41G)(43G,29N)

PASSING	ATT	COM	YARD	PCT.	Avg G	TD	%TD	IN	%IN	LG	SAKS/YDS	RATE
Williams	380	213	2609	56.1	6.87	15	3.9	12	3.2	58	10/88	77.4
Rypien	208	114	1730	54.8	8.32	18	8.7	13	6.3	60t	14/115	85.2
Archer	2	0	0	0.0	0.00	0	0.0	0	0.0	0	0/0	39.6
G. Coleman	1	0	0	0.0	0.00	0	0.0	0	0.0	0	0/0	39.6
Monk	1	0	0	0.0	0.00	0	0.0	0	0.0	0	0/0	39.6
Redskins	592	327	4339	55.2	7.33	33	5.6	25	4.2	60t	24/203	79.6
Opponents	497	261	3744	52.5	7.53	24	4.8	14	2.8	80t	43/305	81.6

AMERICAN FOOTBALL CONFERENCE

BUFFALO BILLS

The Last 5 Seasons

	1984	1985	1986	1987	1988
Won-Lost	2-14	2-14	4-12	7-8	12-4
Percentage	.125	.125	.250	.467	.750
Division Finish	5	5	4	4	1
Games Behind	12	10	7	2	0
Total Points	250	200	287	270	329
Per Game	15.6	12.5	17.9	18.0	20.6
Opponent Points	454	381	348	305	237
Per Game	28.4	23.8	21.8	20.3	14.8
Net Points	-204	-181	-61	-35	92
Predicted Net Wins	-5.1	-4.5	-1.5	-0.9	2.3
Delta Net Wins	-0.9	-1.5	-2.5	0.4	1.7
Total Yards on Offense	4341	4595	5017	4741	5315
Per Game	271.3	287.2	313.6	316.1	332.2
Total Yards Allowed on Defense	5582	5540	5523	4906	4578
Per Game	348.9	346.3	345.2	327.1	286.1
Net Difference	-1241	-945	-506	-165	737
Offensive Turnovers	44	52	39	43	33
Defensive Takeaways	37	35	18	31	32
Net Turnovers	-7	-17	-21	-12	-1
Predicted Net Points	-131	-147	-126	-62	57
Delta Net Points	-73	-34	65	27	35
Net Rushing Yards	1643	1611	1654	1840	2133
Per Game	102.7	100.7	103.4	122.7	133.3
Average Gain	4.1	3.9	3.9	4.0	4.0
Opponent Net Rushing Yards	2106	2462	1721	2052	1854
Per Game	131.6	153.9	107.6	136.8	115.9
Average Gain	4.0	4.3	3.7	3.8	3.9
Net Passing Yards	2698	2984	3363	2901	3182
Per Game	168.6	186.5	210.2	193.4	198.9
Times Sacked	60	42	45	37	30
Passer Rating in Yards	2.4	3.0	5.0	4.1	5.3
Opponent Net Passing Yards	3476	3078	3802	2854	2724
Per Game	217.3	192.4	237.6	190.3	170.3
Times Sacked	26	25	36	34	46
Passer Rating Defense	5.9	4.8	5.9	4.9	4.4
Passer Rating Net	-3.5	-1.8	-0.9	-0.8	0.9
Yards per Drive Offense	20.7	23.3	26.1	24.7	30.2
Yards per Drive Defense	27.6	27.7	28.9	25.0	25.2
Average Time of Possession	28:43	28:21	28:02	28:41	29:54

93

1988 PLAYOFFS
Lost Divisional Playoff to Cincinnati, 10-21

THE 1988 SEASON

DATE	AT	OPPONENT	SCORE	R	SPREAD	Tu	Net YDS	Rush YDS	Pass YDS	TURN
09/04	H	Minnesota	13-10	W	+3	a	300-300	114-130	186-170	1-2
09/11	H	Miami	9- 6	W	-3	a	319-334	104-115	215-219	4-2
09/18	A	New England	16-14	W	+2.5	a	254-264	105-105	149-159	2-3
09/25	H	Pittsburgh	36-28	W	-4	a	398-408	116- 94	282-314	5-5
10/02	A	Chicago	3-24	L	+4	g	218-417	0-157	218-260	1-2
10/09	H	Indianapolis	34-23	W	-4.5	a	456-308	141- 67	315-241	3-3
10/17	A*	N.Y. Jets	37-14	W	+2.5	a	427-199	135- 45	292-154	1-2
10/23	H	New England	23-20	W	-6.5	a	339-223	190-176	149- 47	4-0
10/30	H	Green Bay	28- 0	W	-7	a	261-131	195- 77	66- 54	3-4
11/06	A	Seattle	13- 3	W	-1	a	336-145	142- 72	194- 73	2-2
11/14	A*	Miami	31- 6	W	-1	g	416-257	205- 33	211-224	0-3
11/20	H	N.Y. Jets	9- 6	W	-7	a	341-259	229-140	112-119	2-1
11/27	A	Cincinnati	21-35	L	+3.5	a	353-455	110-232	243-223	4-0
12/04	A	Tampa Bay	5-10	L	-8.5	g	273-253	39-110	234-143	2-0
12/11	H	L.A. Raiders	37-21	W	-6	a	367-318	255-111	112-207	0-3
12/18	A	Indianapolis	14-17	L	-2	a	248-301	53-184	195-117	1-0
						Avg.	332-286	133-116	198-170	2-2

				WINS	LOSSES
Season Record:	12- 4-0	POINTS:		24- 13	11- 22
Vs. Spread:	9- 6-1	Net YDS:	9- 6-1	351-262	273-357
Home:	8- 0-0	Rush YDS:	9- 6-1	161- 97	273-357
On Artificial Turf:	11- 2-0	Pass YDS:	9- 7-0	190-165	223-186
Art. Turf vs. Spread:	8- 4-1	TURN:	7- 6-3	2- 3	2- 1

* Monday Night

180 DEGREES

To hear the comedians tell it, Buffalo is within half a mile of the North Pole. They have two seasons: winter and the Fourth of July. The snow's so deep you need a Saint Bernard to find your shadow. It's so cold all the brass monkeys sing soprano.

Hey, come on! Who wants to live in a place where they decorate palm trees for Christmas and Santa wears a suit cut off at the knees? Snow is just cold sand but not as gritty. And if you're going to buy a thermometer, why not use the whole thing instead of only the top half?

When *Sports Illustrated*'s Frank DeFord said some nice things about playing football the right way in winter at Buffalo, they gave him the key to the city. Or they will, as soon as they dig it out. Hey, we have a friend from Buffalo and he never once invited us over and fed us blubber. Come to think about it, he never once invited us over. Some friend! Well, maybe he was redecorating his igloo. Stop us if you've heard the one about . . .

Anyway, there are lots of colder places than Buffalo. But right now we want to talk about 180 degrees and Buffalo. Not 180 degrees on a thermometer, of course: 180 degrees in the NFL standings.

Back in 1986 the Buffalo Bills were 4–12. Two years later they went 12–4. Get it? A 180-degree turnaround.

Naturally the fans in the fair city of Buffalo were delighted with this reversal of fortunes. When the Bills clinched first place in the AFC East in Week 12 with an overtime win at Rich Stadium, the victory set off a wild celebration by long-suffering Bills fans, who sang, cheered, tore down the goalposts, and generally frightened the players half to death.

Every Bill was a hero that day. But some deserve special mention.

THE QUARTERBACK

When Buffalo signed Jim Kelly in 1986, season ticket sales rose like a bass after a moth. Kelly had been the star quarterback of the USFL, tossing touchdowns like rice at a wedding. Fans predicted he'd do the same thing in the NFL and the Bills' long drought would be over. He didn't and it wasn't.

In three years as the Buffalo quarterback, Kelly has demonstrated three things. First, that there was a wide gulf in overall talent between the NFL and the USFL. (Geez! What d'yuh want for $3?) Second, that he's a good QB; but third, that he can't do it alone. As a matter of fact, Kelly's per-game record for his three Buffalo seasons shows that he threw less often and slightly less effectively with the winning Bills than he did with the losing Bills.

YEAR	TEAM	ATT	COM	YARD	TD	IN	NFL RATE	NEWS* RATE
1986	4-12	30.0	17.8	224.6	1.4	1.1	83.3	6.35
1987†	6- 6	34.9	20.8	233.2	1.6	0.9	83.8	5.94
1988	12-4	28.3	16.8	211.3	0.9	1.1	78.2	6.12

* NEWS Rate - YDS + (10 X TD) - (45 X IN) / Att
(6.48+ = superior performance).
† Strike games not included.

As a passer Kelly seems to have settled comfortably in the upper part of the "average" NFL QB fraternity. That's borne out by first hand observation. He can throw long or short, hard or with "touch," but he doesn't excel at any of them. He reads okay, but once in a while plops one right into the hands of an enemy. A good passer, but not a Hall of Famer.

That said, we still think he's underrated, mostly by those who insist on judging his NFL performance by what he did in the USFL. What Kelly brings to his quarterback position isn't all wrapped up in his arm. He's a tough-guy leader, and though it's a bit early in his career to say for sure, he may be the closest thing to Bobby Layne the league has had in years. (Layne, you'll recall, was the Lions' QB in the fifties who "never lost a game; he just ran out of time.")

Do you know how many games he's missed in three years, not counting the strike? None. That doesn't mean he hasn't been hurt; he just plays through it. Sack him—he gets up. Smash him after he throws—he gets up. When he runs, he looks like a duck, sitting variety—but he gets up.

All Kelly's brothers were linebackers, and everybody says Jim is a quarterback with a linebacker's mentality. We think that's a little narrow; he's just one tough football player who brings a lot of stability to his position.

Still, when you're handing out credit for the Bills' turnaround, you won't find a significant productivity difference between the Kelly-directed offense of '86 and the '88 version. Last year's crew ran a little more, but the average gain per rush climbed only from 3.9 to 4.0 yards. Look.

OFFENSE PER GAME	1986	1987	1988
	4-12	7-8	12-4
Total Yards	313.6	316.1	332.2
Net Rushing Yards	103.4	122.7	133.3
Net Passing Yards	210.2	193.4	198.9

There's no way that 18.6 net yards more per game translates into eight more wins.

THE COACH

After the ninth game of '88, when Buffalo was 8-1, Bills' owner Ralph Wilson termed Marv Levy "the best head coach in the history of the franchise." Well, 8-1 will do that to you. As we recall, Lou Saban was 70-47-4 in two terms

and won a couple of AFL championships back in the 1960s. And Chuck Knox, though only 38-38 overall, won the division title in 1980 and reached the playoffs in '81. Levy is 22-18 since replacing Hank Bullough for the tenth game in '86. He's only had one winning season at Buffalo and was 31-42 with the Chiefs from 1978-82. We're not disputing Wilson, just saying he had a premature accolation.

Levy is a fine enough coach, who at age sixty finally has the players to prove it. He won't knock you on your prat with a bold innovation. However, he won't come up with something harebrained either. He's not the world's greatest motivator, but his players work hard for him and respect him. They call him "Professor."

"I don't think I'm too pedantic," Levy said, confirming the diagnosis with a bit of humor that was surely intentional.

The rap on Levy—and you started to hear it even while the Bills were winning the division—was that his offense was as exciting as watching ice melt. For much of the season, Levy's most reliable weapon was placekicker Scott Norwood, who made 32 of 37 field goal attempts and the Pro Bowl. Interestingly the Bills scored exactly one more rushing touchdown and one more passing touchdown than the opposition, 15-14 in each case, but *twenty* more field goals.

Realistically Levy didn't have that much to work with on offense: a no-frills quarterback, a committee of ordinary runners, solid receivers without a burner, and a decent offensive line. Razzle-dazzle with that group and the Bills might have finished a lot worse than the -9 in takeaways that they did, which would have been disastrous. The Bills' offense was predicated on the proposition that the defense could keep opponents out of the endzone if the offense didn't do anything dumb. That's why the field goal differential was so great. When the Bills gave up the ball, it was usually far downfield and stayed there. When the opposition gave up the ball in close, Norwood delivered.

BVD'S

The Bills' valuable defenders won Buffalo's division title. It may not rank with Chicago's or Minnesota's yet, but there are twenty-four NFL teams that could have had winning records had they been able to field the Bills' defense.

The lineup is a good blend of youth and experience. NT Fred Smerlas, entering his eleventh season, used to be a regular at the Pro Bowl, but was sort of forgotten while the Bills were so terrible. Last season he was rediscovered and picked for the Hawaii trip as an alternate. At thirty-two, he should have another good season or two ahead of him.

The Bills acquired right defensive end Art Still in training camp. Still was one of the AFC's best defenders for years at Kansas City. However, he was not an admirer of Coach Frank Gansz, whom he would imitate to the amusement of his teammates. Somehow the humor was lost on Gansz. When Art had to depart, Buffalo was lucky to be standing in line. With the Bills, he was reunited with defensive coordinator Walt Corey. The 6'7" Still contributed 6 sacks and played particularly well early in the season while left defensive end Bruce Smith was under drug suspension.

Smith is the best DE in the AFC. In only twelve games, he racked up 11 sacks. Bruce is twenty-six, with perhaps his best years ahead of him. Still is thirty-two and on the downside, but if he slips, remember that third-year pro Leon Seals filled in ably last season while Smith was suspended.

The Bills' linebacking corps is even stronger than the front three. After only a year and a half, left outside linebacker Cornelius Bennett is regarded as the AFC's answer to Lawrence Taylor. His strong suit is pass rushing, as witness his 9.5 sacks last season. The Bennett trade in mid-1987—known as the Dickerson trade in Indianapolis—was the pivotal move for this defense. (For more on the particulars of that immense deal, see the essay on the Rams.) Cornelius, the Colts' unsigned number one draft choice, arrived without benefit of training camp and immediately turned the defense into one of the best. In four nonstrike games B.B. (Before Bennett), Buffalo had allowed an average of 29.8 points. In eight games A.B. (After Bennett), the average dropped to 15.3.

The combination of Bennett and Smith gives the Bills a powerful one-two pass rushing duo.

	BRUCE SMITH				CORNELIUS BENNETT		
	GM	SACKS	P/GM		GM	SACKS	P/GM
1985	16	6.5	0.41				
1986	16	15.0	0.94				
1987	12	12.0	1.00	1987	8	8.5	1.06
1988	12	11.0	0.92	1988	16	9.5	0.59
	56	44.5	0.79		24	18.0	0.75

Bennett's arrival allowed the Bills' number one choice, Shane Conlan, to move from OLB, where he was overmatched on pass coverage, to ILB, where he became a Pro Bowl starter. Conlan's ability to close down the run gives Bennett the freedom to blitz or roam. When Shane was injured and out of the lineup at the end of the regular season last year, Bennett's effectiveness was reduced because he had to stay home and attend more to stopping the run. LILB Ray Bentley and ROLB Darryl Talley are solid pros at the peak of their game. Backup Scott Radecic is another Kansas City escapee who knows Corey's system.

The defensive backs are not up to the all-pro level of the front men, but they are adequate. Right cornerback Nate Odomes, entering his third season, is quite good. The left corner, Derrick Burroughs, played better last season than in his three previous years. Leonard Smith, acquired from Phoenix after the season began, filled a hole at strong safety. Mark Kelso isn't the fastest free safety in the league, but he does have the proverbial knack for being in the right place at the right time.

Even when Buffalo was nigh unto the worst team in the league in 1986, their defense wasn't the worst. Bruce Smith, Smerlas, Talley, Bentley, Kelso, and Burroughs were already on the scene—though most of them were not playing up to last year's level. The additions of Bennett, Conlan, Still, Seals, Odomes, Radecic, Leonard Smith, and def-co Corey changed d to D.

DEFENSE PER GAME	1986	1987	1988
	4-12	7-8	12-4
Opponent Points	21.8	20.3	14.8
Opponent Net Yards Allowed	345.2	327.1	286.1
Opponent Net Rushing Yards	107.6	136.8	115.9
Opponent Net Passing Yards	237.6	190.3	170.3
Sacks	2.3	2.3	2.9

The turnaround from the 4–12 mark in 1986 wasn't due *exclusively* to the defense, of course. But when they start handing out laurel wreaths in Buffalo, the defense could look like a jungle.

BUFFALO BILLS STATISTICS

1988 TEAM STATISTICS	BB	OPP
TOTAL FIRST DOWNS	313	299
Rushing	137	114
Passing	161	146
Penalty	15	39
3rd Down Made/Att.	88/207	69/192
Pct.	42.5%	35.9%
4th Down Made/Att.	9/13	6/17
Pct.	69.2%	35.3%
TOTAL NET YARDS	5315	4578
Avg. per Game	332.2	286.1
Total Plays	1012	971
Avg. per Play	5.3	4.7
NET YARDS RUSHING	2133	1854
Avg. per Game	133.3	115.9
Total Rushes	528	477
NET YARDS PASSING	3182	2724
Avg. per Game	198.9	170.3
Tackled/Yards Lost	30/229	46/322

(Continued)

1988 TEAM STATISTICS	BB	OPP
Gross Yards	3411	3046
Attempts/Completions	454/271	448/250
Pct. of Completions	59.7%	55.8%
Had Intercepted	15	17
PUNTS/AVERAGE	62/39.5	75/39.7
NET PUNTING AVG.	35.3	34.5
PENALTIES/YARDS	109/824	90/713
FUMBLES/BALL LOST	26/16	28/17
TOUCHDOWNS	33	29
Rushing	15	14
Passing	15	14
Returns	3	1
TIME OF POSSESSION	—	—

SCORE/PERIODS	1	2	3	4	OT	TOTAL
Bills	71	83	81	91	3	329
Opponents	44	104	27	62	0	237

SCORING	TDR	TDP	TDRt	PAT	FG	S	TP
Norwood				33/33	32/37		129
Riddick	12	1	1				84
Reed		6					36
Harmon	1	3					24
Rolle		2					12
Thomas	2						12
Burkett		1					6
F. Johnson		1					6
Kelso			1				6
Metzelaars		1					6
Seals			1				6
B. Smith						1	2
Bills	15	15	3	33/33	32/37	1	329
Opponents	14	14	1	27/29	12/24	0	237

RUSHING	NO	YDS	AVG	LG	TD
Thomas	207	881	4.3	37t	2
Riddick	111	438	3.9	21	12
Mueller	81	296	3.7	20	0
Harmon	57	212	3.7	32	1
Kelly	35	154	4.4	20	0
Byrum	28	91	3.3	11	0
Reedon	6	64	10.7	36	0
Reich	3	-3	-1.0	-1	0
Bills	528	2133	4.0	37t	15
Opponents	477	1854	3.9	58t	14

RECEIVING	NO	YDS	AVG	LG	TD
Reed	71	968	13.6	65t	6
T. Johnson	37	514	13.9	49	0
Harmon	37	427	11.5	36	3
Metzelaars	33	438	13.3	35	1
Riddick	30	282	9.4	26	1
Burkett	23	354	15.4	34	1
Thomas	18	208	11.6	34	0
F. Johnson	9	170	18.9	66t	1
Mueller	8	42	5.3	17	0
Rolle	2	3	1.5	2t	2
Byrum	2	0	0.0	3	0
Kelly	1	5	5.0	5	0
Bills	271	3411	12.6	66t	15
Opponents	250	3046	12.2	63t	14

INTERCEPTIONS	NO	YDS	AVG	LG	TD
Kelso	7	180	25.7	78t	1
Bennett	2	30	15.0	30	0

(Continued)

INTERCEPTIONS	NO	YDS	AVG	LG	TD
L. Smith, P-B	2	29	14.5	15	0
L. Smith, B	1	14	14.0	14	0
Cocroft	1	17	17.0	17	0
Davis	1	3	3.0	3	0
Bentley	1	0	0.0	0	0
Conlan	1	0	0.0	0	0
Odomes	1	0	0.0	0	0
Bills	15	244	16.3	78t	1
Opponents	17	202	11.9	40t	1

PUNTING	NO	YDS	AVG	TB	In 20	LG	Blk
Kidd	62	2451	39.5	2	13	60	0
Bills	62	2451	39.5	2	13	60	0
Opponents	75	2977	39.7	12	21	64	2

PUNT RETURNS	NO	FC	YDS	AVG	LG	TD
F. Johnson	16	3	72	4.5	16	0
Tucker	10	5	80	8.0	24	0
Bills	26	8	152	5.8	24	0
Opponents	36	10	222	6.2	18	0

KICKOFF RETURNS	NO	YDS	AVG	LG	TD
Tucker	15	310	20.7	30	0
F. Johnson	14	250	17.9	24	0
Harmon	11	249	22.6	37	0
Riddick	6	100	16.7	23	0
Byrum	2	9	4.5	9	0
Pike	1	5	5.0	5	0
Rolle	1	12	12.0	12	0
Bills	50	935	18.7	37	0
Opponents	69	1117	16.2	30	0

FIELD GOALS	1-19	20-29	30-39	40-49	50+	TOTAL
Norwood	1-1	10-10	15-16	6-9	0-1	32-37
Bills	1-1	10-10	15-16	6-9	0-1	32-37
Opponents	0-0	5-7	3-4	3-8	1-5	12-24

FIELD GOALS BY Norwood: 32 of 37
(27G,42N,26G)(41G,35G,28G)(38G,44G,41G)
(38G,39G,39G,48G,49G)(28G,45N)(52N,45G,
19G)(30G,34G,28G)(30G,35G,33G)( )(27G,23G)
(30G,39N)(47N,25G,26G,30G)( )(30G)(30G,30G,22G)

PASSING	ATT	COM	YARD	PCT.	Avg G	TD	%TD	IN	%IN	LG	SAKS/YDS	RATE
Kelly	452	269	3380	59.5	7.48	15	3.3	17	3.8	66t	30/229	78.2
Riddick	2	2	31	100.0	15.50	0	0.0	0	0.0	26	0/0	118.8
Bills	454	271	3411	59.7	7.51	15	3.3	17	3.7	66t	30/229	78.5
Opponents	448	250	3046	55.8	6.80	14	3.1	15	3.3	63t	46/322	73.4

CINCINNATI BENGALS

The Last 5 Seasons

	1984	1985	1986	1987	1988
Won-Lost	8-8	7-9	10-6	4-11	12-4
Percentage	.500	.438	.625	.267	.750
Division Finish	2	2-t	2	4	1
Games Behind	1	1	2	6	0
Total Points	339	441	409	285	448
Per Game	21.2	27.6	25.6	19.0	28.0
Opponent Points	339	437	394	370	329
Per Game	21.2	27.3	24.6	24.7	20.6
Net Points	0	4	15	-85	119
Predicted Net Wins	0.0	0.1	0.4	-2.1	3.0
Delta Net Wins	0.0	-1.1	1.6	-1.4	1.0
Total Yards on Offense	5480	5900	6490	5377	6057
Per Game	342.5	368.8	405.6	358.5	378.6
Total Yards Allowed on Defense	5259	5663	5274	4697	5182
Per Game	328.7	353.9	329.6	313.1	323.9
Net Difference	221	237	1216	680	875
Offensive Turnovers	39	29	36	32	27
Defensive Takeaways	40	38	28	26	36
Net Turnovers	1	9	-8	-6	9
Predicted Net Points	22	56	69	33	109
Delta Net Points	-22	-52	-54	-118	10
Net Rushing Yards	2179	2183	2533	2164	2710
Per Game	136.2	136.4	158.3	144.3	169.4
Average Gain	4.0	4.3	4.9	4.0	4.8
Opponent Net Rushing Yards	1868	1999	2122	1641	2048
Per Game	116.8	124.9	132.6	109.4	128.0
Average Gain	3.9	4.3	4.1	3.7	4.2
Net Passing Yards	3301	3717	3957	3213	3347
Per Game	206.3	232.3	247.3	214.2	209.2
Times Sacked	45	41	28	32	30
Passer Rating in Yards	4.6	6.2	6.3	4.9	7.1
Opponent Net Passing Yards	3391	3664	3152	3056	3134
Per Game	211.9	229.0	197.0	203.7	195.9
Times Sacked	40	40	42	40	42
Passer Rating Defense	4.3	5.5	4.8	5.4	4.1
Passer Rating Net	0.2	0.7	1.5	-0.5	3.0
Yards per Drive Offense	28.8	29.5	32.6	29.1	33.1
Yards per Drive Defense	27.2	29.0	27.0	25.7	28.0
Average Time of Possession	30:50	31:18	28:48	30:24	29:31

1988 PLAYOFFS
Won Divisional Playoff from Seattle, 21-13
Won AFC Championship Game from Buffalo, 21-10
Lost Super Bowl XXIII to San Francisco, 16-20

THE 1988 SEASON

DATE	AT	OPPONENT	SCORE	R	SPREAD	Tu	Net YDS	Rush YDS	Pass YDS	TURN
09/04	H	Phoenix	21-14	W	-5.5	a	403-374	152-167	251-207	1-2
09/11	A	Philadelphia	28-24	W	+5	a	431-415	78-190	353-225	3-1
09/18	A	Pittsburgh	17-12	W	+2.5	a	302-319	116-124	186-195	1-6
09/25	H	Cleveland	24-17	W	-3.5	a	393-322	213- 68	180-254	0-1
10/02	A	L.A. Raiders	45-21	W	-1.5	g	496-405	164- 96	332-309	1-5
10/09	H	N.Y. Jets	36-19	W	-6	a	402-226	206-109	196-117	2-1
10/16	A	New England	21-27	L	-5.5	a	365-311	140-158	225-153	6-0
10/23	H	Houston	44-21	W	-5	a	353-205	222-104	131-101	4-5
10/30	A	Cleveland	16-23	L	+3.5	g	281-302	128- 99	153-203	0-2
11/06	H	Pittsburgh	42- 7	W	-7.5	a	559-198	221-101	338- 97	2-0
11/13	A	Kansas City	28-31	L	-6.5	a	307-418	150-142	157-276	2-0
11/20	A	Dallas	38-24	W	-4.5	a	410-355	214-179	196-176	1-2
11/27	A	Buffalo	35-21	W	-3.5	a	455-353	232-110	223-243	0-4
12/04	H	San Diego	27-10	W	-13.5	a	352-211	207- 88	145-123	2-4
12/11	A	Houston	6-41	L	+1.5	a	226-396	132-147	94-249	2-2
12/17	H	Washington	20-17	W	-7	a	318-372	135-166	183-206	0-2
						Avg.	378-324	169-128	209-196	2-2

				WINS	LOSSES
Season Record:	12- 4-0	POINTS:		31- 17	18- 31
Vs. Spread:	11- 5-0	Net YDS:	11- 5-0	406-313	295-357
Home:	8- 0-0	Rush YDS:	10- 6-0	180-125	138-137
On Artificial Turf:	11- 3-0	Pass YDS:	9- 7-0	226-188	157-220
Art. Turf vs. Spread:	10- 4-0	TURN:	10- 5-1	1- 3	3- 1

WICKY-WACKY WINNER

We've never been big Bengals blasters. When people said the Cincinnati headgear looked like Browns' helmets that had been run over front to back by a semi, we merely nodded and mentioned they were in keeping with the uniform stripes that seemingly had been subjected to a bullwhip. When other, more cynical souls were calling them the "Bungles," we just smiled and kept our counsel. Well, maybe we said it once or twice, but just to show we were regular guys. We didn't get any real fun out of it. To be honest, we didn't much care whether Cincinnati won or lost or how they played the game. They were just another football team. So they dressed funny. So what? Ho-hum.

But a few years ago Cincy hired this coach who was kind of interesting. An ex-quarterback who never made it big. They said the best part of his game back then had been that he kept a beautiful playbook. He was no great shakes at X's and O's on the field, but on paper he was Rembrandt van Staubach. What we liked about him as a coach was that he was willing to try new things. Most of the NFL coaching fraternity looks on anything new the way the Vatican looks at birth control, so right away this guy was an outsider. And when in the fullness of time, some of his new ideas didn't pan out, a lot of people started making fun of him. They

called him "Wicky-Wacky," which was a play on his last name. Cute. "Wicky-Wacky and the Bungles." Sounds like a sixties rock group.

If we remember correctly, one of his screwy ideas that went by the boards was to have his offensive team hold hands before they went on the field. We think the design was to make sure everybody was up and ready and within the sound of the coach's voice, but you just couldn't have that kind of thing. Grown men holding hands! What would people think?

Another thing he'd do was run the ball sometimes on fourth down when everyone in the ballpark knew the *correct* call was to punt. You could prove by mathematics that a team was better off running—that the success rate of making the first down in certain situations was better than the odds on punting and then keeping the other team from scoring. And he *did* have a pretty good offense and a pretty bad defense. Didn't matter. As soon as his team missed the first down and the opposition came back to score, people said, "Wicky-Wacky."

When he started running his offense without a huddle and *not* just in the last two minutes, people made little circle motions by their temples. Obviously his team would wear themselves out.

Call us perverse. We liked the guy for trying new stuff.

And we didn't buy the NFL Coach's Equation: if a thing doesn't work every time, don't use it. Sometimes his team crushed teams it shouldn't have even edged. And sometimes it lost games it figured to win. Those were the ones everyone remembered.

Wacky got himself in trouble sometimes with his candor, too. When the media types who really should have been coaching the team asked questions that all but began, "How stupid can you get—?" he would sometimes say things that suggested they couldn't distinguish a certain part of their anatomy from a hole in the ground. They didn't like that. Few of us do.

So when the Bengals really went to pieces in 1987, the media types started predicting his next press conference would be in the employment line. Did you ever see a wolf gloat? It's not a pretty sight. But we read and listened to those media seers, and naturally believed every word. These guys *know*, right? So we started looking for the announcement that Wacky was history. We thought we'd maybe send him a card. Thanks for the memories or something.

But the ax didn't fall.

It was all Paul Brown's fault, said the media. Wicky-Wacky had another year on his contract and Old Man Brown, the Bengals' head man, was too cheap to pay him off. It was already established that Brown was a miser of the first grasp because he didn't want to pay raw rookies sums that could run the state government of Ohio for six years. Where were his priorities?

Golly gee, we said. Keeping a screwy coach just to save a few bucks? That doesn't sound like the Paul Brown we remembered. It's been a while, but the *Coach* Brown we recalled always put the best prepared team on the field of just about anyone. And we remembered how they used to snicker at his careful playbooks and dissection of game films. And—wow!—his idea of sending plays in from the bench instead of letting the quarterback guess on the field, now *there* was a really nutty idea!

About that time we began to wonder if Old Man Brown might be keeping Wicky-Wacky around because he thought he was a lot smarter than the media types said. Maybe one of those people like Landry or Shula or Walsh or, well, Brown that others end up imitating. Maybe Old Man Brown didn't get his ideas from the newspapers.

Well, a year has passed. The Bengals went all the way to the Super Bowl. Old Man Brown is smiling. A little cold, but a smile. And Wacky—well, they don't call him that anymore. Now, he's "Coach."

THE KEY PLAY WAS "PASS THE ORANGE JUICE."

Looking back over Sam Wyche's five years, there's been a lot of missing the forests because the trees were in the way. For his first three seasons the Bengals were supposed to be a powerhouse, and when they didn't win, everybody figured it was his innovations that ruined them. Look at the weapons! people said. Then they'd start naming the quarter-back, the runners, the linemen, and the receivers. Nobody ever said much about the defense. Just as well; there wasn't much to speak of. The Bengals were never as good as their offensive stats said they were.

But they weren't as bad as they looked in '87 either. What killed them more than anything was the strike. The QB, Boomer Esiason, was the player rep. He believed in the NFLPA cause with all his heart. One time he even lay down in front of the bus bringing the sca—whoops—replacement players into the ballpark. (The bus was parked at the time. Boomer was symbolic, not stupid.) Meanwhile Wyche was with management and loyal. It was the classic blue-collar dilemma: one man fighting for workers' rights and the other pledging allegiance to the people who paid his salary. Two men who honestly believe in the rightness of their causes are a disaster on a collision course.

The disaster came when the strike ended. Esiason and Wyche found it impossible to go back to business as usual. Things had been said, then more things. Trust was shattered. With a coach whose strength was his offensive thinking and a quarterback charged with implementing that thinking, barely speaking, the Bengals' offense fell apart. And the defense, which had been mediocre at best, couldn't pick up the slack. The Bengals got out of 1987 with four wins and may have been lucky at that.

The talent was there for a better season, but only if everyone had pulled in the same direction.

Esiason was the key. He could have sulked until Cincy got a new coach or traded him. Instead, he went to the owners' meeting in Phoenix in the spring at his own expense. For those of a symbolic bent, the phoenix was a bird that was destroyed in a fire and then rose anew from the ashes. The Rocky of birddom. Except this time it was a Bengal tiger that had been destroyed.

Boomer sat down over breakfast with Wyche and told him that he still believed in the NFLPA, but he was giving up his job as player rep because it was in the way of winning football games. Boomer wasn't surrendering or even apologizing. But he was saying that maybe both men had lost sight of the thing that was most important. They could agree to disagree during the off season, but from the first kickoff to the last gun, it would be football only. When they stood up, they shook hands and meant it. In effect the Bengals' championship was decided over ham and eggs.

THE GOOD SIDE OF THE BALL

The Bengals have to be favored to win their division and maybe their conference in '89. They're good, but we have some reservations.

None of them (except health) apply to their quarterback, however. We've always been high on the Boomer as a passer. What really impressed us last season was how well he ran the team.

The running game got most of the late-season ink, but Boomer's passes accounted for the first nine Cincinnati touchdowns in '88. WR's Eddie Brown and Tim McGee were streaking downfield and Boomer was hitting them for 65- and 75-yard scores.

Esiason's early-season success with long-distance passes scared opponents' defensive coordinators half to death. Cincy foes became "deep-conscious" and put LBs and DBs into reverse any time they sniffed a bomb. Boomer had fun firing under the coverage, but the RBs benefited more. Once they passed the line of scrimmage, they had several unhindered yards before the defenders could shift gears and come up.

We have two worries concerning the running game. RB James Brooks is entering his ninth season, and that's a long time for a running back. He's also on the small side, so we worry about injuries. FB Ickey Woods, everybody's favorite shuffler, may be the new Eric Dickerson as the hype would have you believe. He's a personable sort, so we wouldn't mind seeing him stay around and prosper. But the Bengals have traditionally had big fullbacks, the late Boobie Clark, Pete Johnson, and Larry Kinnebrew. They all started out setting the league on fire and then got too big for their britches—literally. Ickey lists at 232 but looks bigger already. Let's hope he can avoid the Cincinnati Fat Fullback Jinx or the Ickey Shuffle may end up being that old standard *The Cincinnati Dancing Pig*.

Esiason's chief targets, Brown and McGee, had great seasons. They need to stay healthy because Cris Collingsworth, who used to be the most charming great receiver in the league, looks to be well on his way to being the most charming member of NFL alumni. TE Rodney Holman made the Pro Bowl and deserved it. He's not spectacular, just all-around good—blocking, receiving, and getting open.

The Cincy offensive line is the best. They give up a few more sacks than you'd expect, but on a good day they can crumble anyone. Only OG Max Montoya is getting along in years, and only OT Joe Walter is coming off a serious injury. OT Anthony Munoz will be in the Hall of Fame five years after he retires.

THE BAD SIDE OF THE BALL

We still don't believe in the Bengals' defense. It gave up over 20 points a game despite playing with an offense that could control the ball.

Granted Tim Krumrie is a great NT. It bothers us that he's led the team in tackles two years in a row. Yes, he's quick, and yes, there's a certain amount of funneling taking place, but we still have to wonder why the rest of the D leaves those runners available to Krumrie.

Cincy was one of the few teams to have linemen as their top three sackers. Jim Skow (9.5) and Jason Buck (6) are quick. They're also a bit small.

The linebackers are okay but not outstanding. Unless you count David Fulcher, a linebacker playing strong safety. Fulcher had an outstanding year against the run and blitzing. His pass coverage man-to-man is suspect. The DBs—Fulcher, Lewis Billups, Eric Thomas, and Solomon Wilcots—are given most of the credit for the improvement on defense. Well, the Cincy D is better than it used to be when it was lousy. But we think a lot of that improvement would evaporate if the offense wasn't controlling the football and scoring points at a clip that forced the opposition into catch-up situations.

As it was, the defense only ranked in the middle of the AFC. Any slip by the offense, and it will be looking up at most of the conference.

Any game that comes down to special-teams play will probably be lost by the Bengals. They aren't very special. The punt team allowed two blocked punts last season, and the punting in general was poor. PK Jim Breech has had a nice career, but he can't hit the long ones anymore.

PUTTING IT TOGETHER

We may be wrong. Maybe everything will go great for the Bengals again in '89. That would be nice for Wyche and Paul Brown and Boomer and the fans in Cincinnati.

However, we think the Bengals were lucky last year in avoiding any key injuries. With quarterbacks falling like flies all over the league, Boomer boomed right along. If he gets hurt, or there are a couple of line injuries, or Eddie Brown goes down, or if anything else costs this team some of its offense, the season is over as far as repeating is concerned.

And when was a team that lucky two years in a row?

CINCINNATI BENGALS STATISTICS

1988 TEAM STATISTICS	CB	OPP
TOTAL FIRST DOWNS	350	321
Rushing	159	125
Passing	164	177
Penalty	27	19
3rd Down Made/Att.	78/179	97/221
Pct.	43.6%	43.9%
4th Down Made/Att.	8/11	12/26
Pct.	72.7%	46.2%

(Continued)		
1988 TEAM STATISTICS	CB	OPP
TOTAL NET YARDS	6057	5182
Avg. per Game	378.6	323.9
Total Plays	985	1059
Avg. per Play	6.1	4.9
NET YARDS RUSHING	2710	2048
Avg. per Game	169.4	128.0
Total Rushes	563	493

(Continued)

(Continued)

1988 TEAM STATISTICS	CB	OPP
NET YARDS PASSING	3347	3134
Avg. per Game	209.2	195.9
Tackled/Yards Lost	30/245	42/374
Gross Yards	3592	3507
Attempts/Completions	392/225	524/283
Pct. of Completions	57.3%	54.0%
Had Intercepted	14	22
PUNTS/AVERAGE	64/36.7	65/39.9
NET PUNTING AVG.	30.2	35.6
PENALTIES/YARDS	82/647	93/863
FUMBLES/BALL LOST	28/13	28/14
TOUCHDOWNS	59	37
Rushing	27	18
Passing	28	19
Returns	4	2
TIME OF POSSESSION	—	—

SCORE/PERIODS	1	2	3	4	OT	TOTAL
Bengals	99	147	107	92	3	448
Opponents	67	79	95	88	0	329

SCORING	TDR	TDP	TDRt	PAT	FG	S	TP
Woods	15						90
Breech				56/59	11/15		48
Brooks	8	6					84
Brown		9					54
McGee		6					36
Holman		3					18
Wilson	2	1					18
Jennings	1		1				12
Barker			1				6
Billups			1				6
Collinsworth		1					6
Esiason	1						6
Fulcher			1				6
Hillary		1					6
Martin		1					6
Johnson					1/3		3
Bengals	27	28	4	56/59	12/18	1	448
Opponents	18	19	2	38/39	17/24	3	329

RUSHING	NO	YDS	AVG	LG	TD
Woods	203	1066	5.3	56	15
Brooks	182	931	5.1	51t	8
Wilson	112	398	3.6	19	2
Esiason	43	248	5.8	24	1
Jennings	17	47	2.8	9	1
Logan	2	10	5.0	9	0
Schonert	2	10	5.0	7	0
Norseth	1	5	5.0	5	0
Brown	1	-5	-5.0	-5	0
Bengals	563	2710	4.8	56	27
Opponents	493	2048	4.2	48	18

RECEIVING	NO	YDS	AVG	LG	TD
Brown	53	1273	24.0	86t	9
Holman	39	527	13.5	33	3
McGee	36	686	19.1	78t	6
Brooks	29	287	9.9	28t	6
Woods	21	199	9.5	25	0
Collinsworth	13	227	17.5	36	1

(Continued)

RECEIVING	NO	YDS	AVG	LG	TD
Wilson	9	110	12.2	28	1
Riggs	9	82	9.1	16	0
Hillary	5	76	15.2	31	1
Jennings	5	75	15.0	31	0
Martin	2	22	11.0	15t	1
Logan	2	20	10.0	17	0
Kattus	2	8	4.0	11	0
Bengals	225	3592	16.0	86t	28
Opponents	283	3507	12.4	65t	19

INTERCEPTIONS	NO	YDS	AVG	LG	TD
Thomas	7	61	8.7	37	0
Fulcher	5	38	7.6	16t	1
Billups	4	47	11.8	29	0
Horton	3	13	4.3	11	0
Dixon	1	13	13.0	13	0
Wilcots	1	6	6.0	6	0
Zander	1	3	3.0	3	0
Bengals	22	181	8.2	37	1
Opponents	14	185	13.2	46	0

PUNTING	NO	YDS	AVG	TB	In 20	LG	Blk
Johnson Cl	31	1237	39.9	2	9	61	0
Johnson Ci	13	594	42.4	1	3	52	0
Fulhage	44	1672	38.0	5	13	53	2
Breech	3	64	21.3	1	1	30	0
Esiason	1	21	21.0	0	0	21	0
Bengals	64	2351	36.7	7	17	53	2
Opponents	65	2596	39.9	2	12	53	0

PUNT RETURNS	NO	FC	YDS	AVG	LG	TD
Hillary	17	5	166	9.8	20	0
Brown	10	7	48	4.8	13	0
Martin	5	5	30	6.0	10	0
Bengals	32	17	244	7.6	20	0
Opponents	32	7	280	8.8	26	0

KICKOFF RETURNS	NO	YDS	AVG	LG	TD
Jennings	32	684	21.4	98t	1
Hillary	12	195	16.3	24	0
Bussey	7	83	11.9	22	0
Logan	4	80	20.0	24	0
Brooks	1	-6	-6.0	-6	0
Dixon	1	18	18.0	18	0
Riggs	0	0	—	0	0
Bengals	57	1054	18.5	98t	1
Opponents	61	1335	21.9	84	0

FIELD GOALS	1-19	20-29	30-39	40-49	50+	TOTAL
Breech	1-1	5-5	3-4	2-4	0-1	11-15
Johnson Ci	0-0	0-0	0-0	0-0	0-1	0-1
Johnson Cl	0-0	0-0	0-0	0-1	1-2	1-3
Bengals	1-1	5-5	3-4	2-5	1-3	12-18
Opponents	1-1	4-5	7-7	5-10	0-1	17-24

FIELD GOALS BY Breech: 11 of 15
(42N)( )(32G)(34G)(28G)(30N,25G)( )( )(19G,32G,22G)
( )( )(41G)(51N)(46N)(45G,27G)(20G)
Johnson, Clev-Cin: ( )( )( )( )( )( )( )( )
( )( )( )( )( )( )(50N)(50G,40N)

PASSING	ATT	COM	YARD	PCT.	Avg G	TD	%TD	IN	%IN	LG	SAKS/YDS	RATE
Esiason	388	223	3572	57.5	9.21	28	7.2	14	3.6	86t	30/245	97.4
Schonert	4	2	20	50.0	5.00	0	0.0	0	0.0	17	0/0	64.6
Bengals	392	225	3592	57.3	9.13	28	7.1	14	3.6	86t	30/245	97.0
Opponents	524	283	3507	54.0	6.69	19	3.6	22	4.2	65t	42/374	74.0

CLEVELAND BROWNS

The Last 5 Seasons

	1984	1985	1986	1987	1988
Won-Lost	5-11	8-8	12-4	10-5	10-6
Percentage	.313	.500	.750	.667	.625
Division Finish	3	1	1	1	2-t
Games Behind	4	0	0	0	2
Total Points	250	287	391	390	304
Per Game	15.6	17.9	24.4	26.0	19.0
Opponent Points	297	294	310	239	288
Per Game	18.6	18.4	19.4	15.9	18.0
Net Points	-47	-7	81	151	16
Predicted Net Wins	-1.2	-0.2	2.0	3.8	0.4
Delta Net Wins	-1.8	0.2	2.0	-1.3	1.6
Total Yards on Offense	4828	4921	5394	5200	5011
Per Game	301.8	307.6	337.1	346.7	313.2
Total Yards Allowed on Defense	4641	4958	5269	4264	4767
Per Game	290.1	309.9	329.3	284.3	297.9
Net Difference	187	-37	125	936	244
Offensive Turnovers	39	36	24	29	33
Defensive Takeaways	35	27	37	36	31
Net Turnovers	-4	-9	13	7	-2
Predicted Net Points	0	-39	62	106	12
Delta Net Points	-47	32	19	45	4
Net Rushing Yards	1696	2285	1650	1745	1575
Per Game	106.0	142.8	103.1	116.3	98.4
Average Gain	3.5	4.3	3.5	3.7	3.6
Opponent Net Rushing Yards	1945	1851	1981	1433	1920
Per Game	121.6	115.7	123.8	95.5	120.0
Average Gain	3.9	3.7	4.0	3.6	3.9
Net Passing Yards	3132	2636	3744	3455	3436
Per Game	195.8	164.8	234.0	230.3	214.8
Times Sacked	55	36	39	29	36
Passer Rating in Yards	4.1	4.9	5.9	6.2	5.0
Opponent Net Passing Yards	2696	3107	3288	2831	2847
Per Game	168.5	194.2	205.5	188.7	177.9
Times Sacked	43	44	35	34	37
Passer Rating Defense	3.9	4.5	4.9	3.9	4.1
Passer Rating Net	0.2	0.5	1.1	2.3	0.9
Yards per Drive Offense	25.3	25.0	27.2	28.0	27.8
Yards per Drive Defense	24.3	26.7	26.3	23.8	26.6
Average Time of Possession	30:53	28:53	29:42	31:44	30:49

1985 PLAYOFFS
Lost Divisional Playoff to Miami, 21-24

1986 PLAYOFFS
Won Divisional Playoff from Jets, 23-20 OT
Lost AFC Championship Game to Denver, 20-23 OT

1987 PLAYOFFS
Won Divisional Playoff from Indianapolis, 38-21
Lost AFC Championship Game to Denver, 33-38

1988 PLAYOFFS
Lost Wild Card Game to Houston, 23-24

THE 1988 SEASON

DATE	AT	OPPONENT	SCORE	R	SPREAD	Tu	Net YDS	Rush YDS	Pass YDS	TURN
09/04	A	Kansas City	6- 3	W	-4	a	337-149	142- 60	195- 89	1-2
09/11	H	N.Y. Jets	3-23	L	-9.5	g	218-402	27-154	191-248	3-1
09/19	H*	Indianapolis	23-17	W	-2	g	356-282	101-128	255-154	2-3
09/25	A	Cincinnati	17-24	L	+3.5	a	322-393	68-213	254-180	1-0
10/02	A	Pittsburgh	23- 9	W	+2.5	a	299-183	168- 89	131- 94	1-5
10/09	H	Seattle	10-16	L	-4	g	334-227	160-126	174-101	4-1
10/16	H	Philadelphia	19- 3	W	+0	g	361-119	182- 71	179- 48	1-2
10/23	A	Phoenix	29-21	W	-1	g	369-330	68-169	301-161	4-4
10/30	H	Cincinnati	23-16	W	-3.5	g	302-281	99-128	203-153	2-0
11/07	A*	Houston	17-24	L	+0	a	253-330	44-148	209-182	1-1
11/13	A	Denver	7-30	L	-3	g	227-335	87-120	140-215	4-0
11/20	H	Pittsburgh	27- 7	W	-8.5	g	262-285	70-118	192-167	0-4
11/27	A	Washington	17-13	W	+1	g	324-227	158-103	166-124	1-2
12/04	H	Dallas	24-21	W	-10.5	g	302-410	27-163	275-247	1-1
12/12	A*	Miami	31-38	L	-5	g	353-497	87- 93	266-404	3-4
12/18	H	Houston	28-23	W	-3	g	388-317	78- 37	310-280	4-1
						Avg.	313-298	98-120	215-178	2-2

					WINS	LOSSES
Season Record:	10- 6-0		POINTS:		22- 13	14- 26
Vs. Spread:	8- 8-0		Net YDS:	9- 7-0	330-258	285-364
Home:	6- 2-0		Rush YDS:	6-10-0	109-107	79-142
On Artificial Turf:	2- 2-0		Pass YDS:	13- 3-0	221-152	206-222
Art. Turf vs. Spread:	1- 3-0		TURN:	7- 6-3	2- 2	3- 1

* Monday Night

NO OSCAR ON THE ERIE

Have you seen the generic Goldie Hawn movie? You must have. At the beginning, there's Goldie as Miss Spoiled-Rich Bitch. She has everything she could possibly want. In triplicate. Money to use as Kleenex, friends to lie to her, servants to hate her, possessions to possess her, an unlisted telephone company. Goldie has the world by its prehensile. Then, through an unbelievable set of setbacks, she's set on hard times. Suddenly, she's overboard with nothing but her own shapely bottom and bottomless reservoir of pluck to get her through. Of course, in the movie, that's all she needs, and she wins the day and our hearts by the last reel.

The Browns must have thought they were in a Goldie Hawn movie last year.

On September 3, 1988, the day before the season began, the Las Vegas line had them 9-2 to win the Super Bowl. After coming within a wasp's waist of winning the AFC two years in a row, they were poised to humble the little folk in '88. They possessed, among other boons, a set of matched cornerbacks who yielded receptions like McAuliffe yielded Bastogne, an RB duo who'd both known 1,000-yard seasons, a flock of willing and able receivers, and veterans in the line.

Best of all they had a brilliant young quarterback, backed two-deep by a crafty old quarterback *and* another former NFL starter. Sooner would Cleveland become the frolic spot of the jet set than would the Browns be without a passer.

And then the unbelievable set of setbacks.

Minor unlikelies to set the stage: Webster Slaughter, the only deep-threat receiver, broke his arm in Game 7; RB Kevin Mack forgot how to stay healthy, RB Earnest Byner forgot how to block, and they both forgot how to run; CB Hanford Dixon limped through the season like Grampa McCoy; and at times the veteran line blocked with the rigidity of Play-Doh.

Now, for the major plot twist:

Eight passes into the schedule, QB Bernie Kosar was sacked and knocked out for nearly two months with a strained right elbow. In Game 2, QB Gary Danielson went down for the season with a broken leg. Four games later, QB Mike Pagel was lost with a shoulder separation. After advertising in the *Cleveland Plain Dealer* classifieds, the Browns signed longtime Miami backup Don Strock, who was so old he was born before the Indians won their last pennant.

Just like Goldie, the Browns were down to pluck.

And just like Goldie, as the final reel began to unwind,

they could still win with that golden last-ditch effort. Kosar had returned in Week 8. If they could just get in the play-offs, then . . . but wait! Someone started the film over! In Game 15, Kosar's knee lost a one-on-one to John Offerdahl's shoulder. To make the playoffs, the Browns needed a final-game win over Houston, the football equivalent of Dirty Harry. For quarterback, Cleveland wheeled out Strock, soon to star in *Cocoon III*.

He certainly didn't star in the first half: three interceptions and a fumble. But Don must have got his Geritol at halftime, because he brought the Browns back from a 23–7 deficit to win 28–23. Rocky, eat your heart out!

We had a week of "Can Don Do It Again?" newspaper stories before Cleveland hosted Houston again in the Wild Card. It turned out he couldn't, mainly because he injured his wrist on the Browns' second series and spent the rest of the game watching Pagel throw his first passes since October. Rex Reed thought losing a fifth QB strained credibility. The Oilers, whose game films are derivative of Sam Peckinpaugh, took the win over the closing credits.

Siskel and Ebert might have loved the twist ending, but Clevelanders gave it a pan. When the writer concocted this Goldie script, he put in plenty of pluck. What he left out was luck.

PARTING SCHOTT

When a coach has his team in the playoffs four years in a row, you figure his job is pretty safe. When the team goes to the championship game in two of those four years, you can bet your season tickets that he'll be around for another season. He can put up a permanent mailbox, run a tab at the Boron station, plant a tree in his backyard. If he gets arrested, he won't have to post bail.

That's why it was such a shock to hear Marty Schottenheimer was out as the Cleveland coach. He was near the bottom of our list of potentially unemployed NFL coaches. We'd just written his Cleveland address in ink on our Christmas card list.

Technically Marty left of his own volition. It was his idea, see? There were several secondary reasons given and some rumored, but the basic circumstance was this. The boss, Art Modell, wanted him to do a certain thing. Marty said no. The next thing, Marty resigned.

The major certain thing that Modell wanted him to do was go get a new offensive coordinator. Marty was more than satisfied with his old coordinator, who happened to be himself. He gave himself an "A" for coordinating the Browns to the Wild Card Game. Modell put the grade a bit lower and thought the time spent coordinating took away Marty's "E" for effort in several other areas. Art didn't demand a total reconstruction, like go to the single wing. But he was firmer than the Cleveland defense that he wanted someone else running his team's offense. He liked Marty as his coach; he just didn't like where he was spending most of his coaching time.

Every news story we saw mentioned prominently that Marty had been a *defensive* coordinator before he became a head coach. (And when Modell went shopping for a new head coach, he again looked to the ranks of the def-cos, selecting Bud Carson of the Jets.) Written between the lines was a suggestion that defensive types were out of their element when they started telling offensive types where to shove their football. Oddly one of the people rumored as a candidate for Cleveland's off-co was Jim Shofner, who held that position for Phoenix in '88. Shofner was a defensive back for the Browns from 1957 to 1963.

Anyway, the Schottenheimer denouement presented an interesting philosophical question: should a team owner meddle in his head coach's choice of assistants? No question he has the *right* as owner, but *should* he?

Answer number one: A guy who makes millions manufacturing collar buttons may know how to run his business at a profit but not how to get his football team to a touchdown. His team is his hobby. The average owner knows as much about the science of football as your next-door neighbor does. Would you want the guy who borrows your lawnmower every June telling your team's coach what to do in November?

Answer number two: Modell isn't your average owner. His only job is the Cleveland Browns. He's paid attention for thirty years and has been supportive of his players and coaches. He doesn't meddle. When he wants something changed, he doesn't seek out the nearest reporter to tell him first. He sits down with his coach and explains what and why. Rest assured that he's not just repeating the latest gripe he heard on some talk show.

The only real question worth investigating is whether Modell made a good decision in insisting on a change in the offensive coordinating.

The first item of interest is Marty's record as a coordinator. Some of his calls drew criticism during the season, but that doesn't mean much. You can call the perfect play and look like an idiot when somebody misses a block.

What an off-co has to be good at mostly is designing the offense before the kickoff. He has to be able to deploy his team's strengths to take best advantage of the other team's weaknesses. He makes the plan. His second most important thing is to figure out what's not working during a game and fix it. He tinkers with the plan. Play-calling—choosing when to use the pieces of the plan (or the tinkered plan)—is only third in the off-co's job jar. Most of the time there are a dozen possible choices and even the off-co never knows if he made the best pick, only whether the one he called worked. So instead of carping that a guy ordered a run instead of a pass on a particular play, look at his record for a game or a season.

The Browns' offensive coordinator two years ago was Lindy Infante, who was so good at it he was given the head coach job at Green Bay. Below are Schottenheimer's and Infante's records. We used Marty's offensive record in 1988 only for the eight games when he had Kosar, his real quarterback, available for most of the minutes. And we used

Lindy's '87 record for only the twelve nonstrike games when he had his real team on the field. All records are given on a per-game basis.

Per Game	Infante 12 Gms	Schott. 8 Gms	+ / - Diff.
W-L	8-4	5-3	—
Plays	64.6	58.3	-6.3
Net Yards	355.9	299.0	-56.9
Avg. Gain	5.5	5.1	—
First Downs	20.8	17.8	-3.0
TD, Off.	3.2	2.3	-0.9
Off. Points	25.0	19.9	-5.1
3rd Down Plays	13.2	12.3	-0.9
Converted	5.4	5.6	0.2
% Converted	41.1	45.9	—
% Rushing	46.4	38.4	—
Rushing Att.	30.0	22.4	-7.6
Net Yards	112.9	80.0	-32.9
Avg. Gain	3.8	3.6	—
FD Rushing	7.1	5.4	-1.7
TD Rushing	1.2	0.6	-0.6
% Passing	53.6	61.6	—
Pass Att.	32.7	32.9	0.2
Completions	20.2	20.0	-0.2
Comp. Pct.	61.6	60.8	—
Sacks	1.8	3.0	-1.2
Sack Pct.	5.3	8.4	—
Yds Lost	16.4	21.1	-4.7
Net Yards	243.0	219.0	-24.0
Gain per Pass	7.4	6.7	—
Gain per Comp.	12.0	11.0	—

(Continued)

Per Game	Infante 12 Gms	Schott. 8 Gms	+ / - Diff.
FD Passing	11.7	11.0	-0.7
Interceptions	0.8	0.9	-0.1
Int. Pct.	2.3	2.7	—
TD Passing	1.8	1.6	-0.2
Penalties	6.7	6.5	0.2
Yards Pen.	56.9	48.9	8.0
FD Penalty	2.1	1.4	-0.7
Fumbles	1.7	2.0	-0.3
Fum. Lost	0.8	1.1	-0.3
% Lost	45.0	56.3	—
FG Att.	2.1	1.6	-0.5
Made	1.3	1.4	0.1
% Made	64.0	84.6	—

You have to give the nod to Infante. His offensive coordinating averaged more plays, more yards, and more points per game. On the other hand, Webster Slaughter was out for all but one of Schottenheimer's games and Kevin Mack missed five, so he didn't have as many weapons as Infante.

The biggest point the numbers make is that Infante passed 53.6 percent of the time, which is a balanced attack, and Schottenheimer threw 61.6 percent, which is too high. However, there seems to be a reason for that. If we look at the Browns' scoring (all points) in each quarter for those games, we can see that they had to score a lot of fourth-quarter points. When you're trailing in the final frame, that's pass time. On the other hand, did Marty's troops trail late because his offense had misfired for three quarters?

	1Q	2Q	3Q	4Q	OT	TOT.
Infante	3.3	11.9	8.1	3.9	—	27.2
Schottenheimer	2.9	5.9	5.1	8.0	—	21.9

All things considered, it's close. Marty trails Lindy but there's no guarantee that a new man will do any better. Had Schottenheimer been judged strictly on his record with the offense, Modell wouldn't have insisted on a change. Art's point wasn't that the offense was suffering. At worst, it had slight distress. Two aspirin, maybe. Modell prescribed an emetic because he felt that Marty had devoted so much time to his coordinating that other areas weren't getting his full attention.

Rumors of dissension among the troops surfaced near the end of the season, particularly when Kosar was quoted after his knee injury in Week 15: "This really was inevitable. I've been taking hits for several games." Bernie was frustrated and burned his offensive linemen, who didn't take his comments in good grace. That the incident was indicative of full-scale disharmony, however, seems unlikely. Dissension rumors always swirl around a team fighting adversity. Reporters comb every locker room after a tough loss, sniffing for any statement that can be blown into a lurid headline,

and young men sometimes say things in the emotion of the moment that they might never say publicly after they've had a little time to cool off. Rather than a team at war with itself, the '88 Browns might better be classified as a group less unified in its focus than in previous years. Of course keeping everyone on the same page is the head coach's responsibility.

The Browns' special-teams play was criticized several times during the season, a situation exacerbated by the fact that Marty's special-teams coach was his brother Kurt. Any coach who hires kin can expect to take some raps for it, as Don Shula has learned in Miami. No matter how well the guy does his job, everybody figures he'd be selling used cars if you didn't carry him on the payroll.

Cleveland's record on kickoffs was actually improved in 1988. They increased their runbacks by an average of 3.5 yards and decreased their opponents' returns by an average of 1.9 yards. Punt coverage slipped. Opponents upped their average return from 5.5 in '87 to 9.5 with a TD return in '88.

The Browns' punt-return average dropped by three yards. Cleveland's punting, lousy in 1987, was only slightly less so in 1988 and they had a punt blocked. Overall, the special teams weren't a strong point.

Where ex-defensive coordinator Marty might have better spent some of his time was with the defense, particularly in improving the rushing defense. The Browns fell from an excellent 95.5 yards per game against the run in '87 to a so-so 120.0 yards. And at times the pass rush hibernated.

Certainly no one of these things caused Modell's stance. But taken as a whole they seem to justify his point that the Browns needed a full-time head coach more than they needed a part-time offensive coordinator.

CLEVELAND BROWNS STATISTICS

1988 TEAM STATISTICS	CB	OPP
TOTAL FIRST DOWNS	294	300
Rushing	93	113
Passing	177	162
Penalty	24	25
3rd Down Made/Att.	92/213	67/197
Pct.	43.2%	34.0%
4th Down Made/Att.	4/15	8/17
Pct.	26.7%	47.1%
TOTAL NET YARDS	5011	4767
Avg. per Game	313.2	297.9
Total Plays	1013	1009
Avg. per Play	4.9	4.7
NET YARDS RUSHING	1575	1920
Avg. per Game	98.4	120.0
Total Rushes	440	498
NET YARDS PASSING	3436	2847
Avg. per Game	214.8	177.9
Tackled/Yards Lost	36/250	37/255
Gross Yards	3686	3102
Attempts/Completions	537/313	474/245
Pct. of Completions	58.3%	51.7%
Had Intercepted	17	20
PUNTS/AVERAGE	67/38.5	69/39.4
NET PUNTING AVG.	33.0	32.4
PENALTIES/YARDS	110/875	100/789
FUMBLES/BALL LOST	32/16	23/11
TOUCHDOWNS	33	30
Rushing	10	13
Passing	19	13
Returns	4	4
TIME OF POSSESSION	8:13:18	7:46:42

SCORE/PERIODS	1	2	3	4	OT	TOTAL
Browns	46	81	63	114	0	304
Opponents	46	137	44	61	0	288

SCORING	TDR	TDP	TDRt	PAT	FG	S	TP
Bahr				32/33	24/29		104
Langhorne	1	7					48
Byner	3	2					30
Slaughter		3					18
Mack	3						18
Manoa	2						12
Newsome		2					12
Fontenot	1	1					12
Tennell		1					6
Washington			1				6
Kosar	1						6
Brennan		1					6
Perry			1				6
Minnifield			1				6
Weathers		1					6
Bolden		1					6

(Continued)

SCORING	TDR	TDP	TDRt	PAT	FG	S	TP
Buchanan						1	2
Browns	10	19	4	32/33	24/29	1	304
Opponents	13	13	4	30/30	26/34	0	288

RUSHING	NO	YDS	AVG	LG	TD
Byner	157	576	3.7	27t	3
Mack	123	485	3.9	65	3
Manoa	99	389	3.9	34	2
Fontenot	28	87	3.1	17	0
Langhorne	2	26	13.0	20t	1
Baker	3	19	6.3	13	0
Danielson	4	3	0.8	5	0
Pagel	4	1	0.3	5	0
Runager	1	0	0.0	0	0
Kosar	12	-1	-0.1	13	1
Strock	6	-2	-0.3	5	0
Bahr	1	-8	-8.0	-8	0
Browns	440	1575	3.6	65	10
Opponents	498	1920	3.9	41t	13

RECEIVING	NO	YDS	AVG	LG	TD
Byner	59	576	9.8	39t	2
Langhorne	57	780	13.7	77t	7
Brennan	46	579	12.6	33	1
Newsome	35	343	9.8	28	2
Slaughter	30	462	15.4	41	3
Weathers	29	436	15.0	49	1
Fontenot	19	170	8.9	15	1
Mack	11	87	7.9	25	0
Manoa	10	54	5.4	9	0
Tennell	9	88	9.8	26	1
McNeil	5	74	14.8	23	0
Young	2	34	17.0	25	0
Bolden	1	3	3.0	3t	1
Browns	313	3686	11.8	77t	19
Opponents	245	3102	12.7	54	13

INTERCEPTIONS	NO	YDS	AVG	LG	TD
Wright	5	126	25.2	53	0
Minnifield	4	16	4.0	13	0
Washington	3	104	34.7	75t	1
Johnson	2	36	18.0	31	0
Dixon	2	24	12.0	24	0
Harper	2	13	6.5	8	0
Johnson	2	0	0.0	0	0
Browns	20	319	15.9	75t	1
Opponents	17	190	11.2	36t	2

PUNTING	NO	YDS	AVG	TB	In 20	LG	Blk
Runager	48	1935	40.3	2	13	52	0
Johnson	17	643	37.8	1	6	61	0

(Continued)

(Continued)

PUNTING	NO	YDS	AVG	TB	In 20	LG	Blk
Team	2	0	0.0	0	0	0	2
Browns	67	2578	38.5	3	19	61	2
Opponents	69	2722	39.4	8	17	62	2

PUNT RETURNS	NO	FC	YDS	AVG	LG	TD
McNeil	38	6	315	8.3	32	0
Weathers	2	0	10	5.0	9	0
Browns	40	6	325	8.1	32	0
Opponents	32	11	304	9.5	73t	1

KICKOFF RETURNS	NO	YDS	AVG	LG	TD
Young	29	635	21.9	34	0
Fontenot	21	435	20.7	84	0
McNeil	2	38	19.0	22	0
Braggs	1	27	27.0	27	0

(Continued)

KICKOFF RETURNS	NO	YDS	AVG	LG	TD
Perry	1	13	13.0	13	0
Tennell	1	11	11.0	11	0
Browns	55	1159	21.1	84	0
Opponents	58	973	16.8	29	0

FIELD GOALS	1-19	20-29	30-39	40-49	50+	TOTAL
Bahr	1-1	10-12	8-10	5-6	0-0	24-29
Browns	1-1	10-12	8-10	5-6	0-0	24-29
Opponents	2-2	7-7	12-15	5-7	0-3	26-34

FIELD GOALS BY Bahr: 24 of 29
(40N,19G,38G)(47G)(21G,29G,40G)(27G)
(22G,21G,40G)(25N,23G)(24G,39N,37G)
(46G,23G)(34G,39G,29G)(40G)( )(32G,28N,
34G)(37N,37G)(25G)(33G)

PASSING	ATT	COM	YARD	PCT.	Avg G	TD	%TD	IN	%IN	LG	SAKS/YDS	RATE
Kosar	259	156	1890	60.2	7.30	10	3.9	7	2.7	77t	25/172	84.3
Strock	91	55	736	60.4	8.09	6	6.6	5	5.5	41	4/26	85.2
Pagel	134	71	736	53.0	5.49	3	2.2	4	3.0	28	1/9	64.1
Danielson	52	31	324	59.6	6.23	0	0.0	1	1.9	26	6/43	69.7
Fontenot	1	0	0	0.0	0.00	0	0.0	0	0.0	00	0/0	39.6
Browns	537	313	3686	58.3	6.86	19	3.5	17	3.2	77t	36/250	77.9
Opponents	474	245	3102	51.7	6.54	13	2.7	20	4.2	54	37/255	64.0

DENVER BRONCOS

The Last 5 Seasons

	1984	1985	1986	1987	1988
Won-Lost	13-3	11-5	11-5	10-4-1	8-8
Percentage	.813	.688	.688	.700	.500
Division Finish	1	2	1	1	2
Games Behind	0	1	0	0	1
Total Points	353	380	378	379	327
Per Game	22.1	23.8	23.6	25.3	20.4
Opponent Points	241	329	327	288	352
Per Game	15.1	20.6	20.4	19.2	22.0
Net Points	112	51	51	91	-25
Predicted Net Wins	2.8	1.3	1.3	2.3	-0.6
Delta Net Wins	2.2	1.7	1.7	0.7	0.6
Total Yards on Offense	4935	5496	5216	5624	5506
Per Game	308.4	343.5	326.0	374.9	344.1
Total Yards Allowed on Defense	5687	5179	4947	4813	5471
Per Game	355.4	323.7	309.2	320.9	341.9
Net Difference	-752	317	269	811	35
Offensive Turnovers	34	31	29	36	34
Defensive Takeaways	55	36	35	47	29
Net Turnovers	21	5	6	11	-5
Predicted Net Points	21	46	46	112	-17
Delta Net Points	91	5	5	-21	-8
Net Rushing Yards	2076	1851	1678	1970	1815
Per Game	129.8	115.7	104.9	131.3	113.4
Average Gain	4.1	3.7	3.7	3.9	3.9
Opponent Net Rushing Yards	1664	1973	1651	2017	2538
Per Game	104.0	123.3	103.2	134.5	158.6
Average Gain	3.8	4.2	3.8	4.4	4.6
Net Passing Yards	2859	3645	3538	3654	3691
Per Game	178.7	227.8	221.1	243.6	230.7
Times Sacked	35	38	38	30	32
Passer Rating in Yards	4.5	4.3	5.2	5.4	4.8
Opponent Net Passing Yards	4023	3206	3296	2796	2933
Per Game	251.4	200.4	206.0	186.4	183.3
Times Sacked	57	47	49	31	36
Passer Rating Defense	4.1	3.9	4.5	3.5	4.8
Passer Rating Net	0.5	0.4	0.6	2.0	0.0
Yards per Drive Offense	23.3	25.6	25.2	28.8	27.8
Yards per Drive Defense	26.3	23.2	24.0	25.2	28.6
Average Time of Possession	28:56	31:19	30:30	31:52	29:46

1984 PLAYOFFS
Lost Divisional Playoff to Pittsburgh, 17-24

1986 PLAYOFFS
Won Divisional Playoff from New England, 22-17
Won AFC Championship from Cleveland, 23-20 OT
Lost Super Bowl XXI to New York Giants, 20-39

1987 PLAYOFFS
Won Divisional Playoff from Houston, 34-10
Won AFC Championship from Cleveland, 38-33
Lost Super Bowl XXII to Washington, 10-42

THE 1988 SEASON

DATE	AT	OPPONENT	SCORE	R	SPREAD	Tu	Net YDS	Rush YDS	Pass YDS	TURN
09/04	H	Seattle	14-21	L	-4	g	302-330	76-178	226-152	3-1
09/11	H	San Diego	34- 3	W	-12.5	g	443-244	184-133	259-111	0-2
09/18	A	Kansas City	13-20	L	-4.5	a	283-380	70-130	213-250	3-0
09/26	H*	L.A. Raiders	27-30	L	-6	g	398-363	189-128	209-235	5-1
10/02	A	San Diego	12- 0	W	-4	g	291-190	129- 20	162-170	1-2
10/09	A	S. Francisco	16-13	W	+6.5	g	314-417	147-246	167-171	3-4
10/16	H	Atlanta	30-14	W	-13	g	406-311	104-174	302-137	1-3
10/23	A	Pittsburgh	21-39	L	-3.5	a	323-386	45-256	278-130	4-2
10/31	A*	Indianapolis	23-55	L	+1.5	a	397-464	131-244	266-220	4-1
11/06	H	Kansas City	17-11	W	-8	g	308-273	131- 90	177-183	2-3
11/13	H	Cleveland	30- 7	W	+3	g	335-227	120- 87	215-140	0-4
11/20	A	New Orleans	0-42	L	+4.5	a	258-385	52-196	206-189	1-0
11/27	H	L.A. Rams	35-24	W	+0	g	368-484	98-132	270-352	1-3
12/04	A	L.A. Raiders	20-21	L	+1.5	a	347-216	50-129	297- 87	3-2
12/11	A	Seattle	14-42	L	+3.5	a	402-450	101-230	301-220	1-0
12/17	H	New England	21-10	W	+0	g	331-351	188-165	143-186	2-2
						Avg.	344-342	113-159	231-183	2-2

				WINS		LOSSES	
Season Record:	8- 8-0	POINTS:		24- 10		17- 34	
Vs. Spread:	8- 8-0	Net YDS:	7- 9-0	350-312		339-372	
Home:	6- 2-0	Rush YDS:	6-10-0	138-131		89-186	
On Artificial Turf:	0- 5-0	Pass YDS:	9- 7-0	212-181		250-185	
Art. Turf vs. Spread:	0- 5-0	TURN:	7- 8-1	1- 3		3- 1	

* Monday Night

THE DENVER DECLINE

We haven't trusted simple answers since they tried to palm that stork story off on us when we were five. We knew darned well there was more to it than some big bird with a bundle in its beak. One of these days we plan to look into the real story. But right now we have our hands full with the Broncos.

For a two-time Super Bowl team, the Broncs looked awful at times last season. Oh, sure, you're going to say they looked pretty bad in those Super Bowls too. Listen, anyone's entitled to one really bad game a year. The Broncos *got* to the Big Watermelon two seasons in a row, and twenty-seven teams didn't. But last year it wasn't just *one* game. It was too many. And too bad. They lost some games by scores that wouldn't have looked out of place on the slates of the original Broncos, the ones with vertically striped socks and wretched records: 16-38-2 in four years. The '88 Broncos were a far better team than that—except sometimes. Like 21-39 to Pittsburgh . . . 23-55 to Indianapolis . . . 0-42 to New Orleans. And, in a game they had to win to have a

chance for the division title, 14-42 to Seattle. The only good thing about games like that is they're easy on headline writers: ORANGE CRUSHED!

Truthfully, the Broncs weren't exactly championship-caliber in most of their games. So the natural question asked was, "What's wrong with the Broncos?"

IT'S ALL IN THEIR HEADS

The most intriguing explanation we heard was that they suffered delayed-stress syndrome from the two Super Bowl years. The idea was that the pressure from two extra-long seasons and the disillusion of the ugly endings finally got to them—sort of a Rocky Mountain low. That excuse appealed to our love of complicated answers. In fact, teams have suffered through worse seasons after one trip to the Psyper Bowl. Washington, f'rinstance, had a worse record than Denver in '88. Maybe instead of handing out rings they should give them coupons for the psychiatrist of their choice.

The problem with blaming Super Bowl Psychosis for the Broncos' problems is that you need to examine every player's psyche and then compare his Rorschach with those of all the other Big-SB participants. And that would take years! And money! Funding anyone?

Another problem with the psychiatric approach—it opens up every mistake to Freudian analysis. "Honest, Coach, my shrink says I fumble 'cause I wet the bed in kindergarten." Why, before you know it, the idea would spread to other walks of life, like courts and things. Well, that sure would be a mess, wouldn't it?

Laying aside the Broncs' mental state, we regretfully moved on to some of the simpler explanations.

TONY DID IT

Like, blame it on Tony Dorsett.

Touchdown Tony has been one of the great runners in football history, but he's always been someone sportswriters raised ink-stained eyebrows at when things came apart. Maybe it's because Dorsett has a knack for saying approximately what he means, with little regard for tact. (We hasten to add that he's never said an unkind word to us.)

Even though we've never spoken with Dorsett, we'd like to semi-defend him. Tony was thirty-four last season. Nevertheless when the Broncs got him from Dallas, some folks expected him to run as he did at twenty-four. Actually he gave a pretty good imitation for the first four games, twice gaining over 100 yards. You know how many 100-yard rushing games Denver had in 1987? One! By Joe Dudek, in a strike game. Dorsett had a career-high of 32 carries against the Raiders in Week 4. Then, after a poor fifth game, he all but disappeared from the Denver attack for most of the remaining games.

DORSETT'S RUSHING IN 1988

WEEK	ATT	YDS	AVG	TD
1	9	32	11	0
2	23	113	21	1
3	10	35	8	1
4	32	119	20	2
5	19	46	8	0
6	5	12	13	0
7	17	86	16	0
8	12	24	6	0
9	6	22	15	0
10	10	44	16	0
11	14	42	13	0
12	2	3	3	0
13	8	21	6	0
14	5	18	5	0
15	0	0	0	0
16	10	86	26	1

By midway through the season, Dorsett was fourth in rushing in the AFC with 467 yards, and a possibility of another 1,000-yard season. He ended up thirteenth.

Supposedly Dorsett didn't really fit into the Broncos' passing game. He never was the greatest receiver in the world, but that argument makes it a little hard to blame him for the Denver decline. After all, he fit pretty snugly into a wide open Dallas attack for years. If he wasn't right for Denver, they certainly must have known that when they got him. A more likely explanation is that Coach Reeves decided not to commit to a ground attack featuring Dorsett. He tried it for a few games, didn't like it, and dropped it. It wasn't necessarily a bad decision, considering that Denver's strength is its air game. But it wasn't Dorsett's fault, either.

Finally, it's a little hard to see that the Denver running game, no great shakes before, suffered greatly by the addition of Dorsett.

LEADERS	1987					LEADERS	1988				
	ATT	YDS	AVG	LG	TD		ATT	YDS	AVG	LG	TD
Winder	196	741	3.8	19	6	Dorsett	181	703	3.9	26	5
Elway	66	304	4.6	29	4	Winder	149	543	3.6	35	4
Lang	89	303	3.4	28	2	Elway	54	234	4.3	26	1
Dudek	35	154	4.4	16	2	Sewell	32	135	4.2	26	1
	510	1970	3.9	29	18		464	1815	3.9	35	13

ELWAY'S WING

If you weren't paying close attention in '88, you might have thought Elway had become an ordinary mortal. Once the nonpareil of quarterbackdom, Denver's John got no more support for last year's Pro Bowl than John Denver. Elway had arm surgery after the season, explaining why he wasn't up to his '87 par. If we compare his '88 season with the two Super Bowl years on a per-game basis, we find . . .

	TEAM RECORD	GAME	RUSH	YARDS	PASS	COMP	NET PASS YARDS	TD	INT
1986	10-4-1	16	3.3	16.1	31.5	17.5	203.3	1.2	0.8
1987	8-3-1	12	5.5	25.3	34.2	18.7	255.0	1.6	1.0
1988	8-7-0	15	3.6	15.6	33.1	18.3	204.8	1.1	1.3

Although he was definitely down from 1987, his '88 record was about the same as '86, except for interceptions. The Denver people claim turnovers were crucial in two losses (and one win), so Elway's last-season stats do not explain the decline or the blowouts.

COLLIER
DONE IT

As soon as the season was over, so was defensive coordinator Joe Collier after a twenty-year reign. The sudden firing was a little embarrassing to Reeves and the Broncos, although it had been rumored for weeks. When the firing was announced on NBC during the final game, Reeves had little choice but to follow through with the *fait accompli*.

Collier has long been regarded as an *artiste* among defensive coordinators, and there's some disagreement whether his *fait* came from his style or his material. He's sometimes criticized for running defenses that live by finesse rather than muscle. The counterpoint was that the available manpower wasn't very muscular. Or healthy.

One really important factor in last year's defensive problems was an injury to LB Karl Mecklenburg. He missed four games, which was bad enough. But he played about a half dozen with his right hand in a big cast that looked like he was palming a basketball. Mecklenburg has been an All-Pro at 230 pounds, but he needs both hands to fight off defenders. He was definitely at a disadvantage for most of the season. And Reeves has said that Mecklenburg is as important to the defense as Elway is to the offense.

Whether Collier did a good or bad job doesn't really matter—it wasn't the kind of job that Reeves *wanted*. It was like he put racing stripes on when Dan wanted the gears ground. Dan wants to see his team be more physical. It's possible that the Denver defenders may slip a little more in '89. But in a couple of years, when they get some meat-eating monsters in there, the then-beefy Broncos will be able to avoid the sudden blowouts that were so embarrassing. At least that's the plan.

DOWN WITH WEIGHT-WATCHERS!

The most common explanation is that the Broncos were just too small. We heard so often how Denver's upfront defenders were so teeny that we expected to see Snow White at free safety. It can't be just a matter of little guys against big guys! What ever happened to "the harder they fall"? We hate simple explanations, but we decided to take a look.

Right away we saw that the Broncs gave up an average of 158.6 rushing yards per game and their opponents averaged 4.5 per carry. Both figures were among the league's worst.

One thing we wondered was whether there was any correlation between the size of an opponent's offensive line from tackle to tackle and the number of rushing yards given up by Denver.

WK	WGT. LINE	OPPONENT	RUSH YARD	OPP. SCORE	
1	279.8	Seattle	178	14-21	
2	290.2	San Diego	133	34- 3	
3	289.0	Kansas City	130	13-20	
4	278.0	Raiders	128	27-30	OT
5	290.2	San Diego	20	12- 0	
6	269.2	San Francisco	246	16-13	OT
7	279.4	Atlanta	174	30-14	
8	267.8	Pittsburgh	256	21-39	
9	295.8	Indianapolis	244	23-55	
10	289.9	Kansas City	90	17-11	
11	284.0	Cleveland	87	30- 7	
12	272.0	New Orleans	196	0-42	
13	272.2	L.A. Rams	132	35-24	
14	278.0	L.A. Raiders	129	20-21	
15	279.8	Seattle	230	14-42	
16	278.4	New England	165	21-10	

Well, we couldn't see that it worked out. In fact, the two smallest offensive lines they faced all season crunched them for the most yards. 'Splain that!

However, when we compared the weight averages of the most-used Denver down linemen and linebackers with those of the AFC playoff teams, we saw just how tiny they were. And, yes, it seems to have made quite a difference.

RANK	RUSH YARD	RANK	RUSH AVG	TEAM	LINE	LBACK	AVG
13	2538	14	4.6	Denver	259.0	228.0	241.3
1	1592	2	3.7	Houston	273.7	234.8	251.4
3	1854	5	3.9	Buffalo	273.3	235.0	251.4
5	1920	4	3.9	Cleveland	270.0	231.3	247.9
6	2048	9	4.2	Cincinnati	266.0	235.8	248.7
11	2286	13	4.5	Seattle	265.0	239.3	250.3

We still insist on some reservations. Bigger isn't always better. Remember the Titanic? Denver needs to add pounds—but *talented* pounds.

Look to the later sections in this book devoted to Team Previews and the draft to see what additional free-agent and collegiate tonnage the Broncos were able to take on.

DENVER BRONCO STATISTICS

1988 TEAM STATISTICS	DB	OPP
TOTAL FIRST DOWNS	338	316
Rushing	106	141
Passing	196	160
Penalty	36	15
3rd Down Made/Att.	84/210	81/214
Pct.	40.0%	37.9%
4th Down Made/Att.	4/13	9/17
Pct.	30.8%	52.9%
TOTAL NET YARDS	5506	5471
Avg. per Game	344.1	341.9
Total Plays	1077	1055
Avg. per Play	5.1	5.2
NET YARDS RUSHING	1815	2538
Avg. per Game	113.4	158.6
Total Rushes	464	552
NET YARDS PASSING	3691	2933
Avg. per Game	230.7	183.3
Tackled/Yards Lost	32/250	36/235
Gross Yards	3941	3168
Attempts/Completions	581/324	467/262
Pct. of Completions	56%	56%
Had Intercepted	22	16
PUNTS/AVERAGE	68/43.8	84/43.4
NET PUNTING AVG.	37.9	36.3
PENALTIES/YARDS	84/717	116/956
FUMBLES/BALL LOST	34/12	23/13
TOUCHDOWNS	37	41
Rushing	13	21
Passing	24	18
Returns	0	2
TIME OF POSSESSION	—	—

SCORE/PERIODS	1	2	3	4	OT	TOTAL
Broncos	43	127	64	90	3	327
Opponents	85	112	96	56	3	352

SCORING	TDR	TDP	TDRt	PAT	FG	S	TP
Karlis				36/37	23/36		105
Sewell	1	5					36
Jackson		6					36
Dorsett	5						30
Winder	4	1					30
Johnson		5					30
Kay		4					24
Willhite	2						12
Mobley		2					12
Elway	1						6
Nattiel		1					6
Broncos	13	24	0	36/37	23/36	0	327
Opponents	21	18	2	41/41	21/27	1	352

RUSHING	NO	YDS	AVG	LG	TD
Dorsett	181	703	3.9	26	5
Winder	149	543	3.6	35	4
Elway	54	234	4.3	26	1
Sewell	32	135	4.2	26	1
Kubiak	17	65	3.8	13	0
Nattiel	5	51	10.2	29	0
Willhite	13	39	3.0	7	2
Bell	9	36	4.0	6	0
Jackson	1	5	5.0	5	0
Johnson	1	3	3.0	3	0

(Continued)

RUSHING	NO	YDS	AVG	LG	TD
Johnson	1	1	1.0	1	0
Thomas	1	0	0.0	0	0
Broncos	464	1815	3.9	35	13
Opponents	552	2538	4.6	64	21

RECEIVING	NO	YDS	AVG	LG	TD
Johnson	68	896	13.2	86	0
Jackson	46	852	18.5	63	0
Nattiel	46	574	12.5	74	1
Sewell	38	507	13.3	68T	5
Kay	34	352	10.4	27	4
Willhite	32	238	7.4	15	0
Mobley	21	218	10.4	28	2
Winder	17	103	6.1	14	1
Dorsett	16	122	7.6	16	0
Massey	3	39	13.0	21	0
Graddy	1	30	30.0	30	0
Johnson	1	6	6.0	6	0
Kelley	1	4	4.0	4	0
Broncos	324	3941	12.2	86	24
Opponents	262	3168	12.1	55	18

INTERCEPTIONS	NO	YDS	AVG	LG	TD
Harden	4	36	9.0	34	0
Castille	3	51	17.0	33	0
Robbins	2	66	33.0	39	0
Braxton	2	6	3.0	6	0
Dennison	1	29	29.0	29	0
Wilson	1	7	7.0	7	0
Fletcher	1	4	4.0	4	0
Bowyer	1	1	1.0	1	0
Haynes	1	0	0.0	0	0
Broncos	16	200	12.5	39	0
Opponents	22	344	15.6	86	1

PUNTING	NO	YDS	AVG	TB	In 20	LG	Blk
Horan	65	2861	44.0	2	19	70	-
Elway	3	117	39.0	0	2	40	-
Broncos	68	2978	43.8	2	21	70	-
Opponents	83	3643	43.9	7	20	68	1

PUNT RETURNS	NO	FC	YDS	AVG	LG	TD
Nattiel	22	0	218	9.9	24	0
Clark	13	0	115	8.8	16	0
Willhite	13	2	90	6.9	12	0
Harden	2	2	14	7.0	14	0
Massey	1	0	5	5.0	5	0
Johnson	1	0	5	5.0	5	0
Bell	1	0	4	4.0	4	0
Johnson	0	1	0	0.0	0	0
Broncos	53	5	451	8.5	24	0
Opponents	33	4	364	11.0	66	1

KICKOFF RETURNS	NO	YDS	AVG	LG	TD
Johnson	14	285	20.4	34	0
Nattiel	6	124	20.7	25	0
Winder	1	11	11.0	11	1
Harden	1	9	9.0	9	0
Broncos	58	1191	20.5	38	0
Opponents	53	965	18.2	40	0

(Continued)

FIELD GOALS	1-19	20-29	30-39	40-49	50+	TOTAL
Karlis	1-1	9-10	6-13	5-8	2-4	23-36
Broncos	1-1	9-10	6-13	5-8	2-4	23-36
Opponents	0-0	9-10	9-12	2-4	1-1	21-27

FIELD GOALS BY KARLIS: 23 of 36
(51G,38G) (23G,42G) (39G,25G) (30G,43G,37N,
30G,32N,28G,21N) (27G,27G,34N,22G) (35N,47G,41G,
50G) (47N) (27G) (42G) (18G,22G,32G,42N,36N)
(35N,50N) (46N) (29G,36G) (52N,37N)

PASSING	ATT	COM	YARD	PCT.	Avg G	TD	%TD	IN	%IN	LG	SAKS/YDS	RATE
Karcher	12	6	128	.500	10.67	1	8.3	0	0.0	74	0/0	115.8
Dorsett	2	1	7	.500	3.50	1	50.0	0	0.0	7T	0/0	97.8
Kubiak	69	43	497	.623	7.20	5	7.2	3	4.3	68T	2/13	90.0
Elway	496	274	3309	.552	6.67	17	3.4	19	3.8	86	30/237	71.3
Sewell	1	0	0	.000	0.00	0	0.0	0	0.0	0	0/0	39.5
Nattiel	1	0	0	.000	0.00	0	0.0	0	0.0	0	0/0	39.5
Broncos	581	324	3941	.558	6.78	24	4.1	22	3.8	86	32/250	74.6
Opponents	467	262	3168	.561	6.78	18	3.9	16	3.4	55	36/235	75.8

HOUSTON OILERS

The Last 5 Seasons

	1984	1985	1986	1987	1988
Won-Lost	3-13	5-11	5-11	9-6	10-6
Percentage	.188	.313	.313	.600	.625
Division Finish	4	4	4	2	2-t
Games Behind	6	3	7	1	2
Total Points	240	284	274	345	424
Per Game	15.0	17.8	17.1	23.0	26.5
Opponent Points	437	412	329	349	365
Per Game	27.3	25.8	20.6	23.3	22.8
Net Points	-197	-128	-55	-4	59
Predicted Net Wins	-4.9	-3.2	-1.4	-0.1	1.5
Delta Net Wins	-0.1	0.2	-1.6	1.6	0.5
Total Yards on Offense	4884	4652	5149	5223	5205
Per Game	305.3	290.8	321.8	348.2	325.3
Total Yards Allowed on Defense	5968	6155	5034	4993	4858
Per Game	373.0	384.7	314.6	332.9	303.6
Net Difference	-1084	-1503	115	230	347
Offensive Turnovers	31	37	43	37	35
Defensive Takeaways	24	35	32	37	42
Net Turnovers	-7	-2	-11	0	7
Predicted Net Points	-118	-133	-34	19	57
Delta Net Points	-79	5	-21	-23	2
Net Rushing Yards	1656	1570	1700	1923	2249
Per Game	103.5	98.1	106.3	128.2	140.6
Average Gain	3.8	3.7	3.5	4.0	4.0
Opponent Net Rushing Yards	2789	2814	2035	1848	1592
Per Game	174.3	175.9	127.2	123.2	99.5
Average Gain	4.7	4.8	3.8	4.1	3.7
Net Passing Yards	3228	3082	3449	3300	2956
Per Game	201.8	192.6	215.6	220.0	184.8
Times Sacked	49	58	48	30	24
Passer Rating in Yards	5.0	4.0	3.7	4.9	5.2
Opponent Net Passing Yards	3179	3341	2999	3145	3266
Per Game	198.7	208.8	187.4	209.7	204.1
Times Sacked	32	41	32	35	42
Passer Rating Defense	5.9	5.9	4.8	4.5	4.5
Passer Rating Net	-0.9	-1.9	-1.2	0.4	0.7
Yards per Drive Offense	26.0	22.8	24.6	25.7	25.5
Yards per Drive Defense	32.8	31.4	24.6	25.2	23.9
Average Time of Possession	28:02	28:07	30:33	30:17	31:10

1987 PLAYOFFS	1988 PLAYOFFS
Won Wild Card Game from Seattle, 23-20 (OT)	Won Wild Card Game from Cleveland, 24-23
Lost Divisional Playoff to Denver, 34-10	Lost Divisional Playoff to Cincinnati, 10-17

THE 1988 SEASON

DATE	AT	OPPONENT	SCORE	R	SPREAD	Tu	Net YDS	Rush YDS	Pass YDS	TURN
09/04	A	Indianapolis	17-14	W	+3.5	a	348-291	174-111	174-180	3-3
09/11	H	L.A. Raiders	38-35	W	-2.5	a	406-158	156- 74	250- 84	3-3
09/18	A	N.Y. Jets	3-45	L	-2	a	237-391	140- 89	97-302	4-1
09/25	H	New England	31- 6	W	-3.5	a	328-184	172- 51	156-133	3-6
10/02	A	Philadelphia	23-32	L	+4	a	194-455	55-190	139-265	3-1
10/09	H	Kansas City	7- 6	W	-5	a	230-184	206- 65	24-119	4-3
10/16	A	Pittsburgh	34-14	W	+0	a	309-344	124- 93	185-251	0-4
10/23	A	Cincinnati	21-44	L	+5	a	205-353	104-222	101-131	5-4
10/30	H	Washington	41-17	W	+1	a	336-250	152- 29	184-221	2-6
11/07	H*	Cleveland	24-17	W	+0	a	330-253	148- 44	182-209	1-1
11/13	A	Seattle	24-27	L	+1.5	a	419-365	237-177	182-188	1-1
11/20	H	Phoenix	38-20	W	-6.5	a	385-314	124- 60	261-254	0-2
11/24	A	Dallas	25-17	W	-5.5	a	355-282	145- 79	210-203	0-2
12/04	H	Pittsburgh	34-37	L	-10.5	a	403-426	134- 94	269-332	4-1
12/11	H	Cincinnati	41- 6	W	-1.5	a	396-226	147-132	249- 94	2-2
12/18	A	Cleveland	23-28	L	+3	g	317-388	37- 78	280-310	1-4
						Avg.	325-304	141- 99	184-205	2-3

				WINS	LOSSES
Season Record:	10- 6-0	POINTS:	30- 15	21- 36	
Vs. Spread:	9- 7-0	Net YDS:	10- 6-0	342-249	296-396
Home:	7- 1-0	Rush YDS:	13- 3-0	155- 74	118-142
On Artificial Turf:	10- 5-0	Pass YDS:	5-11-0	188-175	178-255
Art. Turf vs. Spread:	9- 6-0	TURN:	6- 5-5	2- 3	3- 2

* Monday Night

JOKER . . .

Jerry Glanville isn't everyone's cup of tea. He's not bland enough. In an age when most NFL coaches would rather cut off their nose tackles than say anything that might be construed as controversial, Jerry shoots from the hip. If the projectile threatens to traumatize his own foot, so be it.

He's not the only NFL mentor who's good for a laugh or a barb, of course. In fact, he had to work overtime in '88 to wrest the title of King of Coaching Comedy from Buddy Ryan. What does it matter that even Mike Ditka would rate Ryan ahead of Jerry in coaching acumen—Glanville is ahead on one-liners. Ditka himself made a valiant try for the title until a heart attack added a sobering note to his routine. In the long view we might treasure Mike more, but Jerry gets the quick laughs. Sam Wyche, once a promising zany, played it straight last year.

Jerry's main act was his tickets-at-the-window gag. It began innocently enough when the Oilers played a preseason game in Memphis right at the time when those "Elvis Is Alive and Well and Living in Bayonne" (or wherever) stories were crowding "Sterile Aliens Mate with Twin Towers: Produce No Trump" off the front page of the *Star*. Well, Jerry's a real Elvis buff, and so he left two tickets for the King at the gate.

It would have been a better story if Elvis had shown, but it still got a national giggle. Hey, that was all Jerry needed. Anything that could get him three lines of type in the *Wheeling News Register* was okay by him. In succeeding weeks he left tickets for James Dean, Buddy Holly, and the Phantom of the Opera. Occasionally the joke needed explaining, like W. C. Fields at Veterans Stadium (his tombstone reads: "On the whole, I'd rather be in Philadelphia") or Elliott Ness at Lakefront Stadium (he was born in Cleveland).

For a while there was a rumor that Oilers owner Bud Adams had sent down word for Jerry to cool it on leaving tickets for dead people. Supposedly Adams was afraid that Jerry might do something tasteless when Houston played in RFK Stadium on the twenty-fifth anniversary of the assassination of JFK. Well, Jerry might be a "pull-my-finger" kind of guy, but let's give him more credit than that! Besides, the Oilers played the Redskins in the Astrodome, not at RFK.

Sometimes he ran out of dead people. Loni Anderson (formerly of the TV-show "WKRP in Cincinnati") got only one ticket at Riverfront because Jerry didn't want Burt Reynolds to show up. For the playoff game at Buffalo, he left a ticket for Dabney Coleman, the star of the canceled "Buffalo Bill," and Jay Silverheels, famous as the Lone

Ranger's sidekick Tonto. We *think* that was a reference to old nickels. Well, it's a long season.

All in all, the ticket gag was okay. If it sometimes got the same icy smile you see when somebody breaks wind at High Mass, it still ranked ahead of the endless reports on sore knees and turf toes that usually make up the between-game news.

Once in a while Jerry's choice of target for his one-liner was a little dated, like when he said his team had an advantage in Cleveland because "after the game we can get on a plane and leave." Jerry, *bubela*, Cleveland jokes have been out since their river caught on fire. And Buffalo was two years ago. Now the "in" place to knock is Des Moines.

Oiler cornerback Patrick Allen was widely quoted for calling Jerry "a rebel without a pause," but at the rate he zings folks' hometowns, he'll end up a Rebel Without Applause. What happens when, as happens with all coaches, he's fired at Houston? Who will he ask for a job?

"Geez, Jerry, we'd love to have you, but your picture's still up at our post office."

But that's far in the future. For now the NFL's "life of the parity" is riding high, wide, and handsome. Well, anyway, he's wide. Jerry, *sweetheart*! Basic black adds twenty *pounds*!

Just between us, we think there's a method to Jerry's madcapness. By grabbing the spotlight and wringing its neck, he takes a lot of pressure off his players. Some teams need to be protected because they lack talent or experience or the ability to cope. Through the years the Oilers have been categorized, sometimes unfairly, as chronic underachievers. Supposedly they could do less with more than any organization except Congress. They were especially bad when they were allowed off the block to visit any place but Houston. We read somewhere that they'd won only one regular season game on the road against a team with a winning record since 1979. We were going to look it up, but finally decided, wot-the-hell! Everybody knows the Oilers are lousy out of the Astrodome. Why quantify it?

Anyway, we think Jerry uses his comedy act to keep his team from getting uptight by a media blitz.

And he kind of likes being quoted in the papers, too.

...AND HYDE

It's kind of hard to reconcile good ol' Jere the Jokesmith with Glanville Khan, the leader of the Luv-Ya-Black-and-Blue Oilers. Yet at the same time Jerry's been rolling them in the aisles, his band of merry men have been riling those who think of football as something less than a blood sport. The Oilers, they say, are the epitome of the brutish side of the game. They like to play with pain—the other guy's. More than intimidate, they seek to injure. And they don't even do it with style!

Columnist Jerry Magee put it thusly: "If you hang out in saloons, you probably know somebody who personifies the Houston Oilers. He is all mouth, see, a braggart, full

of bluster, a fat, opinionated oaf who, in the presence of women, says things he shouldn't.

"Not the type of fellow you would invite into your home." Perhaps that's a trifle harsh. Most of us would allow most of the Oilers access to our houses.

The news first made headlines when, after an Oiler win over Pittsburgh in 1987, Steelers' Coach Chuck Noll berated Glanville on the field for Houston's alleged dirty tactics. Noll, who seldom bothers with the obligatory postgame handshake, surprised Jerry by grabbing his mitt as they left the field. Then he held on and yelled at the embarrassed Glanville in sight of God and the TV cameras.

Once alerted, news hawks began looking for cheap shots, punches, gouges, clips, kicks, and such whenever the Oilers "played." They counted quite a few, as Glanville's bunch gave new meaning to the phrase "winning ugly." Particularly notable was LB Ross Grimsley's late hit on Denver's Vance Johnson in the '87 playoffs.

The irrepressible Glanville continued to defend his troops as physical rather than foul. At the same time he turned the criticism to his advantage by stressing the "them versus us" aspects to his team. The Astrodome's alter-nickname, "The House of Pain," added to the image.

There are problems in blanket condemnations of the Oilers. For one thing they are certainly not all blood-smeared ruffians. As has been pointed out by a number of writers, QB Warren Moon is one of the finest gentlemen in the game. We would hazard a guess that three-fourths of the roster plays hard but clean. After watching the Oilers in four '88 games and looking closely for signs of illegality, we have the impression that the degree of swinishness is inversely proportional to the degree of talent.

You see it most openly on the coverage teams, many of whom seem to think it's illegal to tackle below the neck. Once an opponent is down, the Oiler tacklers are adept at the swipe at the mouth, the shoulder in the spine, the finger in the eye, and the kick in the groin. If the fellow cannot rise, the mission has been accomplished. If he does get up, he is bombarded from all sides with verbal assaults, euphemistically described as "taunts," but which we gather would make a Marine D.I. blanch. An alternate strategy is the surreptitious sucker punch, often eliciting a penalized retaliation.

Dirty these tactics may be. Coarse, disgusting, mean-spirited, crude, and improper. But physical, in the football sense, they are not. The Bears are physical. So are the Vikings; the old Raiders—even Noll's Steelers of a decade ago. They came straight at you and flattened you. Occasionally one of them stepped over the line into the red zone, but it was an excess of enthusiasm rather than a planned sneak attack. They punished by hitting harder—the intimidating tactics of strong men, not the furtive cruelties of dirty little boys in a schoolyard.

The trouble with Glanville is that he seems unwilling to recognize the difference. He has been quoted that his team seldom wins unless it racks up at least ten penalties in a game. The number is off, but the idea holds up.

WK	OPPONENT	SCORE	HOUSTON PEN	HOUSTON YDS	OPPONENT PEN	OPPONENT YDS	W-L	NET
1	Colts	17-14	7	70	5	56	W	-14
2	Raiders	38-35	15	184	7	45	W	-139
3	Jets	3-45	10	95	11	95	L	0
4	Patriots	31- 6	5	69	5	45	W	-24
5	Eagles	23-32	12	66	19	147	L	81
6	Chiefs	7- 6	12	121	9	90	W	-31
7	Steelers	34-14	10	105	10	58	W	-47
8	Bengals	21-44	4	27	3	31	L	4
9	Redskins	41-17	9	117	8	61	W	-56
10	Browns	24-17	6	35	1	5	W	-30
11	Seahawks	24-27	9	59	8	60	L	1
12	Cardinals	38-20	5	35	7	55	W	20
13	Cowboys	25-17	4	30	2	10	W	-20
14	Steelers	34-37	6	46	8	103	L	57
15	Bengals	41- 6	7	75	8	45	W	-30
16	Browns	23-28	4	25	4	35	L	10

Except for the Cardinals game, the Oilers were penalized more yards than each of the opponents they defeated. On the other hand, of the seven games in which opponents were penalized more than Houston, the Oilers lost six.

The numbers would seem to indicate Glanville is on the right track with his men. But is he? Most of the objectionable things the Oilers do don't draw penalties. Late hits, spearing, and things like that happen, but not to the extent of ten a game. A more likely explanation is that Jerry's troops get up for certain games and commit the usual infractions to excess: offsides, motion, ineligible man downfield. But despite a certain sloppiness, the Oilers win when aroused because they have more ability than most of their opponents.

The most telling quote came from Moon: "Whenever we lose, it seems to be because we beat ourselves with a lot of stupid penalties and not playing smart. When we do the things we're supposed to do, we pretty much out-talent people."

THE MOUNTAIN MAN

Oilers' General Manager Ladd Herzeg resigned after the season, saying he had "other mountains to climb." It was an odd statement. Usually when somebody talks about "other mountains," he's already climbed one. If he's just moving to something else without completing his task, he's more likely to have "other fish to fry" or some similar saw. As GM, Herzeg's task was to win a Super Bowl, or the AFC title, or the Central Division. The Oilers finished third in the Central. Was Herzeg making a mountain out of his molehill?

We think not. Herzeg could say he put a championship-*caliber* team on the field, even if it didn't win the championship. His job was to assemble the team.

Take the three Central Division powers position by position:

At wide receiver, Cincinnati had Eddie Brown, who had the best year of any WR in the league, but Houston's combination of Drew Hill and Ernest Givens ranks slightly ahead of the Bengals' twosome of Brown and Tim McGee. Cleveland, with Webster Slaughter out half the season, wasn't even close. The Oilers' Curtis Duncan was a solid backup, and Haywood Jeffires began to come on in the playoffs.

Cincy's Rodney Holman is a better tight end than Jamie Williams, who is used mostly to block. However, Williams could be ranked ahead of Cleveland's great Ozzie Newsome, who never blocked a whole lot and wasn't the receiver in '88 that he used to be.

In the offensive line Cincinnati is number one with Anthony Munoz and Company, but Houston isn't far behind with a pair of Pro Bowl guards in Mike Munchak and Bruce Matthews. Bruce Davis is a good tackle and Dean Steinkuhler is okay. Again Cleveland isn't even a close third.

Boomer Esiason was the AFC's top quarterback, but Warren Moon was also named to the Pro Bowl. When Bernie Kosar was in there, Cleveland had good quarterbacking, but he was only available half the season.

At running back the Bengals' duo of Ickey Woods and James Brooks was terrific, but Houston might be better when depth is figured into the equation. Probably no team can match the total talent of Mike Rozier, Alonzo Highsmith, Allen Pinkett, and Lorenzo White. Cleveland's best, Kevin Mack, was injured much of '88.

Overall you'd have to rank the Cincinnati offense as superior, but the Oilers come surprisingly close to matching them in talent. The Oilers' offense scored 47 touchdowns to Cincinnati's 55. The Browns managed 29.

On the defensive line, the Bengals have Tim Krumrie and a bunch of other guys, all of whom rank behind the Oilers' Ray Childress, Doug Smith, Richard Byrd, William Fuller, and Sean Jones. Cleveland has a good NT in Bob Golic, but not a whole lot more.

None of the three teams sparkled at linebacker. Give Cleveland the edge because of Clay Matthews. Houston's Robert Lyles, John Grimsley, Al Smith, and Johnny Meads played better than expected in '88. We'll rank them third in a very close matchup.

Cleveland has a real edge in the secondary. Neither of the other two teams can match Frank Minnifield, or even Hanford Dixon on one leg. FS Felix Wright is good too. The Oilers' corners are weak, but their safeties are strong. The Bengals' David Fulcher (against the run) and Eric Thomas put their secondary slightly ahead of the Oilers'.

Overall on defense the Oilers come in behind the Browns and maybe behind the Bengals. Nevertheless it's a close call, with Houston definitely stronger up front.

Special teams were erratic for all three teams, but Houston did block five punts. Eugene Seale was outstanding. Moreover Tony Zendejas was a better long distance kicker than either Matt Bahr or Jim Breech.

The Oilers had at the very least the second-most talent in the division last season, and probably the second-most in the conference. And that's being conservative.

Herzeg could leave, secure that *he* wasn't why they only finished third.

HOUSTON OILERS STATISTICS

1988 TEAM STATISTICS	HO	OPP
TOTAL FIRST DOWNS	308	304
Rushing	141	94
Passing	148	170
Penalty	19	40
3rd Down Made/Att.	84/202	82/207
Pct.	41.9%	39.6%
4th Down Made/Att.	7/13	8/14
Pct.	53.8%	57.1%
TOTAL NET YARDS	5205	4858
Avg. per Game	325.3	303.6
Total Plays	1010	985
Avg. per Play	5.2	4.9
NET YARDS RUSHING	2249	1592
Avg. per Game	140.6	99.5
Total Rushes	558	431
NET YARDS PASSING	2956	3266
Avg. per Game	184.8	204.1
Tackled/Yards Lost	24/210	42/353
Gross Yards	3166	3619
Attempts/Completions	428/218	512/281
Pct. of Completions	50.9%	54.9%
Had Intercepted	18	22
PUNTS/AVERAGE	65/38.8	80/37.2
NET PUNTING AVG.	34.1	31.9
PENALTIES/YARDS	125/1150	118/947
FUMBLES/BALL LOST	33/17	33/20
TOUCHDOWNS	51	46
Rushing	26	20
Passing	21	22
Returns	4	4
TIME OF POSSESSION	28:45	31:15

SCORE/PERIODS	1	2	3	4	OT	TOTAL
Oilers	84	137	100	100	3	424
Opponents	85	112	71	97	0	365

SCORING	TDR	TDP	TDRt	PAT	FG	S	TP
Zendejas				48/50	22/34		114
Rozier	10	1					66
Hill		10					60
Pinkett	7	2					54
Givins		5					30
Moon	5						30
Highsmith	2						12
Brown			1				6
Bryant			1				6
Carlson	1						6
Dishman			1				6

(Continued)							
SCORING	TDR	TDP	TDRt	PAT	FG	S	TP
Drewrey		1					6
Duncan		1					6
Jeffires		1					6
Pease	1						6
White			1				6
Fairs						1	2
Seale						1	2
Oilers	26	21	4	48/51	22/34	2	424
Opponents	20	22	4	43/46	14/18	2	365

RUSHING	NO	YDS	AVG	LG	TD
Rozier	251	1002	4.0	28	10
Pinkett	122	513	4.2	27	7
Highsmith	94	466	5.0	42	2
White	31	115	3.7	16	0
Moon	33	88	2.7	14	5
Carlson	12	36	3.0	10	1
Givins	4	26	6.5	10	0
Tillman	3	5	1.7	2	0
Pease	8	-2	-0.3	4t	1
Oilers	558	2249	4.0	42	26
Opponents	431	1592	3.7	44t	20

RECEIVING	NO	YDS	AVG	LG	TD
Hill	72	1141	15.8	57t	10
Givins	60	976	16.3	46	5
Duncan	22	302	13.7	36	1
Highsmith	12	131	10.9	28	0
Pinkett	12	114	9.5	51t	2
Drewrey	11	172	15.6	55	1
Rozier	11	99	9.0	18	1
Harris	10	136	13.6	42	0
Williams	6	46	7.7	10	0
Jeffires	2	49	24.5	42	1
Oilers	218	3166	14.5	57t	21
Opponents	281	3619	12.9	80t	22

INTERCEPTIONS	NO	YDS	AVG	LG	TD
Donaldson	4	29	7.3	23	0
Bryant	3	56	18.7	36t	1
R. Johnson	3	0	0.0	0	0
Brown	2	48	24.0	44t	1
Lyles	2	3	1.5	3	0
K. Johnson	1	51	51.0	51	0
Seale	1	46	46.0	46	0
Allen	1	23	23.0	21	0

(Continued)

(Continued)

INTERCEPTIONS	NO	YDS	AVG	LG	TD
D.Smith	1	20	20.0	20	0
Fuller	1	9	9.0	9	0
Grimsley	1	9	9.0	9	0
Bostic	1	7	7.0	7	0
Byrd	1	1	1.0	1	0
Oilers	22	302	13.7	51	2
Opponents	18	289	16.1	73	1

PUNTING	NO	YDS	AVG	TB	In 20	LG	Blk
Montgomery	65	2523	38.8	5	12	61	0
Oilers	65	2523	38.8	5	12	61	0
Opponents	80	2973	37.2	10	14	60	5

PUNT RETURNS	NO	FC	YDS	AVG	LG	TD
K. Johnson	30	6	170	5.7	16	0
Duncan	4	2	47	11.8	26	0
Drewrey	2	2	8	4.0	8	0
Oilers	36	10	225	6.3	26	0
Opponents	35	9	206	5.9	18	0

KICKOFF RETURNS	NO	YDS	AVG	LG	TD
Harris	34	678	19.9	56	0
White	8	196	24.5	90t	1
Pinkett	7	137	19.6	29	0
K. Johnson	6	157	26.2	56	0
Donaldson	1	5	5.0	5	0
Drewrey	1	10	10.0	10	0
Duncan	1	34	34.0	34	0
R. Johnson	1	2	2.0	2	0
Tillman	1	13	13.0	13	0
Oilers	60	1232	20.5	90t	1
Opponents	69	1362	19.7	92t	1

FIELD GOALS	1-19	20-29	30-39	40-49	50+	TOTAL
Zendejas	1-1	3-5	7-8	9-16	2-4	22-34
Oilers	1-1	3-5	7-8	9-16	2-4	22-34
Opponents	0-0	4-4	1-2	8-10	1-2	14-18

FIELD GOALS BY ZENDEJAS: 22 of 34
(47N,26N,35G)(19G)(30G,26N,48N)(46N,
46N,49G)( )(37N,50N)(50G,27G)(45N)(41G,
39G)(52N,47G)(52G)(46N,37G)(28G.49G,47G,
22G)(36G,41G,41N)(43G,48G)(39G,42G,35G)

PASSING	ATT	COM	YARD	PCT.	Avg G	TD	%TD	IN	%IN	LG	SAKS/YDS	RATE
Moon	294	160	2327	54.4	7.91	17	5.8	8	2.7	57t	12/120	88.4
Carlson	112	52	775	46.4	6.92	4	3.6	6	5.4	51t	10/72	59.2
Pease	22	6	64	27.3	2.91	0	0.0	4	18.2	21	2/18	0.0
Oilers	428	218	3166	50.9	7.40	21	4.9	18	4.2	57t	24/210	74.2
Opponents	512	281	3619	54.9	7.07	22	4.3	22	4.3	80t	42/353	73.7

INDIANAPOLIS COLTS

The Last 5 Seasons

	1984	1985	1986	1987	1988
Won-Lost	4-12	5-11	3-13	9-6	9-7
Percentage	.250	.313	.188	.600	.563
Division Finish	4	4	5	1	2-t
Games Behind	10	7	8	0	3
Total Points	239	320	229	300	354
Per Game	14.9	20.0	14.3	20.0	22.1
Opponent Points	414	386	400	238	315
Per Game	25.9	24.1	25.0	15.9	19.7
Net Points	-175	-66	-171	62	39
Predicted Net Wins	-4.4	-1.6	-4.3	1.5	1.0
Delta Net Wins	0.4	-1.4	-0.7	-0.0	0.0
Total Yards on Offense	4132	5006	4700	4995	4870
Per Game	258.3	312.9	293.8	333.0	304.4
Total Yards Allowed on Defense	5577	5599	5701	4550	5296
Per Game	348.6	349.9	356.3	303.3	331.0
Net Difference	-1445	-593	-1001	445	-426
Offensive Turnovers	38	34	44	34	30
Defensive Takeaways	31	33	35	45	35
Net Turnovers	-7	-1	-9	11	5
Predicted Net Points	-148	-53	-119	81	-16
Delta Net Points	-27	-13	-52	-19	55
Net Rushing Yards	2025	2439	1491	2143	2249
Per Game	126.6	152.4	93.2	142.9	140.6
Average Gain	4.0	5.0	3.7	4.3	4.1
Opponent Net Rushing Yards	2007	2145	1962	1790	1694
Per Game	125.4	134.1	122.6	119.3	105.9
Average Gain	3.6	4.0	3.8	3.9	3.8
Net Passing Yards	2107	2567	3209	2852	2621
Per Game	131.7	160.4	200.6	190.1	163.8
Times Sacked	58	35	53	24	34
Passer Rating in Yards	2.7	3.6	3.6	4.9	4.1
Opponent Net Passing Yards	3570	3454	3739	2760	3602
Per Game	223.1	215.9	233.7	184.0	225.1
Times Sacked	42	36	24	39	30
Passer Rating Defense	5.5	5.5	6.2	3.8	5.5
Passer Rating Net	-2.9	-1.9	-2.6	1.1	-1.4
Yards per Drive Offense	20.5	25.4	23.5	25.5	26.8
Yards per Drive Defense	27.3	28.6	29.4	23.8	29.1
Average Time of Possession	27:24	28:49	29:12	30:10	30:19

121

1987 PLAYOFFS
Lost Divisional Playoff to Cleveland, 21-38

THE 1988 SEASON

DATE	AT	OPPONENT	SCORE	R	SPREAD	Tu	Net YDS	Rush YDS	Pass YDS	TURN
09/04	H	Houston	14-17	L	-3.5	a	291-348	111-174	180-174	3-3
09/11	H	Chicago	13-17	L	+2	a	173-332	108-154	65-178	3-1
09/19	A*	Cleveland	17-23	L	+2	g	282-356	128-101	154-255	3-2
09/25	H	Miami	15-13	W	-2.5	a	304-323	213- 71	91-252	1-2
10/02	A	New England	17-21	L	+2	a	267-298	107-105	160-193	1-2
10/09	A	Buffalo	23-34	L	+4.5	a	308-456	67-141	241-315	3-3
10/16	H	Tampa Bay	35-31	W	-5.5	a	343-483	103- 39	240-444	2-2
10/23	A	San Diego	16- 0	W	+0	g	453-239	198-118	255-121	3-1
10/31	H*	Denver	55-23	W	-1.5	a	464-397	244-131	220-266	1-4
11/06	H	N.Y. Jets	38-14	W	-3.5	a	336-273	140- 91	196-182	3-2
11/13	A	Green Bay	20-13	W	-4.5	g	247-297	136- 98	111-199	1-4
11/20	A	Minnesota	3-12	L	+4.5	a	213-274	103- 82	110-192	2-0
11/27	H	New England	24-21	W	-5	a	241-285	81-105	160-180	2-3
12/04	A	Miami	31-28	W	-2.5	g	322-362	221- 58	101-304	0-2
12/10	A	N.Y. Jets	16-34	L	-3	a	331-329	109-171	222-158	3-3
12/18	H	Buffalo	17-14	W	+2	a	301-248	184- 53	117-195	0-1
						Av.	305-33	141-106	164-226	2-2

			WINS	LOSSES
		POINTS:	28- 17	15- 23
Season Record:	9- 7-0	Net YDS: 5-11-0	335-323	266-342
Vs. Spread:	6-10-0	Rush YDS: 11- 5-0	169- 85	105-133
Home:	6- 2-0	Pass YDS: 4-12-0	166-238	162-209
On Artificial Turf:	6- 6-0	TURN: 7- 5-4	1- 2	3- 2
Art. Turf vs. Spread:	3- 9-0			

* Monday Night

TEAM TURMOIL

The weekly standings said "Indianapolis Colts," but around the league they were called "Team Turmoil." The Hoosiers sailed through the '88 season with all the serenity of H.M.S. *Bounty*. The reasons:

REASON NO. 1: PAY ME OR TRADE ME

Like everything else with the Colts, you start with the Dickerson trade. When GM Jim Irsay obtained the Great Ground Gobbler from the Rams on Halloween '87, most of the Colts players gave him huzzahs. You heard things like "a real commitment to winning" and "he sent a message." It worked great. The team jumped from last in the division in '86 to first in '87. You couldn't ask for more, except maybe a playoff win.

But 'tween seasons several Colts began to examine Irsay's message a little more closely and—using their bankbooks as Rosetta Stones—decoded it a little differently. Hey, Dickerson was making a lot of money! *A lot!* And while none of the colts-with-a-small-c rated their contributions to be the equal of Eminent Eric's, they figured they were worth something. Like *more!*

Probably the one most directly affected by the arrival of Eric the Green (as in greenbacks) was RB Albert Bentley, who went from the busiest Indianapolis runner to someone with time on his hands and splinters in his butt. To Albert's credit he didn't make a fuss.

At first the dissatisfaction was most prevalent in the offensive line, without whose estimable efforts Dickerson would have trouble earning his next birthday, much less his salary. They let their feelings be known in preseason. OT Kevin Call held out for a month. OT Chris Hinton walked out of training camp for four days over some bonus dough. Irsay said the bonus was bogus. Hinton decided it would only cost him more money to eat at home and returned, full of grump. OG Ron Solt was the champion sitter, still at home when the season started.

Another holdout was WR Matt Bouza, the possession receiver of 42 passes in '87. He returned just in time for the opening regular-season game—for $100,000 less than what would have made him a happy camper. He even caught a twenty-three-yard pass from QB Gary Hogeboom to score the Colts' first official '88 points.

In the fourth week of the season, Solt finally signed for $2.6 million over five years and bitched all the way to the bank. He figured the Colts hadn't given him the respect due a millionaire. A week later he was dealt to the Eagles, but refused to report until he got a raise.

REASON NO. 2: PAY HIM BUT PLAY ME

Indianapolis had barely lost its opener to Houston on a fumble in overtime when they picked up Pro Bowl LB Fredd Young from Seattle for two first-round draft choices. Young was available to the highest bidder because he was loudly unhappy in Seattle being paid less than the Boz. The Colts already HAD a Pro Bowl LB in Duane Bickett and a couple of other guys who might get there some day. So, even though linebacker was considered one the strongest areas on the team, the Colts signed Young for $4.5 million-plus-incentives, in an apparent effort to make their veteran linebackers as contented as their offensive linemen.

Young had gotten to the Pro Bowl playing inside linebacker for the Seahawks, so naturally the Colts decided to put him at outside linebacker right off. Rusty from his holdout and out of position, he bombed and was benched in favor of rookie O'Brien Alston. The Colts now had a very unhappy 4.5-Million-Dollar Man.

A week later Young replaced Cliff Odom at ILB—although Odom was the team's leading tackler and defensive captain. Hey, you can't leave that kind of money on the bench! Odom didn't quite agree and jumped the team. He came back forty-eight hours later rather than face a $1,000-a-day fine and asked to be traded. He wasn't. The growing Disenchanted Colt Club enrolled a new member.

REASON NO. 3: PLAY ME OR PLAY ME

QB Gary Hogeboom was 15-of-20 for 219 yards in the opener, one of his better marks in a Colt uniform. So for the second game he was demoted in favor of Jack Trudeau. He took it with the grace of a shrew with boils. There were rumors that Coach Ron Meyer really preferred Hogeboom, but the team wouldn't play for Gary because they thought he'd dogged it with some of his injuries the year before. Other rumors had Owner Bob Irsay ordering the change. Of course any time anything happens short of fire, famine, or flood there are rumors among the Colts that Tiger Bob ordered it. It's called the Irsay Hearsay.

The most credible gossip had Meyer upset over Hogeboom's key fumble in the opener. Anyway, Hogeboom was as consistent as March weather and brittle as toast besides. Since arriving in Coltsville in 1986, he'd been sidelined five times, making him an annual candidate for the McMahon Award.

On the other hand, in two years as the Colts' sometime QB, Trudeau had impressed only those fans who thought he drew *Doonesbury*. Whether a contingent of Colts players wanted him, or Irsay wanted him, or anybody in Indianapolis wanted him didn't matter as much as the fact that the Bears didn't want him. They kayoed him in the second half of the Colts' second loss. In came rookie Chris Chandler, while Hogeboom sat and steamed.

Trudeau was back for the third game but not for long.

This time he was knocked out for the season. Chandler played fireman again. And again the Colts lost.

REASON NO. 4: PLAY *SOMEBODY* WHO CAN WIN

Indianapolis lost four of its first five games by less than a TD-plus-PAT. That kind of start would have had the Osmonds nipping at each other—and with all their money gripes, the Colts were more like the Karamazovs.

For the one game they won, Chandler was at QB and Dickerson ran for 125 yards. Meyer called it a "team victory," but they'd have been down the chute again without PK Dean Biasucci. After no practice for two weeks because of a hip injury, Biasucci hit five field goals—50, 34, 41, 51, and 25 yards—for all of the Colt points.

Then they lost the next two.

You expect a 1–5 team to make changes, even a former playoff team. In the first six games, twelve noninjury-related switches took place. That was a bit much for the veterans, some of whom were positive the front office was looking to cut some salaries after investing so heavily in Dickerson and Young.

"You think, 'My God, who's next?'" said ILB Barry Krauss.

DE Donnell Thompson added, "I'm always looking over my shoulder anymore."

REASON NO. 5: THERE IS NO REASON

GM Jim Irsay expounded, "The differences between winning and losing are very small. Right now our cylinders aren't clicking. We feel we have a very fine football team. Why do these things happen?"

HALT!

Everybody but Irsay had a reason why the Colts were flopping around the bottom of the team standings—the dissension, the quarterback(s).

In pure football terms, leaving egos aside, the main culprit was the defense. Even though Buffalo and Tampa Bay were the only teams to blitz the Colts for more than 23 points in the first-half swoon, the D just wasn't stopping anyone when it counted.

Opponents had 13 drives of 70 or more yards in the first seven games. For all the talent at linebacker, the job wasn't getting done. The secondary was a shambles, allowing nearly 60 percent completions. And they weren't being helped much up front; the Colts had only 14 sacks.

The sad thing was watching Joe Klecko operate at NT as a shadow of what he'd been. A courageous, hard-working shadow, true. But still a shadow. The longtime Jets star had been cut by New York for medical reasons after the '87 season. He disagreed with the diagnosis and signed with the Colts for a last hurrah, hoping for one more playoff shot. But the old quickness wasn't there.

Things looked up when the Colts shut out San Diego in Week 8. But then, San Diego usually scored about as often as a fat man in a singles bar.

BOO!

For Halloween only eighty-four Hoosiers no-showed their chance to appear on "Monday Night Football," as 60,544 set an H-Dome record. Most of the show-ups showed off Al Michaels, Frank Gifford, and Dan Dierdorf masks. As cameras panned the crowd, the ABC broadcasting crew enjoyed a narcissistic high known to very few. Rameses II, Louis XIV, Brian Bosworth. It was grand!

The Colts set their own record in the 55–23 win over Denver, topping the old Monday Night mark of 50 points scored by the Chargers in 1983. (Does anyone keep records for Saturday afternoon games? How about Sunday Night ESPN?)

Dickerson celebrated the anniversary of his arrival in Indiana with 159 yards and four touchdowns. The big Indianapolis line simply rolled the little Bronco defenders into a ball and stomped on them.

THE OLD COLLEGE TRY

Also for Halloween, Coach Meyer introduced a collegiate wrinkle by running a wishbone offense much of the time. All those people who've been saying for years the pros should run a wishbone finally got their wish. But in a year when QBs were an endangered species, Meyer seemed to be tempting fate. Trudeau was on the injured reserve list, Hogeboom was on Blue Cross's Don't-Call-Us list, and Chandler had already been knocked out of games with a sternum injury and a concussion.

On November 4, two days before the Jets game, the Colts signed free-agent QB Rick Turner out of a construction job in Washington to run their wishbone. That gave them four quarterbacks on the roster—Turner, Chandler, Hogeboom, and Bill Ransdell—and only three running backs.

Turner knew full well he was expendable. He'd run the wishbone and save the other QBs until he got broken.

THE MAGIC IS GONE

Give Ron Meyer credit. He brought his team back from the abyss to challenge for a playoff berth. He did it with a rookie at quarterback, a faulty defense, and more team paranoia than the Nixon White House. The Colts moved to 6–5 with a win over the Packers in Week 11. But when the Vikings defense stuffed them the next week, they were back teetering.

The challenge was to go into Sullivan Stadium and beat the Patriots and Doug Flutie. The Miracle Midget had brought New England from ten points down in the fourth quarter to top the Colts at Indy in Week 5.

The Patriots started with a bang. Sammy Martin took the opening kickoff back 95 yards for a New England touchdown. Dickerson, having one of his worst days, tied the game with a two-yard TD at 6:42 of the first quarter. But New England went back in front on Rob Perryman's touchdown plunge on the first play of the second period.

New England held Dickerson to only 45 yards on 20 carries for the day, and his longest run was a mere five yards. Nevertheless when the Colts got to the Patriots' two-yard-line with less than two minutes in the half, Chandler handed to Eric. His second TD of the day made it a 14–14 tie at the half.

The Colts had trouble with third quarters all season. This time they barely got through it with the tie intact. Two seconds into the final quarter New England's Mosi Tatupu plunged over from the one for the go-ahead TD. For the third time the Colts came back to tie, scoring at 4:25 of the final period on Chandler's 18-yard pass to TE Mark Boyer.

With six minutes remaining, the Patriots tried to take the lead again, but PK Jason Staurovsky's 43-yard field goal try missed.

The Colts got a huge break when the Pats' Irving Fryar fumbled a punt at his own twenty. Rookie FS Michael Ball recovered—"I thought it was an early Christmas gift. I said to myself, 'Thank you, Santa.'" With 2:22 left, Biasucci put the Colts ahead for the first time in the game with a 28-yard field goal.

Down came Flutie and the Patriots, driving 71 yards to a first down at the Indianapolis nine. It looked like Flutie Magic Time again. In the earlier Patriot win, Li'l Doug had topped them with a 13-yard naked bootleg with twenty-three seconds on the clock.

"We remembered what happened the last time," Meyer said later. "We were prepared for that and anything else he might try."

What Flutie tried was three straight passes, all incomplete. Staurovsky set up at the twenty-seven for the field goal that would put the game into overtime. And missed! The Colts had survived, 24–21.

COLT NOTABLE

Ray Donaldson was named AFC Pro Bowl center for the second year in a row. With Miami's Dwight Stephenson gone with an injury and Pittsburgh's Mike Webster on the wane, Donaldson figures to be the conference starter for several years to come. At one time ideal NFL centers were quick and relatively small, like Jim Ringo and Jim Otto. Four-man defensive lines left them uncovered, and most of their run blocking was downfield. Now, most defenses put a monster over center and the snapper has to have the muscle to take him on. At 6'3" and 288 pounds, Donaldson's plenty big.

He's also durable. The '87 strike ended his string of 91 straight starts. Durability is particularly crucial at center, where replacing a man in the middle of a game or a season usually leads to fumbles.

Did you hear any griping by Ray when most of the other Colts line was leading the league in grumbles? We didn't.

LET'S ALL PULL TOGETHER

In a move interpreted as aimed at improving team harmony, Meyer fired six assistant coaches as soon as the season ended. The six had all been on the staff when Meyer was hired in 1986.

INDIANAPOLIS COLTS STATISTICS

1988 TEAM STATISTICS	IC	OPP
TOTAL FIRST DOWNS	311	315
Rushing	153	109
Passing	130	184
Penalty	28	22
3rd Down Made/Att.	64/186	88/204
Pct.	34.4%	43.1%
4th Down Made/Att.	11/20	9/16
Pct.	55.0%	56.3%
TOTAL NET YARDS	4870	5296
Avg. per Game	304.4	331.0
Total Plays	982	1016
Avg. per Play	5.0	5.2
NET YARDS RUSHING	2249	1694
Avg. per Game	140.6	105.9
Total Rushes	545	447
NET YARDS PASSING	2621	3602
Avg. per Game	163.8	225.1
Tackled/Yards Lost	34/244	30/201
Gross Yards	2865	3803
Attempts/Completions	403/222	539/321
Pct. of Completions	55.1%	59.6%
Had Intercepted	22	15
PUNTS/AVERAGE	64/43.5	68/39.4
NET PUNTING AVG.	34.5	33.6
PENALTIES/YARDS	89/657	118/965
FUMBLES/BALL LOST	20/8	32/20
TOUCHDOWNS	40	38
Rushing	23	14
Passing	15	21
Returns	2	3
TIME OF POSSESSION	—	—

SCORE/PERIODS	1	2	3	4	OT	TOTAL
Colts	44	135	61	81	0	354
Opponents	55	88	48	121	3	315

SCORING	TDR	TDP	TDRt	PAT	FG	S	TP
Biasucci				39/40	25/32		114
Dickerson	14	1					90
Verdin		4	1				30
Bouza		4					24
Bentley	2	1					18
Brooks		3					18
Chandler	3						18
Boyer		2					12
Turner	2						12
Daniel			1				6
Hogeboom	1						6
Wonsley	1						6
Colts	23	15	2	39/40	25/32	0	354
Opponents	14	21	3	36/38	17/25	0	315

RUSHING	NO	YDS	AVG	LG	TD
Dickerson	388	1659	4.3	41t	14
Bentley	45	230	5.1	20	2

(Continued)

RUSHING	NO	YDS	AVG	LG	TD
Chandler	46	139	3.0	29t	3
Verdin	8	77	9.6	44	0
Brooks	5	62	12.4	38	0
Wonsley	26	48	1.8	4	1
Turner	16	42	2.6	14	2
Hogeboom	11	-8	-0.7	6	1
Colts	545	2249	4.1	44	23
Opponents	447	1694	3.8	29	14

RECEIVING	NO	YDS	AVG	LG	TD
Brooks	54	867	16.1	53t	3
Dickerson	36	377	10.5	50t	1
Boyer	27	256	9.5	24t	2
Bentley	26	252	9.7	21	1
Beach	26	235	9.0	23	0
Bouza	25	342	13.7	28	4
Verdin	20	437	21.9	54	4
Bellini	5	64	12.8	25	0
Pruitt	2	38	19.0	19	0
Baldinger	1	37	37.0	37	0
Hinton	1	1	1.0	1	0
Donaldson	1	-3	-3.0	-3	0
Colts	222	2865	12.9	58	15
Opponents	321	3803	11.8	58	21

INTERCEPTIONS	NO	YDS	AVG	LG	TD
Tullis	4	36	9.0	20	0
Prior	3	46	15.3	23	0
Bickett	3	7	2.3	4	0
Goode	2	53	26.5	35	0
Daniel	2	44	22.0	41t	1
Krauss	1	3	3.0	3	0
Colts	15	189	12.6	41t	1
Opponents	22	291	13.2	44t	1

PUNTING	NO	YDS	AVG	TB	In 20	LG	Blk
Stark	64	2784	43.5	8	15	65	0
Colts	64	2784	43.5	8	15	65	0
Opponents	68	2677	39.4	7	25	74	0

PUNT RETURNS	NO	FC	YDS	AVG	LG	TD
Verdin	22	7	239	10.9	73t	1
Brooks	3	0	15	5.0	8	0
Prior	1	5	0	0.0	0	0
Colts	26	12	254	9.8	73t	1
Opponents	37	3	418	11.3	59t	1

KICKOFF RETURNS	NO	YDS	AVG	LG	TD
Bentley	39	775	19.9	40	0
Verdin	7	145	20.7	32	0
Banks	4	56	14.0	20	0
Beach	1	35	35.0	35	0

(Continued)

(Continued)

KICKOFF RETURNS	NO	YDS	AVG	LG	TD
Wright	1	22	22.0	22	0
Colts	52	1033	19.9	40	0
Opponents	67	1480	22.1	95t	1

FIELD GOALS	1-19	20-29	30-39	40-49	50+	TOTAL
Biasucci	0-0	8-8	5-6	6-10	6-8	25-32
Colts	0-0	8-8	5-6	6-10	6-8	25-32
Opponents	1-1	7-9	4-6	5-7	0-2	17-25

FIELD GOALS BY Biasucci: 25 of 32
(57N)(38G,53G)(30G)(50G,34G,41G,51G,
51N,25G)(20G)(31G,49N,40G,22G)( )(20G,
44G,51G)(31G,39N,27G)(48N,51G)(20G,25G)
(44N,42G)(28G)(47G)(45G)(52G,48N)

PASSING	ATT	COM	YARD	PCT.	Avg G	TD	%TD	IN	%IN	LG	SAKS/YDS	RATE
Chandler	233	129	1619	55.4	6.95	8	3.4	12	5.2	54	18/128	67.2
Hogeboom	131	76	996	58.0	7.60	7	5.3	7	5.3	58	12/88	77.7
Trudeau	34	14	158	41.2	4.65	0	0.0	3	8.8	48	2/13	19.0
Turner	4	3	92	75.0	23.00	0	0.0	0	0.0	37	2/15	116.7
Bentley	1	0	0	0.0	0.00	0	0.0	0	0.0	00	0/0	39.6
Colts	403	222	2865	55.1	7.11	15	3.7	22	5.5	58	34/244	67.3
Opponents	539	321	3803	59.6	7.06	21	3.9	15	2.8	58	30/201	82.5

KANSAS CITY CHIEFS

The Last 5 Seasons

	1984	1985	1986	1987	1988
Won-Lost	8-8	6-10	10-6	4-11	4-11-1
Percentage	.500	.375	.625	.267	.281
Division Finish	4	5	2-t	5	5
Games Behind	5	6	1	6.5	4.5
Total Points	314	317	358	273	254
Per Game	19.6	19.8	22.4	18.2	15.9
Opponent Points	324	360	326	388	320
Per Game	20.3	22.5	20.4	25.9	20.0
Net Points	-10	-43	32	-115	-66
Predicted Net Wins	-0.3	-1.1	0.8	-2.9	-1.6
Delta Net Wins	0.3	-0.9	1.2	-0.6	-1.9
Total Yards on Offense	5095	4877	4218	4418	4844
Per Game	318.4	304.8	263.6	294.5	302.8
Total Yards Allowed on Defense	5625	5658	4934	5639	5026
Per Game	351.6	353.6	308.4	375.9	314.1
Net Difference	-530	-781	-716	-1221	-182
Offensive Turnovers	37	34	35	41	33
Defensive Takeaways	41	41	49	28	31
Net Turnovers	4	7	14	-13	-2
Predicted Net Points	-28	-37	-4	-154	-23
Delta Net Points	18	-6	36	39	-43
Net Rushing Yards	1527	1486	1468	1799	1713
Per Game	95.4	92.9	91.8	119.9	107.1
Average Gain	3.7	3.5	3.4	4.3	3.8
Opponent Net Rushing Yards	1980	2169	1739	2333	2592
Per Game	123.8	135.6	108.7	155.5	162.0
Average Gain	3.8	4.2	3.6	4.4	4.3
Net Passing Yards	3568	3391	2750	2619	3131
Per Game	223.0	211.9	171.9	174.6	195.7
Times Sacked	33	43	50	48	43
Passer Rating in Yards	4.5	4.7	3.8	4.2	4.1
Opponent Net Passing Yards	3645	3489	3195	3306	2434
Per Game	227.8	218.1	199.7	220.4	152.1
Times Sacked	50	37	44	26	23
Passer Rating Defense	3.9	4.1	3.3	6.0	4.0
Passer Rating Net	0.5	0.6	0.5	-1.8	0.1
Yards per Drive Offense	23.8	24.0	19.3	24.5	28.0
Yards per Drive Defense	25.7	27.3	22.5	31.3	27.3
Average Time of Possession	27:25	28:06	28:29	27:11	28:30

1986 PLAYOFFS
Lost Wild Card Game to New York Jets, 15-35

THE 1988 SEASON

DATE	AT	OPPONENT	SCORE	R	SPREAD	Tu	Net YDS	Rush YDS	Pass YDS	TURN
09/04	H	Cleveland	3- 6	L	+4	a	149-337	60-142	89-195	2-1
09/11	A	Seattle	10-31	L	+7.5	a	286-263	50-156	236-107	6-1
09/18	H	Denver	20-13	W	+4.5	a	380-283	130- 70	250-213	0-3
09/25	H	San Diego	23-24	L	-6.5	a	331-303	94-165	237-138	2-1
10/02	A	N.Y. Jets	17-17	T	+5.5	a	385-542	124-272	261-270	2-4
10/09	A	Houston	6- 7	L	+5	a	184-230	65-206	119- 24	3-4
10/16	H	L.A. Raiders	17-27	L	-3.5	a	334-233	93-114	241-119	4-0
10/23	H	Detroit	6- 7	L	-6.5	a	171-215	61-127	110- 88	2-3
10/30	A	L.A. Raiders	10-17	L	+6.5	g	208-404	145-156	63-248	0-2
11/06	A	Denver	11-17	L	+8	g	273-308	90-131	183-177	3-2
11/13	H	Cincinnati	31-28	W	+6.5	a	418-307	142-150	276-157	0-2
11/20	H	Seattle	27-24	W	+1.5	a	365-313	162-105	203-208	2-2
11/27	A	Pittsburgh	10-16	L	+2	a	366-336	88-214	278-122	2-1
12/04	H	N.Y. Jets	38-34	W	-1.5	a	430-371	163-179	267-192	2-2
12/11	A	N.Y. Giants	12-28	L	+9.5	a	258-244	107-159	151- 85	1-1
12/18	A	San Diego	13-24	L	+1.5	g	306-337	139-246	167- 91	2-2
						Avg.	303-314	107-162	196-152	2-2

			WINS	LOSSES
Season Record:	4-11-1	POINTS:	29- 25	11- 19
Vs. Spread:	8- 8-0	Net YDS: 9- 7-0	398-319	261-292
Home:	4- 4-0	Rush YDS: 2-14-0	149-126	90-165
On Artificial Turf:	4- 8-1	Pass YDS: 12- 4-0	249-193	170-127
Art. Turf vs. Spread:	7- 6-0	TURN: 6- 6-4	1- 2	2- 2

THE FIRST PROBLEM

The Chiefs have a lot of problems, but most of them could be solved by doing something about the run—coming and going.

Everybody in the league knew they could run on Kansas City, and almost everybody did. Only once did the Chiefs hold an opponent to under 100 yards rushing. Only five times were foes held under 140. Yet eight opponents passed for fewer than 140 yards. That's impressive, but it ain't the way it's supposed to work.

Injuries were part of it, of course. Six players started at nose tackle during the season, and three of them ended on injured reserve. Bill Maas, the incumbent, was an '87 Pro Bowler and the anchor of the line. Linebacking was hit hard too, and—except for ILB Dino Hackett—that area was weak to start with. By December the regular outside backers were a couple of Charger castoffs, and we all know what defensive paradigms the Chargers have been for the last few years. The Chiefs gave up an average of 199.5 rushing yards in their last four games—and lost three of the four. Coach Frank Gansz was not long for Kansas City after that season-end collapse (he was replaced by Marty Schottenheimer); but come to think of it, the collapse may have come with the season's opening.

DE Neal Smith, the first draft choice, never played like it. DE Mike Bell missed thirty days for violating the league's drug policy. This was perhaps a step up; after all, Bell missed the whole '86 season when he served time for violating the nation's drug policy—like in dealing. Longtime Chief standout DE Art Still didn't get along with (that's a euphemism) the coach, so Gansz shuffled him off to Buffalo in training camp. If any of the other Kansas City players compared the Bills' record with the Chiefs', they probably started picking fights with Gansz the next day.

Anyway, KC opponents ran away from Hackett and right at everybody else. They could be sure of a nice chunk of yardage until they met up with somebody from the secondary, which ironically was one of the best in the business.

The Chiefs' defensive record was misleading. They didn't give up points in great gobs, just enough to lose. It takes longer to score by running the ball, but it also kept the Chiefs' impotent offense off the field. Three opponents scored seven or fewer points (all before Maas was kayoed, by the way) and *still* won. Each opponent had the same excuse for its point paucity: its regular QB was sidelined. Kansas City had no excuse.

The first order of business in Kansas City should be to find some help for Hackett, Maas (hopefully), and the secondary. If they could (a) stop the run and (b) pressure the opposing quarterback, they'd find their offense might climb all the way up to adequate.

THE INDISPENSABLE MAN

About the only thing the Chiefs did worse than defend against the run was run the ball themselves. They haven't had a real running game for years, and 1988 was no exception. They *thought* they could get by with Paul Palmer,

Herman Heard, and Christian Okoye. They were wrong. Palmer could be a useful runner-receiver if he can get back in the coaching staff's good graces, but he'll never be a heavy-duty guy. Heard is ordinary. Okoye isn't, but he missed nearly half the season with injuries. When he was available—and when the Chiefs used him—he gave the team a solid runner. In only four games did Okoye carry more than ten times. The Chiefs won three of them and tied the other one.

We all know the phony stat "When Stumblefoot gains 100 yards, his team wins 94.7 percent of the time." And we all know that Stumblefoot gained most of his yards in the fourth quarter, protecting a 20-point lead. We can say that the Chiefs won when Okoye ran the ball at least sixteen times. And those weren't fourth-quarter, run-out-the-clock jobs. The Chiefs trailed at the end of the third quarter in each.

WEEK	OKOYE ATTEMPTS	OKOYE YARDS	SCORE AT END 3rd Q	FINAL SCORE
5	12	51	3-10	17-17
7	10	55	7-14	17-27
8	9	33	6- 7	6- 7
9	9	32	7-14	10-17
10	7	22	8-14	11-17
11	16	102	19-28	31-28
12	17	52	14-17	27-24
13	9	58	7-10	10-16
14	16	68	21-27	38-34
	105	473		

Only once did Okoye gain over 100 yards in a game himself. But by giving the Chiefs a bona fide power runner, he pulled the defenses in and opened the way for Palmer or Heard to run wide. Even more important, he made the secondary conscious of run support, allowing QB Steve De-Berg to hit some long passes. In the "big four games," where Okoye ran at least 12 times, DeBerg threw 6 TD passes for 8, 17, 33, 40, 41, and 80 yards. DeBerg's passes gained 1,067 yards in those four games—an 8.74 yard-per-pass average, over two yards better than his average in the rest of the season.

In fairness, the Chiefs' offensive line was cut up a bit in 1988, but those things happen. The point is, everybody looked better when Okoye was used.

Just how far Okoye can go is hard to figure. He's huge—over 250 pounds—and fast. Moreover, he's still learning. A Nigerian native, he's only been playing football for five years. When he gets the hang of it, he could be something to behold. But did his '88 injuries signal a brittle ballplayer?

A healthy Okoye is a must in '89, though he needs help. With another dependable ground gainer and Palmer doing spot duty, the quarterbacks might begin looking pretty good.

THE DISPENSABLE MAN

One of the strong points on the team is wide receiver, where Stephone Paige and Carlos Carson are both fine—

when they get the ball. Bill Kenney started the season at QB and was benched because he couldn't get the ball into the endzone. Brought back later, he still couldn't. At midseason he had a streak of ten quarters without a touchdown of any kind and he never did throw a TD pass.

By comparison, the thirty-four-year-old DeBerg was a ball of fire. DeBerg has had an eleven-year career that gives new meaning to the term "checkered." Every place he's gone—San Francisco, Denver, Tampa Bay, and Kansas City—he's played reasonably well, with good stats. But he's been saddled with losing teams in all but two of those seasons. And in each case his team drafted a "franchise" quarterback who was handed the job over incumbent De-Berg. With the 49ers it was Joe Montana; in Denver it was John Elway; and in Tampa Bay Vinny Testaverde.

When he signed with Kansas City, he said, only half joking, "It means the next quarterback here will be the next Joe Namath out of college. It's almost guaranteed."

DeBerg won't make anybody forget Namath (or in KC, Len Dawson), but he's savvy, durable, enthusiastic, and a fair passer. He probably has two or three more years left, and if the Chiefs get him some support (like a running game), he can do the job.

THE WIN OF THE YEAR

The Chiefs were 1–8–1 after ten games, and the Bengals were 8–2. The only people who should have shown up were the ones who drove over from Cincinnati and the Kansas City undertakers. The 34,614 who actually did make it to Arrowhead Stadium saw just what they expected to for almost three quarters.

The Chiefs trailed 16–28 thirteen minutes into the third period when Nick Lowery kicked a 47-yard field goal, his fourth of the game. They were behind 19–28 with only 6:06 remaining when CB Albert Lewis blocked a Cincy punt out of the endzone for a safety; still behind 21–28 at 1:11 to go, when Okoye plunged for the tying touchdown.

With the Bengal offense, 1:11 was a lifetime to break the tie. But then reserve RB James Saxon knocked the ball loose from Cincy's Marc Logan on the kickoff and Lewis recovered. "I could almost see the red ribbons and the gift wrapping," Lewis said. With two seconds left Lowery kicked a 39-yard field goal. The Chiefs had—wait a minute, let's double check this—YES!

THE DISPENSED-WITH MAN

An unfunny thing happened to the Chiefs on their way to Pittsburgh. Palmer made a joke. A not-funny joke—actually a dumb joke—about fumbling a kickoff return to get the coaches fired. Pretty dumb, huh? But wait, instead of a fine, or a dressing down, or even a screaming tirade, Coach Gansz sent Palmer back to KC under suspension. So an incident that might have been minuscule became a THING. And by explaining the suspension was for unspecified "conduct detrimental to the team,'' Gansz left the situation open to wild guesses.

Naturally the story eventually came out. Palmer looked dumb. Gansz looked dumber for overreacting. Well, the only way it could have gotten worse was for Palmer to be reinstated the next week for the Jets game and then fumble a kickoff.

He was. He did. Twice!

THE CHIEF CHIEF

The whole Kansas City defensive secondary is exceptional. CB Albert Lewis is a major opportunist and partner Kevin Ross does a good job. SS Lloyd Burruss has been a Pro Bowler, and when he went down with shoulder and knee injuries in '88, rookie Kevin Porter was just fine as a fill-in.

The best of a very good lot is FS Deron Cherry, who made the Pro Bowl for the seventh season in a row. Not bad for an undrafted free agent who came to the Chiefs hoping to make it as a punter. At twenty-nine, he's still at the top of his game. In '88, he led the team in interceptions (7), fumble recoveries (6), and forced fumbles (4). In fact, he led the NFL in takeaways with his combined interceptions and recovered fumbles. He's *some* player.

Cherry also set a career high with 151 tackles. Of course, that's partly a reflection of the Chiefs' weakness up front— he shouldn't *have* to make that many tackles. The people at Cystic Fibrosis didn't complain; Deron donates money to them every time he drops an opponent.

KANSAS CITY CHIEFS STATISTICS

1988 TEAM STATISTICS	KC	OPP
TOTAL FIRST DOWNS	289	318
Rushing	104	162
Passing	161	136
Penalty	24	20
3rd Down Made/Att.	88/224	94/208
Pct.	39.3%	45.2%
4th Down Made/Att.	12/18	6/13
Pct.	66.7%	46.2%
TOTAL NET YARDS	4844	5026
Avg. per Game	302.8	314.1
Total Plays	1019	1042
Avg. per Play	4.8	4.8
NET YARDS RUSHING	1713	2592
Avg. per Game	107.1	162.0
Total Rushes	448	609
NET YARDS PASSING	3131	2434
Avg. per Game	195.7	152.1
Tackled/Yards Lost	43/353	23/157
Gross Yards	3484	2591
Attempts/Completions	528/282	410/214
Pct. of Completions	53.4%	52.2%
Had Intercepted	21	18
PUNTS/AVERAGE	76/40.3	63/40.2
NET PUNTING AVG.	31.9	34.2
PENALTIES/YARDS	85/636	106/854
FUMBLES/BALL LOST	21/12	30/13
TOUCHDOWNS	24	39
Rushing	8	23
Passing	16	12
Returns	0	4
TIME OF POSSESSION	28:31	32:26

SCORE/PERIODS	1	2	3	4	OT	TOTAL
Chiefs	51	74	47	82	0	254
Opponents	77	118	52	73	0	320

SCORING	TDR	TDP	TDRt	PAT	FG	S	TP
Lowery				23/23	27/32		104
Paige		7					42
Palmer	2	4					36
Carson		3					18
Okoye	3						18
Saxon	2						12

(Continued)

SCORING	TDR	TDP	TDRt	PAT	FG	S	TP
DeBerg	1						6
Harry		1					6
Hayes		1					6
Hackett						1	2
Lewis						1	2
Maas						1	2
Chiefs	8	16	0	23/24	27/32	3	254
Opponents	23	12	4	38/39	16/24	0	320

RUSHING	NO	YDS	AVG	LG	TD
Okoye	105	473	4.5	48	3
Palmer	134	452	3.4	26t	2
Heard	106	438	4.1	20	0
Saxon	60	236	3.9	14	2
Moriarty	20	62	3.1	9	0
DeBerg	18	30	1.7	13	1
Goodburn	1	15	15.0	15	0
Kenney	2	4	2.0	2	0
Taylor	1	2	2.0	2	0
Carson	1	1	1.0	1	0
Chiefs	448	1713	3.8	48	8
Opponents	609	2592	4.3	36	23

RECEIVING	NO	YDS	AVG	LG	TD
Paige	61	902	14.8	49	7
Palmer	53	611	11.5	71t	4
Carson	46	711	15.5	80t	3
Harry	26	362	13.9	38	1
Hayes	22	233	10.6	25	1
Heard	20	198	9.9	32	0
Saxon	19	177	9.3	22	0
Roberts	10	104	10.4	20	0
Taylor	9	105	11.7	36	0
Okoye	8	51	6.4	12	0
Moriarty	6	40	6.7	12	0
Colbert	1	-3	-3.0	-3	0
Gamble	1	-7	-7.0	-7	0
Chiefs	282	3484	12.4	30t	16
Opponents	214	2591	12.1	42t	12

INTERCEPTIONS	NO	YDS	AVG	LG	TD
Cherry	7	51	7.3	24	0
Burruss	2	57	28.5	32	0

(Continued)

INTERCEPTIONS	NO	YDS	AVG	LG	TD
J.Pearson	2	8	4.0	7	0
Hill	1	24	24.0	24	0
Lewis	1	19	19.0	19	0
Stensrud	1	5	5.0	5	0
Gamble	1	2	2.0	2	0
Cofield	1	0	0.0	0	0
Del Rio	1	0	0.0	0	0
Ross	1	0	0.0	0	0
Chiefs	18	166	9.2	32	0
Opponents	21	206	9.8	31	1

PUNTING	NO	YDS	AVG	TB	In 20	LG	Blk
Goodburn	76	3059	40.3	8	10	59	0
Chiefs	76	3059	40.3	8	10	59	0
Opponents	63	2531	40.2	8	17	61	1

PUNT RETURNS	NO	FC	YDS	AVG	LG	TD
Taylor	29	6	187	6.4	16	0
Hollis	3	0	28	9.3	15	0
Chiefs	32	6	216	6.7	16	0
Opponents	48	3	473	9.9	31	0

KICKOFF RETURNS	NO	YDS	AVG	LG	TD
Palmer	23	364	15.8	23	0
Gamble	15	291	19.4	31	0
Hollis	6	106	17.7	28	0
Taylor	5	80	16.0	19	0
Ingram	2	16	8.0	9	0
Jenkins	2	12	6.0	12	0
Saxon	2	40	20.0	27	0
Porter	1	16	16.0	16	0
Chiefs	56	925	16.5	31	0
Opponents	57	1380	24.2	98t	2

FIELD GOALS	1-19	20-29	30-39	40-49	50+	TOTAL
Lowery	0-0	7-8	9-11	8-10	3-3	27-32
Chiefs	0-0	7-8	9-11	8-10	3-3	27-32
Opponents	2-2	5-5	4-6	5-9	0-2	16-24

FIELD GOALS BY Lowery: 27 of 32
(33G)(27G)(50G,29G)( )(34G)(28G,51G)(43G)
(38G,43G)(39N,45G)(46G,29G,34G)(37G,35G,
23G,47G,39G)(34G,40G)(26G)(43N,21G)(29N,
31G,51G,46G,41G)(48N,35N)

PASSING	ATT	COM	YARD	PCT.	Avg G	TD	%TD	IN	%IN	LG	SAKS/YDS	RATE
DeBerg	414	224	2935	54.1	7.09	16	3.9	16	3.9	80t	30/246	73.5
Kenney	114	58	549	50.9	4.82	0	0.0	5	4.4	25	13/107	46.3
Chiefs	528	282	3484	53.4	6.60	16	3.0	21	4.0	80t	43/353	67.6
Opponents	410	214	2591	52.2	6.32	12	2.9	18	4.4	42t	23/157	63.4

LOS ANGELES RAIDERS

The Last 5 Seasons

	1984	1985	1986	1987	1988
Won-Lost	11-5	12-4	8-8	5-10	7-9
Percentage	.688	.750	.500	.333	.438
Division Finish	3	1	4	4	3
Games Behind	2	0	3	5.5	2
Total Points	368	354	323	301	325
Per Game	23.0	22.1	20.2	20.1	20.3
Opponent Points	278	308	346	289	369
Per Game	17.4	19.3	21.6	19.3	23.1
Net Points	90	46	-23	12	-44
Predicted Net Wins	2.3	1.1	-0.6	0.3	-1.1
Delta Net Wins	0.8	2.8	0.6	-2.8	0.1
Total Yards on Offense	5244	5408	5299	5267	4961
Per Game	327.8	338.0	331.2	351.1	310.1
Total Yards Allowed on Defense	4644	4603	4804	4364	5379
Per Game	290.3	287.7	300.3	290.9	336.2
Net Difference	600	805	495	903	-418
Offensive Turnovers	48	38	49	31	33
Defensive Takeaways	34	30	38	28	34
Net Turnovers	-14	-8	-11	-3	1
Predicted Net Points	-6	35	-3	63	-31
Delta Net Points	96	11	-20	-51	-13
Net Rushing Yards	1886	2262	1790	2197	1852
Per Game	117.9	141.4	111.9	146.5	115.8
Average Gain	3.7	4.3	3.8	4.6	3.8
Opponent Net Rushing Yards	1892	1605	1728	1637	2208
Per Game	118.3	100.3	108.0	109.1	138.0
Average Gain	3.7	3.5	3.9	3.5	4.1
Net Passing Yards	3358	3146	3509	3070	3109
Per Game	209.9	196.6	219.3	204.7	194.3
Times Sacked	54	43	64	53	46
Passer Rating in Yards	4.2	4.1	4.5	4.8	4.5
Opponent Net Passing Yards	2752	2998	3076	2727	3171
Per Game	172.0	187.4	192.3	181.8	198.2
Times Sacked	64	65	63	44	40
Passer Rating Defense	3.6	4.3	3.8	5.0	5.0
Passer Rating Net	0.7	-0.1	0.7	-0.1	-0.6
Yards per Drive Offense	23.7	24.8	24.8	28.8	23.1
Yards per Drive Defense	20.4	21.1	21.8	24.0	25.9
Average Time of Possession	29:26	30:26	30:40	30:45	29:30

1984 PLAYOFFS
Lost Wild Card Game to Seattle, 7-13

1985 PLAYOFFS
Lost Divisional Playoff to New England, 20-27

THE 1988 SEASON

DATE	AT	OPPONENT	SCORE	R	SPREAD	Tu	Net YDS	Rush YDS	Pass YDS	TURN
09/04	H	San Diego	24-13	W	-6	g	277-263	94-111	183-152	1-1
09/11	A	Houston	35-38	L	+2.5	a	158-406	74-156	84-250	3-3
09/18	H	L.A. Rams	17-22	L	+1	g	408-313	103-140	305-173	1-1
09/26	A*	Denver	30-27	W	+6	g	363-398	128-189	235-209	1-5
10/02	H	Cincinnati	21-45	L	+1.5	g	405-496	96-164	309-332	5-1
10/09	H	Miami	14-24	L	-2	g	356-266	78- 91	278-175	5-1
10/16	A	Kansas City	27-17	W	+3.5	a	233-334	114- 93	119-241	0-4
10/23	A	New Orleans	6-20	L	+4.5	a	367-317	185-190	182-127	3-0
10/30	A	Kansas City	17-10	W	-6.5	g	404-208	156-145	248- 63	2-0
11/06	A	San Diego	13- 3	W	-3	g	306-216	149- 63	157-153	2-3
11/13	A	S. Francisco	9- 3	W	+7	g	251-219	159- 83	92-136	1-2
11/20	H	Atlanta	6-12	L	-7.5	g	212-280	65-130	147-150	3-2
11/28	A*	Seattle	27-35	L	+3	a	257-459	113-247	144-212	2-5
12/04	H	Denver	21-20	W	-1.5	g	216-347	129- 50	87-297	2-3
12/11	A	Buffalo	21-37	L	+6	a	318-367	111-255	207-112	3-0
12/18	H	Seattle	37-43	L	-2.5	g	441-490	110-101	331-389	1-3
						Avg.	311-336	117-138	194-198	2-2

			WINS	LOSSES
Season Record:	7- 9-0	POINTS:	20- 13	20- 31
Vs. Spread:	6-10-0	Net YDS: 7- 9-0	293-284	325-377
Home:	3- 5-0	Rush YDS: 6-10-0	133-105	104-164
On Artificial Turf:	1- 4-0	Pass YDS: 8- 8-0	160-179	221-213
Art. Turf vs. Spread:	1- 4-0	TURN: 7- 6-3	1- 3	3- 2

* Monday Night

AL, AS IN H(AL)L

As you know, Al Davis is a genius. It says that in various words in the Raiders' *Press Guide,* and the sentiment's been writ by so many news scriveners that it must be true. Of course since the Raiders have fallen on hard times of late, a few of those fair-weather sycophants have chosen to flank genius by quotation marks, as in "genius," the printed equivalent of a knowing wink.

An alternate theory holds that Davis *was* a genius but *is* no longer. He's spent so much time in the courts of our land that his IQ has dipped. Maybe they should extend the inscription over the door: "Justice for All; Caution, may prove hazardous to mental health."

It used to be whether Al belonged in MENSA or a lite beer commercial was secondary to whether his team belonged in Oakland or Los Angeles or Irwindale. Or wherever the grass was greener. It was suggested the Raiders would someday become the NFL's first Brazilian franchise. The team's odyssey in search of peace, contentment, and big bucks colored the way just about everybody thought of Al. If he was coming to your burg, he was Mr. Nice Guy. If he was leaving, he was the Prince of Darkness. If your town wasn't involved, you took sides anyway. Who knew where he'd be next year?

Well, the last we heard, the Raiders were going to live and die in L.A. for the foreseeable future. And in that

they've been mostly dying, at least in the standings, this seems like a good time to ruminate on whether Al belongs in the Hall of Fame. After all, we are unlikely to be swayed in the next few seasons by the emotional high of watching Al accept another Lombardi Trophy.

A bust of Al in Canton is anathema to people who'd prefer to bust him in the nose, but he has indeed been under consideration for the last couple of years. Whether he finally makes it will be up to the consideration of the thirty electors who choose for the Hall. But whether he *should* make it, or is *worthy*, must be left to someone with Solomon-like objectivity.

Us.

We've given this question our deepest consideration for hours on end and sometimes standing up. We've come to a conclusion. But first let us tell you how judiciously we arrived at it.

Just being a genius won't get Al in. The smartest guys in football are agents. They make the most dollars for the least sweat. At the same time there are busts in the Hall of Fame with sharper brainwaves than ever undulated through the craniums of the guys they depict.

Owning a winning team won't get him in either. No owner ever had a better year than Miami's Joe Robbie in 1972, but so far there've been no grassroots "Go-for-Joe" rallies. The fact that the Raiders are 261–130–11 since Davis took over (do you remember he started as their coach in 1963?) won't get him in the same Hall with Charley Bidwill, whose Cardinals were 38–107–8 back when they were the *Chicago* Cardinals.

Challenging the system and beating it won't elect Al. When he shoved the NFL into court and proved he could take his team anywhere he damned well pleased, a lot of crack-of-doom types said he'd destroy the game. He didn't. Whether the Davis revolt will ultimately prove good or bad for the NFL won't really be known until the next century, but it did change things some. Nevertheless if changing things got you in the Hall of Fame, they'd elect Fred Gehrke, who designed the first helmet logo (for the Rams). Think how those little team emblems have changed merchandising!

We'd just about decided that what *would* get Davis or anybody else into the Hall was one of those Great Unanswered Questions of the NFL, like why do the Steelers have their logo on only one side? Or why don't the Browns have any at all?

And then it hit us. Hall of *Fame!*

Not Hall of Great or Hall of Good or even Hall of Adequate. Fame! In the past twenty-five years, what NFL type has been most often in our minds? Al Davis! Players and coaches have their seasons, but they retire or get fired. How many owners have there been who were around for a quarter century? And how many could you name anyway? In the realm of "Fame," only Rozelle compares—and he's already in.

We know the difference between *famous* and *infamous.* Benedict Arnold isn't in the Hall of Great Americans and Joe Jackson has been excluded from Cooperstown. But Davis never gave away West Point or threw a World Series.

And so, as pro football's most legendary, compelling, visible, and famous personality of his time, Davis certainly belongs in the Hall of Fame. In fact the place is a little less credible without him.

Our next project will be George Steinbrenner for Cooperstown.

THE COST OF CATCHING

We wonder if anyone is sitting around Raiders headquarters right now saying, "Hey, Al, you know what we oughta do? Go out and spend some more money on wide receivers!"

Last season it looked like the Raiders were going to corner the market on expensive pass catchers. In the WR class, they started with Canadian star Mervyn Fernandez and Chris Woods on the roster from '87. Then they drafted Heisman Trophy winner Tim Brown from Notre Dame and later Penn State's Mike Anderson. Next they got James Lofton from Green Bay, and finally they signed Willie Gault away from the Bears. We forgot to mention Todd Christensen among those previously present. Although listed as a tight end, when viewed from the back the 230-pound Chris-

tensen qualifies as a very wide receiver. Add in TE's Trey Junkin and Andy Parker.

For most folks the big question regarding the employment of all this pass catching talent was where would they find enough footballs to satisfy them? Not for us. We had a better question: how much were the Raiders going to pay per catch?

Well, the tallies are in. You probably want to know which Raider receiver was the biggest bargain. Would you believe Steve Smith?

Who? In case you've forgotten, Smith is a running back. All right, he's easy to miss in there with the likes of Bo Jackson and Marcus Allen. Smith was the third-most-used runner, with 38 carries. But his running was just a bonus, like a hobby. Considered strictly as a pass receiver, Smith caught 26, for which he received a 1988 salary of $147,000. That's $5,653.85 per catch, practically bargain-basement.

Oh, you think that it's unfair to lump running backs, who do other important things, in with people who are paid strictly to catch. Okay, let's only count them.

Alexander and Woods were paid $270,000 between them and didn't catch any. It wasn't their fault; they spent the season on IR.

The tight ends cost like hell. But they also threw some blocks. Probably. Christensen was hurt much of the season, but Coach Mike Shanahan had already lessened the TE's pass-catching role in the Raider attack.

PLAYER	PC	SALARY	PER CATCH
Todd Christensen	15	$750,000	$50,000.00
Trey Junkin	4	185,000	46,250.00
Andy Parker	4	175,000	43,750.00

PLAYER	PC	SALARY	PER CATCH
Willie Gault	16	$ 700,000	$43,750.00
Tim Brown	43	1,200,000	27,906.98
James Lofton	28	725,000	25,892.86
Mervyn Fernandez	31	350,000	11,290.32

By comparison the WRs (real ones) came pretty cheap. The cumulative figures? The envelope, please.

Not counting Smith or Jackson or Allen or a couple of others whose job descriptions come under RB, the Raiders paid $4,344,000.00 last year for people who were supposed to catch passes. For the money, the Raiders got 141 pass receptions. That's an average of $30,808.51 per catch. Maybe Al Davis should have asked for bids.

The most valuable people in the Raiders organization were the quarterbacks who contrived to save the organization scads of money by completing only 44.2 percent of their passes. If they'd been more accurate, the team might have gone broke.

BO'S HOBBY

After two years of it, we kind of take Bo Jackson's double career for granted. When he first announced his decision to try both, there was a lot of comment, most of it leading to the conclusion that it couldn't be done. Or if it could be done, it couldn't be done very well.

Bo proved them wrong. His baseball career is progressing nicely, thank you. He strikes out a lot—someone said he "plays hit-or-miss baseball"—but he's slugged 20-plus home runs in each of his two full seasons. He only plays half seasons in football because the baseball season runs into October now. Every year Al Davis prays the Kansas City Royals don't win the pennant. But when he's in a Raider uniform he's sensational. Davis isn't the only one who longs to see what he might do over a sixteen-game schedule.

We took his 1987 season, when he played in seven games, and his '88 season, when he played in ten, and projected his figures over sixteen games for each year.

	RUSHING				PASSING				SCORE
	ATT	YDS	AVG	TD	PC	YDS	AVG	TD	PTS
1987	185	1266	6.8	9	37	311	8.4	5	84
1988	218	928	4.3	5	14	126	9.0	0	30
	403	2194	5.4	14	51	437	8.6	5	114

Okay, we didn't allow for injuries, but don't you think he'd have done a little better with the benefit of training camp? It strikes us that he might be well on his way to a Hall of Fame career.

It's been many years since an athlete attempted to play major league baseball and football in the same year. The last time was in 1954, when Vic Janowicz, the only other Heisman Trophy winner to play major league baseball, was a substitute third baseman for the Pittsburgh Pirates. He batted only .151 in 41 games. He performed better as a halfback for the Washington Redskins, but certainly did not star that year.

Jim Thorpe did it as a regular thing in the years before the NFL was formed, but his last major league baseball season was 1919. Of the approximately sixty athletes who played both major league baseball and football since 1920, a surprising twenty-three did it in the same year. Almost all of these multiple efforts were made in the early decades, when the baseball and football seasons did not overlap as much as they do now.

MAJOR LEAGUE BASEBALL AND FOOTBALL IN THE SAME SEASON

				TOTAL			TOTAL
		BASEBALL		ML BB	FOOTBALL		ML FB
YEAR	PLAYER	POS	TEAM, LG	YEARS	POS	TEAM, LG	YEARS
1920	Al Pierotti	P	Boston NL	2	C-Q	Cleveland APFA	7
1920	Tom Whelan	1B	Boston NL	1	E	Canton APFA	2
1921	Joe "Nig" Berry	2B	New York NL	2	HB	Rochester APFA	1
1922	John Mohardt	2B	Detroit AL	1	HB	Chi. Cards NFL	5
1923	Dick Reichle	OF	Boston AL	2	E	Milwaukee NFL	1
1924	Hoge Workman	P	Boston AL	1	HB	Cleveland NFL	3
1925	Bill Bedford	2B	Cleveland AL	1	E	Rochester, NFL	1
1925	Charlie Berry	C	Philadelphia AL	11	E	Pottsville NFL	2
1925	Walter French	OF	Philadelphia AL	6	HB	Pottsville NFL	2
1925	Chuck Corgan	IF	Brooklyn NL	-	E	Kans. City NFL	-
1927	" "	"	" "	2	E	N.Y. Giants NFL	4
1925	Ernie Vick	C	St. Louis NL	4	C	Detroit NFL	3
1926	Garland Buckeye	P	Cleveland AL	5	G	Chicago AFL	6
1926	Ernie Nevers	P	St. Louis AL	-	FB	Duluth NFL	-
1927	" "	"	" "	3	"	" "	5
1927	Pid Purdy	OF	Chicago AL	4	B	Green Bay NFL	2
1927	Richard Smith	C	New York NL	1	B	Green Bay NFL	5
1928	Bruce Caldwell	OF	Cleveland AL	2	HB	N.Y. Giants NFL	1
1930	Red Badgro	OF	St. Louis AL	2	E	N.Y. Giants NFL	9
1931	John Scalzi	PH	Boston NL	1	B	Brooklyn NFL	1
1937	Ace Parker	SS	Philadelphia AL	-	QB	Brooklyn NFL	-
1938	" "	"	" "	2	"	" "	7
1943	Bert Kuczynski	P	Philadelphia AL	1	E	Detroit NFL	2
1945	Steve Filipowicz	OF	New York NL	3	QB	N.Y. Giants NFL	2
1948	Pete Layden	OF	St. Louis AL	1	HB	New York AAFC	3
1954	Vic Janowicz	3B	Pittsburgh NL	2	HB	Washington NFL	2

This list reminds us of our favorite baseball trivia question. The next time the guy at the end of the bar is going on about who was on deck when Bobby Thomson hit his home run and who played shortstop for the St. Louis Browns in 1944, you can stop him dead with this one: What *three* Hall of Fame members hit home runs in their first major league at bat?

He'll probably know slugging outfielder Earl Averill and knuckleball pitcher Hoyt Wilhelm, both of whom are ensconced in Cooperstown, but he'll never come up with Clarence "Ace" Parker, an enshrinee in the *Pro Football* Hall of Fame.

LOS ANGELES RAIDERS STATISTICS

1988 TEAM STATISTICS	LAR	OPP
TOTAL FIRST DOWNS	283	310
Rushing	116	124
Passing	145	165
Penalty	22	21
3rd Down Made/Att.	71/220	88/232
Pct.	32.3%	37.9%
4th Down Made/Att.	10/18	8/11
Pct.	55.6%	72.7%
TOTAL NET YARDS	4961	5379
Avg. per Game	310.1	336.2
Total Plays	1035	1056
Avg. per Play	4.8	5.1
NET YARDS RUSHING	1852	2208
Avg. per Game	115.8	138.0
Total Rushes	493	—
NET YARDS PASSING	3109	3171
Avg. per Game	194.3	198.2
Tackled/Yards Lost	46/394	40/300
Gross Yards	3503	3471
Attempts/Completions	496/219	483/265
Pct. of Completions	44.2%	54.9%
Had Intercepted	20	17
PUNTS/AVERAGE	91/41.8	94/41.4
NET PUNTING AVG.	35.7	34.7
PENALTIES/YARDS	102/762	94/823
FUMBLES/BALL LOST	33/13	31/17
TOUCHDOWNS	39	41
Rushing	15	17
Passing	21	23
Returns	3	1
TIME OF POSSESSION	—	—

SCORE/PERIODS	1	2	3	4	OT	TOTAL
Raiders	56	91	68	107	3	325
Opponents	58	138	73	100	0	369

SCORING	TDR	TDP	TDRt	PAT	FG	S	TP
Bahr				37/39	18/29		91
Smith	3	6					54
Allen	7	1					48
T. Brown	1	5	1				42
Fernandez		4					24
Jackson	3						18
Gault		2					12
Junkin		2					12
Townsend			2				12
Schroeder	1						6
Strachan		1					6
Raiders	15	21	3	37/39	18/29	0	325
Opponents	17	23	1	40/41	27/29	1	369

RUSHING	NO	YDS	AVG	LG	TD
Allen	223	831	3.7	32	7
Jackson	136	580	4.3	25	3

(Continued) RUSHING	NO	YDS	AVG	LG	TD
Smith	38	162	4.3	21	3
Schroeder	29	109	3.8	12	1
Mueller	17	60	3.5	13	0
T. Brown	14	50	3.6	12	1
Beuerlein	30	35	1.2	20	0
Strachan	4	12	3.0	5	0
Fernandez	1	9	9.0	9	0
Gault	1	4	4.0	4	0
Raiders	493	1852	3.8	32	15
Opponents	533	2208	4.1	73	17

RECEIVING	NO	YDS	AVG	LG	TD
T. Brown	43	725	16.9	65	5
Allen	34	303	8.9	30	1
Fernandez	31	805	26.0	85	4
Lofton	28	549	19.6	57	0
Smith	26	299	11.5	45	6
Gault	16	392	24.5	57	2
Christensen	15	190	12.7	22	0
Jackson	9	79	8.8	27	0
Mueller	5	63	12.6	28	0
Parker	4	33	8.3	12	0
Junkin	4	25	6.3	9	2
Strachan	3	19	6.3	13	1
Beuerlein	1	21	21.0	21	0
Raiders	219	3503	16.0	85	21
Opponents	265	3471	13.1	86	23

INTERCEPTIONS	NO	YDS	AVG	LG	TD
Haynes	3	30	10.0	30	0
McElroy	3	17	5.7	13	0
Price	2	18	9.0	18	0
Fellows	2	14	7.0	14	0
Anderson	2	-6	-3.0	2	0
Townsend	1	86	86.0	86	1
Long	1	73	73.0	73	0
McKenzie	1	26	26.0	26	0
Lee	1	20	20.0	20	0
Washington	1	2	2.0	2	0
Raiders	17	278	16.4	86	1
Opponents	20	219	11.0	48	0

PUNTING	NO	YDS	AVG	TB	In 20	LG	Blk
Gossett	91	3804	41.8	8	26	58	0
Raiders	91	3804	41.8	8	26	58	0
Opponents	94	3889	41.4	7	22	70	0

PUNT RETURNS	NO	FC	YDS	AVG	LG	TD
T. Brown	49	10	444	9.1	36	0
Adams	6	0	45	7.5	17	0
Raiders	55	10	489	8.9	36	0
Opponents	47	19	397	8.4	30	0

KICKOFF RETURNS	NO	YDS	AVG	LG	TD
T. Brown	41	1098	26.8	97	1
Adams	8	132	16.5	21	0
Mueller	5	97	29.4	25	0
Smith	3	46	15.3	16	0
Toran	2	0	0.0	0	0
Woods	1	20	20.0	20	0
Carter	1	14	14.0	14	0
Raiders	62	1407	22.7	97	1
Opponents	61	1299	21.3	65	0

FIELD GOALS	1-19	20-29	30-39	40-49	50+	TOTAL
Bahr	1-1	7-7	3-7	6-10	1-4	18-29
Raiders	1-1	7-7	3-7	6-10	1-4	18-29
Opponents	1-1	7-7	9-10	9-9	1-2	27-29

FIELD GOALS BY Bahr: 18 of 29
(41N,25G)(48N)(30N,49N,29G)(28G,44G,35G)
( )(55N)( )(50N)(42G,32N)(36G,47N,29G)(45G,
50G,19G)(49N,42G,31G)(46G,46G,31N)( )(53N)
(26G,28G,24G)

PASSING	ATT	COM	YARD	PCT.	Avg G	TD	%TD	IN	%IN	LG	SAKS/YDS	RATE
Schroeder	256	113	1839	44.1	7.18	13	5.1	13	5.1	85	19/178	64.6
Beuerlein	238	105	1643	44.1	6.90	8	3.4	7	2.9	57	26/215	66.6
Allen	2	1	21	50.0	10.50	0	0.0	0	0.0	21	1/1	87.5
Raiders	496	219	3503	44.2	7.06	21	4.2	20	4.0	85	46/394	65.6
Opponents	483	265	3471	54.9	7.19	23	4.8	17	3.5	86	40/300	79.0

MIAMI DOLPHINS

The Last 5 Seasons

	1984	1985	1986	1987	1988
Won-Lost	14-2	12-4	8-8	8-7	6-10
Percentage	.875	.750	.500	.533	.375
Division Finish	1	1	3	2-t	5
Games Behind	0	0	3	1	6
Total Points	513	428	430	362	319
Per Game	32.1	26.8	26.9	24.1	19.9
Opponent Points	298	320	405	335	380
Per Game	18.6	20.0	25.3	22.3	23.8
Net Points	215	108	25	27	-61
Predicted Net Wins	5.4	2.7	0.6	0.7	-1.5
Delta Net Wins	0.6	1.3	-0.6	-0.2	-0.5
Total Yards on Offense	6936	5843	6324	5538	5721
Per Game	433.5	365.2	395.3	369.2	357.6
Total Yards Allowed on Defense	5420	5767	6050	5445	5781
Per Game	338.8	360.4	378.1	363.0	361.3
Net Difference	1516	76	274	93	-60
Offensive Turnovers	28	41	37	37	35
Defensive Takeaways	36	41	27	32	31
Net Turnovers	8	0	-10	-5	-4
Predicted Net Points	158	6	-17	-12	-21
Delta Net Points	57	102	42	39	-40
Net Rushing Yards	1918	1729	1545	1662	1205
Per Game	119.9	108.1	96.6	110.8	75.3
Average Gain	4.0	3.9	4.4	4.1	3.6
Opponent Net Rushing Yards	2155	2256	2493	2198	2506
Per Game	134.7	141.0	155.8	146.5	156.6
Average Gain	4.7	4.4	4.6	4.4	4.5
Net Passing Yards	5018	4114	4779	3876	4516
Per Game	313.6	257.1	298.7	258.4	282.3
Times Sacked	14	19	17	13	7
Passer Rating in Yards	8.0	5.8	6.4	5.5	6.0
Opponent Net Passing Yards	3265	3511	3557	3247	3275
Per Game	204.1	219.4	222.3	216.5	204.7
Times Sacked	42	38	33	21	24
Passer Rating Defense	4.1	5.1	6.2	5.3	5.3
Passer Rating Net	4.0	0.7	0.2	0.2	0.7
Yards per Drive Offense	36.5	29.8	34.4	30.6	32.1
Yards per Drive Defense	29.5	29.6	32.5	30.6	32.3
Average Time of Possession	30:18	30:17	29:24	29:43	27:01

THE 1988 SEASON

DATE	AT	OPPONENT	SCORE	R	SPREAD	Tu	Net YDS	Rush YDS	Pass YDS	TURN
09/04	A	Chicago	7-34	L	+3.5	g	163-427	45-262	118-165	2-0
09/11	A	Buffalo	6- 9	L	+3	a	334-319	115-104	219-215	2-4
09/18	H	Green Bay	24-17	W	-10	g	354-338	98- 78	256-260	3-0
09/25	A	Indianapolis	13-15	L	+2.5	a	323-304	71-213	252- 91	2-1
10/02	H	Minnesota	24- 7	W	+3	g	342-353	78- 58	264-295	3-4
10/09	H	L.A. Raiders	24-14	W	+2	g	266-356	91- 78	175-278	1-5
10/16	H	San Diego	31-28	W	-9.5	g	375-396	46-113	329-283	1-4
10/23	H	N.Y. Jets	30-44	L	-6.5	g	584-333	63-159	521-174	6-1
10/30	A	Tampa Bay	17-14	W	-4	g	309-362	43- 79	266-283	0-5
11/06	H	New England	10-21	L	+3.5	a	437-277	78-203	359- 74	2-1
11/14	H*	Buffalo	6-31	L	+1	g	257-416	33-205	224-211	3-0
11/20	H	New England	3- 6	L	-3	g	293-236	124-170	169- 66	0-0
11/27	A	N.Y. Jets	34-38	L	+2.5	a	440-597	87-171	353-426	1-2
12/04	H	Indianapolis	28-31	L	+2.5	g	362-322	58-221	304-101	2-0
12/12	H*	Cleveland	38-31	W	+5	g	497-353	93- 87	404-266	4-3
12/18	A	Pittsburgh	24-40	L	+2.5	a	385-404	82-305	303- 99	3-1
						Avg.	358-362	75-157	282-205	2-2

					WINS	LOSSES
Season Record:	6-10-0		POINTS:		26- 19	16- 27
Vs. Spread:	4-11-1		Net YDS:	8- 8-0	357-360	358-364
Home:	4- 4-0		Rush YDS:	5-11-0	75- 82	76-201
On Artificial Turf:	0- 5-0		Pass YDS:	10- 6-0	282-278	282-162
Art. Turf vs. Spread:	1- 3-1		TURN:	6- 9-1	2- 4	2- 1

* Monday Night

THE LESSER EVIL

If you took Woody Hayes' old three-yards-and-a-cloud-of-dust offense and turned it upside down, you'd have the Miami Dolphins. The Dolphs threw 65 percent of the time in 1988 and nearly 80 percent of their offensive yards came via the air. Never before was there an NFL team with its attack so skewed toward the pass. There still hasn't been a *successful* NFL team that passed so much.

The '88 Dolphs had a record that sounds like a basketball player, 6–10, and generally were referred to as Don Shula's poorest team even by their friends. Among other things they had a five-game losing streak and did not win a game in their division—both firsts for Shula.

So what was wrong with Shula? Is the old fox, long regarded as the best coach in pro football, finally losing it? Along with the other legends, Landry and Noll, he was trashed a bit last year. Maybe not so much as the other two, but still . . .

We'll get to that later. For now we'll just say that you'd have to look far and near to find a coach who could have done as well with the pass-happy Dolphins of '88. What other coach would have had the courage to throw caution to the winds and—uh—throw? See, Miami doesn't pass the ball *instead* of running it; they pass *because of the way* they run it.

Lousy!

Oh, sure, you're saying. The Miami rushers had low yardage totals because they almost never had a chance to run. Well, you're wrong. Think about it. Every Miami opponent had to look for the pass on nearly every down. They read the figures. They knew that the Dolphins would throw two passes for every once they ran. Now in that situation, you expect Miami to have low rushing *totals* but high rushing *averages*. Remember, the secondary doesn't dare come up fast, the linebackers are backing up at the snap, and the line has its mind set on sacking the quarterback. You should be able to hand off to a palm tree and have it gain five yards. The Miami runners averaged 3.5 yards. Actually, "runners" is hyperbole.

Just imagine what those guys would have averaged if the defense had been looking for them!

Here's an example: in the last game of the season, Pittsburgh's defenders were going in reverse on every snap, so on the Dolphs' second series, Miami RB Ron Davenport ran around right end. He was 64 yards downfield before the Steelers took him seriously and tackled him on the four. On the next play, Lorenzo Hampton bumped into the endzone while nine Steelers covered receivers. The Dolphins had 68 rushing yards with more than fifty-six minutes to go. Do you know how much they rushed for in the entire rest of the whole game? Fourteen yards! For a sparkling 0.8 average per carry.

So there was Shula, lumbered with the worst running game since the invention of the gauntlet. At the same time he happened to have on his team the best football thrower ever. An ordinary coach would have thrown half the time, maybe 55 percent. And would have lost twelve games.

WHY AN EVIL?

Of course, just because Shula chose to pass most of the time doesn't mean it was a good choice. He didn't have any good choices. One of the things they make you do before you get your NFL coach's license is sign a Balanced Offense Oath. In it you swear that, whenever possible, you'll run about as often as you pass. Well, naturally, it's always *possible* to do that (until you get fired), but the survivors have learned to interpret "possible" as "reasonable." It wasn't reasonable for Miami in 1988 to run half the time. How many third-and-eights could they take?

In the best-of-all-possible-offenses, a team would run about 65–75 percent of the time. The running attack controls the ball, drives are sustained, and when the occasional pass is used, it usually goes for a long gain. To make it work, you need a big, versatile line, whippet wide receivers who can go deep, a tight end who can block and catch, a quarterback with excellent accuracy on long or short passes, one versatile running back who can run wide, catch, and occasionally nip through the line, and a powerful fullback who can get the necessary short yardage. If it sounds like we're describing the Cincinnati Bengals of last year or the Miami Dolphins of fifteen years ago, we are. The X's and O's for those two teams were different, but the offensive personnel matched up very similarly.

Before we go on, a quick word about some of those big college teams from out where it's flat. They can run on almost every play—85–90 percent of the time—because (1) they far outclass most of their opponents, (2) they have about seven guys lined up to play every position, and (3) they never, ever face a defense as big and fast as any second-rate pro defense. Oh, and (4) they don't have to worry much about the other side getting a couple of touchdowns ahead.

But back to Miami '88. They just didn't have the full complement to run a best-of-all-possible-offenses offense. Few pro teams do. So most of the NFL teams hope for a nicely balanced offense, with both running and passing somewhere in the 45–55 percent range. Given adequacy at all points and better-than-average performances from one or two parts, they can be successful.

Alas! Miami didn't have adequacy at all points. The Dolphins had a great quarterback, excellent receivers, a line that was only fair, and inadequate runners. So, backed up against a wall, Shula skewed his offense to passing 65 per-

cent of the time. The sad fact is that a run-skewed offense or a balanced offense, when they have the right personnel, will score more points than a pass-skewed offense with the best passer in the world.

PROVING THE POINT(S)

We'll bet you find that a little bit hard to swallow. You probably figured it was an immutable law of nature (except in Nebraska and Oklahoma) that throwing passes equaled points and running the ball equaled scoreless ties. That's what Daddy taught you when you sat at his knee.

Maybe you heard him wrong. A pass-skewed attack, in the right hands, produces one helluva lot of OFFENSE. But most of it is between the two 30-yard-lines. A pass-skewed offense coupled with an average defense will typically outgain an opponent while losing to him. Even Miami, which had a definitely below-average defense, outgained half of its opponents.

One way to rate the efficiency of an attack is to see how many plays it takes, on average, to score a touchdown. The fewer plays-per-TD, the more efficient the offense. It's a simple calculation. Take all the plays from scrimmage—rush attempts, pass attempts, and sacks—and divide by the number of touchdowns scored rushing and passing. Throw out field goals because they are most often a surrender by the offense.

We haven't checked every NFL team that ever was, but of those we've looked at, the record seems to be the 1941 Chicago Bears, with 14.1 plays-per-touchdown. The Bears ran 495 times (71 percent), threw 196 passes (sacks were counted as rushing attempts at that time), and scored 49 touchdowns in an eleven-game season. They were definitely a run-skewed team, but that was long ago, when only a few teams passed much at all.

By comparison, in 1981, when Air-Coryell was at its height in San Diego, the Chargers ran 481 times (43 percent), passed (including sacks) 648 times, and scored 60 touchdowns in a sixteen-game season. Their plays-per-touchdown was 18.8. You're probably astonished to learn that Air-C only passed about 57 percent of the time. It seemed like more at the time. Perhaps you forgot that the Chargers had two outstanding runners that year in Chuck Muncie and James Brooks. Muncie rushed for over 1,000 yards.

Before we get to the '88 Dolphins, here are the numbers for the '88 Best-of-All-Possible-Run-Skewed-Offense Bengals: 17.9. In personnel, the Bengals match up well with the '81 Chargers, except for tight end, where San Diego had Kellen Winslow at his best, and the line, where the Cincinnati behemoths are way ahead. Both teams had a strong pair of running backs: give the Chargers an edge in speed (Muncie) and the Bengals an edge in power (Ickey Woods). James Brooks was a regular with both teams.

Finally, here's the Dolphins: 23.9.

Not so hot, huh?

If any of this surprises you, let us assure you that none of it surprises Don Shula. If he had his druthers, he'd happily even up his running and passing. But when he looked at what he had to work with, he had to opt for passing. And thus was he skewed.

DAN THE MAN

Earlier in this piece we referred to Dan Marino as "the best football thrower ever." That's a conclusion that will not be greeted with universal agreement. To tell the truth, until this last season we wouldn't have gone quite that far. We always hedged around Marino with phrases like "one of the best" or "possibly the best," but if you'd stripped us naked, tied us down on an anthill, covered us with honey, and said, "All right, confess! Who is the greatest passer of all time?" we'd have named Sonny Jurgensen.

Sorry, Sonny. Take solace in your Hall of Fame bust (or some other bust), you've slipped to second in our estimation.

What finally convinced us to enthrone Marino was his performance this past season. And, please note, it was for him a *poor* season!

Below we've averaged (to the nearest whole number) his passing record for his first five years (1983–87) on line one and then put his 1988 stats on line two:

	ATT	COM	PCT.	YARD	Avg G	TD	%TD	IN	%IN	RATE
5 years	499	302	60.6	3884	7.79	34	6.7	16	3.2	94.1
1988	606	354	58.4	4434	7.32	28	4.6	23	3.8	80.8

You can see that his totals were up for attempts, completions, and yardage, but everything else was down. He wasn't as *efficient* a thrower in '88 as he usually had been. That's what the NFL's Passer Rating System measures—efficiency. This isn't the place for a dissertation on the virtues and defects of the system. You don't have to agree with it to believe that it is better to complete a pass than not to complete one, better to gain more yards per pass, better to make touchdowns, and worse to throw interceptions. In all those categories, Dan was down (or up, in the case of interceptions). So the AFC players looked at the stats and the won-lost records and picked Boomer Esiason and Warren Moon as their Pro Bowl quarterbacks.

With all due respect to Esiason and Moon (and a great deal is due), Marino was still the number one man. The numbers that prove it are: 2,710, 2,249, and 1,205. The first is the Bengals' net yards rushing, the second the Oilers' net yards rushing, and the third is the Dolphins' pitiful total. Cincinnati and Houston had powerful running games and Boomer boomed and Moon was luminous. They took advantage, sometimes brilliantly, of defenses that had to beware of their teams' runners. Marino had no such attack to keep the defense honest and still put up formidable figures.

We should remember, of course, that one hand washes the—er—foot. Bengals and Oilers runners benefited from their quarterbacks' sharpshooting. So did the Dolphins' runners, but you can't make chicken salad out of chicken something-or-other.

Something else on Marino's side. He's had years with more help from his receivers. Early in the season they were dropping his passes at such a clip that it was noted in the national press. We figure if the press said it, it must be true. In the games we saw him play, some of his receivers must have thought they were playing volleyball. Then, late in the season, he lost Mark Duper on a drug suspension.

Okay, one other thing. The guy is nearly impossible to sack. Don't let that minuscule, NFL record, 7 sacks given up by Miami fool you (only 6 of which were Marino's).

Esiason and Moon both had better lines in front of them. A lot better. Marino is just faster in delivering the ball than anyone who ever lived.

Pro Bowl honors are certainly not meaningless. For all the faults in the selection process, they help identify players who have had outstanding seasons. Esiason and Moon fill that bill. But we wonder how many AFC-ers thought of it in these terms: "Who would I want at quarterback for a game that really means something?"

Curiously it was a game that didn't mean anything for the Dolphins except an end of their five-game losing streak that finally convinced us that Marino was beyond any other passer. In fact we can even identify the pass.

On December 12, a Monday night, the Browns came to Miami in a must-win situation. The Dolphins, as they say, were "playing for pride" (plus some pretty hefty salaries if they're asked back next year).

Marino was spectacular all night. His 404 yards (on 30-of-50) put him over 4,000 for a record fourth time and extended his NFL record for 400-plus games to nine. Despite his efforts, Cleveland rallied to tie the score at 31–31 with fifty-nine seconds left.

Okay, crunch time. Marino drove his team 65 yards in twenty-five seconds, to snatch victory from the jaws of overtime. Oh, sure, you've seen it done before by other QBs. But, did you ever see a twenty-five-second-drill pass like the one he lofted from about his own forty-five? He was in the middle of the field. His WR Fred Banks was running full out toward the left corner, and he was covered. *Zing!* The ball arched up, then down—a perfect spiral—and right into Banks' outstretched hands at the five. A couple of inches farther and he couldn't have caught it. A couple of inches shorter and it would have been blocked. Marino had shaved a peach at fifty yards! Banks stepped out of bounds at the one, and Miami ran for the touchdown. We forget how many tries that took; we were in shock.

What a pass! What a passer!

MIAMI DOLPHINS STATISTICS

1988 TEAM STATISTICS	MD	OPP
TOTAL FIRST DOWNS	321	359
Rushing	77	155
Passing	218	173
Penalty	26	31
3rd Down Made/Att.	71/184	101/207
Pct.	38.6%	48.8%
4th Down Made/Att.	7/16	6/13
Pct.	43.8%	46.2%
TOTAL NET YARDS	5721	5781
Avg. per Game	357.6	361.3
Total Plays	963	1072
Avg. per Play	5.9	5.4
NET YARDS RUSHING	1205	2506
Avg. per Game	75.3	156.6
Total Rushes	335	557
NET YARDS PASSING	4516	3275
Avg. per Game	282.3	204.7
Tackled/Yards Lost	7/41	24/167
Gross Yards	4557	3442
Attempts/Completions	621/363	491/298
Pct. of Completions	58.5%	60.7%
Had Intercepted	23	16
PUNTS/AVERAGE	64/43.0	58/41.8
NET PUNTING AVG.	35.3	35.0
PENALTIES/YARDS	99/845	103/734
FUMBLES/BALL LOST	26/12	31/15
TOUCHDOWNS	41	45
Rushing	11	22
Passing	29	19
Returns	1	4
TIME OF POSSESSION	—	—

SCORE/PERIODS	1	2	3	4	OT	TOTAL
Dolphins	72	97	88	62	0	319
Opponents	51	159	69	101	0	380

SCORING	TDR	TDP	TDRt	PAT	FG	S	TP
Clayton		14					84
Hampton	9	3					72
Reveiz				31/32	8/12		55
Jensen		5					30
Edmunds		3					18
Franklin				6/7	4/11		18
Stradford	2	1					18
Banks		2					12
Duper		1					6
Hobley			1				6
Dolphins	11	29	1	37/41	12/23	0	3 19
Opponents	22	19	4	44/45	22/28	0	3 80

RUSHING	NO	YDS	AVG	LG	TD
Hampton	117	414	3.5	33	9
Stradford	95	335	3.5	18	2
Davenport	55	273	5.0	64	0
Bennett	31	115	3.7	12	0
Jensen	10	68	6.8	23	0
Cribbs	5	21	4.2	11	0
Clayton	1	4	4.0	4	0
Edmunds	1	-8	-8.0	-8	0

(Continued)

RUSHING	NO	YDS	AVG	LG	TD
Marino	20	-17	-0.9	6	0
Dolphins	335	1205	3.6	64	11
Opponents	557	2506	4.5	44	22

RECEIVING	NO	YDS	AVG	LG	TD
Clayton	86	1129	13.1	45t	14
Jensen	58	652	11.2	31	5
Stradford	56	426	7.6	36	1
Duper	39	626	16.1	56	1
Edmunds	33	575	17.4	80t	3
Davenport	30	282	9.4	27	0
Banks	23	430	18.7	55	2
Hampton	23	204	8.9	39t	3
Schwedes	6	130	21.7	42	0
Hardy	4	46	11.5	19	0
Pruitt	2	38	19.0	19	0
Bennett	2	16	8.0	12	0
Kinchen	1	3	3.0	3	0
Dolphins	363	4557	12.6	80t	29
Opponents	298	3442	11.6	47	19

INTERCEPTIONS	NO	YDS	AVG	LG	TD
Williams	4	62	15.5	23	0
Judson	4	57	14.3	52	0
M. Brown	2	13	6.5	13	0
Offerdahl	2	2	1.0	2	0
Thomas	1	48	48.0	48	0
McNeal	1	23	23.0	23	0
Graf	1	14	14.0	14	0
Lankford	1	0	0.0	0	0
Dolphins	16	219	13.7	52	0
Opponents	23	399	17.3	78t	4

PUNTING	NO	YDS	AVG	TB	In 20	LG	Blk
Roby	64	2754	43.0	9	18	64	0
Dolphins	64	2754	43.0	9	18	64	0
Opponents	58	2427	41.8	7	14	66	1

PUNT RETURNS	NO	FC	YDS	AVG	LG	TD
Schwedes	24	7	230	9.6	36	0
Williams	3	3	29	9.7	14	0
Dolphins	27	10	259	9.6	36	0
Opponents	35	10	318	9.1	31	0

KICKOFF RETURNS	NO	YDS	AVG	LG	TD
Cribbs	41	863	21.0	44	0
Hampton	9	216	24.0	37	0
Williams	8	159	19.9	27	0
Schwedes	3	49	16.3	25	0
Davenport	2	41	20.5	21	0
Edmunds	1	20	20.0	20	0
Hardy	1	17	17.0	17	0
Hill	1	1	1.0	1	0
Dolphins	65	1365	21.0	44	0
Opponents	53	1109	20.9	57	0

FIELD GOALS	1-19	20-29	30-39	40-49	50+	TOTAL
Reveiz	0-0	4-4	3-4	1-2	0-2	8-12
Franklin	0-0	1-2	2-4	0-1	1-4	4-11
Dolphins	0-0	5-6	5-8	1-3	1-6	12-23
Opponents	0-0	6-6	10-11	4-7	2-4	22-27

FIELD GOALS BY Reveiz: 8-12 25
( )(31G,27G,50N)(29G)( )(38G)(45G)(22G,
48N)( )( )( )( )( )( )( )(55N,37N,35G)(20G)
Franklin: ( )( )( )( )( )( )( )(36G,37N)(42N,52N,
31G,38N)(51G)( )(27G,54N,50N,23N)

PASSING	ATT	COM	YARD	PCT.	Avg G	TD	%TD	IN	%IN	LG	SAKS/YDS	RATE
Marino	606	354	4434	58.4	7.32	28	4.6	23	3.8	80t	6/31	80.8
Jaworski	14	9	123	64.3	8.79	1	7.1	0	0.0	22	1/10	116.1
Stradford	1	0	0	00.0	0.00	0	0.0	0	0.0	00	0/0	39.6
Dolphins	621	363	4557	58.5	7.34	29	4.7	23	3.7	80t	7/41	81.5
Opponents	491	298	3442	7.01		19	3.9	16	3.3	47	24/167	81.2

NEW ENGLAND PATRIOTS

The Last 5 Seasons

	1984	1985	1986	1987	1988
Won-Lost	9-7	11-5	11-5	8-7	9-7
Percentage	.563	.688	.688	.533	.563
Division Finish	2	2-t	1	2-t	2-t
Games Behind	5	1	0	1	3
Total Points	362	362	412	320	250
Per Game	22.6	22.6	25.8	21.3	15.6
Opponent Points	352	290	307	293	284
Per Game	22.0	18.1	19.2	19.5	17.8
Net Points	10	72	105	27	-34
Predicted Net Wins	0.3	1.8	2.6	0.7	-0.9
Delta Net Wins	0.8	1.2	0.4	-0.2	1.9
Total Yards on Offense	5263	5499	5327	4454	4293
Per Game	328.9	343.7	332.9	296.9	268.3
Total Yards Allowed on Defense	5100	4714	5181	4877	4681
Per Game	318.8	294.6	323.8	325.1	292.6
Net Difference	163	785	146	-423	-388
Offensive Turnovers	29	42	24	31	38
Defensive Takeaways	25	47	40	42	35
Net Turnovers	-4	5	16	11	-3
Predicted Net Points	-2	85	76	9	-44
Delta Net Points	12	-13	29	18	10
Net Rushing Yards	2032	2331	1373	1771	2120
Per Game	127.0	145.7	85.8	118.1	132.5
Average Gain	4.2	4.1	2.9	3.5	3.6
Opponent Net Rushing Yards	1886	1655	2203	1778	2099
Per Game	117.9	103.4	137.7	118.5	131.2
Average Gain	3.8	3.6	4.3	3.6	4.2
Net Passing Yards	3231	3168	3954	2683	2173
Per Game	201.9	198.0	247.1	178.9	135.8
Times Sacked	66	39	47	33	23
Passer Rating in Yards	5.1	4.8	6.1	4.4	2.5
Opponent Net Passing Yards	3214	3059	2978	3099	2582
Per Game	200.9	191.2	186.1	206.6	161.4
Times Sacked	55	51	48	43	29
Passer Rating Defense	4.8	3.8	4.2	4.1	3.9
Passer Rating Net	0.3	1.0	1.9	0.3	-1.4
Yards per Drive Offense	26.7	25.2	25.5	22.8	21.8
Yards per Drive Defense	24.5	21.1	23.7	24.1	23.4
Average Time of Possession	29:51	31:07	30:29	29:37	31:03

1985 PLAYOFFS
Won Wild Card Game from New York Jets, 26-14
Won Divisional Playoff from Los Angeles Raiders, 27-20
Won AFC Championship from Miami, 31-14
Lost Super Bowl XX to Chicago, 10-46

1986 PLAYOFFS
Lost Divisional Playoff to Denver, 17-22

THE 1988 SEASON

DATE	AT	OPPONENT	SCORE	R	SPREAD	Tu	Net YDS	Rush YDS	Pass YDS	TURN
09/04	H	N.Y. Jets	28- 3	W	-6.5	a	343-179	94- 87	249- 92	2-2
09/11	A	Minnesota	6-36	L	+6.5	a	214-415	103-150	111-265	5-2
09/18	H	Buffalo	14-16	L	-2.5	a	264-254	105-105	159-149	3-2
09/25	A	Houston	6-31	L	+3.5	a	184-328	51-172	133-156	6-3
10/02	H	Indianapolis	21-17	W	-2	a	298-267	105-107	193-160	2-1
10/09	A	Green Bay	3-45	L	-2.5	g	269-399	76-207	193-192	5-0
10/16	H	Cincinnati	27-21	W	+5.5	a	311-365	158-140	153-225	0-6
10/23	A	Buffalo	20-23	L	+6.5	a	223-339	176-190	47-149	0-4
10/30	H	Chicago	30- 7	W	+5	a	350-208	185-134	165- 74	1-3
11/06	H	Miami	21-10	W	-3.5	a	277-437	203- 78	74-359	1-2
11/13	A	N.Y. Jets	14-13	W	+2	a	255-298	177-189	78-109	3-3
11/20	A	Miami	6- 3	W	+3	g	236-293	170-124	66-169	0-0
11/27	A	Indianapolis	21-24	L	+5	a	285-241	105- 81	180-160	3-2
12/04	H	Seattle	13- 7	W	-3.5	a	212- 65	177- 20	35- 45	3-1
12/11	H	Tampa Bay	10- 7	W	-9	a	223-262	76-131	147-131	2-2
12/17	A	Denver	10-21	L	+0	g	351-331	165-188	186-143	2-2
						Avg.	268-293	133-131	136-161	2-2

			WINS		LOSSES	
Season Record:	9- 7-0	POINTS:		19- 10		11- 28
Vs. Spread:	10- 6-0	Net YDS:	7- 9-0	278-264		256-330
Home:	7- 1-0	Rush YDS:	7- 8-1	149-112		112-156
On Artificial Turf:	8- 5-0	Pass YDS:	8- 8-0	129-152		144-173
Art. Turf vs. Spread:	9- 4-0	TURN:	4- 7-5	2- 2		3- 2

BAIT AND SWITCH

Raymond Berry is pretty cool, so he probably doesn't wake up at three in the morning in a cold sweat regretting his end-of-season quarterback switch. He had his reasons. No one can prove the Patriots would have made it to the playoffs with Doug Flutie at quarterback. Of course it's a cinch to prove they *didn't* make it with Tony Eason. Just trot out the final standings.

It'll be hard to say that New England was better off in the long run even if Eason makes a spectacular comeback next season. After all, no matter what the future brings, last season's chance is gone. If it *was* a chance.

Certainly the Patriots thought they had a chance. And their fans thought they had a chance. And Berry thought they had a chance. Which is why he decided to forgo the last dance with the one what brung him.

We think Berry is a smart coach. In fact, we think he's smarter than a lot of people think he is. We don't buy what some people always say—that the Patriots have the best personnel in the AFC. For as long as we can remember, the Patriots have been called underachievers—talented guys who never live up to their advance billing. Sooner or later, when somebody keeps falling short of expectations, we begin to wonder if the expectations weren't too high to start with. Sure, there's a lot of talent on this club, but it's not

wall-to-wall. We thought the Patriots played over their heads a couple of years ago when they got to the Super Bowl.

What profiteth a team to have great foot soldiers and not a great general?

If you're going to look for lacks on this ball club, start at quarterback. Steve Grogan has been in New England so long he must talk like a native by now. For about the first half of his career, he put up good stats and lost big games. He had us absolutely convinced that he was the kind of quarterback who, against all odds, would find a way to snatch defeat from victory. Then, bless him, he changed. Suddenly, for a while, he had a deserved reputation as a come-through player. He earned most of his esteem by rescuing the messes left by other QBs, like an updated Earl Morrall. Every once in a while you see that happen. A QB sticks around long enough, learns all the ins and outs, and gains the confidence of his team and coaches. Maybe it gives him a little confidence lift too.

Grogan went into the '88 season anticipating the best year of his career, perhaps even a Pro Bowl selection. Okay, he was thirty-five or forty-five or fifty-five or something like that. In the NFL they're all about the same. But he was in great shape and nobody knew the offense better, it was said. But after a strong performance in the opener, he started throwing interceptions like he was being paid by the turnover. To be fair, he had a neck injury. He was replaced after the fourth game by Tom Ramsey, who's earned a good living for years by holding a clipboard. Ramsey lasted three quarters, and Berry sent in Doug Flutie, sometimes referred to west of Massachusetts as the world's tallest dwarf. There have been lots of funnier things said about Flutie's lack of height. Let us direct you to the collected sayings of a certain Chicago quarterback. Funny as hell! Probably because he has plenty of time to polish his *bon mots*; he only works six or eight Sundays a year.

The Patriots were 7–3 with Flutie. So Tony Eason started the last two games. On the surface this may have seemed like a curious turn of events. To understand it, you must first make a leap of faith and actually believe that Eason was at that moment in time a capable NFL quarterback. All else makes sense, once you accept that fact (or once you swallow that fiction).

We don't.

THE THREE OFFENSES

To go back to the beginning, under Grogan the Pats ran an offense that might be conservatively described as "bombs away." Well, Steve knew his capabilities. He's certainly had long enough to learn them. It was his judgment that he would be able to outpitch Ken O'Brien, Tommy Kramer, Jim Kelly, and Cody Carlson. As it turned out, he was right once.

In the fifth game, Ramsey made his brief, unsatisfactory appearance. Then Flutie came in and got two fourth-quarter touchdowns to give the Pats their second win.

That week you heard all kinds of stuff about the magic being back and so forth. In New England Li'l Doug ranks with Nathan Hale.

So he started against Green Bay. Three interceptions and three batted back in his face mask. The Patriots lost 45–3. To Green Bay! Who-in-hell did the Packers think they were playing? Minnesota?

If nothing else, the game proved that Flutie couldn't run the Grogan offense. Reportedly it was then that OT Bruce Armstrong, the leader of the line, went to Coach Berry and begged that they use a power-running attack, featuring rookie John Stephens. Somehow we have to believe that Berry was already leaning that way. Unlike most NFL coaches, Raymond is willing to listen to suggestions from his players, but we can't imagine him saying something like, "Well, gee, Bruce, I dunno. I guess we'll try it Sunday, if you really want to. It's only another game."

The Flutie offense was as ground-bound as a Chuck Knox pipedream. Stephens and Rob Perryman ran between the tackles. Flutie rolled out and threw passes like he was eking out blood. At first everybody loved it. Well, everyone who remembers the 1930s as the "good old days." Some fans found it dull. Maybe they couldn't wait for the excitement of getting blown out 45–3 again.

The problem with the Flutie offense was Flutie. And no, the problem with Flutie was not that he's short. NFL defensive linemen are so tall they make every quarterback seem short. When Ed Jones slams one back in the face of Randall Cunningham, no one says, "Gosh, if Randall was just a little taller!" Flutie can roll out and find a passing lane between the defenders. He just didn't demonstrate that he could hit his targets consistently, even when he was given a lane as wide as Jim McMahon's mouth.

Knowing this, Berry worried as his team approached playoff possibilities. Although the Patriots were winning, the Flutie offense wasn't putting up many points. It wasn't just a question of what to do with a grind-it-out offense if his team got a couple of scores behind. Defenses were wise to what New England was doing. A good NFL team will usually find a way to limit the damage a running attack can do unless it's coupled with a threat of the pass. And that's why Berry went to Tony Eason.

Before his injury over a year before, Eason had been a very accurate passer. But according to him, the treatment to restore his shoulder had damaged his wrist. When he was moved off IR at midseason, he complained that he still couldn't throw with any accuracy.

By Game 15, Berry decided Eason was ready and went to the Eason offense.

In one sense the move was a success. Eason *was* more accurate than Flutie. He certainly threw more often and completed more. But what he apparently left in the shop was his arm strength. His passes took forever to get to the receivers. Normally those slow boats lead to a pile of interceptions, but Tony managed to avoid them. He just couldn't throw long. And in the finale, a must-win at Denver, this was painfully obvious.

A short-pass attack coupled with an up-the-gut running game can be successful if you can keep the defense honest with the threat of a long pass. You don't even have to complete any. Just let 'em know it's there. Denver never saw it from Eason. They moved in on the runners, let Tony throw little four-or-five-yard dinks out to the sides, and then nailed the receivers. Near the end Eason was injured again. Grogan came in and threw bombs, but it was too late to surprise anybody.

Below is a comparison of the three offenses.

	GROGAN OFFENSE	FLUTIE OFFENSE	EASON OFFENSE
Win-Loss	2-4	6-2	1-1
Points Scored	13.0	19.0	10.0
Rushing Attempts	27.7	44.4	33.0
% Rushing Plays	44.7	71.9	48.8
Rushing Yards	89.0	168.9	120.5
Avg. Gain per Attempt	3.2	3.8	3.7
Fumbles Lost	0.7	0.8	0.0
Pass Attempts	32.3	16.1	33.0
Sacks Against	1.8	1.4	1.5
% Passing Plays	55.3	28.1	51.2
Passing Yards	172.7	99.8	166.5

(Continued)

	GROGAN OFFENSE	FLUTIE OFFENSE	EASON OFFENSE
Avg. Gain per Pass (+Sacks)	5.1	5.7	4.8
Passes had Intercepted	3.2	0.6	2.0
Total Offense Attempts	61.8	61.8	67.5
Total Yards Gained	261.7	268.6	287.0
Avg. Gain per Play	4.2	4.4	4.3
Turnovers	4.2	1.4	2.0

The most notable figures are the rushing yards, passing yards, average gain per play, and turnovers. Note that the Eason offense outgained the other two (although two games limits the comparison) but shows no improvement in average gain.

We may get a better understanding if we think of the three offenses as *defenses*. What do they let the other team do?

	GROGAN DEFENSE	FLUTIE DEFENSE	EASON DEFENSE
Points Scored Against	24.7	13.5	14.0
Rushing Attempts Against	35.0	26.5	36.5
% Rushing Plays	53.6	47.6	58.9
Rushing Yards	138.0	119.5	159.5
Avg. Gain per Attempt	3.9	4.5	4.4
Fumbles Lost	0.7	1.8	0.0
Pass Attempts Against	27.3	28.0	24.0
Sacks Against	3.0	1.1	1.5
% Passing Plays	46.4	52.4	41.1
Passing Yards	169.0	161.3	137.0
Avg. Gain per Pass (+Sacks)	5.6	5.5	5.4
Passes Had Intercepted	1.0	1.5	1.0
Total Plays Defensed	65.3	55.6	57.0
Total Yards	307.0	280.8	296.5
Avg. Gain per Play	4.7	5.0	4.8
Takeaways	1.3	3.3	2.0

The main difference is that the Grogan and Eason offenses give the other side nine or ten more plays. That's nine or ten more shots at your goal line. If you're running a low-scoring offense (all three), with little quick-strike ability (both Flutie and Eason), the last thing you want to give your opponent is extra downs.

What's in the future for the Patriots? They may win one more than they lose again this year. Maybe two more. But to be a championship team, they need one of three things, listed here in descending order of likelihood.

1. Eason gets his arm strength back.
2. Flutie improves his accuracy (greatly).
3. A clerk in a records office in Kansas comes up with Grogan's birth certificate, proving that he's really twenty-five and became an NFL quarterback about the same time he got zits.

ONE YARD AT A TIME

In training camp, they started calling John Stephens "S.S." for "Something Special." He lived up to the nickname by being a sure gainer in almost every game. He's what they mean when they say "north-south runner." No dancing or juking a play into a three-yard loss. Just BAM! Into the line. Pick up four or five and go back to the huddle.

However, he *wasn't* a breakaway threat. Through fifteen games, his longest run was 22 yards. Gale Sayers used to do one of those every quarter. FB Perryman and number one sub Reggie Dupard were also pluggers, not burners. Perryman is a terrific blocker, but Stephens might benefit if a couple of times each game he had someone who can blaze.

Funny thing, against Denver in the finale, Stephens broke away once for 52 yards before he was hauled down and another time went 23 yards for a touchdown. You can study the films, but what we *think* happened was that Denver overcommitted in close, and Stephens was past them before they could react. In a sense, on those two plays, the Pats benefited from their lack of a deep passing capability.

They can't count on that happening often enough to win. In fact they didn't win at Denver.

We knew you'd be on pins and needles wondering when we'd show you how the three main runners did in the various offenses.

Now:

			JOHN STEPHENS				ROB PERRYMAN				REG DUPARD			
WK	OPP	SCORE	AT	YDS	LG	TD	AT	YDS	LG	TD	AT	YDS	LG	TD
(Grogan Offense)														
1	NYJ	28- 3	10	41	17	0	11	38	6	0	10	-4	3	0
2	Min	6-36	7	40	13	0	5	23	8	0	3	9	3	0
3	Buf	14-16	24	81	11	0	7	23	16	0	1	1	1	0
4	Hou	6-31	8	23	11	0	6	16	7	0	3	6	2	0
5	Ind	21-17	16	52	10	0	5	15	5	1	7	20	6	0
6	GB	3-45	7	21	9	0	3	5	4	0	4	31	13	0
(Flutie Offense)														
7	Cin	27-21	16	56	17	0	13	29	9	0	5	32	15	2
8	Buf	20-23	25	134	17	1	6	16	6	1	9	18	5	0
9	Chi	30- 7	35	124	11	0	8	28	6	0	1	0	0	0
10	Mia	21-10	25	104	13t	1	11	42	8	1	-	-	-	-

(Continued)

(Continued)

WK	OPP	SCORE	JOHN STEPHENS AT	YDS	LG	TD	ROB PERRYMAN AT	YDS	LG	TD	REG DUPARD AT	YDS	LG	TD
11	NYJ	14-13	21	87	22	1	16	53	12	0	-	-	-	-
12	Mia	6- 3	20	88	15	0	10	38	7	0	4	16	14	0
13	Ind	21-24	23	56	11	0	5	10	6	1	1	9	9	0
14	Sea	13- 7	31	131	21	0	14	49	8	1	-	-	-	-
(Eason Offense)														
15	TB	10- 7	12	10	6	0	17	47	7	0	-	-	-	-
16	Den	10-21	17	130	52	1	9	16	4	0	4	13	5	0

WHAT WILL HE BE WHEN HE GROWS UP?

No, that's not another swipe at Flutie. It refers to John Stephens' excellent rookie season. We know a lot of folks are saying, "Gosh, a thousand today; tomorrow two."

We took a quick squint at all the other runners who've gained over 1,000 yards rushing in their first seasons. Frankly it's not a sure indication of a full-scale great career.

Some of the very best football movers anybody'd ever want to see ran for a thou right off the bat. Yet only six made it to the All-Time Top Twenty Rushers List.

What does that presage for Stephens (and Ickey Woods)? We don't know, but here's the list. To make for better comparisons, we added Attempts-per-Scheduled-Game (APSG) and Yards-per-Scheduled-Game (YPSG) as the last two columns.

ROOKIES

	YEAR	SG	ATT	YARD	AVG	LG	TD	APSG	YPSG
John Stephens, New England	1988	16	297	1168	3.9	52	4	18.6	73.0
Ickey Woods, Cincinnati	1988	16	203	1066	5.3	56	15	12.7	66.6
Reuben Mayes, New Orleans	1986	16	286	1353	4.7	50	8	17.9	84.6
Kevin Mack, Cleveland	1985	16	222	1104	5.0	61	7	13.9	69.0
Greg Bell, Buffalo	1984	16	262	1100	4.2	85	7	16.4	68.8
*Eric Dickerson, L.A. Rams	1983	16	390	1808	4.6	85	18	24.4	113.0
Curt Warner, Seattle	1983	16	335	1449	4.3	60	13	20.9	90.6
*George Rogers, New Orleans	1981	16	378	1674	4.4	79	13	23.6	104.6
Joe Delaney, Kansas City	1981	16	234	1121	4.8	82	3	14.6	70.3
Billy Sims, Detroit	1980	16	313	1303	4.2	52	13	19.6	81.4
Joe Cribbs, Buffalo	1980	16	306	1185	3.9	48	11	19.1	74.1
*Ottis Anderson, St. Louis	1979	16	331	1605	4.8	76	8	20.7	100.3
William Andrews, Atlanta	1979	16	239	1023	4.3	23	3	14.9	63.9
*Earl Campbell, Houston	1978	16	302	1450	4.8	81	13	18.9	90.6
Terry Miller, Buffalo	1978	16	238	1060	4.5	60	7	14.9	66.3
*Tony Dorsett, Dallas	1977	14	208	1007	4.8	84	12	14.9	71.9
Don Woods, San Diego	1974	14	227	1162	5.1	56	7	16.2	83.0
*Franco Harris, Pittsburgh	1972	14	188	1055	5.6	75	10	13.4	75.4
John Brockington, Green Bay	1971	14	216	1105	5.1	52	4	15.4	78.9
Paul Robinson, Cincinnati	1968	14	238	1023	4.3	87	8	17.0	73.1
Cookie Gilchrist, Buffalo	1962	14	214	1096	5.1	44	13	15.3	78.3
Beattie Feathers, Chi. Bears	1934	13	101	1004	9.9	82	8	7.8	77.2

* Among the Top Twenty in All-Time Rushing

NEW ENGLAND PATRIOTS STATISTICS

1988 TEAM STATISTICS	NEP	OPP
TOTAL FIRST DOWNS	264	272
Rushing	126	119
Passing	112	138
Penalty	26	15
3rd Down Made/Att.	79/219	58/199
Pct.	36.1%	29.1%
4th Down Made/Att.	9/14	9/18
Pct.	64.3%	50.0%
TOTAL NET YARDS	4293	4681
Avg. per Game	268.3	292.6

(Continued)

1988 TEAM STATISTICS	NEP	OPP
Total Plays	1000	961
Avg. per Play	4.3	4.9
NET YARDS RUSHING	2120	2099
Avg. per Game	132.5	131.2
Total Rushes	588	496
NET YARDS PASSING	2173	2582
Avg. per Game	135.8	161.4
Tackled/Yards Lost	23/160	29/219
Gross Yards	2333	2801

(Continued)

1988 TEAM STATISTICS

	NEP	OPP
Attempts/Completions	389/199	436/234
Pct. of Completions	51.2%	53.7%
Had Intercepted	28	30
PUNTS/AVERAGE	91/38.3	86/42.2
NET PUNTING AVG.	34.1	35.5
PENALTIES/YARDS	87/665	108/858
FUMBLES/BALL LOST	19/10	29/15
TOUCHDOWNS	31	33
Rushing	17	20
Passing	12	13
Returns	2	0
TIME OF POSSESSION	—	—

SCORE/PERIODS

	1	2	3	4	OT	TOTAL
Patriots	49	87	50	61	3	250
Opponents	48	77	57	102	0	284

SCORING

	TDR	TDP	TDRt	PAT	FG	S	TP
Perryman	6						36
Staurovsky				14/15	7/11		35
Fryar		5					30
Stephens	4		1				30
Garcia				11/16	6/13		29
Morgan		4					24
Dawson		2					12
Dupard	2						12
Tatupu	2						12
Flutie	1						6
Grogan	1						6
C. James	1						6
Jones		1					6
Martin			1				6
Partiots	17	12	2	25/31	13/24	0	250
Opponents	20	13	0	33/33	17/26	1	284

RUSHING

	NO	YDS	AVG	LG	TD
Stephens	297	1168	3.9	52	4
Perryman	146	448	3.1	16	6
Flutie	38	179	4.7	16	1
Dupard	52	151	2.9	15	2
Tatupu	22	75	3.4	22	2
Allen	7	40	5.7	12	0
Eason	5	18	3.6	10	0
C. James	4	15	3.8	8t	1
Fryar	6	12	2.0	6	0
Grogan	6	12	2.0	6	1
Ramsey	3	8	2.7	9	0
Feagles	1	0	0.0	0	0
Morgan	1	-6	-6.0	-6	0
Patriots	588	2120	3.6	52	17
Opponents	496	2099	4.2	36	20

RECEIVING

	NO	YDS	AVG	LG	TD
Dupard	34	232	6.8	15	0
Fryar	33	490	14.8	80t	5
Morgan	31	502	16.2	32	4
Jones	22	313	14.2	41t	1
Perryman	17	134	7.9	18	0

(Continued)

RECEIVING

	NO	YDS	AVG	LG	TD
C. James	14	171	12.2	32	0
Stephens	14	98	7.0	17	0
Francis	11	161	14.6	51	0
Dawson	8	106	13.3	38	2
Tatupu	8	58	7.3	17	0
Martin	4	51	12.8	21	0
Scott	1	8	8.0	8	0
Johnson	1	5	5.0	5	0
Farrell	1	4	4.0	4	0
Patriots	199	2333	11.7	80t	12
Opponents	234	2801	12.0	51t	13

INTERCEPTIONS

	NO	YDS	AVG	LG	TD
Clayborn	4	65	16.3	31	0
Marion	4	47	11.8	22	0
R. James	4	30	7.5	22	0
McSwain	2	51	25.5	42	0
Rembert	2	10	5.0	6	0
Jordan	1	31	31.0	31	0
McGrew	1	6	6.0	6	0
Lippett	1	4	4.0	4	0
Bowman	1	0	0.0	0	0
Patriots	20	244	12.2	42	0
Opponents	28	286	10.2	40	0

PUNTING

	NO	YDS	AVG	TB	In 20	LG	Blk
Feagles	91	3482	38.3	8	24	74	0
Patriots	91	3482	38.3	8	24	74	0
Opponents	86	3633	42.2	9	19	70	0

PUNT RETURNS

	NO	FC	YDS	AVG	LG	TD
Fryar	38	8	398	10.5	30	0
Bowman	0	1	0	—	0	0
Patriots	38	9	398	10.5	30	0
Opponents	38	9	398	10.5	30	0

KICKOFF RETURNS

	NO	YDS	AVG	LG	TD
Martin	31	735	23.7	95t	1
Allen	18	391	21.7	30	0
Davis	6	106	17.7	24	0
Fryar	1	3	3.0	3	0
Tatupu	1	13	13.0	13	0
Patriots	57	1248	21.9	95t	1
Opponents	45	888	19.7	51	0

FIELD GOALS

	1-19	20-29	30-39	40-49	50+	TOTAL
Staurovsky	0-0	3-4	4-5	0-2	0-0	7-11
Garcia	0-0	2-3	1-3	2-5	1-2	6-13
Patriots	0-0	5-7	5-8	2-7	1-2	13-24
Opponents	0-0	6-7	5-5	5-11	1-3	17-26

FIELD GOALS BY Staurovsky: 7 of 11
( )( )( )( )( )( )( )( )(35G)( )( )(22G,34G)(43N,27N)
(34G,22G)(36N,27G)(32G,40N)
Garcia: 6 of 13
(47N,39G,24G,47G)(50G,23G)( )( )(31N)(43G,42N)
(43N)(25N,52N,39N)

PASSING

	ATT	COM	YARD	PCT.	Avg G	TD	%TD	IN	%IN	LG	SAKS/YDS	RATE
Flutie	179	92	1150	51.4	6.42	8	4.5	10	5.6	80t	11/65	63.3
Grogan	140	67	834	47.9	5.96	4	2.9	13	9.3	41t	8/77	37.6
Eason	43	28	249	65.1	5.79	0	0.0	2	4.7	26	2/12	61.1
Ramsey	27	12	100	44.4	3.70	0	0.0	3	11.1	23	2/6	15.0
Patriots	389	199	2333	51.2	6.00	12	3.1	28	7.2	80t	23/160	50.0
Opponents	436	234	2801	53.7	6.42	13	3.0	20	4.6	51t	29/219	64.4

NEW YORK JETS

The Last 5 Seasons

	1984	1985	1986	1987	1988
Won-Lost	7-9	11-5	10-6	6-9	8-7-1
Percentage	.438	.688	.625	.400	.531
Division Finish	3	2-t	2	5	4
Games Behind	7	1	1	3	3.5
Total Points	332	393	364	334	372
Per Game	20.8	24.6	22.8	22.3	23.3
Opponent Points	364	264	386	360	354
Per Game	22.8	16.5	24.1	24.0	22.1
Net Points	-32	129	-22	-26	18
Predicted Net Wins	-0.8	3.2	-0.6	-0.6	0.4
Delta Net Wins	-0.2	-0.2	2.6	-0.9	0.1
Total Yards on Offense	5148	5896	5375	4630	5215
Per Game	321.8	368.5	335.9	308.7	325.9
Total Yards Allowed on Defense	5566	4772	6050	5041	5633
Per Game	347.9	298.3	378.1	336.1	352.1
Net Difference	-418	1124	-675	-411	-418
Offensive Turnovers	34	29	37	34	27
Defensive Takeaways	33	42	38	29	40
Net Turnovers	-1	13	1	-5	13
Predicted Net Points	-39	146	-52	-54	17
Delta Net Points	7	-17	30	28	1
Net Rushing Yards	2189	2312	1729	1671	2132
Per Game	136.8	144.5	108.1	111.4	133.3
Average Gain	4.3	4.1	3.5	3.6	4.1
Opponent Net Rushing Yards	2064	1516	1661	1835	2124
Per Game	129.0	94.8	103.8	122.3	132.8
Average Gain	4.2	3.5	3.7	3.9	4.1
Net Passing Yards	2959	3584	3646	2959	3083
Per Game	184.9	224.0	227.9	197.3	192.7
Times Sacked	52	62	45	66	42
Passer Rating in Yards	4.1	6.2	5.1	4.2	4.8
Opponent Net Passing Yards	3502	3256	4389	3206	3509
Per Game	218.9	203.5	274.3	213.7	219.3
Times Sacked	44	49	28	29	45
Passer Rating Defense	5.5	4.4	6.1	5.2	5.2
Passer Rating Net	-1.4	1.8	-1.0	-0.9	-0.4
Yards per Drive Offense	26.5	29.3	26.2	23.6	25.9
Yards per Drive Defense	29.3	24.0	30.0	25.7	28.2
Average Time of Possession	30:02	31:11	29:51	30:28	30.55

1985 PLAYOFFS
Lost Wild Card Game to New England, 14-26

1986 PLAYOFFS
Won Wild Card Game from Kansas City, 35-15
Lost Divisional Playoff to Cleveland, 20-23 OT

THE 1988 SEASON

DATE	AT	OPPONENT	SCORE	R	SPREAD	Tu	Net YDS	Rush YDS	Pass YDS	TURN
9/ 4	A	New England	3-28	L	+6.5	a	179-343	87- 94	92-249	2-2
9/11	A	Cleveland	23- 3	W	+9.5	g	402-218	154- 27	248-191	1-3
9/18	H	Houston	45- 3	W	+2	a	391-237	89-140	302- 97	1-4
9/25	A	Detroit	17-10	W	-2	a	316-183	86- 86	230- 97	1-1
10/ 2	H	Kan. City OT	17-17	T	-5.5	a	542-385	272-124	270-261	4-2
10/ 9	A	Cincinnati	19-36	L	+6	a	226-402	109-206	117-196	1-2
10/17	H*	Buffalo	14-37	L	-2.5	a	199-427	45-135	154-292	2-1
10/23	A	Miami	44-30	W	+6.5	g	333-584	159- 63	174-521	1-6
10/30	H	Pittsburgh	24-20	W	-4.5	a	196-352	84-143	112-209	1-4
11/ 6	A	Indianapolis	14-38	L	+3.5	a	273-336	91-140	182-196	2-3
11/13	H	New England	13-14	L	-2	a	298-255	189-177	109- 78	3-3
11/20	A	Buffalo OT	6- 9	L	+7	a	259-341	140-229	119-112	1-2
11/27	H	Miami	38-34	W	-2.5	a	597-440	171- 87	426-353	2-1
12/ 4	A	Kansas City	34-38	L	+1.5	a	371-430	179-163	192-267	2-2
12/10	H	Indianapolis	34-16	W	+3	a	331-331	173-109	158-222	3-3
12/18	H	N.Y. Giants	27-21	W	+6.5	a	298-367	100-197	190-170	0-1
						Avg.	326-352	133-133	192-219	

			WINS	LOSSES
Season Record:	8- 7-1	POINTS:	32- 17	15- 29
Vs. Spread:	8- 8-0	Net YDS: 6- 9-1	358-339	258-362
Home:	5- 2-1	Rush YDS: 7- 8-1	127-107	120-163
On Artificial Turf:	6- 7-1	Pass YDS: 8- 8-0	230-233	137-199
Art. Turf vs. Spread:	6- 8-0	TURN: 8- 3-5	10- 23	13- 15

* Monday Night

THERE WE DON'T GO AGAIN

When the Jets lost three straight in November, they seemed well on their way to another end-of-season swoon. Since 1983, when Joe Walton became head coach, they'd gone 26–12 in the first half of the season and 15–25 in the second half. Low points had been 1–7 after a 6–2 start in 1984, and the 0–5 collapse for the 10–1 division leaders in 1986. In 1987 they threw away a chance for a winning season with an ugly 0–4 finish. You could set your calendar by it. Are the Jets falling to earth? Well, then, it must be November.

For once the doomsayers who've made a living off the Jets for years were wrong. Walton's crew righted itself to win three of their last four. The comeback finale over the Giants knocked New York's other New Jersey team out of the playoffs. And the previous week's demolition of the Indianapolis Colts denied that turbulent team a return trip to the postseason tourney.

The improvement from 1987's disaster earned Walton a new three-year contract—a side effect nearly as welcome to many Jets as hives.

WHERE'S WESLEY?

An important factor in the closing drive was the rediscovery of WR Wesley Walker. The Jets' best—make that, *only*—burn threat hit midseason with 16 catches and 5 touchdowns, then disappeared completely for three games.

Just how important Mr. Walker has been to the New York attack throughout his career is best illustrated by the chart on the following page.

Even with three seasons truncated by injuries (1979, 1980, 1986), Wesley has better than a fifth of the Jets' passing yardage and nearly a third of the touchdown receptions since 1977. Throw out '80 and '86 and it's better than a third.

The Jets have Al Toon and Mickey Shuler for the short-passing game—they both averaged under 12 yards per catch. Walker is the deep threat. And of course by pulling the secondary back, he opens up the running game. He'll be thirty-four in 1989. How long can he go on? Director of Player Personnel Mike Hickey thought not much longer, and so exposed him to the free agent draft; but even if Walker returns to the Jets in 1989, they have to find someone to replace him soon.

	PC	TPC%	YDS	TYD%	AVG	TAVG	TD	TTD%
1977	35	20.6	740	32.4	21.1	11.5	3	21.1
1978	48	24.9	1169	39.5	24.4	12.3	8	42.1
1979	23	12.1	569	19.9	24.7	13.7	5	31.3
1980	18	6.8	376	11.3	20.9	12.0	1	5.9
1981	47	16.6	770	23.5	16.4	10.6	9	34.6
1982	39	23.6	620	29.4	15.9	11.8	6	37.5
1983	61	18.5	868	23.2	14.2	10.7	7	33.3
1984	41	15.1	623	18.6	15.2	11.8	7	35.0
1985	34	11.2	725	18.2	21.3	12.1	5	20.0
1986	49	14.7	1016	25.2	20.7	10.6	12	44.4
1987	9	3.0	190	5.6	21.1	11.0	1	5.6
1988	26	8.7	551	16.3	21.2	10.3	7	35.0
	430	13.8	8217	21.2	18.8	11.4	71	29.7

Legend: PC — passes caught by Walker; TPC% — percentage of team's receptions by Walker; YDS — receiving yards by Walker; TYD% — percentage of team's receiving yards by Walker; AVG — Walker's yards-per-catch average; TAVG — average yards per catch by all other Jets receivers combined; TD — Walker's receiving touchdowns; TTD% — percentage of team's receiving touchdowns by Walker.

HOLD IT!

When the Jets skidded in November, QB Ken O'Brien was benched in favor of perennial backup Pat Ryan. He may have won his job back with some good relief work and a strong finish against the Giants. To keep it, however, he must improve his 6.05 average gain per pass. That doesn't necessarily mean a return to the mad-bomber persona he showed early in his career, but he must move the ball.

Back in 1983, when the NFL held the Great Quarterback Sweepstakes, O'Brien was drafted on the first round, along with John Elway, Dan Marino, Tony Eason, Jim Kelly, and Todd Blackledge. Although there were some who said, "Who he?", many thought O'Brien might be the best of the lot. So far he ranks ahead of only Blackledge and maybe Eason.

Even when O'Brien used to throw long, he was intercepted about as often as you can find a cabbie who speaks English. The rap on him has always been that he will take a sack rather than put the ball at risk. Very macho, but it kills drives.

Think of it this way. Using the 1988 figures for Dan Marino and O'Brien, we'll put them head to head. If O'Brien and Marino square off and try to throw 50 passes each in a game, it's fifty-fifty that Marino will throw one more interception than O'Brien. But Ken will be sacked four times to Dan's once (maybe). So in reality, Marino throws 49 passes and gains 359 yards, and O'Brien throws 46 for 278 yards. But wait! Marino loses 6 yards on his sack, and O'Brien loses 29 yards on his four. The net passing yardage becomes Miami 353, Jets 249. Will that one more interception make up a 104-yard difference? Especially when at least three of the four O'Brien sacks probably stopped drives?

Incidentally we ran the same 50-pass exercise with Pat Ryan. Again there'd be an extra interception, but Ryan would gain 332 yards.

Here are the sack-interception records for the QBs drafted in 1983:

Todd Blackledge

YEAR	Gm	ATT	SAKS	%SAK	SYDS	AY/S	INT	%IN
1983	4	38	4	10.5	50	12.5	0	0.0
1984	15	308	14	4.5	136	9.7	11	3.6
1985	12	187	15	8.0	112	7.5	14	7.5
1986	10	236	25	10.6	192	7.7	6	2.5
1987	3	38	7	18.4	43	6.1	1	2.6
1988	3	83	4	4.8	25	6.3	3	3.6
6 YR	47	890	69	7.8	558	8.1	35	3.9

Tony Eason

YEAR	Gm	ATT	SAKS	%SAK	SYDS	AY/S	INT	%IN
1983	16	111	16	14.4	139	8.7	5	4.5
1984	16	490	59	12.0	409	6.9	8	1.6
1985	16	327	28	8.6	229	8.2	17	5.2
1986	15	491	43	8.8	336	7.8	10	2.0
1987	4	87	8	9.2	70	8.8	2	2.3
1988	2	45	2	4.4	12	6.0	2	4.4
6 YR	69	1551	156	10.1	1195	7.7	44	2.8

Legend: YEAR — season; Gm — games played; ATT — pass attempts plus sacks; SAKS — sacks; %SAK — percentage of sacks (sacks divided by pass attempts plus sacks); SYDS — yards lost to sacks; AY/S — average yards lost to sack; INT — number of interceptions; %IN — percentage of interceptions (interceptions divided by pass attempts plus sacks).

John Elway

YEAR	Gm	ATT	SAKS	%SAK	SYDS	AY/S	INT	%IN
1983	11	287	28	9.8	218	7.8	14	4.9
1984	15	404	24	5.9	158	6.6	15	3.7
1985	16	643	38	5.9	307	8.1	23	3.6
1986	16	536	32	6.0	233	7.3	13	2.4
1987	12	430	20	4.7	138	6.9	12	2.8
1988	15	526	30	5.7	237	7.9	19	3.6
6 YR	85	2826	172	6.1	1291	7.5	96	3.4

Jim Kelly

YEAR	Gm	ATT	SAKS	%SAK	SYDS	AY/S	INT	%IN
1986	16	523	43	8.2	330	7.7	17	3.3
1987	12	446	27	6.1	239	8.9	11	2.5
1988	16	482	30	6.2	229	7.6	17	3.5
3 YR	44	1451	100	6.9	798	8.0	45	3.1

Dan Marino

YEAR	Gm	ATT	SAKS	%SAK	SYDS	AY/S	INT	%IN
1983	11	306	10	3.3	80	8.0	6	2.0
1984	16	577	13	2.3	120	9.2	17	2.9
1985	16	585	18	3.1	157	8.7	21	3.6
1986	16	640	17	2.7	119	7.0	23	3.6
1987	12	453	9	2.0	77	8.6	13	2.9
1988	16	613	7	1.1	41	5.9	23	3.8
6 YR	87	3174	74	2.3	594	8.0	103	3.2

Ken O'Brien

YEAR	Gm	ATT	SAKS	%SAK	SYDS	AY/S	INT	%IN
1983	0	—	—	—	—	—	—	—
1984	10	225	22	9.8	168	7.6	7	3.1
1985	16	550	62	11.2	399	6.4	8	1.5
1986	15	522	40	7.7	353	8.8	20	3.8
1987	12	443	50	11.3	364	7.3	8	1.8
1988	TK	461	37	8.0	267	7.2	7	1.5
6 YR		2201	211	9.6	1551	7.4	50	2.3

THE BALLAD OF GASTINEAU

(An epic poem found in a locker room in East Rutherford, N.J., possibly written by the former Jet, along with a learned historical gloss that may aid in interpreting some of the more obscure passages.)

> Roses are red. Violets are blue.
> Write of my love, ere I bid adieu.

Much of the Jets' preseason news centered on the romance of Gastineau and actress Brigitte Nielsen. Walton said it was a distraction for the team, but it was certainly more upbeat than Mark's prospects. The one-time dancing star of the "New York Sack Exchange" was considered an end near the end. After setting the NFL record with 22 sacks in 1985, he totaled only 20 for the next three seasons. An injury and a messy divorce were part of the problem. Then, when he crossed the picket line during the '87 strike, he became as popular with his teammates as psoriasis.

> Roses are red. All is not black.
> I have returned to break-dance each sack.

Gastineau looked hopeless in the first two preseason games and was widely expected to be cut. Then he came on in the last two games to win his old job back.

> Roses are red. Jetsters are green.
> I fell in love. Now I'm so mean!

With 7 sacks in the first five games, Gastineau moved out to an early lead in the AFC. He credited his 1988 rejuvenation to the "serenity" he'd found with Brigitte.

> Roses are red. My heart is cornflower.
> Brigitte is ill. Football's gone sour.

On Tuesday, October 18, after the Jets' Monday night loss to Buffalo, Gastineau walked into Walton's office and told him he didn't much feel like playing football anymore and was retiring. Asked to reconsider for a couple of days, Gastineau waited until Thursday to let the world know he was giving up football for love. He would spend his time with his girlfriend, who had cancer of the uterus. A quick check with medical experts revealed that cancer of the uterus was serious but not normally fatal when discovered early, as it was in this case.

> Roses are red. Newsprint grows yellow.
> ("A bleepity-bleepity-bleep sort of fellow!")

Most of the Jets were publicly sympathetic. A few told reporters what they really felt. Gastineau's ears may have been burning as brightly as his bridges.

> Roses are red. Jets' clouds are gray.
> Whatever the reason, I'm going away.

Speculation was rife. Was it love of Nielsen, apathy toward football, or spite for the teammates who shunned him in '87 that caused Gastineau to give up more than half of his $875,000 salary and leave the already-hurting Jets in the lurch?

> Roses are red. I've rung my last bell.
> I'll dance with m' darlin'. Jets go to
> a successful season. I wish them well.

A PAT FOR PAT

We were listening to one of the TV announcers tch-tching that Pat Leahy has never been in a Pro Bowl, and it started us wondering why. No, not why we were listening. We were wondering why Leahy has been passed over so often. He's a fine kicker, and he's been doing it forever. Wasn't his first holder Red Grange?

We decided to put Leahy's year-by-year record side by side with the record of the kicker who booted for the AFC in the Pro Bowl in each season since Pat entered the league.

	PAT LEAHY		AFC PRO BOWL KICKER		
YEAR	FG-ATT	PCT.	FG-ATT	PCT.	
1974	6- 11	.545	*20- 29	.689	Roy Gerela, Pittsburgh
1975	13- 21	.619	*22-*32	.688	Jan Stenerud, Kansas City
1976	11- 16	.688	20- 27	*.740	Toni Linhart, Baltimore
1977	15- 25	.600	17- 26	.654	Toni Linhart, Baltimore
1978	*22-*30	.733	19- 23	*.826	Garo Yepremian, Miami
1979	8- 13	.615	21- 25	*.840	Toni Fritsch, Houston
1980	14- 22	.636	*26- 34	.765	John Smith, New England
1981	25-*36	.694	*26-*36	.722	Nick Lowery, Kansas City
1982	11- 17	.647	16- 22	.727	Rolf Benirschke, San Diego
1983	16- 24	.667	27- 31	.871	Gary Anderson, Pittsburgh
1984	17- 24	.708	20- 24	*.833	Norm Johnson, Seattle
1985	26- 34	.765	*33-*42	.785	Gary Anderson, Pittsburgh
1986	16- 19	.842	*32-*41	.780	Tony Franklin, New England
1987	18- 22	.818	*24- 27	*.889	Dean Biasucci, Indianapolis
1988	23- 28	.821	*32-*37	*.864	Scott Norwood, Buffalo
	241-342	.705			

* Led AFC

We think we've got it. Leahy's great virtue is consistency over the long haul. But as good as he's been, there was always someone a little bit better every year. By "better" we mean in the selectable sense. As near as we can figure, the things that get a kicker to the Pro Bowl are (1) a big field goal total, (2) a high success percentage, (3) kicking for a successful team, and (4) several winning last-second boots.

Leahy's best shot at the Pro Bowl would seem to have been 1978, when he led in the number of field goals and

Garo Yepremian led in percentage. Garo also had a teeny edge in the average length of his successful kicks—35.8 to 33.8—if anyone really studied the stats. We suspect that Yepremian was selected because Miami (11–5) qualified as a Wild Card playoff team and the Jets (8–8) didn't.

Now we understand why Leahy doesn't get to go to the Pro Bowl. Next, we'll try to understand why the NFL plays it.

NEW YORK JETS STATISTICS

1988 TEAM STATISTICS	NYJ	OPP
TOTAL FIRST DOWNS	331	310
Rushing	118	123
Passing	181	162
Penalty	32	25
3rd Down Made/Att.	97/233	87/214
Pct.	41.6%	40.7%
4th Down Made/Att.	7/17	11/21
Pct.	41.2%	52.4%
TOTAL NET YARDS	5215	5633
Avg. per Game	325.9	352.1
Total Plays	1094	1038
Avg. per Play	4.8	5.4
NET YARDS RUSHING	2132	2124
Avg. per Game	133.3	132.8
Total Rushes	514	517
NET YARDS PASSING	3083	3509
Avg. per Game	192.7	219.3
Tackled/Yards Lost	42/291	45/314
Gross Yards	3374	3823
Attempts/Completions	538/299	476/244
Pct. of Completions	55.6%	51.3%
Had Intercepted	11	24

(Continued) 1988 TEAM STATISTICS	NYJ	OPP
PUNTS/AVERAGE	85/38.9	72/38.1
NET PUNTING AVG.	34.2	30.9
PENALTIES/YARDS	115/931	89/757
FUMBLES/BALL LOST	32/16	35/16
TOUCHDOWNS	43	43
Rushing	19	15
Passing	20	28
Returns	4	0
TIME OF POSSESSION	—	—

SCORE/PERIODS	1	2	3	4	OT	TOTAL
Jets	78	125	72	97	0	372
Opponents	86	64	104	97	3	354

SCORING	TDR	TDP	TDRt	PAT	FG	S	TP
Leahy				43/43	23/28		112
Hector	10						60
McNeil	6	1					42
Walker		7					42
Shuler		5					30

(Continued)

SCORING	TDR	TDP	TDRt	PAT	FG	S	TP
Toon		5					30
Vick	3						18
McMillan			2				12
Sohn		2					12
Townsell			1				6
Zordich			1				6
Lyons						1	2
Jets	19	20	4	43/43	23/28	1	372
Opponents	15	28	0	36/43	20/30	0	354

RUSHING	NO	YDS	AVG	LG	TD
McNeil	219	944	4.3	28	6
Hector	137	561	4.1	19	10
Vick	128	540	4.2	17	3
O'Brien	21	25	1.2	17	0
Ryan	5	22	4.4	15	0
Faaola	1	13	13.0	13	0
Walker	1	12	12.0	12	0
Leahy	1	10	10.0	10	0
Toon	1	5	5.0	5	0
Jets	514	2132	4.1	28	19
Opponents	517	2124	4.1	38	15

RECEIVING	NO	YDS	AVG	LG	TD
Toon	93	1067	11.5	42	5
Shuler	70	805	11.5	42t	5
McNeil	34	288	8.5	25	1
Walker	26	551	21.2	50t	7
Hector	26	237	9.1	30	0
Vick	19	120	6.3	17	0
Griggs	14	133	9.5	21	0
Sohn	7	66	9.4	17	2
Dunn	6	67	11.2	26	0
Townsell	4	40	10.0	19	0
Jets	299	3374	11.3	50t	20
Opponents	244	3823	15.7	80t	28

INTERCEPTIONS	NO	YDS	AVG	LG	TD
McMillan	8	168	21.0	55t	2
Hasty	5	20	4.0	16	0
Booty	3	0	0.0	0	0
Howard	2	0	0.0	0	0

(Continued)

INTERCEPTIONS	NO	YDS	AVG	LG	TD
Miano	2	0	0.0	0	0
Zordich	1	35	35.0	35t	1
McArthur	1	3	3.0	3	0
Benson	1	2	2.0	2	0
Humphery	1	0	0.0	0	0
Jets	24	228	9.5	55t	3
Opponents	11	126	11.5	35	0

PUNTING	NO	YDS	AVG	TB	In 20	LG	Blk
Prokop	85	3310	38.9	10	26	64	0
Jets	85	3310	38.9	10	26	64	0
Opponents	72	2742	38.1	5	13	66	1

PUNT RETURNS	NO	FC	YDS	AVG	LG	TD
Townsell	35	9	409	11.7	59t	1
Sohn	3	1	9	3.0	5	0
Jets	38	10	418	11.0	59t	1
Opponents	34	9	201	5.9	24	0

KICKOFF RETURNS	NO	YDS	AVG	LG	TD
Humphery	21	510	24.3	48	0
Townsell	31	601	19.4	40	0
Sohn	9	159	17.7	27	0
Harper	7	114	16.3	32	0
Faaola	2	9	4.5	7	0
Barber	1	11	11.0	11	0
Rose	1	0	0.0	0	0
Jets	72	1404	19.5	48	0
Opponents	70	1491	21.3	56	0

FIELD GOALS	1-19	20-29	30-39	40-49	50+	TOTAL
Leahy	0-0	9-9	7-8	7-10	0-1	23-28
Jets	0-0	9-9	7-8	7-10	0-1	23-28
Opponents	0-0	8-9	8-11	3-9	1-1	20-30

FIELD GOALS BY Leahy: 23 of 28
(29G)(22G,29G,49N,23G)(47G)(39G,33N)
(23G,44N)(30G)( )(33G,38G,28G)(41G)(51N)
(47G,48G)(23G,40G,40N)(29G)(33G,32G)
(35G,46G)(41G,20G)

PASSING	ATT	COM	YARD	PCT.	Avg G	TD	%TD	IN	%IN	LG	SAKS/YDS	RATE
O'Brien	424	236	2567	55.7	6.05	15	3.5	7	1.7	50t	37/267	78.6
Ryan	113	63	807	55.8	7.14	5	4.4	4	3.5	42t	5/24	78.3
Hector	1	0	0	0.0	0.00	0	0.0	0	0.0	0	0/0	39.6
Jets	538	299	3374	55.6	6.27	20	3.7	11	2.0	50t	42/291	78.4
Opponents	476	244	3823	51.3	8.03	28	5.9	24	5.0	80t	45/314	76.9

PITTSBURGH STEELERS

The Last 5 Seasons

	1984	1985	1986	1987	1988
Won-Lost	9-7	7-9	6-10	8-7	5-11
Percentage	.563	.438	.375	.533	.313
Division Finish	1	2-t	3	3	4
Games Behind	0	1	6	2	7
Total Points	387	379	307	285	336
Per Game	24.2	23.7	19.2	19.0	21.0
Opponent Points	310	355	336	299	421
Per Game	19.4	22.2	21.0	19.9	26.3
Net Points	77	24	-29	-14	-85
Predicted Net Wins	1.9	0.6	-0.7	-0.3	-2.1
Delta Net Wins	-0.9	-1.6	-1.3	0.9	-0.9
Total Yards on Offense	5420	5350	4811	4410	5204
Per Game	338.8	334.4	300.7	294.0	325.3
Total Yards Allowed on Defense	4916	4659	5252	4920	5805
Per Game	307.3	291.2	328.3	328.0	362.8
Net Difference	504	691	-441	-510	-601
Offensive Turnovers	40	36	36	33	39
Defensive Takeaways	42	34	33	44	33
Net Turnovers	2	-2	-3	11	-6
Predicted Net Points	50	50	-49	2	-74
Delta Net Points	27	-26	20	-16	-11
Net Rushing Yards	2179	2177	2223	2144	2228
Per Game	136.2	136.1	138.9	142.9	139.3
Average Gain	3.8	4.0	3.9	4.1	4.5
Opponent Net Rushing Yards	1617	1876	1872	1610	1864
Per Game	101.1	117.3	117.0	107.3	116.5
Average Gain	3.6	4.0	4.0	3.5	3.6
Net Passing Yards	3241	3173	2588	2266	2976
Per Game	202.6	198.3	161.8	151.1	186.0
Times Sacked	35	33	20	27	42
Passer Rating in Yards	4.9	4.0	3.6	2.8	4.2
Opponent Net Passing Yards	3299	2783	3380	3310	3941
Per Game	206.2	173.9	211.3	220.7	246.3
Times Sacked	47	36	43	26	19
Passer Rating Defense	3.7	4.0	4.7	4.6	6.0
Passer Rating Net	1.2	0.0	-1.0	-1.8	-1.8
Yards per Drive Offense	25.7	26.2	23.1	23.1	26.3
Yards per Drive Defense	24.2	21.9	25.3	25.8	29.2
Average Time of Possession	30:33	29:45	30:52	29:45	28:31

156

1984 PLAYOFFS
Won Divisional Playoff from Denver, 24-17
Lost AFC Championship Game to Miami, 28-45

THE 1988 SEASON

DATE	AT	OPPONENT	SCORE	R	SPREAD	Tu	Net YDS	Rush YDS	Pass YDS	TURN
09/11	A	Washington	29-30	L	-3.5	g	341-515	83- 93	258-422	1-3
09/18	H	Cincinnati	12-17	L	+8	a	319-302	124-116	195-186	6-1
09/25	A	Buffalo	28-36	L	-2.5	a	408-398	94-116	314-282	5-5
10/02	H	Cleveland	9-23	L	+4	a	183-299	89-168	94-131	5-1
10/09	A	Phoenix	14-31	L	-2.5	g	203-388	78-103	125-285	2-3
10/16	H	Houston	14-34	L	+6	a	344-309	93-124	251-185	4-0
10/23	H	Denver	39-21	W	+0	a	386-323	256- 45	130-278	2-4
10/30	A	N.Y. Jets	20-24	L	+3.5	a	352-196	143- 84	209-112	4-1
11/06	A	Cincinnati	7-42	L	+4.5	a	198-559	101-221	97-338	0-2
11/13	H	Philadelphia	26-27	L	+7.5	a	361-358	164-106	197-252	1-3
11/20	A	Cleveland	7-27	L	+3	g	285-262	118- 70	167-192	4-0
11/27	H	Kansas City	16-10	W	+8.5	a	336-366	214- 88	122-278	1-2
12/04	A	Houston	37-34	W	-2	a	426-403	94-134	332-269	1-4
12/11	A	San Diego	14-20	L	+10.5	g	302-324	130-180	172-144	3-0
12/18	H	Miami	40-24	W	+1	a	404-385	305- 82	99-303	1-3
						Avg.	323-359	139-115	184-244	3-2

				WINS	LOSSES
Season Record:	4-11-0	POINTS:		33- 22	16- 28
Vs. Spread:	7- 8-0	Net YDS:	9- 6-0	388-369	300-355
Home:	3- 4-0	Rush YDS:	7- 8-0	217- 87	111-126
On Artificial Turf:	4- 7-0	Pass YDS:	6- 9-0	171-282	189-230
Art. Turf vs. Spread:	6- 5-0	TURN:	8- 6-1	1- 3	3- 2

THE BIGGEST LOSS

On August 25, 1988, Art Rooney, the beloved "Chief" of the Steelers, died. Often called one of the "Founding Fathers of the NFL," Rooney wasn't quite that. He bought his franchise in 1933, fourteen years into the league's history. Supposedly he paid $2,500 with one day's winnings from the race track.

Never an innovator nor particularly ambitious for himself, Rooney became one of the league's most important leaders, even though his team was usually lousy in the 1930s. And 1940s. And 1950s. And 1960s. His greatest skill was as a mediator among volatile personalities like George Halas, Curly Lambeau, and George Preston Marshall. He didn't make pronouncements, or even statements. He just talked to people.

In Pittsburgh, even during the most frustrating seasons, fans could hate the Steelers and still like Art Rooney. He was a down-to-earth guy who just happened to own the local football team. He lived near Three Rivers Stadium and walked to his office nearly every day, stopping to chat with folks along the way. When he asked a grocer about his family, it was no act.

When the Steelers won Super Bowl IX, just about everyone in football rejoiced for Rooney (with certain Minnesotan exceptions). By then, Art's sons were running the day-to-day operations, but it was still Art's trophy. Of course after three more, he didn't have quite so many people rooting for him outside western Pennsylvania.

In Pittsburgh they all but canonized him once that first silver Super Bowl football was in the trophy case. The affection no doubt pleased him, perhaps even embarrassed him, but it never overwhelmed him. He was a man who always knew exactly who he was. And what he was was perfect for blue-collar Pittsburgh.

FOLK WISDOM

Whenever a team has a bad year, a lot of dumb things are going to be said around town. The Steelers had a poor and sometimes atrocious season in 1988, and fans' prescriptions for turning the local pros around saturated radio talk shows. Sometimes it seems only nutsos call these programs to air their strange opinions (presumably because their friends won't listen to them any longer). But sometimes certain opinions are so pervasive, even persuasive, that those of us who retain our sanity (note, we're including you) must give pause, or better yet, the back of our paws.

Let us examine some of this folk wisdom.

Fire Noll!

Numerous loyal Steeler rooters realized in 1988 that the only thing keeping Pittsburgh from its fifth Super Bowl was Chuck Noll. Although Noll was generally to blame, few fans realized his most insidious schemes. First he schooled his blockers and tacklers to avoid opponents and his runners and receivers to seek them out. Then before each game he put lead in his players' shoes and butter on their fingers. It was rumored that he endlessly lectured his punt squad on the battle tactics of General Custer.

They've Drafted Bums Since 1974

Actually they haven't had a super-great draft since 1974 (Lynn Swann, Jack Lambert, John Stallworth, and Mike Webster), but neither has anyone else. Considering that they drafted at or near the top for the rest of the seventies and in the top half for most of the eighties, the Steelers did pretty well. They chose some good players who kept them winning enough games to continue to draft high.

Where Pittsburgh really fell down was from 1983 to 1985. In '83, the top pick was NT Gabe Rivera, who gave indications he could do a fair imitation of Mean Joe Greene until he was paralyzed in an auto accident midway through his rookie season. None of the other '83 choices were of any real use to the team, making that draft a total washout.

The '84 draft was a considerable improvement: Louis Lipps, the present team's best pass receiver; Terry Long, a short but useful guard; and sub-WR Weegie Thompson. One or two more regulars or potential regulars would have made this one okay.

Only reserve LB Greg Carr and punter Harry Newsome came out of the '85 draft, when DE Darryl Sims was the first pick and a complete flop.

By getting only two regulars out of those three drafts, the Steelers were forced to do two things. First, hang on to some fading stars a season or two past their primes when they might otherwise have been traded away for future draft choices. And second, force-feed newcomers from the 1986-through-1988 drafts into regular positions when they might better have ripened on the bench. What had been broken in the '83–'85 drafts was the replacement continuity that allows a team to supplant a fading veteran with a seasoned youngster.

Instead of the four-to-six year veterans who make up the bulk of most successful teams' lineups, the '88 Steelers were largely inexperienced. The eleven offensive starters who saw the most action totaled fifty-two seasons of experience, but thirty-three of those seasons were tied up in players who were with the team prior to 1983. The eleven busiest defensive players totaled forty-one seasons, with twenty-five in pre-'83 Steelers. In other words, the Steelers normally had sixteen players starting who averaged 2.18 years experience.

As for the 1986–88 drafts, it's too soon to tell about many of them, but twenty-one of those draftees were either on the end-of-season roster or on injured reserve. That hardly constitutes bad drafting.

Fire Noll!!

Among Noll's most vocal critics was his former QB Terry Bradshaw: "I have to question his commitment." When Bradshaw was elected to the Hall of Fame, he didn't ask Noll to be his presenter. And when Noll is elected, he won't ask Terry.

They Only Have Six NFL-Quality Players

We don't understand the significance of the number six, but it was the usual number given—followed by player lists that named different half-dozen combinations. The truth is that the Pittsburgh roster is made up mostly of average NFL-quality players, something that might even be said about championship teams. What they really lack is blue-chip stars. They have perhaps six who have been or might someday be Pro Bowl quality. They need another six or so, and suddenly the average players will look pretty good.

Fire Noll!!!

Team President Dan Rooney, who obviously had learned nothing after spending his life with the Steelers, said he had "never even considered" firing Noll. But many experts whose understanding of the game was deepened by trips to the fridge during commercials considered it at the top of their lungs.

Use the Top Draft Choice on a QB . . . RB . . . WR . . .

Bubby Brister won the QB slot in training camp after playing in only four games in his first two seasons. Sometimes he looked good and at other times he was obviously inexperienced. He has a strong, fairly accurate arm, scrambles well, and is a leader-type. Whether he can put that together to become a Super Bowl type only time will tell. Right now the best bet would be to ride with him and pray, rather than starting from scratch with a rookie.

Sophomore Merril Hoge and freshman Warren Williams actually produced a solid, if unspectacular, running game once they became regulars at midseason. Unless they know they can get a young Franco Harris, the Steelers should use their top draft pick elsewhere.

And "elsewhere" isn't WR. Pittsburgh desperately needs someone to take double coverage off Lipps, but they'd better hope for a late-round pick to come through or one of their present kids to develop because there is an even more dire need.

Fire Noll!!!!

Better yet, have him and assistant coach Joe Greene put on pads again and rush the passer. They'll be in their dotage before they do a worse job than the guys who played in '88.

Human communication cannot describe the inadequacy of the Pittsburgh pass rush. A feather landing on a cloud exerts more pressure. It wouldn't hurry the White Rabbit, much less sack him. Well, in truth, there were 19 sacks for the whole season by the whole defense, but that whole 19 just proves what a hole is there. Not that the Steelers haven't tried to find someone. Starting in 1978, the last Super Bowl season, they began looking for replacements for L. C. Greenwood and Dwight White.

1978 No. 2: Willie Fry (DE) Notre Dame—too brittle, never played.
1979 No. 2: Zack Valentine (LB) East Carolina—too slow for LB, too small for DE (but No. 5 Dwaine Board was let go to San Francisco).
1980 No. 2: John Goodman (DE) Oklahoma—okay against the run.
1981 No. 1: Keith Gary (DE) Oklahoma—ditto.
1982 No. 2: John Meyer (OT) Arizona State—tried at DE; always hurt.
1983 No. 1: Gabe Rivera (NT-DE) Texas Tech—paralyzed; career over.
1984 (no one)
1985 No. 1: Darryl Sims (DE) Wisconsin—ker-plunk!
1986 No. 2: Gerald Williams (DT) Auburn—the present NT.
1987 No. 6: Tim Johnson (DE) Penn State—started at DE.
1988 No. 1: Aaron Jones (DE) East Kentucky—started at DE.

Although at one point the hot-headed Jones had nearly as many penalties as tackles, the Steelers still hold out hope for him. But his 1.5 sacks were pretty poor stuff. Johnson had 4 and Williams 3.5.

Anybody Can Pass Them Silly

This was mostly true.

The patty-cake pass rush doomed the Steelers' young secondary. As a consequence the team's strongest defensive area ended up looking like the weakest—last in the league in pass defense.

Unfortunately the Steelers' history of failure in finding a pass rusher might cause the fans to storm Three Rivers Stadium like the Bastille if another high pick is devoted to this need.

Fire Noll!!!!!

And hire whom? According to Pittsburgh newspaperman Pat Livingston, "Since Lombardi won Super Bowl I, NFL teams have hired 178 coaches, every one of whom had the golden credentials when chosen to reach for the brass ring.

"It is shocking to think that only 17 of those 178 achieved their goal."

The man makes his point without mentioning pigs in pokes or birds in hands. When you fire someone, you had better have a better replacement ready and willing to step in.

Lombardi's dead.

They Aren't Trying

This particular bit of wisdom was usually voiced in connection with the Steelers' sometimes amazing faculty for doing the wrong thing at the wrong time. Their 38 turnovers put them near the bottom of the league. Their 6 punts blocked set a league record. As for penalties, in one series they had Cleveland third-and-17 and jumped offsides three straight times. Third-and-2, the Browns made a first down and went on to score. They also had bad center snaps that cost one game by messing up an extra point and another over the punter's head that produced a turnover after a 47-yard loss.

Some bad things happen to good teams, of course, but the accumulation by the Steelers was indeed rare. About the only place you can find collections of goofs like the Steelers' assortment is with an extremely young team that tries too hard and lets its anxiety overcome its ability.

Fire Noll!!!!!!

The only known remedy for the above-named condition is experience. But there are all kinds of experiences. Young teams seem to reach maturity best when coached by men who are solid on fundamentals, able teachers, and possessed of almost infinite patience. Let's see, do we know a coach who fits that description?

Get a New Punter

Harry Newsome's sixth blocked punt of the season added to the NFL record he had set earlier with his third. He now has 11 for his career, another record. When he first took over the Steeler punting in 1985, Newsome was painfully slow in getting his kicks off. He worked at it and had his time down to 2.0 from snap to kick, not the best but acceptable—with decent snaps and reliable blocking. This year he had neither.

A stranger Newsome stat: his average yards per punt (which did not include the blocked kicks) was 45.4, the best in the NFL. But his net average (which subtracts the runbacks and touchbacks) was 31.8, the second-worst among regular punters.

Fire Noll!!!!!!!

Call back tomorrow night when we'll be talking about fananasia.

They Won't Win Another Game All Season

This was heard from Week 1 on. It became almost a wish by those who considered the Steelers' position in the draft.

In a Steeler season that was mostly lumps of coal, their win at Houston in Week 14 was a gem. Lipps scored on 80- and 65-yard touchdown passes. Brister threw for 311 yards. RB Dwight Stone returned a kickoff 92 yards for a TD. Most important, the underdog Steelers matched muscle with the Oilers and came out ahead. Still it looked like another close loss when Houston took a 34–31 lead with 1:30 to go. But Brister led the team on an 80-yard march to the winning touchdown.

Hardly anyone in Pittsburgh seemed to notice or care that Gary Anderson missed the final extra point, his first flub in 203 tries—the third-longest streak in NFL history.

For a week there was only a little folk wisdom on the radio. It was the nicest week in Pittsburgh all fall.

PITTSBURGH STEELERS STATISTICS

1988 TEAM STATISTICS	PS	OPP
TOTAL FIRST DOWNS	292	319
Rushing	120	110
Passing	150	181
Penalty	22	28
3rd Down Made/Att.	78/216	98/225
Pct.	36.1%	43.6%
4th Down Made/Att.	5/17	4/13
Pct.	29.4%	30.8%
TOTAL NET YARDS	5204	5805
Avg. per Game	325.3	362.8
Total Plays	1030	1067
Avg. per Play	5.1	5.4
NET YARDS RUSHING	2228	1864
Avg. per Game	139.3	116.5
Total Rushes	499	516
NET YARDS PASSING	2976	3941
Avg. per Game	186.0	246.3
Tackled/Yards Lost	42/331	19/145
Gross Yards	3307	4086
Attempts/Completions	489/226	532/309
Pct. of Completions	46.2%	58.1%
Had Intercepted	20	20
PUNTS/AVERAGE	71/41.5	67/40.7
NET PUNTING AVG.	32.8	35.0
PENALTIES/YARDS	99/803	79/705
FUMBLES/BALL LOST	40/19	35/13
TOUCHDOWNS	46	49
Rushing	17	20
Passing	15	25
Returns	4	4
TIME OF POSSESSION	—	—

SCORE/PERIODS	1	2	3	4	OT	TOTAL
Steelers	85	94	47	110	0	336
Opponents	64	138	103	116	0	421

SCORING	TDR	TDP	TDRt	PAT	FG	S	TP
Anderson				34/35	28/36		118
Brister	6						36
Hoge	3	3					36
Lipps	1	5					36
Carter	3	2					30
E. Jackson	3						18
Stone		1	1				12
Blackledge	1						6
Gothard		1					6
Jordan			1				6
Lockett		1					6
Thompson		1					6
W. Williams		1					6
Woodruff			1				6
Woodson			1				6
Steelers	17	15	4	34/36	28/36	1	336
Opponents	20	25	4	47/49	26/32	1	421

RUSHING	NO	YDS	AVG	LG	TD
Hoge	170	705	4.1	20	3
W. Williams	87	409	4.7	33	0
E. Jackson	74	315	4.3	29t	3
Carter	36	216	6.0	64t	3
Brister	45	209	4.6	20	6
Lipps	6	129	21.5	39t	1
Stone	40	127	3.2	11	0
Pollard	31	93	3.0	7	0
Blackledge	8	25	3.1	10	1
Newsome	2	0	0.0	0	0
Steelers	499	2228	4.5	64t	17
Opponents	516	1864	3.6	64	20

RECEIVING	NO	YDS	AVG	LG	TD
Lipps	50	973	19.5	89t	5
Hoge	50	487	9.7	40	3
Carter	32	363	11.3	33	2
Lockett	22	365	16.6	44	1
Thompson	16	370	23.1	50	1
Gothard	12	121	10.1	26	1
Stone	11	196	17.8	72t	1
W. Williams	11	66	6.0	21	1
Tr. Jackson	10	237	23.7	70	0
E. Jackson	9	84	9.3	24	0
Pollard	2	22	11.0	19	0
Hinnant	1	23	23.0	23	0
Steelers	226	3307	14.6	89t	15
Opponents	309	4086	13.2	86t	25

INTERCEPTIONS	NO	YDS	AVG	LG	TD
Woodruff	4	109	27.3	78t	1
Woodson	4	98	24.5	29	0
Everett	3	31	10.3	29	0
Griffin	2	63	31.5	33	0
Jordan	1	28	28.0	28t	1
Carr	1	27	27.0	27	0
Gowdy	1	24	24.0	24	0
Hinkle	1	1	1.0	1	0
Little	1	0	0.0	0	0
Nickerson	1	0	0.0	0	0
Sanchez	1	0	0.0	0	0
Steelers	20	381	19.1	78t	2
Opponents	20	367	18.4	75t	1

PUNTING	NO	YDS	AVG	TB	In 20	LG	Blk
Newsome	65	2950	45.4	10	9	62	6
Steelers	71	2950	41.5	10	9	62	6
Opponents	67	2726	40.7	3	16	63	0

PUNT RETURNS	NO	FC	YDS	AVG	LG	TD
Woodson	33	6	281	8.5	28	0
Lipps	4	2	30	7.5	11	0

(Continued)

PUNT RETURNS	NO	FC	YDS	AVG	LG	TD
Steelers	39	12	322	8.3	28	0
Opponents	40	9	418	10.5	32	0

KICKOFF RETURNS	NO	YDS	AVG	LG	TD
Woodson	37	850	23.0	92t	1
Stone	29	610	21.0	92t	1
Sanchez	4	71	17.8	19	0
Blankenship	1	5	5.0	5	0
Boyle	1	19	19.0	19	0
J. Jackson	1	10	10.0	10	0
W. Williams	1	10	10.0	10	0
Steelers	74	1575	21.3	92t	2
Opponents	63	1351	21.4	90t	1

FIELD GOALS	1-19	20-29	30-39	40-49	50+	TOTAL
Anderson	1-1	11-11	9-10	6-12	1-2	28-36
Steelers	1-1	11-11	9-10	6-12	1-2	28-36
Opponents	3-3	6-7	9-10	7-10	1-2	26-32

FIELD GOALS BY Anderson: 28 of 36
(32G,46N)(33G,24G,43G)(48N,19G)(49N)(49G,
35G,45G)(47N)( )(30G,32G,21G,37G,22G,30G)
(25G,21G)( )(52G,21G,29G,41G,57N)( )(23G,20G,
22G,47N)(39N,45G,48N)( )(34G,43G,34G,22G)

PASSING	ATT	COM	YARD	PCT.	Avg G	TD	%TD	IN	%IN	LG	SAKS/YDS	RATE
Brister	370	175	2634	47.3	7.12	11	3.0	14	3.8	89t	36/292	65.3
Blackledge	79	38	494	48.1	6.25	2	2.5	3	3.8	34	4/25	60.8
Bono	35	10	110	28.6	3.14	1	2.9	2	5.7	15	1/8	25.9
Carter	3	2	56	66.7	18.67	0	0.0	0	0.0	40	0/0	109.7
Lipps	2	1	13	50.0	6.50	1	50.0	1	50.0	13t	1/6	70.8
Steelers	489	226	3307	46.2	6.76	15	3.1	20	4.1	89t	42/331	62.0
Opponents	532	309	4086	58.1	7.68	25	4.7	20	3.8	86t	19/145	82.5

SAN DIEGO CHARGERS

The Last 5 Seasons

	1984	1985	1986	1987	1988
Won-Lost	7-9	8-8	4-12	8-7	6-10
Percentage	.438	.500	.250	.533	.375
Division Finish	5	3-t	5	3	4
Games Behind	6	4	7	2.5	3
Total Points	394	467	335	253	231
Per Game	24.6	29.2	20.9	16.9	14.4
Opponent Points	413	435	396	317	332
Per Game	25.8	27.2	24.8	21.1	20.8
Net Points	-19	32	-61	-64	-101
Predicted Net Wins	-0.5	0.8	-1.5	-1.6	-2.5
Delta Net Wins	-0.5	-0.8	-2.5	2.1	0.5
Total Yards on Offense	6297	6535	5356	4588	4429
Per Game	393.6	408.4	334.8	305.9	276.8
Total Yards Allowed on Defense	5936	6265	5366	4953	5418
Per Game	371.0	391.6	335.4	330.2	338.6
Net Difference	361	270	-10	-365	-989
Offensive Turnovers	38	49	49	43	32
Defensive Takeaways	36	42	37	28	26
Net Turnovers	-2	-7	-12	-15	-6
Predicted Net Points	22	-6	-49	-90	-106
Delta Net Points	-41	38	-12	26	5
Net Rushing Yards	1654	1665	1576	1308	2041
Per Game	103.4	104.1	98.5	87.2	127.6
Average Gain	3.6	3.8	3.3	3.3	4.7
Opponent Net Rushing Yards	1851	1972	1678	2171	2133
Per Game	115.7	123.3	104.9	144.7	133.3
Average Gain	4.1	4.2	3.5	4.2	4.1
Net Passing Yards	4643	4870	3780	3280	2388
Per Game	290.2	304.4	236.3	218.7	149.3
Times Sacked	36	39	32	39	31
Passer Rating in Yards	5.7	5.8	3.9	4.3	3.2
Opponent Net Passing Yards	4085	4293	3688	2782	3285
Per Game	255.3	268.3	230.5	185.5	205.3
Times Sacked	33	40	62	45	34
Passer Rating Defense	6.2	5.4	5.7	4.9	5.1
Passer Rating Net	-0.5	0.4	-1.8	-0.6	-1.9
Yards per Drive Offense	31.3	30.8	25.4	23.1	23.6
Yards per Drive Defense	30.3	28.5	25.4	24.6	29.9
Average Time of Possession	31:43	29:21	30:32	28:08	28:22

THE 1988 SEASON

DATE	AT	OPPONENT	SCORE	R	SPREAD	Tu	Net YDS	Rush YDS	Pass YDS	TURN
09/04	A	L.A. Raiders	13-24	L	+6	g	263-277	111- 94	152-183	1-1
09/11	A	Denver	3-34	L	+12.5	g	244-443	133-184	111-259	2-0
09/18	H	Seattle	17- 6	W	+8	g	237-299	159-105	78-194	1-4
09/25	A	Kansas City	24-23	W	+6.5	a	303-331	165- 94	138-237	1-2
10/02	H	Denver	0-12	L	+4	g	190-291	20-129	170-162	2-1
10/09	H	New Orleans	17-23	L	+4.5	g	206-365	93-134	113-231	2-1
10/16	A	Miami	28-31	L	+9.5	g	396-375	113- 46	283-329	4-1
10/23	H	Indianapolis	0-16	L	+0	g	239-453	118-198	121-255	1-3
10/30	A	Seattle	14-17	L	+8.5	a	299-235	136-126	163-109	3-0
11/06	H	L.A. Raiders	3-13	L	+3	g	216-306	63-149	153-157	3-2
11/13	A	Atlanta	10- 7	W	+5.5	g	355-245	185- 57	170-188	2-3
11/20	H	L.A. Rams	38-24	W	+11	g	297-363	101-151	196-212	1-2
11/27	H	S. Francisco	10-48	L	+7	g	312-475	136-203	176-272	3-0
12/04	A	Cincinnati	10-27	L	+13.5	a	211-352	88-207	123-145	4-2
12/11	H	Pittsburgh	20-14	W	-1	g	324-302	180-130	144-172	0-3
12/18	H	Kansas City	24-13	W	-1.5	g	337-306	246-139	91-167	2-2
						Avg.	277-339	128-134	149-205	2-2

				WINS	LOSSES
Season Record:	6-10-0	POINTS:		22- 15	10- 25
Vs. Spread:	8- 8-0	Net YDS:	5-11-0	309-308	258-357
Home:	3- 5-0	Rush YDS:	8- 8-0	173-113	101-147
On Artificial Turf:	1- 2-0	Pass YDS:	2-14-0	136-195	157-210
Art. Turf vs. Spread:	2- 1-0	TURN:	6- 8-2	1- 3	3- 1

THE SAGA OF SAUNDERS

Each NFL season is like a gigantic book of short stories, with humorous, suspenseful, absurd, heroic, and tragic tales intermingled. Some stories demonstrate moral truths; others are slice-of-life.

This is a story with a happy ending.

Our Protagonist and His Nemesis

Did you happen to catch Al Saunders in a TV closeup near the end of the season? When we saw him, he was getting that Don Coryell look. You know the one: a crease down his forehead you could plant corn in, nostrils flared wider than '65 slacks, and a look in his eyes like his jock was filled with ground glass. Maybe it's something you catch in San Diego. Didn't Sid Gillman get ulcers there? Whatever Saunders caught, it was exacerbated by the Air-Coryell aftertaste.

The song ended a couple of years ago, but the melody—or the memory—lingered on. Sometimes that happens to a team with a strong personality. Their fans still expect them to be the "old" whatevers, long after the footballers who gave the whatevers their particular persona have moved on to their life's work. In Dallas there are folks who still expect razzle-dazzle, even though the Cowboys' dazzle razzled out when Staubach retired. In Green Bay they never got over Lombardi. Maybe some Cajuns still go to the Superdome with bags over their heads. They haven't gotten over Air-Coryell in San Diego. It *was* great fun to watch. A scoring machine: insert football, withdraw touchdowns. You could say that about the offense *or* the defense.

Now only the defense reminds you of the old days. You can't have Air-Coryell with Hindenburg talent.

Setting the Scene

When Saunders took over in mid-1986 as the NFL's then-youngest head coach and the only one born in London, England, he could see that the old TD makers were becoming the old, *old* TD makers. So he started reshaping the team in the image of the talent, if that's the right word, coming up. Henceforth, he decreed, the Chargers would run a balanced offense and some of them would do admirable labor on defense. Ah, if wishing could make it so! Maybe it helped. Saunders looked like a genius when the '87 team won eight of its first nine (including three strike games). Then reality set in and Al's Chargers charged into the toilet in their last six contests.

Buoyed by the first half of that season (and perhaps out of town for the last six weeks), Owner Alex Spanos let it be bruited about that he expected an 8-8 season in '88. Or better. His enthusiasm led him to add $3 to his ticket prices. Or perhaps he simply wanted to get closer to his team by emulating its nickname. Either way, he assured himself of a San Diego fandom that expected improvement with a capital W.

The Plot Thickens

But when Saunders began constructing his '88 juggernaut, he found that his bricks lacked some straws. Take your pick as to which missing straw broke his back.

The defense, which had improved by 3.7 points in '87, was hamstrung by the holdout of star LB Chip Banks. At first, everybody thought Banks just wanted to skip camp, since he'd never been known for his spartan dedication to training rituals. But then it turned ugly and Banks allowed that he'd just as soon not play for San Diego again. This may not have been altogether a catastrophe in view of Banks' later drug bust in Georgia.

The Kellen Winslow incident was much uglier, anyway. The great tight end—perhaps no longer as great as of yore but nevertheless an '87 Pro Bowler—believed that his chronic knee injury rendered him unsuitable for '88 combat. He also believed that he should be paid his full salary in that his affliction had been honorably acquired in service to the Chargers. The powers-that-be believed otherwise, arguing that Winslow had passed his physical and should get back to work. Eventually, Kellen retired and accepted a monetary settlement that made neither side happy.

Most puzzling was the Jim Lachey trade. The OT was regarded as the Chargers' best blocker. So they shipped him to the Raiders for RB Napoleon McCallum, who will be doing his R-ing for the U.S. Navy in the foreseeable future, and fat John Clay, an OT who outperformed Lachey only on the Toledo scales. Shortly after his arrival in San Diego, Clay was knocked out for the season, as was his sub and regular center Don Macek. The Chargers went through most of the season with an offensive line made up of four free agents and a rookie.

Are we setting too many obstacles in our protagonist's path? Wait, there's more.

Rising Action

Veteran WR Wes Chandler was also sent packing. This left San Diego with four WRs whose pre-'88 NFL time totaled one season. And though they are in fact a talented and speedy crew, they too often verified their inexperience by running slants when fly patterns were called or by posting when they should have hooked.

None of these developments endeared Director of Operations Steve Ortmayer to Saunders. Which mattered not a whit to Ortmayer, who wasn't a Saunders booster to start with. Among other annoyances was Saunders' apparent belief that he was not coaching the next Super Bowl winner. In preseason when the coach was asked if he anticipated any cuts, Saunders answered, "Only my wrists."

Introduction of New and Fascinating Characters

But pouring oil on troubled fires, there were the quarterbacks and the coordinator. Ever since the Chargers were ponies their passes were performed by the estimable Dan Fouts. However, by the end of the '87 season, Fouts had become long in the tooth, short in the wind, and a stationary target for enemy sackers. He decided to take his body to the broadcasting booth while he still had a body to take. No problem! The Chargers obtained the services of Mark Malone for 1988.

Before we continue, you should be reminded that Malone had earlier been the Pittsburgh quarterback. He possesses many admirable traits: loyalty, tact, compassion, and wit being among them. He has not, however, up to this point in his career demonstrated a particular knack for passing the football. His NFL-low, 46.7 passer rating in 1987 brought him so many unkind remarks that even his best friends think his full name is Much Maligned Mark Malone. The idea that 4-M would replace Fouts struck many observers as laughable.

But to improve the offense, the Chargers hired a new offensive coordinator of broad experience, one Jerry Rhome, formerly of the Washington Redskins. It chanced that during preseason, backup QB Babe Laufenberg outperformed Malone. At Rhome's urging, Babe opened the regular season as the starting QB, a situation that struck many observers as laufable.

Up to that point in his career, Babe had been cut seven (yes, seven) times by various NFL clubs. In his wanderings he had earlier spent some time under the tutelage of Rhome. This led some to the conclusion that his uncharacteristic success, albeit preseason, had come only because he already knew Rhome's system. And when the Chargers crawled out of the gate with an offense that was truly offensive, there were calls for Malone, something not heard on an NFL gridiron since 1981. The coordinator counseled patience, reminding the nervous that any new offensive system would take time to construct and certainly Rhome's wasn't built in a day.

Heightening of the Conflict

Before a game with the Raiders, Saunders casually mentioned that the coming opponent had more talent on its roster than did the Chargers. It's hard to believe that anyone within the continental United States, Hawaii, or any of the territories would disagree with that assessment. Surprisingly there were two: Messrs. Spanos and Ortmayer. Ortmayer, the man responsible for assembling the Chargers' talent, had held a similar job with the Raiders before coming to San Diego. Saunders had to back down, hem, haw, and take refuge in having been "misunderstood." He'd been on everybody's list of Coaches Most Likely to Be Fired; now he moved to the top.

It was at about this time that a strong suspicion arose that the offensive coordinator fancied himself deserving of a different place in the Chargers' organization—a place like Saunders'. The phrase "stab in the back" gained popularity. If yon Jerry had a lean and hungry look, the inability of his system to generate any offense made him an unlikely candidate to succeed Saunders.

After the sixth game Malone became the starter. After the tenth game, second-year pro Mark Vlasic, who had thrown all of six passes in NFL competition, was handed the keys. When the Chargers won his first start, he was hailed as *the answer* by some, but the 10–7 victory belonged to the defense. In Game 12, Vlasic's season ended with a knee injury. Malone started the last four games.

The Chargers' 231 points were the lowest season total in the AFC. But the offense only scored 196 of those points— an average of 12.25 a game. As a starter in eight games, Malone (2–6) generated 102 points (12.75). Vlasic put 20 points up in his pair of starts. The second win of his 2–0 record was saved by a two-touchdown relief job by Malone. Laufenberg (2–4) engendered 60 points in six starts.

The Climax

Nevertheless the defense was mostly good, particularly in view of having LB Billy Ray Smith available for only half the season. DE Lee Williams was the only Charger to make the Pro Bowl, but FS Vencie Glenn and CB Gil Byrd wouldn't have looked out of place. Leslie O'Neal, an outstanding DE rookie in '86, showed strong signs of a comeback.

The defense, and RB Gary Anderson's 662 rushing yards in the last six games, including a Charger record 217 in the season finale, helped Saunders end a frustrating season on an up note. The 6–10 mark was less than Spanos' 8–8 but better than most people figured for the Chargers.

And a Not-Very Surprising Resolution

The day after the last game, Saunders was fired.
We said this story had a happy ending. Saunders will

coach again. Hopefully it will be some place where the owner has realistic expectations, his immediate superior is sympathetic, his assistants are loyal, the fans are patient, and the ghost of the previous administration isn't hanging over his shoulder. He wasn't a bad coach at San Diego, but he'll be better next time. Particularly if he has the horses.

The stable isn't empty in San Diego, of course. Those kid receivers improved as the season wore on. Jamie Holland and Quinn Early have terrific speed. If they harness it to crisp patterns, they can burn defenses. TE Rod Bernstine is okay.

The Chargers could use a power back. Gary Anderson ran for over 1,000 yards, but he's on the frail side and would benefit by being the second runner in the backfield instead of the main man. Lionel "Little Train" James is the same kind of spot-runner-cum-pass-receiver.

M. M. M. Malone made an effective quarterback in the last two games by handing off most of the time. He threw only ten times in the finale. Vlasic is still the hope.

The line will be better, if only because it will have been there awhile. Maybe Clay will lose weight and gain credibility as a tackle. Maybe Macek will come back from his career-threatening rotator cuff injury.

The defense needs further upgrading. Having LB Billy Ray Smith for sixteen games is the first order of business. In '88 he missed the first four games with a calf injury and then broke his leg in Game 12. A couple of defensive backs would help a lot.

The happiest ending for this story belongs to Charger fans. There's still hope. While they wait till next year, they can dream about the maturation of young talent, the healing of injuries, and how the new coach will make it all work.

SAN DIEGO CHARGERS STATISTICS

1988 TEAM STATISTICS	SDC	OPP
TOTAL FIRST DOWNS	255	335
Rushing	115	135
Passing	116	173
Penalty	24	27
3rd Down Made/Att.	70/203	97/221
Pct.	34.5%	43.9%
4th Down Made/Att.	7/19	6/11
Pct.	36.8%	54.5%
TOTAL NET YARDS	4429	5418
Avg. per Game	276.8	338.6
Total Plays	937	1072
Avg. per Play	4.7	5.1
NET YARDS RUSHING	2041	2133
Avg. per Game	127.6	133.3
Total Rushes	438	521
NET YARDS PASSING	2388	3285
Avg. per Game	149.3	205.3
Tackled/Yards Lost	31/240	34/240
Gross Yards	2628	3525
Attempts/Completions	468/241	517/274
Pct. of Completions	51.5%	53.0%
Had Intercepted	20	16
PUNTS/AVERAGE	86/43.5	71/39.3

(Continued)

1988 TEAM STATISTICS	SDC	OPP
NET PUNTING AVG.	34.5	32.9
PENALTIES/YARDS	118/1039	74/619
FUMBLES/BALL LOST	26/12	25/10
TOUCHDOWNS	27	38
Rushing	11	15
Passing	11	22
Returns	5	1
TIME OF POSSESSION	—	—

SCORE/PERIODS	1	2	3	4	OT	TOTAL
Chargers	72	57	37	65	0	231
Opponents	69	105	57	101	0	332

SCORING	TDR	TDP	TDRt	PAT	FG	S	TP
Abbott				15/15	8/12		39
DeLine				12/12	6/8		30
Early		4					24
A. Miller		3	1				24
Malone	4						24
Anderson	3						18
Redden	3						18

(Continued)

(Continued)

SCORING	TDR	TDP	TDRt	PAT	FG	S	TP
Flutie		2					12
Holland		1	1				12
Adams	1						6
Bennett			1				6
Browner			1				6
James		1					6
Seale			1				6
Chargers	11	11	5	27/27	14/20	0	231
Opponents	15	22	1	36/38	22/36	1	332

RUSHING	NO	YDS	AVG	LG	TD
Anderson	225	1119	5.0	36	3
Spencer	44	169	4.9	24	0
Malone	37	169	4.6	36t	4
Adams	38	149	3.9	14	1
Laufenberg	31	120	3.9	23	0
James	23	105	4.6	23	0
Early	7	63	9.0	37	0
A. Miller	7	45	6.4	20	0
Redden	19	30	1.6	5t	3
Holland	3	19	6.3	10	0
Bernstine	2	7	3.5	5	0
Vlasic	2	0	0.0	0	0
Chargers	438	2041	4.7	37	11
Opponents	521	2133	4.1	37t	15

RECEIVING	NO	YDS	AVG	LG	TD
Holland	39	536	13.7	45	1
A. Miller	36	526	14.6	49	3
James	36	279	7.8	31	1
Anderson	32	182	5.7	20	0
Early	29	375	12.9	38t	4
Bernstine	29	340	11.7	59	0
Flutie	18	208	11.6	28	2
Cox	18	144	8.0	20	0
Jones (W)	3	21	7.0	11	0
Jones (SDC)	1	11	11.0	11	0
Spencer	1	14	14.0	14	0
Redden	1	11	11.0	11	0
Sievers	1	2	2.0	2	0
Chargers	241	2628	10.9	59	11
Opponents	274	3525	12.9	96t	22

INTERCEPTIONS	NO	YDS	AVG	LG	TD
Byrd	7	82	11.7	42	0
Browner	2	65	32.5	55t	1

(Continued)

INTERCEPTIONS	NO	YDS	AVG	LG	TD
Coleman	2	0	0.0	0	0
Bennett	1	21	21.0	21	0
Smith	1	9	9.0	9	0
Faucette	1	2	2.0	2	0
Glenn	1	0	0.0	0	0
Patterson	1	0	0.0	0	0
Chargers	16	179	11.2	55t	1
Opponents	20	307	15.4	44	0

PUNTING	NO	YDS	AVG	TB	In 20	LG	Blk
Mojsiejenko	85	3745	44.1	11	22	62	1
Chargers	86	3745	43.5	11	22	62	1
Opponents	71	2792	39.3	7	16	65	1

PUNT RETURNS	NO	FC	YDS	AVG	LG	TD
James	28	11	278	9.9	24	0
Flutie	7	5	36	5.1	10	0
Chargers	35	16	314	9.0	24	0
Opponents	56	5	558	10.0	36	0

KICKOFF RETURNS	NO	YDS	AVG	LG	TD
Holland	31	810	26.1	94t	1
A. Miller	25	648	25.9	93t	1
Adams	1	13	13.0	13	0
Flutie	1	10	10.0	10	0
Jones	1	13	13.0	13	0
Spencer	1	16	16.0	16	0
Chargers	60	1510	25.2	94t	2
Opponents	47	1055	22.4	97t	1

FIELD GOALS	1-19	20-29	30-39	40-49	50+	TOTAL
Abbott	0-0	3-3	2-4	3-5	0-0	8-12
DeLine	0-0	3-3	1-1	2-4	0-0	6-8
Chargers	0-0	6-6	3-5	5-9	0-0	14-20
Opponents	0-0	8-9	7-10	5-14	2-3	22-36

FIELD GOALS BY Abbott: 8 of 12
(23G,33G)(20G)(48G,30N)(47G)(34N)
(35G)( )( )(49N)(40G)(43N,23G)
DeLine: ( )( )( )( )( )( )( )( )( )( )(38G)(23G)
(26G,41N)(24G,42G)(45G,45N)

PASSING	ATT	COM	YARD	PCT.	Avg G	TD	%TD	IN	%IN	LG	SAKS/YDS	RATE
Malone	272	147	1580	54.0	5.81	6	2.2	13	4.8	59	9/45	58.8
Laufenberg	144	69	778	47.9	5.40	4	2.8	5	3.5	47t	18/155	59.3
Vlasic	52	25	270	48.1	5.19	1	1.9	2	3.8	57	3/32	54.2
James	0	0	0	—	—	0	—	0	—	0	1/8	0.0
Chargers	468	241	2628	51.5	5.62	11	2.4	20	4.3	59	31/240	58.4
Opponents	517	274	3525	53.0	6.82	22	4.3	16	3.1	96t	34/240	75.9

SEATTLE SEAHAWKS

The Last 5 Seasons

	1984	1985	1986	1987	1988
Won-Lost	12-4	8-8	10-6	9-6	9-7
Percentage	.750	.500	.625	.600	.563
Division Finish	2	3-t	2-t	2	1
Games Behind	1	4	1	1.5	0
Total Points	418	349	366	371	339
Per Game	26.1	21.8	22.9	24.7	21.2
Opponent Points	282	303	293	314	329
Per Game	17.6	18.9	18.3	20.9	20.6
Net Points	136	46	73	57	10
Predicted Net Wins	3.4	1.1	1.8	1.4	0.3
Delta Net Wins	0.6	-1.1	0.2	0.1	0.8
Total Yards on Offense	5068	5007	5409	4735	4842
Per Game	316.8	312.9	338.1	315.7	302.6
Total Yards Allowed on Defense	4963	5160	5341	5159	5639
Per Game	310.2	322.5	333.8	343.9	352.4
Net Difference	105	-153	68	-424	-797
Offensive Turnovers	39	41	27	36	34
Defensive Takeaways	63	44	36	38	40
Net Turnovers	24	3	9	2	6
Predicted Net Points	105	-1	42	-27	-42
Delta Net Points	31	47	31	84	52
Net Rushing Yards	1645	1644	2300	2023	2086
Per Game	102.8	102.8	143.8	134.9	130.4
Average Gain	3.3	3.6	4.5	4.1	4.0
Opponent Net Rushing Yards	1789	1837	1759	2201	2286
Per Game	111.8	114.8	109.9	146.7	142.9
Average Gain	3.8	3.9	3.7	4.7	4.5
Net Passing Yards	3423	3363	3109	2712	2756
Per Game	213.9	210.2	194.3	180.8	172.3
Times Sacked	42	53	39	36	29
Passer Rating in Yards	4.8	4.2	5.5	4.7	4.5
Opponent Net Passing Yards	3174	3323	3582	2958	3353
Per Game	198.4	207.7	223.9	197.2	209.6
Times Sacked	55	61	47	37	30
Passer Rating Defense	2.9	4.4	4.8	5.0	4.8
Passer Rating Net	1.9	-0.3	0.7	-0.3	-0.4
Yards per Drive Offense	23.1	22.7	27.7	26.6	25.2
Yards per Drive Defense	22.0	23.7	26.7	28.7	30.2
Average Time of Possession	30:46	30:13	29:47	30:35	28:37

1984 PLAYOFFS
Won Wild Card Game from L.A. Raiders, 13-7
Lost Divisional Playoff to Miami, 10-31

1987 PLAYOFFS
Lost Wild Card Game to Houston, 20-23 (OT)

1988 PLAYOFFS
Lost Divisional Playoff to Cincinnati, 13-21

THE 1988 SEASON

DATE	AT	OPPONENT	SCORE	R	SPREAD	Tu	Net YDS	Rush YDS	Pass YDS	TURN
09/04	A	Denver	21-14	W	+4	g	330-302	178- 76	152-226	1-3
09/11	H	Kansas City	31-10	W	-7.5	a	263-286	156- 50	107-236	1-6
09/18	A	San Diego	6-17	L	-8	g	299-237	105-159	194- 78	4-1
09/25	H	S. Francisco	7-38	L	+2	a	154-580	29-239	125-341	5-1
10/02	A	Atlanta	31-20	W	-4	g	317-385	168-140	149-245	1-3
10/09	A	Cleveland	16-10	W	+4	g	227-334	126-160	101-174	1-4
10/16	H	New Orleans	19-20	L	-2.5	a	434-318	93-141	341-177	2-3
10/23	A	L.A. Rams	10-31	L	+4.5	g	296-465	153-154	143-311	5-3
10/30	H	San Diego	17-14	W	-8.5	a	235-299	126-136	109-163	0-3
11/06	H	Buffalo	3-13	L	+1	a	145-336	72-142	73-194	2-2
11/13	H	Houston	27-24	W	-1.5	a	365-419	177-237	188-182	1-1
11/20	A	Kansas City	24-27	L	-1.5	a	313-365	105-162	208-203	2-2
11/28	H*	L.A. Raiders	35-27	W	-3	a	459-257	247-113	212-144	5-2
12/04	A	New England	7-13	L	+3.5	a	65-212	20-177	45- 35	1-3
12/11	H	Denver	42-14	W	-3.5	a	450-402	230-101	220-301	0-1
12/18	A	L.A. Raiders	43-37	W	+2.5	g	490-441	101-110	389-331	3-1
						Avg.	303-352	130-144	172-209	2-2

				WINS	LOSSES
Season Record:	9- 7-0	POINTS:		29- 19	11- 23
Vs. Spread:	8- 8-0	Net YDS:	6-10-0	348-347	244-359
Home:	5- 3-0	Rush YDS:	5-11-0	168-125	82-168
On Artificial Turf:	5- 5-0	Pass YDS:	7- 9-0	181-222	161-191
Art. Turf vs. Spread:	4- 6-0	TURN:	8- 5-3	1- 3	3- 2

* Monday Night

THREE LETTERS DELIVERED HERE BY MISTAKE

January 1989

Mr. Dave Krieg
Quarterback
c/o Seattle Seahawks
Seattle, WA

Dear Mr. Krieg:

I regret to inform you that I must cancel our sessions for the next month. You explained that this is the most convenient time for you as it is inappropriate to expect the Seahawks' schedule to be extended through the Super Bowl. Nevertheless a recent fiscal setback necessitates my being out of town temporarily. I should have listened when you said take the points and the Seahawks.

Now as to my progress on your case.

First, I wanted to satisfy myself that your problem is not physical. I studied the enclosed X-ray of your 1988 season. It's obvious to my trained eye that you have made a complete recovery from the shoulder injury suffered in the third game. As a matter of fact, I don't believe you've ever thrown better than you did upon your return. Perhaps you are unfamiliar with the rating system noted on the right side of the X-ray. It is the NEWS system advocated by some statisticians whose names escape me at this moment. Basically it takes the yards gained, adds 10 for each touchdown pass, subtracts 45 for each interception, and divides by the number of attempts. A score of 6.48 or better is in the upper 25 percent (W), a score below 5.11 is in the lower 25 percent (L), and in between is an average grade (T). As you can see, in the final six games, you had three above-average performances, two average, and only one below-average.

Excellent.

Despite your fine record, you still have this continuing paranoid feeling. I believe we agreed on your last visit that part of this stems from the surprisingly able work done by young Kelly Stouffer during the time you were sidelined. We also agreed on the likelihood that Mr. Stouffer will eventually become the Seahawks' regular quarterback. We couldn't settle on a timetable. Your suggestion concerning the freezing over of hell seems an unrealistic projection.

Additionally my notes of our first session include "authority figure—hates passers." We will have to investigate this mysterious, unnamed figure.

Looking below the surface, I must suggest that some of

WK	OPP	SCORE	R	ATT	COM	YDS	TD	IN	RATE	W-L-T
1	Denver	21-14	W	30	14	168	2	0	6.26	T
2	Kansas City	31-10	W	22	14	114	1	0	5.64	T
3	San Diego	6-17	L	18	9	134	0	3	-0.05	L
	(shoulder separation)									
11	Houston	27-24	W	26	14	188	1	1	5.88	T
12	Kansas City	24-27	L	30	20	225	2	1	6.66	W
13	Raiders	35-27	W	28	16	220	5	2	6.43	T
14	New England	7-13	L	20	9	62	1	0	3.60	L
15	Denver	42-14	W	22	19	220	2	0	10.91	W
16	Raiders	43-37	W	32	19	410	4	0	14.06	W
	9 Gms (6-3)			228	134	1741	18	8	6.84	3-2-4

your feelings of inadequacy are related to events in 1980. As you'll recall, you were not drafted by any of the teams in the National Football League and you signed with Seattle as a free agent. You seem to blame yourself for this early rejection. It is obvious to me that this snub was inevitable in that you played for Milton College. Are you aware that Milton no longer fields a football team? Are you aware that Milton no longer exists?

Eliminating your negative feelings will undoubtedly take many sessions. We will begin a lengthy period of treatment upon my return. In the meantime I am reminded of a story I once heard of a quarterback who, though drafted on a late round, was cut from the squad in training camp. After a year he was signed as a free agent by another team and went on to some success. When you feel a severe attack coming on, perhaps you should repeat to yourself "Johnny Unitas."

Yours in good health,
Dr. Cash N. Couch, Psych.

January 1989

Mr. Chuck Knox
Head Coach
c/o Seattle Seahawks
Seattle, WA

Dear Chuck:

Well for the first time in the sixteen seasons you've been going with The Plan, I think you messed up. Everything was in place right up to the end, and then you got away from The Plan. I don't mind telling you, Chuck, I'm very disappointed in you.

I remember as if it were yesterday that day in 1973 when you'd just become coach of the Rams. I can still recall there was almost some expression on your face as you leaned back in your chair and told me the bad part of the job.

"I can see it coming," you said. "I win most of my games, and they'll want to keep me on here year after year. I just don't think I want to stay here more than five years. I don't want to stay *anywhere* more than six."

"Maybe you could lose a lot," I said.

You shook your head once. I almost fell off my chair at the show of animation. "I can't do that," you said. "I don't know how."

"Then you don't have any choice," I said.

"What's that?"

"You'll just have to make your teams so boring that they'll be happy to see you leave."

You looked at me with, I think, some pain in your eyes. Well, maybe one of your eyes. The left one. "Run the ball? Golly, that'd be awfully hard!"

"There's no other way," I said.

"But you *know* how I love to see those passes whizzing through the air. Especially the long ones. I was hoping they'd call me Air-Chuck."

"They'll think of something else to call you if you keep the ball on the ground."

"And what about flea-flickers? And hook-and-ladders? I love that wide open stuff! Long bombs, wow!"

"Chuck, you do that and you'll be coach of the Rams for twenty years."

"God, no!"

So right there we thought up The Plan. How you'd run, run, run until Rams fans couldn't take it anymore. I heard they were still shaking ticket holders awake three days after your last game. You won five straight division titles and they couldn't wait to see you go.

In Buffalo you had to be more careful. Put those fans sound asleep on a December day and they might freeze to death. But by then you'd refined The Plan beautifully. I didn't understand when early in your stay you had a season when you threw more than you ran. Of course your idea was that if you showed them passes at the beginning the contrast would be that much greater when you went to your run mode. Brilliant! Five years and they let you resign.

Things started fine is Seattle. You pulled that trick of passing more in your second year there. Then, in 1985, you let yourself go and passed nearly 60 percent. You really loved it, Chuck, but I knew right then that you'd have to stay an extra year. You just can't afford to indulge your natural bent toward throwing the ball, my friend. You could end up being *popular*.

Oh, by the way, Chuck, I'm enclosing the cumulative stats as I do every year. As you can see, you're still comfortably above the league average in percent of rushing attempts.

YEAR	TEAM	W	L	T	FIN	PLAY	OFFENSE %RUSH	%PASS	LEAGUE %RUSH	%PASS	RUSH Vs Lg
1973	Rams	12	2	0	1	0-1	69.6	30.4	56.6	43.4	13.0
1974	Rams	10	4	0	1	1-1	61.2	38.8	54.3	45.7	6.9
1975	Rams	12	2	0	1	1-1	61.6	38.4	54.5	45.5	7.1
1976	Rams	10	3	1	1	1-1	63.9	36.1	55.9	44.1	6.4
1977	Rams	10	4	0	1	0-1	63.0	37.0	57.5	42.5	5.5
5 seasons		54	15	1	-	3-5	63.9	36.1	55.8	44.2	8.1
1978	Bills	5	11	0	4t		57.1	42.9	55.5	44.5	1.6
1979	Bills	7	9	0	4		48.3	51.7	52.1	47.9	-3.8
1980	Bills	11	5	0	1	0-1	55.6	44.4	49.2	50.8	6.4
1981	Bills	10	6	0	3	1-1	50.2	49.8	48.9	51.1	1.3
1982	Bills	4	5	0	8t		52.8	47.2	47.2	52.8	5.6
5 seasons		37	36	0	-	1-2	52.8	47.2	50.9	49.1	1.9
1983	Seahawks	9	7	0	2	2-1	52.4	47.6	48.1	51.9	4.3
1984	Seahawks	12	4	0	2	1-1	47.9	52.1	46.9	53.1	1.0
1985	Seahawks	8	8	0	3		42.4	57.6	46.6	53.4	-4.2
1986	Seahawks	10	6	0	2t		51.0	49.0	46.1	53.9	4.9
1987	Seahawks	9	6	0	2	0-1	52.9	47.1	47.3	52.7	5.6
1988	Seahawks	9	7	0	1	0-1	52.6	47.4	47.1	52.9	5.5
6 seasons		57	38	0	-	3-4	49.7	50.3	47.0	53.0	2.7
16 seasons		148	89	1	-	7-11	55.0	45.0	50.7	49.3	4.3

Anyway, as I was saying, I'm very disappointed. I heard all last season how this was your last year with the Seahawks. You were right on schedule. And then you messed up.

Just one game, Chuck! You were just one game away! And what did you do? You turned Krieg loose in that last game against the Raiders and let him pass for 410 yards. What was it? A going-away present? Well, you shouldn't have done it, Chuck. He won the game and, with it, the Western Division championship. They aren't used to championships in Seattle, Chuck. They'd never won one before. It's not like L.A. or even Buffalo, where the fans want to have fun while watching.

Well, I don't know how much longer you'll have to stay out there, Chuck. Just remember, it's your own damned fault.

Your friend,
Bartleby

January 1989

Mr. Wright Hack
Rocky Road
Seattle, WA

Dear Mr. Hack:

We have received with interest your proposal for *The Curt Warner Story.* You suggest in your letter that the book might be more uplifting than *The Boz,* published by another house last year. We must agree that Mr. Warner's story is an inspiring one, in that he overcame a career-threatening knee injury in 1984 to rush for over 1,000 yards in three of his next four seasons. And it is certainly true that his contributions to the Seattle team have certainly exceeded those of Mr. Bosworth up to this time.

However, what you have overlooked is that it matters not that Mr. Bosworth elicits no more interest this season than cabbage-patch dolls; he was "hot" last year. Unfortunately Mr. Warner is not "hot." Our research department was unable to come up with any bizarre behavior, braggadocio, or narcissism on his part.

They also suggested that Mr. John L. Williams had an even better season in 1988 than Mr. Warner. Their game-by-game comparison is printed below with their choice for the recipient of the "game ball" printed to the right. Their choices seem arbitrary, but they assure me that they looked carefully at rushing attempts (ATT), rushing yards (YDS), rushing touchdowns (TD), total rushing and receiving yards (+REC), and points scored (PT).

Should Mr. Williams both continue to excel and at the same time develop a particularly cloddish personality, we might be interested in publishing *his* story. Actually, he need only be an average player so long as he's a "character." Our readers are more interested in the outlandish than the outstanding. Tentative title: *The Great John L.*

Sincerely,
Barry Banal
Hype House

			CURT WARNER					JOHN L. WILLIAMS					
WK	OPP	SCORE	ATT	YDS	TD	+REC	PT	ATT	YDS	TD	+REC	PT	
1	Denver	21-14	22	72	1	86	12	16	79	0	161	0	Williams
2	Kansas City	31-10	20	72	2	72	12	14	65	0	67	0	Warner
3	San Diego	6-17	18	60	0	72	0	9	42	0	96	0	Williams
4	San Fran.	7-38	9	29	0	43	0	2	-1	0	-1	0	Warner
5	Atlanta	31-20	22	110	1	129	6	14	50	3	54	18	Warner
6	Cleveland	16-10	24	96	1	125	6	9	29	0	35	0	Warner
7	New Orleans	19-20	11	26	0	45	0	11	35	0	103	0	Williams
8	Rams	10-31	16	81	0	98	0	9	27	0	58	0	Warner
9	San Diego	17-14	14	52	0	52	0	15	73	0	107	6	Williams
10	Buffalo	13- 3	11	33	0	33	0	5	33	0	51	0	Williams
11	Houston	27-24	18	72	1	76	6	13	102	1	112	6	Williams
12	Kansas City	24-27	14	35	0	35	0	11	50	0	82	0	Williams
13	Raiders	35-27	27	130	0	137	6	17	105	0	124	0	Warner
14	New England	7-13	7	10	0	1	0	10	20	0	57	0	Williams
15	Denver	42-14	23	126	4	136	24	20	109	0	183	6	Williams
16	Raiders	43-37	10	21	0	40	0	14	59	0	239	6	Williams

SEATTLE SEAHAWKS STATISTICS

1988 TEAM STATISTICS	SS	OPP
TOTAL FIRST DOWNS	291	321
Rushing	125	134
Passing	139	171
Penalty	27	16
3rd Down Made/Att.	83/211	96/219
Pct.	39.3%	43.8%
4th Down Made/Att.	7/16	10/16
Pct.	43.8%	62.5%
TOTAL NET YARDS	4842	5639
Avg. per Game	302.6	352.4
Total Plays	983	1040
Avg. per Play	4.9	5.4
NET YARDS RUSHING	2086	2286
Avg. per Game	130.4	142.9
Total Rushes	517	509
NET YARDS PASSING	2756	3353
Avg. per Game	172.3	209.6
Tackled/Yards Lost	29/223	30/265
Gross Yards	2979	3618
Attempts/Completions	437/245	501/280
Pct. of Completions	56.1%	55.9%
Had Intercepted	20	22
PUNTS/AVERAGE	70/40.8	66/42.1
NET PUNTING AVG.	36.8	35.7
PENALTIES/YARDS	89/790	111/861
FUMBLES/BALL LOST	29/14	31/18
TOUCHDOWNS	39	38
Rushing	14	14
Passing	22	21
Returns	3	3
TIME OF POSSESSION	—	—

SCORE/PERIODS	1	2	3	4	OT	TOTAL
Seahawks	58	124	83	74	0	339
Opponents	75	90	72	92	0	329

SCORING	TDR	TDP	TDRt	PAT	FG	S	TP
W. Johnson				39/39	22/28		105
Warner	10	2					72
Blades		8					48
Williams	4	3					42

SCORING	TDR	TDP	TDRt	PAT	FG	S	TP
Butler		4					24
Largent		2					12
Clark		1					6
Dean			1				6
Green			1				6
Skansi		1					6
Spagnola		1					6
Taylor			1				6
Seahawks	14	22	3	39/39	22/28	0	339
Opponents	14	21	3	38/38	21/32	0	329

RUSHING	NO	YDS	AVG	LG	TD
Warner	266	1025	3.9	29	10
Williams	189	877	4.6	44t	4
Krieg	24	64	2.7	17	0
Kemp	6	51	8.5	21	0
Stouffer	19	27	1.4	17	0
Blades	5	24	4.8	12	0
Harmon	2	13	6.5	8	0
Morris	3	6	2.0	5	0
Agee	1	2	2.0	2	0
Rodriguez	1	0	0.0	0	0
Largent	1	-3	-3.0	-3	0
Seahawks	517	2086	4.0	44t	14
Opponents	509	2286	4.5	42	14

RECEIVING	NO	YDS	AVG	LG	TD
Williams	58	651	11.2	75t	3
Blades	40	682	17.1	55	8
Largent	39	645	16.5	46	2
Tice	29	244	8.4	26	0
Skansi	24	238	9.9	21	1
Warner	22	154	7.0	17	2
Butler	18	242	13.4	46t	4
Kane	6	32	5.3	9	0
Spagnola	5	40	8.0	16	1
Agee	3	31	10.3	13	0
Clark	1	20	20.0	20t	1
Seahawks	245	2979	12.2	75t	22
Opponents	280	3618	12.9	69t	21

(Continued)

(Continued)

INTERCEPTIONS	NO	YDS	AVG	LG	TD
Moyer	6	79	13.2	34	0
Taylor	5	53	10.6	27t	1
Jenkins	3	41	13.7	21	0
Hollis	2	32	16.0	30	0
Glasgow	2	19	9.5	19	0
Dean	1	31	31.0	31	0
Comeaux	1	18	18.0	18	0
Miller	1	7	7.0	7	0
Robinson	1	0	0.0	0	0
Seahawks	22	280	12.7	34	1
Opponents	20	195	9.8	55t	1

PUNTING	NO	YDS	AVG	TB	In 20	LG	Blk
Rodriguez	70	2858	40.8	4	14	68	-
Seahawks	70	2858	40.8	4	14	68	-
Opponents	66	2778	42.1	4	22	59	0

PUNT RETURNS	NO	FC	YDS	AVG	LG	TD
Edmonds	35	8	340	9.7	41	0
Glasgow	1	0	0	0.0	0	0
Hunter	1	0	0	0.0	0	0

(Continued)

PUNT RETURNS	NO	FC	YDS	AVG	LG	TD
Seahawks	37	8	340	9.2	41	0
Opponents	36	14	202	5.6	16	0

KICKOFF RETURNS	NO	YDS	AVG	LG	TD
Edmonds	40	900	22.5	65	0
Hollis	7	155	22.1	35	0
Morris	11	218	19.8	30	0
Harmon	3	62	20.7	30	0
Tice	1	17	17.0	17	0
Seahawks	61	1352	21.8	65	0
Opponents	66	1207	18.3	95	0

FIELD GOALS	1-19	20-29	30-39	40-49	50+	TOTAL
N. Johnson	1-1	4-4	7-9	10-14	0-0	23-28
Seahawks	1-1	4-4	7-9	10-14	0-0	23-28
Opponents	0-0	10-11	6-10	4-6	1-5	21-32

FIELD GOALS BY JOHNSON: 23 of 28
( )(18G)(44N,40G,42G)(41N)(44G)(31G,38G,22G)
(22G,47G,46G,36N,42G)(33N,33G)(26G)(41G)(40G,
46G)(32G)( )(47N,41N)( )(39G,24G,40G,35G,32G)

PASSING	ATT	COM	YARD	PCT.	Avg G	TD	%TD	IN	%IN	LG	SAKS/YDS	RATE
Krieg	228	134	1741	58.8	7.64	18	7.9	8	3.5	75t	12/92	94.6
Stouffer	173	98	1106	56.6	6.39	4	2.3	6	3.5	53	13/110	69.2
Kemp	35	13	132	37.1	3.77	0	0.0	5	14.3	19	3/21	9.2
Agee	1	0	0	0.0	0.00	0	0.0	1	100.0	0	0/0	0.0
Blades	0	0	0	—	—	0	—	0	—	0	1/0	0.0
Seahawks	437	245	2979	56.1	6.82	22	5.0	20	4.6	75t	29/223	74.9
Opponents	501	280	3618	55.9	7.22	21	4.2	22	4.4	69t	30/265	74.4

PLAYER AND COACH RATINGS

A glossary of statistical terms and list of abbreviations used in this book can be found on pages 293–295.

QUARTERBACKS

Playing quarterback in the NFL is feast or famine. When the team wins, the quarterback is every fan's idol, the Top Gun. When it loses, he's a bum, the Bottom Rung. They get the big bucks, the big cheers, and the big boos. No quarterback can win singlehandedly, but no team can win consistently without a reasonably accomplished quarterback.

The QB's job involves leadership, reading defenses, calling some plays, and handling the ball on nearly every play. None of those are measurable skills. We may believe that QB Smith lacks leadership or calls poor plays. We may even be right. But we can't quantify those things in relation to other QBs except in the most general sense.

The NFL doesn't rate quarterbacks; it rates passers with its infamous NFL Passer Rating System (PRS). Although many curse the system because it doesn't yield quick, easy answers, it's actually a good way of doing what it sets out to do—tell us who the most *efficient* passers are.

We have three reservations about the NFL PRS.

Because it's tied to average and record performances of two decades ago, it tends to punish most of the great throwers of the past when career stats are compiled. For example, twenty years ago 50 percent was an average completion percentage. Today, most passers are up to 55 percent. They are not necessarily throwing more accurately than the oldsters. The rules have changed, allowing less bumping in the secondary and giving blockers the right to use their hands. Additionally, QBs throw more short passes into the flat today, and these are nearly automatic completions.

That first reservation doesn't particularly concern us here. This isn't a history lesson. However, it's something you might keep in mind the next time you're browsing through Y. A. Tittle's passing stats.

Something that does concern us here is the weighting of the NFL's system. In effect, it's based on yardage and then awards bonuses and penalties that can be translated into more yardage: twenty yards for each completion (even if the play results in a net loss), eighty yards bonus for each touchdown pass, and a hundred-yard penalty for each interception. We think these bonuses and penalties are out of proportion. A completion is only worth what the play gains, few TD passes go for eighty yards, and an interception costs the passers' team 45 yards on average, a figure derived from the extensive computer analysis of hundreds of NFL games that we did for *The Hidden Game of Football* (Warner, 1988). For those reasons, our preferred passing stat is NEWS (for New System). It awards ten yards for a TD, subtracts forty-five for an interception, and gives no reward for a completion other than the actual yards gained. It's also a much easier system to figure:

NEWS yields a rating in yards, such as 8.30, instead of the NFL PRS's rating points. It doesn't flip-flop the rankings, putting poor passers at the top and good ones at the bottom; that would make you distrust the measure, and rightfully so. Only a few passers will change their order, but we think those changes reflect more accurate measuring.

A third factor that has always bothered us about the NFL PRS is that it treats 210 pass attempts (the minimum to qualify for the passing title) the same as 606 attempts (the number Dan Marino threw in 1988). Obviously a QB who handles nearly all of his team's passing is more important to his team's success than a part-timer who only plays half the schedule.

We recognize that some teams pass a lot more than others. Miami, for example, threw 621 times in 1988 and Cincinnati only 392. Yet Marino and Esiason handled nearly every throw for their respective teams. We decided to give what, for lack of a better name, we'll call a Durability Rating (DURA). It's nothing more than the percentage of a team's passes thrown by each QB.

Once we'd done that, we were inspired to tie the NEWS and DURA marks together in a Total Rating by multiplying one times the other. In effect, the Total Rating rewards those quarterbacks who were truly number one on their teams in 1988. Part-timers are dropped lower. Also reduced in rank are the quarterbacks who missed significant parts of the schedule because of injuries. No, we don't believe in kicking a man when he's down. But we'd all have thought it silly if, say, Bernie Kosar had led the NFL in passing last year while playing less than half a season. We think the world and all of Bernie, but through no fault of his own, he wasn't as valuable to the Browns in 1988 as he had been in previous seasons.

A final word before we get to the individual QBs. They are ranked on their combination of passing and durability, not their ability to lead or to come through in the clutch or to give haircuts—or any other unmeasurable. The comments that follow each passer's record often reflect those things, but don't ask us to quantify them.

Boomer Esiason, Cincinnati   NFL

ATT	COM	PCT	YARD	Avg G	TD	%TD	IN	%IN	RATE	NEWS	DURA	TOTAL
388	223	57.5	3572	9.21	28	7.2	14	3.6	97.4	8.30	99.0	821.70

Last year Boomer moved into the ranks of the very top QBs. He's always had talent. In 1988 he had great support, but there's no question he was the key man in the Bengals' offense. An interesting thought is that left-handed quarterbacks may have a slight advantage over righthanders, similar to what you find with boxers. Defenses see few lefties, who roll out the "wrong" way more easily. Also defenders may have problems intercepting passes that rotate "backwards."

Jim Everett, L.A. Rams   NFL

ATT	COM	PCT	YARD	Avg G	TD	%TD	IN	%IN	RATE	NEWS	DURA	TOTAL
517	308	59.6	3964	7.67	31	6.0	18	3.5	89.2	6.70	99.0	663.30

Although he tailed off at the end, Everett justified the investment the Rams made in him by trading Dickerson. QBs keep getting taller; Everett is 6'5". Roger Staubach is the only quarterback in the Hall of Fame over 6'2".

Jim Kelly, Buffalo   NFL

ATT	COM	PCT	YARD	Avg G	TD	%TD	IN	%IN	RATE	NEWS	DURA	TOTAL
452	269	59.5	3380	7.48	15	3.3	17	3.8	78.2	6.12	99.6	609.55

Kelly's durability is his greatest asset. There are plenty of better passers around. Check the IRs. He'll probably never lead the league in passing, but he might lead the Bills to a Super Bowl.

Dan Marino, Miami   NFL

ATT	COM	PCT	YARD	Avg G	TD	%TD	IN	%IN	RATE	NEWS	DURA	TOTAL
606	354	58.4	4434	7.32	28	4.6	23	3.8	80.8	6.07	97.6	592.43

The best passer in the world, and maybe the best ever. He's *not* the best quarterback in mechanics, but who cares? If he had a line and some runners, he could throw a hundred fewer passes and still gain as many yards.

Phil Simms, N.Y. Giants   NFL

ATT	COM	PCT	YARD	Avg G	TD	%TD	IN	%IN	RATE	NEWS	DURA	TOTAL
479	263	54.9	3359	7.01	21	4.4	11	2.3	82.1	6.42	91.2	585.50

Weird! A New York quarterback who is *under*publicized. He's better than most of the cover boys, and without him the Giants would finish last.

Randall Cunningham, Philadelphia   NFL

ATT	COM	PCT	YARD	Avg G	TD	%TD	IN	%IN	RATE	NEWS	DURA	TOTAL
560	301	53.8	3808	6.80	24	4.3	16	2.9	77.6	5.94	96.4	572.62

The single most irreplaceable (to his team) man in football. He would rank higher if we factored in his running, even if we don't approve of so much of it.

Neil Lomax, Phoenix   NFL

ATT	COM	PCT	YARD	Avg G	TD	%TD	IN	%IN	RATE	NEWS	DURA	TOTAL
443	255	57.6	3395	7.66	20	4.5	11	2.5	86.7	7.00	78.8	551.60

After a couple of poor seasons, he's been excellent the last two years. The only things standing between him and All-Pro status are his arthritic hip and the Cardinals' inalienable right of mediocrity.

Joe Montana, San Francisco   NFL

ATT	COM	PCT	YARD	Avg G	TD	%TD	IN	%IN	RATE	NEWS	DURA	TOTAL
397	238	59.9	2981	7.51	18	4.5	10	2.5	87.9	6.83	79.1	540.25

When healthy, which he wasn't always in 1988, he's still the best all-around quarterback in football. Without a doubt, the "Quarterback of the Eighties" and a certain Hall of Famer.

Bobby Hebert, New Orleans   NFL

ATT	COM	PCT	YARD	Avg G	TD	%TD	IN	%IN	RATE	NEWS	DURA	TOTAL
478	280	58.6	3156	6.60	20	4.2	15	3.1	79.3	5.61	96.0	538.56

An effective QB of the "Don't-Make-a-Disastrous-Mistake" School. Very good with a short-passing game when he can couple it with a strong running attack. Not very stylish, but he gets it done.

Warren Moon, Houston   NFL

ATT	COM	PCT	YARD	Avg G	TD	%TD	IN	%IN	RATE	NEWS	DURA	TOTAL
294	160	54.4	2327	7.91	17	5.8	8	2.7	88.4	7.27	68.7	499.45

The jury may always be out on Moon. He has a reputation, not necessarily earned, for losing big games. After so long he may have to win so many big ones to get rid of the rep that he'd have to play into his sixties. The playoff win at Cleveland helped a little, but only a Super Bowl victory would really quiet the critics.

Wade Wilson, Minnesota   NFL

ATT	COM	PCT	YARD	Avg G	TD	%TD	IN	%IN	RATE	NEWS	DURA	TOTAL
332	204	61.4	2746	8.27	15	4.5	9	2.7	91.5	7.50	63.8	478.50

Terrific numbers in '88, but he still must show he can put them up against the tough teams.

John Elway, Denver   NFL

ATT	COM	PCT	YARD	Avg G	TD	%TD	IN	%IN	RATE	NEWS	DURA	TOTAL
496	274	55.2	3309	6.67	17	3.4	19	3.8	71.4	5.29	85.4	451.77

He played while hurt in '88 and then was blamed for Denver's off year. An arm operation after the season is supposed to make him whole in '89. Magnificent talent, but sometimes he tries to do too much.

Steve DeBerg, Kansas City   NFL

ATT	COM	PCT	YARD	Avg G	TD	%TD	IN	%IN	RATE	NEWS	DURA	TOTAL
414	224	54.1	2935	7.09	16	3.9	16	3.9	73.5	5.74	78.4	450.02

Has he finally found a home? A solid, unspectacular quarterback who has never had the team to move up in class.

Ken O'Brien, N.Y. Jets   NFL

ATT	COM	PCT	YARD	Avg G	TD	%TD	IN	%IN	RATE	NEWS	DURA	TOTAL
424	236	55.7	2567	6.05	15	3.5	7	1.7	78.6	5.67	78.8	446.80

Gets sacked too often but doesn't throw interceptions. It's a mixed blessing. On balance, he's been a disappointment. Two magic words that make us think better of him: Richard Todd.

Steve Pelluer, Dallas   NFL

ATT	COM	PCT	YARD	Avg G	TD	%TD	IN	%IN	RATE	NEWS	DURA	TOTAL
435	245	56.3	3139	7.22	17	3.9	19	4.4	73.9	5.64	78.4	442.18

Still makes too many mistakes. He would benefit from a change of scenery.

Bubby Brister, Pittsburgh   NFL

ATT	COM	PCT	YARD	Avg G	TD	%TD	IN	%IN	RATE	NEWS	DURA	TOTAL
370	175	47.3	2634	7.12	11	3.0	14	3.8	65.3	5.71	75.7	432.25

Made good progress in '88. Ran the offense (such as it was) very well, considering his lack of experience. A bit too anxious to force his passes or to run.

Doug Williams, Washington   NFL

ATT	COM	PCT	YARD	Avg G	TD	%TD	IN	%IN	RATE	NEWS	DURA	TOTAL
380	213	56.1	2609	6.87	15	3.9	12	3.2	77.4	5.84	64.2	374.93

Just when he figured it was safe to settle in as the regular, he had that appendectomy. When he came back, he had a new rival in Rypien. Not the most consistent thrower in the world, but when he's on, he can devastate an opponent. Throws deep very well, and the Redskins have the speedy receivers he needs.

Dave Krieg, Seattle   NFL

ATT	COM	PCT	YARD	Avg G	TD	%TD	IN	%IN	RATE	NEWS	DURA	TOTAL
228	134	58.8	1741	7.64	18	7.9	8	3.5	94.6	6.85	52.2	357.57

Great half-season. We can now start counting the days until Stouffer replaces him. Not appreciated, but better than most.

Chris Miller, Atlanta   NFL

ATT	COM	PCT	YARD	Avg G	TD	%TD	IN	%IN	RATE	NEWS	DURA	TOTAL
351	184	52.4	2133	6.08	11	3.1	12	3.4	67.3	4.85	73.0	354.05

Started to come on last year. Some think he may become the top QB of the nineties.

Vinny Testaverde, Tampa Bay   NFL

ATT	COM	PCT	YARD	Avg G	TD	%TD	IN	%IN	RATE	NEWS	DURA	TOTAL
466	222	47.6	3240	6.95	13	2.8	35	7.5	48.8	3.85	91.0	350.35

Considering the expectations and his surroundings, he's done okay. Everybody's down on him right now because of his interceptions, but there's not a team that wouldn't like to have him. Would you believe "The Passing Duel of 1994—Miller vs. Testaverde"?

Bernie Kosar, Cleveland   NFL

ATT	COM	PCT	YARD	Avg G	TD	%TD	IN	%IN	RATE	NEWS	DURA	TOTAL
259	156	60.2	1890	7.30	10	3.9	7	2.7	84.3	6.47	48.2	311.85

The worst-looking quarterback above the Pop Warner League. Looks awkward and throws funny sidearm passes. However, he can beat you with his arm or his mind. In a healthy year Bernie belongs in the top five QBs.

Don Majkowski, Green Bay   NFL

ATT	COM	PCT	YARD	Avg G	TD	%TD	IN	%IN	RATE	NEWS	DURA	TOTAL
336	178	53.0	2119	6.31	9	2.7	11	3.3	67.8	5.10	57.7	294.27

Inconsistent and not as stylish as Wright, with whom he shared time, but probably the Packers' best bet.

Chris Chandler, Indianapolis   NFL

ATT	COM	PCT	YARD	Avg G	TD	%TD	IN	%IN	RATE	NEWS	DURA	TOTAL
233	129	55.4	1619	6.95	8	3.4	12	5.2	67.2	4.97	57.8	287.27

Showed promise, but needs a full season to prove anything.

Steve Beuerlein, Raiders   NFL

ATT	COM	PCT	YARD	Avg G	TD	%TD	IN	%IN	RATE	NEWS	DURA	TOTAL
238	105	44.1	1643	6.90	8	3.4	7	2.9	66.6	5.92	48.0	284.16

The Raiders seem to be committed to Schroeder.

Jay Schroeder, Raiders   NFL

ATT	COM	PCT	YARD	Avg G	TD	%TD	IN	%IN	RATE	NEWS	DURA	TOTAL
256	113	44.1	1839	7.18	13	5.1	13	5.1	64.6	5.41	51.6	279.16

He should put up better numbers in 1989, but can he win? We're impressed by his arm, but so far not by much else. If he's benched, he'll lead the league in Pout.

Mike Tomczak, Chicago   NFL

ATT	COM	PCT	YARD	Avg G	TD	%TD	IN	%IN	RATE	NEWS	DURA	TOTAL
170	86	50.6	1310	7.71	7	4.1	6	3.5	75.4	6.53	36.9	240.96

Not outstanding in any area, but he can win as long as the defense holds up. Could go either way: a perennial backup or a gutty leader who gets the job done with a minimum of flourish.

Jim McMahon, Chicago   NFL

ATT	COM	PCT	YARD	Avg G	TD	%TD	IN	%IN	RATE	NEWS	DURA	TOTAL
192	114	59.4	1346	7.01	6	3.1	7	3.6	76.0	5.68	41.6	236.29

The world's most famous benchwarmer.

Rusty Hilger, Detroit   NFL

ATT	COM	PCT	YARD	Avg G	TD	%TD	IN	%IN	RATE	NEWS	DURA	TOTAL
306	126	41.2	1558	5.09	7	2.3	12	3.9	48.9	3.56	64.2	228.55

If Long is healthy, Hilger may throw ten passes in 1989.

Mark Malone, San Diego NFL

ATT	COM	PCT	YARD	Avg G	TD	%TD	IN	%IN	RATE	NEWS	DURA	TOTAL
272	147	54.0	1580	5.81	6	2.2	13	4.8	58.8	3.88	58.1	225.43

Everybody's favorite whipping boy. We'd love to see him win a Super Bowl. We'd also love to see Kirstie Alley beating down our door. Still, for all the criticism, he's won more games than a lot of higher-rated passers.

Mark Rypien, Washington NFL

ATT	COM	PCT	YARD	Avg G	TD	%TD	IN	%IN	RATE	NEWS	DURA	TOTAL
208	114	54.8	1730	8.32	18	8.7	13	6.3	85.2	6.37	35.1	223.59

Needed to throw two more passes to qualify in the NFL's Passer Rating System. He would have finished eighth after leading earlier. That tells you he wasn't throwing real well at the end.

Doug Flutie, New England NFL

ATT	COM	PCT	YARD	Avg G	TD	%TD	IN	%IN	RATE	NEWS	DURA	TOTAL
179	92	51.4	1150	6.42	8	4.5	10	5.6	63.3	4.36	46.0	200.56

When they stop knocking his height, they complain about his arm or his mechanics. But the Pats played best with him at QB. If Eason isn't 100 percent in 1989, they should go with Flutie. And maybe even if Eason *is* 100 percent.

Kelly Stouffer, Seattle NFL

ATT	COM	PCT	YARD	Avg G	TD	%TD	IN	%IN	RATE	NEWS	DURA	TOTAL
173	98	56.6	1106	6.39	4	2.3	6	3.5	69.2	5.06	39.6	200.38

The Seahawks' QB of the future, but he has yet to prove he's better than reliable Krieg.

Tommy Kramer, Minnesota NFL

ATT	COM	PCT	YARD	Avg G	TD	%TD	IN	%IN	RATE	NEWS	DURA	TOTAL
173	83	48.0	1264	7.31	5	2.9	9	5.2	60.5	5.25	33.3	174.83

He may be nearing the end of a mixed career.

Randy Wright, Green Bay NFL

ATT	COM	PCT	YARD	Avg G	TD	%TD	IN	%IN	RATE	NEWS	DURA	TOTAL
244	141	57.8	1490	6.11	4	1.6	13	5.3	58.9	3.87	41.9	162.15

Now entering his sixth season as the Packers' "next Bart Starr." Any odds?

Nobody asked us, but if we could have our pick of any young quarterback who's not yet an established star in the NFL, we'd take them in this order:

1. Chris Miller
2. Vinny Testaverde
3. Bubby Brister
4. Kelly Stouffer
5. Chris Chandler
6. Chuck Long
7. Mark Rypien
8. Don Majkowski
9. Steve Beuerlein
10. Cody Carlson
11. Jim Harbaugh

RUNNING BACKS

The denotation of offensive players reveals an eccentric wit. No wide receiver has ever caught a wide, an offensive tackle will be penalized if he does precisely that to the man opposite him, tight ends are sober, an offensive guard is a contradiction in terms, and a quarterback sounds like what you get when you give your kid a ten and tell him to go get you a newspaper. Sanity returns with the center who is indeed located there. But running backs are a special case. Oh, sure, they all run, and they all start from a reasonable distance back, but they are not interchangeable.

Years of study (or two minutes of reflection) will allow you to distinguish among the various species of the genus *running back*.

For example, some are in the backfield for their blocking. Examples are San Francisco's Tom Rathman, Houston's Alonzo Highsmith, New England's Robert Perryman, and the Giants' Maurice Carthon. They are easily recognizable because they play regularly but seldom carry the ball. It's not that they can't run; it's just that someone else in their backfield runs better—and runs a whole lot better with these men blocking.

Another popular model is the short-yardage specialist. He is called into action when his team desperately needs a yard or two for a first down or a touchdown. It's the latter situation that gives short-yardage men their most distinguishing characteristic: a low number of carries and a high number of touchdowns. Buffalo's Robb Riddick carried only 111 times in 1988 and scored 12 touchdowns, an average of 1 TD for every 9.25 carries.

Related to the short-yardage man is the third-down specialist. He plays mainly on third-and-long and is considered a better pass receiver than runner. His number of receptions rivals and sometimes surpasses his rushing attempts. Pittsburgh's Rodney Carter ran only 36 times in 1988 but caught 32 passes.

The complete statistical profile of a return specialist—yet another sort of running back—is generally confined to the category of returns, but much of this traditional work is being taken over by defensive backs and wide receivers.

All of these running backs are useful, even critical, to a team's success, but they seem almost second bananas to the kings of running backdom—the heavy-duty runners.

Heavy-duty men bear the main burden of a team's running attack. Early in the game they must establish the run so defenses cannot concentrate exclusively on stopping passes. A strong runner can force the defense to restrain its blitz and keep its defensive backs up where they become vulnerable to speedy pass receivers. Late in the game, if his team is ahead, the heavy-duty back becomes the key to wearing down the clock and grinding out lead-protecting first downs.

Heavy-duty runners may block, catch passes, smash for short yardage, and even return kicks, but they are paid—and very well, too—to execute a preponderance of their team's ball carrying. When fans look at the weekly stat lists, their eyes go immediately to the "YDS" column. Next, they might take in "AVG" and "TD." They almost totally ignore "ATT," the stat that makes everything possible and the one that separates the men from the menials.

In the following grouping, we ranked only the heavy-duty runners of 1988—the RBs who ran at least 160 times (a minimum average of 10 carries a game). The other species are not unimportant, but their jobs are situational and secondary. Since every team carries four to six RBs on its roster, we had to draw the line somewhere or this chapter would be longer than Dorsett's Monday Night run against the Vikings in the '83 season.

In working out grades for the runners, we didn't try to estimate speed or power or change of pace. We're interested in relative numbers. We tied the runner's attempts, yards, and touchdowns to his team's total and then compared that with the league leader to get a rating for each category. For example, Herschel Walker's yardage was the highest percentage of his team's of any runner, so every other runner's percentage was compared to his. The average gain for each runner was compared with John L. Williams' mark and weighted twice (as the most revealing figure within the group) in coming up with an overall rushing rating (TOTAL).

We didn't want to ignore total rushing yards completely, but we didn't want to weight it too heavily. We found that by inserting a decimal point in the runner's total rushing yards (i.e. Dickerson's 1,659 becomes 16.59) and adding that number to the total before we divided, we got the right mix.

We also gave a pass receiving rating, based on figures arrived at from all backs with 32 or more catches. Because many of those were third-down specialists, the receiving rating (TOTAL) for the heavy-duty runners usually lowered the combined rating (in parentheses after the runner's name). This didn't matter, because we were only rating within the group. Because the heavy-duty runner's main job is to run, we weighted his rushing TOTAL five-to-one in arriving at the combined rating.

1. Eric Dickerson, Indianapolis (81.8)

	ATT	Att R	YARD	Yds R	AVG	Avg R	TD	Td R	TOTAL
Rushing	388	92.5	1659	97.2	4.3	91.2	14	60.9	86.0

	PC	Pc R	YARD	Yds R	AVG	Avg G	TD	Td R	TOTAL
Receiving	36	59.6	377	60.2	10.5	78.5	1	26.7	60.7

Legend: Att R = Attempt Percentage Rating; Yds R = Yardage Percentage Rating; Avg R = Average/Carry Percentage Rating; Td R = Touchdown Percentage Rating; Pc R = Pass Catching Percentage Rating; Avg G= Average/Reception Percentage Rating

Dickerson remains the greatest runner in football. In fact, had someone else finished on top, we would have doubted our system. In 1988 he improved two areas that had been questionable. He cut down on his occasional fumbles and began catching passes. The touchdown pass he scored against the Jets was his first since 1983.

2. Herschel Walker, Dallas (81.1)

	ATT	Att R	YARD	Yds R	AVG	Avg R	TD	Td R	TOTAL
Rushing	361	100.0	1514	100.0	4.2	79.9	5	50.0	85.0

	PC	Pc R	YARD	Yds R	AVG	Avg G	TD	Td R	TOTAL
Receiving	53	63.5	505	62.0	9.5	71.4	2	38.1	61.3

Although he was ignored on most All-NFL teams because the Cowboys' record was so bad, Walker is probably the most dangerous running back in football at this point. He's close to Dickerson as a runner, with possibly a slight edge in breakaway potential, and he's a better pass receiver.

3. Roger Craig, San Francisco (77.0)

	ATT	Att R	YARD	Yds R	AVG	Avg R	TD	Td R	TOTAL
Rushing	310	76.4	1502	78.4	4.8	92.3	9	50.0	80.9

	PC	Pc R	YARD	Yds R	AVG	Avg G	TD	Td R	TOTAL
Receiving	76	95.4	534	66.5	7.0	52.7	1	19.0	57.2

As great as he is, Craig ranks just under Dickerson and Walker. However, one thing the ratings do not show is his propensity for coming up with big plays at opportune moments, something he did a lot of in 1988, when many considered him the most valuable player in the NFL.

4. Greg Bell, L.A. Rams (76.0)

	ATT	Att R	YARD	Yds R	AVG	Avg R	TD	Td R	TOTAL
Rushing	288	73.8	1212	79.7	4.2	80.1	16	100.0	85.2

	PC	Pc R	YARD	Yds R	AVG	Avg G	TD	Td R	TOTAL
Receiving	28	32.9	124	14.1	5.2	38.9	2	25.8	30.0

Bell had a super year in '88, but his numbers look a little higher than they really are. He rushed for 16 touchdowns (which was terrific), but no other Ram runner had even one. Because of the imbalance, every other league runner's Td R is reduced. We're not quarreling with our own system; we're simply pointing out that an unusual record can make a runner appear better than he really is. Bell is a fine back when he's healthy, but he'll have to match most of last year's figures this season before we'll concede he is the fourth best runner in football.

5. John Settle, Atlanta (73.5)

	ATT	Att R	YARD	Yds R	AVG	Avg R	TD	Td R	TOTAL
Rushing	232	63.1	1024	66.9	4.4	84.1	7	63.6	74.4

	PC	Pc R	YARD	Yds R	AVG	Avg G	TD	Td R	TOTAL
Receiving	68	100.0	570	89.5	8.4	62.8	1	30.8	69.2

Settle is another runner who came out of nowhere to tear up the league. With Gerald Riggs back and healthy in '89, Settle may have to share his carries and his figures could drop. He may be every bit as good in 1989; it just may not be so obvious.

6. Ickey Woods, Cincinnati (67.6)

	ATT	Att R	YARD	Yds R	AVG	Avg R	TD	Td R	TOTAL
Rushing	203	46.8	1066	51.8	5.3	100.0	15	55.6	73.0

	PC	Pc R	YARD	Yds R	AVG	Avg G	TD	Td R	TOTAL
Receiving	21	34.3	199	25.3	9.5	70.9	0	0.0	40.3

No question Ickey was strong and tricky an jus' plain great in '88, and we know he'll be fine in '89, but before we rejoice, one quiet voice says a couple of others (if they'd had their druthers) could have done it all behind the Cincy front wall, cha-cha-cha!

7 (tie). Neal Anderson, Chicago (66.7)

	ATT	Att R	YARD	Yds R	AVG	Avg R	TD	Td R	TOTAL
Rushing	249	58.3	1106	62.8	4.4	84.6	12	48.0	69.9

	PC	Pc R	YARD	Yds R	AVG	Avg G	TD	Td R	TOTAL
Receiving	39	57.8	371	53.5	9.5	71.3	0	0.0	50.8

Anderson had a season that wouldn't look out of place on Walter Payton's chart, but because he *isn't* Payton, he'll probably never get the recognition he might someplace else. Anderson had some fumble problems.

7 (tie). Gary Anderson, San Diego (66.7)

	ATT	Att R	YARD	Yds R	AVG	Avg R	TD	Td R	TOTAL
Rushing	225	66.7	1119	62.8	5.0	94.7	3	27.3	73.4

	PC	Pc R	YARD	Yds R	AVG	Avg G	TD	Td R	TOTAL
Receiving	32	48.8	182	31.5	5.7	42.4	0	0.0	33.0

The average is fine, even if most of it came in four games. A very dangerous back, but we question whether he can stand the pounding of another 225 rushing attempts in one season. If the Chargers had someone else who could slam into the line for three quarters, Gary Anderson could win some games in the final period.

9. John L. Williams, Seattle (66.5)

	ATT	Att R	YARD	Yds R	AVG	Avg R	TD	Td R	TOTAL
Rushing	189	47.5	877	55.4	4.6	88.4	4	28.6	63.4

	PC	Pc R	YARD	Yds R	AVG	Avg G	TD	Td R	TOTAL
Receiving	58	87.0	651	100.0	11.2	84.1	3	54.5	82.0

Expect the great John L. to run the ball more in 1989. He only needs a 1,000-yard season to certify him as one of the best.

10. Curt Warner, Seattle (65.5)

	ATT	Att R	YARD	Yds R	AVG	Avg R	TD	Td R	TOTAL
Rushing	266	66.8	1025	64.7	3.9	73.4	10	71.4	72.0

	PC	Pc R	YARD	Yds R	AVG	Avg G	TD	Td R	TOTAL
Receiving	22	33.0	154	23.6	7.0	52.5	2	36.3	33.0

We heard that Seattle is shopping Warner around. There's not a great market for seventh-year running backs with a history of knee problems, and we doubt if the Seahawks could get what he'll be worth if he can last two more years.

11. Earl Ferrell, Phoenix (65.3)

	ATT	Att R	YARD	Yds R	AVG	Avg R	TD	Td R	TOTAL
Rushing	202	54.7	924	60.0	4.6	87.1	7	46.7	69.0

	PC	Pc R	YARD	Yds R	AVG	Avg G	TD	Td R	TOTAL
Receiving	38	43.4	315	34.4	8.3	62.1	2	30.8	46.6

When a veteran who's been around for six years without raising a fuss suddenly has his best season by far, you've got to think of those suns that burn brightest just before they go out.

12. James Brooks, Cincinnati (64.1)

	ATT	Att R	YARD	Yds R	AVG	Avg R	TD	Td R	TOTAL
Rushing	182	42.0	931	57.5	5.1	97.4	8	29.6	64.2

	PC	Pc R	YARD	Yds R	AVG	Avg G	TD	Td R	TOTAL
Receiving	29	47.3	287	36.5	9.9	74.1	6	85.7	63.5

It would be sacrilege to say that Brooks was more valuable than teammate Woods, but Brooks was a more versatile threat.

13. Garry James, Detroit (63.4)

	ATT	Att R	YARD	Yds R	AVG	Avg R	TD	Td R	TOTAL
Rushing	182	60.5	552	58.5	3.0	57.8	5	71.4	62.3

	PC	Pc R	YARD	Yds R	AVG	Avg G	TD	Td R	TOTAL
Receiving	39	67.3	382	68.0	9.8	73.4	2	61.5	68.7

At first we were shocked that James ranked so high. We thought he'd had a terrible rushing season. However, after thinking about the Detroit offense (or lack of it) in general, James may have been better than we gave him credit for being.

14. Joe Morris, N.Y. Giants (62.7)

	ATT	Att R	YARD	Yds R	AVG	Avg R	TD	Td R	TOTAL
Rushing	307	80.9	1083	84.5	3.5	67.2	5	33.3	68.8

	PC	Pc R	YARD	Yds R	AVG	Avg G	TD	Td R	TOTAL
Receiving	22	27.8	166	20.4	7.5	56.2	0	0.0	32.1

One-third of Little Joe's yards came in the last three games, after the Giants got their line together. He wasn't that good at the end, but he certainly wasn't as bad as he looked up until then.

15. Dalton Hilliard, New Orleans (62.3)

	ATT	Att R	YARD	Yds R	AVG	Avg R	TD	Td R	TOTAL
Rushing	204	51.8	823	53.0	4.0	76.8	5	55.6	64.4

	PC	Pc R	YARD	Yds R	AVG	Avg G	TD	Td R	TOTAL
Receiving	34	43.7	335	47.1	9.9	73.8	1	19.0	51.5

Hilliard's marks are all the more impressive considering that he shared time as the Saints' main runner with Reuben Mayes and Ironhead Heyward.

16 (tie). Marcus Allen, L.A. Raiders (60.8)

	ATT	Att R	YARD	Yds R	AVG	Avg R	TD	Td R	TOTAL
Rushing	223	58.8	831	59.1	3.7	71.0	7	46.7	63.0

	PC	Pc R	YARD	Yds R	AVG	Avg G	TD	Td R	TOTAL
Receiving	34	57.1	303	39.6	3.7	66.8	1	19.0	49.9

Allen isn't the back he was four years ago. On the other hand, he holds down the fort for half a season until Bo Jackson arrives (flourish of trumpets!) and then becomes mostly a blocker. And he did it in '88 with an injured wrist. This is a very valuable football player.

16 (tie). Freeman McNeil, N.Y. Jets (60.8)

	ATT	Att R	YARD	Yds R	AVG	Avg R	TD	Td R	TOTAL
Rushing	219	55.4	944	58.3	4.3	82.1	6	31.6	63.8

	PC	Pc R	YARD	Yds R	AVG	Avg G	TD	Td R	TOTAL
Receiving	34	41.8	288	39.1	8.5	63.5	1	20.0	45.6

A dangerous slasher when healthy, but probably out of place as a heavy-duty runner. Even if McNeil's not injured, look for him to run only half as often in '89.

18. Mike Rozier, Houston (59.1)

	ATT	Att R	YARD	Yds R	AVG	Avg R	TD	Td R	TOTAL
Rushing	251	58.4	1002	58.7	4.0	76.0	10	38.5	63.5

	PC	Pc R	YARD	Yds R	AVG	Avg G	TD	Td R	TOTAL
Receiving	11	18.5	99	14.3	9.0	67.4	1	19.0	37.3

The totals look better than they are because he runs behind a strong line. When he was injured Allen Pinkett ran just as well. Lorenzo White, the number one draft choice in '88, wants equal time. Also we're tired of hearing that Rozier shouldn't be blamed for poor pass receiving because he went to Nebraska and they never passed there. Roger Craig went to Nebraska.

19. John Stephens, New England (58.0)

	ATT	Att R	YARD	Yds R	AVG	Avg R	TD	Td R	TOTAL
Rushing	297	65.6	1168	72.6	3.9	74.9	4	23.5	64.6

	PC	Pc R	YARD	Yds R	AVG	Avg G	TD	Td R	TOTAL
Receiving	14	25.8	98	19.2	7.0	52.4	0	0.0	25.0

How come this terrific runner ranks so low? Well, he didn't become a regular until the season was underway, his average gain was 0.3 below his team's, and fullback Rob

Perryman usually got the TD plunges in close. Whether Stephens is a receiver or not is impossible to tell from the way the Patriots threw the ball in '88. We expect him to improve all his figures in '89 and move up. Maybe a lot.

20. Thurman Thomas, Buffalo (57.3)

	ATT	Att R	YARD	Yds R	AVG	Avg R	TD	Td R	TOTAL
Rushing	207	50.9	881	54.4	4.3	81.0	2	13.3	57.9

	PC	Pc R	YARD	Yds R	AVG	Avg G	TD	Td R	TOTAL
Receiving	18	24.4	354	47.4	15.4	100.0	0	0.0	54.4

The Bills' best runner, but in the games we saw him it looked like Buffalo was spotting him so that when he ran, he could tear off a good gain. That may be what he's best at, indicating that the Bills still need a heavy-duty man to handle the main load.

21. Merril Hoge, Pittsburgh (57.2)

	ATT	Att R	YARD	Yds R	AVG	Avg R	TD	Td R	TOTAL
Rushing	170	44.3	705	41.7	4.1	79.0	3	17.6	53.7

	PC	Pc R	YARD	Yds R	AVG	Avg G	TD	Td R	TOTAL
Receiving	50	81.3	487	67.4	9.7	73.0	3	80.0	74.9

Hoge became the regular only in the last half of the season. Until then, he was a third-down back (note his receiving record). He must learn that fumbling is bad, bad, bad!

22. Stump Mitchell, Phoenix (55.5)

	ATT	Att R	YARD	Yds R	AVG	Avg R	TD	Td R	TOTAL
Rushing	164	44.4	726	47.2	4.4	84.3	4	26.7	58.8

	PC	Pc R	YARD	Yds R	AVG	Avg G	TD	Td R	TOTAL
Receiving	25	28.5	214	23.3	8.6	64.4	1	15.3	39.2

A good, solid pro who always contributes.

23. Tony Dorsett, Denver (54.1)

	ATT	Att R	YARD	Yds R	AVG	Avg R	TD	Td R	TOTAL
Rushing	181	50.7	703	41.2	3.9	74.0	5	38.5	59.0

	PC	Pc R	YARD	Yds R	AVG	Avg G	TD	Td R	TOTAL
Receiving	16	18.1	122	14.1	7.6	57.1	0	0.0	29.3

The 1988 season was awful for a back with 12,739 career yards. Dorsett didn't adjust well to the Denver attack and vice versa. He may have one more great season left, but it may not be with the Broncos.

24. Reuben Mayes, New Orleans (49.7)

	ATT	Att R	YARD	Yds R	AVG	Avg R	TD	Td R	TOTAL
Rushing	170	43.1	628	40.4	3.7	70.3	3	33.3	52.8

	PC	Pc R	YARD	Yds R	AVG	Avg G	TD	Td R	TOTAL
Receiving	11	14.1	103	14.4	9.4	70.4	0	0.0	33.9

The question is knees. If Mayes's are okay, he can be very good. If Heyward's is okay (and he doesn't weigh more than the Queen Mary when he comes to camp), the Saints will have trouble finding a place for him. If both knees are okay and GM Jim Finks asked us, we'd say trade Mayes or Hilliard for some draft choices or some live bodies to give the Saints depth.

The following players caught 32 or more passes but did not average 10 rushing attempts per game. They are ranked as receivers only.

	PC	Pc R	YARD	Yds R	AVG	Avg G	TD	Td R	TOTAL
Palmer, KC	52	67.8	608	79.9	11.7	87.6	4	100.0	84.6
Sewell, Den	38	43.1	507	58.9	13.3	100.0	5	83.3	77.1
Byars, Phil	72	85.7	705	82.2	9.8	73.4	4	64.0	75.7
Harmon, Buf	37	50.2	427	57.3	11.5	86.5	3	80.0	72.1
Byner, Clev	59	69.3	576	71.5	9.8	73.2	2	42.1	65.9
Carter, Pitt	32	52.1	363	50.2	6.0	85.0	2	53.3	65.1
Bryant, Wash	42	47.2	447	47.1	10.6	79.8	5	60.6	62.9
Lang, Atl	37	54.4	398	62.5	10.8	80.6	1	30.8	61.8
Woodside, GB	39	44.9	352	44.6	9.0	67.6	2	61.5	57.3
Rathman, SF	42	52.7	382	47.6	9.1	68.2	0	0.0	47.3
Stradford, Mia	56	56.7	426	42.8	7.6	57.0	1	13.8	45.5
Dupard, NE	34	62.8	232	45.5	6.8	51.1	0	0.0	42.1
Toney, Phil	34	40.5	256	29.8	7.5	56.4	1	16.0	39.8
Willhite, Den	32	36.3	238	27.6	7.4	55.7	0	0.0	35.1

PASS RECEIVERS

There are more outstanding pass receivers in the NFL today than ever before. Virtually every team has a burner who can outrun a pass fifty yards downfield or take a short flip all the way for a touchdown. Many teams have two of them and some have three. If you're looking for a reason, go back to the 1977 rule changes that cut down on the bump-and-run crunching by defensive backs. That opened the door for 170- and 180-pound speedsters at WR, the kind that defenders like Mel Blount and Willie Brown used to turn into rubble. The age of the smurfs is upon us.

The NFL lumps all pass receivers together—WRs, TEs, and RBs—and then ranks them in two ways: by number of catches and by yards gained. This has led to a number of running backs leading the league in pass receptions by catching scads of little checkoffs that were maybe a foot shy of being laterals. In fact it was the absurdity of having running backs lead the NFL in receptions from 1974 through 1979—with only one gaining as much as 750 yards—that caused the league to begin keeping a separate yards' listing. The catch leader is still considered the champion.

Of the four important stats kept on receivers—total catches, total yards, average gain, and total touchdowns—the best measurement of the modern receiver's value is average gain. The other three are almost completely dependent upon the team's offensive style. When Miami throws 621 passes in a season and Cincinnati throws 392, you might assume that there are going to be a couple of Dolphins with more receptions than any Bengal. Yardage and touchdown figures would normally be higher for Dolphin receivers, too. Only an exceptional season by Cincinnati's Eddie Brown allowed him to top the AFC in catch yardage. But how can we be certain his season was exceptional? We need to look at his average gain.

In the two sections that follow, we've separated the wide receivers from the tight ends (RB receivers will be found in the discussion of rating rushers).

WIDE RECEIVERS

We wanted to rank the receivers statistically, but independently of their team's offensive style—and we think we've found a way to do it. First we converted each receiver's number of catches into his percentage of his team's pass receptions; then we changed that percentage into a rating with 100.00 for the receiver with the highest percentage—Drew Hill, with 33.02 percent of Houston's 218 completions—and worked out ratings for the other wide receivers with at least 32 catches (an average of 2 per scheduled game) by dividing their percentages by Hill's 33.02 percent. For example, Anthony Carter's 24.48 percent becomes a 74.1 rating. In the stat line after each receiver, you'll find PC (passes caught) and Pc R (passes caught percentage rating).

We did the same with yards, dividing the receiver's yards by his team's and converting to a rating, and for touchdowns, dividing the individual's TDs by his team's TDs and again converting to a rating. We think these marks, when taken together, give a better picture of the individual's accomplishments in the context of his team situation.

We did not adjust average gain to the player's team situation. Although it's true that some teams emphasize long passes more than others, a talented receiver can take a short flip 90 yards. All average gains were rated against leader Eddie Brown's 24.01.

In putting the total rankings together, we emphasized average gain (the most important figure) by counting it twice. The formula:

Rate = (PC/Tm PC + YDS/Tm YDS + 2 X [Avg/Top Avg] + TD/Tm TD) / 5

1. Eddie Brown, Cincinnati

PC	Pc R	YARD	Yds R	AVG	Avg R	TD	Td R	RATE
53	71.3	1273	98.3	24.0	100.0	9	57.1	85.4

Brown's long gains early in the season not only got the Bengals started on a great season, but also opened defenses to the dominating rushing attack Cincinnati developed later.

2. Drew Hill, Houston

PC	Pc R	YARD	Yds R	AVG	Avg R	TD	Td R	RATE
72	100.0	1141	100.0	15.8	66.0	10	84.7	83.3

The most dangerous weapon in a well-stocked arsenal.

3. Jerry Rice, San Francisco

PC	Pc R	YARD	Yds R	AVG	Avg R	TD	Td R	RATE
64	66.1	1306	98.6	20.4	85.0	9	76.2	82.2

Generally rated the top receiver in football, Rice was bothered by an ankle injury for much of the year, but was still terrific.

4. Bruce Hill, Tampa Bay

PC	Pc R	YARD	Yds R	AVG	Avg R	TD	Td R	RATE
58	69.4	1040	80.0	17.9	74.7	9	100.0	79.7

Entering his third season, Hill looks like he'll be a star for years.

5. Henry Ellard, L.A. Rams

PC	Pc R	YARD	Yds R	AVG	Avg R	TD	Td R	RATE
86	83.5	1414	98.0	16.4	68.5	10	57.3	75.2

The year 1988 was easily the best season of Ellard's career. His previous high in receptions, 54, and in yards, 811, came in '85.

6. Louis Lipps, Pittsburgh

PC	Pc R	YARD	Yds R	AVG	Avg R	TD	Td R	RATE
50	67.0	973	81.6	19.5	81.0	5	59.3	74.0

Although few noticed because the Steelers played so badly most of the year, Lipps made a great comeback after two nothing seasons.

7. Anthony Carter, Minnesota

PC	Pc R	YARD	Yds R	AVG	Avg R	TD	Td R	RATE
72	74.1	1225	82.9	17.0	70.8	6	53.3	70.4

A great receiver who is particularly dangerous over the middle, Carter's '88 TD total was lower than one would expect.

8. Eric Martin, New Orleans

PC	Pc R	YARD	Yds R	AVG	Avg R	TD	Td R	RATE
85	90.0	1083	92.3	12.7	53.0	7	59.3	69.5

Martin's average gain was probably hurt by the Saints' short game, but he's more an all-around catcher than a burner.

9. Ernest Givens, Houston

PC	Pc R	YARD	Yds R	AVG	Avg R	TD	Td R	RATE
60	83.3	976	85.5	16.3	67.7	5	42.3	69.3

The Oilers were the only team with two receivers in the top ten. Givens, ranked behind Hill, is entering his fourth season; Hill his tenth. They could reverse slots in 1989.

10. Andre Reed, Buffalo

PC	Pc R	YARD	Yds R	AVG	Avg R	TD	Td R	RATE
71	79.3	968	78.7	13.6	56.8	6	71.1	68.5

Underrated. The essential receiver in the Bills' passing game. The Buffalo attack was nuts-and-bolts, but Reed was a step above that.

11. Mark Carrier, Tampa Bay

PC	Pc R	YARD	Yds R	AVG	Avg R	TD	Td R	RATE
57	68.2	970	74.6	17.0	70.9	5	55.6	68.0

Like his teammate Hill, only entering his third season. As the two WRs continue to improve, so do Testaverde's chances of living up to the hype.

12. Stephone Paige, Kansas City

PC	Pc R	YARD	Yds R	AVG	Avg R	TD	Td R	RATE
62	66.6	905	72.1	14.6	60.8	7	77.8	67.6

If you want to keep an outstanding player a secret, there are few better places to do it than Kansas City. Paige is probably the most dangerous Chiefs' receiver since Otis Taylor. And if you don't know about O.T., we've made our point about secrets.

13. Ricky Sanders, Washington

PC	Pc R	YARD	Yds R	AVG	Avg R	TD	Td R	RATE
73	67.6	1148	73.4	15.7	65.5	12	64.6	67.3

For much of the season, Sanders started behind Monk and Clark (who are fine). Sanders was the "hot" receiver this year and was the top threat by season's end.

14. Mark Clayton, Miami

PC	Pc R	YARD	Yds R	AVG	Avg R	TD	Td R	RATE
86	71.7	1129	68.7	13.1	54.7	14	85.8	67.1

Despite his totals, this wasn't one of Clayton's best seasons. He dropped some and was covered more heavily than before because of Duper's off year.

15. Bill Brooks, Indianapolis

PC	Pc R	YARD	Yds R	AVG	Avg R	TD	Td R	RATE
54	73.6	867	84.0	16.1	66.8	3	35.6	65.4

Considering the Colts' turnstile at QB, this was a fine performance.

16. Al Toon, N.Y. Jets

PC	Pc R	YARD	Yds R	AVG	Avg R	TD	Td R	RATE
93	94.2	1067	87.7	11.5	47.8	5	44.4	64.4

Toon is an excellent possession receiver. However, it's hard to see why he would rate any higher than this when you look at his yards, average, and TDs.

17. Brian Blades, Seattle

PC	Pc R	YARD	Yds R	AVG	Avg R	TD	Td R	RATE
40	49.4	682	63.5	17.1	71.0	8	64.6	63.9

An impact rookie for the Seahawks.

18. Roy Green, Phoenix

PC	Pc R	YARD	Yds R	AVG	Avg R	TD	Td R	RATE
68	63.9	1097	72.6	16.1	67.2	7	47.9	63.8

Green has been one of the top receivers of the eighties. He's slowing down a bit but is still dangerous.

19. Lionel Manuel, N.Y. Giants

PC	Pc R	YARD	Yds R	AVG	Avg R	TD	Td R	RATE
65	67.9	1029	76.8	15.8	65.9	4	32.3	61.8

Free of injuries in '88, he had his best year.

20. Irving Fryar, New England

PC	Pc R	YARD	Yds R	AVG	Avg R	TD	Td R	RATE
33	50.2	490	58.3	14.8	61.8	5	74.1	61.2

Fryar's receiving record is better than the totals would suggest. The Pats passed less than anybody. His major problems seem to occur off the field.

21. Mark Jackson, Denver

PC	Pc R	YARD	Yds R	AVG	Avg R	TD	Td R	RATE
46	43.0	852	60.0	18.5	77.1	6	44.4	60.3

Jackson came within 40 of fellow "Amigo" Johnson's yardage total on 22 fewer catches.

22. Pete Mandley, Detroit

PC	Pc R	YARD	Yds R	AVG	Avg R	TD	Td R	RATE
44	62.5	617	66.6	14.0	58.4	4	54.7	60.1

Mandley did about as well as you could hope for in an awful Detroit season.

23. Hassan Jones, Minnesota

PC	Pc R	YARD	Yds R	AVG	Avg R	TD	Td R	RATE
40	41.2	778	52.7	19.5	81.0	5	44.4	60.0

24. Tim Brown, L.A. Raiders

PC	Pc R	YARD	Yds R	AVG	Avg R	TD	Td R	RATE
43	59.4	725	57.4	16.9	70.2	5	42.3	59.9

25. Tim McGee, Cincinnati

PC	Pc R	YARD	Yds R	AVG	Avg R	TD	Td R	RATE
36	48.4	686	53.0	19.1	79.3	6	38.1	59.6

26. Cris Carter, Philadelphia

PC	Pc R	YARD	Yds R	AVG	Avg R	TD	Td R	RATE
39	38.2	761	53.8	19.5	81.2	6	42.7	59.4

If you rate Tim Brown strictly as a receiver and leave out his kick returns, you could put a hat over Jones, Brown, McGee, and Carter and call the first one to break free the best of the group.

27. Reggie Langhorne, Cleveland

PC	Pc R	YARD	Yds R	AVG	Avg R	TD	Td R	RATE
57	55.1	780	58.7	13.7	57.0	7	65.5	58.7

28. Michael Irvin, Dallas

PC	Pc R	YARD	Yds R	AVG	Avg R	TD	Td R	RATE
32	31.6	654	48.7	20.4	85.1	5	42.3	58.6

29. Dennis McKinnon, Chicago

PC	Pc R	YARD	Yds R	AVG	Avg R	TD	Td R	RATE
45	54.9	704	61.6	15.6	65.1	3	41.0	57.6

30 (tie). Ray Alexander, Dallas

PC	Pc R	YARD	Yds R	AVG	Avg R	TD	Td R	RATE
54	53.3	788	58.7	14.6	60.8	6	50.8	56.8

30 (tie). Stephen Baker, N.Y. Giants

PC	Pc R	YARD	Yds R	AVG	Avg R	TD	Td R	RATE
40	41.8	656	49.0	16.4	68.3	7	56.6	56.8

32. Lonzell Hill, New Orleans

PC	Pc R	YARD	Yds R	AVG	Avg R	TD	Td R	RATE
66	69.9	703	59.9	10.7	44.3	7	59.3	55.5

Langhorne is basically a third-down type. McKinnon is bidding to replace Willie Gault in Chicago. The rest are young and fast. One of them—perhaps Irvin—will emerge as a full-blown star in the next couple of years.

33. J. T. Smith, Phoenix

PC	Pc R	YARD	Yds R	AVG	Avg R	TD	Td R	RATE
83	78.0	986	65.3	11.9	49.5	5	34.2	55.3

A late bloomer, Smith is going into his twelfth season. He doesn't beat you deep, but he's caught 172 passes in the last two years, and that adds up to a lot of first downs.

34. Gary Clark, Washington

PC	Pc R	YARD	Yds R	AVG	Avg R	TD	Td R	RATE
59	54.6	892	57.0	15.1	62.9	7	37.7	55.1

35. Vance Johnson, Denver

PC	Pc R	YARD	Yds R	AVG	Avg R	TD	Td R	RATE
68	63.5	896	63.1	13.2	54.9	5	37.0	54.7

36. Anthony Miller, San Diego

PC	Pc R	YARD	Yds R	AVG	Avg R	TD	Td R	RATE
36	45.2	526	55.5	14.6	60.8	3	48.5	54.2

37. Carlos Carson, Kansas City

PC	Pc R	YARD	Yds R	AVG	Avg R	TD	Td R	RATE
46	49.4	711	56.6	15.5	64.4	3	33.3	53.6

38. Art Monk, Washington

PC	Pc R	YARD	Yds R	AVG	Avg R	TD	Td R	RATE
72	66.7	946	60.5	13.1	54.7	5	26.9	52.7

Monk, who caught 106 passes in 1984, is bigger than Clark or Sanders. The 'Skins' possession man, he now has 576 career receptions.

39. Steve Largent, Seattle

PC	Pc R	YARD	Yds R	AVG	Avg R	TD	Td R	RATE
39	48.2	645	60.1	16.5	68.9	2	16.2	52.4

Largent may be retired by the time you read this. He suffered through an un-Largent season in '88 because of injuries. Never the fastest, he's been a sure Hall of Famer because of hands, moves, and hard work. He finished last season with 791 catches, 12,686 yards, and 97 touchdowns.

40 (tie). Dennis Gentry, Chicago

PC	Pc R	YARD	Yds R	AVG	Avg R	TD	Td R	RATE
33	40.3	486	42.5	14.7	61.3	3	41.0	49.3

40 (tie). Sterling Sharpe, Green Bay

PC	Pc R	YARD	Yds R	AVG	Avg R	TD	Td R	RATE
55	52.2	791	60.8	14.4	59.9	1	13.7	49.3

42. Jamie Holland, San Diego

PC	Pc R	YARD	Yds R	AVG	Avg R	TD	Td R	RATE
39	49.0	536	56.6	13.7	57.2	1	16.2	47.2

43. Kevin Martin, Dallas

PC	Pc R	YARD	Yds R	AVG	Avg R	TD	Td R	RATE
49	48.3	622	46.3	12.7	52.8	3	25.4	45.1

44. Mark Duper, Miami

PC	Pc R	YARD	Yds R	AVG	Avg R	TD	Td R	RATE
39	32.5	626	38.1	16.1	66.8	1	6.1	42.1

Even before his suspension, Duper was having a poor year. Through 1987 he'd averaged nearly 7 touchdowns a season.

45. Brian Brennan, Cleveland

PC	Pc R	YARD	Yds R	AVG	Avg R	TD	Td R	RATE
46	44.5	579	43.6	12.6	52.4	1	9.4	40.4

46. Perry Kemp, Green Bay

PC	Pc R	YARD	Yds R	AVG	Avg R	TD	Td R	RATE
48	45.6	620	47.7	12.9	53.8	0	0.0	40.2

47. Trumaine Johnson, Buffalo

PC	Pc R	YARD	Yds R	AVG	Avg R	TD	Td R	RATE
37	41.3	514	41.8	13.9	57.8	0	0.0	39.8

48. Ricky Nattiel, Denver

PC	Pc R	YARD	Yds R	AVG	Avg R	TD	Td R	RATE
46	43.0	574	40.4	12.5	52.0	1	7.4	38.9

49. Mike Wilson, San Francisco

PC	Pc R	YARD	Yds R	AVG	Avg R	TD	Td R	RATE
33	34.1	405	30.6	12.3	51.1	3	25.4	38.5

50. Lionel James, San Diego

PC	Pc R	YARD	Yds R	AVG	Avg R	TD	Td R	RATE
36	45.2	279	29.5	7.8	32.3	1	16.2	31.1

Technically "Little Train" is a running back, but he has been mainly a receiver for the Chargers for the last couple of years.

Philadelphia's Mike Quick missed eight games in '88 with a fractured left leg. His figures for his half-season: 22 receptions, 4 touchdowns, 508 yards, and a 23.1 average. That would give him a 53.5 total rate here.

TIGHT ENDS

A tight end is a hybrid: half receiver, half blocker. Some teams emphasize the receiver side, other teams the blocking. An interesting changeover began in Los Angeles last season. Todd Christensen, a tight end who'd been among the league's top catchmakers for five years, found himself in a changed offense. Under new coach Mike Shanahan, the Raiders deemphasized the TE's role as a receiver in favor of a larger blocking responsibility. Even before he was injured, Christensen was being eased out for younger, huskier TEs.

The pass catchers make the All-Star teams and the Pro Bowl, but several good TEs, who are primarily blockers, didn't make enough catches to be ranked here. As we have no way to compare the blocking abilities of TEs across the league, the following are ranked strictly as receivers. We did set up a different set of standards for tight ends, using only the maximums by TEs. Although there are some exceptions, TEs are used primarily for possession receiving, and their yardages and average gains reflect that.

1. Mickey Shuler, N.Y. Jets

PC	Pc R	YARD	Yds R	AVG	Avg R	TD	Td R	RATE
70	89.3	805	100.0	11.5	66.0	5	100.0	84.3

The Jets' veteran has moved into the plus-400 range in catches. His 1988 figures are typical of his career.

2. Keith Jackson, Philadelphia

PC	Pc R	YARD	Yds R	AVG	Avg R	TD	Td R	RATE
81	100.0	869	92.7	10.7	61.6	6	96.0	82.4

At Oklahoma, Jackson caught few passes in the ground-based attack. As a rookie last year he proved he was an exceptional receiver. Although his average gain was nothing special, he's fast enough to get free deep.

3. Steve Jordan, Minnesota

PC	Pc R	YARD	Yds R	AVG	Avg R	TD	Td R	RATE
57	74.0	756	77.3	13.3	76.1	5	100.0	80.7

One of the best, both as a receiver and as a blocker. Jordan has usually been ranked behind the Giants' Bavaro, but Jordan had a better season than Bavaro did in '88.

4. Mark Bavaro, N.Y. Giants

PC	Pc R	YARD	Yds R	AVG	Avg R	TD	Td R	RATE
53	69.7	672	75.8	12.7	72.8	4	72.7	72.8

Generally considered the best tight end in the NFL, Bavaro had a poor (for him) '88 season. His catches fell only 2 from 1987, but his yardage was down nearly 200 and his TDs were cut in half.

5. Jay Novacek, Phoenix

PC	Pc R	YARD	Yds R	AVG	Avg R	TD	Td R	RATE
38	45.0	569	56.9	15.0	85.9	4	61.5	67.1

An All-Star in the first half of '88 but tailed badly in the second half.

6. Ferrell Edmunds, Miami

PC	Pc R	YARD	Yds R	AVG	Avg R	TD	Td R	RATE
33	34.7	575	52.9	17.4	100.0	3	41.4	65.8

At 6'6" and 241, Edmunds has the size. A third-round draft choice last year, he split time with handyman Jim Jensen. It remains to be seen if Edmunds can maintain that average, the best among TEs and the source of this rating.

7. Rodney Holman, Cincinnati

PC	Pc R	YARD	Yds R	AVG	Avg R	TD	Td R	RATE
39	66.1	527	61.5	13.5	77.6	3	42.9	65.1

A fine blend of blocker-receiver, Holman was one of the Bengals' most valuable players and was picked for the Pro Bowl behind Shuler.

8. Jim Jensen, Miami

PC	Pc R	YARD	Yds R	AVG	Avg R	TD	Td R	RATE
58	61.0	652	60.0	11.2	64.5	5	69.0	63.8

At 215 pounds, Jensen is too small to be a true tight end, but the Dolphins didn't run much anyway. He also plays WR, RB, and, in a pinch, QB. Simply a good, useful football player.

9. Pete Holohan, L.A. Rams

PC	Pc R	YARD	Yds R	AVG	Avg R	TD	Td R	RATE
59	72.1	640	67.0	10.8	62.3	3	38.7	60.5

A bargain pickup for the Rams from San Diego, where he was stagnating behind Kellen Winslow. Solid year.

10. Robert Awalt, Phoenix

PC	Pc R	YARD	Yds R	AVG	Avg R	TD	Td R	RATE
39	46.2	454	45.4	11.6	66.8	4	61.5	57.4

11. Ron Hall, Tampa Bay

PC	Pc R	YARD	Yds R	AVG	Avg R	TD	Td R	RATE
39	58.8	555	64.5	14.2	81.7	0	0.0	57.3

12. Pete Metzelaars, Buffalo

PC	Pc R	YARD	Yds R	AVG	Avg R	TD	Td R	RATE
33	46.5	438	53.8	13.3	76.2	1	26.7	55.9

13. Clarence Kay, Denver

PC	Pc R	YARD	Yds R	AVG	Avg R	TD	Td R	RATE
34	40.0	352	37.4	10.4	59.4	4	66.7	52.6

14. Damone Johnson, L.A. Rams

PC	Pc R	YARD	Yds R	AVG	Avg R	TD	Td R	RATE
42	51.4	350	36.7	8.3	47.8	6	77.4	52.2

15. Ozzie Newsome, Cleveland

PC	Pc R	YARD	Yds R	AVG	Avg R	TD	Td R	RATE
35	42.7	343	39.0	9.8	56.2	2	42.1	47.3

Newsome slowed down greatly in '88, but moved his career receptions to 610, sixth all-time and the record for tight ends.

OFFENSIVE LINES

Offensive linemen have to jump offsides to get noticed, but nobody wins without them. When it comes to picking the good ones, it's mostly guesswork unless you happen to be playing opposite one. A coach may extol his right guard as the greatest protector since Right Guard, but he hasn't seen all of the league's guards in action. Scouts see only a couple of games a year for rivals. Line coaches grade their own men with differing systems, so you can't even compare one team's records with another team's (if they'd ever let you see them).

A couple of years ago we decided to try to rate linemen statistically. Don't worry, we know there aren't any official-type numbers kept on individual linemen. But we saw some possibilities for whole lines from tackle to tackle. That made more sense anyway. A line isn't as strong as its best man; it's closer to being as weak as its poorest. If you had four great starters and one klutz, you'd have trouble making your offense go, because one missed block can lose a play or a quarterback. An offensive line must work as a unit, which is one reason they usually take a couple of years to reach peak efficiency.

The two things every line must do is open holes for its runners and close them for its passer.

We decided to use a team's Average Gain per Rushing Attempt as an index of its line's ability to run block. That figure isn't affected quite so much as Total Rushing Yards and Rushing Yards per Game by the score or by a team's ability to pass. Obviously it helps to be opening holes for Roger Craig and hurts to be opening them for Lenny Leadfoot. But it makes just as much sense to credit yards to the line as it does to give them all to the runner.

To measure pass blocking, we used the Sack Average, which is nothing more than the number of sacks, divided by pass attempts plus sacks. Total sacks allowed isn't a good measure because one team may attempt 200 more passes than another.

We took Average Gain, which is better if it's high, and Sack Average, which is better if it's low, and turned them into ratings so they can be compared side by side. Then we combined the two marks to get a Total Grade. This is not a perfect system, but we don't know of any other that isn't totally subjective.

When we first invented the system, we skewed it toward whatever a team did the most of. If it ran more often than it passed, we weighted its total grade toward running by the percentage of rushing plays. Then someone pointed out that a team just might run more often because its pass blocking was lousy. So this year we gave the two numbers equal weight in arriving at the Total Grade.

Another new thing this year was to add some bonus points, between zero and five, for a team's performance on third downs. We assumed that whether a team ran on short yardage or passed on long yardage, the line had its greatest challenges on third-and-whatever. The bonus points changed the rank of a couple of lines, in most cases lifting the ones who are thought of as being the better combinations.

We've tinkered with our old formula slightly in the numbers used to change the Rush Average and Sack Average into Ratings. Our original formula gave too big a spread to the pass blocking grade.

Some of the results sorely need further explanation. And, besides, by taking the lines one at a time, we get to name people you've seen many times but probably never heard of.

1988 OFFENSIVE LINE GRADES

Team	Rush Att	Rush Avg	Rush Grade	Pass +Sack Att	Tot Sack	Pct Sack	Sack Grade	3rd-D Eff.	TOTAL GRADE
Cin	563	4.81	100.23	422	30	7.11	80.84	43.6	94.79
SD	438	4.66	96.76	499	31	6.21	84.21	34.5	91.32
Chi	555	4.18	85.69	485	24	4.95	88.94	41.9	90.93
SF	527	4.79	99.77	549	47	8.56	75.40	41.2	90.93
NO	512	4.00	81.54	522	24	4.60	90.25	45.6	90.90
Dal	469	4.25	92.50	580	35	6.03	84.89	37.6	90.69
Mia	335	3.60	72.31	628	7	1.11	103.34	38.7	90.24
Hous	558	4.03	82.23	452	24	5.30	87.63	40.4	87.98
Rams	507	3.95	80.38	550	28	5.09	88.41	39.7	87.18
Buff	528	4.04	82.46	484	30	6.20	84.25	42.0	87.01
Clev	440	3.58	81.08	573	36	6.28	83.95	43.7	86.81
Denv	464	3.91	79.46	613	32	5.22	87.93	40.2	86.67
Pitt	499	4.46	92.15	531	42	7.91	77.84	36.6	86.62
Wash	437	3.53	71.17	616	24	3.90	92.88	42.9	86.01
NY J	514	4.15	85.00	580	42	7.24	80.35	40.9	85.91
Seat	517	4.03	82.23	466	29	6.22	84.18	38.4	85.50
Atl	478	4.22	86.62	524	43	8.21	76.71	37.0	83.44
TB	452	3.88	78.77	546	34	6.23	84.14	34.5	82.28
Ind	545	4.13	84.54	437	34	7.78	78.32	34.2	82.14
Phoe	480	4.22	86.62	622	60	9.65	71.31	40.1	81.90
Phil	464	4.19	85.92	638	57	8.93	74.01	36.7	81.62
KC	448	3.82	77.38	571	43	7.53	79.26	39.7	81.10
NE	588	3.61	72.54	412	23	5.58	86.58	35.9	80.91
Minn	501	3.60	72.31	567	47	8.29	76.41	37.4	76.28
GrB	385	3.58	71.85	633	51	8.06	77.28	36.0	75.96
Raid	493	3.76	76.00	542	46	8.49	75.66	32.3	75.83
NY G	493	3.43	68.38	585	60	10.26	69.03	36.7	70.36
Det	391	3.18	62.62	529	52	9.83	70.64	33.2	66.97

The Formulas:

RG (Rush Grade) = [(RA - 3.5) / 1.3] X 30 + 70
SG (Sack Grade) = 100 - [(SA - 2) / 8 X 30]
Bonus up to 5 points for Third-Down Efficiency (3rd-D Eff)

CINCINNATI BENGALS

Run Blocking: 100.23	LT Anthony Munoz
Pass Blocking: 80.84	LG Bruce Reimers
3rd-Down Eff.: 43.6	C Bruce Kozerski
TOTAL GRADE: 94.79	RG Max Montoya
	RT Joe Walter

What the Maginot Line was *supposed* to be. Munoz and Montoya were picked for the Pro Bowl, and Walter probably should have been. Reimers and Kozerski are solid and keep 295-pound Brian Blados, a number one draft choice in '84, on the bench. The pass blocking grade is surprisingly ordinary. Nobody's perfect.

SAN DIEGO CHARGERS

Run Blocking: 96.76	LT Ken Dallafior
Pass Blocking: 84.21	LG Broderick Thompson
3rd-Down Eff.: 34.5	C Dan Rosado
TOTAL GRADE: 91.32	RG Dennis McKnight
	RT David Richards

Not even the Chargers would rate this line as the second best in the NFL. The grades are astonishing for a 6–10 team. Even more surprising, Richards was a rookie and the other four were free agents. McKnight, who's been around since 1982, is very good. The Chargers didn't score much and were blown out a couple of times, so this group faced a lot of prevent defenses, helping the old averages. They're still underrated and played very well at season's end.

CHICAGO BEARS

Run Blocking: 85.69	LT Jimbo Covert
Pass Blocking: 88.94	LG Mark Bortz
3rd-Down Eff.: 41.9	C Jay Hilgenberg
TOTAL GRADE: 90.93	RG Tom Thayer
	RT Keith Van Horne

Covert missed over half the season with a back injury and John Wojciechowski filled in. If Jimbo's healthy, this is the best NFC line. If he's not, it's still probably the best. Hilgenberg is one of the two best centers in the NFL. Bortz and Thayer are excellent. Van Horne is steady. Okay, McMahon keeps getting hurt, but he'd find a way to do that behind a wall of titanium.

SAN FRANCISCO 49ERS

Run Blocking:	99.77	LT	Steve Wallace
Pass Blocking:	75.40	LG	Jesse Sapolu
3rd-Down Eff.:	41.2	C	Randy Cross
TOTAL GRADE:	90.93	RG	Guy McIntyre
		RT	Harris Barton

Roger Craig and sometimes Steve Young helped the rushing average, but this bunch did an okay job except for too many sacks. Aside from thirteen-year vet Cross, this is a young group that replaced the guys the 49ers used to send to the Pro Bowl. Young tackles Wallace and Barton should improve.

NEW ORLEANS SAINTS

Run Blocking:	81.54	LT	Jim Dombrowski
Pass Blocking:	90.25	LG	Brad Edelman
3rd-Down Eff.:	45.6	C	Steve Korte
TOTAL GRADE:	90.90	RG	Steve Trapilo
		RT	Daren Gilbert

The Saints' 45.6 rating in third-down efficiency was easily the best in the NFL, but it was 50.8 at midyear and dropped off in must-win games. Korte and Edelman are excellent, and Dombrowski and Trapilo are getting better. The line was badly hurt when RT Stan Brock, one of the best, went out with an injured knee. He missed over half the season.

DALLAS COWBOYS

Run Blocking:	92.50	LT	Dave Widell
Pass Blocking:	84.89	LG	Nate Newton
3rd-Down Eff.:	37.6	C	Tom Rafferty
TOTAL GRADE:	90.69	RG	Crawford Ker
		RT	Kevin Grogan

This could be the NFL's next premier line. They are huge. Newman and Grogan top 300 pounds, as does guard Jeff Zimmerman, who was injured all season. Widell, a rookie last year, is 6'6" and Grogan 6'7". The rub is experience. When Bob White replaced Rafferty at center, the line averaged 2.2 years in the NFL. Right now, Ker is the most consistent.

MIAMI DOLPHINS

Run Blocking:	72.31	LT	Jon Geisler
Pass Blocking:	103.34	LG	Roy Foster
3rd-Down Eff.:	38.7	C	Jeff Dellenbach
TOTAL GRADE:	90.24	RG	Harry Galbreath
		RT	Ronnie Lee

You could shoot a cannon from the press box at the snap and Marino would still get his pass off before impact, so don't hand out too many medals to the line for the record-low sack total. Even Pittsburgh, who couldn't rush a freshman at a frat party, hurried Dan a couple of times. And they couldn't open holes for the runners (who might not have found them anyway). Foster didn't play up to his par. Geisler and Lee are both thirty-three and are not going to get any better. If Dwight Stephenson can come back at 80 percent, center will be improved.

HOUSTON OILERS

Run Blocking:	82.23	LT	Bruce Davis
Pass Blocking:	87.63	LG	Mike Munchak
3rd-Down Eff.:	40.4	C	Jay Pennison
TOTAL GRADE:	87.98	RG	Bruce Matthews
		RT	Dean Steinkuhler

Very good, but it should be even better. Pro Bowlers Matthews and Munchak are a great guard duo, and Davis is very underrated. Steinkuhler, number one draft choice in '84, hasn't earned that rank. Pennison is nothing special.

LOS ANGELES RAMS

Run Blocking:	80.38	LT	Irv Pankey
Pass Blocking:	88.41	LG	Tom Newberry
3rd-Down Eff.:	39.7	C	Doug Smith
TOTAL GRADE:	87.18	RG	Duval Love
		RT	Jackie Slater

Newberry and Slater started in the Pro Bowl and Smith was a backup. The Rams said Pankey belonged there. So why was their rushing average so low? And how come the Viking defense handled them in the Wild Card game? This group is probably slightly overrated (except for Newberry) by most; these grades seem about right. Good, not great.

BUFFALO BILLS

Run Blocking:	82.46	LT	Will Wolford
Pass Blocking:	84.25	LG	Jim Ritcher
3rd-Down Eff.:	42.0	C	Kent Hull
TOTAL GRADE:	87.01	RG	Tim Vogler
		RT	Joe Devlin

Hull made Pro Bowl squad, but ranks in a pack far behind Indy's Donaldson. Wolford is developing into a very good tackle. Overall, a slightly above average wall. Age may be a problem on the right side: Devlin is thirty-five, Vogler thirty-three.

CLEVELAND BROWNS

Run Blocking:	81.08	LT	Paul Farren
Pass Blocking:	83.95	LG	Larry Williams
3rd-Down Eff.:	43.7	C	Gregg Rakoczy
TOTAL GRADE:	86.81	RG	Dan Fike
		RT	Cody Risien

Fike is highly respected, as is former Pro Bowler Risien, but the Browns lost five quarterbacks during the season and in the Wild Card game. It can't *all* be dumb luck. The running game was sporadic, to put it charitably. The left side needs a lot of upgrading. Did Cleveland make a mistake in letting veteran center Mike Baab go and keeping Rakoczy?

DENVER BRONCOS

Run Blocking:	79.46	LT	Dave Studdard
Pass Blocking:	87.93	LG	Keith Bishop
3rd-Down Eff.:	40.2	C	Billy Bryan
TOTAL GRADE:	86.67	RG	Jim Juriga
		RT	Ken Lanier

Like the Bronco defense, this group is undersized. Juriga, at 275 pounds, is the only one close to NFL-size. This hurts most on the run blocking. Part of the good pass blocking grade is due to Elway's ability to escape. Studdard and Bryan are both thirty-four; Bishop and Lanier are thirty. Look for changes.

PITTSBURGH STEELERS

Run Blocking:	92.15	LT	Craig Wolfley
Pass Blocking:	77.84	LG	Brian Blankenship
3rd-Down Eff.:	36.6	C	Mike Webster
TOTAL GRADE:	86.62	RG	Terry Long
		RT	Tunch Ilkin

Unsung hero Wolfley, a 6'1" guard, had to play tackle all season because there was no one else. DEs would laugh when he lined up. The Steelers had the smallest line in the NFL. Trap blocks very well, but can be outmuscled. Ilkin gives few sacks. Fifteen-year-vet Webster retired, then un-retired with Kansas City.

WASHINGTON REDSKINS

Run Blocking:	71.17	LT	Jim Lachey
Pass Blocking:	92.88	LG	Raleigh McKenzie
3rd-Down Eff.:	42.9	C	Jeff Bostic
TOTAL GRADE:	86.62	RG	Mike May
		RT	Joe Jacoby

Run blocking grade would be higher if RB Kelvin Bryant had stayed healthy. Russ Grimm and R. C. Thielmann also started at times and the shuffling hurt cohesiveness. Former All-Pro Jacoby was shifted from LT after a rash of sacks. May was outstanding.

NEW YORK JETS

Run Blocking:	85.00	LT	Jeff Criswell
Pass Blocking:	80.35	LG	Ted Banker
3rd-Down Eff.:	40.9	C	Jim Sweeney
TOTAL GRADE:	85.91	RG	Dan Alexander
		RT	Reggie McElroy

Number one draft choice OT Dave Cadigan was injured all season and Alexander spent time on IR. Sweeney is the best here. Actually, they graded pretty well, considering that any line blocking for Hold-'Em-and-Fold-'Em O'Brien will give up more sacks than one blocking for a normal QB.

SEATTLE SEAHAWKS

Run Blocking:	82.23	LT	Ron Mattes
Pass Blocking:	84.18	LG	Edwin Bailey
3rd-Down Eff.:	38.4	C	Blair Bush
TOTAL GRADE:	85.50	RG	Bryan Millard
		RT	Mike Wilson

Millard is a standout. Steady Bailey tied the Seahawks' record for most career starts in the season's final game. Otherwise, your generic NFL line. Wilson is getting up in years. And Bush signed with Green Bay.

ATLANTA FALCONS

Run Blocking:	86.62	LT	Mike Kenn
Pass Blocking:	76.71	LG	John Scully
3rd-Down Eff.:	37.0	C	George Yarno
TOTAL GRADE:	83.44	RG	Bill Fralic
		RT	Houston Hoover

Fralic is the best in the business, and Kenn is still fine at thirty-three. Scully is a journeyman. Rookie Hoover was okay after he took over in the fifth game. A very uneven group that averages out as average.

TAMPA BAY BUCCANEERS

Run Blocking:	78.77	LT	Paul Gruber
Pass Blocking:	84.14	LG	Rick Mallory
3rd-Down Eff.:	34.5	C	Randy Grimes
TOTAL GRADE:	82.28	RG	John Bruhn
		RT	Rob Taylor

Number one draft choice Gruber is already ranked as one of the best in the NFC. Grimes is an okay center. C-G Dan Turk started at RG much of the season, but rookie Bruhn ended the season there. The run blocking grade will go up if the young backs improve.

INDIANAPOLIS COLTS

Run Blocking:	84.54	LT	Chris Hinton
Pass Blocking:	78.32	LG	Randy Dixon
3rd-Down Eff.:	34.2	C	Ray Donaldson
TOTAL GRADE:	82.14	RG	Ben Utt
		RT	Kevin Call

The Colts' line should have done better, considering their reputation and that they were blocking for Eric Dickerson. The unsettled quarterback situation may have hurt. Hinton was named a Pro Bowl starter, but it wasn't one of his better years. Donaldson is the best center in the AFC by a wide margin.

PHOENIX CARDINALS

Run Blocking:	86.82	LT	Luis Sharpe
Pass Blocking:	71.31	LG	Todd Peat
3rd-Down Eff.:	40.1	C	Derek Kennard
TOTAL GRADE:	81.90	RG	Lance Smith
		RT	Tootie Robbins

Sharpe is rated as one of NFL's top OTs, and Kennard and Smith have their advocates. But this group gave up seven sacks to the 49ers, six to the Browns (!), five in two other games, and four in five *other* games. They opened holes for the runners and the gates for the quarterbacks.

PHILADELPHIA EAGLES

Run Blocking:	85.92	LT	Matt Darwin
Pass Blocking:	74.01	LG	Dave Alexander
3rd-Down Eff.:	36.7	C	Dave Rimington
TOTAL GRADE:	81.62	RG	Ron Baker
		RT	Ron Heller

The addition of the so-so Rimington and former 49ers TE Heller improved this line from unmitigated disaster to mitigated. Expensive OG Ron Solt, injured all season, might have helped. Sacks went down after '87 regular Baker rejoined the lineup in Week 10. QB Cunningham caused some extra sacks by holding the ball too long, but his running saved the run blocking grade. He averaged 6.7 yards, but none of the regular runners got above 3.6. This is perhaps the weakest line ever to win a division.

KANSAS CITY CHIEFS

Run Blocking:	77.38	LT	John Alt
Pass Blocking:	79.26	LG	Rich Baldinger
3rd-Down Eff.:	39.7	C	Gerry Feehery
TOTAL GRADE:	81.10	RG	Mark Adickes
		RT	Irv Eatman

The Chiefs used eight line combos in the first eleven weeks, as Alt, Adickes, and Baldinger suffered various hurts. Feehery came from Philadelphia on waivers in late October. After this group took over in Week 12, they gave up only six sacks to the season's end, and the Chiefs' per-game rush average went up forty yards.

NEW ENGLAND PATRIOTS

Run Blocking:	72.54	LT	Danny Villa
Pass Blocking:	86.58	LG	Sean Farrell
3rd-Down Eff.:	35.9	C	Mike Baab
TOTAL GRADE:	80.91	RG	Ron Wooten
		RT	Bruce Armstrong

Despite the low grade, the Pats' line can run block. The lack of a breakaway runner and the grind-it-out offense used for half the season pulled the grade down, but they couldn't have gone to that offense if these people didn't do the job. Armstrong is terrific now and he's a mere twenty-three. When he grows up, he'll really be something. The 305-pound Villa is only entering his third year. Farrell is very good. The whole line picked up when Baab took over at center.

MINNESOTA VIKINGS

Run Blocking:	72.31	LT	Gary Zimmerman
Pass Blocking:	76.41	LG	Randy McDaniel
3rd-Down Eff.:	37.4	C	Kirk Loudermilk
TOTAL GRADE:	76.28	RG	Terry Tausch
		RT	Tim Irwin

This line gave up ten more sacks than the vaunted defense produced. The rush average was way down, too. You have to believe they're better than the grades suggest—

especially after watching them handle the Rams' rush in the NFC Wild Cards—but it's not up to the level of the rest of the team. Zimmerman held out, then had an off year, although he was still named to the Pro Bowl. McDaniel broke Mick Tinglehoff's 1962 Viking rookie record by starting in fifteen regular season games. Loudermilk is the best Vike center since Mick retired.

GREEN BAY PACKERS

Run Blocking:	71.85	LT	Ken Ruettgers
Pass Blocking:	77.28	LG	Rich Moran
3rd-Down Eff.:	36.0	C	Mark Cannon
TOTAL GRADE:	75.96	RG	Ron Hallstrom
		RT	Keith Uecker

Ruettgers, probably the best of this group, was bothered with an injury last season and missed time. The other four started every game. Hallstrom is above average, but Cannon was rated as lower caliber. A better line than its grades, which were hurt by backfield inexperience and ineptitude.

LOS ANGELES RAIDERS

Run Blocking:	76.00	LT	Don Mosebar
Pass Blocking:	75.66	LG	Chris Riehm
3rd-Down Eff.:	32.2	C	Bill Lewis
TOTAL GRADE:	75.83	RG	Bruce Wilkerson
		RT	Rory Graves

The switch of center Mosebar to RT helped counter some early-season problems. He's the best here. This group is the lowest rated in the AFC, but it's young—Graves was a rookie, Riehm and Wilkerson were only sophomores, and Lewis was in his third year.

NEW YORK GIANTS

Run Blocking:	68.38	LT	William Roberts
Pass Blocking:	69.03	LG	Bill Ard
3rd-Down Eff.:	36.7	C	Bart Oates
TOTAL GRADE:	70.36	RG	Eric Moore R
		RT	Doug Riesenberg

A weak unit, although Oates is okay and Ard is reliable. Moore, the first draft pick, was shoved into a starting role and showed promise. Second pick John Elliott flunked his first trial at RT. Roberts and Riesenberg would be subs on a better team.

DETROIT LIONS

Run Blocking:	62.62	LT	Lomas Brown
Pass Blocking:	70.64	LG	Kevin Glover
3rd-Down Eff.:	33.2	C	Steve Mott
TOTAL GRADE:	66.97	RG	Joe Milinchik
		RT	Harvey Salem

Thought to be the strongest area on the team at the beginning of the '88 season, it didn't do the job. On the other hand, the Lions lack so much that the line can't be blamed for the entire season. Brown has been a standout tackle before. One thing is sure, when someone made a crisp block in the Silver Dome, you could hear it. The sound reverberated off the empty seats.

THE DEFENDERS

WHY WE CAN'T RATE THEM

A team game like football, with twenty-two guys racing every which way on each play, is as hard to measure in its individual parts as calibrating an avalanche rock by rock. The only possible way to get every bit of it is to study each game film and run every play at least twenty-two times. We could have 1988 figured out sometime in October 1997, which might be a tad late to interest anyone but historians. As a reasonable compromise, we'll settle for measuring the contributions of the people who get their hands and feet on the ball. Nevertheless, most of us feel a little queasy in crediting Joe Montana with a pass completion for 20 yards. We know that someone had to catch the ball, several some-ones had to block to make it possible, and even the other receiver, who ran an out pattern away from where the pass was thrown, contributed by drawing off a defender. But there it is: Montana, completion +20.

The problem is compounded on the other side of the football. What few individual stats we have may be mislead-ing. That cornerback who intercepts six passes may simply be the one that all the quarterbacks pick on. For every one he gets in front of, ten sail over his head. Another corner-back may go through a season with nary an interception because he covers so well that few passes come in his direc-tion. The lineman who makes a sack may have been able to do it only because another defender tied up two or three blockers. Certainly interceptions and sacks are not mean-ingless; it's just that we never know their *whole* meaning.

Most teams publish unofficial lists of tackles made. These are usually compiled in the press box and are often of dubious accuracy. What's worse, there's no telling the cir-cumstances of the tackle. A linebacker who makes all his tackles ten yards down the field won't be starting for long. Defensive backs are usually high on the "Tackles Made"

lists because they pull a lot of receivers down *after* the catch has been made. If a receiver catches a pass and his momen-tum carries him out of bounds, in some lists the defensive man nearest him will be credited with a tackle even if he's ten yards away.

We noticed that the left-inside linebacker in many 3-4 defenses makes a lot of tackles. On reflection, we realized that most offenses run "right-handed," giving the LILB the most opportunities to make tackles. Without a percentage the totals don't mean much. Even when the nose tackle leads his team in tackles, and a few have, we have to make allowances for the likelihood that the defense is set up to contain all runs to the inside.

Some teams publish a "Passer Hurried" column. Does a lineman get credit if he hurries a quarterback who *still* completes his pass? As nearly as we can learn, no.

Adding to all the problems in rating defenders, all teams use situational substitutions. Certain players play only in "passing" situations. Others play only against expected runs. The modern defensive unit has fifteen to eighteen "regulars."

TAKE REGGIE WHITE . . . PLEASE!

We wanted to rate defensive players based on statistics, but no really valid stats exist. For example, we may *believe* that Reggie White is the best defensive end in the world. We note that he had 18 sacks in 1988. That still leaves 1,068 plays run against the Eagles' defense unaccounted for. In theory, White could have played well 18 times last year and lousy the other 98.3 percent.

But wait! Unofficially, he made 133 tackles, 96 unas-sisted. We can't tell whether the Eagles' unofficial stats count sacks as tackles or not, so we'll assume they don't for the sake of argument. Also, let's assume that he didn't make any tackles on passing plays. Okay, he was in on 133 tackles out of 466 rushing plays against Philadelphia. That's 28.5 percent.

Unfortunately it's not that simple. Offenses try to run away from White, so Buddy Ryan moves him along the line to surprise places, increasing his opportunities. Nevertheless he finished only fourth in total tackles on his team (behind a linebacker and two defensive backs). We *know* he's the best, but darned if we can prove it.

SO WE DID IT THIS WAY . . .

Though individuals can't be rated objectively, defenses can. In fact there are numerous ways—total yards against, total points against, average yards per attempt, takeaways, and sacks. None of them alone gives a complete picture, but taken together they do.

On the following pages we've ranked the twenty-eight NFL defenses by combining and weighting the most important team defensive stats. First we divided the defense into two sections, the line/linebackers, whose main concerns are stopping the run and rushing the passer, and the defensive secondary, whose main concern is pass defense.

To get a rating for the line/linebackers, we used the following:

1. % RUSH = Opponent Rushing Attempts/Opponent Total Plays (Rush Attempts + Pass Attempts + Times Sacked). Over the course of a season, offenses will attack the weakest part of a defense more often than the strongest. If a team stops the run, as Chicago did, it will have a lower percentage of rushing attempts against it.

2. AVG RUSH = Opponent Rush Yards/Opponent Rush Attempts. Because of the wide difference in number of rushing attempts by opponents, the Average Gain per Rush is a better gauge of a defense's skill in stopping the running game than total yards.

3. SACK % = Opponent Times Sacked/Opponent Total Pass Plays (Pass Attempts + Times Sacked). Again, the Sack Percentage is a better gauge than the total number for the same reason.

4. COMP % = Opponent Pass Completions/Opponent Pass Attempts. The pass completion percentage by opponents is at least partially a result of how well or how poorly the passer was rushed.

5. FUM/PLAY = Opponent Total Plays/Opponent Fumbles Lost. Opponents' Fumbles Lost per Opponents' Plays is an interesting stat, and some teams do seem to excel at this. We have two reservations. Special-teams fumbles are included, and there's a lot of luck involved.

We weighted the categories to get a Total Rate for line/linebackers, using the following formula:

```
LINE/LINEBACKERS (Total Rate) = [2(% Rush) + 3(AVG GAIN, RUSH) + 3 (SACK %) + COMP % + FUM/PLAY] / 10
```

In effect the front seven are rated 50 percent on their ability to stop the run, 40 percent on their ability to rush the passer, and 10 percent on opportunism (though we know full

well that defensive backs also cause and recover fumbles). The final rate is given as a grade between 70 and 100.

We ranked the defensive secondaries with the following stats:

1. AVG PASS = Opponent Net Passing Yards/Opponent Total Pass Plays. This is a different Average Gain per Pass figure than the one normally published. We used Opponents' Net Passing Yards, rather than Gross Passing Yards, because we wanted the sack yardage subtracted. A secondary must cover long enough to allow most sacks. We also divided by total pass plays (which includes sacks) instead of simply passes attempted.

2. COMP %. Same as item 4 for line/linebackers.

3. INT/PLAY = Opponent Total Plays/Opponent Passes Intercepted. The number of interceptions per play involves slightly less luck than fumbles.

4. INVERTED SACK %. No secondary can cover for long enough if the rush is really weak, so we turned the Sack % upside down to help those crews like Pittsburgh and Miami, who had virtually no help.

We weighted the secondaries' Total Rate as follows:

```
LINE/LINEBACKERS (Total Rate) = [2(% Rush) + 3(AVG GAIN, RUSH) + 3 (SACK %) + COMP %  + FUM/PLAY] / 10
```

Again the rate is given as a 70–100 grade.

Finally we put together a Total Defense Rate for each team by using the Line/Linebackers Rate, the Defensive Secondary Rate, and Points Allowed per Game (by the offense only):

```
DEF. SECONDARY (Total Rate) = [2(AVG GAIN, PASS) + 3(COMP %) + 2 (INT/PLAY) + INVERTED SACK %] / 8
```

As you can see, we weighted it 3–2–1 in favor of the front seven. We believe the key to any successful defense starts there.

In addition to rating the defenses, we listed for your information the most-used (or, in some cases, the healthiest) eleven by position. Rookies are marked with * after their names, and we remind you of the old saying that "a rookie on defense costs a touchdown a game." We also added sack and interception leaders for ready reference.

```
TOTAL  DEFENSE (Rate) = [3(LINE/LINEBACKERS) + 2 (DEF. SECONDARY) + POINTS PER GM] / 6
```

Certainly no one can be surprised to find the Bears ranked at the top. We covered The Defense in the discussion of Chicago. The one figure that we weren't expecting was the low rate on fumbles. Okay, a lot of it is luck, but these guys hit so hard you'd expect a higher number.

1. CHICAGO BEARS

% RUSH	39.8	% PASS	60.2	LINE/BACKERS	95.0
AVG RUSH	3.4	AVG PASS	5.2	DEF SECONDARY	94.4
SACK %	7.3	COMP %	45.0	POINTS PER GM	12.5
FUM/PLAY	108.6	INT/PLAY	37.6	TOTAL DEFENSE	95.6

LE	Al Harris	LLB	Ron Rivera	LCB	Mike Richardson
LT	Steve McMichael	MLB	Mike Singletary	SS	Dave Duerson
RT	Dan Hampton	RLB	Jim Morrissey	FS	David Tate*
RE	Richard Dent			RCB	Vestee Jackson

SACK LEADERS: McMichael 11.5, Dent 10.5, Hampton 9.5, Harris 3.5
INTERCEPTIONS: Jackson 8, Tate* 4, Morrissey 3

Close on the Bears' heels (and maybe trampling over them in '89) come the Vikings. Millard, Doleman, Lee, and Browner are among the best in the NFL, but there aren't any weaknesses. We rank the secondary as better than Chicago's.

2. MINNESOTA VIKINGS

% RUSH	45.7	% PASS	54.3	LINE/BACKERS	93.2
AVG RUSH	3.7	AVG PASS	4.8	DEF SECONDARY	97.4
SACK %	7.2	COMP %	45.6	POINTS PER GM	13.6
FUM/PLAY	56.0	INT/PLAY	26.4	TOTAL DEFENSE	95.3

LE	Doug Martin	LLB	David Howard	LCB	Carl Lee
LT	Henry Thomas	MLB	Scott Studwell	SS	Joey Browner
RT	Keith Millard	RLB	Jesse Solomon	FS	Brad Edwards*
RE	Chris Doleman			RCB	Reggie Rutland

SACK LEADERS: Doleman 8, Millard 8, Thomas 6, Al Baker 5.5, Martin 3
INTERCEPTIONS: Lee 8, Browner 5, Solomon 4

3. LOS ANGELES RAMS

% RUSH	39.8	% PASS	60.2	LINE/BACKERS	92.1
AVG RUSH	4.1	AVG PASS	5.3	DEF SECONDARY	88.7
SACK %	8.9	COMP %	53.8	POINTS PER GM	15.7
FUM/PLAY	69.4	INT/PLAY	47.3	TOTAL DEFENSE	91.0

LE	Doug Reed	LOLB	Kevin Greene	LCB	Jerry Gray
NT	Alvin Wright	LILB	Carl Ekern	SS	Michael Stewart
RE	Shawn Miller	RILB	Jim Collins	FS	Johnnie Johnson
		ROLB	Mike Wilcher	RCB	LeRoy Irvin

SACK LEADERS: Greene 16.5, Gary Jeter 11.5, Wilcher 7.5, Mel Owens 5
INTERCEPTIONS: Johnson 4, Gray 3, Irvin 3

The Rams' defense was at its best in the first half of the season, when Greene and Jeter were sacking everything in sight. The front line is light, but the linebacking is excellent and deep. Good corners, too.

4. SAN FRANCISCO 49ERS

% RUSH	43.5	% PASS	56.5	LINE/BACKERS	92.9
AVG RUSH	3.6	AVG PASS	5.2	DEF SECONDARY	89.8
SACK %	4.1	COMP %	55.1	POINTS PER GM	17.8
FUM/PLAY	63.3	INT/PLAY	40.5	TOTAL DEFENSE	90.9

LE	Larry Roberts	LOLB	Charles Haley	LCB	Tim McKyer
NT	Michael Carter	LILB	Jim Fahnhorst	SS	Jeff Fuller
RE	Kevin Fagan	RILB	Mike Walter	FS	Ronnie Lott
		ROLB	Keena Turner	RCB	Don Griffen

SACK LEADERS: Haley 11.5, Carter 6.5, Roberts 6, Daniel Stubbs* 6, Pierce Holt* 5
INTERCEPTIONS: McKyer 7, Lott 5, Fuller 4, Tom Holmoe 2, Wright 2

This crew came on like mad in the second half of the season and continued right through the Super Bowl. Carter, Haley, and Lott are the best known. McKyer and Griffen held out at the beginning of the season and got off to a slow start. By the end they were fine. This is a very deep unit that uses a lot of situational substitutions. Among others, Bill Romanowski* was starting over veteran All-Pro Turner in running situations at season's end. Holt replaced Fagan in passing situations. Holmoe was the nickel back.

5. BUFFALO BILLS

% RUSH	49.1	% PASS	50.9	LINE/BACKERS	90.8
AVG RUSH	3.9	AVG PASS	5.5	DEF SECONDARY	85.8
SACK %	9.3	COMP %	55.8	POINTS PER GM	14.5
FUM/PLAY	57.1	INT/PLAY	64.7	TOTAL DEFENSE	89.8

LE	Art Still	LOLB	Cornelius Bennett	LCB	Derrick Burroughs
NT	Fred Smerlas	LILB	Ray Bentley	SS	Leonard Smith
RE	Bruce Smith	RILB	Shane Conlan	FS	Mark Kelso
		ROLB	Darryl Talley	RLB	Nate Odomes

SACK LEADERS: B. Smith 11, Bennett 9.5, Still 6, Jeff Wright* 5, Smerlas 4
INTERCEPTIONS: Kelso 7, Bennett 2, L.Smith 2

We commented on this best-of-AFC crew in the Buffalo team discussion. Let us just add that we don't think Derrick Burroughs lost the playoff when he lost his cool. If you have to blame it on anything, blame the injuries to Bruce Smith and Shane Conlan.

6. NEW YORK GIANTS

% RUSH	42.3	% PASS	57.7	LINE/BACKERS	93.0
AVG RUSH	3.9	AVG PASS	5.4	DEF SECONDARY	86.9
SACK %	8.4	COMP %	51.9	POINTS PER GM	18.3
FUM/PLAY	59.6	INT/PLAY	71.5	TOTAL DEFENSE	89.7

LE	Eric Dorsey	LOLB	Carl Banks	LCB	Mark Collins
NT	Jim Burt	LILB	Pepper Johnson	SS	Kenny Hill
RE	Leonard Marshall	RILB	Harry Carson	FS	Terry Kinard
		ROLB	Lawrence Taylor	RCB	Perry Williams

SACK LEADERS: Taylor 15.5, Marshall 8, George Martin 7.5, Johnson 4, Dorsey 3.5
INTERCEPTIONS: Sheldon White* 4, Kinard 3, Carson 2

Harry Carson may be retired by '89—a loss. Banks, who looked like Taylor's equal in '87, had a disappointing year but should come back strong. The front seven are miles better than the pedestrian secondary.

7. CLEVELAND BROWNS

% RUSH	49.4	% PASS	50.6	LINE/BACKERS	88.6
AVG RUSH	3.9	AVG PASS	5.6	DEF SECONDARY	89.5
SACK %	7.2	COMP %	51.7	POINTS PER GM	16.3
FUM/PLAY	91.7	INT/PLAY	50.5	TOTAL DEFENSE	89.3

LE	Sam Clancy	LOLB	David Grayson	LCB	Frank Minnifield
NT	Bob Golic	LILB	Mike Johnson	SS	Brian Washington*
RE	Carl Hairston	RILB	Mike Junkin	FS	Felix Wright
		ROLB	Clay Matthews	RCB	Hanford Dixon

SACK LEADERS: Matthews 6, Michael Dean Perry* 6, Charles Buchanan* 5, Grayson 5, Clancy 4.5
INTERCEPTIONS: Wright 5, Minnifield 4, Washington* 3

The secondary is better than the rating. At times, they had no rush to help and many of the sacks were of the "coverage" variety. Buchanan, who provided some rush until he was hurt, will probably replace Clancy, one of the NFL's most interesting players in that he played basketball at college instead of football. It will be interesting to see if Junkin can keep his position now that Marty Schottenheimer (who drafted him) is gone. Many thought Marty played him only to justify his selection as a number one draft choice. No one will replace Golic, Matthews, Minnifield, or Dixon (if he's not limping).

8. HOUSTON OILERS

% RUSH	43.7	% PASS	56.3	LINE/BACKERS	93.1
AVG RUSH	3.7	AVG PASS	5.9	DEF SECONDARY	86.7
SACK %	7.6	COMP %	54.9	POINTS PER GM	21.0
FUM/PLAY	49.3	INT/PLAY	44.8	TOTAL DEFENSE	88.6

LE	Ray Childress	LOLB	Robert Lyles	LCB	Steve Brown
NT	Richard Byrd	LILB	John Grimsley	SS	Keith Bostic
RE	William Fuller	RILB	Al Smith	FS	Jeff Donaldson
		ROLB	Johnny Meads	RCB	Patrick Allen

SACK LEADERS: Childress 8.5, Fuller 8.5, Meads 8, Sean Jones 7.5, Doug Smith 3
INTERCEPTIONS: Donaldson 4, Domingo Bryant 3, Kenny Johnson 3

An "A+" for Childress. NT Doug Smith couldn't win his starting position back after his return from suspension. The linebackers are overrated, as are the corners.

9. PHILADELPHIA EAGLES

% RUSH	42.9	% PASS	57.1	LINE/BACKERS	92.1
AVG RUSH	3.5	AVG PASS	6.7	DEF SECONDARY	84.9
SACK %	6.8	COMP %	53.5	POINTS PER GM	18.6
FUM/PLAY	90.5	INT/PLAY	33.9	TOTAL DEFENSE	88.5

LE	Reggie White	LLB	Seth Joyner	LCB	Roynell Young
LT	Mike Pitts	MLB	Mike Reichenbach	SS	Andre Waters
RT	Jerome Brown	RLB	Todd Bell	FS	Wes Hopkins
RE	Clyde Simmons			RCB	Eric Allen*

SACK LEADERS: White 18, Simmons 8.5, Brown 5, Joyner 3, Terry Hoage 2
INTERCEPTIONS: Terry Hoage 8, Allen* 5, Hopkins 5, Joyner 4

White is great, Brown and Simmons are both above average, and everybody else is middling. Hopkins once was exceptional but he missed a season-and-a-half with an injury and has slowed. Bell is a FS out of place. This should be just a "C" unit, but it plays at "B."

10. GREEN BAY PACKERS

% RUSH	50.5	% PASS	49.5	LINE/BACKERS	86.5
AVG RUSH	4.1	AVG PASS	5.4	DEF SECONDARY	90.2
SACK %	6.0	COMP %	54.0	POINTS PER GM	17.3
FUM/PLAY	48.5	INT/PLAY	50.9	TOTAL DEFENSE	88.0

LE	Shawn Patterson	LOLB	John Anderson	LCB	Mark Lee
NT	Blaise Winter	LILB	Brian Noble	SS	Mark Murphy
RE	Robert Brown	RILB	Johnny Holland	FS	Ken Stills
		ROLB	Tim Harris	RCB	David Brown

SACK LEADERS: Harris 13.5, Winter 5, Patterson 4
INTERCEPTIONS: Murphy 5, Chuck Cecil 4, Lee 3, Stills 3, D.Brown 3

Some of their success should be credited to Def-co Hank Bullough, but Tim Harris was a great player all season. The secondary worked very well together, with Lee and Murphy both having good years. How long can David Brown go on? A great example of a quick mind over slow feet.

11. CINCINNATI BENGALS

% RUSH	46.6	% PASS	53.5	LINE/BACKERS	88.0
AVG RUSH	4.2	AVG RUSH	5.5	DEF SECONDARY	88.7
SACK %	7.4	COMP %	54.0	POINTS PER GM	19.4
FUM/PLAY	75.6	INT/PLAY	48.1	TOTAL DEFENSE	87.4

LE	Skip McClendon	LOLB	Leon White	LCB	Lewis Billups
NT	Tim Krumrie	LILB	Carl Zander	SS	David Fulcher
RE	Jim Skow	RILB	Joe Kelly	FS	Solomon Wilcots
		RILB	Reggie Williams	RCB	Eric Thomas

SACK LEADERS: Skow 9.5, Jason Buck 6, David Grant* 5, Barney Bussey 4
INTERCEPTIONS: Thomas 7, Fulcher 5, Billups 4, Ray Horton 3

Except for Fulcher against the run and Krumrie against anything, this is only an average group. It played over its head in the playoffs until the last drive of the Super Bowl. More beef at the DEs and more talent at LB and CB would help.

12. NEW ORLEANS SAINTS

% RUSH	45.2	% PASS	54.8	LINE/BACKERS	87.7
AVG RUSH	4.0	AVG PASS	6.2	DEF SECONDARY	85.1
SACK %	5.8	COMP %	54.9	POINTS PER GM	16.4
FUM/PLAY	65.2	INT/PLAY	57.5	TOTAL DEFENSE	87.3

LE	Frank Warren	LOLB	Rickey Jackson	LCB	Dave Waymer
NT	Jim Wilks	LILB	Sam Mills	SS	Antonio Gibson
RE	James Geathers	RILB	Vaughan Johnson	FS	Brett Maxie
		ROLB	Pat Swilling	RCB	Reggie Sutton

SACK LEADERS: Jackson 7, Swilling 7, Gaethers 3.5, Wilks 3.5
INTERCEPTIONS: Gene Atkins 4, Waymer 3, Van Jakes 3, Reggie Sutton 3

One of the best linebacking crews in the NFL. Many thought Johnson should have made the Pro Bowl instead of Mills, but they're all good. The pass rush from the front three wasn't much, but Jackson and Swilling helped out.

13. NEW ENGLAND PATRIOTS

% RUSH	51.6	% PASS	48.4	LINE/BACKERS	85.1
AVG RUSH	4.2	AVG RUSH	5.6	DEF SECONDARY	89.9
SACK %	6.2	COMP %	53.7	POINTS PER GM	17.6
FUM/PLAY	64.1	INT/PLAY	48.1	TOTAL DEFENSE	87.1

LE	Brent Williams	LOLB	Andre Tippett	LCB	Ronnie Lippett
NT	Tim Goad*	LILB	Ed Reynolds	SS	Roland James
RE	Garin Veris	RILB	Johnny Rembert	FS	Fred Marion
		ROLB	Lawrence McGrew	RCB	Raymond Clayborn

SACK LEADERS: Williams 8, Tippett 7, Tim Jordan 3, Rembert 3
INTERCEPTIONS: Clayborn 4, Marion 4, James 4

An outstanding secondary bogged down by a weak pass rush from the DEs. Losing Kenneth Sims in the first game of the year and Veris for a couple of games hurt. Rembert and Tippett are terrific.

14. INDIANAPOLIS COLTS

% RUSH	44.0	% PASS	56.0	LINE/BACKERS	88.8
AVG RUSH	3.8	AVG RUSH	6.3	DEF SECONDARY	81.9
SACK %	5.3	COMP %	59.6	POINTS PER GM	18.5
FUM/PLAY	50.8	INT/PLAY	67.7	TOTAL DEFENSE	85.9

LE	Donnell Thompson	LOLB	O'Brien Alston*	LCB	Willie Tullis
NT	Joe Klecko	LILB	Fredd Young	SS	Freddie Robinson
RE	Jon Hand	RILB	Barry Krauss	FS	Mike Prior
		ROLB	Duane Bickett	RCB	Eugene Daniel

SACK LEADERS: Hand 5, Bickett 3.5, Alston* 3, Ezra Johnson 3, Thompson 3
INTERCEPTIONS: Tullis 4, Prior 3, Bickett 3

Thompson is a good run-stopper, but the only real strength here is the LB crew. Young improved after he was moved inside and Bickett is fine. The secondary is weak.

15. DETROIT LIONS

% RUSH	47.7	% PASS	52.3	LINE/BACKERS	88.8
AVG RUSH	4.0	AVG RUSH	5.9	DEF SECONDARY	80.3
SACK %	8.4	COMP %	65.7	POINTS PER GM	19.1
FUM/PLAY	51.0	INT/PLAY	71.4	TOTAL DEFENSE	85.1

LE	Eric Williams	LOLB	George Jamison	LCB	Jerry Holmes
NT	Jerry Ball	LILB	Chris Spielman*	SS	Bennie Blades*
RE	Keith Ferguson	RILB	Dennis Gibson	FS	Devon Mitchell
		ROLB	Michael Cofer	RCB	Bruce McNorton

SACK LEADERS: Cofer 12, Ferguson 8.5, Williams 6.5, Jamison 5.5
INTERCEPTIONS: Mitchell 3, Jamison 3

Good linebacking with big problems in front and behind. There is hope that Blades will develop into a star, but more help is needed.

16. NEW YORK JETS

% RUSH	49.8	% PASS	50.2	LINE/BACKERS	89.0
AVG RUSH	4.1	AVG RUSH	6.7	DEF SECONDARY	83.9
SACK %	4.3	COMP %	51.3	POINTS PER GM	22.6
FUM/PLAY	64.9	INT/PLAY	43.3	TOTAL DEFENSE	85.0

LE	Paul Frase*	LOLB	Alex Gordon	LCB	Bobby Humphrey
NT	Scott Mersereau	LILB	Troy Benson	SS	Rich Miano
RE	Marty Lyons	RILB	Kyle Clifton	FS	Erik McMillan*
		ROLB	Kevin McArthur	RCB	James Hasty*

SACK LEADERS: Lyons 7.5, Mark Gastineau 7, Ken Rose 5, Mersereau 4.5
INTERCEPTIONS: McMillan* 8, Hasty* 5, John Booty* 3

A study in the domino effect. The kid secondary was doing okay until Gastineau quit. Then, without a good pass rush, they got bombed. Rookie mistakes also hurt. Still, they have a future. Lyons had a strong year.

17 (tie). KANSAS CITY CHIEFS

% RUSH	58.4	% PASS	41.6	LINE/BACKERS	81.0
AVG RUSH	4.3	AVG RUSH	5.6	DEF SECONDARY	90.5
SACK %	5.3	COMP %	52.2	POINTS PER GM	18.3
FUM/PLAY	48.5	INT/PLAY	57.9	TOTAL DEFENSE	84.9

LE	Leonard Griffin	LOLB	Jack Del Rio	LCB	Albert Lewis
NT	Bill Maas	LILB	Aaron Pearson	SS	Lloyd Burruss
RE	Mike Bell	RILB	Dino Hackett	FS	Deron Cherry
		ROLB	Tim Cofield	RCB	Kevin Ross

SACK LEADERS: Maas 4, Cofield 3.5, Hackett 3, Neil Smith 2.5, Mike Stensrud 2.5
INTERCEPTIONS: Cherry 7, Burruss 2, J. C. Pearson 2

The secondary would be the scourge of the league if it got any help up front. Despite Hackett, the Chiefs have the weakest LB group in the NFL. The real key is Maas. If he comes back from his injury, the whole front seven will improve. Can Marty Schottenheimer, an excellent defensive coach, help? Definitely.

17 (tie). PHOENIX CARDINALS

% RUSH	46.1	% PASS	53.9	LINE/BACKERS	88.3
AVG RUSH	4.1	AVG RUSH	5.9	DEF SECONDARY	86.3
SACK %	7.1	COMP %	52.0	POINTS PER GM	23.9
FUM/PLAY	78.0	INT/PLAY	63.4	TOTAL DEFENSE	84.9

LE	Freddie Joe Nunn	LLB	Anthony Bell	LCB	Carl Carter
LT	Bob Clasby	MLB	Niko Noga	SS	Tim McDonald
RT	Steve Alvord	RLB	E.J. Junior	FS	Lonnie Young
RE	Rod Saddler			RCB	Cedric Mack

SACK LEADERS: Nunn 14, Ken Harvey 6*, Clasby 5
INTERCEPTIONS: Mack 3, Carter 3, McDonald 2, Lester Lyles 2

A healthy DE in David Galloway, paired with Nunn, would make a solid front four. The linebackers must produce more. See the Phoenix chapter for what happened when Young was injured.

19. SAN DIEGO CHARGERS

% RUSH	48.6	% PASS	51.4	LINE/BACKERS	85.3
AVG RUSH	4.1	AVG RUSH	6.0	DEF SECONDARY	86.2
SACK %	6.2	COMP %	53.0	POINTS PER GM	20.3
FUM/PLAY	107.2	INT/PLAY	67.0	TOTAL DEFENSE	84.8

LE	Lee Williams	LLB	Keith Browner	LCB	Gill Byrd
LT	Mike Charles	MLB	Cedric Figaro	SS	Pat Miller
RT	Mike Phillips	RLB	Gary Plummer	FS	Vencie Glenn
RE	Leslie O'Neal			RCB	Sam Seale

SACK LEADERS: Williams 11, O'Neal 4, Joe Campbell* 3, George Hinkle* 3, Tyrone Keys 3
INTERCEPTIONS: Byrd 7, Browner 2, Leonard Coleman 2

Okay. Maybe *this* is a worse group of LBs, but Billy Ray Smith will be back to help. If Chip Banks were to return with a different head, the Chargers' LB corps would be outstanding. Williams and O'Neal (if he's really over his injury) are fine, as are Byrd and Glenn.

20 (tie). LOS ANGELES RAIDERS

% RUSH	50.5	% PASS	49.5	LINE/BACKERS	87.5
AVG RUSH	4.1	AVG RUSH	6.1	DEF SECONDARY	84.8
SACK %	7.6	COMP %	54.9	POINTS PER GM	22.6
FUM/PLAY	62.1	INT/PLAY	45.9	TOTAL DEFENSE	84.5

LE	Greg Townsend	LOLB	Linden King	LCB	Ron Fellows
NT	Bill Pickel	LILB	Matt Millen	SS	Russell Carter
RE	Howie Long	RILB	Jerry Robinson	FS	Vann McElroy
		ROLB	Rod Martin	RCB	Mike Haynes

SACK LEADERS: Townsend 11.5, Scott Davis* 5.5, Pickel 5, Mike Wise 5, Long 3
INTERCEPTIONS: Haynes 3, McElroy 3

While we were napping, the Raiders got old. Haynes had a good year, but it was his thirteenth. Townsend became a strong DE and picked up some of the slack for Long, who was hurt most of the season.

20 (tie). TAMPA BAY BUCCANEERS

% RUSH	46.6	% PASS	53.4	LINE/BACKERS	86.3
AVG RUSH	3.2	AVG RUSH	6.6	DEF SECONDARY	84.5
SACK %	3.7	COMP %	57.7	POINTS PER GM	20.9
FUM/PLAY	85.4	INT/PLAY	48.8	TOTAL DEFENSE	84.5

LE	Reuben Davis*	LOLB	Kevin Murphy	LCB	Ricky Reynolds
NT	Curt Jarvis	LILB	Eugene Marve	SS	Mark Robinson
RE	Robert Goff*	RILB	Sidney Coleman*	FS	Harry Hamilton
		ROLB	Winston Moss	RCB	Bobby Futrell

SACK LEADERS: Ron Holmes 4, John Cannon 3, Davis* 3, Jarvis 2.5
INTERCEPTIONS: Hamilton 6, Reynolds 4, Donnie Elder 3

The Bucs did a better job than expected, but they are vulnerable to a good passing attack. Robinson and Hamilton are Jets rejects. Mostly a young crew that should improve.

20 (tie). WASHINGTON REDSKINS

% RUSH	45.0	% PASS	55.0	LINE/BACKERS	88.6
AVG RUSH	3.9	AVG RUSH	6.4	DEF SECONDARY	82.5
SACK %	8.0	COMP %	52.5	POINTS PER GM	22.1
FUM/PLAY	122.8	INT/PLAY	70.1	TOTAL DEFENSE	84.5

LE	Charles Mann	LLB	Monte Coleman	LCB	Barry Wilburn
LT	Dave Butz	MLB	Neal Olkewicz	SS	Alvin Walton
RT	Darryl Grant	RLB	Wilbur Marshall	FS	Todd Bowles
RE	Dexter Manley			RCB	Darrell Green

SACK LEADERS: Manley 9, Mann 5.5, Ravin Caldwell 4, Grant 4, Marshall 4
INTERCEPTIONS: Wilburn 4, Marshall 3, Walton 3

The problems are injuries and age. Butz will probably retire, and two of the LBs may be replaced. But strong years by Manley, Mann, Marshall, and the CBs could move this crew way up.

23. ATLANTA FALCONS

% RUSH	49.2	% PASS	50.8	LINE/BACKERS	82.6
AVG RUSH	4.5	AVG RUSH	6.3	DEF SECONDARY	86.0
SACK %	5.6	COMP %	55.8	POINTS PER GM	18.4
FUM/PLAY	75.1	INT/PLAY	43.8	TOTAL DEFENSE	84.2

LE	Mike Gann	LOLB	Andray Bruce*	LCB	Bobby Butler
NT	Tony Casillas	LILB	Joel Williams	SS	Robert Moore
RE	Rick Bryan	RILB	Jessie Tuggle	FS	Bret Clark
		ROLB	John Rade	RCB	Scott Case

SACK LEADERS: Bruce* 6, Bryan 5, Marcus Cotton* 5, Gann 4, Tim Green 4
INTERCEPTIONS: Case 10, Moore 5, Clark 4, Bruce* 2, Tim Gordon 2

We thought the Falcons would rate higher. At times they did, but the front three didn't do much. If Cotton is as good as he looked on occasion and Bruce keeps improving, the LBs will be very strong.

24. SEATTLE SEAHAWKS

% RUSH	48.9	% PASS	51.1	LINE/BACKERS	83.4
AVG RUSH	4.5	AVG RUSH	6.3	DEF SECONDARY	85.6
SACK %	5.6	COMP %	55.9	POINTS PER GM	19.3
FUM/PLAY	57.8	INT/PLAY	47.3	TOTAL DEFENSE	84.1

LE	Jacob Green	LOLB	Bruce Scholtz	LCB	Terry Taylor
NT	Joe Nash	LILB	Brian Bosworth	SS	Paul Moyer
RE	Jeff Bryant	RILB	David Wyman	FS	Eugene Robinson
		ROLB	Tony Woods	RCB	Melvin Jenkins

SACK LEADERS: Green 9, Woods 5, Bryant 3.5, Alonzo Mitz 3, Wyman 2.5
INTERCEPTIONS: Moyer 6, Taylor 5, Jenkins 3

It seems that the front three have been there forever. They can be outmuscled. Even when he was healthy, Bosworth didn't justify his hype. He's not a washout, but Woods may be better.

25. DALLAS COWBOYS

% RUSH	44.4	% PASS	55.6	LINE/BACKERS	88.6
AVG RUSH	4.1	AVG RUSH	6.2	DEF SECONDARY	80.6
SACK %	8.1	COMP %	50.5	POINTS PER GM	23.3
FUM/PLAY	113.7	INT/PLAY	102.3	TOTAL DEFENSE	83.4

LE	Ed Jones	LLB	Ron Burton	LCB	Everson Walls
LT	Kevin Brooks	MLB	Eugene Lockhart	SS	Bill Bates
RT	Danny Noonan	RLB	Garry Cobb	FS	Michael Downs
RE	Jim Jeffcoat			RCB	Robert Williams

SACK LEADERS: Cobb 7.5, Noonan 7.5, Jones 7, Jeffcoat 6.5, Brooks 5
INTERCEPTIONS: Williams 2, Downs 2, Walls 2

Amazing how long they went between takeaways! If it was just dumb luck, there'll be some improvement in '89, just because the ball bounces funny. However, no area is either strong or uniformly young. Help!

26. DENVER BRONCOS

% RUSH	52.3	% PASS	47.7	LINE/BACKERS	82.4
AVG RUSH	4.6	AVG RUSH	5.8	DEF SECONDARY	85.7
SACK %	7.2	COMP %	56.1	POINTS PER GM	21.0
FUM/PLAY	81.2	INT/PLAY	65.9	TOTAL DEFENSE	82.9

LE	Walt Bowyer	LOLB	Simon Fletcher	LCB	Mark Haynes
NT	Greg Kragen	LILB	Karl Mecklenburg	SS	Dennis Smith
RE	Andre Townsend	RILB	Rick Dennison	FS	Mike Harden
		ROLB	Michael Brooks	RCB	Jeremiah Castille

SACK LEADERS: Fletcher 9, Rulon Jones 5, Townsend 5, Jim Ryan 3.5, Kragen 2.5
INTERCEPTIONS: Harden 4, Castille 3

Kragen and Fletcher are okay. Having Mecklenburg for sixteen games would help. So would about twenty pounds per man up front. It's probably time to try some new people in the secondary.

27. PITTSBURGH STEELERS

% RUSH	48.4	% PASS	51.6	LINE/BACKERS	82.5
AVG RUSH	3.6	AVG RUSH	7.2	DEF SECONDARY	81.4
SACK %	3.4	COMP %	58.1	POINTS PER GM	24.6
FUM/PLAY	82.1	INT/PLAY	53.4	TOTAL DEFENSE	80.1

LE	Aaron Jones*	LOLB	Bryan Hinkle	LCB	Dwayne Woodruff
NT	Gerald Williams	LILB	David Little	SS	Cornell Gowdy
RE	Tim Johnson	RILB	Hardy Nickerson	FS	Thomas Everett
		ROLB	Darin Jordan*	RCB	Rod Woodson

SACK LEADERS: Johnson 4, Greg Carr 3.5, Nickerson 3.5, Williams 3.5
INTERCEPTIONS: Woodruff 4, Woodson 4, Everett 3

You could time how long it took them to get to a quarterback with a sundial. There were games when no one got close enough to read his number. Woodson is a star, and Nickerson may become one. Little and Hinkle are solid.

28. MIAMI DOLPHINS

% RUSH	52.0	% PASS	48.0	LINE/BACKERS	79.3
AVG RUSH	4.5	AVG RUSH	6.4	DEF SECONDARY	82.8
SACK %	4.7	COMP %	60.7	POINTS PER GM	22.1
FUM/PLAY	71.5	INT/PLAY	67.0	TOTAL DEFENSE	79.9

LE	T. J. Turner	LOLB	Rick Graf	LCB	Paul Lankford
NT	Brian Sochia	LILB	Mark Brown	SS	Liffort Hobley
RE	Jackie Cline	RILB	John Offerdahl	FS	Jarvis Williams*
		ROLB	Hugh Green	RCB	William Judson

SACK LEADERS: Turner 5, Sochia 4.5, Cline 4, Tim Kumerow* 3, Green 2.5
INTERCEPTIONS: Williams* 4, Judson 4, Brown 2, Offerdahl 2

Offerdahl stood out, but the rest of the cupboard was bare. Run on 'em; pass on 'em—it didn't matter. The secondary actually gave up completions at a higher rate than Marino could complete them on offense!

Just so we'll be on record. Here are the defenders we'd put highest if we were going to rank them subjectively.

Defensive Ends

1. Reggie White, Philadelphia
2. Bruce Smith, Buffalo
3. Ray Childress, Houston
4. Richard Dent, Chicago
5. Chris Doleman, Minnesota
6. Dexter Manley, Washington
7. Lee Williams, San Diego
8. Freddie Joe Nunn, Phoenix
9. Charles Mann, Washington
10. Marty Lyons, N.Y. Jets

Defensive Tackles-Nose Tackles

1. Tim Krumrie, Cincinnati
2. Keith Millard, Minnesota
3. Dan Hampton, Chicago
4. Steve McMichael, Chicago
5. Michael Carter, San Francisco
6. Fred Smerlas, Buffalo
7. Jerome Brown, Philadelphia
8. Henry Thomas, Minnesota
9. Tim Goad, New England
10. Bob Golic, Cleveland

Outside Linebackers

1. Lawrence Taylor, N.Y. Giants
2. Cornelius Bennett, Buffalo
3. Tim Harris, Green Bay
4. Charles Haley, San Francisco
5. Andre Tippett, New England
6. Clay Matthews, Cleveland
7. Duane Bickett, Indianapolis
8. Mike Cofer, Detroit
9. Rickey Jackson, New Orleans
10. Kevin Greene, L.A. Rams

Inside Linebackers

1. Mike Singletary, Chicago
2. Shane Conlan, Buffalo
3. Johnny Rembert, New England
4. Vaughan Johnson, New Orleans
5. Mike Walter, San Francisco
6. John Offerdahl, Miami
7. Dino Hackett, Kansas City
8. Sam Mills, New Orleans
9. Chris Spielman, Detroit
10. Scott Studwell, Minnesota

Cornerbacks

1. Frank Minnifield, Cleveland
2. Carl Lee, Minnesota
3. Albert Lewis, Kansas City
4. Raymond Clayborn, New England
5. Jerry Gray, L.A. Rams
6. Scott Case, Atlanta
7. Rod Woodson, Pittsburgh
8. Hanford Dixon, Cleveland
9. Tim McKyer, San Francisco
10. Gil Byrd, San Diego

Safeties

1. Deron Cherry, Kansas City
2. Joey Browner, Minnesota
3. Ronnie Lott, San Francisco
4. Dave Duerson, Chicago
5. Jeff Fuller, San Francisco
6. David Fulcher, Cincinnati
7. Fred Marion, New England
8. Mark Kelso, Buffalo
9. Erik McMillan, N.Y. Jets
10. Keith Bostic, Houston

SOME RANDOM THOUGHTS ON PUNTERS

We're fans of the Elias Sports Bureau. They're the people who compile all the stats that we drool over every season. We spend a lot of time thinking up new ways to crunch the numbers so that they'll give us a better picture, but one thing we never question about the numbers the Elias people put out is their accuracy. Seymour Sywoff, Steve Hirdt, and the other folks at Elias won't stand for shoddy work. It's hard to imagine anything harder to measure than a football game, or anybody who could measure it better. We'll even bet that between the time we write this and the time next season begins, the Elias people will have gone back over all the numbers a dozen times and found a yard missing here or added there. And they'll get it perfect.

Anyway, because we admire the Elias people, we wondered about the way they ranked punters. There are two things that bother us, and we tried to reason them through.

The first question we had was why punters aren't charged with blocked punts in their punting average. The prime case in point was Harry Newsome of Pittsburgh last season. To remind you, the Pittsburgh punt team was choreographed by the Marx Brothers last year and Harry had six punts blocked. He happened to lead the NFL in punting by compiling an average of 45.4 yards per punt on 65 kicks. But Harry tried to punt 71 times. Well, actually, he tried 72, but one snap at Cleveland sailed so far over his head they picked it up on radar in Akron. Okay, Harry never got a foot on that one, but what about the six that were blocked? Had he been charged with them, and they *do* appear in the team averages, Harry's average would have been 41.5.

But even if we knocked Newsome off the top perch, the punting champ wouldn't have been San Diego's Ralf Mojsiejenko, who finished second, either. He had one blocked and his average would have slipped to 43.5. Denver's Mike Horan with no blocks and a 44.0 average would have won. Whenever there's any doubt, they should give the punting title to a Denver guy anyway. The Broncos have had seven league or conference champs since 1960. Amazing how legs get stronger as air gets thinner!

Well, we tried to reason through why the individual punters don't have blocked kicks charged against their averages. We can only assume that a blocked punt is considered a team error. To that we say pshaw.

If a punter is so hurried he shanks one off his knee for a net six inches, he's charged with the punt. The "team" let those guys in on him, but he kicked it. He's charged with his bad kick because it's part of his job to know when he can get a kick away and when he can't. The same thing applies to blocked kicks. The punter can't stop that guy who's flying in from his left, but he must see him. And he has to know before his foot hits the ball whether he's going to get that ball back in his face. When he misjudges, charge him.

The other thing we wondered about punters was why they were ranked by how far they kicked the ball. You'll find the Net Average in the stats and that's what nearly everybody looks at first. For those of you who may not know, the Net Average is figured by subtracting the runbacks and 20 yards for each touchback from the gross yards and dividing by the number of punts, including the blocked ones. For example, Harry Newsome kicked the ball 2,950 yards last season. Subtract 418 yards in runbacks and 200 yards on ten touchbacks. Then divide by 71, not 65, and Harry's Net Average was 32.8.

We've already told you why we think punters should be charged with blocks. We're even more aghast that they're not charged with touchbacks in figuring the league champ. When the kick goes into the endzone, the ball is brought back to the twenty. Yet the punter is given credit for 20 yards that don't exist!

The argument against including the runbacks is the old "team error" concept. Why charge the poor kicker if his coverage team is lousy? Well, we'll tell you why. Any punter who knows he's got a poor coverage bunch had better concentrate on making his punts unreturnable. The good ones will do it.

And let us throw in one other thing about using the Gross Average as the yardstick for punters. Anybody who's ever kicked a football knows he can get the most distance with a line drive, which is the way a lot of people kicked them years ago. The problem, of course, is a line drive right at the return man gets returned a long way before anybody gets downfield to him. So, coaches started looking for hang time. If you get the ball high enough to bring rain, the most leadfooted coverage team can get downfield and force a fair catch. The punter loses the distance of the line drive but improves the net. The NET!

See what we're saying? The punters are being graded on a standard of fifty years ago, but they're all shooting for something else. The net. No punter will hold his job because he gives great gross.

In the following chart, we'll give you the qualifying NFL punters from 1988 in the order of their Net Average. We're also adding three stats. The NFL gives you an "Inside the Twenty" total (kicks that rolled dead or out of bounds between the goal line and twenty or that were not returned to the twenty. We added a percent inside the twenty by dividing by the total number of punts. It's not as meaningful as we'd like because there's no way to be certain how many real chances the punter had at an inside-the-twenty shot. The other new stats relate to returns. The NFL gives you the number returned; we switched to number *not* returned because that's what the punter actually wants. We subtracted returns, touchbacks, and blocks from the total punts. Admittedly, a guy gets credit for a "not returned" if he shanks one out of bounds two yards upfield, but that's no worse than giving you return numbers and letting you try to guess what happened to the other kicks. We also added a *percent* not returned, which is more meaningful than the total.

We think there's some significance to the fact that Horan, who led in Net Average, was also near the top in Not Returned Percentage. At the same time, New England's Feagles led in Not Returned Percentage but had a much lower net because his distance was lower to start with.

	NO	GROSS YARDS	GROSS AVG	TOT	TB	BK	NOT RET	NOT RET%	RET YDS	IN 20	IN 20%	NET AVG
Horan, Den	65	2861	44.0	65	2	0	30	46.1	364	19	29.2	37.8
Rodriguez, Sea	70	2858	40.8	70	4	0	30	42.9	202	14	20.0	36.8
Arnold, Det	97	4110	42.4	97	7	0	33	34.0	483	22	22.7	35.9
Donnelly, Atl	98	3920	40.0	98	6	0	41	41.8	297	26	26.5	35.74
Gossett, Raid	91	3804	41.8	91	8	0	35	38.5	397	26	28.6	35.68
Kidd, Buf	62	2451	39.5	62	2	0	24	38.7	222	12	19.4	35.31
Roby, Mia	64	2754	43.0	64	9	0	20	31.3	318	18	28.1	35.25
Camarillo, Rams	40	1579	39.5	40	2	0	12	30.0	145	11	27.5	34.8
Mojsiejenko, SD	85	3745	44.1	86	11	1	18	20.9	558	22	25.6	34.5
Stark, Ind	64	2784	43.5	64	8	0	19	29.6	418	15	23.4	34.46
Hansen, NO	72	2913	40.5	73	8	1	25	34.2	248	19	26.0	34.3
Prokop, NYJ	85	3310	38.9	85	10	0	41	48.2	201	26	30.6	34.22
Saxon, Dal	80	3271	40.9	80	15	0	28	35.0	239	24	30.0	34.15
Feagles, NE	91	3482	38.3	91	8	0	46	50.5	217	24	26.4	34.12
Montgomery, Hou	65	2523	38.8	65	5	0	25	38.5	206	12	18.5	34.11
Teltschik, Phi	98	3958	40.4	101	8	3	45	44.6	375	28	27.7	33.9
Runager, Cle	49	1959	40.0	47	2	2	20	42.5	201	13	27.7	33.7
Buford, NYG	73	3012	41.3	75	10	2	27	36.0	296	13	17.3	33.5
Hatcher, Rams	36	1424	39.6	36	1	0	18	50.0	202	13	36.1	33.38
Wagner, Chi	79	3282	41.5	79	10	0	29	36.7	447	18	22.8	33.35
Horne, Pho	79	3228	40.9	80	9	1	29	36.3	416	16	20.0	32.9
Newsome, Pit	65	2950	45.4	71	10	6	15	21.1	418	9	12.6	32.8
Scribner, Min	84	3387	40.3	86	9	2	36	41.9	405	23	26.7	32.6
Criswell, TB	68	2477	36.4	68	0	0	30	44.1	273	20	29.4	32.4
Helton, SF	78	3069	39.3	79	5	1	26	32.9	426	22	27.8	32.2
Goodburn, KC	76	3059	40.3	76	8	0	20	26.3	473	10	13.7	31.9
Bracken, GB	85	3287	38.7	86	12	1	34	39.5	314	20	23.3	31.8
Fulhage, Cin	44	1672	38.0	46	5	2	17	36.9	220	13	28.3	29.4
Coleman, Was	39	1505	38.6	39	3	0	12	30.8	305	8	20.5	29.2

Incidentally our old pal Harry Newsome would have finished with a 35.8 Net Average—good for fourth place—if he'd just taken the losses when he was rushed instead of trying to kick and getting them blocked.

COACHES

FIRE THE BUM

The easiest way to set a football team on its rightful way to the championship it richly deserves is to fire the coach. He's the guy who, most fans will tell you, *in spite of whom* a team wins but *because of whom* it loses. It's a rule that all *other* coaches are brilliant motivators, strategists, and innovators, and *our* coach knows less about football than you or the guy sitting on the bar stool next to you. A lot less.

But, just for the sake of argument, let's say that all the coaches in the NFL are up for grabs and you can go out and hire any one of them to coach your team for five seasons only. After that, you'll have to get someone else. Which one do you take? Let's exclude the guy on the bar stool; he promised his wife he'd be home by midnight. So pick one. You're looking for the coach who'll get the most out of his material for five seasons and give you a winner.

What's the matter, cat got your tongue?

Well, we'll tell you which one we'd choose—and the order in which we would choose them right down the line. We'll even show you their résumés. (Note: Head Coach=(HC); all other coaching positions are assistants.)

DON SHULA, Miami Dolphins

Born: 1/4/30 Painesville, Ohio. College: John Carroll 1949-50 (HB).
Pro Playing Experience: Cleveland NFL 1951-52; Baltimore NFL 1953-56; Washington NFL 1957.
Other Coaching Experience: Virginia 1958; Kentucky 1959; Detroit NFL 1960-62.

YEAR	TEAM	W- L-T	FIN	PLAY	
1963	Balt	8- 6-0	3	-	
1964	Balt	12- 2-0	1	0-1	
1965	Balt	10- 3-1	1t	0-1	

YEAR	TEAM	W- L-T	FIN	PLAY	
(Continued)					
1966	Balt	9- 5-0	2	-	
1967	Balt	11- 1-2	2	-	
1968	Balt	13- 1-0	1	2-1	
1969	Balt	8- 5-1	2	-	
1970	Miami	10- 4-0	2	0-1	
1971	Miami	10- 3-1	1	2-1	
1972	Miami	14- 0-0	1	3-0	VII
1973	Miami	12- 2-0	1	3-0	VIII
1974	Miami	11- 3-0	1	0-1	
1975	Miami	10- 4-0	2	-	
1976	Miami	6- 8-0	3	-	
1977	Miami	10- 4-0	2	-	
1978	Miami	11- 5-0	2	0-1	
1979	Miami	10- 6-0	1	0-1	
1980	Miami	8- 8-0	3	-	
1981	Miami	11- 4-1	1	0-1	
1982	Miami	7- 2-0	2	3-1	
1983	Miami	12- 4-0	1	0-1	
1984	Miami	14- 2-0	1	2-1	
1985	Miami	12- 4-0	1	1-1	
1986	Miami	8- 8-0	3	-	
1987	Miami	8- 7-0	3	-	
1988	Miami	6-10-0	5	-	
Balt Total		71-23-4		2-3	
Miami Total		190-88-2		14-10	
NFL Total		261-111-6		16-13	

One of the myths about Shula is that he took over an already strong team at Baltimore in 1963. What he really did was get an aging team that had gone 6–6–0, 8–6–0, and 7–7–0 before he was hired. Two years later, he had them playing for the NFL Championship. But that was nothing compared to what he did in Miami, where he transformed a losing expansion team (4–10–0, 5–8–1, and 3–10–1) immediately into one of the league's strongest teams. He has rebuilt the Dolphins twice "on the run" and can be expected to do it again, although his present club is extremely weak. He could have been Coach of the Year in '88 for getting them six wins. The rumor that Shula was considering quitting after '88 didn't jibe with the thought that he'd never leave on his own with the team losing. He'll go out a winner.

Despite his poor '88 season, Shula will go down in history as possibly the best coach ever to set foot in the NFL. Well, at least he will in *our* history book.

JOE GIBBS, Washington Redskins

Born: 11/25/40 Mocksville, N. C. College: Cerritos, Calif. Jr. Coll. 1959-60; San Diego St. 1961-62 (E-LB-G).
Pro Playing Experience: None.
Other Coaching Experience: San Diego State 1964-66; Florida State 1967-68; USC 1969-70; Arkansas 1971-72; St. Louis NFL 1973-77; Tampa Bay NFL 1978; San Diego NFL 1979-80.

YEAR	TEAM	W- L-T	FIN	PLAY	
1981	Wash	8- 8-0	4	-	
1982	Wash	8- 1-0	1	4-0	XVII
1983	Wash	14- 2-0	1	2-1	
1984	Wash	11- 5-0	1	0-1	
1985	Wash	10- 6-0	3	-	
1986	Wash	12- 4-0	2	2-1	
1987	Wash	11- 4-0	1	3-0	XXII
1988	Wash	7- 9-0	3	-	
NFL Total		81-39-0		11-3	

Those who were ready to enshrine Gibbs in the Hall of Fame after Super Bowl XXII were caught short last season when he had some tough luck and, by his own admission, made some mistakes. Nevertheless he has only to bounce back from his first losing season to prove that he does belong in Canton. We expect him to do it, if not in '89 then in '90. The Redskins were 6-10-0 in 1980, the year before he got the job, but 10-6 in '79. If history repeats itself, Gibbs will have them righted this year and on top the year after.

CHUCK NOLL, Pittsburgh Steelers

Born: 1/5/32 Cleveland, Ohio. College: Dayton 1950-51 (G).
Pro Playing Experience: Cleveland NFL 1953-59.
Other Coaching Experience: L.A./S.D. Charger AFL 1960-65; Baltimore NFL 1966-68.

YEAR	TEAM	W- L-T	FIN	PLAY
1969	Pitt	1-13-0	4	-
1970	Pitt	5- 9-0	4	-
1971	Pitt	6- 8-0	2	-
1972	Pitt 1	1- 3-0	1	1-1
1973	Pitt 1	0- 4-0	2	0-1

(Continued)

YEAR	TEAM	W- L-T	FIN	PLAY	
1974	Pitt 1	0- 3-1	1	3-0	IX
1975	Pitt 1	2- 2-0	1	3-0	X
1976	Pitt 1	0- 4-0	1	1-1	
1977	Pitt	9- 5-0	1	0-1	
1978	Pitt 1	4- 2-0	1	3-0	XIII
1979	Pitt 1	2- 4-0	1	3-0	XIV
1980	Pitt	9- 7-0	3	-	
1981	Pitt	8- 8-0	2	-	
1982	Pitt	6- 3-0	4	0-1	
1983	Pitt 1	0- 6-0	1	0-1	
1984	Pitt	9- 7-0	1	1-1	
1985	Pitt	7- 9-0	3	-	
1986	Pitt	6-10-0	3	-	
1987	Pitt	8- 7-0	3	-	
1988	Pitt	5-11-0	4	-	
NFL Total		168-125-1		15-7	

Last year a Pittsburgh newspaperman asked, "How long is Noll going to be measured by those four Super Bowls?" One answer might be, "Until somebody else gets that many." The revisionists have been busy explaining that Noll simply won those Super Bowls because he had the best players, as though *good* coaches won them with a handful of pebbles. If Noll gets more credit than he deserves for taking a team that was 5-8-1, 4-9-1, and 2-11-1 before he was put in charge and had never won even a division title and turning it into "the team of the 1970s," he probably doesn't get enough credit for keeping the aging team competitive well into the 1980s.

The announcement by owner Dan Rooney that Noll would "end his career with the Steelers" was taken as equivocal in that Rooney didn't say Noll would continue coaching until he retired. For right now, however, it looks as though this very stubborn man will stay at the helm unless the Steelers experience an even worse season than in '88.

CHUCK KNOX, Seattle Seahawks

Born: 4/27/32 Sewickley, Pa. College: Juniata 1950-53 (T).
Pro Playing Experience: None.
Other Coaching Experience: Juniata 1954; high school 1955; Wake Forest 1959-60; Kentucky 1961-62; N.Y. Jets AFL 1963-66; Detroit NFL 1967-72.

(See the Seattle article for Knox's NFL record as head coach.)

Knox doesn't run the most exciting show, but he wins consistently. In a sense, it's a curse. He's brought his teams to contending status almost immediately but has never gotten them over the hump into the Super Bowl. After a while, that kind of close-but-no-cigar finish leads fans to call for his head, feeling certain that a new broom will sweep them to Valhalla. The knocks probably don't bother Knox a whole lot. He knows there are plenty of franchises that would look at a plus-.500 record as tall clover. If he's fired by the Seahawks, he'll probably have the next NFL head coaching job that opens up.

MIKE DITKA, Chicago Bears

Born: 10/18/39 Carnegie, Pa. College: Pittsburgh
  1958-60 (E).
Pro Playing Experience: Chicago NFL 1961-66;
  Philadelphia NFL 1967-68; Dallas NFL 1969-72.
Other Coaching Experience: Dallas NFL 1973-81.

YEAR	TEAM	W- L-T	FIN	PLAY	
1982	Chi	3- 6-0	12	-	
1983	Chi	8- 8-0	3	-	
1984	Chi	10- 6-0	1	1-1	
1985	Chi	15- 1-0	1	3-0	XX
1986	Chi	14- 2-0	1	0-1	
1987	Chi	11- 4-0	1	0-1	
1988	Chi	12- 4-0	1	1-1	
NFL Total		73-31-0		5-4	

Ditka brings more volatility and tumult to his job than is good for him or the Bears, but it's hard to quarrel with five straight double-digit victory totals and a Super Bowl ring. He's the second most successful coach in the Bears' long history, the first being George Halas, of course. Will Ditka play it cooler after his heart attack? Can he keep winning if he does? Will McMahon show up without a bandage? Will half the team keep from attacking the other half? There are only Bears in this zoo.

Regardless of what Ditka does, his team is getting older. He probably faces his greatest challenge to keep it at the top this year. One good move was to declare the quarterback job open in '89 training camp.

JIM MORA, New Orleans Saints

Born: 5/24/35 Glendale, Calif. College: Occidental
  1957 (E).
Pro Playing Experience: None.
Other Coaching Experience: Occidental 1960-63, (HC)
  1964-67; Colorado 1968-73; UCLA 1974; Washington
  1975-77; Seattle NFL 1978-81; New England NFL 1982;
  Philadelphia-Baltimore USFL 1983-85.

YEAR	TEAM	W- L-T	FIN	PLAY
1986	New Or	7- 9-0	4	-
1987	New Or	12- 3-0	2	0-1
1988	New Or	10- 6-0	3	-
NFL Total		29-18-0		0-1

Mora has been a terrific coach in his first three years in the NFL, and every sign says he'll continue to be. But, of course, he has to *do* it. The Saints were 8-8-0, 7-9-0, and 5-11-0 in the three seasons before Mora was hired, so there's no question he can turn a team around. Having Jim Finks as a GM don't hurt none, neither.

BUDDY RYAN, Philadelphia Eagles

Born: 2/17/34 Frederick, Okla. College: Oklahoma
  State 1952-55 (G).
Pro Playing Experience: None.
Other Coaching Experience: Buffalo 1961-65; Vanderbilt
  1966; Pacific 1967; N.Y. Jets NFL 1968-75;
  Minnesota NFL 1976-77; Chicago NFL 1978-85.

YEAR	TEAM	W- L-T	FIN	PLAY
1986	Phil	5-10-1	4	-
1987	Phil	7- 8-0	4	-
1988	Phil	10- 6-0	1	0-1
NFL Total		22-24-1		0-1

Buddy would put himself higher on this list. We will too if he gets the Eagles into the playoffs this year. It's hard to think of anyone in the NFC who accomplished so much with so little in 1988, but doing it again may be even beyond the abilities that Ryan says he has.

JOHN ROBINSON, Los Angeles Rams

Born: 6/25/35 Chicago, Ill. College: Oregon 1955-58
  (E).
Pro Playing Experience: None
Other Coaching Experience: Oregon 1960-71; USC
  1972-74; Raiders NFL 1975; USC (HC) 1976-82.

YEAR	TEAM	W- L-T	FIN	PLAY
1983	Rams	9- 7-0	2	1-1
1984	Rams	10- 6-0	2	0-1
1985	Rams	11- 5-0	1	1-1
1986	Rams	10- 6-0	2	0-1
1987	Rams	6- 9-0	3	-
1988	Rams	10- 6-0	2	0-1
NFL Total		56-39-0		2-5

Robinson seems to get taken for granted. After all, he's been one of the best coaches in the country since 1976. But since he came to the Rams (who were 6-10 and 2-7 before he arrived), some very good coaching by Robinson has been overshadowed by what was happening up the coast. Not to put the kiss of death on them, but look for the Rams to be *the* West Coast team in the early nineties and Robinson to be proclaimed a genius.

MARV LEVY, Buffalo Bills

Born: 8/3/28 Chicago, Ill. College: Coe 1948-50 (RB).
Pro Playing Experience: None.
Other Coaching Experience: High school 1951-52; Coe
1953-55; New Mexico 1956-57, (HC) 1958-59;
California (HC) 1960-63; William and Mary (HC)
1964-68; Philadelphia NFL 1969; L.A. Rams NFL 1970;
Washington NFL 1971-72; Montreal CFL (HC) 1973-77;
Chicago USFL (HC) 1984.

YEAR	TEAM	W- L-T	FIN	PLAY
1978	KC	4-12-0	5	-
1979	KC	7- 9-0	5	-
1980	KC	8- 8-0	3	-
1981	KC	9- 7-0	3	-
1982	KC	3- 6-0	11	-
1986	Buff	2- 5-0	4	-
1987	Buff	7- 8-0	4	-
1988	Buff	12- 4-0	1	1-1
Buff Total		21-17-0		1-1
KC Total		31-42-0		-
NFL Total		52-59-0		1-1

Levy, coming off his best NFL year, has shown an ability to improve a team. In three seasons before his arrival at Kansas City, the Chiefs were 5-9-0, 5-9-0, and 2-12-0. At Buffalo the Bills had gone 8-8-0, 2-14-0, 2-14-0, and were 2-7-0 when he took over in 1986. He also won two Grey Cups in Canada. Whether he can sustain a winner hasn't been proved. His last season in KC was the strike-torn '82 mess.

Professorial in both the good and bad senses of the description, he appears to have been underrated by everyone but Bills' owner Ralph Wilson.

JERRY BURNS, Minnesota Vikings

Born: 1/24/27 Detroit, Mich. College: Michigan
1949-50 (QB).
Pro Playing Experience: None.
Other Coaching Experience: Hawaii 1951; Whittier 1952;
high school 1953; Iowa 1954-60, (HC) 1961-65; Green
Bay NFL 1966-67; Minnesota 1968-85.

YEAR	TEAM	W- L-T	FIN	PLAY
1986	Minn	9- 7-0	2	-
1987	Minn	8- 7-0	2	2-1
1988	Minn	11- 5-0	2	1-1
NFL Total		28-17-0		3-2

Burns paid his dues—thirty-five years of coaching, including eighteen as a Viking assistant—before he finally got his shot as an NFL head coach. Sometimes when that happens, the successful head coach steps out and leaves his trusted assistant with a team ready to go into the toilet. But Bud

Grant retired when the Vikings were ready to move up. Because of that, Burns doesn't get a lot of credit for turning around a loser, but he's improved the team since he's been the boss. The Vikings have to be favored in the Central Division in 1989.

MARTY SCHOTTENHEIMER, Kansas City Chiefs

Born: 9/23/43 Canonsburg, Pa. College: Pittsburgh
1962-64 (LB).
Pro Playing Experience: Buffalo NFL 1965-68; New
England NFL 1969-70.
Other Coaching Experience: Portland Storm WFL 1974;
N.Y. Giants NFL 1975-77; Detroit NFL 1978-79;
Cleveland 1980-84.

YEAR	TEAM	W- L-T	FIN	PLAY
1984	Clev	4- 4-0	3	-
1985	Clev	8- 8-0	1	0-1
1986	Clev	12- 4-0	1	1-1
1987	Clev	10- 5-0	1	1-1
1988	Clev	10- 6-0	2	0-1
NFL Total		44-27-0		2-4

Schottenheimer was the defensive coordinator of the Browns when Cleveland gave him his first head coaching job midway through 1984, after a 1-7-0 start. Although he turned that around immediately, the Browns had appeared to be a team on the rise prior to '84, having gone 5-11-0, 4-5-0, and 9-7-0.

He will not be his own offensive coordinator at Kansas City.

DAN REEVES, Denver Broncos

Born: 1/19/44 Rome, Ga. College: South Carolina
1962-64 (QB).
Pro Playing Experience: Dallas NFL 1965-71 (RB).
Other Coaching Experience: Dallas NFL 1970-80.

YEAR	TEAM	W- L-T	FIN	PLAY
1981	Denv	10- 6-0	2	-
1982	Denv	2- 7-0	12	-
1983	Denv	9- 7-0	3	0-1
1984	Denv	13- 3-0	1	0-1
1985	Denv	11- 5-0	2	-
1986	Denv	11- 5-0	1	2-1
1987	Denv	10- 4-1	1	2-1
1988	Denv	8- 8-0	2	-
NFL Total		74-45-1		4-4

Although Reeves is the most successful coach in Bronco history, Denver wasn't exactly a disaster zone before he took over, going 10-6-0, 10-6-0, and 8-8-0 in the immediately preceding seasons. And a .500 record got preceder Red Miller fired.

SAM WYCHE, Cincinnati Bengals

Born: 1/5/45 Atlanta, Ga. College: Furman 1962-66
(QB).
Pro Playing Experience: Cincinnati NFL 1968-70;
Washington NFL 1971-73; Detroit NFL 1974-75; St.
Louis NFL 1976; Buffalo NFL 1977.
Other Coaching Experience: South Carolina 1967; San
Francisco NFL 1979-82; Indiana (HC) 1983.

YEAR	TEAM	W- L-T	FIN	PLAY
1984	Cin	8- 8-0	2	-
1985	Cin	7- 9-0	2	-
1986	Cin	10- 6-0	2	-
1987	Cin	4-11-0	4	-
1988	Cin	12- 4-0	1	2-1
NFL Total		41-38-0		2-1

Before Wyche took over the Bengals, they appeared to be a team on the slide. From a Super Bowl appearance in 1981 (12–4–0), they'd dropped to 7–9–0 in '83. He didn't turn them around overnight, but he did seem to have them moving in the right direction until he was torpedoed by the strike in '87. Everyone but Bengals' boss Paul Brown was amazed at the '88 turnaround, which earned Wyche a new five-year contract.

Brilliantly innovative but sometimes mercurial in the past, he appears to be settled in for a long run, so get used to him.

RAYMOND BERRY, New England Patriots

Born: 2/27/33 Corpus Christi, Texas. College: SMU
1951-54 (WR).
Pro Playing Experience: Baltimore NFL 1955-67.
Other Coaching Experience: Dallas NFL 1968-69; Detroit
NFL 1973-75; Cleveland NFL 1976-77; New England NFL
1978-81.

YEAR	TEAM	W- L-T	FIN	PLAY
1984	NE	4- 4-0	2	-
1985	NE	11- 5-0	3	3-1
1986	NE	11- 5-0	1	0-1
1987	NE	8- 7-0	2	-
1988	NE	9- 7-0	3	-
NFL Total		43-28-0		3-2

One of the few great players to make a successful transition to coaching (Ditka is another), Berry made himself into a Hall of Fame receiver by hard work. He applies the same ethic as a coach. The year after he took over the Patriots from Ron Meyer in 1984, the team went all the way to the Super Bowl. If he can straighten out his quarterback situation in 1989, he could get the Pats past the Bills in the AFC East. Second place and a Wild Card berth in the playoffs isn't an unrealistic goal.

RON MEYER, Indianapolis Colts

Born: 2/17/41 Westerville, Ohio. College: Purdue
1959-62 (DB).
Pro Playing Experience: None
Other Coaching Experience: High school 1964; Purdue
1965-70; Nevada-Las Vegas (HC) 1973-75; SMU (HC)
1976-81.

YEAR	TEAM	W- L-T	FIN	PLAY
1982	NE	5- 4-0	7	0-1
1983	NE	8- 8-0	2	-
1984	NE	5- 3-0	2	-
1986	Ind	3- 0-0	5	-
1987	Ind	9- 6-0	1	0-1
1988	Ind	9- 7-0	2	-
NE Total		18-15-0		0-1
Ind Total		21-13-0		0-1
NFL Total		39-28-0		0-2

Meyer looked like a wonder-worker when he gained three straight victories for the until-then winless Colts in 1986 and put them in the playoffs the next year. Some of the luster wore off last season, but most of the problems couldn't be blamed on him. The Colts had gone 7–9–0, 4–12–0, and 5–11–0 in the full seasons before he took over and appeared to be floundering. At New England, he inherited a team with good talent that had been 9–7–0, 10–6–0, and then dived to 2–14–0. He got them back on track but was fired in a controversial move when he precipitously canned defensive coordinator Rod Rust (the Steelers' new def-co) in midyear. With the players on the verge of a revolt, the Patriots opted to keep Rust and drop Meyer.

BILL PARCELLS, New York Giants

Born: 8/22/41 Englewood, N.J. College: Wichita State
1961-63 (LB).
Pro Playing Experience: None.
Other Coaching Experience: Hastings 1964; Wichita
State 1965; Army 1966-69; Florida State 1970-72;
Vanderbilt 1973-74; Texas Tech 1975-77; Air Force
(HC) 1978; New England NFL 1980; N.Y. Giants
1981-82.

YEAR	TEAM	W- L-T	FIN	PLAY	
1983	NYG	3-12-1	5	-	
1984	NYG	9- 7-0	2	1-1	
1985	NYG	10- 6-0	2	1-1	
1986	NYG	14- 2-0	1	3-0	XXI
1987	NYG	6- 9-0	5	-	
1988	NYG	10- 6-0	2	-	
NFL Total		52-42-1		5-2	

Don't get us wrong. We're not saying Parcells is a bad coach. We thought he was terrific, riding a winner home in 1986. Still, we have to believe that few of the coaches named above him here would have let his team collapse as far as Parcells did in '87. And, given the Giants' soft schedule in

'88, we think most of the coaches named here could have found some way to win the NFC East. The Giants aren't a real good team, but Parcells had more horses than Ryan in Philadelphia. If he can overtake Buddy and hold off Joe in '89, we'll be happy to move him up a notch. But if the Giants finish third or worse, remember you read it here first.

GENE STALLINGS, Phoenix Cardinals

Born: 3/2/35 Paris, Texas. College: Texas A & M 1954-57 (E).
Pro Playing Experience: None.
Other Coaching Experience: Texas A & M 1957, (HC) 1965-71; Alabama 1958-64; Dallas NFL 1972-85.

YEAR	TEAM	W- L-T	FIN	PLAY
1986	StL	4-11-1	5	-
1987	StL	7- 8-0	3	-
1988	Phoe	7- 9-0	4	-
NFL Total		18-28-1		-

Although Stallings took over a 5–11 team in 1986, the Cardinals had actually been just over .500 for Jim Hanifan in 1983–84, so Stallings hasn't exactly turned them around. Of course no one has ever turned the Cards around for long. Stallings is their thirtieth coach since 1920, and most of them left with losing records.

Stallings is respected as a football man and gets plenty of votes in the "nice guy" league. Maybe that's the problem. Maybe the Cardinals would do better with a real bastard as coach. They've tried everything else, including moving out of town twice.

JOE WALTON, New York Jets

Born: 12/15/35 Beaver Falls, Pa. College: Pittsburgh 1953-56 (E).
Pro Playing Experience: Washington NFL 1957-60; N.Y. Giants NFL 1961-63.
Other Coaching Experience: N.Y. Giants NFL 1969-73; Washington NFL 1974-80; N.Y. Jets NFL 1981-82.

YEAR	TEAM	W- L-T	FIN	PLAY
1983	NYJ	7- 9-0	5	-
1984	NYJ	7- 9-0	3	-
1985	NYJ	11- 5-0	1	0-1
1986	NYJ	10- 6-0	2	1-1
1987	NYJ	6- 9-0	5	-
1988	NYJ	8- 7-1	4	-
NYJ Total		49-45-1		1-2

Walton isn't regarded as one of the elite among NFL coaches and he'll probably never satisfy a majority in New York. However, he did a fine job in '88. Further improvement by the Jets, which doesn't seem likely, could bring some reevaluation of his capabilities. At any rate, he's got a

new contract, which cuts him some slack. The Jets were a team on the rise when he replaced Walt Michaels in 1983 (4–12–0, 10–5–1, and 6–3–0), but they peaked in 1985.

JERRY GLANVILLE, Houston Oilers

Born: 10/14/41 Detroit, Mich. Colleges: Montana State 1960; Northern Michigan 1961-63 (LB).
Pro Playing Experience: None.
Other Coaching Experience: High school 1964-66; Western Michigan 1967; Georgia Tech 1968-73; Detroit NFL 1974-76; Atlanta NFL 1977-82; Buffalo NFL 1983; Houston NFL 1984-85.

YEAR	TEAM	W- L-T	FIN	PLAY
1985	Hous	0- 2-0	4	-
1986	Hous	5-11-0	4	-
1987	Hous	9- 6-0	2	1-1
1988	Hous 1	0- 6-0	3	1-1
NFL Total		24-25-0		2-2

Although we are not among the admirers of Glanville's coaching style, he must get some credit for bringing one of the NFL's worst teams into contention. Before he took over the 5–9–0 Oilers with two games remaining in 1985, the team had struggled to 1–8–0, 2–14–0, and 3–13–0. It would be crass to suggest that those losing years gave the Oilers a jereboam of high draft choices, or even crasser to mention that the Oilers finished third in their division last year with at least the second-best talent in the AFC.

RAY PERKINS, Tampa Bay Buccaneers

Born: 11/6/41 Mt. Olive, Miss. College: Alabama 1964-66 (WR).
Pro Playing Experience: Baltimore 1967-71.
Other Coaching Experience: Mississippi State 1973; New England NFL 1974-77; San Diego NFL 1978; Alabama (HC) 1983-86.

YEAR	TEAM	W- L-T	FIN	PLAY
1979	NYG	6-10-0	4	-
1980	NYG	4-12-0	5	-
1981	NYG	9- 7-0	3	1-1
1982	NYG	4- 5-0	10	-
1987	TB	4-11-0	4	-
1988	TB	5-11-0	3	-
NYG Total		23-34-0		1-1
TB Total		9-22-0		-
NFL Total		32-56-0		1-1

Perkins wasn't what you'd call a ball of fire in New York, where he got one good season out of four. And though he was Bear Bryant's handpicked successor at Alabama, he was only 32-15-1 in four years, which was not as good as 'Bama was used to. He's stockpiled some pretty good young talent at Tampa Bay, but it's time for him to show he can do something with it—a break-even season at least. Otherwise maybe he should begin looking for another opportunity.

MARION CAMPBELL, Atlanta Falcons

Born: 5/25/29 Chester, S.C. College: Georgia 1948-51 (T).

Pro Playing Experience: San Francisco NFL 1954-55; Philadelphia NFL 1956-61

Other Coaching Experience: Boston AFL 1962-63; Minnesota NFL 1964-66; L.A. Rams 1967-68; Atlanta NFL 1969-74; Philadelphia NFL 1977-82; Atlanta NFL 1986.

YEAR	TEAM	W- L-T	FIN	PLAY
1974	Atl	1- 5-0	4	-
1975	Atl	4-10-0	3	-
1976	Atl	1- 4-0	3	-
1983	Phil	5-11-0	4	-
1984	Phil	6- 9-1	5	-
1985	Phil	6- 9-0	4	-
1987	Atl	3-12-0	4	-
1988	Atl	5-11-0	4	-
Atl-1 Total		6-19-0		-
Phil Total		17-29-1		-
Atl-2 Total		8-23-0		-
NFL Total		31-71-1		-

Campbell has been an outstanding defensive assistant for years, but 1989 should answer whether he can really handle the head coach job. Supposedly, he "wasn't ready" when he took over a slipping Atlanta team the first time, but he didn't show much progress in his three seasons at Philadelphia, either. Again, however, the team was already in a nose dive before he was given the reins.

The knocks are that he's "too nice" (which isn't the worst thing a man can be accused of) and that he doesn't know offense. He has surrounded himself with an excellent staff in his second tour at Atlanta, which should cool the second criticism. He's made some headway but probably needs at least an 8-8-0 mark in '89 to hang on.

LINDY INFANTE, Green Bay Packers

Born: 5/27/40 Miami, Fla. College: Florida 1960-62 (RB-DB).

Pro Playing Experience: None.

Other Coaching Experience: High school 1965; Florida 1966-71; Memphis State 1972-74; Charlotte WFL 1975; Tulane 1976, 1979; N.Y. Giants 1978; Cincinnati NFL 1980-82; Jacksonville USFL (HC) 1984-85; Cleveland NFL 1986-87.

YEAR	TEAM	W- L-T	FIN	PLAY
1988	GB	4-12-0	5	-

You couldn't call Infante's first year a rip-roaring success, but they haven't had much of any kind of success in Green Bay of late. The Pack was 5-9-1 in '87 and 4-12 in '86. The defense did a decent job in '88 and that's something. Now if Infante can get the offense, which is his specialty, working, well . . . there's hope.

MIKE SHANAHAN, Los Angeles Raiders

Born: 8/24/52 Oak Park, Ill. College: East Illinois State 1972 (Q).

Pro Playing Experience: None.

Other Coaching Experience: East Illinois State 1973-74; Oklahoma 1975-76; North Arizona 1977; E. Illinois St. 1978; Minnesota NFL 1979; Florida 1980-83; Denver NFL 1984-87.

YEAR	TEAM	W- L-T	FIN	PLAY
1988	Raid	7- 9-0	3	-

The Raiders look like a team in a slide (12-4-0, 8-8-0, and 5-10-0) and Shanahan, who wasn't Al Davis' first choice anyway, could get buried in it. He was roundly criticized as unprepared by fired assistant Charley Sumner after the '88 season, but no one loves the guy who ties a can to you. This season should show whether he's head coach material or just a talented assistant.

On the plus side, he installed a completely new offensive philosophy and still won two more games in '88 than the Raiders had managed under Tom Flores in '87.

WAYNE FONTES, Detroit Lions

Born: 2/17/40 New Bedford, Mass. College: Michigan State 1959-61 (DB).

Pro Playing Experience: N.Y. Titans AFL 1962.

Other Coaching Experience: Dayton 1967-68; Iowa 1969-70; USC 1971-75; Tampa Bay NFL 1976-84; Detroit NFL 1985-88.

YEAR	TEAM	W- L-T	FIN	PLAY
1988	Det	2- 3-0	4	-

Who knows? Were those two wins at the end of the season the beginning of a comeback for Detroit or just a salary drive? Things can't get much worse in the Silver Dome, so Fontes will have some time. And almost any improvement in the won-lost record will make him look good. Right now, all we can say for certain is he's been a good defensive assistant and he's enthusiastic.

BUD CARSON, Cleveland Browns

Born: 4/28/31 Brackenridge, Pa. College: North
  Carolina 1948-52 (DB).
Pro Playing Experience: None.
Other Coaching Experience: North Carolina 1957-64; S.
  Carolina 1965; Georgia Tech (HC) 1966-71;
  Pittsburgh NFL 1972-77; L.A. Rams NFL 1978-81;
  Baltimore NFL 1982; Kansas City NFL 1983-84; N.Y.
  Jets NFL 1985-87.

Carson has been an outstanding defensive coach for
years. He's getting his first shot at an NFL head job at age
fifty-eight, inheriting a team that's been in the playoffs four
straight years and has had 12, 12, and 10 wins in its last
three seasons. The Browns look to be definitely in decline,
making Carson's job that much harder. The good news is
that he can expect to have QB Bernie Kosar back healthy;
the bad news is that the Browns are springing leaks just
about everywhere else.

GEORGE SEIFERT, San Francisco 49ers

Born: 1/22/40 San Francisco, Calif. College: Utah
  1960-62 (LB).
Pro Playing Experience: None
Other Coaching Experience: Westminster (HC) 1965; Iowa
  1966; Oregon 1967-71; Stanford 1972-74,1977-79;
  Cornell (HC) 1975-76; San Francisco NFL 1980-88.

Seifert is another longtime assistant getting his first
chance at the top job when the Master steps aside. Every
time that happens, we remember Phil Bengtson, who got
the Packers from Lombardi just as they were deteriorating.
Bengtson was a good coach, but he never had a prayer.
Seifert was Walsh's defensive coordinator. He knows the
system. He's highly regarded around the league. And the
49ers look like they'll be solvent for several more years. But
if they don't win the Super Bowl next year—and they probably won't—a lot of people are going to say that Walsh would
have done it.

DAN HENNING, San Diego Chargers

Born: 6/21/42 Bronx, N.Y. College: William & Mary
  1960-63 (QB).
Pro Playing Experience: San Diego AFL 1964-67.
Other Coaching Experience: Florida State 1968-70,
  1974; Virginia Tech 1971, 1973; Houston NFL 1972;
  N.Y. Jets NFL 1976-78; Miami NFL 1979-80;
  Washington NFL 1981-82, 1987.

YEAR	TEAM	W- L-T	FIN	PLAY
1983	Atl	7- 9-0	4	-
1984	Atl	4-12-0	4	-
1985	Atl	4-12-0	4	-
1986	Atl	7- 8-1	3	-

Atl Total   22-41-1

This is the second time Henning was hired off Joe Gibbs'
staff to take over as head coach of an NFL loser. He couldn't
make Atlanta a winner in four years, and when he finally
nudged them out of last place, he was fired. Henning is a
former quarterback known as an offensive coach, but his
Falcon teams did their best playing on defense.

JIMMY JOHNSON, Dallas Cowboys

Born: 7/16/43 Port Arthur, Tex. College: Arkansas
  1962-64 (DT).
Pro Playing Experience: None
Other Coaching Experience: Louisiana Tech 1965; high
  school 1966; Wichita State 1967; Iowa State
  1968-69; Oklahoma 1970-72; Arkansas 1973-76;
  Pittsburgh 1977-78; Oklahoma State (HC) 1979-83;
  Miami (HC) 1984-88.

Johnson comes into an uncomfortable position, with all
the pro-Landry people rooting against him. But the Cowboys are a lead-pipe cinch to improve in 1989, and that will
help his popularity (in Dallas if not Miami). He got great
results with the Hurricanes, but a lot of college geniuses
have flunked their NFL tests. Has an owner's "best friend"
ever been a success as a coach? We don't remember any.

ESSAYS

A glossary of statistical terms and list of abbreviations used in this book can be found on pages 293–295.

THE THREE BEST GAMES OF
THE YEAR: WIN PROBABILITY
IN ACTION

Everything that occurs on a football field happens in relation to three things—the time, the score, and the field position. Every second used by a team's offense is one less second the other team can use. Both teams aim for the same thing—to be ahead when there is no more time for an opponent to catch up. How much is enough? A touchdown scored with three minutes left and one team up by thirty points is meaningless, no matter which team scores it. But if the score is 21–17 with three minutes left, a touchdown—again by either team—completely changes the game. So the score of the game becomes meaningful within the context of time. Field position, which we can think of as *potentiality to score,* also has meaning only when we relate it to the time left and the score.

We can call the three dimensions the *game situation.*

The game situation—time, score, and field position—is so unyielding that it is possible to calculate the probability of a team's winning at any moment in a game.

Maybe you should reread that last sentence. Yes, that's exactly what we said. For example, if a team trails 13–7 and has a first down at its own twenty-nine-yard line with 6:50 left in the second quarter, it will probably go on to win the game 32 percent of the time; 68 percent of the time it will lose.

Questions?

How do we know this?

Simple. Feed enough games—with all their possible game situations—into a computer, punch the right keys, and it will tell you exactly how many times teams in the same situation as the one we just described have eventually won or lost. We started a few years ago with over five hundred games and have continued to add to our sample. It holds up.

So what? What good does it do to know the probability *of winning?*

If you're hung up on predicting the outcome of the game, none. This isn't a tool for predicting; it's a tool for evaluating.

How so?

Let's use an example of a twelve-yard pass completion. What does it mean—aside from twelve yards? Its real meaning depends on the game situation. With thirty seconds left, down by fifteen, and at your own thirty-five, it means nothing. With ten seconds left, down by two, at the opponent's forty-one, it could be the most important pass of the game. If the twelve-yard completion came in the first quarter of a tied game, it has meaning, but how do we measure it?

Easy. We look to see how much that first-quarter completion has raised a team's probability of winning the game. Suppose that before the play the offensive team had a Win Probability of 462 (46.2 percent). And after the play, the WP was raised to 468 (46.8 percent). The play was worth six Win Probability Points (0.6 percent). It also cost the defensive team six WP points.

What if the same pass happened near the end and scored the winning points?

Depending on the exact game situation, it might be worth 700 to 999 WP points.

So Win Probability Points are a way of calculating the real value of a play, rather than simply noting the yards?

Exactly.

Tell us more.

Glad to. We decided to look at three important games—by our lights, the best—from the 1988 season, to analyze them in terms of WP points. Obviously play-by-play accounts would take too much space and show mostly minute changes, so we'll use Drive Charts.

What's a Drive Chart?

A Drive Chart shows the results of each team's "possessions" in a game. A "possession" simply begins with the time a team gets the ball and ends when it gives it up. If you'll look below, we'll explain the first drive of the first game we're going to look at.

DR SE	GM PR	SCORE START	HOW OBTAINED PLAY	YDS	RET	SCRIMM BEG	END	NET TOT	YDS PEN	NO PL	FD —	CLOCK START	TIME END	TIME POSS	HOW GIVEN UP PLAY	YDS	RET	SCORE END	WIN PROBAB BEG	END	NOR	WIN OFF	TEAM TYPE	WIN SPE
																							kor	-7
PAT 1	1	0- 0	ko	73	28	p20	p25	5	0	4	0	15:00	13:51	1:09	punt	33	0	0- 0	493	470	473	-20	punt	-3

Indianapolis kicked off to the Patriots. Okay, reading the chart's stacked column heads from left to right, we find:

DR/SE (drive/series) = Patriots' first drive. GM/PR (game/period) = drive started in the first quarter. SCORE/START = the score was 0–0. HOW OBTAINED/PLAY YDS RET = Patriots received kickoff (ko) 8 yards deep in the endzone (73-yard ko) and the ball was brought out to the 20, via a touchback (28).

SCRIMM/BEG END = the drive began on the Patriots' 20 (p20) and ended at the Pats' 25 (p25). NET/TOT = the drive totaled 5 yards. YDS/PEN = there were no penalties in the drive. NO/PL = 4 plays in the drive (the punt at the end is counted). FD/— = no first downs in the drive.

CLOCK/START = there were 15:00 minutes left in the first quarter at the beginning of the drive. TIME/END = 13:51 left at the end. TIME/POSS = 1:09 was the elapsed time of possession.

HOW GIVEN UP/PLAY YDS RET = the Pats gave up the ball on a 33-yard punt that was not returned. SCORE/END = the score was still 0–0 at the end of the drive.

Up to here, it's a normal drive chart. But here we add the Win Probability part.

WIN PROBAB/BEG END NOR = here is the Win Probability at the beginning (BEG) of the drive (493 or 49.3 percent), the end (END) of the drive (470), and NOR, which is what the WP would be if we counted only the offense (473); this allows us to calculate the contributions of special

teams. WIN/OFF = how many WP points the Pats' offense gets or loses for its poor 5-yard drive (493 – 473 = –20). Remember that the Colts' defense receives a +20 for stopping the Pats. TEAM/TYPE and WIN/SPE refers to special teams and their WP points. Note that the kickoff return (kor) is counted separately.

We could say that the Pats' chance of winning was 50.1 when they won the coin flip, 49.3 percent when they only got the kickoff out to the twenty, 47.3 percent after their first drive gained only five yards, and 47.0 percent when their punt was downed only thirty-three yards upfield.

Okay, now let's look at three important games from 1988.

THE FLUTIE GAME

Both the Patriots and the Colts needed wins badly when they met on October 2 at Sullivan Stadium. They had each been rated a strong challenger going into the season. But Indianapolis had dropped its first three decisions before finally edging Miami 15–13 in Week 4; New England had won its opener and then lost three straight. They were coming off a 31–6 blowout by the Oilers. Another loss would just about end either team's chances for '88.

The Colts had Eric Dickerson. The Patriots didn't have Steve Grogan, who was sidelined with a neck injury. Tom Ramsey opened at quarterback.

First Quarter

DR SE	GM PR	SCORE START	HOW OBTAINED PLAY	YDS	RET	SCRIMM BEG	END	NET TOT	YDS PEN	NO PL	FD —	CLOCK START	TIME END	TIME POSS	HOW GIVEN UP PLAY	YDS	RET	SCORE END	WIN PROBAB BEG	END	NOR	WIN OFF	TEAM TYPE	WIN SPE
																							kor	-7
PAT 1	1	0- 0	ko	73	28	p20	p25	5	0	4	0	15:00	13:51	1:09	punt	33	0	0- 0	493	470	473	-20	punt	-3
IND 1	1	0- 0	punt	33	0	i42	p49	9	0	4	0	13:51	11:40	2:11	punt	49	20	0- 0	530	507	516	-14	punt	-9
PAT 2	1	0- 0	punt	49	20	p20	p20	0	0	4	0	11:40	9:56	1:44	punt	53	0	0- 0	493	495	464	-29	punt	31
IND 2	1	0- 0	punt	53	0	i27	i22	-5	0	4	0	9:56	8:41	1:15	punt	51	26	0- 0	505	450	467	-38	punt	-17
PAT 3	1	0- 0	punt	51	26	i47	i49	-2	0	2	0	8:41	8:23	0:18	int	45	16	0- 0	550	507	507	-43		0
IND 3	1	0- 0	int	45	16	i20	i15	-5	-10	4	0	8:23	6:29	1:54	punt	59	11	0- 0	493	476	454	-39	punt	22
PAT 4	1	0- 0	punt	59	11	p37	i14	49	1	11	3	6:29	1:02	5:27	FGA	14	20	0- 0	524	508	566	42	FG	-58
IND 4	1	0- 0	FGA	14	20	i20	i43	23	0	5	1	1:02	14:54	1:08	punt	38	0	0- 0	492	510	504	12	punt	6

The first quarter had to be one of the dullest in the NFL all year. Neither team could even register a first down until its fourth possession. Finally the Patriots' Irving Fryar returned a punt eleven yards to New England's thirty-seven. From there the Pats moved haltingly downfield, aided by a

third-down penalty when the Colts' Eugene Daniel grabbed John Stephens' face mask.

The drive stalled at the fourteen. Rookie kicker Teddy Garcia booted wide to the left to end the only scoring threat of the first period.

Second Quarter

DR SE	GM PR	SCORE START	HOW OBTAINED PLAY	YDS	RET	SCRIMM BEG	END	NET TOT	YDS PEN	NO PL	FD —	CLOCK START	TIME END	TIME POSS	HOW GIVEN UP PLAY	YDS	RET	SCORE END	WIN PROBAB BEG	END	NOR	WIN OFF	TEAM TYPE	WIN SPE
PAT 5	2	0- 0	punt	38	0	p19	i 0	81	10	13	6	14:54	6:48	8:06	TD	1	0	7- 0	490	739	736	245	XP	3
																							kor	-10
IND 5	2	0- 7	ko	75	30	i20	i35	15	-5	6	1	6:48	4:40	2:08	punt	55	15	0- 7	251	251	241	-10	punt	10
PAT 6	2	7- 0	punt	55	15	p25	p16	1	-5	4	0	4:40	2:53	1:47	punt	74	20	7- 0	749	766	734	-15	punt	32
IND 6	2	0- 7	punt	74	20	i20	p 0	80	5	12	6	2:53	0:10	2:43	TD	1	0	7- 7	234	504	500	265	XP	4
																							kor	4
PAT 7	2	7- 7	ko	53	22	p34	p34	0	0	1	0	0:10	0:00	0:10	EOH	0	0	7- 7	500	504	504	4		0

The Patriots put together a nice eighty-one-yard drive early in the second quarter. Ramsey, who was only two for seven until then, completed four of four and Reggie Dupard carried five times for fifteen tough yards. Robert Perryman scored on a one-yard leap over the top. The extra point put the Pats' WP at 73.9 percent.

Indianapolis didn't get anything started until there were less than three minutes remaining in the half. Then they drove eighty yards to tie the score. Dickerson gained forty-three of the yards, including the final yard over left guard for the TD.

The game was close but not particularly exciting. Ramsey was only six for thirteen for sixty-six yards. Chris Chandler of Indianapolis was even worse, five for twelve for thirty-four yards. Dickerson had ninety-three yards, with nearly half of them on the long drive to tie the score.

Third Quarter

DR SE	GM PR	SCORE START	HOW OBTAINED PLAY	YDS	RET	SCRIMM BEG	END	NET TOT	YDS PEN	NO PL	FD —	CLOCK START	TIME END	TIME POSS	HOW PLAY	GIVEN UP YDS	RET	SCORE END	WIN PROBAB BEG	END	NOR	WIN OFF	TEAM TYPE	WIN SPE
																							kor	-12
IND 7	3	7- 7	KO	73	30	120	122	2	0	4	0	15:00	13:44	1:16	punt	41	0	7- 7	491	469	456	-35	punt	13
																							kor	4
PAT 8	3	7- 7	punt	41	0	p37	p49	12	-5	6	1	13:44	9:58	3:46	punt	49	0	7- 7	531	559	520	-11	punt	39
IND 8	3	7- 7	punt	49	0	i 2	115	13	0	6	1	9:58	7:03	2:55	punt	28	0	7- 7	441	415	432	-3	punt	-17
PAT 9	3	7- 7	punt	28	0	143	142	1	0	4	0	7:03	5:58	1:05	punt	38	0	7- 7	585	558	525	-60	punt	33
IND 9	3	7- 7	punt	38	0	i 4	113	9	5	6	1	5:58	1:57	4:01	punt	45	14	7- 7	442	405	417	-25	punt	-12
PAT 10	3	7- 7	punt	45	14	145	149	-4	-10	4	0	1:57	1:05	0:52	punt	49	20	7- 7	593	512	528	-65	punt	-16
IND 10	3	7- 7	punt	49	20	120	128	8	0	4	0	1:05	0:00	1:05	punt	42	0	7- 7	488	479	457	-31	punt	22

The offensive brownout continued through the third quarter, with neither team able to sustain a drive. The Colts punted four times, the Pats three. Ramsey missed on five passes in a row. Indianapolis' offense totaled a −94 in WP points during the quarter. New England's offense totaled −136.

As the final quarter began, Coach Berry put Doug Flutie in at quarterback.

Fourth Quarter (A)

DR SE	GM PR	SCORE START	HOW OBTAINED PLAY	YDS	RET	SCRIMM BEG	END	NET TOT	YDS PEN	NO PL	FD —	CLOCK START	TIME END	TIME POSS	HOW PLAY	GIVEN UP YDS	RET	SCORE END	WIN PROBAB BEG	END	NOR	WIN OFF	TEAM TYPE	WIN SPE
PAT 11	4	7- 7	punt	42	0	p30	i 0	70	5	6	3	15:00	10:58	4:02	TD	26	0	14- 7	521	866	861	340	XP	5
																							kor	-10
IND 11	4	7-14	ko	75	30	120	138	18	0	5	1	10:58	8:26	2:32	punt	48	12	7-14	124	100	98	-25	punt	2
PAT 12	4	14- 7	punt	48	12	p26	p29	3	0	3	0	8:26	7:32	0:54	int	9	18	14- 7	900	714	714	-186		0
IND 12	4	7-14	int	9	18	p20	p 2	18	0	5	1	7:32	5:57	1:35	FG	2	0	10-14	286	148	145	-141	FG	3

Flutie took the Patriots seventy yards to a touchdown in six plays. His first pass was called back on a penalty, but he followed with four completions in a row, the last going twenty-six yards down the middle to Stanley Morgan for the TD. The Pats suddenly had an 86.6 percent Win Probability.

After another Colts' drive fizzled, Flutie went from potential hero to potential goat with an interception that was returned to the Patriots' twenty. But when the Colts could only cash it for Dean Biasucci's twenty-yard field goal, they actually lost 145 WP points.

Fourth Quarter (B)

DR SE	GM PR	SCORE START	HOW OBTAINED PLAY	YDS	RET	SCRIMM BEG	END	NET TOT	YDS PEN	NO PL	FD —	CLOCK START	TIME END	TIME POSS	HOW PLAY	GIVEN UP YDS	RET	SCORE END	WIN PROBAB BEG	END	NOR	WIN OFF	TEAM TYPE	WIN SPE
																							kor	19
PAT 13	4	14-10	ko	52	28	p31	p46	15	0	7	1	5:57	3:47	2:10	punt	35	0	14-10	871	923	923	52	punt	0
IND 13	4	10-14	punt	35	0	119	p 0	81	5	5	3	3:47	2:23	1:24	TD	48	0	17-14	77	970	969	892	XP	1

Flutie led New England on a short drive to the forty-six, where Jeff Fleagles punted to the Colts' nineteen. Indianapolis had 3:47 remaining and a Win Probability of only 7.7 percent. But Chandler passed twelve yards to Pat Beach and nineteen yards to Dickerson. Then, with the ball at the Pats' forty-eight, he arched a deep pass down the left sideline to Bill Brooks for a touchdown. The Colts jumped to a 97.0 percent Win Probability.

Fourth Quarter (C)

DR SE	GM PR	SCORE START	HOW OBTAINED PLAY	YDS	RET	SCRIMM BEG	END	NET TOT	YDS PEN	NO PL	FD —	CLOCK START	TIME END	TIME POSS	HOW PLAY	GIVEN UP YDS	RET	SCORE END	WIN PROBAB BEG	END	NOR	WIN OFF	TEAM TYPE	WIN SPE
																							kor	-7
PAT 14	4	14-17	ko	75	30	p20	i 0	80	15	9	5	2:23	0:23	2:00	TD	13	0	21-17	23	988	988	965	XP	0
																							kor	2
IND 14	4	17-21	ko	30	0	135	135	0	0	1	0	0:23	0:15	0:08	int	51	0	17-21	14	0	0	-14		0
PAT 15	4	21-17	int	51	0	p14	p12	-2	0	1	0	0:15	0:00	0:15	EOG	0	0	21-17	1000	1000	1000	0		0

Flutie had 2:23 to turn it around. Six passes, a fifteen-yard penalty for roughness, and one run by John Stephens brought the ball to the Colts' twenty. On the eighth play of the drive, Flutie ran up the middle for seven. Then, on the play of the game, he bootlegged left for thirteen yards and the winning touchdown.

The Colts still had a minuscule chance (1.4 percent), but Chandler's first pass attempt was intercepted.

TEAM	PAT WP PTS	IND WP PTS
Offensive	+1220	+788
Defensive	-788	-1220
Kickoff	+30	-9
Kickoff Return	+9	-30
Punting	+116	+20
Punt Returns	-20	-116
Field Goal	-58	+3
FG Return (or Block)	-3	+58
Extra Points	+8	+5
XP Return (or Block)	-5	-8
Totals	509	-509

If we total up the Win Probability points, we find that the New England offense had 1,220 WP points—including 965

on that final drive. The winning team will always total about 500 points for its offense, defense, and various special teams, no matter what the score. The losing team—the mirror image—will have a negative total that matches the winner's positive number.

The game itself proved important to both teams. The Colts' loss came back to haunt them at the end of the season. Though they rallied down the stretch, they couldn't make up the ground to get into the playoffs. Flutie won the starting QB spot for the Patriots. Once they switched to a ground-oriented attack that complemented his skills, the Patriots made a good if unsuccessful run at the playoffs.

THE FIELD GOAL THAT WASN'T THAT WAS

When the Giants sat home watching the playoffs on TV, they must have thought of this game a lot. And gnashed their teeth.

The Eagles had won the first meeting between the two teams on an exceptional performance by Randall Cunningham. This one—played on November 20 at Giants Stadium—was a must-win for New York.

First Quarter

DR SE	GM PR	SCORE START	HOW PLAY	OBTAINED YDS	RET	SCRIMM BEG	END	NET TOT	YDS PEN	NO PL	FD —	CLOCK START	TIME END	TIME POSS	HOW PLAY	GIVEN UP YDS	RET	SCORE END	WIN PROBAB BEG	END	NOR	WIN OFF	TEAM TYPE	WIN SPE
																							kor	-2
NYG	1 1	0- 0	ko	65	23	n23	n35	12	0	5	1	15:00	12:41	2:19	int	-3	30	0- 0	498	324	324	-174		0
PHI	1 1	0- 0	int	-3	30	n 2	n 0	2	0	3	1	12:41	11:16	1:25	TD	1	0	7- 0	676	704	702	26	XP	2
																							kor	-8
NYG	2 1	0- 7	ko	73	23	n20	p 0	80	0	5	2	11:16	8:57	2:19	TD	62	0	7- 7	288	498	495	207	XP	3
																							kor	-13
PHI	2 1	7- 7	ko	52	5	p18	p34	16	0	7	1	8:57	5:37	3:20	punt	41	0	7- 7	489	498	487	-2	punt	11
NYG	3 1	7- 7	punt	41	0	n25	p44	31	0	9	2	5:37	2:15	3:22	punt	44	20	7- 7	502	508	518	16	punt	-10
PHI	3 1	7- 7	punt	44	20	p20	p21	1	0	4	0	2:15	1:21	0:54	punt	37	0	7- 7	492	466	462	-30	punt	4
NYG	4 1	7- 7	punt	37	0	n42	n39	-3	0	4	0	1:21	14:49	1:32	punt	-6	0	7- 7	534	415	496	-38	punt	-81

The Eagles' Seth Joyner intercepted Phil Simms' second pass of the game and ran it back thirty yards to the New York two. It took Philadelphia three plays to score from there, with Cunningham going over. Philadelphia already had a 70.4 percent WP, with less than five minutes gone.

The Giants came back immediately, going eighty yards to tie. Simms passed sixty-two yards to Stacy Robinson for the touchdown.

Second Quarter

DR SE	GM PR	SCORE START	HOW PLAY	OBTAINED YDS	RET	SCRIMM BEG	END	NET TOT	YDS PEN	NO PL	FD —	CLOCK START	TIME END	TIME POSS	HOW PLAY	GIVEN UP YDS	RET	SCORE END	WIN PROBAB BEG	END	NOR	WIN OFF	TEAM TYPE	WIN SPE
PHI	4 2	7- 7	punt	-6	0	n33	p44	-23	0	4	0	14:49	14:05	0:44	punt	36	0	7- 7	585	508	506	-79	punt	2
NYG	5 2	7- 7	punt	36	0	n20	n21	1	0	4	0	14:05	12:44	1:21	punt	44	0	7- 7	492	478	461	-31	punt	17
PHI	5 2	7- 7	punt	44	0	p35	n20	45	0	10	3	12:44	7:46	4:58	FG	20	0	10- 7	522	597	561	39	FG	36
																							kor	-17
NYG	6 2	7-10	ko	63	15	n17	p 4	79	0	15	4	7:46	1:10	6:36	FG	4	0	10-10	386	504	495	109	FG	9
																							kor	4
PHI	6 2	10-10	ko	30	0	p35	p37	2	-5	5	0	1:10	0:36	0:34	punt	45	0	10-10	500	508	503	3	punt	5
NYG	7 2	10-10	punt	45	0	n18	n17	-1	0	1	0	0:36	0:00	0:36	EOH	0	0	10-10	492	504	504	12		0

Both teams exchanged field goals in the second quarter. Although the score was tied at the half, Cunningham had not been nearly as effective as in the first Giants game (five of twelve for 45 yards). In this game Simms was nine of sixteen for 159 yards.

Third Quarter

DR SE	GM PR	SCORE START	HOW PLAY	OBTAINED YDS	RET	SCRIMM BEG	END	NET TOT	YDS PEN	NO PL	FD	CLOCK — START	TIME END	TIME POSS	HOW PLAY	GIVEN YDS	UP RET	SCORE END	WIN BEG	PROBAB END	NOR	WIN OFF	TEAM TYPE	WIN SPE
																							kor	21
PHI 7	3	10-10	ko	53	22	p34	p41	7	5	7	1	15:00	11:53	3:07	punt	53	0	10-10	524	546	499	-25	punt	47
NYG 8	3	10-10	punt	53	0	n6	p0	94	0	15	7	11:53	5:37	6:16	TD	9	0	17-10	454	798	794	340	XP	4
																							kor	-8
PHI 8	3	10-17	ko	53	19	p21	p25	4	0	4	0	5:37	4:07	1:30	punt	46	0	10-17	194	179	160	-34	punt	19
NYG 9	3	17-10	punt	46	0	n29	p47	24	0	5	1	4:07	2:21	1:46	punt	35	0	17-10	821	846	841	20	punt	5
PHI 9	3	10-17	punt	35	0	p12	n41	47	0	5	1	2:21	0:30	1:51	punt	25	0	10-17	154	188	190	35	punt	-2
NYG 10	3	17-10	punt	25	0	n16	n48	32	0	9	3	0:30	11:21	4:09	int	18	3	17-10	812	840	840	28		0

Simms continued hot into the third quarter, leading a brilliant fifteen-play, ninety-four-yard drive that put New York in front 17–10. His nine-yard pass to Stephen Baker tied the score. But on the next possession Simms was injured and replaced by Jeff Hostetler.

Fourth Quarter

DR SE	GM PR	SCORE START	HOW PLAY	OBTAINED YDS	RET	SCRIMM BEG	END	NET TOT	YDS PEN	NO PL	FD	CLOCK — START	TIME END	TIME POSS	HOW PLAY	GIVEN YDS	UP RET	SCORE END	WIN BEG	PROBAB END	NOR	WIN OFF	TEAM TYPE	WIN SPE
PHI 10	4	10-17	int	18	3	p37	n32	31	-5	8	2	11:21	8:39	2:42	int	23	4	10-17	160	139	139	-21		0
NYG 11	4	17-10	int	23	4	n13	n19	6	0	4	0	8:39	6:28	2:11	punt	43	6	17-10	861	874	869	8	punt	5
PHI 11	4	10-17	punt	43	6	p44	n0	56	0	6	2	6:28	4:28	2:00	TD	18	0	17-17	126	499	481	355	XP	18
																							kor	-17
NYG 12	4	17-17	ko	61	18	n22	p49	29	0	5	1	4:28	2:08	2:20	punt	49	20	17-17	484	530	543	59	punt	-13
PHI 12	4	17-17	punt	49	20	p20	p25	5	-5	5	0	2:08	1:04	1:04	punt	40	10	17-17	470	488	495	25	punt	-7
NYG 13	4	17-17	punt	40	10	n45	50	5	0	4	0	1:04	0:01	1:03	punt	50	20	17-17	512	517	523	11	punt	-6
PHI 13	4	17-17	punt	50	20	p20	p19	-1	0	1	0	0:01	0:00	0:01	EOH	0	0	17-17	500	497	497	-3		0

With 6:28 remaining, Cunningham started at his own forty-four. The Giants flushed him out of the pocket but he scrambled for six yards. After an incomplete pass, he scrambled again—this time for twenty-nine yards down to the Giants' twenty-one. Three plays later he passed to TE Keith Jackson, who was hit and fumbled at the two. Philadelphia's Cris Carter recovered in the endzone, and Luis Zendejas' PAT tied the score with 4:28 left.

Neither team could mount a threat and the game went into overtime.

Overtime

DR SE	GM PR	SCORE START	HOW PLAY	OBTAINED YDS	RET	SCRIMM BEG	END	NET TOT	YDS PEN	NO PL	FD	CLOCK — START	TIME END	TIME POSS	HOW PLAY	GIVEN YDS	UP RET	SCORE END	WIN BEG	PROBAB END	NOR	WIN OFF	TEAM TYPE	WIN SPE
																							kor	0
PHI 14	5	17-17	ko	65	25	p25	n41	34	0	7	1	15:00	12:58	2:02	punt	41	20	17-17	489	517	523	34	punt	-6
NYG 14	5	17-17	punt	41	20	n20	n25	5	0	3	0	12:58	11:59	0:59	int	27	11	17-17	483	427	427	-56		0
PHI 15	5	17-17	int	27	11	n41	n13	28	0	6	2	11:59	8:50	3:09	FGA	13	-13	23-17	573	1000	863	290	FG	137

The Eagles won the toss, but, after a twenty-five-yard pass to Keith Byers, they ran out of gas. The Giants started at their twenty following the punt. Hostetler passed for five, then went incomplete. His third pass of the overtime was grabbed off by the Eagles' Terry Hoage at the Philadelphia forty-eight and returned to the Giants' forty-one.

The Eagles' Win Probability jumped to 57.3 percent with the interception. Cunningham passed for twelve and scrambled for eleven. Two running plays put the ball at the New York thirteen, as Philadelphia set up to try a field goal on third down.

New York cornerback Sheldon White blocked Zendejas' kick, but in a one-in-a-million shot, Eagles DE Clyde Simmons, who was in to block, picked up the ball and raced into the endzone to win the game.

TEAM	PHI WP PTS	NYG WP PTS
Offensive	+614	+511
Defensive	-511	-614
Kickoff	+44	-4
Kickoff Return	+4	-44
Punting	+73	-83
Punt Returns	+83	-73
Field Goal	+173	+9
FG Return (or Block)	-9	-173
Extra Points	+20	+7
XP Return (or Block)	-7	-20
Totals	+484	-484

THE COMEBACK

Talk about comebacks! It would be hard to top what ancient Don Strock did in Cleveland last year. Signed as an emergency replacement when the Browns' first three quarterbacks went out injured, he took Cleveland to a win, then retired to the bench to watch a recovered Bernie Kosar do the quarterbacking. But in Week 15, Kosar was hurt again at Miami. Strock nearly pulled the Browns through that one. Only a great pass from Dan Marino beat the Browns. They had only one chance left to make the playoffs. For the season finale they had to beat Houston at Cleveland.

The Oilers' proclivity for losing on the road was more than matched by the Browns being forced to go with, in effect, their fourth-string quarterback in their season's biggest game.

First Quarter

DR SE	GM PR	SCORE START	HOW PLAY	OBTAINED YDS	RET	SCRIMM BEG	END	NET TOT	YDS PEN	NO PL	FD —	CLOCK START	TIME END	TIME POSS	HOW PLAY	GIVEN YDS	UP RET	SCORE END	WIN BEG	PROBAB END	NOR	WIN OFF	TEAM TYPE	WIN SPE
																							kor	24
CLE	1 1	0- 0	ko	61	34	c38	c38	0	0	3	0	15:00	13:10	1:50	int	15	20	0- 0	524	424	424	-100		0
HOU	1 1	0- 0	int	15	20	c38	c22	16	0	6	1	13:10	9:58	3:12	FG	22	0	3- 0	563	583	548	-15	FG	35
																							kor	-6
CLE	2 1	0- 3	ko	58	15	c22	h42	36	-15	5	1	9:58	6:24	3:34	int	9	0	0- 3	411	396	396	-15		0
HOU	2 1	3- 0	int	9	0	h42	c49	9	0	3	0	6:24	5:57	0:27	punt	36	3	3- 0	619	603	604	-15	punt	-1
CLE	3 1	0- 3	punt	36	3	c16	c18	2	0	3	0	5:57	4:53	1:04	int	18	36	0-10	397	207	207	-190		0
																							kor	13
CLE	4 1	0-10	ko	45	13	c33	c49	16	-5	7	2	4:53	14:46	5:07	punt	41	0	0-10	220	220	210	-10	punt	10

Strock couldn't have been much worse in the first quarter. His first pass was intercepted by Domingo Bryant and turned into a thirty-nine-yard field goal by Tony Zendejas. His sixth pass was intercepted by Richard Johnson. Houston couldn't convert, but as soon as the Browns got the ball back, Strock threw his third interception. Bryant took this one thirty-six yards for a touchdown. The Browns were down 10–0 and had only a 20.7 percent Win Probability with nearly five minutes left in the opening period.

Second Quarter

DR SE	GM PR	SCORE START	HOW PLAY	OBTAINED YDS	RET	SCRIMM BEG	END	NET TOT	YDS PEN	NO PL	FD —	CLOCK START	TIME END	TIME POSS	HOW PLAY	GIVEN YDS	UP RET	SCORE END	WIN BEG	PROBAB END	NOR	WIN OFF	TEAM TYPE	WIN SPE
HOU	3 2	10- 0	punt	41	0	h10	h14	4	0	5	1	14:46	11:42	3:04	fumb	-7	14	10- 7	780	597	597	-183		0
																							kor	-10
HOU	4 2	10- 7	ko	65	20	h20	c24	56	0	10	3	11:42	6:50	4:52	FG	24	0	13- 7	587	688	645	58	FG	43
																							kor	8
CLE	5 2	7-13	ko	47	11	c29	c25	-4	0	3	0	6:50	4:54	1:56	punt	35	15	7-13	320	244	273	-47	punt	-29
HOU	5 2	13- 7	punt	35	15	c44	c17	27	-10	7	2	4:54	2:16	2:38	FG	17	0	16- 7	757	823	785	28	FG	38
																							kor	1
CLE	6 2	7-16	ko	56	17	c26	h 6	68	0	14	5	2:16	0:13	2:03	fumb	-9	22	7-16	178	180	180	2		0
HOU	6 2	16- 7	fumb	-9	22	h37	h48	11	0	2	1	0:13	0:00	0:13	EOH	0	0	16- 7	820	823	823	3		0

The Browns got a big break early in the second quarter. Houston QB Warren Moon went back to pass at his own twenty-one. Cleveland's David Grayson sacked him at the fourteen and he fumbled. Michael Dean Perry picked up the ball at the ten and raced to a touchdown.

Despite the help from the defense, Strock and the offense could do nothing as Houston tagged on two field goals to make the score 16–7 at the half. On Cleveland's only good drive before intermission, the Browns reached the Oilers' six, but Strock was sacked, fumbled, and Houston's Keith Bostic took the bobble out to the thirty-seven-yard-line. The Oilers had an 82.3 percent Win Probability when the whistle blew.

Third Quarter (A)

DR SE	GM PR	SCORE START	HOW PLAY	OBTAINED YDS	RET	SCRIMM BEG	END	NET TOT	YDS PEN	NO PL	FD —	CLOCK START	TIME END	TIME POSS	HOW PLAY	GIVEN YDS	UP RET	SCORE END	WIN BEG	PROBAB END	NOR	WIN OFF	TEAM TYPE	WIN SPE
																							kor	2
HOU	7 3	16- 7	ko	58	19	h26	c 0	74	0	11	4	15:00	9:03	5:57	TD	7	0	23- 7	825	954	953	128	XP	1

The Oilers widened their lead and their Win Probability with a strong seventy-four-yard drive to a touchdown to open the third quarter. Moon's seven-yard pass to little-used rookie wide receiver Haywood Jeffires brought the score.

Leading 23–7 with 21:03 to go, the Oilers had a 95.4 percent Win Probability. In review, this means that a team in that position will win 954 games out of a thousand. A team in Cleveland's position will lose all but 4.6 percent of the time. Of course, most games don't get so far out of hand by ten minutes into the third quarter, so you might have to watch for four or five seasons to see a team come back from this game situation to win.

But this was one of those times.

Third Quarter (B)

DR SE	GM PR	SCORE START	HOW PLAY	OBTAINED YDS	RET	SCRIMM BEG END	NET TOT	YDS PEN	NO PL	FD —	CLOCK START	TIME END	TIME POSS	HOW PLAY	GIVEN UP YDS	RET	SCORE END	WIN PROBAB BEG	END	NOR	WIN OFF	TEAM TYPE	WIN SPE
																						kor	8
CLE	7 3	7-23	ko	42	14	c37 h 0	63	0	8	5	9:03	6:06	2:57	TD	2	0	14-23	54	132	130	75	XP	2
																						kor	-2
HOU	8 3	23-14	ko	55	14	c24 h37	39	0	6	2	6:06	2:47	3:19	punt	20	5	23-14	866	891	902	36	punt	-11
CLE	8 3	14-23	punt	20	5	c22 h 0	78	5	13	6	2:47	13:17	4:30	TD	2	0	21-23	109	345	342	233	XP	3

Strock suddenly began to hit his short passes. He drove the Browns sixty-three yards for their first offensive touchdown. One of his completions was to Ozzie Newsome for the veteran tight end's 143rd consecutive game with at least one reception. Strock's two-yard pass to Earnest Byner brought the score.

Houston drove thirty-seven yards, but on fourth-and-nine Greg Montgomery punted short to Gerald McNeil, who returned to the Cleveland twenty-two. Strock mixed short passes and sweeps by Herman Fontenot to reach the Houston twenty-nine. There his fourth-down pass was broken up by Steve Brown and Keith Bostic—but Houston was offsides and the drive continued. At 1:47 into the final quarter, Byner plunged over from two yards out. The score was 23–21.

Fourth Quarter

DR SE	GM PR	SCORE START	HOW PLAY	OBTAINED YDS	RET	SCRIMM BEG END	NET TOT	YDS PEN	NO PL	FD —	CLOCK START	TIME END	TIME POSS	HOW PLAY	GIVEN UP YDS	RET	SCORE END	WIN PROBAB BEG	END	NOR	WIN OFF	TEAM TYPE	WIN SPE
																						kor	49
HOU	9 4	23-21	ko	53	23	h41 c47	12	-5	5	1	13:17	10:54	2:23	punt	36	0	23-21	704	719	704	0	punt	15
CLE	9 4	21-23	punt	36	0	c11 h 0	89	0	11	4	10:54	6:23	4:31	TD	22	0	28-23	281	844	843	562	XP	1
																						kor	12
HOU	10 4	23-28	ko	50	13	h28 h39	11	0	5	1	6:23	4:46	1:37	punt	25	0	23-28	168	92	121	-47	punt	-29
CLE	10 4	28-23	punt	25	0	c36 h28	36	5	10	2	4:46	0:20	4:26	down	0	0	28-23	908	988	988	80		0
HOU	11 4	23-28	down	0	0	h28 c35	37	0	2	2	0:20	0:00	0:20	EOG	0	0	23-28	12	0	0	-12		0

The snow was falling on Cleveland Stadium and the Oilers were falling apart. Allen Pinkett brought Matt Bahr's short kickoff back twenty-nine yards to the Houston forty-one, but the Oilers could gain only to the Cleveland forty-two before another penalty knocked them back five yards. Montgomery's punt went out of bounds at the Cleveland eleven.

Eighty-nine yards, big deal! Cleveland was unstoppable. Strock's short tosses and a few Fontenot sweeps brought them to the Houston twenty-two in ten plays. Then Ancient Don, the Comeback King, threw to Webster Slaughter for the touchdown that made it 28–23, Browns.

The Oilers still had plenty of time to come back, but Moon missed on three straight passes at his own thirty-nine. Cleveland held the ball for four minutes and twenty seconds before handing it over on downs at the Houston twenty-eight with only twenty seconds left. Cleveland coach Marty Schottenheimer could have called for a forty-five-yard field goal attempt, but decided against it. A blocked kick could have cost him the game. For once the prevent defense prevented. Houston completed two passes before time and their chances ran out.

TEAM	CLEV WP PTS	HOUS WP PTS
Offensive	+591	-19
Defensive	+19	-591
Kickoff	-51	-48
Kickoff Return	+48	+51
Punting	-19	-26
Punt Returns	+26	+19
Field Goal	0	+119
FG Return (or Block)	-119	0
Extra Points	+6	+1
XP Return (or Block)	-1	-6
Totals	+510	-510

The win put Cleveland into the playoffs, just ahead of the Oilers as the two Wild Cards. By the time that game was played the next week at Cleveland, Strock's luck had run out. He was injured in the opening quarter. His replacement, Mike Pagel, did a good job, but the Oilers finally won one on the road. Cleveland fans were left to wonder what might have been had Comeback Don played the whole game.

THE PLAYOFFS

"DIDN'T WE WATCH THIS LAST WEEK, RALPH?"

In a game replete with repeats, the one new development was that the Oilers finally won a big game on the road. Houston's consistent application of the Humpty-Dumpty maneuver whenever out of sight of the Astrodome was a popular lead item in pregame hype. And no news story about the game failed to observe that the same two teams had played each other six days before on the same field, with the Browns winning. Also up front was mention that the Browns had been knocked from the playoffs two years in a row by heartbreaking losses. The third time was less than charming to the Brownies—another heartbreaker—though the game wasn't quite as close as the final score.

At the top of the second quarter, after Houston had taken a 7–3 lead on Allen Pinkett's TD catch of a Warren Moon pass, Cleveland discovered still another repetition—a quarterback injury. Veteran QB Don Strock, playing in place of injured Bernie Kosar, suffered a sprained wrist in a pileup, the fifth time this season the Browns had lost a starting quarterback because of an injury. Houston came out of the pileup with a fumble recovery, and Pinkett scored his second touchdown in twenty-two seconds, with a darting run on the next play.

In for Cleveland came Mike Pagel, who had been sidelined since October with a shoulder separation. He led the Browns to a pair of Matt Bahr field goals before the half to pull Cleveland back to 14–9. Despite the close score, there was so much taunting and shoving by both sides after every play that a neutral observer might have preferred adjourning to an alley to watch younger adolescents at their games and thus save the price of an NFL ticket. Nearly as truant as sportsmanship was any benefit from Instant Replay. The instants were long and unproductive, as inadvertent whistles and inconclusive pictures left several questionable calls dubious.

Pagel put the Browns in the lead, 16–14, late in the third quarter on a fourteen-yard toss to Webster Slaughter. That was the cue for Moon to take the Oilers on a seventy-six-yard drive—perhaps his finest moment in the NFL—to regain the lead. Lorenzo White scored, crashing over from a yard out. Tony Zendejas stretched the Houston lead to 24–16 with 1:54 left. Pagel's second score to Slaughter, at 14:29, was only cosmetic when the Browns couldn't execute an onside kick.

Houston Coach Jerry Glanville was magnanimous as always in victory, reminding everyone that his road record had been unfairly criticized and instructing the world press that it could now write about something else.

AFC WILD CARD

December 24, 1988, at Cleveland, Ohio
Attendance: 74,977

Houston Oilers	0	14	0	10	—	24
Cleveland Browns	3	6	7	7	—	23

SCORING:

CLE: Bahr 33 FG (5:17, 1Q)
HOU: Pinkett 14 pass from Moon; Zendejas PK (0:07, 2Q)
HOU: Pinkett 16 run; Zendejas PK (0:22, 2Q)
CLE: Bahr 26 FG (6:27, 2Q)
CLE: Bahr 28 FG (11:41, 2Q)
CLE: Slaughter 14 pass from Pagel; Bahr PK (12:24, 3Q)
HOU: White 1 run; Zendejas PK (2:35, 4Q)
HOU: Zendejas 49 FG (13:06, 4Q)
CLE: Slaughter 2 pass from Pagel; Bahr PK (14:29, 4Q)

"RALPH, DOES IT MAKE A DIFFERENCE WHICH SIDE CATCHES A PASS?"

The Vikings defense put the Rams in a hole early, then covered them over, and stomped on the mound. The high-scoring L.A. offense never materialized. All-NFC Wide Receiver Henry Ellard spent most of the game as an observer, blanketed and all but blanked by the Minnesota secondary. Quarterback Jim Everett posted a completion percentage that could have won a batting title but not a football game. And Greg Bell, whose running on draw plays was the only highlight of the first half, was extinguished in the second.

The leader of Minnesota's secondary—make that "firstary"—was All-Pro SS Joey Browner. His two first-quarter interceptions led to Viking touchdowns and a 14-0 lead, at which point Minnesota fans could have ordered their air tickets to San Francisco for the next playoff. Nor did Browner coast the rest of the afternoon. On that day, he had seven solo tackles, two passes defensed (that awful but useful TV announcers' coinage), and the Vikes' only sack—a −12 on Everett. After the game Everett declared, "Joey Browner is the best." It was unclear whether he meant SS, DB, defensive man, or football player, since they all applied for the day.

Ably aiding Browner in discouraging the Rams from throwing passes with happy results were Carl Lee, who finished with six passes defensed, Reggie Rutland, and Brad Edwards. Meanwhile, LBs Scott Studwell and Ray Berry, in for injured Jesse Solomon, cauterized Bell's running.

The Minnesota offense that put up two more touchdowns before the end of the game actually gained thirty-two fewer yards than L.A. Of course they seldom had as far to go. QB Wade Wilson threw no interceptions, while completing 17 of 28 passes for 253 yards. His most important completion was a fourth-quarter, third-down, forty-six-yard throw to WR Anthony Carter after the Rams had pulled within shouting distance at 21-10. Minnesota went on to a touchdown that put the already-iced game in the deep freeze.

Years ago the Rams were famous for coming to Minnesota from sunny Cal and freezing, both on the field and on the scoreboard. They couldn't blame the weather in climate-controlled Hubert H. Humphrey Metrodome. For while it snowed plowfuls outside, L.A. was burned by Browner & Co. inside. Just like sacrificial rams.

NFC WILD CARD

December 26, 1988, at Minneapolis, Min.
Attendance: 57,666

L.A. Rams	0	7	3	7	— 17
Minnesota Vikings	14	0	7	7	— 28

SCORING:

MIN: Anderson 7 run; C. Nelson PK (8:13, 1Q)
MIN: Rice 17 run; C. Nelson PK (8:34, 1Q)
LA : D.Johnson 3 pass from Everett;
    Lansford PK (7:42, 2Q)
MIN: Anderson 1 run; C. Nelson PK (5:35, 3Q)
LA : Lansford 33 FG; (13:22, 3Q)
MIN: Hilton 5 pass from Wilson; C.Nelson PK (2:22, 4Q)
LA : Holohan 11 pass from Everett;
    Lansford PK (13:43, 4Q)

"IF THE POOR MAN'S HURT, RALPH, WHY ARE YOU LAUGHING?"

All you had to do was look at the two head coaches and you knew how this game would be played. On the Cincinnati side was Sam Wyche, Mr. Innovation, always ready with a clever new wrinkle to spice up a game. Even when they backfired, his gimmicks were fun to talk about for weeks afterward. On the Seattle side was Chuck Knox, Ground Chuck himself, the meat-and-potatoes traditionalist whose rush-oriented philosophy could bring to a football game all the excitement of watching dust settle. So you knew how it would go, but you tuned in anyway.

And there was that one team running, running, running. Funny thing! They were Bengals. Ground Sam?

Boomer Esiason, the NFL's leading passer, only threw 19 times for a mere 91 yards, but it didn't matter. His tosses were only the fourth wheel on the Cincy tricycle that ground Chuck and the Seahawks into the Riverfront Stadium artificial turf. The Big Wheels were Ickey Woods, with 23 attempts for 126 yards and a touchdown; James Brooks, with 13 attempts for 72 yards and Stanley Wilson, 7 attempts, 45 yards, and 2 touchdowns. Altogether, 254 rushing yards.

Most of the credit belonged to the huge Cincinnati line, which simply pushed the smallish Seahawks defenders wherever the playbook suggested, like a big fork moving peas around a plate. Although OT Joe Walter was out with a knee injury and OG Bruce Reimers nursed a sprained ankle, the Bengal Bullies put Seattle's Smallfry in need of a doctor. But all the visitors got was a prescription for more rushing from the Wyche doctor. Cincinnati built up a 21-0 halftime lead with their ground game. Meanwhile Tim Krumrie and the Cincy defense stuffed the Seahawks like master taxidermists. When a fumble on a punt return gave the 'Hawks the ball at the Bengals' twenty-five, it was Krumrie who moments later crunched John L. Williams at the six to force a score-averting fumble.

That missed opportunity loomed bigger in the fourth quarter. The Bengals gained but didn't score in the second half and Seattle, abandoning its ground attack—if a net of eighteen yards can be called an "attack"—went to Dave Krieg's arm for a pair of TDs. The second, with 6:05 remaining, brought the score to 20-13, but when Norm Johnson

AFC DIVISIONAL PLAYOFF

December 31, 1988, at Cincinnati, Ohio
Attendance: 58,560

Seattle Seahawks	0	0	0	13	— 13
Cincinnati Bengals	7	14	0	0	— 21

SCORING:

CIN: Wilson 3 run; Breech PK (5:49, 1Q)
CIN: Wilson 3 run; Breech PK (3:25, 2Q)
CIN: Woods 1 run; Breech PK (7:20, 2Q)
SEA: Williams 7 pass from Krieg; Johnson PK (3:20, 4Q)
SEA: Krieg 1 run; Johnson PK failed (8:55, 4Q)

missed his first extra point in 132 attempts, the Seahawks were done.

The game's one exciting new innovation came from Knox—the dreaded Oh-My-Knee-Fake. To stop the Cincy no-huddle offense and get the right subs on for Seattle, the Seahawks' nose tackles developed an astonishing string of knee injuries in the second half. All just before third down, all stopping play, and all miraculously cured as soon as the player reached the sideline. Of course, it *might* have been simply a fortuitous combination of coincidence and spontaneous regeneration.

"SHOULD I CALL THE TV-MAN, RALPH?"

At Chicago 65,534 fans saw the Bears forge a lead in the first half and heard them protect it to the end of the game. The "Fog Bowl" will go into history as one of the most memorable games never seen.

Three minutes into the game, when the day was bright and clear, the Bears' Mike Tomczak lofted a pass to Dennis McKinnon that resulted in a sixty-four-yard touchdown. The Eagles came back on their third possession to score two touchdowns and a field goal, but only the three-pointer counted. Both TDs were nullified by penalties. Philadelphia closed to 7–6 in the second period on Luis Zendejas' second field goal, but again they blew an opportunity for more when TE Keith Jackson dropped a Randall Cunningham pass while he stood alone in the endzone.

Chicago got all the points they would really need shortly after that. Glenn Kozlowski brought a short kickoff back to the Philadelphia forty-four. Tomczak passed twenty-seven yards to Ron Morris, and moments later, Neal Anderson went in from four yards out.

Thomas Sanders' fifty-eight-yard sweep put the Bears into position for Kevin Butler's forty-six-yard field goal—his longest of the season—with only a little over two minutes remaining in the half.

Zendejas' third field goal made the score 17–9 at the half. By then the fog had rolled in on little cat feet and stomped all over Soldier Field. The situation was, if anything, worse in the second half. The only scoring came on Butler and Zendejas field goals that sounded good. The crowd in the stands was limited to looking down on a white blanket while the field announcer described what he thought he could see. TV watchers had the benefit of field-level cameras, but nevertheless most of what they saw remained quick, gray blobs. Jim McMahon was said to have gone in at quarterback for the Bears after Tomczak was injured, but it may have been only a rumor.

Several Eagles, including Owner Norman Braman, complained later about the conditions, but their principle nemesis was their own early mistakes. Some of their justification for blaming the fog for their inability to score touchdowns was blunted by the 430 total yards they stacked up against the famed Bear defense. Philadelphia moved the ball all day. They just didn't move it legally into the endzone.

Referee Jim Tunney insisted that he could see both goal-posts all during the game, indicating his eyes were more eaglelike than any Philadelphian's. If nothing else, the game proved the NFL will not call a game because of fog until it starts deflecting passes.

NFC DIVISIONAL PLAYOFF

December 31, 1988, at Chicago, Ill.
Attendance: 65,534

Philadelphia Eagles	3	6	3	0	—	12
Chicago Bears	7	10	0	3	—	20

SCORING:

CHI: McKinnon 64 pass from Tomczak; Butler PK (3:02, 1Q)
PHI: L. Zendejas 42 FG (7:56, 1Q)
PHI: L. Zendejas 29 FG (5:43, 2Q)
CHI: Anderson 4 run; Butler PK (8:39, 2Q)
CHI: Butler 46 FG; (12:57, 2Q)
PHI: L. Zendejas 30 FG (14:28, 2Q)
PHI: L. Zendejas 35 FG (13:02, 3Q)
CHI: Butler 27 FG (2:26, 4Q)

"RALPH . . . DO YOU THINK *I* LOOK FAT IN BLACK?"

Hmmmm, le'ssee, Mr. Glanville, suh. It couldn'a been the Buffalo weather. The day come up sunny with tempachers in the thirties. An' we know it wuzn't that yer team can't win them big games on the road. Yuh tol' us last week that wuz all over. An' yer guys tackled necks an' pushed people in the face an' pointed fingers an' yelled, jus' like yuh wanted. Yuh wore black. Yuh lef' tickets. We jus' can't figger whut went wrong.

Mebbe the Bills jus' played better.

Like, did yuh notice how they come out passin', when ever'one was sure they wuz gonna run all'a time? An' did yuh see whut they done when their first drive went a-glimmerin' 'cause of a bad snap? They come right down ag'in. An' this time they went fer a touchdown 'stead o' the field goal—an' they failed. But that didn' stop 'em neither. They jes' blocked ol' Greg Montgomery's punt, an' that there Robb Riddick run fer a TD. Well, shucks, yuh musta' seen whut heppened when yer Oilers got to the two-yard-line at the top o' the secon' half. There they was, trailin' only 7–3 an' all hankerin' t' score. So then that Warren Moon fella whut plays quarterback fer y'all pitched out, only the ball went clean out o' bounds at the fourteen. An' *then* Tony Zendejas shanked his ol' field goal try.

But them Buffaloes, they jes' kep' on a-comin'. Scored another touchdown an' a field goal a'fore your'n got that bitty TD in the las' quarter.

Yuh know whut we saw, Mr. Glanville, suh? Them Buffaloes tackled funny. Like that special-teams fella, Steve Tasker, who used t' play fer y'all. Well, he jes' didn' learn nothin'. We seen him tackle the *football*! Doan' he know about necks? Oh, sure, it made yore fellas fumble a li'l, but that ain't real football. *Real* football is runnin' into guys after th' whistle an' then yellin' at 'em an' callin' names. Ain't that so, Mr. Glanville, suh?

Well, anyhow, that ol' 17–10 victory sure made them Buffalo fans happy. But that's jes' your way, Mr. Glanville, suh. Spreadin' happiness all over the league. Ankle deep.

AFC DIVISIONAL PLAYOFF

January 1, 1989, at Orchard Park, N.Y.
Attendance: 79,532

Houston Oilers	0	3	0	7 —	10
Cincinnati Bengals	0	7	7	3 —	17

SCORING:

BUF: Riddick 1 run; Norwood PK (4:25, 2Q)
HOU: Zendejas 35 FG (10:28, 2Q)
BUF: Thomas 11 run; Norwood PK (12:02, 3Q)
BUF: Norwood 27 FG (3:25, 4Q)
HOU: Rozier 1 run; Zendejas PK (9:48, 4Q)

"WELL, IF YOU'RE NOT GOING TO WATCH, YOU *COULD* DO THE DISHES!"

If you were feeling a little logy after three other weekend NFL Division Championships, this was the one to fall asleep during. All you had to do was wait a little longer after Chuck Nelson put the Vikings temporarily in front midway through the first quarter with a forty-seven-yard field goal, and you would have seen the 49ers' Jerry Rice catch a touchdown pass from Joe Montana. Certainly touchdown catches by Rice have become so repetitious in the past few years that this one, a dinky two-yarder, would hardly move your adrenaline off idle. But the fact that Rice continues to catch them would have assured you that all was right with the world. And so, safe and secure, you could nuzzle down into your sofa to sleep off any lingering effects from your celebration of the advent of 1989.

While in slumberland your dreams might have been invaded by the announcer exclaiming that Rice had caught a touchdown pass. No doubt you thought it a trick of the mind. Actually it was a trick of the Rice, who twice more received touchdown passes from Joe Montana. As Mr. Rice seems capable of running into the endzone at San Francisco and catching a pass thrown from the *state* of Montana, these two were no more than generic four- and eleven-yard touchdowns. Their significance lay in building the 49ers' halftime lead to 21–3, and in the astonishing fact that Mr. Rice had never before this game caught a TD pass in postseason play.

Perchance you awakened from your stupor during the second half in time to see the Vikings awaken from theirs to score a touchdown, cutting the lead to 21–9. And, as the third quarter closed, you may have believed for a split second that it might become closer still. For there was Viking CB Reggie Rutland leaping for a hanging Montana pass with only California atmosphere 'twixt him and the goal line. The split second went "*poof!*" as the ubiquitous Mr.

Rice appeared from his phone booth, cut in front of Rutland, and flew down the sideline for a twenty-eight-yard gain to the Minnesota twenty-nine. As the final period began, Roger Craig raced over for another San Francisco touchdown. Several minutes later Craig vented his high spirits by running 80 yards for still another TD in celebration of his earlier one. Some observers found Craig's a more productive ceremony than the Ickey Shuffle. Heroic as Roger's runs were, they merely iced the cake provided by Rice, whose mundane number "80" might be properly replaced by a large red "S."

But if you slept through it all, we'll give you the short version: Minnesota left its kryptonite at home.

NFC DIVISIONAL PLAYOFF

January 1, 1989, at San Francisco, Cal.
Attendance: 61,848

Minnesota Vikings	3	0	6	0 —	9
San Francisco 49ers	7	14	0	13 —	34

SCORING:

MIN: Nelson 47 FG (6:22, 1Q)
SF : J. Rice 2 pass from Montana; Cofer PK (13:11, 1Q)
SF : J. Rice 4 pass from Montana; Cofer PK (0:04, 2Q)
SF : J. Rice 11 pass from Montana; Cofer PK (14:22, 2Q)
MIN: H. Jones 5 pass from Wilson;
      Nelson PK failed (5:18, 3Q)
SF : Craig 4 run; Cofer PK (1:19, 4Q)
SF : Craig 80 run; Cofer PK failed (5:56, 4Q)

"ARE YOU *SURE* IT'S NOT A RERUN, RALPH?"

The final results of the study aren't in yet, but there was a versus virus going around in the playoffs last season. One team caught it when it played another. The symptom was that the newly infected team began to play like the team that had infected it. Although several had noted the Bengals performed more in the manner of the Ground Chuck Seahawks than the Seahawks themselves in the Divisional Playoff, it seemed only a temporary contamination until Cincinnati continued to be groundbound against Buffalo in the Championship Game.

For the second week in a row, QB Boomer Esiason passed little and to little effect, content to hand off. And again Ickey Woods gained over 100 yards and the rest of the Bengals' runners contributed their mite with might. Meanwhile the Cincinnati defense exhibited certain signs that they had caught the disease which had run rampant among the Bills all season—*stoppus drivus quicklea*—better known as the "Shutdown Syndrome." The fever racing through the Bengal defenders led them to abandon their normally mediocre performance and limit the Buffaloes to a meager 181 yards and only 45 on the ground. The curious combination of a Buffalo Shuffle and an Ickey Stampede gave Cincinnati a 14–10 lead by midway through the second half.

It is a testimony to the Bills' iron constitution that their defense kept Buffalo's vital signs intact until then, despite more mundane ills such as a thigh injury that made Bruce Smith just another DE, a lingering arch malady that reduced LB Shane Conlan's effectiveness and playing time, and an ankle injury that put FS Mark Kelso on the sideline for most of the second half. Then Cincinnati cleared its head long enough to revert to its former persona and ran a fake punt for a first down. Moments later Conlan dumped Woods on his ick for an apparent three-yard loss, just like the old Buffalo.

But on the same play that Conlan deposited Woods, Bills' CB Derrick Burroughs attempted oral surgery with his elbow on Cincy WR Tim McGee. The referee prescribed ejection for Burroughs, and the ensuing penalty put the Bengals first-and-goal at the one instead of third-and-eight at the fifteen. When Ickey shuffled over from there, the game was over.

AFC CHAMPIONSHIP GAME

January 8, 1989, at Cincinnati, Ohio
Attendance: 59,747

Buffalo Bills	0	10	0	0 —	10
Cincinnati Bengals	7	7	0	7 —	21

SCORING:

CIN: Woods 1 run; Breech PK (13:09, 1Q)
BUF: Reed 9 pass from Kelly; Norwood PK (1:39, 2Q)
CIN: Brooks 10 pass from Esiason; Breech PK (12:39, 2Q)
BUF: Norwood 39 FG (14:38, 2Q)
CIN: Woods 1 run; Breech PK (0:04, 4Q)

"RALPH, DID THEY NAME THE WHOLE STATE AFTER HIM?"

In Chicago the 49ers' defense played like that of the Vikings, the 49ers' offensive line played like the Bears', and the Bears played like they were still in a fog. But Jerry Rice and Joe Montana played like nobody else in the world. The result was a blowout that wasn't as close as the score.

Chicago's starting quarterback was one Jim McMahon, a hitherto shadowy figure often seen since midseason lurking on the sideline beneath a headband. In the final quarter, after he had passed for a whole 121 yards in twenty-nine tries, McMahon was replaced by Mike Tomczak, who did better in his short span but also neglected to produce a touchdown.

Meanwhile, Montana, hereafter referred to as The Quarterback, completed seventeen of his twenty-eight passes for 288 yards and three touchdowns. Appendixes have been removed with scalpels less sharp.

Montana's most telling pass came late in the first quarter, when he connected with Rice for a sixty-one-yard touchdown. Rice later explained the play's intricacies: "Joe told me he'd throw the ball and I should just go and get it." Though we can't be that technical in our recitation, it appeared that Rice got Bears CB Mike Richardson in single coverage (hereafter known as Sheer Suicide), leaped in front

of him to recover the ball on his Velcro fingertips, performed a *pas de trois* as Richardson was bumped aside by Chicago teammate Vestee Jackson, and sprinted unhindered into the endzone.

In the second quarter Rice took a Montana pass aimed at his shoelaces and repeated his journey into the endzone. A third TD pass to Rice was called back in the third quarter. However, Montana got *his* third on a five-yard lob to TE John Frank. This one completed a thirteen-play, seventy-three-yard drive from the kickoff. It was executed with such unerring skill by Montana that one had the feeling should it ever become necessary to drive a great distance, say, in the last three minutes of a game, Montana would be the ideal man to do it.

Foremost among the San Francisco defensive heroes was SS Jeff Fuller. His name was mentioned so often as he made ten tackles, deflected two passes, and intercepted one that brush sales no doubt rose all over America for the next week.

NFC CHAMPIONSHIP GAME

January 8, 1989, at Chicago, Ill.
Attendance: 64,830

San Francisco 49ers	7	7	7	7 —	28
Chicago Bears	0	3	0	3 —	3

SCORING:

SF : Rice 61 pass from Montana; Cofer PK (11:42 1Q)
SF : Rice 27 pass from montana; Cofer PK (7:35 2Q)
CHI: Butler 25 FG (11:54, 2Q)
SF : Frank 5 pass from Montana; Cofer PK (5:27 3Q)
SF : Rathman 4 run; Cofer PK (8:07 4Q)

"NOW DON'T GET YOUR HOPES UP, RALPH. YOU KNOW WHAT ALWAYS HAPPENS."

When the euphoria wears off in a couple of years, no one will pretend that this was the greatest Super Bowl ever played. Too much of the highlight film will be devoted to the final sixteen minutes to call it the greatest *game*. What it might rank as is the greatest last quarter-plus in Super Bowl history. Up until then, it was an interesting game and that rarest of all Super Bowl achievements—a close game. It should have been more exciting.

The Bengals came in with, supposedly, the NFL's best offense, but QB Boomer Esiason was more out of rhythm than the Ickey Shuffle. The Ick himself ran well in the first half, but Cincinnati seemed unwilling to commit to a consistent running game, and Boomer kept intruding with off-target passes. James Brooks might as well have been home watching the game on TV for all he was used. Perhaps the shocking news of the night before—that RB Stanley Wilson had been suspended for drug use—threw off the Cincinnati timing. Or maybe the Miami riots earlier in the week, when unaccountably some of the locals insisted on putting food, shelter, and civil rights ahead of the Super Bowl, contributed to the Cincy out-of-kilterness. Most likely it was jitters. *Shucks, guys, it's only the most important game you've ever played and one that your whole career might be judged by—to say nothing of the money. But relax.*

San Francisco's offense gained a few more yards than Cincinnati's over the first three quarters but was just as inefficient in getting to the endzone. They had an excuse for a while when OT Steve Wallace went out with a broken ankle on the third play, but that was more than made up for a few minutes later when the Bengals' All-Pro NT Tim Krumrie suffered a double break in his left leg. Only one time did the TV cameras show Krumrie planting his leg, and then, as his momentum brought him around, the upper leg and knee following naturally and from midshin down the lower leg trailing like a wind sock. Once was plenty to start fans retching all over America. This one will definitely not make any of those humorous "follies" films.

Without Krumrie, the Bengals' defense should have collapsed like a souffle in a boiler factory. Give them credit. They gutted it up and held the 49ers to field goals for three quarters, just as the Bengals' offense was holding themselves to the same thing. LB Reggie Williams, the Councilman, earned a lot of votes with his efforts, including a few for MVP.

Of course if you really groove on field goals, you had a ball. And so did San Francisco's Mike Cofer, who kicked one for a forty-one-yard fielder and another for thirty-two yards. And he set a Super Bowl record that may never be broken by missing a nineteen-yarder. To get any closer some day, the ball will have to be snapped from the endzone. It wasn't really Cofer's fault. Randy Cross, the San Francisco center, gave him a snap that would have been perfect if Cofer was left-footed and standing five yards to his right and two yards closer. Cofer also missed a 49er forty-nine-yarder in the second half, but what the hell.

Cincy kicker Jim Breech, who'd had trouble all season hitting for distances that didn't begin with one or two, was fine. He had a thirty-four-yarder to tie the game in the second quarter and a forty-three-yarder to put the Bengals ahead in the third quarter. Even more exciting were the punts by Lee Johnson, who parked three inside the San Fran twenty.

So until about a half minute was left in the third quarter, it was a *great* game for foot fetishists, but only a *close* game for the rest of us. There wasn't even that feeling that you sometimes get that "something" is going to explode. It seemed like we'd just wait around drinking beer and eating popcorn until one or the other got the third field goal. Then they could start the locker room interviews. Bud Bowl I was better.

And then something *did* explode. The 49ers had just tied it at 6–6 with a you-know-what. The kickoff went to Stanford Jennings at the seven. BAR-ROOM! Ninety-three yards. He didn't twist, turn, juke, joke, hop, skip, or jump. He just ex*ploded* straight up the field. And Cincy led 13–6.

It took four plays for San Francisco to tie it up again. Hardly enough time for the Bengals on the sideline to "Hi, Mom" or raise their index fingers. It was almost like the 49ers said, "Oh, if you're gonna be that way about it, take this!" They started at the fifteen. Joe Montana passed thirty-one yards to Jerry Rice. *Yes, Virginia, there is a Jerry Rice. He's just come out to play.* At the San Fran forty-six, Montana threw to Craig, who took it to the Cincy fourteen. Joe's next pass was perfect—for Bengals' CB Lewis Billups—at the goal line. However, Billups had taken a vow of butchery and the interception was incomplete. On the next play, Montana threw where Rice was: 13–13.

The 49ers had moved down the field with such ridiculous ease you had to figure the Bengals needed a pair of touchdowns on their next possession to stay in the game. They didn't get even one, and when San Francisco got the ball at its eighteen, well, eighty-two yards looked like maybe three plays. Two giant steps and a Mother-may-I? *Don't go to the refrigerator NOW, Ralph. You'll miss the touchdown.* On the first play Montana passed to Rice for forty-four yards. Then—wonder of wonders—the 49ers stalled at the thirty-two and Cofer got to miss from the thirty-nine.

Enthused by the turn of events, Cincinnati limped down the field to the San Francisco twenty-two. Then, shocked by their own effrontery, they had Breech kick a forty-yard field goal to make it 16–13. There were three minutes and twenty seconds left.

Rodgers brought the kickoff out to the fifteen, but San Francisco was holding and the penalty put the ball at the eight. *Here we go.* Montana passed over the middle to Craig for eight, then picked up a first down at the twenty-three on a toss to John Frank. Joe flipped one to the right to Rice for seven. Craig dived into the middle for one. And it was time for the two-minute warning.

Now consider for a moment the plight of the sponsors who'd paid $675,000 to get their thirty-second message into that spot. Do you think anybody really watched? Or do you think that just about everyone had his mind on what Montana would do to pick up the two yards he needed for a first down? Well, maybe not *everybody.* We can't be certain about the Bengals.

Joe gave the ball to Craig, who went four yards up the middle. Would Krumrie have stopped it? Would San Francisco have called that play if Krumrie was in there? What is the meaning of life?

Joe passed seventeen yards to Rice for another first down. Then thirteen to Craig to put the 49ers at the Cincy thirty-five. At this point, most S.F. fans were still hoping their guys could get close enough for a tying field goal. *Oh, ye of little faith!* The momentum—the tension—that had been absent all day was crackling in the 49ers' huddle like the last scene of a Frankenstein movie. You couldn't have kept them from a touchdown with the Third Armored Division.

Montana passed incomplete to Rice. *That's it, Joe, wind us tighter.* He threw to Craig, but a lineman was downfield and the play was called back. *Like the juggler who drops a plate to show the audience how hard his trick is. Now!* Twenty-seven yards to Rice over the middle. *Get him!* Too late; he's at the eighteen. The clock is moving. San Fran lines up and Montana—*holy smoke! he didn't waste a pass!*—throws over the middle to Craig at the ten. Time out, San Francisco. *"Sure," said the headsman, "I'll get on with the execution in a bit. But first I shall pause while we all consider the brevity of our time here."*

San Francisco is ten yards from its third Super Bowl win. Cincinnati is thirty-four seconds from its first. Time and space. And momentum.

Montana throws into the center of the endzone, where John Taylor grabs, bounces five feet in the air, with the ball held straight up. And all of a sudden you know what the artist was thinking of when he designed the Super Bowl Trophy.

The 1988 season is over.

SUPER BOWL XXIII

January 22, 1989, at Miami, Fla.
Attendance: 75,179

Cincinnati Bengals	0	3	10	3	— 16
San Francisco 49ers	3	0	3	14	— 20

SCORING:

SF : Cofer 41 FG (11:46, 1Q)
CIN: Breech 34 FG (13:45, 2Q)
CIN: Breech 43 FG (9:21, 3Q)
SF : Cofer 32 FG (14:10, 3Q)
CIN: Jennings 93 kickoff return; Breech PK (14:26, 3Q)
SF : Rice 14 pass from Montana; Cofer PK (0:57, 4Q)
CIN: Breech 40 FG (11:40, 4Q)
SF : Taylor 10 pass from Montana; Cofer PK (14:26, 4Q)

TEAM STATISTICS

	CIN	SF
First Downs/Rush-Pass-Penalty	13/7-6-0	23/6-16-1
Average Gain-1st Down	4.1	8.5
1st Down Passes-Avg. Gain	10-5.9	19-11.8
1st Down Rushes-Avg. Gain	14-2.9	12-3.3
3rd Down Efficiency	4-13	4-13
4th Down Efficiency	0-1	0-0
Total Plays-Net Yards-Avg.Gain	64-229-3.6	67-454-6.8
Rushes-Yards-Avg. Gain	28-106-3.8	28-111-4.0
Pass Comp.-Att.-Avg. Gain-Int.	11-25-123-1	23-36-343-0
Net Yards Gain per Pass	3.4	8.8
Sacked-Yards Lost	5-21	3-14
Punt Returns-Yards	2-5	3-56
Kickoff Returns-Yards	3-132	5-77
Fumbles-Lost	1-0	4-1
Penalties-Yards	7-65	4-32
Punts-Average Yards	5-44.6	4-37.0
Time of Possession	32:43	27:17

INDIVIDUAL STATISTICS

CINCINNATI						SAN FRANCISCO					
RUSHING	ATT	YDS	AVG	LG	TD	RUSHING	ATT	YDS	AVG	LG	TD
Woods	20	79	4.0	10	0	Craig	17	74	4.4	16	0
Brooks	6	24	4.0	11	0	Rathman	5	23	4.6	11	0
Jennings	1	3	3.0	3	0	Montana	5	9	1.8	11	0
Esiason	1	0	0.0	0	0	Rice	1	5	5.0	5	0
RECEIVING	NO	YDS	AVG	LG	TD	RECEIVING	NO	YDS	AVG	LG	TD
Brown	4	44	11.0	17	0	Rice	11	215	19.5	44	1
Collinsworth	3	40	13.3	23	0	Craig	8	101	12.6	40	0

(Continued)

INDIVIDUAL STATISTICS

CINCINNATI						SAN FRANCISCO					
McGee	2	23	11.5	18	0	Frank	2	15	7.5	8	0
Brooks	1	20	20.0	20	0	Rathman	1	16	16.0	16	0
Hillary	1	17	17.0	17	0	Taylor	1	10	10.0	10	1

PASSING	AT	CO	YDS	PCT.	TD	IN	PASSING	AT	CO	YDS	PCT	TD	IN
Esiason	25	11	144	44.0	0	1	Montana	36	23	357	63.9	2	0

INTERCEPTIONS	NO	YDS	LG	TD
Romanowski	1	0	0	0

PUNTING	NO	YDS	AVG	LG	In 20	PUNTING	NO	YDS	AVG	LG	In 20
Johnson	5	223	44.6	63	3	Helton	4	148	37.0	55	2

PUNT RET.	NO	FC	YDS	LG	TD	PUNT RET.	NO	FC	YDS	LG	TD
Horton	1	0	5	5	0	Taylor	3	1	56	45	0
Hillary	1	0	0	0	0						

KO RETURNS	NO	YDS	AVG	LG	TD	KO RETURNS	NO	YDS	AVG	LG	TD
Jennings	2	117	58.5	93	1	Rogers	3	53	17.7	22	0
Brooks	1	15	15.0	15	0	Taylor	1	13	13.0	13	0
						Sydney	1	11	11.0	11	0

THE DRAFT

The advance word on the draft was that it was weak after the first half dozen or so picks, but that will only be certified several years from now, when we can look back at the careers of those drafted and know the sure-Hall-of-Famers who fell on their faces and the unknowns who turned themselves into household words.

As usual, the late rounds produced several players whom virtually no one except their mothers and some NFL scout had heard of. Mel Kiper, Jr. and Joel Buchsbaum, two lay experts on drafting, had rated hundreds of college players for *The Sporting News* and *Pro Football Weekly*, and had also authored guides to the draft, but there were still plenty of players picked whom the gurus had missed. Pittsburgh's final pick was a six-time NCAA wrestling champ who never played college football.

Kiper was part of the ESPN broadcasting team. The high point of the telecast for us was the look on his face with each succeeding pick by the Jets. At one point, he cracked, "It's obvious to me the Jets don't know what a draft's all about."

That nettled Jets' personnel chief Mike Hickey so much that he carped about "guys ... on TV working out of their basements." It will be interesting to check the Jets' roster in about five years to see whose face is caked with egg, Kiper's or Hickey's.

Here's how we rate the picks. Whenever possible, we've included the player's height, weight, and time in the 40 based on several sources. The three columns on the right are for comparison purposes:

GRADE: National Football Scouting combined December ratings, as reported in *USA Today* (leaders at each position only).

- 9.0, sure starter.
- 8.0, should start first year.
- 7.0, should start eventually.
- 6.0, backup but will make team.
- 5.0, can make club and contribute.
- 4.0, prospect worth drafting.

MK/RD: Selection round projected by Mel Kiper, Jr. in *The Sporting News*.

JB/RK: Ranking among others at same position by Joel Buchsbaum in *Pro Football Weekly*. Note: the positions listed for the players are those for which Buchsbaum ranked them, not necessarily the position for which they were drafted.

ATLANTA FALCONS

Main Needs: WR, TE, DB, DL

The flamboyant Sanders was rated by many as the best pure athlete in the draft. One of the raters was himself. Baseball's Yankees also think highly of him, creating a possible Bo Jackson situation. But if he plays, he should be an All-Pro within three years. He can also return kicks. Collins was ranked behind several other WRs, but he'll be used as an H-back, for which he's highly suited. Sadowski has a good shot at TE. Norwood may someday replace Kenn.

Grade B: Sanders alone makes it a good draft, but it could have been better.

RND	NO.	PLAYER	SCHOOL	POS	HGT	WGT	40-YD TIME	GRADE	MK RD	JB RK
1	5	Deion Sanders	Florida St.	CB	5-11	188	4.29	8.00	1	1
1	27	Shawn Collins (from Cincinnati)	N. Arizona	WR	6-1	200	4.52	6.20	1-2	9
2	—	to Cincinnati								
2	38	Ralph Norwood (Raiders pick from Washington)	LSU	OT	6-6	273	5.15	6.40	1-2	3
3	62	Keith Jones	Illinois	RB	6-1	205	4.69	5.61	—	7
4	—	to Cincinnati								
5	—	to Raiders, then to Dallas								
6	145	Troy Sadowski	Georgia	TE	6-4	242	4.90	5.60	4-5	6
7	172	Undra Johnson	W. Virginia	RB	5-9	199	4.38	5.31	5-6	18
8	202	Paul Singer	W. Illinois	QB	—	—	—	—	—	30
9	229	Chris Dunn	Cal. Poly-SLO	LB	—	—	—	—	—	—
10	—	to Cincinnati								
11	286	Greg Paterra	Slippery Rock	RB	6-1	200	4.55	—	—	19
12	313	Tony Bowick	Tenn.-Chatt.	NT	—	—	—	—	—	—

BUFFALO BILLS

Main Needs: DB, WR, OL

No picks until the third round put the Bills under the gun. Beebe has heart-stopping speed but little experience; Kolesar is erratic and injury-prone. Late picks of defensive backs are likely to help because at least one should work out.

Grade C+. Higher if Beebe surprises.

RND	NO.	PLAYER	SCHOOL	POS	HGT	WGT	40-YD TIME	GRADE	MK RD	JB RK
1	—	to Rams								
2	—	to Rams								
3	82	Don Beebe	Chadron St.	WR	5-10	175	—	—	—	16
4	109	John Kolesar	Michigan	WR	5-11	185	4.5	3-4	26	
5	137	Michael Andrews	Alcorn St.	CB	5-11	180	4.56	—	—	23
6	164	Sean Doctor	Marshall	FB	6-0	237	4.8	—	—	43
7	173	Brian Jordan (from Tampa Bay)	Richmond	DB	5-11	202	4.70	6.11	3-4	10
7	193	Chris Hale	USC	CB	5-7	160	4.55	—	6	19
8	—	to Kansas City								
9	249	Pat Rabold	Wyoming	DT	6-2	264	5.01	5.12	—	14
10	276	Carlo Cheattom	Auburn	DB	5-11	189	4.56	6.00	—	12
11	305	Richard Harvey	Tulane	LB	6-1	225	4.7	—	—	42
12	332	Derrell Marshall	USC	OT	—	—	—	—	—	27

CHICAGO BEARS

Main Needs: DT, CB, LB, OT

With twenty players picked, there should be a scramble for special teams slots. Woolford will start right away. He was the second-highest-ranked cornerback. Armstrong may be a Pro Bowl tackle someday, but he'll either play at end or will back up Hampton this season. Moreover, there's a lot of Bear-type talent (i.e. hard-nosed overachievers) among the rest.

Grade A.

RND	NO.	PLAYER	SCHOOL	POS	HGT	WGT	40-YD TIME	GRADE	MK RD	JB RK
1	11	Donnell Woolford (from Raiders)	Clemson	CB	5-9	189	4.51	7.00	1	2
1	12	Trace Armstrong (from Washington)	Florida	DE	6-4	263	4.88	5.90	1	2
1	—	to Miami								
2	36	John Roper (from Miami)	Texas A&M	ILB	6-1	228	4.60	7.40	2	8
2	54	Dave Zawatson	California	G-T	6-4	282	5.2	—	—	7
3	65	Jerry Fontenot (from Miami)	Texas A&M	C	6-3	259	5.00	6.40	5-6	2
3	—	to Philadelphia								
4	95	Markus Paul (from Raiders)	Syracuse	S	6-2	200	4.61	5.61	4-5	14
4	—	to Green Bay								
5	130	Mark Green (from Philadelphia)	Notre Dame	RB	5-11	185	4.5	—	3-4	17
5	136	Greg Gilbert	Alabama	LB	6-1	220	4.7	—	6	61

RND	NO.	PLAYER	SCHOOL	POS	HGT	WGT	40-YD TIME	GRADE	MK RD	JB RK
(Continued)										
6	—	to Raiders, then New England								
7	189	Richard Brothers (from Philadelphia)	Arkansas	S	5-11	200	4.52	—	—	23
7	192	Brent Snyder	Utah St.	QB	6-3	225	4.91	5.40	—	11
8	216	Tony Woods (from Philadelphia)	Oklahoma	DT	6-4	290	5.1	—	—	13
8	221	Chris Dyko	Washington St.	OT	6-6	295	5.45	—	6	12
9	243	LaSalle Harper (from Philadelphia)	Arkansas	LB	6-0	240	4.9	—	—	21
9	248	Byron Sanders	Northwestern	RB	5-8	188	4.65	—	5-6	27
10	270	Todd Millikin (from Philadelphia)	Nebraska	TE	6-2	238	4.80	5.40	—	8
10	277	John Simpson	Baylor	WR					—	70
11	297	Joe Nelms (from Philadelphia)	California	DT	6-4	265	5.0	—	—	9
11	304	George Streeter	Notre Dame	S	—	—	—	—	—	64
12	330	Freddy Weygand (from Philadelphia)	Auburn	WR	6-0	195	4.7	—	—	58
12	333	Anthony Phillips	Oklahoma	OG	6-1	277	5.1	—	—	15

CINCINNATI BENGALS

Main Needs: LB, RB, DB, OL

Cincinnati may have ensured the quality of their offensive line with the huge Childress and Woods, but they waited until the fourth round to do anything about the defense, and that may have been too long. Ball is scheduled to be the short-yardage man to replace Stanley Wilson.

Grade C−.

RND	NO.	PLAYER	SCHOOL	POS	HGT	WGT	40-YD TIME	GRADE	MK RD	JB RK
1	—	to Atlanta								
2	35	Eric Ball (from Atlanta)	UCLA	RB	6-1	218	4.56	—	3-4	5
2	55	Fred Childress	Arkansas	OG	6-3	328	5.25	5.60	5-6	6
3	83	Erik Wilhelm	Oregon St.	QB	6-2	215	5.20	5.00	6	7
4	89	Kerry Owens (from Atlanta)	Arkansas	LB	6-2	235	4.9	—	3-4	18
4	111	Rob Woods	Arizona	OT	6-5	275	5.2	—	—	17
5	138	Natu Tuatagaloa	California	DT	6-3	260	4.96	—	4-5	5
6	166	Craig Taylor	W. Virginia	FB	5-11	224	4.63	5.11	4-5	6
7	194	Kendal Smith	Utah St.	WR	5-9	175	4.57	—	—	25
8	222	Chris Chenault	Kentucky	LB	6-1	245	4.7	—	—	36
9	250	Richard Stephens	Tulsa	OT	6-6	290	5.0	—	—	22
10	256	Cornell Holloway (from Atlanta)	Pittsburgh	DB	5-9	175	4.55	—	—	34
10	278	Robert Jean	New Hampshire	QB	6-1	210	4.85	—	—	20
11	306	Dana Wells	Arizona	DT	6-0	269	5.09	4.81	—	19
12	334	Scott Jones	Washington	OL	6-4	265	4.95	—	—	33

CLEVELAND BROWNS

Main Needs: DL, OL, TE, WR

No guts, no glory! Cleveland drafted for the speed to take advantage of Bernie Kosar's arm. Eric Metcalf, the son of former Cards' star Terry, may be a sensational all-purpose back. Tillman is to replace Ozzie Newsome. Getting Stewart on the fourth round may have been a break. Kiper thought this was the best draft among all the teams.

Grade B+. But risky. The Browns are assuming a lot on defense.

RND	NO.	PLAYER	SCHOOL	POS	HGT	WGT	40-YD TIME	GRADE	MK RD	JB RK
1	13	Eric Metcalf (from Denver)	Texas	RB	5-9	177	4.40	7.50	1	2
1	—	to Denver								
2	31	Lawyer Tillman (from Green Bay)	Auburn	WR	6-4	222	4.60	6.11	1	4
2	—	to Denver								
3	—	to Green Bay								
4	107	Andrew Stewart	Cincinnati	DE	6-4	260	5.00	6.00	2	7
5	114	Kyle Kramer (from Green Bay)	Bowling Green	S	6-2	175	4.55	—	5	15
5	116	Vernon Jones (from Kansas City)	Maryland	WR	6-1	195	4.54	—	—	29
5	—	to Denver								
6	160	Gary Wilkerson	Penn State	LB	—	—	—	—	—	—
7	187	Mike Graybill	Boston U.	OT	6-6	255	5.0	—	—	19
8	214	Rick Aeilts	S.E. Mo. St.	TE	—	—	—	—	—	24
9	—	to Denver								
10	274	John Buddenberg	Akron	OT	—	—	—	—	—	—
11	301	Dan Plocki	Maryland	PK	5-7	176	4.95	5.00	9-12	—
12	328	Marlon Brown	Memphis St.	LB	6-2	222	4.6	—	4-5	22

DALLAS COWBOYS

Main Needs: QB, LB, DB, FB, OL

Aikman is supposed to be the franchise, but Johnston and Stepnoski are good picks too. Tolbert may be switched to DE to eventually replace Too Tall. If the first three are as good as expected and Weston comes through, this could be a great draft.

Grade A−. But what might they have gotten by trading the Number One?

RND	NO.	PLAYER	SCHOOL	POS	HGT	WGT	40-YD TIME	GRADE	MK RD	JB RK
1	1	Troy Aikman	UCLA	QB	6-2	218	4.72	7.60	1	1
2	29	(Drafted Steve Wisniewski, then traded his rights to Raiders)								
2	39	Daryl Johnston (Raiders pick from Washington)	Syracuse	FB	6-1	237	4.72	5.30	1-2	2
3	57	Mark Stepnoski	Pittsburgh	OG	6-2	269	4.88	5.52	3	4
3	68	Rhondy Weston (from Raiders)	Florida	DT	6-4	274	4.96	5.71	1-2	3
4	85	Tony Tolbert	UTEP	LB	6-6	230	4.85	—	—	17
5	113	Keith Jennings	Clemson	TE	6-3	235	4.8	—	6	12
5	119	Willis Crockett (Raiders pick from Atlanta)	Georgia Tech	LB	6-2	225	4.8	—	—	54
5	125	Jeff Roth (from Denver)	Florida	DT	6-3	265	4.9	—	—	12
6	—	to Raiders								
7	168	Kevin Peterson	Northwestern	LB	—	—	—	—	—	—
8	196	Charvez Foger	Nevada-Reno	FB	5-10	205	4.65	5.33	—	11

(Continued)

RND	NO.	PLAYER	SCHOOL	POS	HGT	WGT	40-YD TIME	GRADE	MK RD	JB RK
9	224	Tim Jackson	Nebraska	S	5-11	190	4.65	—	—	42
10	252	Rod Carter	Miami (FL)	LB	6-1	230	4.85	—	—	19
11	280	Randy Shannon	Miami (FL)	LB	—	—	—	—	—	—
12	308	Scott Ankrom	TCU	RB	6-0	187	4.63	5.62	—	20

DENVER BRONCOS

Main Needs: DL, DB, LB, OL, RB

The Broncos got some up-front size they desperately need, but the quality isn't certain yet. Widell should start. Powers could be terrific or disappointing, depending on how much he wants it. Atwater will start out playing behind oft-injured incumbent Dennis Smith.

Grade C+ But the grade could go up if Powers or Hamilton performs beyond expectations.

RND	NO.	PLAYER	SCHOOL	POS	HGT	WGT	40-YD TIME	GRADE	MK RD	JB RK
1	—	to Cleveland								
1	20	Steve Atwater (from Cleveland)	Arkansas	S	6-3	212	4.60	6.10	1	3
2	41	Doug Widell	Boston Coll.	OG	6-4	285	5.2	—	2-3	3
2	47	Warren Powers (from Cleveland)	Maryland	DT	6-6	280	5.0	—	2-3	4
3	69	Darrell Hamilton	N. Carolina	OT	6-5	292	5.2	—	3-4	7
4	97	Rich McCullough	Clemson	DE	6-5	265	5.12	—	—	14
5	—	to Dallas								
5	134	Dar. Carrington (from Cleveland)	N. Arizona	CB	6-1	190	4.6	—	—	12
6	152	Anthony Stafford	Oklahoma	RB	5-7	179	4.43	5.34	4-5	16
7	180	Melvin Bratton	Miami (FL)	RB	6-0	225	—	—	—	NR
8	208	Paul Green	USC	TE	6-2	236	4.88	—	—	10
9	236	Monte Smith	N. Dakota	G	6-4	265	5.2	—	—	33
9	241	Wayne Williams (from Cleveland)	Florida	RB	5-9	190	4.55	—	—	24
10	264	Anthony Butts	Mississippi St.	DT	—	—	—	—	—	26
11	292	Richard Shelton	Liberty	DB	5-10	184	4.53	—	—	20
12	320	John Jarvis	Howard	WR	—	—	—	—	—	—

DETROIT LIONS

Main Needs: RB, DE, CB, WR

Anything would have helped, but Sanders should help a lot. Ford too. They got no certain pass rusher, however. Peete is an intriguing pick in that he might be better suited to the Lions' new offense than any of the quarterback incumbents.

Grade C+. The Lions got about what you'd expect for their draft position, maybe a little less.

RND	NO.	PLAYER	SCHOOL	POS	HGT	WGT	40-YD TIME	GRADE	MK RD	JB RK
1	3	Barry Sanders	Oklahoma St.	RB	5-8	193	4.39	—	1	NR
2	30	John Ford	Virginia	WR	6-1	200	4.55	6.80	2	5
3	59	Mike Utley	Washington St.	OT	6-6	286	5.33	6.31	3	5
4	86	Ray Crockett	Baylor	CB	5-9	180	4.60	6.00	—	9
5	115	Lawrence Pete	Nebraska	DT	6-1	180	5.10	4.80	—	23
6	141	Rodney Peete	USC	QB	6-0	197	4.80	6.10	1-2	2
7	170	Jerry Woods	N. Michigan	DB	5-9	182	4.6	—	—	21
8	197	Chris Parker	W. Virginia	DT	—	—	—	—	6	36
9	226	Derek MacCready	Ohio St.	DE	—	—	—	—	—	23
10	253	Jason Phillips	Houston	WR	5-8	170	4.55	—	—	35
11	282	Keith Karpinski	Penn St.	LB	6-3	220	4.7	—	—	52
12	309	James Cribbs	Memphis St.	DL	—	—	—	—	—	—

GREEN BAY PACKERS

Main Needs: QB, DE, DB, PK

Offensive tackle wasn't a main need, but Mandarich was too good to pass up. Brock will help the pass rush. Affholter isn't a burner, but he works hard. Query has rocket speed but will need time to develop. So will Dilweg, who is also a punter. Jacke will solve a glaring need if he can make it as a placekicker.

Grade A.

RND	NO.	PLAYER	SCHOOL	POS	HGT	WGT	40-YD TIME	GRADE	MK RD	JB RK
1	2	Tony Mandarich	Michigan	OT	6-5	305	4.80	8.50	1	1
2	—	to Cleveland								
3	58	Matt Brock	Oregon	DE	6-4	267	4.96	5.80	1-2	
3	74	Anthony Dilweg (from Cleveland)	Duke	QB	6-3	195	4.85	5.51	3-4	3
4	110	Erik Affholter (Drafted by Washington; rights traded to Green Bay)	USC	WR	5-11	180	4.65	—	4-5	14
5	—	to Cleveland								
5	123	Jeff Query (from Washington)	Millikin	WR	5-11	165	4.4	—	—	6
5	127	Vince Workman (New England pick from Cleveland)	Ohio State	RB	5-10	195	4.61	5.32	—	21
6	142	Chris Jacke	Texas-El Paso	PK	5-10	180	—	—	9-12	1
7	169	Mark Hall	S.W. Louisiana	DT	6-4	285	5.15	—	6	31
8	198	Thomas King	S.W. Louisiana	S	6-0	185	4.55	—	—	25
8	206	Brian Shulman (from Washington)	Auburn	P	5-9	185	—	—	—	4
9	225	Scott Kirby	Arizona St.	OT	6-5	290	5.4	—	—	37
10	254	Ben Jessie	S.W. Texas St.	S	—	—	—	—	—	53
11	281	Cedr. Stallworth	Georgia Tech	CB	5-10	180	4.65	—	—	49
12	310	Stan Shiver	Florida St.	S	6-2	210	4.7	—	—	35

HOUSTON OILERS

Main Needs: DB, TE, LB, OL

More than anything, the Oilers had to improve their depth. They seem to have grabbed a smorgasbord. Williams is insurance for Steinkuhler's knees. Kozak helps a so-so

linebacking situation, although he probably won't start. McDowell may move in at safety.

Grade C+. Not outstanding, but it filled the special teams.

RND	NO.	PLAYER	SCHOOL	POS	HGT	WGT	40-YD TIME	GRADE	MK RD	JB RK
1	23	David Williams	Florida	OT	6-4	295	5.14	6.50	1-2	4
2	50	Scott Kozak	Oregon	OLB	6-2	221	4.73	5.90	2	5
3	77	Bubba McDowell	Miami (FL)	DB	6-0	195	4.58	—	2	2
4	104	Rod Harris	Texas A&M	WR	5-10	180	4.60	5.90	5-6	10
5	131	Glenn Montgomery	Houston	DT	6-0	270	4.88	—	—	10
6	157	Bo Orlando	W. Virginia	S	5-9	180	4.7	—	—	59
7	190	Tracy Rogers	Fresno St.	LB	6-1	230	4.88	—	—	10
8	217	Alvoid Mays	W. Virginia	CB	5-10	167	4.55	—	—	42
9	244	Bob Mrosko	Penn St.	TE	6-4	260	5.0	—	—	—
10	271	Tracy Johnson	Clemson	FB	5-11	230	4.85	—	6	9
11	298	Brian Smidler	W. Virginia	OT	6-3	298	5.35	—	—	25
12	325	Chuck Hartlieb	Iowa	QB	6-0	206	4.75	5.02	6-7	12

INDIANAPOLIS COLTS

Main Needs: NT, DB, WR

Rison was a steal as the twenty-second pick. He'll be a boon to Chandler and give the Colts a real bomb threat. Benson is the candidate for NT and considered a "maybe." Tomberlin is huge, but can he play?

Grade B–.

RND	NO.	PLAYER	SCHOOL	POS	HGT	WGT	40-YD TIME	GRADE	MK RD	JB RK
1	—	to Seattle								
1	22	Andre Rison (from Philadelphia)	Michigan St.	WR	5-10	185	4.50	7.30	1	1
2	—	to Rams								
3	72	Mitchell Benson	TCU	DT	6-3	294	5.20	6.10	1-2	2
4	99	Pat Tomberlin	Florida St.	OT	6-3	310	5.41	5.80	6	23
5	—	to Washington								
6	155	Quintus McDonald	Penn St.	LB	6-3	240	4.8	—	6	28
7	182	Ivy Joe Hunter	Kentucky	RB	6-0	216	4.5	—	—	9
7	185	Chas. Washington (from Giants)	Cameron	S	—	—	—	—	—	48
8	212	Kurt Larson	Michigan St.	LB	6-3	226	4.89	5.80	—	62
9	239	William Mackall	Tenn.-Martin	WR	—	—	—	—	—	63
10	266	Jim Thompson	Auburn	OT	6-6	270	5.05	—	4-5	10
11	296	Wayne Johnson	Georgia	QB	—	—	—	—	—	—
12	314	William DuBose (from Tampa Bay)	S. Carolina St.	FB	5-11	220	4.65	—	—	18
12	323	Steve Taylor	Nebraska	QB	5-11	205	4.6	—	—	23

KANSAS CITY CHIEFS

Main Needs: LB, TE, DL

Thomas should be an impact player. Sancho may also help a position that was hurting. And the Chiefs traded for

Cleveland ILB Mike Junkin, whom Schottenheimer was criticized for drafting. Elkins and Worthen are for the future.

Grade A –.

RND	NO.	PLAYER	SCHOOL	POS	HGT	WGT	40-YD TIME	GRADE	MK RD	JB RK
1	4	Derrick Thomas	Alabama	OLB	6-2	227	4.56	7.70	1	1
2	32	Mike Elkins	Wake Forest	QB	6-2	221	4.99	6.50	2-3	4
3	60	Naz Worthen	N.C. State	WR	5-8	172	4.68	5.70	2	11
4	88	Stanley Petry	TCU	CB	5-11	165	—	—	—	13
5	—	to Cleveland								
6	143	Robb Thomas	Oregon St.	WR	5-10	176	4.55	—	—	13
7	171	Ron Sancho	LSU	LB	6-1	223	4.85	5.50	—	25
8	199	Bryan Tobey	Grambling	RB	6-0	240	4.8	—	—	26
8	220	Todd McNair (from Buffalo)	Temple	RB	6-0	190	4.6	—	—	12
9	227	Jack Phillips	Alcorn St.	S	6-0	200	4.68	—	—	49
10	255	Rob McGovern	Holy Cross	LB	—	—	—	—	—	—
11	283	Marcus Turner	UCLA	S	6-0	190	4.55	—	4-5	9
12	311	Bill Jones	S.W. Texas St.	RB	6-1	215	4.6	—	—	NR

LOS ANGELES RAIDERS

Main Needs: OL, LB, DB

Obviously, the Raiders plan to build in ways other than the draft. Wisniewski should help now, but no one else looks like he'll make any impact this year—or maybe ever.

Grade D.

RND	NO.	PLAYER	SCHOOL	POS	HGT	WGT	40-YD TIME	GRADE	MK RD	JB RK
1	—	to Chicago								
2	29	Steve Wisniewski (Dallas drafted Wisniewski, then traded his rights.)	Penn St.	OG	6-3	266	4.91	5.53	1-2	2
2	—	to Dallas								
2	—	to Washington, then to Atlanta								
2	—	Washington pick to Dallas								
3	—	to Dallas								
4	—	to Chicago								
5	—	Atlanta pick to Dallas								
5	—	to San Francisco								
6	140	Jeff Francis (from Dallas)	Tennessee	QB	6-3	206	4.86	5.70	6-7	8
6	—	to Jets								
6	156	Doug Lloyd (from New England)	N. Dakota St.	FB	6-0	217	4.48	5.23	—	4
7	—	to New England								
8	205	Derrick Gainer	Florida A & M	RB	—	—	—	—	—	—
9	235	Gary Gooden	Indiana	DB	—	—	—	—	—	—
10	262	Charles Jackson	Jackson St.	DT	—	—	—	—	—	21
11	—	to San Francisco								
12	—	to San Francisco								

LOS ANGELES RAMS

Main Needs: DL, LB, OL

Except for Gary, the Rams went for defense. Hawkins, Stams, and Smith will probably never get to a Pro Bowl, but they should be useful players. Henley can return kicks, although he may not make it at cornerback. Will Gary be used as a blocker, or is he the big runner the Rams have wanted since Dickerson was traded?

Grade B +.

RND	NO.	PLAYER	SCHOOL	POS	HGT	WGT	40-YD TIME	GRADE	MK RD	JB RK
1	21	Bill Hawkins	Miami (FL)	DE	6-5	260	4.82	6.40	1	4
1	26	Cleveland Gary (from Buffalo)	Miami (FL)	FB	5-11	231	4.82	5.20	1	1
2	45	Frank Stams (from Indianapolis)	Notre Dame	OLB	6-3	238	4.73	—	6	6
2	48	Brian Smith	Auburn	DE	6-6	245	4.7	—	1-2	9
2	53	Darryl Henley (from Buffalo)	UCLA	CB	5-8	160	4.55	—	3	14
3	75	Kevin Robbins	Michigan St.	OT	6-4	293	5.39	5.90	—	8
4	102	Jeff Carlson	Weber St.	QB	6-3	210	4.95	5.50	—	16
5	135	Alfred Jackson	San Diego St.	WR	5-11	175	4.55	—	—	19
6	148	Thom Kaumeyer (from San Diego)	Oregon	S	5-11	185	4.65	—	6	22
6	161	Mark Messner	Michigan	DT	6-2	256	5.2	—	—	7
7	188	George Bethune	Alabama	LB	—	—	—	—	—	69
8	215	Warren Wheat	BYU	OT	6-4	285	5.2	—	—	29
9	242	Vernon Kirk	Pittsburgh	TE	—	—	—	—	—	—
10	269	Mike Williams	Northeastern	WR	5-11	176	4.55	—	—	69
11	—	to Tampa Bay								
12	—	to Tampa Bay								

MIAMI DOLPHINS

Main Needs: DB, LB, DL, OL, RB

Smith was kind of a shock, but he has the potential to be great. Oliver and maybe Holmes will start in the Dolphins' secondary, where the "condemned" sign was posted. Uhlenhake is the hoped-for replacement for Stephenson. Anything would have helped, and the Dolphins got a lot, but they still need tons.

Grade A –. Unless Smith flops.

RND	NO.	PLAYER	SCHOOL	POS	HGT	WGT	40-YD TIME	GRADE	MK RD	JB RK
1	9	Sammie Smith	Florida St.	RB	6-1	222	4.44	—	1	4
1	25	Louis Oliver (from Chicago)	Florida	S	6-2	225	4.35	6.80	1	1
2	—	to Chicago								
3	—	to Chicago								
4	92	David Holmes	Syracuse	S	6-1	195	4.6	—	3-4	8
5	121	Jeff Uhlenhake	Ohio St.	C	6-3	275	4.95	6.50	3-4	4
6	147	Wes Pritchett	Notre Dame	LB	6-4	245	5.0	—	—	16
7	176	Jim Zdelar	Youngstown St.	OT	6-4	290	5.22	—	—	18
8	203	Pete Stoyanovich	Indiana	PK	5-10	178	4.89	5.00	3-4	3
9	232	Dana Batiste	Texas A & M	LB	6-0	230	4.92	—	—	39
10	259	Deval Glover	Syracuse	WR	5-11	184	4.6	—	—	39
10	275	Greg Ross (from Minnesota)	Memphis St.	DE	6-2	270	4.9	—	—	19
11	288	Bert Weidner	Kent St.	DE	—	—	—	—	—	28
12	315	J.B. Brown	Maryland	S	6-0	190	4.52	—	—	13

MINNESOTA VIKINGS

Main Needs: LB, RB, G

Merriweather (in a trade from Pittsburgh) makes this draft, but Braxton can also help. Hunter and Mickel should improve the offensive line. No blue-chip runner, but you can't get egg in your beer.

Grade B+.

RND	NO.	PLAYER	SCHOOL	POS	HGT	WGT	40-YD TIME	GRADE	MK RD	JB RK
1	—	to Pittsburgh								
2	52	David Braxton	Wake Forest	OLB	6-1	227	4.50	5.91	3	11
3	80	John Hunter	BYU	OT	6-7	290	5.4	—	—	13
4	108	Darrl Ingram	California	TE	6-3	230	4.73	5.80	6	9
5	136	exercised in 1988 supplemental draft								
6	163	Jeff Mickel	E. Washington	OL	6-5	285	5.0	—	—	15
7	191	Benji Roland	Auburn	DT	6-2	270	5.00	5.90	5-6	18
8	219	Alex Stewart	Cal. St.-Fuller	DE	6-3	260	4.68	6.20	2-3	7
9	—	to New England								
10	—	to Miami								
11	303	Brad Baxter	Alabama St.	FB	6-1	235	4.8	—	—	8
12	331	Shawn Woodson	James Madison	LB	6-2	218	4.7	—	—	33
12	335	Everett Ross (San Francisco pick from Raiders)	Ohio St.	WR	5-10	184	4.61	5.61	—	22

NEW ENGLAND PATRIOTS

Main Needs: TE, WR, DE, PK

Dykes will give Eason/Flutie/Grogan a terrific target, and Cook gets good marks at TE. Gannon is the needed DE insurance if Sims can't come back. The secondary, already a Pats' strength, gains depth.

Grade B.

RND	NO.	PLAYER	SCHOOL	POS	HGT	WGT	40-YD TIME	GRADE	MK RD	JB RK
1	16	Hart Lee Dykes	Oklahoma St.	WR	6-3	221	4.66	7.40	1	2
2	43	Eric Coleman	Wyoming	CB	5-11	185	4.51	6.20	2	4
3	63	Marv Cook (from Tampa Bay)	Iowa	TE	6-3	243	4.83	6.00	5-6	3
3	73	Chris Gannon	S.W. Louisiana	DE	6-5	254	4.8	—	—	6
4	96	Maurice Hurst (from Washington)	Southern	CB	5-9	185	4.55	—	—	24
4	100	Michael Timpson	Penn St.	WR	5-11	175	—	—	6	8
5	—	to Cleveland								
6	—	to Raiders								
6	165	Eric Mitchel (Chicago pick from Raiders)	Oklahoma	RB	5-11	199	4.55	5.22	4-5	13
7	178	Eric Lindstrom (from Raiders)	Boston Coll.	LB	6-2	231	4.69	5.37	—	14
7	—	to San Diego								
8	210	Rodney Rice	BYU	CB	5-7	175	4.62	—	—	29
8	223	Tony Zackery (San Francisco pick from Raiders)	Washington	S	6-1	200	4.55	—	6	5
9	240	Darron Norris	Texas	FB	5-9	190	4.6	—	—	23

RND	NO.	PLAYER	SCHOOL	POS	HGT	WGT	40-YD TIME	GRADE	MK RD	JB RK
(Continued)										
9	247	Curtis Wilson (from Minnesota)	Missouri	C	6-2	270	4.95	—	4-5	5
10	267	Emanuel McNeil	Tenn.-Martin	DT	6-2	270	4.95	—	—	11
11	294	Tony Hinz	Harvard	FB	6-0	212	4.76	—	—	12
12	324	Aaron Chubb	Georgia	LB	6-3	220	4.7	—	—	43

NEW ORLEANS SAINTS

Main Needs: DE, NT, CB, OL, WR

Martin has been a problem player in college, including a marijuana suspension. He wasn't rated a first-rounder by anyone, apparently, except the Saints, who have been bombing with defensive linemen on recent drafts. Massey needs experience against the big kids, but he could be great. Three straight defensive-back picks tell you how the Saints ranked their incumbents.

Grade C.

RND	NO.	PLAYER	SCHOOL	POS	HGT	WGT	40-YD TIME	GRADE	MK RD	JB RK
1	19	Wayne Martin	Arkansas	DE	6-4	280	5.04	—	2-3	5
2	46	Robert Massey	N.C. Central	CB	5-10	183	4.5	—	1-2	3
3	79	Kim Phillips	N. Texas	CB	5-9	185	4.54	5.40	3	5
4	106	Michael Mayes	Louisiana St.	CB	5-10	180	4.53	—	—	27
5	133	Kevin Haverdink	W. Michigan	OT	6-6	275	5.23	5.54	—	11
6	159	Floyd Turner	NE Louisiana	WR	5-11	185	4.6	—	—	17
7	186	David Griggs	Virginia	LB	6-3	239	4.85	5.31	—	15
8	213	Fred Hadley	Mississippi St.	WR	—	—	—	—	—	28
9	246	Jerry Leggett	Cal. St.-Fuller	DE	6-4	265	4.95	—	—	24
10	273	Joe Henderson	Iowa	FB	6-0	205	4.65	—	—	15
11	300	Calvin Nicholson	Oregon St.	CB	—	—	—	—	—	25
12	327	Mike Cadore	E. Kentucky	WR	—	—	—	—	—	32

NEW YORK GIANTS

Main Needs: RB, DB, OL

The Giants are building a "Save the Whales" line, according to GM George Young. Coupled with last year's picks, they now have the big people for the next decade. It will probably take some time for them to mesh, but New York will benefit next year. Now they need a runner. Tillman is a long shot to be more than average. Jackson will help at safety, where there's a definite need.

Grade B.

RND	NO.	PLAYER	SCHOOL	POS	HGT	WGT	40-YD TIME	GRADE	MK RD	JB RK
1	18	Brian Williams	Minnesota	G-C	6-4	306	4.91	6.60	1-2	1
2	—	to San Diego								
3	64	Bob Kratch (from San Diego)	Iowa	OG	6-3	286	5.10	6.60	2-3	9
3	78	Greg Jackson	LSU	S	6-0	200	4.47	5.60	5	7
4	93	Lewis Tillman (from San Diego)	Jackson St.	RB	5-11	190	4.70	5.60	2-3	10
4	105	Brad Henke	Arizona	DT	6-3	270	5.01	5.10	3-4	6
5	132	Dave Meggett	Towson St.	RB	5-7	175	4.6	—	—	11
6	158	Howard Cross	Alabama	TE	6-5	245	5.15	—	5-6	18
7	175	David Popp (from San Francisco)	E. Illinois	OT	—	—	—	—	—	—
7	—	to Indianapolis								
8	218	Myron Guyton	E. Kentucky	S	—	—	—	—	—	26
9	245	A. J. Greene	Wake Forest	S	5-7	160	4.5	—	—	18
10	272	Rodney Lowe	Mississippi	DE	6-4	255	4.9	—	—	13
11	299	Jerome Rinehart	Tenn.-Martin	DE	—	—	—	—	—	31
12	326	Eric Smith	UCLA	LB	6-2	230	4.74	—	—	55

NEW YORK JETS

Main Needs: DE, LB, WR, OL

Each of the first three picks was a reach. The Jets would appear to have helped the defense, but were these the best defenders available? Few believed they were. Speedy Martin will try to unseat Wesley Walker. Maybe next year.

Grade D. But if Hickey knows a lot more than appears, he'll have the final chuckle.

RND	NO.	PLAYER	SCHOOL	POS	HGT	WGT	40-YD TIME	GRADE	MK RD	JB RK
1	14	Jeff Lageman	Virginia	ILB	6-5	241	4.95	5.52	1-2	7
2	42	Dennis Byrd	Tulsa	DE	6-4	256	4.93	5.50	3-4	11
3	70	Joe Mott	Iowa	LB	6-3	240	4.85	—	—	30
4	98	Ron Stallworth	Auburn	DE	6-4	260	4.95	—	2-3	10
5	126	Tony Martin	Mesa	WR	6-0	175	4.45	—	—	24
6	151	Marv Washington (from Raiders)	Idaho	DE	6-4	240	4.85	—	—	20
6	153	Titus Dixon	Troy St.	WR	5-6	155	4.38	—	—	21
7	181	Stevon Moore	Mississippi	S	5-11	200	4.65	—	—	11
8	209	Anthony Brown	W. Virginia	RB	5-9	210	4.65	—	5-6	8
9	237	Pat Marlatt	W. Virginia	DT	—	—	—	—	—	—
10	265	Adam Bob	Texas A & M	LB	6-1	244	5.0	—	—	41
11	293	Artie Holmes	Washington St.	S	5-11	190	4.65	—	—	29
12	321	Willie Snead	Florida	WR	—	—	—	—	—	—

PHILADELPHIA EAGLES

Main Needs: LB, OL, DB, RB

The Eagles got more than they figured to. Small should allow Bell to move back to safety. Getting Drummond could be a real bonus. A good draft considering the possibilities, but the possibilities were slight. Only having four picks set a new record for fewest.

Grade C –.

RND	NO.	PLAYER	SCHOOL	POS	HGT	WGT	40-YD TIME	GRADE	MK RD	JB RK
1	—	to Indianapolis								
2	49	Jesse Small	E. Kentucky	OLB	6-3	235	4.74	6.20	2	12
3	76	Robert Drummond	Syracuse	RB	6-1	205	4.51	6.00	2	3
3	81	Britt Hager (from Chicago)	Texas	LB	6-0	230	4.65	5.60	3-4	13
4	—	to Seattle								
5	—	to Chicago								
6	162	Heath Sherman	Texas A & I	RB	5-11	198	4.6	—	—	10
7	—	to Chicago								
8	—	to Chicago								
9	—	to Chicago								
10	—	to Chicago								
11	—	to Chicago								
12	—	to Chicago								

PITTSBURGH STEELERS

Main Needs: RB, WR, OT, DL, LB

Worley should become the best Pittsburgh runner since Franco Harris. Hill looks like a steal. Ricketts addresses a specific need. Lake is projected as a big-hit strong safety, but he needs experience. A very good draft that will be great if Lake comes through.

Grade A –.

RND	NO.	PLAYER	SCHOOL	POS	HGT	WGT	40-YD TIME	GRADE	MK RD	JB RK
1	7	Tim Worley	Georgia	RB	6-1	221	4.4	—	1	1
1	24	Tom Ricketts (from Minnesota)	Pittsburgh	OT	6-4	299	5.25	—	1	5
2	34	Carnell Lake	UCLA	DB	6-0	205	4.42	—	2	4
3	61	Derek Hill	Arizona	WR	6-1	180	4.54	6.10	2	3
4	91	Jerrol Williams	Purdue	LB	6-4	240	4.9	—	4-5	9
5	118	David Arnold	Michigan	S	6-2	200	4.58	6.02	5	16
6	144	Mark Stock	VMI	WR	5-11	175	4.61	—	5-6	23
7	174	David Johnson	Kentucky	CB	6-0	190	4.61	—	—	8
8	201	Chris Asbeck	Cincinnati	NT	6-2	265	4.90	4.90	—	15
9	228	A. J. Jenkins	Cal. St.-Fuller	LB	6-1	240	4.78	—	—	27
10	258	Jerry Olsavsky	Pittsburgh	LB	6-0	222	4.9	—	—	38
11	285	Brian Slater	Washington	WR	6-3	200	4.51	5.60	—	15
12	312	Carlton Haselrig	Pitt.-Johnstown	NT	6-1	275	—	—	—	—

PHOENIX CARDINALS

Main Needs: DB, DT, RB, WR, P, K

Although they might have done more for immediate improvement, the Cards picked several players who should help them for years. Hill could replace last year's pick, Harvey. Reeves is a surprise because Cards seemed set at TE. Perhaps the Cards have finally solved their kicking problems. A good draft with few risks.

Grade B.

RND	NO.	PLAYER	SCHOOL	POS	HGT	WGT	40-YD TIME	GRADE	MK RD	JB RK
1	10	Eric Hill	LSU	OLB	6-1	250	4.70	6.70	1	3
1	17	Joe Wolf (from Seattle)	Boston Coll.	OG	6-5	280	5.08	7.00	1	1
2	40	Walter Reeves	Auburn	TE	6-3	251	4.79	5.81	2	2
3	67	Mike Zandofsky	Washington	OG	6-2	267	5.28	6.10	5-6	8
4	94	Jim Wahler	UCLA	DT	6-4	265	5.04	5.20	3-4	8
5	124	Richard Tardits	Georgia	LB	6-1	220	4.75	—	—	40
5	128	David Edeem (from Seattle)	Wyoming	DE	6-3	255	4.73	5.70	4-5	12
6	150	Jay Taylor	San Jose St.	CB	5-9	177	4.50	5.94	3-4	11
7	177	Rickey Royal	S. Houston St.	CB	5-9	186	4.45	—	—	15
8	207	John Burch	Tenn.-Martin	RB	5-10	200	4.55	—	—	33
9	234	Kendall Trainor	Arkansas	PK	6-1	202	4.90	5.50	9-12	2
10	261	Chris Becker	TCU	P	6-1	192	4.90	5.20	9-12	6
11	291	Jeffrey Hunter	Albany St.	DE	6-4	265	4.75	—	—	15
12	318	Todd Nelson	Wisconsin	OG	6-5	290	5.03	—	6	16

SAN DIEGO CHARGERS

Main Needs: QB, LB, DB, OL, DL

Maybe Grossman was too good to pass up, but the Chargers were already strong at DE. Hall is a small reach. Too much was given up for Tolliver, who isn't ready and may never be. Some of the late picks may help. With so many needs, they should have done better.

Grade C.

RND	NO.	PLAYER	SCHOOL	POS	HGT	WGT	40-YD TIME	GRADE	MK RD	JB RK
1	8	Burt Grossman	Pittsburgh	DE	6-5	267	4.8	—	1	1
2	37	Courtney Hall	Rice	C	6-1	266	4.93	5.01	4-5	3
2	51	Billy Tolliver (from Giants)	Texas Tech	QB	6-0	217	4.95	—	5-6	9
3	—	to Giants								
4	—	to Giants								
5	120	Elliot Smith	Alcorn St.	S	6-0	190	4.55	—	—	6
6	—	to Rams								
7	—	to Giants								
7	183	Marion Butts (from New England)	Florida St.	FB	—	—	—	—	—	NR
7	195	Terrence Jones (from San Francisco)	Tulane	QB	6-1	208	4.63	6.00	2-3	5
8	204	Dana Brinson	Nebraska	WR	5-9	167	4.31	5.63	3-4	18
9	231	Pat Davis	Syracuse	TE	6-2	257	4.81	5.01	5	7
10	260	Ricky Andrews	Washington	LB	6-2	235	4.7	—	4-5	23
11	287	Victor Floyd	Florida St.	RB	6-0	200	4.6	—	—	38
12	—	to Washington								

SAN FRANCISCO 49ERS

Main Needs: TE, LB, OL

DeLong and Walls play the right positions, but others do not rate them as highly as the 49ers. Considering where they drafted, an average-to-good draft.

Grade C+.

RND	NO.	PLAYER	SCHOOL	POS	HGT	WGT	40-YD TIME	GRADE	MK RD	JB RK
1	28	Keith DeLong	Tennessee	ILB	6-2	229	4.79	5.32	5-6	4
2	56	Wesley Walls	Mississippi	TE	6-4	245	4.73	5.20	4	5
3	84	Keith Henderson	Georgia	FB	6-2	202	4.6	—	1-2	3
4	112	Mike Barber	Marshall	WR	5-10	170	4.6	—	—	20
5	122	Johnny Jackson (from Raiders)	Houston	DB	6-1	200	4.70	6.01	5	30
5	—	to Raiders, then Washington								
6	167	Steve Hendrickson	California	LB	5-11	240	4.7	—	5-6	29
7	—	to San Diego								
8	—	to Raiders, then New England								
9	251	Rudy Harmon	LSU	LB	6-0	230	4.78	—	—	48
10	279	Andy Sinclair	Stanford	C	6-2	279	5.29	5.00	—	10
11	289	Jim Bell (from Raiders)	Boston Coll.	RB	6-0	205	4.65	—	—	15
11	307	Norm McGee	N. Arizona	WR	6-0	170	4.35	—	—	62
12	319	Antonio Goss (from Raiders)	N. Carolina	LB	6-3	228	4.75	—	4-5	32
12	—	to Raiders, then Minnesota								

SEATTLE SEAHAWKS

Main Needs: TE, DL, OL, DB

Heck will help the beleaguered line, but Tofflemire is a reach. Heck will have to be a heck of a player to make this a really outstanding draft. McNeal is pretty green.

Grade C+.

RND	NO.	PLAYER	SCHOOL	POS	HGT	WGT	40-YD TIME	GRADE	MK RD	JB RK
1	15	Andy Heck (from Indianapolis)	Notre Dame	OT	6-6	268	4.85	6.51	2-3	2
1	—	to Phoenix								
2	44	Joe Tofflemire	Arizona	C	6-1	265	5.14	5.30	—	6
3	71	ES Harris	E. Kentucky	RB	5-9	218	—	—	3-4	6
4	101	Travis McNeal	Tenn.-Chatt.	TE	6-3	235	4.70	5.50	4	4
4	103	James Henry (from Philadelphia)	S. Mississippi	CB	5-9	190	4.6	—	—	21
5	—	to Phoenix								
6	—	to Tampa Bay								
7	184	Mike Nettles	Memphis St.	CB	5-10	190	4.68	—	—	31
8	211	Marlin Williams	W. Illinois	DE	6-3	256	4.85	—	—	25
9	238	David Franks	Connecticut	G	—	—	—	—	—	—
10	268	Derrick Fenner	N. Carolina	RB	—	—	—	—	—	—
11	295	Mike Baum	Northwestern	DE	—	—	—	—	—	—
12	322	R.J. Kors	Long Beach St.	DB	—	—	—	—	—	—

TAMPA BAY BUCCANEERS

Main Needs: DB, DL, P, RB

Thomas may be the best Buc defender since Leroy Selmon. He should provide some desperately needed pass rushing. Several needs were not addressed. A fairly good draft if Florence comes through. Peebles adds speed outside.

Grade B−.

RND	NO.	PLAYER	SCHOOL	POS	HGT	WGT	40-YD TIME	GRADE	MK RD	JB RK
1	6	Broderick Thomas	Nebraska	OLB	6-2	252	4.58	7.60	1	2
2	33	Danny Peebles	N.C. State	WR	5-11	169	4.45	5.62	1-2	7
3	—	to New England								
4	90	Anthony Florence	Beth-Cookman	CB	5-11	185	—	—	—	NR
5	117	Jamie Lawson	Nicholls St.	RB	5-10	250	4.75	—	—	20
6	146	Chris Mohr	Alabama	P	6-4	215	—	—	—	1
6	154	Derrick Little (from Seattle)	S. Carolina	LB	6-3	240	4.80	5.51	—	26
7	—	to Buffalo								
8	200	Carl Bax	Missouri	OG	6-4	275	5.05	—	—	13
9	230	Patrick Egu	Nevada-Reno	WR	5-9	200	4.45	—	—	53
10	257	Ty Granger	Clemson	OT	6-5	275	5.0	—	—	31
11	284	Rod Mounts	Texas A & I	OG	—	—	—	—	—	41
11	290	Willie Griffin (Washington pick from Rams)	Nebraska	DT	6-2	290	5.15	—	—	16
11	302	Herb Duncan (from Rams)	N. Arizona	WR	—	—	—	—	—	—
12	—	to Indianapolis								
12	329	Terry Young (from Rams)	Georgia So.	DB	5-10	175	4.55	—	—	26

WASHINGTON REDSKINS

Main Needs: RB, DT, TE

GM Beathard uses the draft as currency to be spent. By trading future draft choices, he picked up the running backs he needed (Riggs, Byner). Every year critics say he'll pay for it someday, but he hasn't so far. Rocker will be moved inside to fill Butz's DT slot. A good draft.

Grade B+.

RND	NO.	PLAYER	SCHOOL	POS	HGT	WGT	40-YD TIME	GRADE	MK RD	JB RK
1	—	to Chicago								
2	—	Raiders' pick to Atlanta								
2	—	to Raiders, then to Dallas								
3	66	Tracy Rocker	Auburn	DE	6-2	270	4.95	6.80	1-2	1
4	87	Jeff Graham (Drafted by Green Bay; rights traded to Washington.)	Long Beach	QB	6-4	200	4.95	—	3-4	6
4	—	to New England								
5	—	to Green Bay								
5	129	Tim Smiley (from Indianapolis)	Arkansas St.	DB	6-0	190	—	—	—	NR
5	139	Lybrant Robinson	Delaware St.	LB-E	6-4	225	—	—	—	NR

RND	NO.	PLAYER	SCHOOL	POS	HGT	WGT	40-YD TIME	GRADE	MK RD	JB RK
		(Continued)								
6	149	Anthony Johnson	S.W. Texas St.	DB	5-8	171	4.45	—	—	7
7	179	Kevin Hendrix	S. Carolina	LB	6-2	260	4.9	—	—	34
8	—	to Green Bay								
9	233	Charles Darrington	Kentucky	TE	—	—	—	—	—	—
10	263	Mark Schlereth	Idaho	OG	—	—	—	—	—	—
11	—	to Rams, then Tampa Bay								
12	316	Jimmy Johnson (from San Diego)	Howard	TE	—	—	—	—	—	—
12	317	Joe Mickles	Mississippi	FB	5-9	220	4.8	—	—	31

THE CHOICES

We've presented above the draft choices for each team. We present below the draft by rounds for historical purposes, listing the drafting team, player, his college, and position.

ROUND 1

NO.	TEAM		PLAYER	SCHOOL	POS
1	DAL		Troy Aikman	UCLA	QB
2	GB		Tony Mandarich	Michigan	OT
3	DET		Barry Sanders	Okla. St.	RB
4	KC		Derrick Thomas	Alabama	OLB
5	ATL		Deion Sanders	Florida St.	CB
6	TB		Broderick Thomas	Nebraska	OLB
7	PIT		Tim Worley	Georgia	RB
8	SD		Burt Grossman	Pittsburgh	DE
9	MIA		Sammie Smith	Florida St.	RB
10	PHO		Eric Hill	LSU	OLB
11	CHI	f/RAI	Donnell Woolford	Clemson	CB
12	CHI	f/WAS	Trace Armstrong	Florida	DE
13	CLE	f/DEN	Eric Metcalf	Texas	RB
14	NYJ		Jeff Lageman	Virginia	ILB
15	SEA	f/IND	Andy Heck	Notre Dame	OT
16	NE		Hart Lee Dykes	Okla. St.	WR
17	PHO	f/SEA	Joe Wolf	Boston Col.	OG
18	NYG		Brian Williams	Minnesota	G-C
19	NO		Wayne Martin	Arkansas	DE
20	DEN		Steve Atwater	Arkansas	S
21	RAM		Bill Hawkins	Miami (FL)	DE
22	IND	f/PHI	Andre Rison	Michigan St.	WR
23	HOU		David Williams	Florida	OT
24	PIT		Tom Ricketts	Pittsburgh	OT
25	MIA	f/CHI	Louis Oliver	Florida	S
26	RAM	f/BUF	Cleveland Gary	Miami (FL)	FB
27	ATL	f/CIN	Shawn Collins	No. Arizona	WR
28	SF		Keith DeLong	Tennessee	ILB

ROUND 2

NO.	TEAM			PLAYER	SCHOOL	POS
29	RAI	f/DAL		Steve Wisniewski	Penn State	OG
				(Dallas drafted Wisniewski, then traded his rights.)		
30	DET			John Ford	Virginia	WR
31	CLE	f/GB		Lawyer Tillman	Auburn	WR
32	KC			Mike Elkins	Wake Forest	QB
33	TB			Danny Peebles	N.C. State	WR
34	PIT			Carnell Lake	UCLA	DB
35	CIN	f/ATL		Eric Ball	UCLA	RB
36	CHI	f/MIA		John Roper	Texas A&M	ILB
37	SD			Courtney Hall	Rice	C
38	ATL	f/WAS	f/RAI	Ralph Norwood	LSU	OT

NOTE: f/ indicates draft pick came from following team.

(Continued)

NO.	TEAM			PLAYER	SCHOOL	POS
39	DAL	f/RAI	f/WAS	Daryl Johnston	Syracuse	RB
40	PHO			Walter Reeves	Auburn	TE
41	DEN			Doug Widell	Boston Col.	G-T
42	NYJ			Dennis Byrd	Tulsa	DE
43	NE			Eric Coleman	Wyoming	CB
44	SEA			Joe Tofflemire	Arizona	C
45	RAM	f/IND		Frank Stams	Notre Dame	OLB
46	NO			Robert Massey	N.C. Central	CB
47	DEN			Warren Powers	Maryland	DT
48	RAM			Brian Smith	Auburn	DE-LB
49	PHI			Jesse Small	E. Kentucky	OLB
50	HOU			Scott Kozak	Oregon	OLB
51	SD	f/NYG		Billy Tolliver	Texas Tech	QB
52	MIN			David Braxton	Wake Forest	OLB
53	RAM	f/BUF		Darryl Henley	UCLA	CB
54	CHI			Dave Zawatson	California	G-T
55	CIN			Fred Childress	Arkansas	OG
56	SF			Wesley Walls	Mississippi	TE

ROUND 3

NO.	TEAM		PLAYER	SCHOOL	POS
57	DAL		Mark Stepnoski	Pittsburgh	OG
58	GB		Matt Brock	Oregon	DE
59	DET		Mike Utley	Wash. St.	OT
60	KC		Naz Worthen	N.C. State	WR
61	PIT		Derek Hill	Arizona	WR
62	ATL		Keith Jones	Illinois	RB
63	NE	f/TB	Marv Cook	Iowa	TE
64	NYG	f/SD	Bob Kratch	Iowa	OG
65	CHI	f/MIA	Jerry Fontenot	Texas A&M	OG
66	WAS		Tracy Rocker	Auburn	DE
67	PHO		Mike Zandofsky	Washington	OG
68	RAI		Rhondy Weston	Florida	DT
69	DEN		Darrell Hamilton	N.Carolina	OT
70	NYJ		Joe Mott	Iowa	LB
71	SEA		Elroy Harris	E. Kentucky	RB
72	IND		Mitchell Benson	TCU	DE
73	NE		Chris Gannon	SW Louisiana	DE
74	GB	f/CLE	Anthony Dilweg	Duke	QB
75	RAM		Kevin Robbins	Michigan St.	OT
76	PHI		Robert Drummond	Syracuse	RB
77	HOU		Bubba McDowell	Miami (FL)	DB
78	NYG		Greg Jackson	LSU	S
79	NO		Kim Phillips	No. Texas	CB
80	MIN		John Hunter	BYU	OT
81	PHI	f/CHI	Britt Hager	Texas	LB
82	BUF		Don Beebe	Chadron St.	WR
83	CIN		Erik Wilhelm	Oregon St.	QB
84	SF		Keith Henderson	Georgia	FB

ROUND 4

NO.	TEAM		PLAYER	SCHOOL	POS
85	DAL		Tony Tolbert	UTEP	LB
86	DET		Ray Crockett	Baylor	CB
87	WAS	f/GB	Jeff Graham	Long Beach	QB
88	KC		Stanley Petry	TCU	CB
89	CIN	f/ATL	Kerry Owens	Arkansas	LB
90	TB		Anthony Florence	Beth-Cooman	CB
91	PIT		Jerrol Williams	Purdue	LB
92	MIA		David Holmes	Syracuse	S
93	NYG	f/SD	Lewis Tillman	Jackson St.	RB
94	PHO		Jim Wahler	UCLA	DT
95	CHI	f/RAI	Markus Paul	Syracuse	S
96	NE	f/WAS	Maurice Hurst	Southern	CB
97	DEN		Rich McCullough	Clemson	DE
98	NYJ		Ron Stallworth	Auburn	DT
99	IND		Pat Tomberlin	Florida St.	OT
100	NE		Michael Timpson	Penn State	WR
101	SEA		Travis McNeal	Tenn.-Chatt.	TE

(Continued)

NO.	TEAM		PLAYER	SCHOOL	POS
102	RAM		Jeff Carlson	Weber St.	QB
103	SEA	f/PHI	James Henry	So. Miss.	CB
104	HOU		Rod Harris	Texas A&M	WR
105	NYG		Brad Henke	Arizona	DT
106	NO		Michael Mayes	La. State	S
107	CLE		Andrew Stewart	Cincinnati	DE
108	MIN		Darrl Ingram	California	TE
109	BUF		John Kolesar	Michigan	WR
110	GB	f/CHI	Erik Affholter	USC	WR
111	CIN		Rob Woods	Arizona	OT
112	SF		Mike Barber	Marshall	WR

ROUND 5

NO.	TEAM			PLAYER	SCHOOL	POS
113	DAL			Keith Jennings	Clemson	TE
114	CLE	f/GB		Kyle Kramer	Bowling Green	S
115	DET			Lawrence Pete	Nebraska	DT
116	CLE	f/KC		Vernon Jones	Maryland	WR
117	TB			Jamie Lawson	Nicholls St.	RB
118	PIT			David Arnold	Michigan	S
119	DAL	f/RAI	f/ATL	Willis Crockett	Georgia Tech	LB
120	SD			Elliot Smith	Alcorn St.	CB
121	MIA			Jeff Uhlenhake	Ohio State	C
122	SF	f/RAI		Johnny Jackson	Houston	DB
123	GB	f/WAS		Jeff Query	Millikin	WR
124	PHO			Richard Tardits	Georgia	LB
125	DAL	f/DEN		Jeff Roth	Florida	DT
126	NYJ			Tony Martin	Mesa	WR
127	GB	f/CLE	f/NE	Vince Workman	Ohio State	RB
128	PHO	f/SEA		David Edeem	Wyoming	DE
129	WAS	f/IND		Tim Smiley	Arkansas St.	DB
130	CHI	f/PHI		Mark Green	Notre Dame	RB
131	HOU			Glenn Montgomery	Houston	DT
132	NYG			Dave Meggett	Towson St.	RB
133	NO			Kevin Haverdink	W. Michigan	OT
134	DEN	f/CLE		Dar. Carrington	N. Arizona	CB
135	RAM			Alfred Jackson	San Diego St.	WR
—	MIN—exercised choice in 1988 supplemental draft					
136	CHI			Greg Gilbert	Alabama	LB
137	BUF			Michael Andrews	Alcorn St.	CB
138	CIN			Natu Tuatagaloa	California	DT
139	SF			Lybrant Robinson	Delaware St.	LB-E

ROUND 6

NO.	TEAM		PLAYER	SCHOOL	POS
140	DAL	f/RAI	Jeff Francis	Tennessee	QB
141	DET		Rodney Peete	USC	QB
142	GB		Chris Jacke	Texas-El Paso	PK
143	KC		Robb Thomas	Oregon St.	WR
144	PIT		Mark Stock	VMI	WR
145	ATL		Troy Sadowski	Georgia	TE
146	TB		Chris Mohr	Alabama	P
147	MIA		Wes Pritchett	Notre Dame	LB
148	RAM	f/SD	Thom Kaumeyer	Oregon	DB
149	WAS		Anthony Johnson	SW Texas St.	DB
150	PHO		Jim Taylor	San Jose St.	DB
151	NYJ	f/RAI	Marv Washington	Idaho	DE
152	DEN		Anthony Stafford	Oklahoma	WR
153	NYJ		Titus Dixon	Troy St.	WR
154	TB	f/SEA	Derrick Little	S. Carolina	LB
155	IND		Quintus McDonald	Penn State	LB
156	RAI	f/NE	Doug Lloyd	N. Dakota St.	RB
157	HOU		Bo Orlando	W. Virginia	DB
158	NYG		Howard Cross	Alabama	TE
159	NO		Floyd Turner	NW Louisiana	WR
160	CLE		Gary Wilkerson	Penn State	DB
161	RAM		Mark Messner	Michigan	LB
162	PHI		Heath Sherman	Texas A & I	RB

(Continued)

(Continued)

NO.	TEAM			PLAYER	SCHOOL	POS
163	MIN			Jeff Mickel	E. Washington	OL
164	BUF			Sean Doctor	Marshall	RB
165	NE	f/RAI	f/CHI	Eric Mitchell	Oklahoma	RB
166	CIN			Creaig Taylor	W. Virginia	RB
167	SF			Steve Hendrickson	California	LB

ROUND 7

NO.	TEAM		PLAYER	SCHOOL	POS
168	DAL		Kevin Peterson	Northwestern	LB
169	GB		Mark Hall	SW Louisiana	DE
170	DET		Jerry Woods	N. Michigan	DB
171	KC		Ron Sancho	LSU	LB
172	ATL		Undra Johnson	W. Virginia	RB
173	BUF	f/TB	Brian Jordan	Richmond	DB
174	PIT		David Johnson	Kentucky	DB
175	NYG	f/SD	David Popp	E. Illinois	OT
176	MIA		Jim Zdelar	Youngstown St	OT
177	PHO		Rickey Royal	S. Houston St	DB
178	NE	f/RAI	Eric Lindstrom	Boston Col.	LB
179	WAS		Kevin Hendrix	S. Carolina	LB
180	DEN		Melvin Bratton	Miami, (FL)	RB
181	NYJ		Stevon Moore	Mississippi	DB
182	IND		Ivy Joe Hunter	Kentucky	RB
183	SD	f/NE	Marion Butts	Florida St.	RB
184	SEA		Mike Nettles	Memphis St.	DB
185	IND	f/NYG	Chas. Washington	Cameron	DB
186	NO		David Griggs	Virginia	LB
187	CLE		Mike Graybill	Boston U.	OT
188	RAM		George Bethune	Alabama	LB
189	CHI	f/PHI	Richard Brothers	Arkansas	DB
190	HOU		Tracy Rogers	Fresno St.	LB
191	MIN		Benji Roland	Auburn	DT
192	CHI		Brent Snyder	Utah St.	QB
193	BUF		Chris Hale	USC	DB
194	CIN		Kendal Smith	Utah St.	WR
195	SD	f/SF	Terrence Jones	Tulane	QB

ROUND 8

NO.	TEAM		PLAYER	SCHOOL	POS
196	DAL		Charvez Foger	Nevada-Reno	RB
197	DET		Chris Parker	W. Virginia	DT
198	GB		Thomas King	SW Louisiana	DB
199	KC		Bryan Tobey	Grambling	RB
200	TB		Carl Bax	Missouri	G
201	PIT		Chris Asbeck	Cincinnati	NT
202	ATL		Paul Singer	W. Illinois	QB
203	MIA		Pete Stoyanovich	Indiana	PK
204	SD		Dana Brinson	Nebraska	WR
205	RAI		Derrick Gainer	Florida A&M	RB
206	GB	f/WAS	Brian Shulman	Auburn	P
207	PHO		John Burch	Tenn.-Martin	RB
208	DEN		Paul Green	USC	TE
209	NYJ		Anthony Brown	W. Virginia	RB
210	NE		Rodney Rice	BYU	DB
211	SEA		Marlin Williams	W. Illinois	DE
212	IND		Kurt Larson	Mich. State	LB
213	NO		Fred Hadley	Mississippi	WR
214	CLE		Rick Aeilts	SE Mo. St.	TE
215	RAM		Warren Wheat	BYU	OT
216	CHI	f/PHI	Tony Woods	Oklahoma	DT
217	HOU		Alvoid Mays	W. Virginia	DB
218	NYG		Myron Guyton	E. Kentucky	DB
219	MIN		Alex Stewart	Cal.St.-Ful.	DE
220	KC	f/BUF	Todd McNair	Temple	RB

(Continued)

NO.	TEAM			PLAYER	SCHOOL	POS
221	CHI			Chris Dyko	Wash. St.	OT
222	CIN			Chris Chenault	Kentucky	LB
223	NE	f/RAI	f/SF	Tony Zackery	Washington	DB

ROUND 9

NO.	TEAM		PLAYER	SCHOOL	POS
224	DAL		Tim Jackson	Nebraska	DB
225	GB		Scott Kirby	Arizona St.	OT
226	DET		Derek MacCready	Ohio State	DE
227	KC		Jack Phillips	Alcorn State	DB
228	PIT		A.J. Jenkins	Cal.St.-Ful.	DE
229	ATL		Chris Dunn	Cal.Poly-SLO	LB
230	TB		Egu Patrick	Nevada-Reno	RB
231	SD		Pat Davis	Syracuse	TE
232	MIA		Dana Batiste	Texas A&M	LB
233	WAS		Chas. Darrington	Kentucky	TE
234	PHO		Kendall Trainor	Arkansas	PK
235	RAI		Gary Gooden	Indiana	DB
236	DEN		Monte Smith	N. Dakota	G
237	NYJ		Pat Marlatt	W. Virginia	DT
238	SEA		David Franks	Connecticut	G
239	IND		William Mackall	Tenn.-Martin	WR
240	NE		Darron Norris	Texas	RB
241	CLE		Wayne Williams	Florida	RB
242	RAM		Vernon Kirk	Pittsburgh	TE
243	CHI	f/PHI	LaSalle Harper	Arkansas	LB
244	HOU		Bob Mrosko	Penn State	TE
245	NYG		A.J. Greene	Wake Forest	DB
246	NO		Jerry Leggett	Cal.St.-Ful.	LB
247	NE	f/MIN	Curtis Wilson	Missouri	C
248	CHI		Byron Sanders	Northwestern	RB
249	BUF		Pat Rabold	Wyoming	DT
250	CIN		Richard Stephens	Tulsa	OT
251	SF		Rudy Harmon	LSU	LB

ROUND 10

NO.	TEAM		PLAYER	SCHOOL	POS
252	DAL		Rod Carter	Miami (FL)	LB
253	DET		Jason Phillips	Houston	WR
254	GB		Ben Jessie	SW Texas St.	DB
255	KC		Rob McGovern	Holy Cross	LB
256	CIN	f/ATL	Cornell Holloway	Pittsburgh	DB
257	TB		Ty Granger	Clemson	OT
258	PIT		Jerry Olsavsky	Pittsburgh	LB
259	MIA		Deval Glover	Syracuse	WR
260	SD		Ricky Andrews	Washington	LB
261	PHO		Chris Becker	TCU	P
262	RAI		Charles Jackson	Jackson State	DT
263	WAS		Mark Schlereth	Idaho	G
264	DEN		Anthony Butts	Miss. State	DT
265	NYJ		Adam Bob	Texas A&M	LB
266	IND		Jim Thompson	Auburn	OT
267	NE		Emanuel McNeill	Tenn.-Martin	DT
268	SEA		Derrick Fenner	N. Carolina	RB
269	RAM		Mike Williams	Northeastern	WR
270	CHI	f/PHI	Todd Millikin	Nebraska	TE
271	HOU		Tracy Johnson	Clemson	WR
272	NYG		Rodney Lowe	Mississippi	DE
273	NO		Joe Henderson	Iowa State	RB
274	CLE		John Buddenberg	Akron	OT
275	MIA	f/MIN	Greg Ross	Memphis St.	OT
276	BUF		Carlo Cheattom	Auburn	DB
277	CHI		John Simpson	Baylor	WR
278	CIN		Robert Jean	N. Hampshire	QB
279	SF		Andy Sinclair	Stanford	C

ROUND 11

NO.	TEAM			PLAYER	SCHOOL	POS
280	DAL			Randy Shannon	Miami (FL)	LB
281	GB			Cedric Stallworth	Georgia Tech	DB
282	DET			Keith Karpinski	Penn State	LB
283	KC			Marcus Turner	UCLA	DB
284	TB			Rod Mounts	Texas A&I	G
285	PIT			Brian Slater	Washington	WR
286	ATL			Greg Paterra	Slippery Rock	RB
287	SD			Victor Floyd	Florida St.	RB
288	MIA			Bert Weidner	Kent State	DT
289	SF	f/RAI		Jim Bell	Boston Col.	RB
290	TB	f/RAM	f/WAS	Willie Griffin	Nebraska	DE
291	PHO			Jeffrey Hunter	Albany, Ga., St.	DE
292	DEN			Richard Shelton	Liberty	DB
293	NYJ			Artie Holmes	Wash. St.	DB
294	NE			Tony Hinz	Harvard	RB
295	SEA			Mike Baum	Northwestern	DE
296	IND			Wayne Johnson	Georgia	QB
297	CHI	f/PHI		Joe Nelms	California	DT
298	HOU			Brian Smider	W. Virginia	OT
299	NYG			Jerome Rinehart	Tenn.-Martin	LB
300	NO			Calvin Nicholson	Oregon St.	DB
301	CLE			Dan Piocki	Maryland	PK
302	TB	f/RAM		Herb Duncan	N. Arizona	WR
303	MIN			Brad Baxter	Alabama St.	RB
304	CHI			George Streeter	Notre Dame	DB
305	BUF			Richard Harvey	Tulane	LB
306	CIN			Dana Wells	Arizona	DT
307	SF			Norm McGee	N. Dakota	WR

ROUND 12

NO.	TEAM			PLAYER	SCHOOL	POS
308	DAL			Scott Ankrom	TCU	WR
309	DET			James Cribbs	Memphis St.	DL
310	GB			Stan Shiver	Florida St.	DB
311	KC			Bill Jones	SW Texas St.	RB
312	PIT			Carlton Hasselrig	Pitt-Johnstown	NT
313	ATL			Tony Bowick	Tenn.-Chatt.	NT
314	IND	f/TB		William DuBose	S. Carolina St.	RB
315	MIA			J.B. Brown	Maryland	DB
316	WAS	f/SD		Jimmy Johnson	Howard	TE
317	WAS			Joe Mickles	Mississippi	RB
318	PHO			Todd Nelson	Wisconsin	G
319	SF	f/RAI		Antonio Goss	N. Carolina	LB
320	DEN			John Jarvis	Howard	WR
321	NYJ			Willie Snead	Florida	WR
322	SEA			R.J. Kors	Long Beach St.	DB
323	IND			Steve Taylor	Nebraska	QB
324	NE			Aaron Chubb	Georgia	LB
325	HOU			Chuck Hartlieb	Iowa	QB
326	NYG			Eric Smith	UCLA	LB
327	NO			Mike Cadore	E. Kentucky	WR
328	CLE			Marlon Brown	Memphis St.	LB
329	TB	f/RAM		Terry Young	Georgia So.	DB
330	CHI	f/PHI		Freddy Weygand	Auburn	WR
331	MIN			Shawn Woodson	J. Madison	LB
332	BUF			Derrell Marshall	USC	OT
333	CHI			Anthony Phillips	Oklahoma	G
334	CIN			Scott Jones	Washington	OL
335	MIN	f/RAI	f/SF	Everett Ross	Ohio State	WR

TEAM PREVIEWS

NATIONAL FOOTBALL CONFERENCE

ATLANTA FALCONS

"Respectability" wouldn't make a popular objective in San Francisco or Los Angeles. Even New Orleans wouldn't be happy with that anymore. In Atlanta, achieving a measure of respectability was enough to make the Falcons' 1988 season a qualified success. You've got to realize the pits they came from. The 1987 team was last in points allowed, points scored, total defense, and rushing yards. By comparison, baseball's Braves were pennant contenders. When a team is as bad as those Falcons were the year before last, it can regard last year's 5–11 as a breath of fresh air and boast that it was blown out only once.

In truth, the Falcons are on the right track and may well be a lot more than respectable in the 1990. But for right now, it's best not to get carried away with euphoria. There are holes and a serious lack of depth all up and down the roster. The team was hit hard by injuries last season; anything similar could make this season a nightmare. Regardless the Falcons are dead-bang sure to finish last in their division again. A modest record improvement to 7–9 would be a triumph.

THE OFFENSE

Any assessment of the Falcons' future must start with quarterback Chris Miller, the franchise quarterback. However, you must remember that "franchise" is used here in the *potential* sense. He's not made it yet. In fact, his '88 passing figures—2,133 yards and 11 touchdowns—put him only in the middle range of QBs at best. Still, the Falcons and a lot of other observers are convinced Miller is a star

waiting to happen. Whether he happens in '89 or just continues progressing, he'd better be healthy because there's no quality backup behind him.

Miller's job would be a lot easier if the Falcons could give him a couple of big, big-play receivers. Last year's corps is smurfy, unproductive, and prone to injury. Regulars Floyd Dixon and Stacy Bailey caught only 45 passes for 4 touchdowns between them. Rookie Michael Haynes had 4 TDs himself but caught only 13 tosses. Shawn Collins, a 200-pounder drafted late in the first round, should be able to step right in. Regular tight end Ken Whisenhunt and his backup Gary Wilkins have free-agented up in smoke, leaving the position to Alex Higdon, who missed nearly all of his rookie year injured, or one of the four—count 'em, four—free-agent TEs signed.

If Atlanta has a surfeit anywhere, it's at running back, although all the possibilities are inside runners. John Settle was a wonder last year, coming out of nowhere to rush for over a thousand yards and lead the team in receiving. His play enabled the Falcons to deal all-time rushing leader Gerald Riggs to Washington, a move that should pay dividends down the line. Gene Lang is reliable and a good receiver. Kenny Flowers, a bust as an '87 rookie and out all of '88 with an injury, is still considered a prospect. Third-round draft pick Keith Jones is another possibility.

With Bill Fralic at guard and Mike Kenn at tackle, Atlanta has the start of an outstanding line. Kenn is thirty-three but coming off his best season in years. Second-round draft choice Ralph Norwood will replace him one day, but not this year. Fralic is the best guard in the world when he's healthy all the way. He missed some time at the end of last season. Houston Hoover, the ORT, doesn't have the size to be a dominant blocker like Kenn, but he stepped in as a rookie and held his own. He made Brett Miller expendable. Center Wayne Radloff and guard John Scully are adequate. Some depth is a sore need.

SPECIAL TEAMS

Incoming free agent Paul McFadden will replace outgoing free agent Greg Davis as placekicker. That doesn't necessarily bode improvement. Punter Rick Donnelly didn't have a particularly good year either. A big return artist like Deion Sanders will find immediate work, and the coverage teams are okay.

THE DEFENSE

The front three of Mike Gann, Tony Casillas, and Rick Bryan gave up 2,319 rushing yards and a 4.5 average, but Atlanta seems reasonably satisfied. None of them are big pass rushers. And, like just about every area on this team, more depth is an urgency. The only free-agent hopeful is Gary Baldinger, a nose tackle let go by Kansas City . . . which had a nose tackle problem.

If Marcus Cotton can play a full season without injury, the outside linebacking slots should be fine. Aundray Bruce had a successful rookie year, improving as the season went on. Cotton had 5 sacks, while playing only half a season. Bruce had 6. But the middle men—John Rade, Jesse Tuggle, and Joel Williams—are a tad soft.

There's a real problem in the secondary, and it's going to take more than Sanders to solve it. Cornerback Scott Case, who led the NFL with 10 interceptions, is the only dependable defender returning. Bobby Butler, on the other side, is getting up in years and will be replaced by Sanders, if "Prime Time" isn't needed even more at safety. Injuries may end free safety Brett Clark's career. Robert Moore, the strong safety, isn't anything special. Backup Charles Dimry is lacking in experience and it shows.

THE BRAINTRUST

Coach Marion Campbell deserves the chance to stick around while his youngsters mature and some of the holes are plugged. You can only wonder what he would accomplish if he ever got a strong team to lead. Certainly, he's never had that chance before. One or two more good drafts and a little luck should do it.

CHICAGO BEARS

Despite appearances, it is not chiseled in stone that the Bears will win the the NFC Central every year. They may prove it this season. This may be the year the Bruins get caught in a time warp—with their older stars suddenly too old and their younger stars not yet ready to play up to championship level. Don't expect an all-out collapse, of course. There are just too many good Bears for that to happen. A worst-case season would still find Chicago at around .500 and no lower than third in the five-team Central. More likely are ten wins and second place behind the Vikings.

However, the Bears, in addition to waning and waxing talent, have a carload of pride, poise, and guts. If they were to get all the way to Super Bowl XXIV, it wouldn't qualify as the decade's biggest upset.

THE DEFENSE

It's hard to imagine the Bears springing leaks on defense. Nevertheless Randall Cunningham and Joe Montana punctured them readily in the playoffs. But even that aside, there are some real problems looming for what was the best part of the team. The front line that has been the envy of all

it surveyed is going to have to survive eventually without tackles Dan Hampton and Steve McMichael. Both are on the wrong side of thirty with knees more like sixty. Trace Armstrong, one of two first-round draft choices, should be able to do the job in a year or so, but it's unrealistic to expect him to play up to the Hampton-McMichael level in his first year. Big-play DE Richard Dent is coming off a broken ankle, and on the other side William Perry had a broken arm. Will Dent regain the quickness that made him a sack king? Will Perry avoid regaining the weight that made him a pinup for Toledo Scales? Is third-year man Sean Smith ready to step in as a regular? Al Harris came through last year for Perry, but he's been free-agented to Philadelphia.

Linebacker Otis Wilson was also allowed to free-agent away, indicating the Bears didn't think he could come back from the knee injury that kept him out in 1988. Ron Rivera and Jim Morrissey are competent outside linebackers, but Wilson and Wilbur Marshall were a lot more than that in the good old days. The Bears hope second-round draft choice John Roper can grow into something special. Of course, there's no problem at middle LB with Mike Singletary. Yet even he will be less effective if one of the tackles goes down.

Mike Richardson may not have been the greatest cornerback in captivity, but he had a fair year in 1988 and then was let slide awfully easily as a free agent. First-round draft choice Donnell Woolford might be able to step in immediately. Otherwise, the Bruins might go with 165-pound Lemuel Stinson or David Tate, who played mostly at free safety last year. Both are second-year men. Vestee Jackson will handle the other CB and Dave Duerson is still fine at strong safety. Shaun Gayle or Maurice Douglass will probably take on free safety if Tate is moved to the corner. Regardless there are more "ifs" in the secondary than Chicago is used to.

SPECIAL TEAMS

Kevin Butler is a satisfactory placekicker. He hit 15 of 19 field goal tries. The return men, receivers Dennis McKinnon and Dennis Gentry, can fly, but they were only ordinary last year. Punter Bryan Wagner was another free-agent lost. If by now you have the impression the Bears' free-agent movement was pretty one-sided, you're right. Nine Bears went away; none came in. This could present a serious lack of depth and a dearth on the special teams.

THE OFFENSE

You want to hear something weird? The main quarterback question is the health of *Mike Tomczak*! Well, all things come to those who wait, and Tomczak is finally regarded as the Number One guy after so many years of replacing Jim McMahon during his annual sidelinings. Of course Tomczak, who was kayoed at least twice last year, hasn't proved himself Mr. Durable yet. If McMahon, the prototype China doll, makes it to training camp, he'll be number two. Everybody figures Jim Harbaugh is still a year or two away, but this could be the time to throw him into the kettle and see if he floats, especially if the Bears lose a few early on.

McKinnon and Gentry had more speed than catches last year. The Bears pass less than most teams, but the two starters had only 6 TDs between them. Number three man Ron Morris had 28 catches and a better yards-per-catch average than either starter, and Wendell Davis, the Bears' second first-round draft choice last year, was impressive in his few appearances. Rookie tight end Jim Thornton is a blue-collar type who will probably never be in the Pro Bowl but will give you your money's worth.

Neal Anderson learned to hang on to the football better last year and rushed for 1,106 yards. He's a go-all-the-way threat who scored 4 touchdowns from 45-or-more yards out. Another good year and he'll be out from under Walter Payton's shadow. Thomas Sanders is a capable RB backup. Fullback Brad Muster, the *first* first-round draft choice, ended the season as the starter over reliable Matt Suhey, but he still has to prove he can block the way Suhey used to.

Tackle to tackle, the Bears have one of the best offensive lines in the league. Center Jay Hilgenberg was deservedly in the Pro Bowl. OT Jimbo Colbert can get there when he plays a full season. OT Keith Van Horne and OGs Mark Bortz and Tom Thayer are fine. There's nothing wrong here that a season free of injury won't fix. Unfortunately that's long odds. Maybe either Dave Zawatson or Jerry Fontenot, both early-draft choices, can help out as rookies. The team suffered last year when Jimbo Covert was out. Caesar Rentie, who replaced him, was one of the free agents who left.

THE BRAINTRUST

Mike Ditka earned everyone's admiration for bouncing back from his heart attack, but he certainly also deserved it for keeping the Bears on course through a terrific spate of injuries. McMahon doesn't count anymore, but he also lost Perry and Wilson for the season and Covert, Dent, and some lesser mortals for large portions of it. His iron will is one of the Bears' strengths.

DALLAS COWBOYS

After last year's disaster ended with a thirteenth loss, Coach Tom Landry allowed that there would be changes made. But, he said, the overhaul would not be sweeping. Then, in one of the off season's most enduring conversation pieces, he was swept out.

No matter how distastefully some viewed new owner Jerry Jones's quick trigger on the man who'd coached the Cowboys throughout their existence, or the departure ("forced" is perhaps too harsh an adjective) of vice president/architect Tex Schramm, or even the retirement of future Hall of Famer Randy White without a farewell celebration, all will be forgiven in Dallas if the New Order shows more than a millimeter of progress in '89.

But there's progress and then there's Progress. As mentioned elsewhere, we think the 1988 Cowboys were a 6–10 team that stumbled to 3–13 through a combination of faults not entirely of their own making. So *real* progress by Jones and Jimmy Johnson in '89 might properly be measured from win Number Seven on.

THE OFFENSE

More on the spot than even first-year coach Johnson will be the shiny Number One draft pick of all creation, quarterback Troy Aikman. Although many draftniks felt the Cowboys could have benefited by trading the first choice for a couple of hole fillers, there's no doubt that success in the NFL starts at quarterback, and Aikman was the only "franchise QB" Dallas had any hope of getting. Had they attempted to work any other kind of magic with their draft pick, the decision makers might have had a full-scale revolt among the ticket buyers.

So Steve Pelluer, last year's signal caller, has been consigned to the rubbish heap. Now for a little irony. The knock on Pelluer is not that he lacks talent but that he makes bad *decisions*. Aikman may have more talent than Pelluer, but it's hard to imagine that, with no NFL experience and only two years of major college competition, his decision-making apparatus is going to be honed a whole lot sharper than Steve's. And the one criticism you hear about Troy is that he lacks the spontaneity that makes a great leader like—oh, say, Roger Staubach.

Once you get away from quarterback, the Cowboys have a number of offensive pluses. For example, there's Herschel Walker, arguably the most devastating running back in today's world. Whether running or catching, Herschel is a threat to score every time he touches a football. There isn't any reliable backup for Walker, but his durability is well established. New fullback Daryl Johnston will have to be broken in for Timmy Newsome, who's just about broken down.

If anyone can get him the ball, expect wide receiver Michael Irvin to have a big year. Ray Alexander, Kevin Martin, and Kelvin Edwards add more youth and speed to what could be a very strong area. Tight end Thornton Chandler hasn't proved himself, and veteran Doug Cosbie left as a free agent.

In future years, the question will be asked: What if they'd taken Tony Mandarich instead of Aikman? However, it'll be asked a lot less often if the Cowboys' oversized young line plays the way they hope it will. So far the major achiever is guard Crawford Ker, but tackle Dave Widell surprised as a rookie and looks to be a solid performer. Nate Newton is an obscene 315 pounds at one guard, and Jeff Zimmerman outweighs him by a pound at tackle. Zimmerman was out all last season with an injury. Kevin Gogan, another tackle, is "only" 310. Third-round draft choice Mark Stepnoski is a good prospect, though at 270, he's a little small for this crowd. The major worry is whether Bob White can develop into an adequate center.

SPECIAL TEAMS

Punter Mike Saxon and placekicker Roger Ruzek were ordinary last year, as were the rest of the special teams. In Dallas's Year of Hell, "ordinary" was pretty good, but down the line there'll have to be improvement.

THE DEFENSE

The best part of the Dallas defense is the rush line. Okay, you've got to wonder how long Too Tall Jones will go on. (No, he's *not* older than the Alamo; he's just harder to overcome.) And there isn't a devastating, knock-'em-dead pass rusher on the scene, but Jim Jeffcoat, Kevin Brooks, and Danny Noonan are all solid. Mark Walen is a reliable backup. Even last year, running on the Cowboys was no cinch.

The linebacking situation isn't good, but maybe it's better than the abyss it was last year. Eugene Lockhart can do the job in the middle if he's healthy. The best outside man last year was Garry Cobb, who was signed after being cut by the Eagles. Ken Norton, the 1988 second-round draft choice, spent almost the whole season injured and saw only a little special-team action late, but he's the brightest hope for improvement on the outside. A pass rushing backer is needed, since the job won't be done up front.

Everson Walls remains a world-class cornerback but, he needs some help. Robert Williams showed some promise at the other corner but must improve more to hold the job. Strong safety Bill Bates isn't fast enough to rank very high, and free safety Michael Downs is showing his age. There could be several new faces starting in the secondary by the time the season opens.

THE BRAINTRUST

Jones and Johnson have rubbed a lot of people raw with their "now we'll teach you how to do it" attitude. They sure didn't fill up on humble pie at the Arkansas training table when they were roommates there. On the other hand, it's hard to be humble when you've been successful just about every time you've sat down to play. They're not dummies, and it's very likely that they'll raise the Cowboys from the ashes. If that happens, nobody will worry about old-fashioned claptrap like tact, compassion, or class.

DETROIT LIONS

The Lions can be greatly improved in 1989 if they simply lose more interestingly. Their greatest sin last year lay not in being a bad team; it was in being boring. They were so dull they couldn't even be lovable losers.

In drafting last year's most glittering collegian, Heisman Trophy winner Barry Sanders, the Lions upped the excitement factor. Sanders is a bit short at 5'8", but the holes are horizontal, not vertical. The Lions have done rather well with past Heisman winners, including Frank Sinkwich, Doak Walker, Leon Hart, Howard Cassady, Steve Owens, and Billy Sims.

New coach Wayne Fontes seems likely to inject more spirit into the troops than they showed under Daryll Rogers. At least that was the way they played for him in the final five games last year. But to get them to win—and winners are *always* more lovable than even the most cuddly losers—Fontes is going to need a couple of seasons' worth of new bodies.

THE OFFENSE

The worst part of 1988 was the offense—worst by a darn sight. Not a single area of the offense qualified as a bright spot. Fontes plans to go to a run-and-shoot offense in 1989, but if the Lions run or shoot like they ran and shot in 1988, they should be run out of town or shot at dawn.

This should be the year that quarterback Chuck Long either produces or gets off the pot. He didn't look like the Lions' QB of the future last year even before he was hurt. He combined lackluster throwing with indecisiveness. Fontes hopes that hiring a quarterback coach for the first time will help Long progress toward what Detroit expected when they drafted him first in 1986. If Long can't cut it, incumbent Rusty Hilger or ever hopeful Eric Hipple will be under center in 1989, and the Lions will be in the market to draft a new man in 1990.

The running back situation was equally drab until Sanders was drafted. Fullback James Jones may be about finished. He hasn't scored in two years. Running back Garry James has talent, but his numbers were awful. Between them, the two starters gained 866 yards. To find less effective rushing by a pair of Lions, you'd have to check the library steps. Backup Tony Paige wasn't an improvement.

Wide receiver Pete Mandley wasn't bad, considering that he was the only threat and considering that the quarterbacks were scatter-armed much of the time. Mandley isn't a burner, but he'll make a splendid running mate for swift rookie John Ford. Jeff Chadwick, Gary Lee, and Carl Bland were ineffective, but rookie Ray Roundtree, who spent most of the season on the IR, showed flashes in training camp. Rookie tight end Paul Carter was a disappointment.

A bigger disappointment was the offensive line. Rated as the one solid section of the offense in preseason, the line fell in with the general malaise and never delivered. Tackles Lomas Brown and Harvey Salem have to bring more to the Silver Dome than their reputations. Likewise for guards Kevin Glover and Joe Milinchik and center Steve Mott, whose reps aren't all that inflated to start with. If Fontes can get the adrenaline flowing here, the Lions could be in decent shape. All five starters are at an age when they should be playing their best. Moreover, they'll be pushed by huge rookie Mike Utley. And if they don't play better than last year, Utley will push someone aside.

The Lions' offense accounted for 20 touchdowns last year. With accounting like that you don't need a C.P.A.; your grandma can do it on the back of an envelope.

SPECIAL TEAMS

At least the Lions could punt and kick in 1988. Jim Arnold is one of the very best booters, averaging 42.4 per punt. Ed Murray was excellent on his placekicks. He missed only 1 of 23 extra point tries and 1 of 21 field goal attempts. Ironically, both misses were important in the Lions' losses, but that was just dumb luck. Murray is normally a come-through kicker.

The special teams should be even better this year with the signing of free agents Bobby Joe Edmonds and Mel Gray, two of the best returners available.

THE DEFENSE

The Lions gave up 313 points last year, which wasn't bad for a defense that spent thirty-five to forty minutes on the field most games. There are some definite bright spots.

Brightest of all is the linebacking corps. Mike Cofer moved into the ranks of the very best OLBs last year. His 12 sacks helped earn him a Pro Bowl start. On the far side, George Jamison played well enough to make six-year starter Jimmy Williams available to trade. Rookie Chris Spielman was a wonder in the middle, setting a new team record for tackles. Dennis Gibson, the other inside man, has shown steady improvement.

Nose tackle Jerry Ball enters his third year giving every indication that he'll be on the job for a long time to come. The same can't be said for defensive ends Eric Williams or Keith Ferguson. Neither was consistent or gave the Lions a reliable pass rush, although their sack totals, 8.5 for Ferguson and 6.5 for Williams, were not bad. Reggie Rogers was supposed to be the answer to the pass-rush problem until he was involved in a driving accident that cost three lives. Whatever the verdict in his trial for involuntary manslaughter, he seems unlikely ever to play for the Lions again.

The Lions improved at cornerback last year and *still* weren't good enough. Either Bruce McNorton or Jerry Holmes or both could be replaced. Free safety Devon Mitchell returned to play well after missing a season and a half with a knee injury. The one blue-chipper is strong safety Brian Blades. As a rookie, he tackled and covered like a veteran. There has been talk of moving him to free safety to take advantage of his size and speed, and of switching Mitchell to cornerback.

Detroit could live with its present defense, despite the weak spots, but there's very little depth.

THE BRAINTRUST

Fontes will have a more *gung-ho* squad. To move up, however, they'll have to improve the offense. A lot! Sanders,

Ford, and maybe Utley will help, but it all starts with the quarterback. In the long run, the installation of Jerry Vainisi as vice president in charge of player personnel may be more important than who coaches the team. The Lions have a sad history of failed drafts, but Vainisi is a good man to change that.

GREEN BAY PACKERS

Green Bay is the major test for the free-agency crap shoot. The Packers jumped in with both feet, outdoing all the other teams in scouting and evaluating the available horseflesh. Once they had a list of sixty players they thought could help, they went whole hog in signing them. The result is twenty new players. Even if several of them don't make the finals, the Packers' roster is going to see one heckuva turnover. Add in the draft picks and you'll really need a scorecard.

THE OFFENSE

One free agent who got away was the Colts' Gary Hogeboom. The Packers wanted Hogeboom because Randy Wright had off-season elbow surgery, and, if the truth were known, has never lived up to expectations anyway. Of course, you could say that about the brittle Hogeboom too. Apparently Don Majkowski will open the season at QB. "Magic" is world-class erratic, but he's still learning. He could develop into someone special or he could flop like a fish on a rock. With Wright, you get steady, ordinary perform-ance. Rookie Anthony Dilweg is a year away from challeng-ing them.

Of the four free-agent runners signed, the one expected to make the greatest impact is fullback Michael Haddix. He was up and down at Philadelphia but should improve the blocking out of that slot. Brent Fullwood, a two-year bust, will move to running back if he feels whole enough to play. Fullwood was drafted by former coach Forrest Gregg to be a heavy-duty, power-I back, but he had a rocky rookie season. Last year he didn't fit well at fullback in Infante's pass-first-and-ask-questions-later offense—"an octagonal peg in a round hole," Infante called him. The real knock is that he won't play with the slightest hurt. If Fullwood can avoid paper cuts, he still may be a valuable runner. If not, look for the limited Keith Woodside or the fumble-prone Paul Ott Carruth.

By one count, the receivers dropped 53 passes last year. Well, that happens with rookies like Sterling Sharpe, the number one draft choice, and Perry Kemp, a free agent who took over after Walter Stanley went out at midseason with a shoulder injury. Stanley has the most game-breaking poten-tial of the trio. Tight end Ed West caught 30 passes but is mainly a blocker.

The offensive line never jelled last year, but the draft and the free-agent pool showered goodies. F'rinstance, Tony Mandarich is, they swear, the best blocking tackle to arrive in the league since Anthony Munoz. Of course, he wants to be paid like a Saudi prince, but supposedly all they have to do is bury him in money and he'll bury opposing linemen. Returning OLT Ken Ruettgers is a possible Pro Bowler too, but he may be switched to the right side. Ron Hallstrom is a fine returning guard. Bill Ard, a free agent from the Giants, is penciled in at the other guard. Either former Seahawk Blair Bush or former Saint James Campen will take over center, and either is an improvement over Mark Cannon, who was a liability last year. That leaves former regulars Rich Moran, Keith Uecker, and sub Dave Croston to fill in when necessary.

Improved receiving and a greatly improved line could merge with a year's experience in Infante's system to make this a decent offense. If Majkowski becomes steadier and Fullwood begins to play, it could be outstanding.

SPECIAL TEAMS

Who, oh who, will do the placekicking? The Packers went through four placekickers last year, and Curtis Burrow, who ended with the job, missed 2 of his 4 extra-point attempts and his only field goal try. Punter Don Bracken might not make it back after a poor season. The free agents are punter Maury Buford (Giants) and placekicker Kirk Roach (Bills). At least the coverage squads will have a lot of bodies to choose from.

THE DEFENSE

The Pack's defense was smart and opportunistic without being all that talented last year. The kudos belong to defen-sive coordinator Hank Bullough and a dedicated bunch of veterans.

Defensive end Alphonso Carreker was the main free-agent loss, but Shawn Patterson, who has more pass-rush-ing potential, was certain to replace him anyway. Third-round draft choice Matt Brock is another candidate. He was a good pass rusher at Oregon. Robert Brown can stop the running game at the other DE. The nose tackle will be Jerry Boyarski, Blaise Winter, or free agent Toby Williams. None is hopeless, but none is outstanding.

In Tim Harris, Green Bay has one of the best outside linebackers around. His 13.5 sacks were only part of his value. He is an inspirational, never-say-die guy who lifts the level of play of everyone on the unit. John Anderson on the far side is thirty-three, so a replacement is due. Brian Noble and Johnny Holland are okay inside. There are a lot of bodies to back up, but no one stands out.

Right cornerback Dave Brown is thirty-six and left CB Mark Lee is thirty-one. Both played well last year, despite serious deficiencies in speed. Van Jakes, a free agent from New Orleans, will probably replace Brown. Strong safety Mark Murphy had a bang-up year, but he too is over thirty. Chuck Cecil is likely to supplant Ken Stills at free safety. Cecil can make big plays, but he may destroy his body in the process.

The Packers have been hunting a top pass rusher, it seems, since Lombardi left. Patterson could help, but he's not the answer. Can Bullough continue to work miracles?

THE BRAINTRUST

Coach Infante and executive veep Tom Braatz seem to be in synch with each other, and both are committed to moving the Pack out of their twenty-year doldrums. But how far can they go with other teams' rejects?

The preliminary opinion is that they'll move up to average this season, but to move higher, or even stay there, they need more guys like Harris, Ruettgers, and Mandarich.

LOS ANGELES RAMS

The Rams are a team on the rise. Just how far they go is going to depend on how quickly their young players mature and if a few key veterans can hold on for one more stellar season. It's a narrow path, but the club has the necessities to negotiate it. A little luck wouldn't hurt.

The Rams looked like big losers in the free-agent derby, giving up twelve players and gaining only three. Particularly hard hit was the defense, which lost linemen Gary Jeter, Greg Meisner, and Fred Stokes, linebacker Jim Collins, and defensive backs Johnnie Johnson and Mickey Sutton. Only Johnson was a starter, but Jeter was an important pass rushing sub and the others constituted a load of the depth. Looking at it from another point of view, the less satisfactory side of the 1988 Rams was the defense, and changes were scheduled there already, the Rams simply protected what they expected to keep in '89 and beyond. And that included six draft choices out of the first seventy-five players chosen.

THE OFFENSE

Any offense that can score 407 points—an average of more than 25 points per game—has got to satisfy most critics and should come home a winner.

The key man was quarterback Jim Everett, who put up impressive numbers: 3,964 yards gained and 31 touchdowns. More important, he began to assert himself as the leader of the Rams' offense. All signs are that he's ready to set up shop as one of the top QBs—maybe the best—of the 1990s. The only worry is that there's not much behind him. Mark Herrmann has been around for a long time without ever holding a job long anywhere.

Everett got plenty of help from his receiving corps last year, but he figures to get even more in 1989. Henry Ellard is coming off a career year with 86 catches, 1,414 yards, and

10 touchdowns. He's at the top of his game. Ready to blossom are Aaron Cox (21.1 average on 28 catches) and Willie Anderson (29.0 average on 11 catches). The speedy duo came on the first two draft rounds last year, and though Cox dropped a few and Anderson saw only limited action, both should shine this year. Tight ends Damone Johnson and Pete Holohan leave something to be desired as blockers, but they caught 101 passes between them.

Greg Bell, who was considered only a throw-in on the Dickerson trade, had a marvelous season with 1,212 yards and 16 touchdowns. The feeling persists, however, that he's the interim tailback, waiting for someone even better. Charles White, the league's leading rusher in 1987, has retired, clearing the way for Gaston Green, the heralded rookie who carried only 35 times last year. The surprise of last year's excellent rookie crop was fifth-rounder Robert Delpino, who impressed on the special teams and could become the starting fullback over incumbent Buford McGee and heralded rookie Cleveland Gary.

If there's any cause to worry about the Rams' offense, you'll find it at offensive tackle. OLT Irv Pankey has three "overs"—overweight, over thirty and overrated. ORT Jackie Slater is one of the great offensive linemen of the decade, but he's thirty-five. Backup Robert Cox is a trifle small at 258. The seventy-fifth player taken in the draft, OT Kevin Robbins of Michigan State is big enough at 293, but he may not be ready. Tom Newberry is one of the best guards in football, a sure All-Pro. Duval Love is adequate at the other guard. Center Doug Smith is solid, but he too is getting a bit long in the tooth.

SPECIAL TEAMS

The Rams have no particular holes on their special teams, but they aren't exactly sensational either. Delpino, who provided some spark, may be playing regularly instead this year. Mike Lansford scored 117 points but isn't the first name you think of when the subject is placekickers. Punter Dale Hatcher is only so-so. Rookie Darryl Henley, who will be tried at cornerback, was a top college kick returner.

THE DEFENSE

The defense gave up 293 points—not awful, but it definitely needed upgrading. Four of the top six draft choices are defenders. Several of last year's starters are likely to provide the depth that was lost by free agency.

The incumbent three-man line of Shawn Miller, Alvin Wright, and Doug Reed is too light to do the job consistently. All of them come in under 265, and none of them provided a steady pass rush. As a consequence, the Rams had to depend too much on their linebackers to hurry passers. Gary Jeter was used at DE in passing situations and registered 11.5 sacks. No doubt he could have been useful had he not gone the free-agent route, but at thirty-four he had to be sacrificed to protect youth. New on the block are Bill Hawkins and Brian Smith, who is also a linebacker possibility.

Outside linebacker Kevin Greene was the main pass rusher, especially early in the season, and he finished with 16.5 sacks. With a little help up front, he could be less spectacular but more effective. Mike Wilcher is solid on the other side. Fred Strickland played a good deal in the middle as a rookie and should start this season. Rookie Frank Stams played outside at Notre Dame but may be moved inside for the Rams. Last year's regulars, Carl Ekern and Mark Jerue, might both be out. Ekern is thirty-five and Jerue didn't really impress.

Jerry Gray and LeRoy Irvin are okay cornerbacks, but Irvin is thirty-two and may lose out, either to Henley or sophomore, Anthony Newman. Yet another sophomore, James Washington, should take over Johnson's free safety slot. Michael Stewart isn't solid at strong safety either.

There could be three new starters in the Rams' secondary and as many as eight are possible on the defensive unit. That's a tremendous deficit in experience to overcome. Nevertheless the Rams may make it up with added muscle.

THE BRAINTRUST

Coach John Robinson will give up some defense (for future considerations), but his offense should be able to make up the difference. We think he's an underrated coach who will shoehorn his team into first place in the Western Division. However, the Rams always seem to fall on their prats once the playoffs begin, and with so much youth in so many places, that would seem a likely scenario once again.

MINNESOTA VIKINGS

If you have to go out on a thin limb and pick a team to win all the way through the Super Bowl this year, you'll receive the fewest raised eyebrows by tabbing the Vikings. They were a popular pick last year, especially from Week 10 through Week 14, when they won five straight and outscored opponents 167–26. When the Voracious Vikings sacked and pillaged New Orleans 45–3 with two weeks to go in the season, there were some ready to declare the playoffs and Super Bowl superfluous and anoint Minnesota then and there. Of course, the next week the Vikes lost *for the second time* to Green Bay, suggesting that their crowning was a trifle premature. And then there was that sad playoff appearance at San Francisco . . .

Nevertheless, Minnesota has so many good things it should get to the playoffs this year. And then who knows?

THE DEFENSE

Any evaluation of the Vikings' chances has to start with the defense. With a little puttering, it should be every bit as sublime as last year, which means that it's almost certain to surpass the Bears and be the envy of the league.

Two of the four frontmen are legitimate All-Pros. Tackle Keith Millard was regarded by some as the most valuable defensive player in football last year. The Vikes credited him with 86 tackles and 8 sacks, both high numbers for an inside man on a four-man front. DE Chris Doleman tied Millard with 8 sacks. 'Twixt the two of them, they made the right side as impregnable as it gets. Henry Thomas, the other tackle, wasn't bad either with 6 sacks. Al Baker, who closed the season at the left DE, was let slide as a free agent. Al Noga, the rookie starter when last season began, will get another shot. A year's experience should have increased his dependability.

The linebacking was a potential trouble spot, but the Vikings traded their number one draft choice for the Steelers' discontented Mike Merriweather. Unless a year's holdout has atrophied Merriweather's skills, the Vikes got a better player than they were likely to draft. When they finally did draft a player late in the second round, they took another linebacker, Wake Forest's David Braxton. Of last year's starters, middleman Scott Studwell is thirty-five, right LB Jesse Solomon is coming off knee surgery, and left LB David Howard is only so-so. Ray Berry, who filled in well last year, may move in as a regular for one of the three incumbents, but another quality linebacker wouldn't hurt. Backups Sam Anno and Walker Lee Ashley went as free agents.

Two of the best defenders in the league roam the Minnesota secondary. Strong safety Joey Browner is a perennial All-Pro. He was the biggest factor in the Vikings' playoff win over Los Angeles. If anything, Carl Lee had an even better season at cornerback. The other CB, Reggie Rutland, did a fine job, though he was overshadowed by Lee. Brad Edwards should win the strong safety spot in his second year. He started for a stretch in '88 but was replaced by experienced John Harris late. The addition of possible Pro Bowler Merriweather means the Vike D should hold foes to about the same 233 points as last time out.

SPECIAL TEAMS

Placekicker Chuck Nelson doesn't have a lot of distance, but the defense will likely give him plenty of chances from inside the forty, where he's money in the bank. There was nothing special about the rest of the special teams, and punter Bucky Scribner was ordinary at best. In fact, his net of 32.6 was pretty poor. Using Anthony Carter as a return man was just asking for trouble.

THE OFFENSE

Wade Wilson will get a chance to prove that last season was no fluke. Despite his gaudy 91.5 NFL Passer Rating, there are still some who question his ability to lead the team through tough games. Tommy Kramer returns, but unless Wilson flops completely or is injured, he won't see much action.

Wide receiver Anthony Carter is the Vikes' most potent weapon. He caught 72 passes for a 17.0 average and 8 touchdowns last year, and the only complaint was that he wasn't targeted more often. Hassam Jones, who had a 19.5

average on 32 fewer catches, is dangerous too. Ryan Bethea spent last year on the IR, but he could be ready for big things this year. Tight end Steve Jordan is at the top of his game, with the only question being a backup. Sub Mike Mularkey free-agented over to Pittsburgh.

Starting guard Terry Tausch was another lost free agent, but Minnesota thinks Todd Kalis is ready for that spot. OT Gary Zimmerman is one of the best, and Randall McDaniel, a rookie starter last year, could become an All-Pro. The key man is center Kirk Lowdermilk. When he was out for a while last year, the whole offense stumbled.

To scramble anatomy (as well as a metaphor), the Vikings' Achilles' heel is in their legs. Inability to run the ball at key moments makes their offense a thing of beauty when the passing game is hot and junk forever when it's not. To round up the usual suspects: start with Darrin Nelson, a fine little back who isn't robust enough to run fifteen or twenty times a game, and D. J. Dozier, a big back who has been both oft injured and oftener disappointing for two years. Then there's Allen Rice, Alfred Anderson, and Rick Fenney—none of whom threaten to become household words or home run hitters. Because the Minnesota defense shuts down opponent runners so well, the Vikes can outrush a foe and still be inadequate on the ground.

THE BRAINTRUST

Jerry Burns is a good man, but those who wanted him for Coach of the Year last season have a hard time explaining why he couldn't motivate his charges in either Green Bay game or the playoff loss to San Francisco. Actually he did a pretty good job most of the time heading up a strange team with a one-armed offense, possibly the league's best defense, and certainly the NFL's worst drunk-driving record.

Mike Lynn is one of the most visible GMs around, but he seems to have been snookered in the free-agent grab unless WR Anthony Allen, DB Daryl Smith, and DE Curtis Greer are better than they've shown till now.

NEW ORLEANS SAINTS

The Saints were good, but in the final analysis—like in losing three of the last four—they weren't good enough. The verdict that there just weren't enough quality athletes on this ball club and that they were succeeding on over-achievement presents an interesting conundrum. Can over-achievers continue to do so if they begin to doubt that their actions can accomplish their goals? Or, in other words, when do you say to hell with it, it won't work anyway? If the Saints ever reach that point, the bottom could drop out real fast.

Still, based on their first-half play last year, the Saints

have to be given a shot at the NFC West, even if they look inferior to the Rams and 49ers on paper.

THE OFFENSE

Quarterback Bobby Hebert is a solid enough passer within his limitations. He's best at running a careful, take-what-you-can-get kind of offense, and that's just as well. New Orleans doesn't have much big-play potential on offense anyway. Some serious questions were asked about his leadership ability at the end of last season, when he did some ugly finger pointing. That's a tricky business. It can sometimes produce a jump start, but just as often it can split a team into warring factions. The Saints better stay behind Hebert because after him the deluge. Dave Wilson just ain't gonna get it done.

There's competence but not much excitement in the wide receivers. Eric Martin took 85 catches to get 1,083 yards. His longest reception—the longest by any Saint—was 40 yards. Lonzell Hill, the other WR, is pretty much the same. He had 66 catches. Brett Perriman, last year's second-round draft choice, didn't do much spectacular. He does have speed, and with that there's hope. Tight end Hoby Brenner is a good blocker and should be recovered from the hurts that beset him last year. John Tice is an okay backup.

If Ironhead Heywood shows up with his knee healed and he's not as big as all outdoors, the Saints will have a great power runner who can block and break off long dashes. But if he lets his pounds pile up as he has in the past, they'll have the world's most expensive paperweight. Even in that event, New Orleans is solid at running back, with gifted Rueben Mayes seemingly recovered from his knee injury and gutsy Dalton Hilliard still available. Buford Jordan also showed some ability last year. If everyone's healthy, someone will probably get traded.

The offensive line was hurt badly last year when ORT Stan Brock was kayoed at midseason. Even if he comes back all the way, the Saints need at least one more tackle to provide depth. No one, including Brock, is really outstanding, the kind of horse who can open a hole through a battleship. Center Steve Korte, guards Brad Edelman and Steve Trapilo, and OLT Jim Dombrowski are competent, but none of them is likely to go to the Pro Bowl unless he plans to sit in the stands.

SPECIAL TEAMS

The Saints' special teams have been a big part of their success the last two years, but the loss of returner Mel Gray through free agency could hurt. Kicker Morten Andersen had an off-year and missed a couple of important field goals late in the season. Regardless he's still considered the NFL's top booter. Punter Brian Hansen is perfectly serviceable.

THE DEFENSE

Nose tackle is getting to be a real pain in the assault on enemy offenses. In 1987 New Orleans drafted DE Shawn

Knight in the first round with the thought of converting him to the middle. He was such a bust that last year he was converted into a Denver Bronco in exchange for Ted Gregory, Denver's 1988 first-round pick, who so far has been worthless. The Saints drafted Tony Stephens in the third round last year, and he didn't even last through training camp. In the meantime, James Geathers hasn't been able to cut it since he injured a knee two years ago. Regular Tony Elliott irked the coaching staff with his attitude and work habits. He was finally declared *persona non grata* before the draft and was released. The latest plan is to move DE Bruce Clark inside. That would further weaken the flanks, where Frank Warren, Jim Wilks, and Blaine Board are all over thirty and nothing to write home about anyway. First-round pick Wayne Martin figured to go later in the draft and was rated behind several other available DEs.

New Orleans survives with a sub-par front three because they have as good a set of linebackers as anyone in the NFC. Any one of the four could go to the Pro Bowl. Last year it was Sam Mills. Rickey Jackson and Vaughan Johnson may have had even better years, and Pat Swilling topped them on his best days. As long as they stay healthy, the Saints will not be a soft touch for any rival. The only worry is depth. Number one sub Alvin Toles's career may be over because of a knee injury. Joe Kohlbrand is a definite step down.

The secondary is universally slow-footed. One of the starting cornerbacks, Van Jakes, was free-agented off, leaving the way open to Reggie Sutton, who has had drug problems. Dave Waymer, the other corner, is over thirty, and 1988 wasn't one of his better years. Rookie Robert Massey has great natural gifts but is raw as a skinned knee. Antonio Gibson, the strong safety, had a thirty-day drug suspension last year. Gene Atkins, his replacement, led the team with 4 interceptions, but Gibson is the better player. Free safety Brett Maxie is regarded as merely adequate.

THE BRAINTRUST

Coach Jim Mora blamed himself rather than his players for the end-of-season fizzle. That's nice, but more properly credit him for the first-half streak. Rest assured he will continue to get as much and more out of this team as it's possible to get. And that leaves it squarely up to GM Jim Finks, who built the team up to competitive. Now he must find the people to put them over the top. His successful track record with Chicago and Minnesota indicates his recent failure to find an adequate nose tackle is only a momentary glitch.

NEW YORK GIANTS

You can find lots of excuses for the Giants finishing out of the money last year—Lawrence Taylor's forced thirty-day

vacation, the fluke field goal-touchdown against the Eagles, the failure to stop one last drive by the Jets, and so forth.

The fact is, they blew a golden opportunity, and they might not have the chance this time around.

This is basically a veteran team, and maybe too many vets have been around too long. The one place where youth can be found in abundance is in the offensive line, and that's just where most winners stock up on experience. Don't look for the Giants to suddenly go belly up, but a li'l slippage is a distinct possibility. Figure them to hold second place with maybe one fewer win than last year, say 9–7.

THE OFFENSE

Phil Simms is a superior, underrated quarterback, but he'll probably need another Super Bowl win before anyone will admit it. He's gotten better since he won number XXI, and as long as he's in there the Giants have no reason to complain. He passed for 3,359 yards and 21 touchdowns in kind of a generic Simms year. On the downside, he's thirty-two. Even more of a downer is what happens if Simms gets hurt. Jeff Hostetler has as yet to prove he's ready to do the job, and you get the feeling the Giants don't think he ever will be. Might Simms be in danger? New York gave up 60 sacks last year.

Simms has an adequate crew of receivers, with Lionel Manuel the gem of the collection. Manuel had his best year by far with 65 catches and 1,029 yards, although his 4 touchdowns were less than you'd expect. Stephen Baker had 7 TDs on only 40 receptions. The worry is that Baker barely nudges the scales at 165 pounds, and the history of wee little WRs in the NFL is footnoted with numerous IRs. However, Odessa Turner and Mark Ingram had *their* injuries last year, so the Giants are well stocked. Tight end Mark Bavaro was also dogged by injury last year, which is why he failed to repeat as World's Tip-Top TE. Zeke Mowatt is perhaps the best TE not starting in the league.

New York may be putting too much faith in the end-of-season spurt that gave Joe Morris over a thousand rushing yards. Little Joe couldn't do much of anything through the first two-thirds of the sched, and he's definitely not the runner he was three years ago when he was twenty-six. Ottis Anderson has been released and George Adams has been a continual disappointment. Fullback Maurice Carthon earns his money by blocking, and indeed he *does* earn it.

A lot of Morris's problems were caused by an offensive line that didn't jell until late. The number one and two draft choices helped get things together. Eric Moore started all season at guard, and John Elliott finally won a tackle slot. Sophomore Doug Riesenberg was a useful tackle. The Giants' first two draft choices this year again went to linemen. Brian Williams, the 306-pound giant Giant from Minnesota, can play anywhere along the line, with guard being his most likely spot this year. The influx of youth may give New York a fearsome front in a couple of years, but very young lines are seldom terrific right off the bat. Some veterans could add a little know-how, but guard Billy Ard left as a free agent, a move that could prove costly. When center Bart Oates was injured, the Giants had to lure ex-Jet Joe Fields out of retirement. Fields was dropped this year when New York signed free agent Frank Winters from Cleveland. OT Karl Nelson is fighting a return of Hodgkin's disease. Tackle William Roberts is coming off an injury. This is not a solid area of the team yet.

The Giants have to be able to run the ball to make it to the division title. They didn't do it well last year. This year they could find themselves struggling with an offense that looks like Miami's.

SPECIAL TEAMS

Raul Allegre will improve the placekicking if he's healthy, but Paul McFadden was by no means a washout last year. The punting is okay, but the coverage wasn't. And the Giants *really* need a kick returner.

THE DEFENSE

The Giants' defense is still formidable after all these years. Nevertheless the 304 points they gave up in 1988 was 78 more than the 1986 champs let happen. There's no glaring weakness and lots of strengths. More than anything else, though, they could use some more depth.

The front three—DEs Eric Dorsey and Leonard Marshall and NT Jim Burt—make a solid unit. Opponents were held to 1,759 rushing yards last year. The retirement of veteran George Martin may cut into the pass rush a little.

The only question concerning Lawrence Taylor is whether he'll be there. As long as he avoids strike three on substance abuse, the Giants have the premier outside linebacker of the decade. Carl Banks on the other side had a very poor season after his holdout, but he should be up to snuff this year. Pepper Johnson and Gary Reasons are just okay in the middle. Harry Carson's retirement takes away a lot of inspiration. Johnnie Cooks is an adequate backup.

Cornerback, where New York can choose from Mark Collins, Sheldon White, and Perry Williams, will be all right, but there could be a problem at safety. Strong safety Kenny Hill is thirty-one and has never been great on pass coverage. Free safety Terry Kinard is thirty and slumped badly last year. Either is on the bubble, but backup Adrian White has been notable only for his temper thus far.

With an epidemic of good health, this defense can carry the team a long way. However, the way these things usually go, the Giants are going to need some able subs, and right now they're few and far between.

THE BRAINTRUST

Last season left a sour taste. Coach Bill Parcells has to get the team back on the beam, forget the Jets game, and chalk it up to experience. Then he has to find a running game and plug a few other holes. If he can do all that, he'll be showered in Gatorade.

PHILADELPHIA EAGLES

The Eagles shouldn't repeat as Eastern Division champs. Big deal! They shouldn't have won last year, if you go by paper evaluations. Instead they came within a handful of their own errors and a faceful of fog of playing for the NFC title. Buddy Ryan told them they could win, and darned if they didn't believe it. Not even the Shadow knows what wonders lurk in Buddy's bag of tricks this year.

Nevertheless Philadelphia goes into 1989 with two strikes against it. Not having a draft choice until forty-eight other hopefuls had been tagged makes it unlikely any of the choices the Eagles did get will turn the world upside down. And despite the 10–6 record, there were some definite shortcomings on last year's team. Strike one. The schedule will be tougher too. That's the kick in the face the NFL annually awards to its top teams. Strike two.

THE OFFENSE

Anything untoward happening to quarterback Randall Cunningham would be the ultimate strike three. He accounted for better than 70 percent of the Eagles' offense last year. You can admire him all you want, but 70-plus percent out of anybody is too much. Philadelphia (a) relied too much on his passes and (b) far too much on his legs. Running quarterbacks—and Cunningham was the best—make for a questionable offense. Worse, they usually end up with something or other in a cast.

The Eagles are well backed at QB. Matt Cavanaugh is a competent career sub, and Don McPherson, who was taxied last year, has a world of ability. Should Cunningham be sidelined for any lengthy spell, Coach Ryan will have to choose between Cavanaugh's experience and McPherson's more Randall-like talents. But neither *is* Randall.

It seems like only yesterday that Keith Byars was being touted as the next Jim Brown. Then came the foot injuries, and ever since he's run more like James Brown. Owww! He was certainly useful last year catching 72 passes, but his 517 rushing yards weren't at all the kind of production hoped for when he was drafted on the first round in 1986. Behind him is Walter Abercrombie, who never lived up to his advance billing with the Steelers. Fullback Anthony Toney is often injured, and his backup, Michael Haddix, was free-agented to Green Bay. No one in last year's backfield could get around end except Cunningham, but draft choice Robert Drummond may have been a steal on the third round.

One area where the Eagles can expect improvement is in wide receiver. They'll have Mike Quick for a whole season. Healthy, Quick is one of the half dozen best. Cris Carter came on last year in Quick's absence, averaging 19.5 yards per catch. On the down side, Kenny Jackson was lost to free agency. Amid all the huzzahs over rookie tight end Keith Jackson, there were a few clunk notes over his blocking, or rather the lack thereof. There was no question about his receiving, though—81 catches and 6 touchdowns.

The offensive line improved at the end of last season, once veteran guard Ron Baker made it back from injury. Maybe Ron Solt, who cost a number one draft choice, can bounce back from surgery to fill the other guard. Another possibility is that Matt Patchan, a rookie injured all last year, may be ready to move in at one tackle spot. Ron Heller is adequate at the other tackle, and Dave Rimington won't embarrass anyone at center. But even with the best possible scenario, this is just an average group.

SPECIAL TEAMS

You've got to wonder if anybody outside the clan can identify all the kicking Zendejases and which teams they kick for. The Eagles' Zendejas is Luis, and he solved a problem with 16 of 20 field goals. Punter John Teltschik was blocked 3 times, and furthermore his record was a little below par. The Eagles did an okay job covering kicks, but their return crew didn't return for much. They'd like a speedy return man. Who wouldn't?

THE DEFENSE

The Eagles' defense was opportunistic in 1989 with 32 interceptions and a plus-18 turnover differential. Given their druthers, most teams would prefer *talented* over *opportunistic* defenses because talent lasts from season to season. Opportunism can disappear in a puff.

The only absolutely great talent on the Philadelphia defense is Reggie White, the best in the world at his position. His 18 sacks were only one less than the total for Pittsburgh's whole team. But Reggie wasn't a happy camper this spring, disputing his contract. The Birds might be better served to keep White focused on football because, after him, the whole defense is average, overage, or undersize.

Among the average are other frontliners Jerome Brown, Clyde Simmons, and Mike Pitts. Factor in White and this is the best part of the D. Opponents got only 1,652 rushing yards against these four, which was almost 300 fewer yards than Philadelphia managed with its own substandard rushing game. The only concern here is depth, but the Eagles made a good move in signing Bears' free agent Al Harris.

The linebacking needs depth too, but that's not the major problem. Middle linebacker Mike Reichenbach has average size and less-than-average speed. Outside linebacker Seth Joyner is okay on one side, possibly the best defender after White, but Todd Bell is a strong safety playing out of position on the other side. He doesn't lack for courage, but the pounds just aren't there. Moreover, he might be needed more in the secondary this year. Jesse Small, drafted on the second round but the Eagles' first choice, very well might start as a rookie. Paul Butcher, a free agent from Detroit, could also find a spot.

The Eagles were thoroughly vulnerable to passes last year and only survived on their interceptions. Strong safety Andre Waters is likely to be replaced. Cornerback Roynell Young may be near the end too. Terry Hoage, who replaced Wes Hopkins at free safety in passing situations, was the leader in interceptions with eight.

THE BRAINTRUST

For all his yakking, Buddy Ryan came through last year by sneaking up on everybody and then closing with a 6–1 rush. It's going to be a lot harder this time around.

PHOENIX CARDINALS

If you're old enough, you might remember the character who walked around with a rain cloud over his head in the old Li'l Abner comic strip. His name was something like "Joe Btifsplyk," and everything he came near met with disaster. He must have been a Cardinals fan. In every group there's at least one that will be forever jinxed. One that spends its thwarted existence grasping the wrong end of the stick. That's the Cardinals.

Aside from the hope that springs eternal even in the breast of the guy who mounts the gallows and plants his feet on the trapdoor, there seems to be no reason to expect an upturn in the Cards' fate this year. Matching last year's 7–9 would be a real accomplishment. Not that the Cards don't have a few strengths. It's just that nearly all of them are threatened by age or infirmity.

THE OFFENSE

For example, Neil Lomax is all any team could ask for in a passer. His arm accounted for 3,395 yards and 20 touchdowns last year. At thirty-one, he's at an age when many quarterbacks have their greatest years. But he also has an arthritic hip that could end his season or his career at any moment. Behind Lomax there's free agent Gary Hogeboom, a quarterback with a history of injury and underachievement that should make him perfect for this club.

The tight end combination of Robert Awalt and Jay Novacek makes one of the few Cardinals' unmixed blessings, and they added big Walter Reeves on the third round of the draft. Wide receivers J. T. Smith and Roy Green are terrific for guys thirty-three and thirty-two, respectively. Added together that's retirement age for most of us; separately, either is a common end-of-the-line for wideouts. Ernie Jones, who was excellent in limited duty as a rookie, could replace one of them.

Age is part of the worry about the running backs. Earl Ferrell is thirty-one and Stump Mitchell thirty. The other part is Ferrell's substance-abuse situation. Tony Jordan showed some promise last year until he was injured. The saddest thing about the Cardinals' running back condition is that they nearly chose John Stephens in the draft last year, then opted for linebacker Ken Harvey instead. Stephens could have solved any running back problems for the next decade; Harvey didn't nail down a starting position last year.

OT Tootie Robbins is thirty-one and coming off an injury. When the Cards lost his 305 pounds last year, they were hurting. The rest of the offensive line is okay, with OT Luis Sharpe an All-Pro and center Derek Kennard above par. Second-round draft choice Joe Wolf could win a guard spot. But, as Robbins' injury proved, there's an extreme lack of depth.

If Mother Nature heals the injured and Father Time stays away for another season—and if nothing else untoward occurs—the Cardinals should score more than their share of points. They'll have to, because the defense and special teams aren't ready to bail them out.

THE SPECIAL TEAMS

Val Sikahema is still a good return man, and Ron Wolfley is an outstanding special teams guy, but the rest of the return-and-coverage squads leave lots to be desired. Even with Sikahema's 10.3 punt-return average, opponents came out of the season with a higher average return than Phoenix. Punter Greg Horne had a so-so average (40.9) and poor net (32.9), in part because the coverage guys didn't excel. No matter; he jumped ship to sign as a free agent with Washington anyway. Placekicker Al Del Greco doesn't rank with the league's better booters. Teddy Garcia, who flunked with New England last year, will get a trial.

THE DEFENSE

In Freddie Joe Nunn, who led the team with 14 sacks, the Cards have a possible Pro Bowl DE. They'd have a matched set if David Galloway could avoid injury, but that hasn't happened for a while. Linemen like Rod Saddler, Bob

Clasby, and Steve Alford are just sort of there. Curtis Greer, a sub DE, free-agented off to Minnesota. A top-flight tackle and a healthy Galloway could make this a strength.

Last year Phoenix had a raft of former first-round draft choices at linebacker—E. J. Junior in 1981, Ricky Hunley in 1984 (by Cincinnati), Anthony Bell in 1986, and Harvey in 1988. If nothing else, they proved that a first-round selection doesn't ensure an outstanding player. RLB Junior was free-agented away. Hunley couldn't supplant Niko Noga in the middle. Bell and Harvey split time at LLB. Only Noga was good for big plays, but he also made some big mistakes. Well, here we go again! This time the Cards hope to have better luck with LB Eric Hill as their-first round pick.

Strong safety Tim McDonald could break through as a star, and free safety Lonnie Young is okay. Lester Lyles subbed last year, but he's a new San Diego free agent. Cornerback is a bigger problem. Neither Carl Carter nor Cedric Mack is anybody's ultimate answer.

The defense gave up 398 points last year. They are likely to hit 400 before Wade Boggs.

THE BRAINTRUST

The Cardinals have had a long history of front-office ineptitude. Director of pro personnel Larry Wilson hasn't struck out yet, but he hasn't reversed much either. He appears to have lost ground in the free-agent carnival. His drafts haven't been very good. This year he most needed help at cornerback, a defensive tackle, and some heir-apparents at wide receiver and running back. So on the first four rounds, he drafted a linebacker, two offensive linemen, and a tight end. He got some good players, but from their positions you'd think he was drafting for another team.

Coach Gene Stallings is no miracle worker, although he gets good marks from most observers. Last year, when the Cardinals were winning for a while, he didn't get swept away in the euphoria. Maybe he should have because he probably won't get many chances this year. On days when the offense is working, the Cardinals can upset anybody, but a successful season doesn't seem to be in the Cards. Joe Btifsplyk strikes again.

SAN FRANCISCO 49ERS

Strange thing. The 49ers are coming off the Super Bowl win that made them the Team of the Decade in just about every place except Washington. A championship tends to inflate the estimated value of everybody on the roster. Like, if you're the third left cornerback on a championship team, people assume you're better than a lot of the starters on other teams. So how come the Niners lost only two players to free agency? That's right. The roster that was "proved" the best by Super Bowl test was the one least snipped. The only losses were backup tight end Ron Heller and reserve DB Greg Cox. Okay, the 49ers pay well, and there's the chance of more playoff money. Still, it *is* strange.

Meanwhile, San Francisco went out and got some depth in guard Terry Tausch and TE Jamie Williams. They also got what might be the steal of the free-agency circus. Dallas wide receiver Mike Sherrard has been on the IR for a couple of years recovering from a broken leg, but before that he was one of the hottest prospects around. Just imagine what would happen if he came back all the way and paired with Jerry Rice!

THE OFFENSE

Joe Montana now has three Super Bowl victories to his credit, leaving him one behind Pittsburgh Hall of Famer Terry Bradshaw. However, if you'd like to argue that Montana was the key man in all three San Francisco wins while Pittsburgh won its first two with a defense that carried the offense, you'll get no argument here.

Having Steve Young on the roster automatically causes a quarterback controversy, but that's a small price to pay. Montana has never been an oak and now seems likely to miss a few games every year. But with Young ready to relieve, the 49ers are in better shape than just about anybody. Free agent Kevin Sweeney was given a try at Dallas but wasn't ready.

Playing most of the season on one leg, Jerry Rice was still better than all but a handful of NFL pass catchers, and you saw in the playoffs what he could do when he got healthy. The Montana-to-Rice combo is perhaps the most devastating tandem in NFL history. John Taylor played effectively at the end of the season, but the 49ers would like another premier receiver. Talk about greedy! Anyway, it could be Sherrard. Tight end John Frank has decided to retire rather than risk another hand injury such as he had last year (he plans to be a surgeon). Second-round draft choice Wesley Walls should fit in nicely, and free agent Williams will be useful for his blocking.

Roger Craig was a great back all year. Many boosted him for league MVP. He had 2,036 rushing-passing yards and 10 touchdowns! Terrence Flagler has been injured for two years but is still an exciting prospect. Tom Rathman is the ideal blocking-plunging-pass-catching fullback and deserves a lot more credit than he gets.

The offensive line was shaky at the start of last season but improved week to week until it became one of the best. Look for young OTs Steve Wallace and Harris Barton to get even better, and big Bubba Paris is an able backup. The guards, Jesse Sapolu and Guy McIntyre, could be a tad bigger. The big question is who will fill Randy Cross's big shoes at center.

SPECIAL TEAMS

Rookie Mike Cofer replaced Ray Wersching, who was practically a San Francisco landmark, and did a good job. Another rookie, punter Barry Helton, was released, then re-signed, but averaged a paltry 39.3. A new punter is a distinct possibility. Taylor returned 2 of 44 punts for TDs and averaged 12.6. Neither Taylor nor Doug DuBose set the world afire on kickoff returns, but the coverage squads played very well.

THE DEFENSE

Like the rest of the team, the 49ers' defense got stronger as the season wore on. They weren't locked into either a 3–4 or 4–3 and used both. Nose tackle Michael Carter was the best-known and best of the front-liners. Youngsters Larry Roberts and Kevin Fagan started at the DE slots, and both could use a bit more heft. Roberts had 6 sacks. Pierce Holt and Dan Stubbs have potential and played well at times.

Charles Haley is a rising star at left outside linebacker. He led the team with 11.5 sacks. Bill Romanowski played much of the season for ailing Keena Turner at the other OLB slot, but his future seems eventually to be on the inside. Rikki Ellison appears vulnerable there, creating an opening for first-round draft choice Keith DeLong, the son of 1964 Outland Trophy winner Steve DeLong. Michael Walter is solid as the other ILB. Jim Fahnhorst is a satisfactory backup. A lot will depend on whether Turner can gear up for a full season.

All things considered, the starting San Fran secondary is about the best in the NFC. It's also the deepest in the whole league. Free safety Ronnie Lott is an established big-play man as well as the spiritual leader of the D. Strong safety Jeff Fuller is another top gun who is often overlooked because he plays in the same milieu as Lott. Tom Holmoe is one of those people who'd probably play regularly for a lot of people, but is limited to passing situations because of the 49ers' regulars. Cornerbacks Tim McKyer, Don Griffin, and Eric Wright give the team a surfeit of protection.

THE BRAINTRUST

Bill Walsh has moved upstairs, but he'll continue to oversee personnel. George Seifert, the former defensive coordinator, is ready for the head job. And he has a team apparently loaded with talent.

So are we picking the 49ers to repeat? No. We think the combination of reorganization at the top, a tough schedule, postpartum depression, and the Rams are going to bring the 49ers in second.

TAMPA BAY BUCCANEERS

The Bucs could be a real good team in a couple of years and may almost make it to good this year, but that doesn't necessarily mean a winning record. In fact, they could come through 1989 with a won-lost mark not much better than last year's 5–11. There are some weaknesses, and too many Tampa Bay strengths still need another year to mature and to learn how to win. The schedule is going to be tougher this year too. Coach Ray Perkins' team should be respectable, which puts it head and shoulders above a lot of other Bucs teams, but it's still an impact player or two and some overall team speed away from victory in the close ones.

THE OFFENSE

Remember, you read it here first. Vinny Testaverde will not throw 35 interceptions this season. All right, it's a safe bet because if he gets over 30, he might be lynched by Tampa Bay fans. But the truth is he won't throw so many simply because he got a couple of years' worth of experience last season. He learned he can't outmuscle NFL cornerbacks the way he could college defenders. He learned to read defenses better. And he learned his receivers. His education isn't complete—after all, he's only been in the league for one season and a handful of 1986 games. He'll make more mistakes, but not nearly so many. And don't forget, with all his problems last year, he still passed for 3,240 yards in 15 games. The guy can throw. Behind Testaverde is Joe Ferguson, who is older than God.

You can also look for improvement in the young wide receivers. Bruce Hill and Mark Carrier caught 115 passes for 2,010 yards and 14 touchdowns, but they weren't the consummate catchers they are likely to be with another year under their belts. They could fail to match last season's numbers and still be more valuable if they can be more consistent. Second-round draft choice Danny Peebles is a sprinter with agility. Frank Pillow, a rookie last year, looks like a useful backup. Willie Drewery was a free-agent signee but figures to be most useful as a kick returner. Tight end Ron Hall is regarded as a better blocker than catcher, yet he caught 39 passes for a 14.2 average. His sub Calvin Magee was free-agented away.

Rookie runners Lars Tate and William Howard were fair last year. Tate has the most potential as a runner, but that's about all he can do. Howard is a better all-around player who lacks Tate's speed. Together they make the running fair. What the Bucs really need is a super back who can open up defenses for Testaverde's passes. Reliable James Wilder may be nearing the end of an honorable career. Kerry Goode was the major free-agent loss.

The offensive line went from awful to adequate last year, but it's still short of awesome. In tackle Paul Gruber the Bucs have someone to build a line around. Only a rookie last year, he immediately moved to the front ranks of OTs. He'll only get better. Center Randy Grimes is another stalwart. Guards Rick Mallory and John Bruhin, another rookie, are okay, and tackle Rob Taylor improved last year. There's not much depth if anything happens to Gruber or Taylor. Tampa Bay needs more than last year's 261 points to move up. Maturity would seem to favor their getting them.

SPECIAL TEAMS

Drewery and Sylvester Stamps, another free agent, should improve the kick returning, and the coverage squads did okay in 1988. Placekicker Donald Igwebuike will be back from injury. He looked like The Answer until he was hurt. Punter Ray Criswell is The Question. He averaged only 36.4, which is a couple of yards below terrible. Oddly he went through the whole season without a touchback, which prompted critics to sneer that he couldn't kick it that far.

THE DEFENSE

Before the Bucs can move up very far, they need to fill some defensive holes. More than anything, they have to find a pass rush—even a little one. The total of 20 sacks was the worst in the NFC.

The defensive ends were two rookies for most of last year. Eugene Davis started the whole season and played well. Robert Goff moved in after Ron Holmes was hurt. Both youngsters are run-stoppers who showed little inclination to get to rival passers. Holmes has some ability in that direction, but no one has ever registered a sack while on IR. Nose tackle Curt Jarvis works hard within limitations. Shawn Lee was a green rookie with potential last year.

First-round draft choice Broderick Thomas, one of the real blue-chippers in the rookie crop, can be counted on to add some pass rushing from either a DE or outside linebacker spot. The linebackers last year were all run-stoppers. As a matter of fact, the Bucs held opponents to only 1,551 rushing yards all season. Middle man Eugene Marve was the leader of the pack, and Sidney Coleman, yet *another* rookie, was okay. Irvin Randle, hurt part of the year, is a third adequate middle linebacker. The outside men, Kevin Murphy and Winston Moss, had only a single sack between them.

There's a gaping hole at right cornerback. Sherman Cocroft, a free agent who couldn't break into the Kansas City secondary, is the hope. Ricky Reynolds at left CB had some bad moments but came on late. The safeties, Harry Hamilton and Odie Harris, lack the speed to rank any higher than "competent." Without a pass rush, the Bucs will have trouble showing any further improvement.

THE BRAINTRUST

Ray Perkins has gotten together a surprisingly able group of young players in a very short time. Unfortunately the Bucs were so bad when he started that he still needs another good draft to move up. And he still has to prove he can meld them into a solid unit. Aside from filling a few holes and finding a couple more players with Pro Bowl potential, his biggest challenge will be speeding up the maturation process.

WASHINGTON REDSKINS

A lot of people are ready to write the Redskins off because they went from Super Bowl champs to 7-9 losers last year. The burial is premature. It assumes the fall from grace was on merit. The rumor is that the 'Skins are too old, have too many gaps, and have lost their intensity. R.I.P.

Okay, there were and are some liver spots, but most of the flesh is firm. Sure, there are a few holes to be filled, but it ain't the Grand Canyon. And a year in the dumper should put the braves back in a fighting mood. The Redskins are coming back. With a little luck—and after last year they deserve a lot of it—they might make it this season.

THE OFFENSE

Washington has more quarterbacking than just about anybody. Doug Williams, the incumbent, passed for 2,609 yards despite missing four games with an appendectomy. He's never been a model of consistency, but when he's hot he can bomb anyone into submission. Mark Rypien was sensational while Williams recovered. Later, when he got some chances, his inexperience showed. Stan Humphries is regarded as a hot prospect. And fourth round draft choice Jeff Graham has his admirers. Since no team needs four quarterbacks (note: Cleveland fans disregard), one of them can be used as trade bait. Rypien would probably bring the biggest catch.

One gap was at running back, and that's a considerable chasm in the one-back offense favored by coach Joe Gibbs. Timmy Smith, the Super Bowl hero, hit the chocolate eclairs hard but missed his holes and has been free-agented off. Kelvin Bryant proved he was best suited for spot duty by spraining his knee when he was pressed into full service. Jamie Morris is a tough little runner, but the operative word is "little." Then on Draft Day, GM Bobby Beathard came up with a pair of top "picks." Atlanta's Gerald Riggs, a certified bully back who should give the 'Skins the Riggins-Rogers rammer they need. Then, in another deal, Beathard added Cleveland's Earnest Byner, a fine all-purpose guy who'll benefit from new surroundings. In one day a weakness became a strength.

The 'Skins have three of the best wide receivers around in Ricky Sanders, Art Monk, and Gary Clark. Sanders was a wonder in 1988 with 73 catches and an NFC-high 12 touchdowns. He and Clark are the bomb catchers. Monk, who caught 72, is more of the possession type, and also the only one with dangerous mileage on his chart. Tight end and the H-back need to be upgraded. Don Warren is thirty-three and starting to play like it, and Craig McEwen didn't excite anyone. Mike Tice and Ken Whisenhunt, a pair of free agents, could inherit.

There's an age factor in the offensive line, but it's not so pronounced as to cause any panic. There's certainly enough talent to get by. OLT Jim Lachey should have a Pro Bowl year, and ORG Mark May is coming off one. OLG Russ Grimm and ORT Joe Jacoby have to prove they can still make the plays after seasons spoiled by injuries. That leaves Jeff Bostic and Raleigh McKenzie to fight over the center position or, if necessary, Grimm's spot.

The Redskins spent most of 1988 without a running game and the line was chopped up until the last few weeks. Still they put 345 points on the board. With Riggs and Byner adding balance, they could hit 400.

SPECIAL TEAMS

Gibbs's patience with placekicker Chip Lohmiller paid off. After a shaky start, he came on strong at the end. Free agent Greg Horne should be the new punter, the old punter, Greg Coleman, had a net under 30! None of the kick returners excelled, and it seemed that everybody possible was tried.

THE DEFENSE

You could find a lot wrong with the Washington defense last year. Mostly it was at cornerback, where starters Darrell Green and Barry Wilburn *and* number one sub Brian Davis were all ambushed by injury. If only two of them remain healthy, this is a team strength instead of a weakness. Another CB injured all year was rookie Carl Mims, who will add depth. Free safety Todd Bowles is a bit slow, but strong safety Alvin Walton is okay. All things considered, the Redskins should be at least two wins better with a hale-and-hearty secondary.

Dave Butz, the defensive tackle who's been in Washington since Ford was President, probably won't make it through Bush, but Darryl Grant appears ready to settle in for a long stay. Tracy Rocker, the 1988 Outland Trophy winner, wasn't drafted until the sixty-sixth pick, which just happened to be Washington's first. The rumor is Rocker has an arthritis problem, but if he can overcome it, the Redskins have Butz's successor.

Defensive end Charles Mann was another of the '88 wounded who should be fully recovered. And Dexter Manley, for all his excesses, can be a murderous DE. Markus Koch filled in well when Manley was suspended. Mann, Manley, Grant, and Koch should give the 'Skins a better pass rush this year. Even with the problems last year, the team was still tough to run on.

Middle linebacker Neal Olkewicz and LLB Monte Coleman are both on the bad side of thirty and serve mainly as run-stoppers these days. Wilbur Marshall is set at RLB. He didn't have his usual quota of big plays, but then the 'Skins didn't have their usual quota of big-play possibilities. Ravin Caldwell may see more action, and another big play guy would help.

The defense is better than its record suggests. Injuries and a –24 turnover differential were the biggest bugaboos last year. A little healing, a little opportunism, and a little luck could make this a very strong unit.

THE BRAINTRUST

Even in the midst of last year's debacle, Coach Gibbs, his staff, and GM Beathard were all ranked at or near the top in doing what they do by various polls. Those weren't pity votes. A large reason for figuring the 'Skins to bounce back is faith in Beathard, Gibbs, et al.

Washington could have been 10–6 with a few breaks. The Eagles might have been 7–9 without them. Since breaks usually even out, look for the Redskins and Eagles to flip-flop positions this year.

AMERICAN FOOTBALL CONFERENCE

BUFFALO BILLS

Had Denver succeeded in luring Bruce Smith away from Buffalo, it would have just about given the Broncos a lock on their division's championship (with the usual disclaimers about injuries). But by keeping Smith, the Bills haven't assured themselves of a division title. A conundrum? Not really. With Denver, Smith would have shored up the weakest facet of a team in a weak division and given them enough defense to win. With Buffalo, Smith is part of the strongest facet of a team in a strong division. He's a given. But the Bills could slip from their top-o'-the-heap spot if any number of other things go wrong.

On the other hand, with a little luck and a little maturity the Bills could find themselves in a Super Bowl next January. One thing seems certain: Buffalo has most of the parts in place to field a strong contender for several years to come.

THE DEFENSE

Certainly the rosiest side of Buffalo's future is its defense. The Big D got them to the AFC Championship Game last year, but injuries and other catastrophes to the defense kept them out of the Super Bowl.

Everything starts up front, and the Bills are in better shape there than anyone else in the AFC. The three-man front of Smith, Fred Smerlas, and Art Still has no weakness aside from those revealed on Smerlas' and Still's birth certificates. Both are on the wrong side of thirty. However, neither slowed up even a tad last year, so there's no reason to pencil either in for a rocking chair yet. A more legitimate worry is Smith's two earlier substance-abuse busts. One more and he'll be gone for a year. Leon Seals filled in well

when Smith was suspended last year. He'll probably see more playing time this season.

The front line is very good, but the linebackers are even better. Outside linebacker Cornelius Bennett, in only his second year, moved to the head of the AFC class. Only Lawrence Taylor ranks ahead of him at his position, and if you could have any OLB in the business, you'd pick Bennett because he's younger and has no substance-abuse Damocles' sword hanging over his head. The Bennett-Dickerson deal cost the Bills their first two '89 draft choices, but don't look for complaints at Rich Stadium.

Shane Conlan, playing inside, frees Bennett to rush the passer. Conlan clogs the middle as well as anybody in the conference. Injuries to Conlan and Smith were a large part of the title-game loss to Cincinnati. Albert Bentley and Darryl Talley are both good enough to rank as the big men on several clubs, and Scott Radecic is a solid backup.

Cornerback Derrick Burroughs gets some votes as the Achilles' heel of the defense. He's not really a weakness so much as an also-ran. There's always a chance he could be replaced if someone better comes along, but the Bills won't collapse if he plays the whole year. Nate Odomes, the other CB, is solid. Free safety Mark Kelso and strong safety Leonard Smith do a good job. They're not Cherry and Burruss, but who is? The biggest worry in the secondary is injury. There's not a whole lot of talent behind the starters.

SPECIAL TEAMS

Scott Norwood set a Bills' record with 32 field goals and provided the victory-points six times. Punter John Kidd was adequate, with a 35.3 net. Steve Tasker leads good coverage squads. The return men are only so-so.

THE OFFENSE

Buffalo's offense didn't scare anybody last year, and it's the biggest worry this time out. Particularly scary is the age of the offensive line, which is smallish to start with. Tackle Joe Devlin is thirty-five, and guards Tim Vogler and Jim Ritcher are thirty-three and thirty-one, respectively. The best hope here is that free agents John Davis (Houston) or Caesar Rentie (Chicago) can move in. Center Kent Hull and tackle Will Wolford are both entering their fourth years and are beginning to assert themselves.

The Bills' running game usually gets rated adequate, but that's being kind. They couldn't intimidate anyone on the ground. Last year's rookie, Thurman Thomas, was okay in spots, and Robb Riddick is a good short-yardage man. The rest of the crew got few press clippings, which was just about what they deserved. Maybe—just maybe—Kenneth Davis, a free agent who was a constant letdown at Green Bay, will show why he was a second-round draft choice in 1986.

There aren't any complaints about wide receiver Andre Reed; who can find fault with 71 catches and 6 touchdowns? Trumaine Johnson and Chris Burkett aren't chopped liver either, but none of the wideouts has the speed to terrify a cornerback. The lack of speed at WR doesn't just hurt the passing game; it also impacts on the running because it can't stretch opponent defenses. Draft choices Don Beebe and John Kolesar may help, but Beebe is apple-green, and Kolesar always seemed to be hurt in college. Tight end Pete Metzelaars is enormous but no deep threat either.

The Bills' blah offense is led by Jim Kelly, who deserves better. Kelly is no Marino and probably not even an Esiason, but he'd be capable of running a high-tech offense if he had the right microchips. He doesn't have them here, of course, so he'll probably get booed by some of the homers at Rich when the Bills struggle for yardage like a fat lady trying to get into a girdle—lots of huffing and puffing, but the lumps still show. From the reality standpoint, he might be the best of all possible whips to guide a buggy that is seriously deficient in speedy horses. He'll take the failures, the sacks, and the abuse and keep a'comin'.

THE BRAINTRUST

Don't expect any cute innovations from Coach Marv Levy. Just as well, this isn't the kind of team that could make them work very often. He can surprise you once in a while with a strategy switch, like going to his running attack in the playoffs, when the Oilers were primed to squash Kelly's passes. Like Kelly, Levy's probably the right man for the time and place.

CINCINNATI BENGALS

The Bengals were one of two teams to eschew signing any unprotected free agents. Depending on your mindset, that confirms Paul Brown's frugality or his sagacity. Probably it was a bit of both. The Bengals could have found some useful players but not at the price asked. The team lost nine free agents to other clubs, the only regular being linebacker Emmanuel King. They might have lost more, but the possibility of going to another Super Bowl had to weigh on the mind of any temptee. A return trip isn't out of the question. Cincinnati has as many strengths as anyone in the AFC. They also have some weaknesses and two huge question marks.

THE OFFENSE

The biggest "what if?" in the Bengals' prospects is Boomer Esiason. The party line downplayed his finger, shoulder, and ankle injuries, but he obviously couldn't throw right in the playoffs, and it finally caught up with Cincinnati in the Super Bowl. If Boomer's not up to par this year, it could make for long afternoons at Riverfront Stadium. He's the key to the offense. Turk Schonert is a good backup, but that's just it—he's a backup, the kind of quarterback who makes a career out of short relief stints. What he lacks—and what Esiason had until the end of last season—is the ability to throw deep and thus open the running game. And, of course, Boomer is the unquestioned team leader.

Should Esiason's arm be a no-show, the pressure on the running game may be more than enough to grind the Bengals' attack to a screeching halt. The Cincinnati running game was the best in the AFC last year, but a lot of the success stemmed from opponents' panic because of Esiason's deep passes early in the year. *Wunderkind* Ickey Woods still has to prove he wasn't a one-year wonder and that he can avoid the disease that's struck other big Bengal fullbacks: "eatumus too-muchus." James Brooks is thirty, a dangerous age for a running back, and Stanley Wilson is gone. Eric Ball, the Bengals' top draft pick, looks more like a third-down back than a full-time threat. What was one of the strongest areas on the team has become shaky.

Assuming Esiason can throw okay, Eddie Brown and Tim McGee give the Bengals a top pair of wide receivers with long-bomb speed. Cris Collinsworth provides quality depth if he comes back for one more year. Rodney Holman is all you could ask for in a tight end.

The offensive line was the best in the NFL. It will be again, so long as OT Joe Walter's knee surgery worked.

With Walter starting, Brian Blados can go back to being the number one sub. With Walter not starting, the line is a little thin after you get past the regulars. Max Montoya and Anthony Munoz are getting on in years but should have a few more good seasons in them. Draft choice OG Freddie Childress might contribute if he can keep his weight within reasonable limits. It can range from 300 up to numbers that belong on powerful handguns.

SPECIAL TEAMS

Stanford Jennings' touchdown kickoff return in the Super Bowl was his second in 1988. Still, he averaged only a tame 21.4. Jim Breech remains as accurate as ever with his placekicks, but they get shorter every year. Punter Lee Johnson doubles on kickoffs and extra-long field goals, but as a punter, Johnson is inconsistent.

THE DEFENSE

The number one question mark for the team is nose tackle Tim Krumrie. The two-bone break in his leg is going to take a lot of healing, and it's hard to believe he'll be fully recovered by the first kickoff. Yet Krumrie is the key to the entire Bengals' defense. His ability to tie up the middle last year protected the rest of what was otherwise an ordinary front line and linebacking crew. David Grant did a good job subbing for Krumrie in the Super Bowl, but he's more of a pass rusher.

Skip McClendon, Jim Skow, and Jason Buck were effective with Krumrie protecting the middle, but only McClendon has run-stopping size. Subtract Krumrie, and the Bengals are hurting here. They're hurting at linebacker even with a 100 percent Krumrie. Neither Carl Zander nor Joe Kelly is a stuffer in the middle. Outside linebacker Reggie Williams will be thirty-five by mid-September. Emmanuel King was left unprotected and signed with the Raiders. Kevin Walker, an '88 third-round draft choice, may help.

Rickey Dixon, the high-priced number one pick last year, will be somewhere in the secondary. He should develop into a real good player. Most likely he'll be used at cornerback, where Lewis Billups and Eric Thomas were not strong. Billups looks like the one on the bubble, not because he blew that interception in the Super Bowl, but because he didn't get in front of enough other passes. David Fulcher, the linebacker-size safety, could be hurt badly if Krumrie is out. Fulcher made the Pro Bowl as a run-stopper last year, but take away Krumrie and the Bengals' pass rushers can be stopped. And that would mean added pass-coverage duty for Fulcher—not his strong suit. Free safety Solomon Wilcots is all right, although there's a possibility that Dixon could be worked in here.

THE BRAINTRUST

Sam Wyche went from dunce in '87 to genius in '88. He'll have to blow the doors off the IQ test to repeat if Esiason isn't okay. That aside, his defense will be his major concern. Of course, lack of defense is an old story in Cincinnati. They have traditionally tried to outscore everyone, a philosophy that has often led to surprising upsets—for and against. Wyche will go the same route in 1989 if Esiason is Boomerable. Under that hoped-for circumstance, the offense, albeit thinner than last year, has more firepower than anyone else.

CLEVELAND BROWNS

Based on past performance the Browns have to be given a shot at the division title, even if they rank no better than third on paper. Apparently they felt the same way about it and went into the draft determined to give Bernie Kosar the weapons he needs. New Coach Bud Carson won't coordinate his own offense, but there's going to be more of it than Marty Schottenheimer had to work with. However, even with Kosar available for the whole season, Cleveland can't outgun the Bengals or Oilers. The Browns' defense has to make up the difference. But when push has come to shove each time for the past three playoffs, it was the defense that faltered.

Cleveland lost some useful players in the free-agent fun, but on balance they came out ahead. For the most part the new players line up where the biggest holes were.

THE OFFENSE

What happened to the Cleveland quarterbacks last year—five disabling injuries—was surely a one-in-a-million shot. They're counting on a full season from Kosar, and those fans who never look past who's under center figure that's all there is to it. Kosar, the Ugly Duckling of quarterbackdom, ranks right up there with the best throwers in football when he's all in one piece. Moreover, he's smart and a leader. He may look like a guy spending his first day ever in pads, but he is a true "franchise quarterback." The only trouble is that some of the offensive part of the franchise is crumbling around him. After you get past Bernie and his able backups of Don Strock, Mike Pagel, and others, the Browns have to put a lot of faith in rookies.

For example, Reggie Langhorne is solid enough at wide receiver, and Brian Brennan is adequate. However, neither has the speed to burn a secondary to the ground. Webster Slaughter is more dangerous, but he's not the equal of Eddie Brown, Ernest Givens, or Drew Hill. Ray Butler, a free agent, never quite got it all together at Seattle. The big boost is supposed to come from rookies Eric Metcalf and Lawyer Tillman. Metcalf is little and fast. He also is scheduled to be awfully busy, catching passes, running from scrimmage, and returning punts. The worry is that he'll burn out before Week 8. Tillman is big and fast, and will probably be used as a tight end with minimal blocking duties. Ozzie Newsome, the man Tillman's to replace, probably should retire while we can all remember how great he used to be.

Running back Earnest Byner was sent off to Washington. He's a useful all-around back, though not a top-shelfer, but he's been in the wrong place at the wrong time more than once in the last few years and may be happier in new surroundings. That leaves Kevin Mack, the big fullback who was able to play only about half of last season. Again, a healthy Mack is a strong asset, but he's never had to carry the whole running game for a full season. It remains to be seen how much Metcalf will contribute running from scrimmage. Mike Oliphant, acquired in the Byner deal, wasn't the answer for the Redskins.

The offensive line will get some retooling. Any line that gives up five major quarterback injuries in one season is going to fall under suspicion. Shucks, it's likely to get indicted. Cody Risien and Dan Fike are solid. Larry Williams was free-agented out at guard, and the Jets' Ted Banker was free-agented in. Center Larry Rakoczy still has to prove himself and could be ousted by ex-Chief Tom Baugh. A pass-blocking tackle would be appreciated.

SPECIAL TEAMS

Punter Max Runager finally brought some stability to the Browns' awful punting last year, but he's gone to Kansas City as a free agent. Bryan Wagner is the likely choice to replace him. The 147-pound Gerald McNeil does okay returning punts. Metcalf may be worked in here too. Matt Bahr will likely do the placekicking again, although he'll get some competition from eleventh-round draft pick Dan Plocki.

THE DEFENSE

Sorting out the front line will be Carson's major defensive chore. Nose tackle Bob Golic and defensive end Sam Clancy are gone; Golic particularly will be missed. Apparently the Browns thought he would stay in Cleveland come what may, but the Raiders made him an offer he couldn't refuse. In the free-agent exchange, the Browns signed Al Baker from Minnesota, Robert Banks from Houston, and Tom Gibson from New England. Fourth-round draft pick Andrew Stewart is another possibility. The key returnees are Michael Dean Perry, Charles Buchanan, and Chris Pike, all of whom could be significant if they can stay off IR. Darryl Sims has always been a disappointment, and Carl Hairston is nearly old enough to start riding buses at halffare.

The linebacking isn't bad but could be better. Outside man Clay Matthews is fine but thirty-three. David Grayson is okay on the far side. The Johnsons, Eddie and Mike, take care of the middle. Mike Junkin, the number one draft pick of two years ago, was finally written off and sent to Kansas City.

Cornerbacks Frank Minnifield and Hanford Dixon are the best pair in the league when they're healthy. Free safety Felix Wright isn't far behind the dynamic duo, and some thought he moved ahead a bit last year when both CBs were sometimes hurt. Brian Washington started at strong safety all last season as a rookie and should be better in 1989. The strength of the secondary makes a strong defense possible with only a little help up front.

THE BRAINTRUST

Carson, who paid years of dues to get a head coach's cap, is a defensive coach. He worked wonders with the raw Jets' secondary last year. Ironically, the Browns' secondary is the most solid area of their team. The Browns got to the AFC title game in 1986 and 1987 but couldn't make it over the hump to the Super Bowl. You get the feeling they believe they have one last shot to go all the way before overhauling completely. It's not an impossible dream, but so many things could fall apart on them, they may not make it to the playoffs.

DENVER BRONCOS

The Broncos need an outbreak of "largesse" to get back into the thick of the AFC title fight. The undersized defense that got brushed aside for 39 points by Pittsburgh, 42 by both New Orleans and Seattle, and 55 by Indianapolis has to show more muscle in 1989 or they're going to be plowed a mile under at Mile High. Former defensive coordinator Joe

Collier's bend-don't-break defense fractured badly last year, costing Collier and his staff their jobs. Attack-and-destroy will be the new philosophy under Wade Phillips.

Denver bent without breaking successfully for nearly twenty years, but the system had a built-in flaw. Because it put a premium on quickness and agility, the Broncos eventually wound up with defenders a ton or so lighter than just about anyone else. When some of that quickness and agility got old or was injured, the defense bent like a pane of glass bends when you smack it with a four-iron.

THE DEFENSE

You get some idea about how Denver treasures its 1988 defenders when you note that four starters from last year's unit were left unprotected in the free-agent circus—DE Walt Bowyer, LB Rick Dennison, and DBs Mark Haynes and Jeremiah Castille. Four backups could be had for the asking too. Only Bowyer and sub DE Reggie Ware found anyone interested.

The situation is critical but not hopeless. Former All-Pro linebacker Karl Mecklenburg will be back for a full season. A healthy Mecklenburg can search-and-destroy with the best. Simon Fletcher has developed into a first-rate linebacker to pair with him on the strong side. Fletcher, who was too small for a defensive end (even by Denver standards), was probably the best Bronco defender last year and he'll get better as he learns the linebacker position. Nose tackle Greg Kragen is undersized but otherwise adequate. Defensive end Andre Townsend is just undersized. Shawn Knight, acquired even-up from New Orleans for first-round flop Ted Gregory, is a possible tackle. The weakside linebacking needs a partner for Michael Brooks.

The Broncs made a serious, albeit unsuccessful, attempt to sign Buffalo defensive end Bruce Smith—$7.5 million and two number one draft picks. That's as serious as it gets. It was a good move. As valuable as the big DE is to the Bills (who matched Denver's offer), he'd have been more valuable to the Broncos. The addition of Smith (or a Smith clone) would make the Bronco defense instantly respectable and just about guarantee the top spot in the weak AFL West. Two number one draft picks would scare off a lot of teams. Of course, considering the washout that Ted Gregory became, they may not value high-draft picks in Denver the way they do in other places. But they probably have a fair regard for $7.5 mill.

Second-round draft pick Warren Powers will add some beef to the line if he plays. He brings good notices, but the Broncos have been bitten before. The availability of Haynes and Castille as free agents tells you that Denver could use some new cornerbacks of *any* size. Again, though, a strong, Smith-like pass rush would take a lot of pressure off the CBs. Safeties Mike Hardin and Dennis Smith are just okay when healthy, and Smith is unhealthy a lot. *A lot!* That's why Denver made Arkansas' tough Steve Atwater their first pick in the draft.

SPECIAL TEAMS

Several folks expressed surprise that Rich Karlis was left as an unprotected free agent. He hit 23 of 36 field goal tries, but that's only average in this era. Not his distance, his accuracy, or his clutch hitting are likely to get him inundated with offers from other teams. He's tried and reasonably true, though, and should be back. Punter Mike Horan had a 44.0 average and an excellent 37.8 net. He's a good one, although kicking for Denver automatically adds a few yards to his record.

THE OFFENSE

If John Elway comes back at 100 percent as expected, the Broncos will have an offense. His arm operation in the off season was downplayed as minor repair. Even with Elway at 70–80 percent, as he was in 1988, he was still the Western Division's best quarterback over a full season. For all the Broncos' problems—and an underachieving Elway was a biggie—Seattle only nosed them out for the division title because Seahawk QB Dave Krieg was red-hot for the last five weeks. A healthy Elway is still probably the best all-around weapon in the AFC and the prototype "franchise quarterback." Back up Gary Kubiak is considered adequate, but when he had to play a whole game against Pittsburgh in Week 8, the Broncs lost badly, 39–21.

Elway will get plenty of help from the "Three Amigos"— receivers Vance Johnson, Mark Jackson, and Ricky Nattiel—who caught 160 passes among them in 1988. There are better duos in the league, but few trios come close to matching the Denver Three. Tight end Clarence Kay may at last be on the verge of blossoming into something special too.

It remains to be seen if Tony Dorsett can squeeze one more decent season out of his thirty-five-year-old legs. He was widely regarded as a disappointment in '88. On the other hand, 703 yards at his age was a pretty fair achievement. Sammy Winder was useful as usual last year, but it's about time Denver went out and drafted a star runner and developed him. The heyday of Floyd Little and Otis Armstrong was more than a decade ago.

The offensive line suffered from the same lack of size as the defense last year, but second-round pick Doug Widell and third-rounder Darrell Hamilton will add heft if not experience.

THE BRAINTRUST

Coach Dan Reeves will have a defense more to his liking in 1989—at least philosophically. However, how the holdover Broncos will take to Wade Phillips' newthink will depend more on muscle than attitude. Reeves can yell "Sic 'em!" all he wants, but he'll get better results by putting a few pit bulls alongside his terriers. Remember how they used to say "it isn't the size of the dog in the fight; it's the size of the fight in the dog"? They never bet on Denver.

HOUSTON OILERS

To start with the Kiss of Death, the Oilers should win the Central Division this year. To enhance the lethal buss, they could well win the AFC playoffs. They have the talent. Last year you could argue that Houston's abilities were no greater than Cincinnati's. Matched man-for-man, it was a tough call. But whereas the Bengals go into 1989 with serious questions as to the health of several key men, the Oilers have no such problems. And whereas a couple of Bengals are entering the sere-and-yellow stage of their careers, the Oilers are flush with experienced youth. And whereas both the Bengals and Oilers lost heavily in the free-agent market, the Oilers at least got some marginal help back.

However, we'd best not skip the season, declare the Oilers division champs, and go right on to the playoffs: this team has never lived up to its promise previously. You'd have to take a long walk on a short limb to pick them to do it this time.

THE OFFENSE

The only serious injury the Oilers had last year was the shoulder crack that knocked quarterback Warren Moon out for five games. Moon returned to have the best of his five NFL seasons, gaining him a measure of respect he'd not had before. Even though he may not make the Pro Bowl this year, should Esiason, Kosar, and Elway be injury-free and Marino get some help in Miami, there's no reason to believe he won't be just as good. Cody Carlson had some good (and some bad) moments subbing while Moon was in eclipse.

The Oilers are perhaps the only team in football that can afford to trade away a thousand-yard runner without worrying about it. Mike Rozier is at this writing being dangled as trade bait because Houston is deeper than a well at running back. Allen Pinkett was terrific subbing for Rozier last year, and Lorenzo White looked like a coming star in his few opportunities. Meanwhile, they've barely scratched the surface of fullback Alonzo Highsmith's potential.

Drew Hill and Ernest Givens return to give the Oilers a top-notch duo at wide receiver. Haywood Jeffires, who will back them, began to come on at the end of last season. Losing tight end Jamie Williams to the free-agent circus costs them a replaceable blocker.

The offensive line has Pro Bowl pair Mike Munchak and Bruce Matthews. If there's a problem here, it will come at tackle, where Dean Steinkuhler's knees are risky and Bruce Davis will be thirty-three. However, David Williams, the number-one draft choice, should allay fears. The Oilers lost free agents John Davis, David Viane, and Doug Williams, so depth is lacking.

SPECIAL TEAMS

The Oilers' special teams got deserved ink for their five blocks of opponents' punts and some undeserved ink for their nicknames. They were only ordinary covering and returning kicks. For all their strength at running back, the Oilers could use a return specialist. Punter Greg Montgomery was a disappointment as a rookie. Tony Zendejas had a good year. The Oilers did a lot of moaning about how the free-agent market had decimated their special teams, but the draft should put them ahead.

THE DEFENSE

Although Houston's defense isn't as formidable as its offense, it's nothing to sneeze at, especially up front. Ray Childress is a Pro-Bowl quality defensive end; Sean Jones and William Fuller had 16 sacks between them. Nose tackles Doug Smith and Richard Byrd are an imposing duo, although Smith won't win any reliability awards. He missed thirty days for substance abuse last year.

The linebackers overachieved in 1988—a rare happenstance on this ball club. Still, John Grimsley and Johnny Meads are okay. Eugene Seale, the Oilers' best special teams player, may move in here permanently. The odd-man-out would seem to be Al Smith, who's a bit small for the middle. Outside LB Robert Lyles could be replaced, too, possibly by second-round draft choice Scott Kozak.

Free safety Jeff Donaldson is first rate, but losing strong safety Keith Bostic as a free agent put a big hole in the secondary, which was already the weakest part of the defense. It's up to rookie Bubba McDonald to move in here. Cornerbacks Patrick Allen and Steve Brown are vulnerable. In fact, the best way to beat the Oilers last year was to give them a lead and then play catch-up. Four of their six losses came that way, including the final game, when Cleveland bounced back from a 23–7 deficit.

THE BRAINTRUST

It might not be very long before Elvis will have to buy his own tickets. The smart money says it's just a matter of time until Coach Jerry Glanville is replaced by Jackie Sherrill. Jerry is the main whipping boy for the media in explaining why a very good team was only pretty good and just managed to edge into the playoffs while finishing third in its division. According to one critic, "This team is so talented, it'd go 8–8 if it was coached by a mannequin dressed in black."

Glanville will be tested more in 1989. Quarterback coach June Jones, who was given a lot of credit for the Oiler offense, has departed, and the defense may be a tad weaker if something good doesn't happen in the secondary. Nevertheless Houston has the manpower to win. If they get off to a slow start, Glanville could be sacked before the season is over. If they don't get to the AFC Championship Game, he could go anyway.

Sherrill has never coached a pro team—at least not officially, despite all those rumors about his Texas A&M elevens. He has, however, been a winner every place he's gone. And he ranks Oiler owner Bud Adams among his most sincere admirers. And owners of NFL teams in Texas have been known to hire buddies, as Tom Landry knows.

Tick, tick, tick . . .

INDIANAPOLIS COLTS

As long as Eric Dickerson is the main mucketymuck of running backs, the Colts have a chance of winning, as they say, on any given Sunday. A dominant ground attack—and Dickerson is the most overbearing—can control a game far better than the best of passing attacks—using up the clock, scoring a few points, and forcing opponents into offensive errors. And a ground attack will still be there when a passing attack is put in disarray by high winds or heavy rainfall or blizzards—disruptions rare to the Hoosier Dome, of course, but something to be considered on the road.

However, a running game alone, even a Dickersonian ground attack, will not guarantee a win against the real toughies in the NFL. They have their own weapons and will eventually outscore any one-dimensional attack, no matter how stern the defense agin' 'em. So to beat 'em, you have to be able to come after them in diverse ways. All of which leads up to a therefore . . .

Therefore, the Man of the Moment in Indy during 1989 will not be Eric the Dreadnaught. The guy in the cross hairs will be quarterback Chris Chandler.

THE OFFENSE

At times last season, Chandler gave evidence of becoming a top-notch NFL quarterback. But the evidence was circumstantial. In some of his other circumstances, Chandler looked like a rookie thrown into the stew before he was ripe. That was indeed the case, brought about by Gary Hogeboom's various problems and Jack Trudeau's knee injury. Hogeboom was free-agented away, but Trudeau will be back, convinced he should be starting. If he convinces the coach, it will be because Chandler has regressed. Should Chandler's -gress be pro- instead of re-, and the Colts can add an air threat to Dickerson, they have a chance to overtake Buffalo. Naturally, that assumes Dickerson doesn't get hurt (you can just hear everyone in the state of Indiana saying "Bite your tongue!") or decide its time to renegotiate his contract. Actually, backup Albert Bentley is a pretty good runner when he gets the chance, but he may go in a trade to shore up some other pressing needs.

The Colts hit it lucky in the draft when Andre Rison was still available for their twenty-second pick. He can do for the Colts what Anthony Carter does for Minnesota. Wide receiver Bill Brooks is a good grabber but not a gamebreaker. Neither are Matt Bouza or Clarence Verdin, who operate from the other side. Clarence Weathers, the free agent from Cleveland, might help a little. Tight end Pat Beach averaged only 9.0 for his 26 catches with nary a TD last year.

The Colts' offensive line didn't produce the way it was supposed to on paper last year. The holdouts, walkouts, and bitchouts produced a brownout in blocking out. An arch injury to OT Kevin Call was a major problem, and some felt that center Ray Donaldson wasn't up to his usual form. OT Chris Hinton has been pegged as overrated so often that it can't be too long before he's considered underrated. The biggest need is more depth.

SPECIAL TEAMS

Placekicker Dean Biasucci was worth his weight in dollar bills last year. He hit 6 field goals of 50 or more yards, which is nice kicking even in a dome. Punter Rohn Stark had some line-drive problems, but his average of 43.5 and net of 34.5 were strong. Opponents outreturned the Colts on both punts and kickoffs, so some work is needed there.

THE DEFENSE

Indianapolis badly needs a nose tackle. Joe Klecko got through the 1988 season without adding anything positive to his legend. A replacement is critical. They hope it will be second-round draft choice Mitchell Benson. Defensive ends Jon Hand and Donnell Thompson can stop the run. Neither puts a whole lot of pressure on opposing quarterbacks. Hand led the team with 5 sacks. The Colts signed free agents Mitch Willis from Atlanta and Sam Clancy from Cleveland.

The most solid part of the Indy defense is at linebacker. Outside man Duane Bickett is fine. Rookie O'Brien Alston shocked everyone by earning a starting spot as a tenth-round draft choice. He delivered some big plays, though his pass coverage is suspect. Fredd Young and Barry Krauss are able inside. Cliff Odom was and is unhappy in a sub's role and may be traded.

The secondary was the answer to a lot of "what's wrong with the Colts" questions. It was burned for 3,803 yards, which will make any secondary the object of a certain amount of derision. It didn't get a whole lot of help from the pass rush, but it can't lay off all the blame. Cornerback Eugene Daniel is the best of the returnees, though that wasn't necessarily true last year. Most observers figured strong safety Steve Prior had a better season. There's hope for improvement from last year's rookie Michael Ball. And Indianapolis should be able to get some good work from free agent Jeff Bostic, who used to be one of the league's best safeties at Houston.

A full-scale shakeup in the coaching staff supposedly presages a shift in defensive philosophy from bend-don't-break to search-and-destroy. Philosophy, schmilosophy! The real question is whether they have the people. It's hard to search without pass-rushing ends or destroy without a nose tackle.

THE BRAINTRUST

Speaking of philosophy, Coach Meyer fired all six of the assistants hired by previous headman Rod Dowhower. While you expect a head coach to hire his own people, you usually don't see him wait two seasons-plus-three-games to do it. Meyer said he would have changed his staff even if the Colts had gone all the way to the Super Bowl. Sure. Anyway, the massacre should produce a bit more cohesion among the staff, or in Meyer's words, the new men will reflect his personality and philosophy. Is it just our imagination, or do all football coaches talk like corporate vice presidents these days?

KANSAS CITY CHIEFS

It's hard to believe a 4–11–1 team like the Chiefs could have a shot at the division title the next year, but that's the line new coach Marty Schottenheimer is laying down. And it's not as silly as it sounds. The Chiefs have a lot of "ifs" and "buts," and if most of those can be resolved, they have some very talented players, too. Based on his track record at Cleveland, Schottenheimer is a coach who can make things come up roses. He has yet to go a full season without getting to the playoffs.

THE OFFENSE

A couple of seasons from now, Kansas City is going to need a quarterback, so they drafted Wake Forest's Mike Elkins. For now, however, the key man will be a veteran. Steve DeBerg would seem to have a lock on the job after passing for 2,935 yards last year. On the other hand, there's Ron Jaworski, the used-to-be-great with the Eagles, who was a semisurprising free-agent signing after two years in semiretirement as Dan Marino's backup. Whichever way Schottenheimer decides to go, he won't be expecting rookie mistakes.

There's some age at wide receiver too, where Carlos Carson has nine seasons in the till. Stephone Paige is a veteran at the top of his game, but an extra burner wouldn't hurt. Rookie Naz Worthen looks more the possession type. Tight end Jonathan Hayes is adequate only, meaning former Jet free agent Billy Griggs may have a shot.

If Christian Okoye is healthy this year and runs as he did last year on those few occasions when he was, the Chiefs will have the semblance of a rushing game. Paul Palmer is most dangerous as a kick returner-receiver, and Herman Heard is a journeyman. Young James Saxon may see more action.

Injuries chewed up the offensive line last year, but the group that settled in after Game 10 was adequate. Opponents' sacks dropped from an awful 3.6 for the first ten games to a reasonable 1.2 for the last six. Offensive left tackle John Alt looks like a good one. ORT Irv Eatman was first rate in the USFL and still may be okay in the majors. OT Dave Smith, a Bengals' free agent, could work in here. Center Gerry Feehery did a fair job after he was picked up from Philadelphia, but the tipoff here is that the Chiefs signed erstwhile All-Pro Mike Webster as a line coach and then reversed field, with him coming back for another year as a player.

SPECIAL TEAMS

After being the AFC's top kickoff returner in 1987, Palmer had a dreadful 15.8 average last year, mostly because of some fumble muffing. But he's still a talent. Punter Kelly Goodburn hasn't been a world beater in two seasons and might be replaced by free agent Max Runager from Cleveland.

Kicker Nick Lowery had his best season last year. He connected on 27 field goals and accounted for last-second winning points in two of the the Chiefs' four wins. He probably would have been an All-Pro candidate if Kansas City had put up a better record.

DEFENSE

The Chiefs have to do a better job of stopping the run in 1989 if they expect to go anywhere but into the toilet. They gave up more yards rushing than passing last year, which is well nigh impossible to do in this day and age. All right, it was only one more yard—2,592 to 2,591—but it didn't happen anywhere else in the NFL.

Schottenheimer signed several Cleveland free agents, but one of them—surprisingly—wasn't nose tackle Bob Golic. That indicates the Chiefs are pretty certain Bill Maas will be back and okay this year. It was after Maas broke his leg in Week 8 that the Chiefs became really hopeless against the run. Healthy, Maas is a Pro Bowler. If he's not up to par, the Chiefs will go with Rams' free agent NT Greg Meisner.

The Chiefs came out of last season with one real good linebacker—Dino Hackett—and one who played well in the last few games—Jack Del Rio. Not surprisingly they made Alabama's Derrick Thomas their first-draft choice. He's regarded as a future Pro Bowler who will add some punch to the pass rushing right off the bat. Seventh-rounder Ron Sancho is also expected to be useful, and Coach Schottenheimer traded for Mike Junkin, a player he once drafted as a Number One. The weakest part of the defense looks greatly improved going into 1989.

If—there's that word again—a lot of maybe's come through, things could get better on the front line, too. Maybe last year's first-round draft choice, DE Neal Smith, will begin to play like a first-round draft choice should. Maybe DE Mike Bell can bounce back from his lackluster 1988 season. The biggest maybe is Maas.

The strength of the defense is the secondary, of course. You could spend a lifetime looking for a better free safety than Deron Cherry. Strong safety Lloyd Burruss isn't far behind, although he missed five games with injuries last year. Cornerbacks Albert Lewis and Kevin Ross are also fine. What wonders this crew might perform if they ever got a strong pass rush up front!

THE BRAINTRUST

Getting Schottenheimer was a real coup. Former Coach Frank Gansz certainly wasn't to blame for all of last year's faults, but he didn't seem to inspire confidence in the troops and did make some errors. Schottenheimer has always been a "get-it-done" coach.

In the long run, however, the more telling stroke may be the installation of Carl Peterson as president/general manager. Peterson built a winner in the USFL's Philadelphia/Baltimore Stars. Okay, that's not doing it in the big leagues yet, but just about everybody figures Peterson can finally put the Chiefs on the right track. One tipoff is that he signed seventeen unprotected free agents last spring, more than anyone except Green Bay.

The team has been floundering since the early 1970s. Picking them to win the AFC West this year is a bit much. A .500 season is possible and, should most of the "ifs" come up smiling, it could be very interesting. Schottenheimer insists he came to Kansas City to win now. He hasn't missed yet.

LOS ANGELES RAIDERS

The Raiders have gone two losing seasons in a row—unprecedented for an Al Davis team. The smart money says 1989 will make three straight, but it might not take much improvement from last year's 7-9 to put the Silver and Black into the playoffs.

THE OFFENSE

This is going to be the year that Jay Schroeder puts up or shuts up. Only three seasons ago, Schroeder was regarded as one of the coming stars of quarterbackdom. Then his hot-and-cold throwing cost him the Redskins' starting slot and his tantrums cost him a job in Washington. Hailed as the Raiders' savior last year, he produced little to savor. No doubt he has a major league arm; in 1989 he'll have to prove he has a major league head.

Last year ex–Notre Damer Steve Beurelein, with less talent and considerably less experience, was the Raiders'

better quarterback. But, to be fair, Schroeder came to Los Angeles a week after the season opened and was tossed into the breach before he'd had a chance to learn the new system. And, to be fair to both quarterbacks, the whole Raiders' offensive unit was in the midst of learning new coach Mike Shanahan's system—one that stressed taking what was given rather than the traditional banzai Raiders' attack. Ironically, Schroeder has always been the kind of quarterback who lived by the long bomb.

Neither quarterback will hurt for long-distance receivers. Rookie of the Year Tim Brown, Mervyn Fernandez, James Lofton, and Willie Gault are all returning. Last year Gault saw about as much action as Dan Quayle in the Indiana National Guard, but he should be worked into the scheme this season. Lofton may be nearing the end, however. Tight end Todd Christensen may regain his starting slot, but the odds are stacked against his regaining his annual trip to the Pro Bowl. Not only is he coming back from a serious injury, but Shanahan's offense utilizes the TE more as a blocker than a catcher. Christensen always earned his living with his hands, not his shoulders.

The running game can't afford to sit around for half a season waiting for Bo Jackson to finish his baseball duties. As great as Bo is when he finally checks in, you've got to wonder how much his absence during the first half of the season hurts the Raiders psychologically. For example, how does Steve Smith feel knowing that no matter what he does, he'll be shunted to the bench as soon as Bo is a go? Actually, Jackson had less impact on the L.A. running game in his half of 1988 than in his half of 1987, but he's still an awesome talent.

Marcus Allen, who was the number one guy until Jackson arrived, is still one of the NFL's finest all-around backs. He'll benefit by playing without the wrist injury that hurt him both as a runner and receiver last year. Unless some new, destructive persons like rookie Steve Wisniewski can be worked into the offensive line—or unless last year's mediocre bunch improves significantly—nothing that Schroeder, Brown, Allen, or Jackson might do will be good enough to put the Silver and Black into the black.

SPECIAL TEAMS

Tim Brown is the big man on the special teams as long as the Raiders are willing to risk his usefulness as a pass receiver by exposing him to constant danger as a kick returner. Punter Jeff Gossett was okay in '88 but will never make 'em forget Ray Guy—or a lot of other guys. Placekicker Chris Bahr, entering his fourteenth season, was let go to San Diego as an unprotected free agent. He was never one of the league's long kickers, and his range decreased last year.

THE DEFENSE

The 369 points the Raiders gave up last year were the most since 1962, back in the pre-Davis days, when the team was a laughingstock. Defensive coordinator Charlie Sumner and secondary coach Willie Brown were canned as a result, but the problem will have to be solved on the field, not the sideline.

Andre Townsend turned in a fine job at one defensive end, leading the AFC with 11.5 sacks. Howie Long was mostly injured but should bounce back. (He'd better; he's the highest-paid defensive lineman in the league.) Scott Davis, a first-round draft choice last year, didn't make any lasting contributions but is still a prospect. Nose tackle Bill Pickel will fight it out with Bob Golic, a free agent from Cleveland.

Linebacking, long a Raiders strength, is now mostly just long in the tooth. Rod Martin is thirty-five; Matt Millen is thirty-one; Jerry Robinson and Lindon King are in between. The Raiders signed four unprotected free-agent linebackers: Otis Wilson (Chicago), Emmanuel King (Cincinnati), Jackie Shipp (Miami), and Joe Costello (Atlanta). Wilson, who missed all of last season with an injury, used to be a good'un for the Bears, but he's thirty-two. There's a definite "Help Wanted" sign out here. Historically, the Raiders have been successful with other teams' disappointments. Shipp, King, and DL Pete Koch fit that description.

Cornerback Mike Haynes is thirty-six and you've got to worry how much longer he can last. Obviously the Raiders have been worrying too. Terry McDaniel, another of L.A.'s three first-round draft choices last year, looked good up to the second game and then went out with a broken leg. Free agent Mike Richardson was signed away from the Bears and should help. Vann McElroy is still a good free safety, but strong safety Russell Carter is only so-so.

Overall, you can expect—well, anyway, hope—for some improvement on defense.

THE BRAINTRUST

Mike Shanahan is on the spot. He's got his system in place, and his staff is more his own than inherited. There's a lot of experience on the team, particularly on the defense, but last year "experience" turned into "age." The good news is that some key younger players will have a year of experience and (hopefully) their health. The team could be improved without improving its record. Will Al Davis be satisfied with that? Remember this man's most quoted line: "Just win, Baby!"

MIAMI DOLPHINS

Miami signed eleven unprotected free agents, and seven of them were defensive players. That pretty much tells you where the gaping holes are. Make that the *most* gaping; the offense isn't anything to boast about either. The wonder is that a team with so many faults won six games. The Dolphins have so far to go before they are a respectable team that they'd be favored to finish last even if they played in the weak AFC West. In the strong Eastern Division, they're as

mortal a certainty to graze on the bottom as you can get in the NFL. Oh, Shula might pull a half dozen rabbits out of his hat, and Dan Marino's arm always gives them a chance. Or maybe another Eastern foe will collapse under a catastrophic rash of injuries. Anything is possible. But in the realm of the probable, pencil in another long year for Miami fans.

At least fans will have some new faces to look at. A few

days before the draft, Shula opened up his roster by releasing five veterans. Two former All-NFL's, center Dwight Stephenson and linebacker Hugh Green, were both dropped. Neither was able to overcome serious injuries. Also gone will be linebacker Bob Brudzinski, a one-time "Killer B," and runners Woody Bennett and Joe Cribbs.

THE OFFENSE

When Marino casually mentioned that he wouldn't mind playing elsewhere before his career ended, the rumor mill went into overdrive. Not that nearly every other NFL team wouldn't drool over Dan, but what could they offer? Their first-round draft pick through 2016? The World's Greatest Passer will be back under center for the Dolphins, knees willing, and once more he'll prove that even the W.G.P. needs some help. If he needs relief, the only Rolaids in sight right now are free agents Brent Pease and Cliff Stoudt.

Marino got 86 catches worth of help from wide receiver Mark Clayton last year. Mark II became Mark I with 1,129 yards and 14 touchdowns. The heretofore Mark I—Duper—ended up suspended for substance abuse, but he wasn't having much of a year even before that. Tight end Ferrell Edmunds has some pass-catching ability but doesn't block the way you'd expect from a guy who's 6'6" and 246. Then there's Jim Jensen, the TE-WR-RB-QB. Jensen subs so many places, he's a twelfth regular. His 58 catches were second on the team last year.

Runner Sammie Smith was a surprising first-draft pick—until you looked at what the Dolphins were trying to get by with last year. Smith can give them some tough inside running. If he wants to. The best thing that can be said for the returning running backs is that Troy Stradford was hurt last year. Of course, even with Stradford the picture of health, there's no one around to remind us of Eric Dickerson or John Stephens. Lorenzo Hampton has spent four years proving he's a journeyman, and Ron Davenport hasn't even proved that much yet.

Years from now, somebody will be looking through the record book and notice that the Dolphins' line allowed only 7 sacks in 1988. "Gee, they musta been great," that somebody will say. If ever a record needed an asterisk, it's this one. The Miami line is poor. It doesn't run block, and its pass blocking isn't any great shakes either, despite its record. Marino is just well nigh impossible to sack. Rookie guard Harry Galbreath played reasonably well. Maybe guard Roy Foster will hang in there. Tackles Ronnie Lee and Jon Geisler have each been on the scene for ten years. The odds are at least two incumbents won't be starting in '89. Almost certain to be the new center is rookie Jeff Uhlenhake.

SPECIAL TEAMS

Punter Reggie Roby is the gem of the special teams. Fewer than half his punts were returned last year, and his net average was 35.3. Placekicker Faud Reveiz is just okay, and the coverage and return teams are nothing special.

THE DEFENSE

If you were to sweep up the eleven Miami defensive regulars and hand them en masse to any other Eastern Division team, how many would win starting jobs? Well, there are a few who might make it on some clubs, but there's only one who'd be a certainty no matter where he landed: right inside linebacker John Offerdahl. The team leader in tackles and tied for second in interceptions, Offerdahl may not be the best inside LB in the league, but he would place no worse than second on any team, including Buffalo. With three or four more like him, Miami's defense would be respectable—something it isn't with only one of him.

Up front, defensive end John Bosa is the best of the lot, if he can come back from the knee injury that ended his season in the middle last year. Nose tackle Brian Sochia, DE T. J. Turner, and swing man Jackie Cline are big but seldom imposing. Last year's Number One draft choice, Eric Kumerow, is either an undersize DE or an oversize LB, but doesn't seem capable of moving beyond adequate at either position. The Dolphins got only 24 sacks last year and were run on like a failing bank.

Mark Brown is a decent inside linebacker to pair with Offerdahl. Hugh Green's departure opens up one outside linebacking position, and Rick Graf continues to disappoint on the far side. Free agent E. J. Junior should help, even though he never lived up to his clippings while with the Cardinals.

Rookie free safety Jarvis Williams made plenty of rookie mistakes last year but was the best in a bad secondary. Opponent pass catchers looked at the likes of Paul Lankford, Liffort Hobley, et al., and found their mouths watering. That's why you can bet on Louis Oliver, a second first-round draft choice, starting and possibly on David Holmes, a fourth-round pick. Free-agent hopefuls are Ernest Gibson (New England) and Bobby Watkins (Detroit).

THE BRAINTRUST

All right, you can't take any team coached by Don Shula and blithely consign it to the trash heap. If there's a way to get the Dolphins to a .500 season, Shula will find it. We can't, but we'll be happy to defer to the master.

NEW ENGLAND PATRIOTS

Tony Eason opens as the Patriots' quarterback. He announced in the spring that he was completely recovered from the shoulder and wrist injuries that nearly ended his career, but that was after he'd been denoted Numero Uno by Coach Raymond Berry. In point of fact, Berry gave Eason the job with two games left in the 1988 regular season, and, to the thinking of many Patriots' fans, that was why New England was not in the playoffs last year. They'd bet a full membership in the Henry Cabot Lodge that the team would have made it with Doug Flutie in there. If there's a stumble by the Pats coming out of the gate this year, those fans are going to howl like dyspeptic wolves.

The crux of the situation is that Eason looks like a quarterback and used to throw like a quarterback, while Flutie looks like he belongs in the Pop Warner League and throws too many pop flies. All of which should defuse any argument except that (a) Eason has not yet proved he can win NFL football games, (b) Flutie has been on the winning side for most of the league games he's started, and (c) Flutie, win or lose, is one of the most popular athletes ever produced in Massachusetts. So he can afford to be the good soldier and talk peacefully about waiting for his chance because hordes of locals are going to lobby loudly for him.

Steve Grogan, the Pats' third quarterback, started the season as Number One last year, but he may be a coach by the time this season starts. And should Berry really mess up on his quarterback choice, he may not be a coach himself by the time the season ends.

THE OFFENSE

The quarterback situation will never be resolved to everyone's satisfaction. However, if Whosis proves even adequate, the Pats should be able to score more than the paltry 250 points they registered last year.

For one thing, there's John Stephens, who just might be the league's next great runner. He rumbled for 1,168 yards as a rookie, even though he wasn't the starter at the top of the schedule. If Eason/Flutie can take some of the pressure off with an adequate passing attack, Stephens could move up to 1,500 yards. Fullback Rob Perryman is a solid plunger and excellent blocker, and Reggie Dupard is an excellent third-down back.

Quarterback Whosis will have a new receiver to throw to, one with big play potential—Hart Lee Dykes, the Number One draft pick. Everybody figured he'd be gone by the time the Pats got to draft. He arrives just in time. Stanley Morgan has been around almost long enough to have been one of the original Patriots—the Revolutionary War kind. Irving Fryar apparently will never reach his full potential, and Cedric Jones was no world beater last year. Even more worrisome is the tight end situation, where a broken ankle threatens Lin Dawson's career. Dawson is important to both the passing and running attack. Eric Sievers is a free-agent pickup and Marv Cook is a rookie.

The Pats have a good offensive line that can either run or pass block. Tackle Bruce Armstrong is one of the best and keeps getting better. Maybe this year he'll move ahead of Anthony Munoz in the annals of OTdom. Danny Villa brings 305 active pounds to the other side. Guards Sean Farrell and Ron Wooten are seasoned and strong. Center was a problem last year until former Brown Mike Baab took over.

SPECIAL TEAMS

The Pats' poor placekicking cost them several games in 1988. Fourth-round draft choice Teddy Garcia flopped and was picked up as a free agent by Phoenix. Jason Staurovsky got the job by default but didn't kick well enough to hold it against any decent competition. Punter Jeff Feagles had a fair net (34.1) but a poor average (38.3). The coverage teams were fine and deserve much of the credit for Feagle's net. Fryar and rookie Sammy Martin were okay returners.

THE DEFENSE

New England's main losses in the free-agent circus were on defense, where depth could be a problem. If everyone stays healthy, the Pats' will put up one of the half dozen best Ds in the league.

The biggest question mark is DE Kenneth Sims' Achilles tendon. Sims went out for the year in the Pats' first game last year. If he's okay, the front three will be solid, with sophomore nose tackle Tim Goad a possible all-star. Defensive end Garin Veris can be a good pass rusher, as can free-agent signee Gary Jeter. Brent Williams and Sims play the run well. Rookie Chris Gannon may fit in too.

The linebacking is strong. OLB Andre Tippett and ILB Johnny Rembert are both outstanding. Lawrence McGrew and Ed Reynolds are adequate. There's no "Help Wanted" sign, but a good backup or two wouldn't be turned away.

New England's secondary ranks with Kansas City's and Cleveland's, though again, lack of depth could hurt. Cornerback subs Eugene Profit and Ernest Gibson both evaporated as free agents. The starters, Raymond Clayborn and Ronnie Lippett, are two of the best (though Clayborn is getting into his Geritol years). Free safety Fred Marion had perhaps his best year. He may have been the Pats' defensive MVP. Strong safety Roland James is no slouch either.

THE BRAINTRUST

Depending on Berry's making the right choice of quarterback, finding a placekicker, and a spate of good health, the Patriots could catch the Bills. If everything goes kaflooey, they could drop to fourth in the tough Eastern Division. The most likely scenario: second place again, but a playoff berth.

NEW YORK JETS

The Jets improved in 1988, finished with three wins in their last four games, and spoiled the Giants' season in the final game. So Jets' fans have begun to talk championship in '89. Considering this team's past proclivity for falling flat on its face, that's a marvelous leap of faith. It may not be undeserved. The Jets conceivably could win this year; they have no glaring weaknesses going in. And they do have strengths. However, the total pluses and minuses seem to add up to less than a similar accounting for Buffalo, New England, or Indianapolis. And some of those Jets' pluses are a bit fragile. They got a short stick in the unprotected free-agent gala. New York lost ten free agents and signed only five. Mainly the subtraction was in defensive depth.

Perhaps the most serious defensive loss was Coach Bud Carson, who did such a terrific job coordinating the defense that he won the head job in Cleveland. His replacement, Ralph Hawkins, is capable, but it remains to be seen if he can supplant Carson in the hearts and minds of the defensive crew. A transitional period could get the Jets off to a slow start.

THE OFFENSE

During the off season Coach Joe Walton was telling all how Kenny O'Brien came back from his late benching a better quarterback. O'Brien indeed played well in the final two games, but he's had spurts of excellence before. Perhaps this time he's ready to move into the front rank of NFL quarterbacks the way the Jets keep thinking he will. But after so many false starts, he's made Missourians out of all but the most optimistic observers. Pat Ryan will provide his usual able backup.

In Al Toon, who had 93 catches last year, the Jets have the optimal possession receiver. Wesley Walker was injured or ignored at times; he's thirty-four, and with the retirement of Kurt Sohn, there's no proven talent behind him. The Jets need a new burner. Mickey Shuler is an excellent tight end, perhaps the AFC's best, but he's another possession catcher. Billy Griggs, his sub, went as a free agent.

Although none of them qualify as thousand-yard horses, the trio of Freeman McNeil, Johnny Hector, and Roger Vick gave New York a creditable ground game last year. All three were over 500 yards with 4.1 or better averages. The oft-injured McNeil slashed for 944 yards by playing all sixteen games. That he can get through another full season without a sidelining injury is not the kind of bet that prudent investors make.

The Jets felt enough confidence in their young offensive linemen to leave regular guard Ted Banker an unprotected free agent. Last year's Number One draft choice, Dave Cadigan, spent almost the whole season on the IR, but the Jets still believe he'll be a good one at either tackle or guard. Jeff Criswell and Mike Haight played decently last year, and

tackle Reggie McElroy is adequate. Center Jim Sweeney is noteworthy. Veteran Dan Alexander also returns. Despite Cadigan's injury, the line was greatly improved. The Jets count it as one of their strengths, although the only proven commodity is Sweeney.

SPECIAL TEAMS

Pat Leahy may go on kicking field goals until the end of the century. Last season was his fifteenth and one of his best. Punter Joe Prokop didn't have much of an average (38.9), but his net was a commendable 34.2. Bobby Humphery and JoJo Townsell are good return men. The coverage units were fine.

THE DEFENSE

So many nice things were written last year about the Jets' kiddiecorps secondary that it seems sort of curmudgeonly to point out that New York was burned for 3,823 passing yards, 2,124 rushing yards, and 354 points. None of those are championship-caliber numbers. Six times they gave up 30 or more points.

Free safety Erik McMillan was the Defensive Rookie of the Year with an AFC-high 8 interceptions and numerous other big plays. Rookie cornerback James Hasty and nickel back John Booty were also impressive most of the time. The Jets feel set in the secondary, but young defenders sometimes need a couple of seasons to prove they're for real. Cornerback Bobby Humphery and strong safety Rich Milano are all right. Terry Williams, a second-round draft pick last year who missed nearly the whole season with an injury, may find a spot.

The linebacking is competent but nothing special. Kyle Clifton is perhaps the best of the lot. Alex Gordon, Troy Benson, and Kevin McArthur are all early in their careers and may see better days. Whether veteran Robin Cole will return is unclear. His contributions in a backup role were considerable, particularly in the area of inspiration. Tim Cofield was signed as a free agent out of Kansas City. Jeff Lageman was the surprise first-round draft choice, but some question whether he'll start even as a member of this none-too-distinguished group.

Marty Lyons made a rousing comeback at defensive end last season. He can stop the run as well as anyone. Another rookie, Paul Frase, finished the season at the other DE, but he's a run-stomper like Lyons. A pass rusher is a priority, but no one seems likely to beg Mark Gastineau to return. That includes Miss Nielsen, who booted him out of her life in April, alleging cruelty. Looks like Mark has burned his bridges and Brigittes behind him. Scott Mersereau and Gerald Nichols share nose tackle without distinction.

THE BRAINTRUST

According to his contract they'll have Joe Walton to kick around for a while longer. If the Jets went undefeated through the Super Bowl, you'd still hear complaints about Joe. Several Jets commented after the season that he was a kinder, gentler Walton last year, so maybe things are looking up.

PITTSBURGH STEELERS

The Steelers don't have a realistic hope for the division championship this year. Cincinnati, Houston, and Cleveland are all miles ahead on paper. The best Pittsburgh can look for is a return to respectability with a long shot at third place if one of the powers suddenly goes bust. Of course, even respectability is more easily looked for than found. The three victories in the last four 1988 games might give Pittsburgh fans the impression that the corner has been turned. They are likely to find that corner still in front of them once the season starts.

THE OFFENSE

Unlike last year, the Steelers go into this season with their quarterback situation settled. Bubby Brister brought raw talent, enthusiasm, and leadership to the position last year. He won the spot almost from the first day of training camp, and from then on there was never a question of who was Number One. He's still relatively inexperienced, but one year as the starter should help him cut down on some of his more obvious errors. He can also hope for more help from his receivers. Backup Todd Blackledge's stock is low right now.

Most of the time last year, Brister was limited to one deep receiver. Louis Lipps made a strong comeback to return to the ranks of the league's top receivers, averaging 19.5 per catch. Brister and Lipps will both benefit if someone can share the WR load. Charles Lockett has had chances without consistent success. Troy Johnson always seems to be hurt, and Weegie Thompson is tall but that's all. Derek Hill, the third round draft choice, should be able to move in and improve this area. Some say he'll do more than that. If Mike Mularkey, a free agent from Minnesota, can win Preton Gothard's slot, the Steelers may finally work a tight end into the passing attack. Of late Pittsburgh has thrown to its tight end only slightly more often than it's elected a Republican mayor—an event that last occurred before Pittsburgh joined the NFL. The top draft choice, Tim Worley, is being hailed as a sure All-Pro. That's a lot of weight to carry. However, the young man is a good combination of speed and size and can be expected to help out.

Merril Hoge gives the Steelers an old-fashioned fullback who can block, run up the middle, and catch passes. He'll be backed by free agent Ray Wallace. Warren Williams was the Steelers' Rookie of the Year. He's a slasher, not a burner, and no one seems to think Pittsburgh can win with him starting. Elgin Davis, a free agent from New England, has a chance. Rodney Carter is a third-down receiver.

For the first time in sixteen seasons, the center won't be Mike Webster, who went to Kansas City as a free agent. Dermontti Dawson, who showed promise as a rookie guard last year, is penciled in. The Steelers have used a trapping line, undersized and quick, since Chuck Noll arrived. Tunch Ilkin, Terry Long, and Craig Wolfley all fit that mold. John Rienstra, who's been mostly injured for two years, could help beef up the wall. The Steelers traded to be able to draft three-hundred-pound Tom Ricketts, who's slated for left tackle, where natural guard Wolfley was an undersized fill-in last year.

SPECIAL TEAMS

Gary Anderson is all you could ask for in a placekicker, and Harry Newsome punted excellently when he got his kicks away. Where the Steelers' special teams were pathetic was in the nuts-and-bolts stuff like blocking and tackling. Rod Woodson was okay as a kick returner, but Pittsburgh would like to replace him rather than risk their best defensive player.

THE DEFENSE

Cornerback Woodson leads a secondary that was long on promise despite a terrible record in 1988. He went Pro Bowl in his first full season and is the best athlete to put on a Steeler uniform since the Super Bowl years. Delton Hall, who had looked like a comer in 1987, was a liability in an injury-ruined year. Dwayne Woodruff, who played opposite Woodson , may retire. Safeties Cornell Gowdy and Thomas Everett were inconsistent. The party line is that all the secondary's problems can be traced to injuries and a pitiful pass rush, and there's no reason to doubt it.

Rival quarterbacks were in more danger warming up on the sideline than under Pittsburgh's pass rush. There's hope that DE Keith Willis, out all last year with a neck injury, will return. There's also hope that last year's rookie flop DE Aaron Jones will right himself. There's always hope. Keith Gary and Tim Johnson are run-stoppers. Nose tackle Gerald

Williams got generally poor reviews in his first year as the starter.

Linebacking is a mixture of competence—Bryan Hinkle outside and David Little inside—and promise—Hardy Nickerson inside and Darin Jordan outside. Greg Lloyd and Greg Carr back them.

Mike Merriweather, the Steelers' top outside linebacker through the mid 1980s, held out the entire season. He wanted to renegotiate his contract, but the Steelers didn't. Merriweather punctuated his holdout with some nasty comments about his employers, the kind that are usually counterproductive. Two days before the draft, he was traded for the Vikings first-round choice, who turned out to be Ricketts.

THE BRAINTRUST

Although Chuck Noll stayed as head coach, several Steeler assistants were replaced and the front office was reshuffled. In the long run, those moves will help, but right now the team needs more quality players. Counting Webster, only three free agents were signed away from Pittsburgh. Okay, San Francisco only lost two, but their players were coming off Super Bowl money with a chance for more. That's one hope no Steeler can honestly have for '89. Noll announced after the season that he "couldn't take" another year like 1988. He may have to, at least in the won-lost column.

SAN DIEGO CHARGERS

Dan Henning is a bright guy, so it's hard to figure why he wound up in San Diego. Earlier in the decade, he spent four frustrating seasons trying to do something positive with the no-talent Atlanta Falcons. He didn't get very far, but when he went back to assist Joe Gibbs, he still had a good rep. Whenever a head coaching vacancy opened, someone would toss his name on the table. Sooner or later he would have got a shot at a team that only needed a little tinkering to contend. Instead of waiting, he jumped into the San Diego situation, which is possibly worse from a talent standpoint than the Falcons were. Moreover, he faces a front office situation that assassinated Al Saunders and might be lethal to anybody who deigns act like a head coach. Henning could be the first interim coach ever hired in the off season.

THE OFFENSE

With all of a game and a half under his belt, Mark Vlasic goes into the '89 season as the designated Fouts successor. Admittedly the Chargers won both of Vlasic's starts last year, but he didn't put a whole lot of points on the board, and it's yet to be proved that he's recovered from his serious knee injury. If Vlasic fails, falters, or flinches, Plan B is MMM Malone (that's as in Much Maligned Mark, not as in MMM Good!). Malone is a better quarterback than anyone gives him credit for, but that's not saying much. The Chargers have the shakiest quarterback situation in the NFL.

Whoever does the throwing, he'll benefit from the year of experience the wide receivers picked up last season. Youngsters Jamie Holland, Quinn Early, and Anthony Miller have a world of potential. The tight end situation depends mostly on Rod Bernstine's injured knee. A healthy hinge for Bernstine is almost as critical as a ditto for Vlasic.

No one can complain about the season Gary Anderson had. He blossomed as one of the AFC's best in '88. Whether

Anderson, who they *say* weighs 181, can carry another 200-plus times without becoming porridge is another question. San Diego would like to spot Anderson and leave the heavy stuff to someone a little more muscular. The U.S. Navy could help the Chargers a lot by making Napoleon McCallum available this year instead of next. Of course, "helping the Chargers" ranks kind of low in the Navy's list of priorities.

San Diego got far more out of its grab-bag offensive line—four free agents and a rookie—than they had any right to expect. They signed three unprotected free-agent offensive linemen for '89: OTs Brett Miller and Joel Patten and OG Larry Williams. Of the returnees, guard Dennis McKnight is okay and last year's rookie, 305-pound tackle David Richards, is big enough to play for anybody. It's hoped that tackle John Clay will do something besides sit around putting on pounds this year. Last year the Chargers traded Jim Lachey for McCallum and Clay, in effect giving up an All-Pro for a long wait and a dead weight.

SPECIAL TEAMS

Placekicker Vince Abbott may lose his job to free agent Chris Bahr. Neither of them was in top form last year. Punter Rolf Mojsiejenko is one of the very best. He led the AFC in 1986 and averaged 44.1 last season. A good thing, too. He gets a lot of chances with the Chargers. Lionel "Little Train" James returned punts for a creditable 9.9 average in 1988. Holland and Miller were all right on kickoff returns—each ran back one kick for a touchdown—but you hate risking your starting receivers to bring back kicks.

THE DEFENSE

For starters, Chip Banks is likely to play for the Chargers again about as soon as Willard Scott adopts Bryant Gumbel as his godson. San Diego would gladly trade Banks for something, but not even Henny Youngman could get applause from "Take my linebacker—please!"

The defensemen who *will* play for San Diego include some valuable people. Defensive end Lee Williams is among the best at what he does. His 11 sacks last year were only a half off the AFC leadership, and his trip to the Pro Bowl was deserved. Leslie O'Neal is another good one on the far side. And Burt Grossman, the first-round draft pick, was about the best pass rusher in college football last year. If the space in between the ends could be upgraded a bit, the Chargers would have as good a front as anyone in the division.

Linebacking starts with Billy Ray Smith. Out for half of last season, he figures to be fully recovered and fairly fantastic. Alas, one linebacker doth not a defense make. Jim Collins, a free agent from the Rams, should help, but a lot more is needed.

Gil Byrd was fine at one cornerback last season. He led the team with 7 interceptions. After that, though, there are people like Elvis "Toast" Patterson (so called because he's been so often burned) and others who don't even have colorful nicknames. Vencie Glenn is an okay free safety.

Henning goes into the season with half a fair defense. Unfortunately opponents have a nasty habit of picking on the other half, so the Chargers are going to live or die by what he can whip up to fill the holes.

THE BRAINTRUST

As we said, Henning is a bright guy. He can be depended on to get the best out of the hand he's dealt. Doing the dealing is the Chargers' director of football operations, Steve Ortmayer. So far he hasn't done as well as he did when he was with the Raiders. The wild card is owner Alex Spanos, who's shown a predilection to get involved with football decisions but no aptitude for making the right ones. Spanos and Ortmayer talk as if they expect to be right up there contending this season, but the odds favor the Chargers to charge to the rear in the West.

SEATTLE SEAHAWKS

Coming off their first division title and second-straight playoff appearance, the Seahawks should be looking toward 1989 the way a kid looks toward Christmas. They're on the rise, right? Super Bowl coming up, right? Don't bet your Captain Midnight Decoder Ring. The Seahawks didn't rise in 1988; they merely declined less than the rest of a division that crashed in flames. Counting the playoff loss to the Bengals, they won only one more than they lost. Playing in pro football's weakest division made Seattle a moderately corpulent frog in a very shallow pond.

The AFC West is like the AFC Central of 1985. "Putrid" was one of the more complimentary adjectives. But within a season or two, the Browns, Bengals, and Oilers all became formidable. Something like that may happen in the AFC West. But the Seahawks were a middling team in 1988, and it's hard to see where a whole lot of improvement is going to come from.

THE OFFENSE

Most of the Seahawks' positives are on offense. For example, fullback John L. Williams is positively one of the most exciting and all-around valuable people in the NFL. He runs, blocks, catches, and, if they asked him, he'd probably paint the yard-lines on the Kingdome turf. He'd get 'em straight, too. Williams will give the 'Hawks a running game. How much of a running game will depend not on Williams but on teammate Curt Warner. Even though he gained over a thousand yards again, the Seahawks have been shopping Warner around. You don't trade thousand-yard runners unless you (a) are pretty sure they can't do it again, or (b) can get a Ramsian bonanza of draft choices.

Another plus is the quarterback slot, where the ever adequate, never adulated Dave Krieg is coming off the best half-season in his checkered career. The Seahawks would love to see him play a whole year the way he did in the last five games of 1988, but Krieg has never put together a whole All-Pro season up to now. He's been a world beater in some games and world-weary in others. You can almost make book that somewhere in midseason young Kelly Stouffer will be handed the starting keys. And a couple of games later, Krieg will be back. One of these years, Stouffer will get his hand on the tiller and not let go, but it'll more likely happen in 1990.

Either quarterback will miss Steve Largent if he decides to retire—a yes-or-no announcement is due any moment at this writing. Except for the money, you have to wonder why Largent would want to come back for another year. What's he got to prove? He can increase a couple of records—maybe. But it would be a shame to watch a pass catcher who can be mentioned in the same breath with Don Hutson limp through another season like the last one.

Surprisingly the Seahawks protected Largent in the free-agent circus. Out of courtesy maybe. They didn't protect regular tight end Mike Tice or backup wide receiver Ray Butler, who wound up in Washington and Cleveland, respectively. If the Seahawks lose Largent too, they'll miss Butler. Paul Skansi is habitually called a Largent clone, but that's not true. What he is, is a Largent type. You know, like you can get a cheap imitation of an expensive watch; just don't expect it to keep the same time. The 'Hawks got free agent TE Jon Embree from the Rams to replace Tice, but it doesn't look like an even exchange.

The hope of the receiving corps is Brian Blades, the rookie who took 20 percent of his 40 pass receptions for touchdowns. He has speed, moves, and hands, but whether they can overcome the double and triple coverage he's likely to get this year is another matter. Look for him to catch more and score less.

Andy Heck, the first-draft choice, is figured as a starting tackle. He'll help. Otherwise the offensive line will be a lot like it's been for the last couple of years—good enough most of the time but too small to overpower anybody. One missing link will be Blair Bush, who'll be centering for Green Bay.

SPECIAL TEAMS

Also among the missing will be kick returner Bobby Joe Edmonds, who was grabbed as an FA by Detroit. Edmonds is one of the best at bringing back kicks (although 1988 wasn't his best year). On the other hand, kick returners in the NFL have a career expectancy only slightly longer than butterfingered bomb disposers. The other Seahawk specialists, punter Ruben Rodriquez and placekicker Norm Johnson, earned their keep in 1988—Johnson particularly. The seven-year vet was 22 of 28 in field goals and letter-perfect in 39 extra-point tries. Of course, anyone who does most of his kicking on artificial turf indoors should outperform less-blessed mortals.

DEFENSE

Seattle doesn't scare anyone on defense. Last year they tried to induce fear and trembling with the Boz. Golly! Someone with a bestseller and all that time logged on talk shows just had to be really gloryoski, didn't he? Funny thing about the book. No one we talked to would admit to reading it, but everybody knew all about it. So when the season started, everybody knew about Boz, but no one remembered seeing him do much tackling. Actually Bosworth got his share of tackles until he went out with a shoulder injury. He earned the salary of any one of a half-dozen good journeyman NFL linebackers. Of course, he was paid the equivalent of all six of their salaries. Seattle's new across-the-board raise in ticket prices will help pay for the Boz. That should give Seahawk fans a warm glow. Incidentally, Dave Wyman played a better brand of linebacker all season, but no one seems to be writing *The Wy*.

Old reliables Jacob Green and Joe Nash were adequate in 1988. Individually the Seahawks' defense had a lot of okay guys, but collectively they didn't do the job: opponents ran for a 4.5 average. The Seahawks weren't the AFC's worst, mainly because Miami was in the league. Seattle's okay little guys were too often overpowered by opponents' okay big guys. The best the 'Hawks could do in the draft was fourth-round pick Travis McNeal. Any quick, 290-pound stud looking for work should check with the Seahawks.

The secondary had a bad case of Easley-shock, missing the former All-Pro who retired before the 1988 season.

THE BRAINTRUST

We'll take it as an article of faith that Chuck Knox will improve the defense in 1989. A healthy Bosworth will help. Still, it probably won't offset the improvement of some of the other division teams. The 'Hawks won't collapse. No Knox team would ever do that, but it's a long shot to bat plus-.500.

As for what bearing new owner Ken Behring will have on the team's fortunes this year, we can only guess. He says he'll be a "hands-on" owner. Uh oh.

1989 PREDICTIONS

Picking game winners in the NFL is harder than handicapping horse races because there are more moving parts. All the pitfalls are magnified when you take a shot at crystal-balling a whole season. It's sort of like juggling a dozen eggs while playing hopscotch on an escalator.

Funny thing, though, every year various experts can't resist juggling those eggs and telling you who's going to win. It's probably ego (eggo?) on their part. We, on the other hand, are going to reveal next year's winners as a public service.

THE NFC

Eastern Division: We think the Redskins will bounce back on Gerald Riggs's legs to edge the Giants in a close race. New York won't get its running game working until it's too late. Philadelphia will make a game try, but lack of depth will kill them. Everybody will be saying what an improvement Dallas has made, but they'll stop at seven wins. Phoenix will slide. Neither Wild Card will come from the East. Here's the order:

1. Washington Redskins
2. New York Giants
3. Philadelphia Eagles
4. Dallas Cowboys
5. Phoenix Cardinals

Central Division: There'll be a lot of improvement in the bottom three, but by December everyone will be predicting a Super Bowl trophy for the Vikes. Chicago, after some early stumbling, will come roaring down the stretch to capture a Wild Card.

1. Minnesota Vikings
2. Chicago Bears
3. Green Bay Packers
4. Tampa Bay Buccaneers
5. Detroit Lions

Western Division: The Rams beat the 49ers twice and end up with the division crown by a nose. San Francisco still gains a Wild Card berth. The Saints drop to .500 with defensive problems. Atlanta is never a pushover but loses too many close ones.

1. Los Angeles Rams
2. San Francisco 49ers
3. New Orleans Saints
4. Atlanta Falcons

PLAYOFFS

Wild Card: Chicago over the 49ers in a revenge upset.
First Round: The Vikings stop the Rams (yes, again!), and Washington drops Chicago.
NFC Championship: In an upset, Washington shocks the Vikings.

THE AFC

Eastern Division: The order will be the same as last year, but it will be a lot closer. New England will make the Wild Card cut, barely edging the Colts. The Jets, after early success, swoon again. Shula wins seven at Miami on brains.

1. Buffalo Bills
2. New England Patriots
3. Indianapolis Colts
4. New York Jets
5. Miami Dolphins

Central Division: After a bad start the Bengals can't quite catch the Oilers and have to settle for a Wild Card. There's talk of naming Jerry Glanville Coach of the Year. Cleveland starts fast but fades. Pittsburgh shows up for all sixteen games.

1. Houston Oilers
2. Cincinnati Bengals
3. Cleveland Browns
4. Pittsburgh Steelers

Western Division: The Chiefs get out in front early and hold on by their fingernails. You can throw a hat over the top four: 9–7, 8–8, 8–8, and 7–9. Because both Cleveland and Indianapolis are better than the Chiefs, "Nightline" asks if the playoffs should be revamped. Bob Irsay tells Ted Koppel yes, but Lamar Hunt says no.

1. Kansas City Chiefs
2. Denver Broncos
3. Seattle Seahawks
4. Los Angeles Raiders
5. San Diego Chargers

PLAYOFFS

Wild Card: New England over Cincinnati.
First Round: Buffalo beats Kansas City easily. New England surprises Houston in the House of Pain.
AFC Championship: Buffalo ends New England's dream.
Super Bowl XXIV: Buffalo over Washington.

GAMBLING AND GUESSING

We had quite a bit to say on this subject in *The Hidden Game of Football,* which all but a handful of you have surely read by now ... but in the unlikely event that you somehow found something else to do with your $18.95 last year, we'll recap a bit of basic stuff before we get tricky.

Even if you've already placed a few bets, you may not be sure about how everything works.

First of all, you're not going to bet on who wins the game. If it was that easy, even your worthless brother-in-law would get rich betting on football. Almost anyone who reads a sports page knows that the 49ers, Bears, and Bengals are going to win most of the time and Tampa Bay isn't. What you bet on in a football game isn't *who* but *how much they'll do it by*—the margin of victory, called the "point spread," or "spread."

Here's how it works. Let's say the 49ers are playing the Falcons at Atlanta. You decide San Francisco will probably win. They've got Montana and Rice and Craig. And they've got Lott and Fuller and Haley. Atlanta has red uniforms. You *know* San Francisco will win. But by how much? A touchdown? Two touchdowns?

Tuesday the week of the game, just about every newspaper in the country prints the "Line," which is sometimes called the "Las Vegas Line" although it supposedly originates in Miami. The Line is what very astute handicappers—the best in the world—think the margins, or spreads, will be in that week's games. If Hamlet were a handicapper, he'd ask: "2½ or not 2½; that is the question." To look at it from the other side, the purpose of the spread is to make every game appear "even," no matter how strong one team may be. The Line on some games may change during the week, usually because of heavy money bet on one team or sometimes because of late injuries to key players. Also, an individual bookmaker may quote a slightly different line on a game if he wants to encourage bets on one side. For example, a San Francisco bookmaker may make the 49ers heavier favorites if he can't find many 49er fans willing to put their money on the Falcons.

In this scenario, the 49ers are favored by 7 points— written either as Frisco −7 or Atlanta +7. The 49ers are called the "favorites" and the Falcons are "underdogs," or, for bettors in a hurry, "dogs." But the spread theoretically makes the dog as strong as the favorite. A game really rated even, with no points given, is called a "pick 'em."

You can think of it as betting on the teams if you want to, but you're really betting on the spread—and your bookie doesn't much care which way you go so long as he finds somebody who'll bet the other side. If you bet on the 49ers, they not only have to win, they have to win by more than 7 points for you to collect. If you bet on Atlanta and they lose by 6, you win because you had an extra 7 points to add to the Falcons' score. Let's say the real score was 14-9, San Fran. The betting score, with the spread, was 14-16, Atlanta. Those who bet on Atlanta won despite the actual score.

Of course, if the actual score had been 14-7 (14-14 with the spread), everybody gets his money back. A spread-induced tie is called a "push," and no one likes them. To eliminate ties, most spreads have a half-point, like 2½ or 5½. Half-points make the bets more attractive by killing the push. Sometimes a bookie will sell you a half-point and increase his cut.

His cut is in the "vigorish." Lovely word. It sounds like something sweet and sticky. Well, it is: sweet for him and sticky for you.

See, if you go out in your back yard and bet your neighbor $10 on the game, with or without the spread, one of you will end up with another $10 and the other will be out an equal amount. Not so if you bet with a bookie. With him, you have to bet $11 on San Francisco to win $10. Meanwhile, somebody else has bet $11 on Atlanta. When the 14-9 score comes in, the bookie passes $10 of your money on to the Atlanta guy and keeps a dollar for himself. Thus the bookie takes in $22 and pays out $21 to the winner, keeping a dollar (4.5 percent of the total) for himself. That's the vigorish. Another name for it is "juice."

Now think a minute. If you make ten $10 bets and win

half of them, you may think you're even. You're not. You're out $5. You made $50 on your winning teams and lost $55 on your losing teams (assuming you didn't buy a half-point somewhere along the way, which usually puts the vigorish up to 12–10). That's why you must win eleven of twenty-one bets (52.4 percent) just to break even.

And that's why a bookie doesn't care which way you bet. As long as he can keep his bettors balanced on either side, he'll make money. As a matter of fact, he's called a bookmaker because he strives to keep his "book" balanced and thereby be guaranteed a profit.

For you to break even, you have to be right 52.4 percent of the time.

Well, you say, that doesn't sound very hard. You read the sports pages, maybe *The Sporting News*, perhaps a magazine or two. That certainly readies you to do battle against the handicappers who do this full time 365 days a year, study every available piece of football information under a microscope, squeeze every statistic until it burps, and no doubt has someone with an inside pipeline to the teams. Just how smart are you? Because make no mistake, to win you have to outsmart the guys who make the spread, and they're very smart.

But not perfect.

What most intelligent bettors do is look over the spreads for the week and try to find one that doesn't look right. They don't care which team is favored. What they're searching for is a spread that seems all out of proportion to what they expect the final victory margin to be. That's called an "overlay."

Instead of going with gut feelings, these bettors usually look for patterns in past performances. Sometimes these can get pretty elaborate, like: Bet on a home underdog that scored 10 points or less in each of its last two games. Or bet on a home underdog playing a nondivision game after a streak of two or more division games. Or bet against an NFC Central team as a road favorite versus a nondivisional opponent after a point spread loss or tie.

Predicting the future with an example from the past can be intriguing but not always productive. Remember the girl you took out in high school because another guy said he'd gotten somewhere with her? She wouldn't even hold hands! However, certain patterns do have some predictive power. If a team gives up a barrelful of points in three straight games against mediocre teams, don't expect them to imitate Gibraltar when they meet a good team. If a team that has shown a strong passing attack goes against a team that has proved itself vulnerable to the air, expect the pattern to continue.

The best known pattern is the "Home Field Advantage." It's an accepted fact in all sports that a team playing at home has an advantage which can be translated into points in the spread. Various studies bear this out, although the H.F.A. in pro football is thought to be smaller than in college football or any kind of basketball. There's some disagreement as to how much the H.F.A. is actually worth to

a pro football team. It used to be figured at 3 points; some rate it as low as 2.1. We favor 2.2, but remember it's only a general concept.

Among the many suggestions as to why a team has a home field advantage: familiarity, as in playing in Green Bay in December is easier for a Packer than a Ram; internal clocks, as in a 49er in a one o'clock game at Philadelphia is taking the field at his internal ten o'clock in the morning; and the home crowd, as in the visiting quarterback can't call his plays if the home fans scream loud enough.

Incidentally, one theory as to why the home field advantage seems to be narrowing holds that artificial grass is responsible, making many fields more uniform. An offshoot of that is the theory that a team used to playing on one kind of surface will do poorly when they play on the other kind.

At any rate, knowledgeable bettors add in the home field advantage, and often some other frills that they believe are important—including the use of power ratings, which we won't get into here—and come up with their own line. They compare it with the bookie's line, looking for overlays.

You may be surprised to learn that the best place to look for overlays is in the 6 1/2 to 9 1/2 range, but it makes sense if you think about it. A closer spread—say, 3 1/2 points—indicates two teams that are near equals. If the game develops as billed, it may turn on one fluke play, wiping out all your careful analysis. Moreover, a close spread often indicates two strong teams. One of the strengths of a strong team is its consistency.

A big spread—say, 17 points—is a definite blowout but a shaky bet. You may be on the favorite, comfortably ahead by 21 points in the last minute, only to watch the leader's subs give up a "so-what" touchdown. If you're on the dog, trailing by only 14 in the fourth quarter, their desperation passes may end up as interception TD returns. Additionally, a favorite may relax a little and come out flat; or the dog may give up before they leave the locker room and really get murdered.

A middle ground spread—say, 7½ or 8½—shows two teams that are reasonably close to each other in ability. Here you can put your mind to work. If your analysis indicates a strength or weakness that you think the linemakers may have missed, like the dog's excellent rush defense will offset the favorite's superior running, go with it. If you're right only 60 percent of the time, you'll make a profit.

So let's develop some useful stats for analyzing football handicapping, and from that analysis, some concrete betting advice.

We took the point spreads for all regular-season games over the past twelve years and compared them with the actual results. When looking at data like this, it helps to calculate what is called a standard deviation. *Don't run; it's easy.* The difference between the spread and the score for each game is squared and then added up for all games. This total is then divided by the number of games before the square root is taken.

That wasn't so bad, was it? (It *was*? Well, then, just skip the explanation that follows and go directly to the advice printed in italics.)

In this case, the standard deviation is 13½ points. What this means is that if the distribution of differences is normal, which it is, about two-thirds of the scores will be within 13.5 points of the spread, and 95 percent will be within two standard deviations or 27 points. Holy Moly! you say. That's a helluva big difference, but believe us, this is the correct figure.

Out of 2,548 games in the twelve-year period, 136 or 5.3 percent were off by more than 27 points. Honest! This difference has very little to do with mis-handicapping (though it probably got some shnook canned), but is simply a measure of the variation in play in a typical football game. We believe that if you took two evenly matched teams and had them play a number of games against each other, the variation in the scores would be the same 13.5 points.

Take an example in which a game is rated as even, but you know for a fact that one team should be favored by 13.5 points, and therefore the spread is wrong. Okay, it's a hypothetical game: in the real world with your real money this would never happen. We're just using it to illustrate our point. Your team would win by more than 27 points about 16 percent of the time (half of the one-third region beyond one standard deviation) and lose the game just as frequently, the other 16 percent. So if you could spot a 13.5-point error, you would win 84 percent of the time.

But getting down to reasonable levels, an error of 7 points would correspond to a 69 percent advantage, while 4 points is 61 percent. Assuming you have to lay 11 to make 10—the normal vigorish—your break even point is 11/21 or 52.4 percent. In order to win 55 percent of the time, you need without fail to recognize a lot of two-point errors in the spread or, more realistically, recognize four-point errors about half the time.

We have never seen any data showing that any handicapping service is able reliably to pick more than 50 percent winners over any reasonable length of time. Some of the claims are outlandish. We're not saying that some handicappers are barefaced liars. As we recall, at least one has a beard. Anyone claiming 70 percent success must detect errors in the spread of more than 7 points on a consistent basis. The spread is never off by that many points.

What happens is that, like coin flipping, the choices don't come out to exactly half every time. Take a sample of 40 services that pick 64 games a year. The standard deviation in games is equal to the square root of (1/2 X 1/2 X 64), or 4. And 4 over 64 is about 6 percent. So about 7 services will be better than 56 percent and 7 worse than 44 percent. This is the one-third region beyond one standard deviation. One will probably be better than 62 percent, which is the 5 percent region beyond two standard deviations. But this says nothing about their ability in the future. Just when you're impressed enough to stake your kid's tuition on their say-so, they can go sour.

Besides, if these guys were so good, why aren't they betting their own selections, winning a bundle, and going off to buy Tibet or something? Hey, send us a dollar and a stamped, self-addressed envelope and we'll tell you who we think will win next week's games and throw in the whole 2001 season to boot. On second thought, make that two dollars. We wouldn't want to look sleazy. We have principles.

Speaking of principles, there are a couple of handicapping principles to keep in mind.

First, the teams are a lot more evenly matched than they appear to be. In fact, about half the difference in team strength over an entire season is simply due to random variations in game results.

The second is that the handicappers are really handicapping the public, not the teams, and the public likes to bet on teams that have won before.

Both these factors favor underdogs. In fact, over the twelve-year period, the underdogs beat the spread over 53 percent of the time. That's enough of a difference that you'd better have a pretty good reason before you back a favorite.

Okay, if you're with us, you're gonna say it would seem like the secret to winning would simply be to determine if the public hangs onto good teams that are slipping too long and fails to recognize emerging teams quickly enough. If they do, then you just go in the opposite direction, right? Naturally the "public" isn't you; it's all those other jokers.

Unfortunately, because teams change very little from year to year in real strength, but the variation due to chance is large, it's next to impossible to tell if a team is really slipping, or just had a tough-luck year. Looking at teams with win differences of 3 or more in successive seasons, and how they did in the two years following the change, produced what are called "nonsignificant results." Translation: they didn't tell us a damn thing.

A total of 16 teams that declined beat the spread 49 percent of the time over the next pair of seasons, while 14 teams that improved were at exactly 50 percent. Well, there was one significant result. We get the message that the "public" ain't so dumb after all.

However, when we started looking at the point-spread records for each team, we got something worth the effort. *It appears that the public tends to back a team that had a good record versus the spread in the previous season.*

There were 39 teams that beat the spread at least 10 times in a given season, and their record against the spread the following year was 264–288, or 48 percent. Those that lost ten or more times had a 280–258 record the next season, a 52 percent mark. Combining these two—going against the first group and with the second—we get a 52 percent success rate in 1,080 games. This is still slightly below the 52.4 percent we need to come out ahead. But (note the significance of "but"), *if we limit these only to games in which the selected team is an underdog,* we get 334 wins out of 622 games, a 53.7 percent margin. And that would make a tidy profit.

The expected standard deviation for a sample of this size is the square root of (½ X ½ X 622) or 12.5. The expected number of wins, if each game was even, would be 311. Since we got 334, 23 above the expected number, this is almost two standard deviations away from the mean, a figure expected only about 5 percent of the time. As the mathematicians say, "This difference is considered significant."

This theory is based on the premise that the public counts how a team did against the spread in the previous season pretty highly—and will therefore back a team that did well excessively while at the same time staying away from a team that did poorly. *It works for us.*

Here is the yearly record versus the spread for each team (wins-losses, with ties omitted):

Team	1977	1978	1979	1980	1981	1982	1983	1984	1985	1986	1987	1988
Games	14	16	16	16	16	9	16	16	16	16	15	16
NFC												
ATL	8-6	6-9	7-9	13-3	5-9	5-4	9-7	4-12	6-10	9-7	5-9	9-7
CHI	7-6	9-7	8-7	8-8	8-8	4-5	7-7	9-7	12-3	5-11	7-6	11-5
DAL	7-6	8-8	5-11	10-6	9-7	5-4	9-7	7-8	10-6	5-10	7-7	7-9
DET	3-10	8-8	4-12	9-6	10-6	5-4	8-7	6-10	8-8	9-7	6-9	8-8
GB	5-8	8-8	6-9	8-8	8-8	6-3	6-9	8-7	7-8	8-8	7-8	6-10
RAMS	9-5	5-9	6-10	10-5	7-9	3-6	8-5	8-8	9-7	9-7	6-9	9-7
MIN	4-9	6-10	8-8	9-7	8-8	5-4	8-7	5-11	8-8	10-6	6-8	9-7
NO	5-8	10-6	8-8	6-9	6-10	4-5	6-7	7-9	4-12	10-6	11-4	7-9
NYG	7-7	8-7	9-7	6-9	10-6	4-5	5-11	6-10	9-6	9-5	5-10	7-9
PHI	8-6	10-5	8-8	11-5	10-6	3-6	6-10	10-6	7-9	9-7	9-5	9-7
PHOE	—	—	—	—	—	—	—	—	—	—	—	7-9
STL	5-9	7-8	9-7	5-10	7-9	5-4	8-8	9-7	5-11	7-9	9-6	—
SF	5-6	4-10	7-9	8-7	12-4	3-6	9-7	12-4	10-6	9-7	8-6	9-7
TB	8-5	8-7	8-8	5-11	11-5	3-5	6-9	10-5	5-9	6-10	7-8	10-6
WAS	8-5	7-9	11-5	7-8	8-8	7-2	11-4	9-6	8-7	9-7	9-6	5-11
AFC												
BAL	6-8	6-9	7-8	8-8	3-12	4-5	10-6	—	—	—	—	—
BUF	4-10	12-3	9-6	10-6	7-9	3-5	7-9	5-10	5-10	8-8	9-6	9-6
CIN	7-7	7-8	6-8	8-7	11-4	5-4	7-9	9-6	7-9	7-9	3-11	11-5
CLE	8-6	8-7	8-8	9-7	6-10	3-6	8-8	9-6	9-7	9-6	9-6	8-8
DEN	9-5	8-7	8-7	6-9	7-9	3-6	9-7	11-5	9-7	9-6	7-7	8-8
HOU	10-4	6-8	8-7	7-8	6-8	2-7	7-9	4-11	7-9	8-8	8-6	9-7
IND	—	—	—	—	—	—	—	7-9	8-7	6-10	9-6	6-10
KC	8-6	8-8	8-7	8-7	11-5	3-6	9-7	8-8	7-9	8-8	8-7	8-8
RAID	0-0	0-0	0-0	0-0	0-0	6-3	10-5	7-8	10-6	7-9	7-8	6-10
MIA	7-5	9-7	8-7	7-9	11-4	6-3	10-6	10-5	8-7	7-9	7-8	4-11
NE	6-8	6-10	6-9	10-6	3-13	6-3	8-8	6-10	12-4	6-10	6-9	10-6
NYJ	8-5	8-7	9-7	5-11	9-7	5-4	5-11	6-9	8-7	7-9	8-7	8-8
OAK	7-7	6-10	9-7	9-6	6-10	0-0	0-0	0-0	0-0	0-0	0-0	0-0
PIT	6-8	7-7	9-7	3-13	8-7	6-3	8-8	8-8	6-10	9-6	8-7	7-9
SD	7-7	9-7	9-6	7-9	7-9	6-3	5-11	8-8	7-8	7-9	6-9	8-8
SEA	7-7	10-5	10-6	6-10	6-10	5-4	8-8	10-5	7-8	9-7	8-7	8-8

Next is a summary of the results for the past twelve years. The data shows a breakdown by the line for the visiting team. A minus figure indicates that the visiting team was favored by that many points. The first set of columns shows the record versus the spread for that value, and the second set shows the number of straight-up winners, ties, and percentage. The third set gives data on one type of tease.

A tease is a bet in which you get to pick two teams and get extra points, but have to win both games to collect. The reason it is called a tease is because it looks like you can't lose. In reality, though, a 7-point tease wins only about 71 percent of the time, and the chances of going 2-for-2 is just about 50 percent, the same as picking a single game. Data is shown for the number of wins and ties for both the visiting (V) and home (H) teams. Since there is a range of winning scores, it is possible for both teams to win any particular game.

VISITOR VS. SPREAD					STRAIGHT UP			TEASE				
								WINS		TIES		
SPREAD	G	W	L	T	PCT	W	T	PCT	W-V	W-H	T-V	T-H	PCT
-20.0	1	0	1	0	0.00	1	0	100.00	0	1	0	0	50.00
-15.0	1	1	0	0	100.00	1	0	100.00	1	1	0	0	100.00
-14.5	2	0	2	0	0.00	2	0	100.00	1	2	0	0	75.00

(Continued)
VISITOR VS. SPREAD   STRAIGHT UP   TEASE

| | | | | | | | | WINS | | TIES | | |
SPREAD	G	W	L	T	PCT	W	T	PCT	W-V	W-H	T-V	T-H	PCT
-14.0	5	1	4	0	20.00	5	0	100.00	3	5	0	0	80.00
-13.5	3	1	2	0	33.33	3	0	100.00	3	3	0	0	100.00
-13.0	8	2	6	0	25.00	5	0	62.50	3	7	0	0	62.50
-12.5	1	0	1	0	0.00	1	0	100.00	1	1	0	0	100.00
-12.0	3	1	2	0	33.33	3	0	100.00	3	3	0	0	100.00
-11.5	4	1	3	0	25.00	3	0	75.00	3	3	0	0	75.00
-11.0	4	1	2	1	33.33	3	0	75.00	3	3	0	0	75.00
-10.5	10	5	5	0	50.00	8	0	80.00	7	7	0	0	70.00
-10.0	14	5	8	1	38.46	9	1	69.23	7	11	1	0	66.67
-9.5	10	4	6	0	40.00	8	0	80.00	8	7	0	0	75.00
-9.0	12	8	4	0	66.67	10	0	83.33	9	6	1	2	71.43
-8.5	6	1	5	0	16.67	4	0	66.67	4	6	0	0	83.33
-8.0	11	5	5	1	50.00	8	0	72.73	8	8	0	0	72.73
-7.5	23	9	14	0	39.13	18	0	78.26	18	16	0	0	73.91
-7.0	40	24	15	1	61.54	31	1	79.49	31	21	1	2	67.53
-6.5	41	16	25	0	39.02	24	0	58.54	24	33	0	0	69.51
-6.0	43	14	26	3	35.00	29	0	67.44	29	32	0	1	71.76
-5.5	28	16	12	0	57.14	20	0	71.43	21	19	0	0	71.43
-5.0	33	8	24	1	25.00	15	0	45.45	16	28	0	1	67.69
-4.5	45	22	23	0	48.89	29	0	64.44	32	30	0	0	68.89
-4.0	60	22	34	4	39.29	33	0	55.00	36	41	6	3	69.37
-3.5	81	43	38	0	53.09	49	1	61.25	62	56	0	0	72.84
-3.0	104	42	53	9	44.21	57	1	55.34	74	78	1	2	74.15
-2.5	73	32	41	0	43.84	38	0	52.05	46	56	0	0	69.86
-2.0	70	24	41	5	36.92	32	0	45.71	41	55	2	2	70.59
-1.5	28	16	12	0	57.14	16	0	57.14	18	17	0	0	62.50
-1.0	56	32	23	1	58.18	33	0	58.93	38	39	1	1	70.00
0.0	57	27	30	0	47.37	27	0	47.37	38	39	4	2	71.30
1.0	54	20	31	3	39.22	20	0	37.04	36	42	1	1	73.58
1.5	42	23	19	0	54.76	21	1	51.22	32	32	0	0	76.19
2.0	93	53	37	3	58.89	52	0	55.91	73	59	1	6	73.74
2.5	83	46	37	0	55.42	38	0	45.78	64	59	0	0	74.10
3.0	164	76	70	18	52.05	67	1	41.10	115	119	7	7	74.52
3.5	162	82	80	0	50.62	59	0	36.42	118	116	0	0	72.22
4.0	113	55	56	2	49.55	44	0	38.94	77	74	2	4	68.64
4.5	64	31	33	0	48.44	25	1	39.68	46	42	0	0	68.75
5.0	66	34	32	0	51.52	20	0	30.30	49	49	2	0	75.38
5.5	51	24	27	0	47.06	14	1	28.00	35	38	0	0	71.57
6.0	98	50	48	0	51.02	32	2	33.33	63	66	3	2	67.54
6.5	114	64	50	0	56.14	43	0	37.72	81	71	0	0	66.67
7.0	104	56	46	2	54.90	28	0	26.92	77	76	3	0	74.63
7.5	50	28	22	0	56.00	13	0	26.00	38	37	0	0	75.00
8.0	40	22	17	1	56.41	12	0	30.00	28	26	1	2	70.13
8.5	25	15	10	0	60.00	9	0	36.00	18	15	0	0	66.00
9.0	47	26	21	0	55.32	11	0	23.40	32	35	0	0	71.28
9.5	54	27	27	0	50.00	14	0	25.93	40	38	0	0	72.22
10.0	49	27	21	1	56.25	9	0	18.37	33	36	0	3	72.63
10.5	32	15	17	0	46.88	3	0	9.38	23	24	0	0	73.44
11.0	28	14	14	0	50.00	6	0	21.43	18	18	1	0	65.45
11.5	11	4	7	0	36.36	1	0	9.09	7	10	0	0	77.27
12.0	10	6	4	0	60.00	1	0	10.00	7	6	0	0	65.00
12.5	7	3	4	0	42.86	0	0	0.00	5	5	0	0	71.43
13.0	27	13	14	0	48.15	4	0	14.81	16	18	3	0	66.67
13.5	24	12	12	0	50.00	2	0	8.33	17	15	0	0	66.67
14.0	21	12	8	1	60.00	3	0	14.29	17	13	0	0	71.43
14.5	4	4	0	0	100.00	1	0	25.00	4	2	0	0	75.00
15.0	6	4	2	0	66.67	0	0	0.00	5	3	0	0	66.67
15.5	1	1	0	0	100.00	1	0	100.00	1	0	0	0	50.00

(Continued)

(Continued)

SPREAD	G	W	L	T	PCT	W	T	PCT	W-F	W-U	T-F	T-U	PCT
16.0	8	3	5	0	37.50	1	0	12.50	5	6	0	0	68.75
16.5	1	0	1	0	0.00	0	0	0.00	1	1	0	0	100.00
17.0	4	2	1	1	66.67	1	0	25.00	3	2	0	0	62.50
17.5	1	0	1	0	0.00	0	0	0.00	1	1	0	0	100.00
18.0	3	0	2	1	0.00	0	0	0.00	1	3	0	0	66.67
18.5	1	1	0	0	100.00	1	0	100.00	1	0	0	0	50.00
19.0	1	0	0	1	0.00	0	0	0.00	1	1	0	0	100.00
19.5	1	1	0	0	100.00	0	0	0.00	1	0	0	0	50.00
20.0	7	2	4	1	33.33	0	0	0.00	4	6	0	0	71.43
TOTAL	2548	1239	1247	62	49.84	1081	10	42.59	1781	1798	41	41	71.38

The next table combines home and away data for favorites. The format is the same. The main point here is that the overall winning percentage for favorites is only 46.8. Here the tease data is broken down by (F) favorite and (U) underdog, rather than by (H) home and (V) visitor. Even though all spreads do not show exactly even numbers of wins and losses versus the spread, there are no significant differences for any particular point spread. *However, the overall low success rate of all favorites is quite significant. If the games were truly even, then a difference this large would only happen about once in 400 samples of this size.*

The table shows that a team favored by a certain number of points will actually win the game at a predictable rate. A 13.5-point favorite should win the game 84 percent of the time, a 7-point favorite would win 69 percent of the time, and a 3-point favorite would take 58 percent of the games.

Thus there is no reason why odds couldn't be given on games instead of a point spread. The odds method would eliminate the rather curious phenomenon of the public betting on one thing while the team is trying for something else. It is very rare for a team with the ball and the lead to score in the final three minutes of a game. For example, in 1986 there were 80 cases of the team with the lead having the ball in the final three minutes, and 2 ended up with scores. On the other hand, the team behind scored 21 times in 91 tries.

FAVORITE VS. SPREAD STRAIGHT UP TEASE

SPREAD	G	W	L	T	PCT	W	T	PCT	W-F	W-U	T-F	T-U	PCT
-20.0	8	4	3	1	57.14	8	0	100.00	6	5	0	0	68.75
-19.5	1	0	1	0	0.00	1	0	100.00	0	1	0	0	50.00
-19.0	1	0	0	1	0.00	1	0	100.00	1	1	0	0	100.00
-18.5	1	0	1	0	0.00	0	0	0.00	0	1	0	0	50.00
-18.0	3	2	0	1	100.00	3	0	100.00	3	1	0	0	66.67
-17.5	1	1	0	0	100.00	1	0	100.00	1	1	0	0	100.00
-17.0	4	1	2	1	33.33	3	0	75.00	2	3	0	0	62.50
-16.5	1	1	0	0	100.00	1	0	100.00	1	1	0	0	100.00
-16.0	8	5	3	0	62.50	7	0	87.50	6	5	0	0	68.75
-15.5	1	0	1	0	0.00	0	0	0.00	0	1	0	0	50.00
-15.0	7	3	4	0	42.86	7	0	100.00	4	6	0	0	71.43
-14.5	6	0	6	0	0.00	5	0	83.33	3	6	0	0	75.00
-14.0	26	9	16	1	36.00	23	0	88.46	16	22	0	0	73.08
-13.5	27	13	14	0	48.15	25	0	92.59	18	20	0	0	70.37
-13.0	35	16	19	0	45.71	28	0	80.00	21	23	0	3	65.67
-12.5	8	4	4	0	50.00	8	0	100.00	6	6	0	0	75.00
-12.0	13	5	8	0	38.46	12	0	92.31	9	10	0	0	73.08
-11.5	15	8	7	0	53.33	13	0	86.67	13	10	0	0	76.67
-11.0	32	15	16	1	48.39	25	0	78.13	21	21	0	1	66.67
-10.5	42	22	20	0	52.38	37	0	88.10	31	30	0	0	72.62
-10.0	63	26	35	2	42.62	49	1	79.03	43	44	4	0	71.31
-9.5	64	31	33	0	48.44	48	0	75.00	46	47	0	0	72.66
-9.0	59	29	30	0	49.15	46	0	77.97	44	38	1	2	71.30
-8.5	31	11	20	0	35.48	20	0	64.52	19	24	0	0	69.35
-8.0	51	22	27	2	44.90	36	0	70.59	34	36	2	1	70.71
-7.5	73	31	42	0	42.47	55	0	75.34	55	54	0	0	74.66
-7.0	144	70	71	3	49.65	107	1	74.83	107	98	1	5	72.70
-6.5	155	66	89	0	42.58	95	0	61.29	95	114	0	0	67.42

(Continued)

	FAVORITE VS. SPREAD					STRAIGHT UP			TEASE					
									WINS		TIES			
SPREAD	G	W	L	T	PCT	W	T	PCT	W-F	W-U	T-F	T-U	PCT
-6.0	141	62	76	3	44.93	93	2	66.91	95	95	2	4	68.84
-5.5	79	43	36	0	54.43	56	1	71.79	59	54	0	0	71.52
-5.0	99	40	58	1	40.82	61	0	61.62	65	77	0	3	72.82
-4.5	109	55	54	0	50.46	67	1	62.04	74	76	0	0	68.81
-4.0	173	78	89	6	46.71	102	0	58.96	110	118	10	5	68.88
-3.5	243	123	120	0	50.62	152	1	62.81	178	174	0	0	-62.42
-3.0	268	112	129	27	46.47	153	2	57.52	193	193	8	9	-51.90
-2.5	156	69	87	0	44.23	83	0	53.21	105	120	0	0	72.12
-2.0	163	61	94	8	39.35	73	0	44.79	100	128	8	3	72.38
-1.5	70	35	35	0	50.00	36	1	52.17	50	49	0	0	70.71
-1.0	110	63	43	4	59.43	67	0	60.91	80	75	2	2	71.76
0.0	57	27	30	0	47.37	27	0	47.37	38	39	4	2	71.30
TOTAL	2548	1163	1323	62	46.84	1634	10	64.38	1752	1827	42	40	71.38

We heard that 10 billion dollars was bet on football cards last year. We don't believe it. We have unlimited faith in the intelligence of the American people. Maybe there was one guy out there—an oil sheik or something—who bet all 10 billion on one card. Surely by now everybody else knows that betting on football cards is the same thing as tying your money to helium balloons and saying "Bye-bye."

Just in case you know some seventh-grader who is considering investing his allowance in football cards, and you want to explain to him the error of his ways, have him look at the popular ten-team parlay. Here you have to pick ten winners out of ten. Tell him, the odds against this should be 1,023 to 1 (2 raised to the tenth power minus 1), but they aren't. This is because of a very important feature of cards betting. Ties lose. Cards usually have spreads of 3, 7, and 10 points, the most likely game outcomes. The percentage of ties is just about 5 percent (133 out of 2,548 games in the twelve-year sample, or 5.2 percent). So, you say to him, the probability of not getting at least one tie in picking ten games is about 60 percent (0.95 raised to the tenth power). Thus and therefore, you tell your would-be Sky Masterson, the real odds against getting all ten right is about 1,700 to 1 (1,023 divided by 0.6). Tell him he can get better odds that his civics teacher is really Jimmy Hoffa.

Then lower the boom with the really bad news. The typical payoff for winning this exercise is about 300 to 1. And if he says he might be able to get 30 to 1 for nine out of ten, tell him that's something that happens only about ten times as often. For every horse he puts in, he's getting horseshit back. The card man will be able to keep about two-thirds of his money.

Playing fewer teams, perhaps as few as four, is not as bad a deal, but it's still not a very good one. It's sort of like getting kicked in the shins rather than clubbed senseless over the head.

If somebody out there is really hooked on cards, the best way to go about it is to get some friends together in a pool, with the one with the most wins getting the jackpot. You still get the challenge of trying to outdo others and all the money stays in the group.

Another popular bet is called an over-under, where you get to pick whether the number of points scored by both teams is above or below a selected number. The table following shows the results of these bets for over 1,000 games in recent years. The game-average data shows that there is some correlation between the predicted and actual values. The most significant figure here is that the total was less than expected about 52 percent of the time. If you restrict this to totals of 42 or more, then the unders prevailed in almost 55 percent of the games. There seems to be a tendency to score closer to 42 points than the line expects, as most of the total below 42 go over more often than under.

		GAME			
LINE	NO	AVG	OVER	UNDER	TIE
34	6	38.0	4	1	1
35	23	33.3	10	13	0
36	40	39.2	25	15	0
37	70	39.5	37	29	4
38	113	39.7	53	58	2
39	100	39.3	52	48	0
40	119	40.0	53	62	4
41	143	42.8	72	66	5
42	159	40.5	70	88	1
43	116	40.7	47	65	4
44	151	42.4	69	78	4
45	133	43.9	56	75	2
46	60	48.8	38	22	0
47	35	47.8	18	17	0
48	22	45.5	6	16	0
49	17	51.3	8	9	0
50	15	46.9	6	8	1
51	9	42.1	2	7	0
52	7	54.6	3	4	0
53	1	51.0	0	1	0
54	2	48.0	0	2	0
TOTAL	1341		629	684	28

Finally let's look at the home advantage for each team over the twelve-year period, both in point spread and in actual game results. The purpose of this table is not to show that some teams have a higher home advantage than others. Rather it is to show that the actual advantages are pretty much the same. In fact there is no statistically significant difference in home team advantage for any club.

The figures in the final two columns for actual and pre-dicted home team advantage is simply taking the difference of the home and away data and then dividing by two. This is because a team has a positive advantage at home and a negative one on the road.

The data shows the average number of points allowed in the spread for home team advantage is 2.41, while the actual difference in the score is 2.79, meaning that home advantage is underrated by a fraction of a point.

CLUB	GAMES HOME	PTS	SPREAD	GAMES AWAY	PTS	SPREAD	POINTS SCORE	SPREAD
NFC								
ATL	92	-0.8	0.3	90	-4.7	-4.5	2.0	2.4
CHI	91	6.8	4.7	91	0.3	-0.2	3.2	2.5
DAL	91	6.8	6.6	91	1.1	2.0	2.8	2.3
DET	91	1.8	0.9	91	-6.8	-4.6	4.3	2.8
GB	91	-0.1	-0.9	91	-5.7	-4.8	2.8	1.9
RAMS	91	4.5	5.1	91	1.0	0.4	1.7	2.3
MIN	92	1.8	2.6	90	-2.7	-2.4	2.3	2.5
NO	91	-2.2	0.1	91	-3.6	-4.6	0.7	2.3
NYG	92	2.1	0.9	90	-3.8	-3.2	2.9	2.0
PHI	92	2.8	2.4	90	-0.7	-3.4	1.8	2.9
PHO	8	1.0	1.3	8	-7.8	-4.4	4.4	2.8
STL	82	-0.7	0.3	84	-5.8	-3.8	2.5	2.0
SF	91	4.7	3.9	91	2.8	-0.4	1.0	2.2
TB	91	-2.3	-0.8	91	-7.4	-6.5	2.5	2.9
WAS	90	4.6	4.7	92	1.1	-0.3	1.7	2.5

CLUB	GAMES HOME	PTS	SPREAD	GAMES AWAY	PTS	SPREAD	POINTS SCORE	SPREAD
AFC								
BAL	51	-6.5	-0.2	52	-7.2	-5.3	0.4	2.5
BUF	92	0.6	-0.1	90	-7.0	-4.8	3.8	2.3
CIN	91	4.2	2.5	91	-3.2	-1.8	3.7	2.1
CLE	90	2.4	3.0	92	-1.2	-2.0	1.8	2.5
DEN	92	6.4	4.1	90	-1.7	-0.2	4.0	2.2
HOU	91	0.7	0.3	91	-6.9	-4.0	3.8	2.2
IND	40	-1.3	-2.4	39	-6.8	-7.2	2.7	2.4
KC	90	2.5	-0.1	92	-6.6	-5.6	4.6	2.8
RAID	52	2.9	5.6	52	1.8	0.0	0.6	2.8
MIA	90	8.3	6.1	92	1.3	0.8	3.5	2.6
NE	91	5.8	4.8	91	-1.0	0.1	3.4	2.3
NYJ	91	2.7	1.4	91	-3.3	-3.1	3.0	2.2
OAK	39	4.8	6.1	39	-0.6	1.4	2.7	2.4
PIT	90	7.7	5.5	92	-1.6	0.1	4.6	2.7
SD	90	3.6	2.8	92	-1.8	-1.5	2.7	2.1
SEA	92	4.1	1.9	90	-3.8	-4.1	3.9	3.0

AVERAGE VISTOR SPREAD = 2.41 PTS UNDERDOG
AVERAGE VISTOR DEFICIT IN ACTUAL GAME SCORE = 2.789639

BESTOWING IMMORTALITY:
HALL OF FAME CONTENDERS
AND PRETENDERS

Every year the new class for the Pro Football Hall of Fame is presented at the Pro Bowl. That's about the only real reason to tune into this dullest of all bowls—to see which former stars have gotten fat or lost their hair. Once upon a time the Hall of Fame tried to *announce* the new class at the Pro Bowl, but word always got out ahead of time. It wasn't hard to figure. There'd be some former stars smiling and planning a Hawaii trip, and there'd be others grumping around and complaining about the snow. So finally, the Hall gave up and started announcing the winners as soon as it knew who they were.

Which brings us to how someone gets elected.

Well, first off, anyone can nominate anyone. All you have to do is write a letter to Pro Football Hall of Fame, 2121 George Halas Drive, Canton, Ohio 44708 and say something like, "I nominate John Doe for the Hall of Fame." Of course, if John Doe never had anything to do with pro football, you've just wasted a stamp. If he was a player, he has to be retired for five years. Coaches have to be retired for one year. Owners, league executives, and other contributors do not have to be retired at all.

Now if Doe was a player who maybe subbed for two seasons in the USFL and then went on to his life's work, you can bet no one is going to give him a second thought. But each year there are sixty or seventy former players, coaches, or whatever who can make some reasonable claim for consideration.

Thirty people—the Hall of Fame Selectors—vote on the large group by mail. There is one media person for each league team, an "at-large" media veteran, and a representative of the Football Writers of America. And, to answer your question, no, there are no votes taken from members of the NFL hierarchy. That's why it's pretty silly when people mis-refer to the place as the "National Football League Hall of Fame."

The mail vote gets the group of sixty or seventy nominees down to a manageable fourteen. A player who misses this cut isn't a good bet to make it next year unless something happens or is discovered that enhances his reputation. Although there aren't any restrictions on how long a player can be retired to be eligible, for all practical purposes, the fourteen will nearly always have had the bulk of their careers within the last twenty-five years. This is because of several factors, the most obvious being the working careers of most of the selectors. These aren't just guys who watch a game or two on TV every season; they are trained observers who've been covering pro football closely for years. But even so, most of them do not go back far enough to have a good knowledge of the game thirty-five or forty years ago.

A few do. They form an Oldtimers Committee within the board of selectors. Each year they nominate a fifteenth representative from the past—someone who may have been overlooked years ago, but may well belong in the Hall. "Oldtimer" nominees are expected to have had at least 60 percent of their careers twenty-five years before the election. For example, the oldtimer nominee in 1989 was Green Bay defensive tackle Henry Jordan, who played 60 percent before 1964.

The selectors vote on the fifteen remaining nominees to reduce the final list to seven. Procedural rules state that each Hall of Fame class will have at least four and no more than seven members. In the final vote, held the Saturday before the Super Bowl, the seven finalists must receive approximately 82 percent of the selectors' nods to make it.

Making the semifinal fifteen or even the final seven doesn't assure a nominee of eventual Hall of Fame enshrinement. Each year new stars become eligible, elbowing out some of the near-misses. Reputations fade. And while it's not a rule, the odds are against even a supergreat former player if he gets arrested for some heinous crime. Also it's nearly impossible to get elected posthumously. The Hall hasn't elected a deceased player since 1976, a factor that may have weighed heavily against Jordan.

HANDICAPPING THE HALL

Estimating who will and who won't get in the Hall in the future isn't a matter of simply deciding which players are most deserving. What has to be considered is what factors are most likely to impress the selectors. Having followed every election since 1963, we *think* it works somewhat in this order:

Championship Teams

The more Super Bowls, the better. Conference and division titles are okay, but nothing tops a win with a roman numeral after it. This helped the Packers of the 1960s and is helping the Steelers of the 1970s, particularly because mostly the same players won all of those teams' Super Bowls. However, there can be an "overkill" backlash in which the selectors begin to feel that too many players are being elected from one team. The most overlooked great team seems to be the Miami Dolphins of the early 1970s.

All-League Teams

It always helps if a player was honored year after year. The Pro Bowl would appear to be the major criterion. Next come the All-League teams of the Associated Press and Football Writers. *The Sporting News*, United Press International, and others don't carry a whole lot of weight. MVP awards seem to mean very little in themselves, probably because most of the winners have such great careers that they would be named to the Hall anyway.

Career Stats

High numbers help, but not as much as you might think. The top man in interceptions still hasn't been elected. Quarterbacks are ranked more on winning games than winning passing titles. The selectors recognize that anyone who sticks around long enough today will get large totals. Efficiency seems to be more important than quantity.

Career Length

Playing fifteen or even twenty years will not get anyone into the Hall. In fact, sticking around too long as an ordinary player may cause selectors to forget a guy's early years

when he was exceptional. However, there do seem to be some minimums. It's unlikely you'll see anyone elected again with only seven seasons, such as Gale Sayers—unless there's another Gale Sayers.

Other Factors

As mentioned before, a player should stay alive and out of jail. He should also stay visible, either as a coach or as a TV commentator. Another factor is the position played. You seldom see two players who played the same position go into the Hall together. You'll never see three.

We've broken the players becoming eligible in the next four years into four groups: *Sure Shots*, who are likely to be elected in their first year of eligibility; *Probables*, who would seem likely to be elected sometime within five years of becoming eligible, if all goes well; *Possibles*, who might get in if they happen to strike the voters just right some year; and *Long Shots*, who are not likely to make it despite fine careers.

ELIGIBLE FOR THE FIRST TIME IN THE NEXT FOUR YEARS

1990
Sure Shots:
   Franco Harris, Running Back, 1972–84
   Jack Lambert, Linebacker, 1974–84
Probables:
   Bob Kuechenberg, Offensive Guard, 1971–84
   Jack Youngblood, Defensive End, 1971–84
Possibles:
   Harold Carmichael, Wide Receiver, 1971–84
   Dave Casper, Tight End, 1974–84
   Joe DeLamielleure, Offensive Guard, 1973–84
   Ken Stabler, Oakland, Quarterback, 1970–84
Long Shots:
   Robert Brazile, Linebacker, 1975–84
   Tom DeLeone, Center, 1972–84
   Doug Dieken, Offensive Tackle, 1971–84
   Jim Hart, Quarterback, 1966–84
Harris and Lambert rank only behind Bradshaw and Greene as contributors to the Steelers' four Super Bowls. Kuechenberg was with the "perfect" Dolphins and had tons of All-Pro credits. Youngblood may be ranked a little high here, but we're betting that a recent paucity of both ex-Rams and defensive ends will pull him through. Carmichael is hurt by the fact that so many outstanding receivers have become eligible lately. Casper played a couple of years past his prime, and it could hurt his chances. The same applies to Stabler. It would seem unlikely DeLamielleure could get in before Kuechenberg.

And don't forget Tom Landry, who is a certainty, and Bill Walsh, who will also be eligible in the event he stays retired.

1991
Sure Shots:
   Earl Campbell, Running Back, 1978–85
   John Hannah, Offensive Guard, 1973–85
Probables:
   John Riggins, Running Back, 1971–85
   Jan Stenerud, Kicker, 1967–85
Possible:
   Lee Roy Selmon, Defensive End, 1977–85
Long Shots:
   Lyle Alzado, Defensive End, 1972–85
   Robert Jackson, Linebacker, 1975–85
   Wilbert Montgomery, Running Back, 1977–85
   Charle Young, Tight End, 1973–85
   Campbell has all the stats anyone could need. If Hannah doesn't go in on his first try, it will only prove our suspicion that there's a plot against offensive guards. Riggins could be a Sure Shot if enough weight is put on his Super Bowls. Stenerud's only problem is that a pure kicker has never been elected. Selmon's career was a bit short.

1992
Probables:
   Ken Anderson, Quarterback, 1971–86
   Ray Guy, Punter, 1973–86
   Charlie Joiner, Wide Receiver, 1969–86
Possible:
   Tom Jackson, Linebacker, 1973–86
Long Shots:
   Steve Bartkowski, Quarterback, 1975–86
   Rubin Carter, Nose Tackle, 1975–86
   Jeff Van Note, Center, 1969–86
   No Sure Shots. Anderson was a great passer, but he lost his only Super Bowl. If anyone is ever elected for punting, it will be Guy. Joiner played forever and caught 750 passes, but he had few All-League seasons.

1993
Sure Shots:
   Walter Payton, Running Back, 1973–87
   Kellen Winslow, Tight End, 1979–87
Probables:
   Dan Fouts, Quarterback, 1973–87
   Donnie Shell, Safety, 1974–87
   John Stallworth, Wide Receiver, 1974–87
Possible:
   Dwight Clark, Wide Receiver, 1979–87
Long Shots:
   Wes Chandler, Wide Receiver, 1974–87
   Gary Fencik, Safety, 1976–87
   Dennis Harrah, Offensive Guard, 1975–87
   Payton is the surest lock of any player not now in the Hall. Winslow was so unbelievable for a few years it should

override a relatively short career. Fouts is hurt by never getting to a Super Bowl. Shell and Stallworth could run into a Steeler backlash. Clark looks like a good dark horse.

RECENT PLAYERS PASSED OVER BUT STILL STRONG CANDIDATES

Very Strong:
   Dan Dierdorf, Offensive Tackle, 1971–83
   Carl Eller, Defensive End, 1964–79
   Bob Griese, Quarterback, 1967–80
   Ted Hendricks, Linebacker, 1969–83
   Leroy Kelly, Running Back, 1964–73
   Tom Mack, Offensive Guard, 1966–78
   John Mackey, Tight End, 1963–72
Strong:
   Buck Buchanan, Defensive Tackle, 1963–75
   Lynn Swann, Wide Receiver, 1974–82
   Ron Yary, Offensive Tackle, 1968–82
Fair:
   Nick Buonoconti, Linebacker, 1962–76
   Paul Krause, Safety, 1964–79
   Harvey Martin, Defensive End, 1973–83
   Drew Pearson, Wide Receiver, 1973–83
   Jackie Smith, Tight End, 1963–78
   Mick Tingelhoff, Center, 1962–78
Long Shots:
   Chuck Foreman, Running Back, 1973–80
   L. C. Greenwood, Defensive End, 1969–81
   Jimmy Johnson, Defensive Back, 1961–76
   Henry Jordan, Defensive Tackle, 1957–69
   Jerry Kramer, Offensive Guard, 1958–68
   Larry Little, Offensive Guard, 1967–80
   Charlie Sanders, Tight End, 1966–77
   Jim Tyrer, Offensive Tackle, 1961–74
   Rayfield Wright, Offensive Tackle, 1967–79
   We were amazed that Hendricks didn't make it last year. Griese's best years were before the rules were relaxed on pass blocking and defense, and that hurts his stats. It's beginning to look like Kelly and Mackey may have to wait to become "oldtimers."
   And now for those who really like to see us go out on a limb, here are the active players who rank as Sure Shots and Probables at this moment in time. We considered only players with at least six seasons in the till.
Sure Shots:
   Eric Dickerson, Indianapolis, Running Back
   Tony Dorsett, Denver, Running Back
   Mike Haynes, Los Angeles Raiders, Cornerback
   Steve Largent, Seattle, Wide Receiver
   Joe Montana, San Francisco, Quarterback
   Anthony Munoz, Cincinnati, Offensive Tackle
   Ozzie Newsome, Cleveland, Tight End

Mike Singletary, Chicago, Linebacker
Mike Webster, Pittsburgh, Center
Randy White, Dallas, Defensive Tackle

Unless these guys are caught selling Pentagon plans to the Russians, they would all seem likely to go in at the earliest possible opportunity. Coaches Don Shula and Chuck Noll will be in when they retire.

Probables:

Marcus Allen, Oakland, Running Back
Deron Cherry, Kansas City, Safety
Russ Francis, New England, Tight End
Drew Hill, Houston, Wide Receiver
Too-Tall Jones, Dallas, Defensive End
Joe Klecko, Indianapolis, Defensive Tackle
Ronnie Lott, San Francisco, Safety
Dan Marino, Miami, Quarterback
Dwight Stephenson, Miami, Center
Jackie Slater, Los Angeles Rams, Offensive Tackle
Lawrence Taylor, New York Giants, Linebacker

The only thing keeping Taylor from being a Sure Shot is the specter of a drug suspension. Stephenson will be a lock if he comes back from his injury and plays a couple of years. Marino may have to win a Super Bowl sometime. Lott now has three Super Bowl rings.

The following deserve consideration and could move up with a big year or two. (Recent retirees who are not yet eligible are also included on this list.) A couple will make it anyway.

Receivers: Cris Collinsworth, Cincinnati; Todd Christensen, Los Angeles Raiders; Mark Clayton, Miami; Mark Duper, Miami; Stanley Morgan, New England; Mickey Shuler, New York Jets; Wesley Walker, New York Jets; Mike Quick, Philadelphia; Roy Green, Phoenix; Art Monk, Washington

Offensive Linemen: Cody Risien, Cleveland; Ray Donaldson, Indianapolis; Chris Hinton, Indianapolis; Mike Kenn, Atlanta; Doug Smith, Los Angeles Rams; Luis Sharpe, Phoenix; Randy Cross, San Francisco (ret.); Joe Jacoby, Washington

Quarterbacks: Boomer Esiason, Cincinnati; John Elway, Denver; Jim Plunkett, Los Angeles Raiders (ret.); Ron Jaworski, Miami; Phil Simms, New York Giants; Neil Lomax, Phoenix

Running Backs: Curt Warner, Seattle; Gerald Riggs, Atlanta; Ottis Anderson, New York Giants; Joe Morris, New York Giants; Roger Craig, San Francisco

Defensive Linemen: Fred Smerlas, Buffalo; Art Still, Buffalo; Tim Krumrie, Cincinnati; Mark Gastineau, New York Jets (ret.); Richard Dent, Chicago; Dan Hampton, Chicago; Steve McMichael, Chicago; Dave Butz, Washington

Linebackers: Clay Matthews, Cleveland; Karl Mecklenburg, Denver; Rod Martin, Los Angeles Raiders; Andre Tippett, New England; Rickey Jackson, New Orleans

Defensive Backs: Frank Minnifield, Cleveland; Lloyd Burruss, Kansas City; Raymond Clayborn, New England; Everson Walls, Dallas; Nolan Cromwell, Los Angeles Rams; Joey Browner, Minnesota

Specialists: Reggie Roby, Miami; Pat Leahy, New York Jets; Ray Wersching, San Francisco; Morten Andersen, New Orleans; Gary Anderson, Pittsburgh

Coach: Joe Gibbs, Washington

We haven't mentioned Al Davis of the Raiders yet. Certainly he will have to be enshrined someday.

And last, we'd like to make an appeal to the Old-timers Committee to reevaluate the credentials of six veterans from the distant past whose exclusion continues to mystify us:

Lavie Dilweg, End, 1926–34
Benny Friedman, Quarterback, 1927–34
Verne Lewellen, Halfback, 1924–32
Duke Slater, Tackle, 1922–31
Mac Speedie, Receiver, 1946–52
Albert Wistert, Tackle, 1943–51

DO FOOTBALL PLAYERS DIE EARLY?

The headline looks like something out of one of those tabloids you find at the checkout counter, but the question is being asked seriously. Especially by the National Football League Players Association. And it's been asked often enough that articles exploring the subject have turned up during the past year in *USA Today*, the *St. Louis Post-Dispatch*, the *Los Angeles Times*, the *Atlanta Constitution and Journal*, and several other major newspapers. The *Times*, for example, ran a long, two-part article that included the results of a survey of 440 ex-NFL players, quotes by former players, doctors, and NFLPA spokesmen, and a great deal of speculation.

That's the problem. Most of what is available now is speculation. Sixty-six percent of the players answering the *Times* survey believed that playing football had shortened their life span—a frightening statistic. But what does it mean? Obviously the ex-players were still alive to answer. As of March 1988, the NFL Management Council had recorded 79 deaths of former players who had at least four years of playing experience after 1960. The Council didn't believe 79 out of 5,000 was a significant number. The NFLPA thinks otherwise, and adds that the fates of many of the 5,000 presumed-living ex-players are actually unknown. The number of deaths could be much higher than anyone realizes.

Perception is a factor. When a Bobby Layne dies at fifty-nine, it makes headlines everywhere because Layne was a Hall of Famer. But the death of a reserve linebacker who played from 1961 to 1964 might go unnoticed except in his local newspaper. As a rule of thumb, the farther a player is from his last game, the bigger star he had to be to make his death newsworthy. As a consequence, we are likely to read of the passing of a player in his thirties, but less likely to hear about the death of one in his forties or fifties.

The total number of deaths out of the past is not the real issue, says the NFLPA. The real questions are how many more players will die before their time, is football the reason, and can anything be done about it?

Of the seventy-nine player deaths recorded by the Management Council, ten were from auto accidents, two from aircraft accidents, two from accidental drownings, and one by accidental electrocution. One can hardly describe those as "football related." There were several other accidental deaths and at least two murders. Five were listed as "unknown causes."

However, twenty-eight died of heart failure, fourteen of cancer, two from kidney failure, two from Lou Gehrig's disease, and two from respiratory arrest. There have been more in the year since the count was made. Are these deaths by "natural causes" unnaturally high? The NFLPA thinks so. They note that at least three heart attack victims were in their twenties. The average age at death of the deceased players was 38.2 years.

The most common theory suggests that many premature deaths are caused not by football itself but as a byproduct of the weight gains players go through. During their careers they "beef up," trying to add pounds to compete against ever-heavier rookies. Their diets are rich enough to put fat on a tapeworm. Worse, steroids were common for years—today they're an epidemic—with all the concomitant health risks. When the career ends, the combination of excess weight and reduced exercise is sometimes fatal. How much steroids up the odds can only be guessed.

As stupid as steroid use seems to any thinking person on the outside, many players view them as the only way to survive in the football world—even if they may not survive as long out of it.

"I took steroids because I wanted to take steroids," former Rams offensive lineman Russ Bolinger admitted to the *Times*. He said he played seven years in the NFL before he began taking steroids, but finally he found 255 pounds

287

wasn't enough to hold his job. In a ten-year period from 1977 to 1987, the size of opposing defensive linemen went up an average of nineteen pounds per man. Bolinger took the drugs, bulked up to 275 pounds, and stayed in the NFL. "It's like a street fight. If somebody brings a club, you bring a club."

Many are convinced that the physical damage caused by past steroid use will show up more and more in the next decade—often in the obituaries. They believe that many players have swallowed—are still swallowing—time bombs.

Athletes should be healthier than normal folk, but when they stop being athletes, they often put on dangerous pounds. And though advice on diet and exercise is readily available, changing the habits of a lifetime is hard.

Darrell Austin put on twenty pounds almost as soon as he retired. "I think there are a lot of players who never learn to control their lifestyles after the game," he says. "You're working out trying to keep a job every day of the year. Once you're finished, you have nothing to work out for." Austin slimmed down to below his playing weight because he found a reason. "I didn't want to be a statistic."

But proper exercise isn't so easy for an ex-player walking on plastic knees. Fully 78 percent of the ex-players responding to the *Times* survey said they suffered some physical disability directly related to football.

Dick Szymanski, who played for the Colts from 1955 to 1968, says, "Many of the guys I played with and against are breaking down. They're having hips replaced and knees replaced and back surgery. They're having a lot of problems. Some of them can hardly walk."

Ron Mix, the Hall of Fame tackle, is an attorney handling workers' compensation and disability claims in California. After studying death and disability cases of eight hundred ex-NFL players, he estimated that the average ex-player will be 50 to 65 percent disabled because of leg and back injuries. He pegged average life expectancy at fifty-five. The use of more artificial surfaces simply compounds the problem. According to a Ball State study, the number of players who left the game because of a disabling injury jumped from 28 percent before 1970 to 42 percent after 1970.

Mix has evidence that a typical seven-year pro has sustained a minimum of 130,000 full-speed hits. The injuries mount and can be measured, but is there a cumulative price too? How many hits can a body take before it breaks down in ways not seemingly directly related?

A different theory suggests that the fault lies not with football but with football players. The argument is that the body type required for most football positions mitigates against long life. In a study of ex-baseball players by Dr. John Waterbor of the University of Alabama, it was shown that infielders—usually small, wiry people—tended to outlive the national average. But catchers—blocky fellows, built along the lines of football players—tended to die at a younger age than the national average. According to this theory, people built like football players are less likely than others to reach a ripe old age whether they actually play football or not.

As with most theories, little factual evidence exists one way or the other.

Another factor in the premature deaths of pro football players may be the stress involved in playing the game. The 1988 "Jobs Rated Almanac" put being an NFL player in 246th place when ranking 250 jobs from least to most stressful. The only jobs worse were surgeon, astronaut, Indy car driver, and firefighter. Such traditionally stressful occupations as air traffic controller and police officer involved less stress than playing football in the NFL. Playing basketball in the NBA ranked 207th, baseball in the majors 203rd.

Although doctors disagree on the extent of the damage caused by too much stress, no one thinks it's good for you. And some suggest the effects can be wide-ranging and long-term, leading to blood disorders, heart failure, cancer, and other problems.

The stress of playing football is followed by the trauma of *not* playing. Most players have been "stars" since junior high school. The "team" has been the main thrust of their lives. The pay is almost always higher than what they will earn when football ends. They've grown used to the adulation, the discipline, and the lifestyle. Suddenly, after an average NFL "career" of 3.2 years, it's over. Many ex-players reported problems in adjusting to "normal" life afterward. They felt "abandoned," lost their self-esteem, and, of course, many experienced financial difficulties once the big paychecks stopped. At least three suicides can apparently be traced to postcareer trauma.

Perhaps the most tragic was the case of Jim Tyrer, an All-Pro offensive tackle for Kansas City. Few linemen were more honored during their careers, but afterward he suffered several career failures. On September 15, 1980, out of work at the age of forty-one, it became too much for him. He shot his wife, then turned the gun on himself.

While postcareer adjustment for most players is not as difficult as it was for Tyrer, and most players eventually adjust completely, there's no way to measure the health effects caused by the transition.

The early deaths of star athletes are shocking. Two situations add a grotesque note—and pose new questions. Giants Stadium in East Rutherford, N.J., came under scrutiny when four Giants' players developed cancer within a ten-year period. Offensive tackle Karl Nelson was diagnosed as having Hodgkin's disease, a form of lymph cancer, in 1987. Former linebacker Dan Lloyd was found to have a malignant lymphoma in 1980. Doug Kotar, a former Giants running back, died of a malignant brain tumor in 1980. John Tuggle, another runner, died of a rare blood-vessel cancer, angiosarcoma, in 1986. The suspicion was that they might have developed their cancers because of environmental conditions at the stadium, which lies near toxic Superfund sites, radio towers, and polluted marshes and landfills.

A preliminary medical report, released to the NFL in

September last year, concluded that the radio waves and traces of cancer-causing chemicals were well within safe standards and posed no threat to humans. Athough the study was to be continued, the four incidences of cancer were termed a "tragic coincidence."

Equally mystifying—and also so far considered a coincidence—three former members of the San Francisco 49ers in the 1960s developed Lou Gehrig's disease in the 1980s. Two, linebacker Matt Hazeltine and running back Gary Lewis, have died.

Although these strange occurrences may be only coincidences, there does seem to be some truth to the idea that the average life expectancy for football players is falling while the life expectancy for the rest of the population is rising.

However, figures can be misleading. For example, an article by the Scripps Howard News Service, from March 1988, pointed out that thirty-one players in the Pro Football Hall of Fame whose careers were primarily in the 1920s lived to an average age of 72.4 years. Hall of Fame players whose careers were primarily in the 1930s averaged 64.2 years. Players from the 1940s averaged 58.3. From the 1950s—54.3.

Taken at face value, the case would seem to be proved. But a moment's reflection will remind you that most living Hall of Fame players from the 1950s are in their late fifties or early sixties. The average age is about sixty. Each year that they grow older lifts the average age for their group. But the deaths of defensive end Len Ford at forty-six, defensive back Emlen Tunnell at fifty, and linebacker Bill George at fifty-two pull the average down to far more now than they will someday if some other players live to be ninety. There are still Hall of Fame players alive who played in the 1930s.

More to the point, the 148 members of the Hall of Fame, not all of them players, represents too small a group to be statistically significant. What is needed is a full-scale study, following the postcareer lives and deaths of all former NFL players. The players in today's NFL should at least know what risks they're taking. But such a study ranks rather low in priority when measured against other, more pressing health needs in the nation. Dr. Robert Rinsky of the National Intitute for Occupational Safety, a branch of the Department of Health and Human Services, points out, "Everything we do is a matter of priority . . . A project that involves 150,000 people who may be suffering takes priority over a project that involves 10,000."

So for now we are left with circumstantial evidence and speculation. And a strong presumption that footballs should be labeled like cigarette packs: "Warning! May prove hazardous to your health."

ADDRESS TO BE DELIVERED UPON
OUR BEING NAMED
NFL COMMISSIONER:
HOW TO REPAIR THE GAME

Gentlemen and Georgia, we accept your mandate to save the National Football League and we recognize the desperation that has led you to grant us unprecedented dictatorial powers. As the owners of the twenty-eight league teams, relinquishing any degree of control was not an easy step for you to take. But gentlemen and Georgia, the erosion of the American public's love affair with professional football must be stopped—and reversed. Most of the actions we intend to take are merely common sense. If you had been able to set aside your petty grievances, massive egos, and unswerving devotion to wresting as many dollars as possible from the public, you would have already instituted many of these reforms yourselves.

Get your pens ready for note taking, and we will explain our Ten-Point Plan to Save Football. We will start with the structure of the league itself.

1. Clean up the Geography.

This is no longer a joking matter. It's not just because it's silly to lump Atlanta, New Orleans, Los Angeles, and San Francisco together, to name the worst example. It's also economically foolish. We thought that would get your attention, Bill.

Teams spend millions each season on long airplane trips. If we simply realign the divisions along more realistic geographical lines, we can save a bundle. There's nothing wrong with the Falcons flying to the West Coast once every three years, but to do it every season is absurd.

Moreover, you have been ignoring natural rivalries—the heart-and-soul of SRO. Could there be a more natural grouping than Miami, Tampa Bay, Atlanta, and New Orleans? Yet how often are they found on each other's schedules? Such natural geographical rivalries are being wasted all over the league.

That the NFL must expand to thirty-two teams is such a given that we haven't even placed it among our Ten Points. Until the new cities to be embraced are decided upon, we will refrain from suggesting the final, best division setup.

Joe, Hugh, Rankin, and Tom, how about you form the committee?

2. Sweeten the Mix.

Fans enjoy seeing the other teams in the league if they are top clubs. But too often the visitor is a dog and has no drawing power. However, intradivisional games draw well, even when the teams involved are out of the race. We will increase the divisional games. For example, Washington will have three games each with Dallas and the Giants each season. One of those will be a home game and one an away; the third game will be home one year, away the next. Admittedly, Washington fans don't need the extra incentive now, but fans in some of the cities with weaklings do.

An additional benefit will be that teams will stay in the race longer because they can gain a full game on the leader every time they play.

Al, Victor, Alex, and Bill, why don't you take this one?

And, now we'd like to turn to employee relations.

3. Dragoon the Druggies.

We are not so naive as to believe drug addiction is simply a matter of willpower. At the same time, the wrist slaps handed out now are hardly an encouragement for a player to

290

exercise whatever willpower is involved. In any normal walk of life, someone caught using drugs might expect to be fired. In the NFL it takes a second offense before a player is even suspended for thirty days! Absurd. With today's salaries, thirty days without pay is certainly not a hardship.

All right, let's get tough. It's against the law. A full year's suspension for a first offense and two years for the second. If you're worried about what the courts have to say, fine. So are we. But take it to court and fight it. At least you'll get some stronger guidelines instead of today's timid approach.

We think everyone should serve on this committee.

4. Pay Where It Counts.

This practice of paying raw rookies more than established veterans has got to stop. No, we're not talking collusion here. Just common sense. What other business rewards potential more than achievement? Now this may sound visionary, but suppose you set a limit for this year's rookie crop at the amount of money you each laid out for rookies last year. Then announce that any money left over will be divided equally among the members of last year's team. That way no one would accuse you of being cheap, money-grubbing S.O.B.'s. At least not on this.

Oh, sure, if they can't make a million their first year out of college, a few players might opt to skip pro football. So the country benefits by a few more neurosurgeons and rocket scientists.

Rankin, would you check this out for us?

Now, about the way the game is played . . .

5. Tear Up the Turf.

Most of you people have brought cities to their knees every time you wanted a few more luxury boxes or a better stadium deal. All you have to do is mention you're considering a move to Des Moines and every city in this land (except St. Louis, bless 'em) will sell their mothers into white slavery to make you happy. It's time to use that power to do something good. Enough with artificial turf! Every study done has shown it increases injuries. Folks, the players are your game! No one pays to watch you! Okay, you can't do much about indoor stadiums yet. But there's no excuse for the artificial stuff in outdoor stadiums. Sooner or later, OSHA is going to close you down. So use your power to force the stadiums back to grass.

And it might help if you shared some of the cost.

Dan, Wellington, Ralph, Tex, and Lamar, why don't you and some others form a committee on this?

6. Instant Justice.

Every year you go back and forth over Instant Replay. Sure the delays are interminable. And sure sometimes the

officials cop out with "inadvertent" whistles. But for all its warts, the alternative is worse. As long as the networks are going to show those replays in slo-mo, you have to use them.

Do those who dislike the system honestly think that fans are going to watch a goofy call and say, "Oh well, there's nothing to be done"? Everyone knows what to do now.

Art, we know you have some feelings on this subject.

7. No harm—no foul.

You can speed up the game if you simply instruct officials to refrain from flagging infractions that don't affect the play. We are sick to death of watching a terrific pass called back because some goof, who did nothing more than go in motion, turned a split second too soon. It doesn't take a genius to figure out whether a no-no had any bearing on the way the play went. Throw the flag. And then pick it up.

Norman, would you like to be in charge of the committee?

8. Enough with the Kid Crap!

We have grown tired of the shoving and pointing after every play. We won't say anything about the pitiful example it sets for youngsters. We know that doesn't impress you. Maybe you don't care that it slows the game and is esthetically ugly. Perhaps you don't give a thought to the behavior, or lack thereof, it inspires in the stands.

Maybe it's time you started thinking about such things. Do you want hockey's image? We don't want to stifle enthusiasm. But that crap isn't aggressiveness, it's hooliganism.

Here's a simple way to stop it. Review the films. Each time you see one of these thugs holding up the game for five seconds by instituting a shoving match, fine him $1,000 for the first offense, $2,000 for the second, and so on. We can think of at least one team that will end the season with some of its players paying the league to play. Call it "conduct unbecoming a professional." Or a "person."

Bud, maybe you will head the committee to improve this situation?

9. Legalize the Airwaves.

More than thirty years ago those helmet receivers for the quarterback were outlawed. It's time to bring them back and put them in every player's helmet. We pretend that we're offering the best possible brand of football. That makes us duty-bound to take advantage of any technological improvements. The technology is fine now. Plays are called from the sideline anyway, but doing it with hand signals looks horse-and-buggy. If we give the quarterback a cut-in mike, he can still call the signals and audibles.

First of all, we can eliminate huddles and speed up the game. If you think that's going to ruin some of the situational subbing, hold up until you hear our tenth proposal.

The most important benefit of helmet receivers is that we won't have any more of this silliness where the crowd drowns out the visiting quarterback's signals. The occasional penalty for the home team is no more than a band-aid. Who's running this game anyway? You don't listen to the fans when you set ticket prices, but you let them control whole sections of the game. Ridiculous!

Paul, you have the most experience with this idea. You head the committee.

Now, for the most important change in the way the game is played . . .

10. Restrict Substitution.

Yes, we're serious. What we want is for you to go back to pretty much the rules of 1947–48. Except for punters and place-kickers, no substitutions will be made during a possession and only three substitutions can be made when the ball changes hands. Naturally, we'll allow injury substitutions, but those players who leave as injured cannot return until the next quarter.

Now consider the benefits.

First the obvious. All this ludicrous situational substitution will be out the window, and fans can begin to see players as people instead of cogs. Wouldn't it be nice to have a starting lineup that really means something again?

However, the hidden benefits are much more important. If most of the players are forced to play both offense and defense and to stay on the field for an extended time, you're going to quickly lose some of your unnaturally pumped-up capons. Guys who are naturally big will be able to play, but the steroid-impostors won't last.

In general, though, you'll find the size of players will decrease. And that will decrease injuries.

Finally you can expect offense to increase, which always increases revenue. That will be partly because we do away with some of the specialists and partly because fatigue will cause more mistakes.

Now we know you're going to rub your hands in glee at the thought of decreasing rosters. No, you won't save money. Rosters will stay the same, but only thirty-five players will be activated for each game. That's another thing that should cut into injuries; coaches aren't going to activate a semi-healthy player if he may lose him early.

We don't need a committee on this one. This is how it's going to be.

All right, gentlemen and Georgia, that's how we are going to fix the game. We'll expect action before the next kickoff. Now shall we talk about a higher salary for your new commissioner?

GLOSSARY AND ABBREVIATIONS

This Glossary contains definitions of the statistical terms used in this book—generally in the tables—that may be unfamiliar to even the most avid football fan. The basic terminology of the game is not included here; if you don't know a hashmark from a goalpost or a pass from a hole in the ground, you have picked up the wrong book. We have also included at the end of this section a list of abbreviations used in *The Football Abstract*.

STATISTICAL TERMS

Attempt Percentage Rating   Percentage of team rushes by a particular RB, measured in comparison to the top rusher in this category

Average per Carry (or Reception) Percentage Rating   A measure of a rusher's (or receiver's) yards per carry in comparison to the top rusher in this category

Delta Net Points   The difference between the Predicted Net Points (which see) and the actual Net Points (which see).

Delta Net Wins   The difference between the Predicted Net Wins (which see) and the actual Wins.

Drive   The total plays between the time an offense takes possession and the time it yields the ball.

Drive Chart   A schematic representation of the plays that make up a drive, with a degree of detail far greater than that of a standard play-by-play account.

Durability Rating   Applied to quarterbacks; a percentage of a team's passes thrown by a particular QB.

Net Points   The difference between points scored and points allowed.

Net Punting Average   Punting yards minus runbacks and touchbacks, divided by attempts.

NEWS or NEWS Rate   New Passer Rating System, defined as: Yards + (10 times touchdowns) − (45 times interceptions), all divided by attempts.

NEWS Loss   NEWS rating (which see) of 5.10 or less for 1988 season, which put a quarterback in the bottom 25 percent of his NFL peers.

NEWS Tie   NEWS rating (which see) of 5.11 to 6.47 for 1988 season, which put a quarterback in the middle 50 percent of his NFL peers.

NEWS Win   NEWS rating of 6.48 or more for 1988 season, which put a quarterback in the top 25 percent of his NFL peers.

NFL Passer Rating System   The official formula for rating passers, defined as: 100 × [(Completion Pct. − 30)/20 + (Average Gain − 3)/4 + Touchdown Pct./5 + (9.5 − Interception Pct.)/4]/6. And you thought *our* stuff was complicated!

Overall Rusher Rating   A weighted combination of ratings for the following, each meaured against the leading NFL rusher in that category, whose rating is defined as 100: attempts, yards per carry, touchdowns, total rushing yards, and pass catching; explained in detail in the "Running Backs" chapter of the Player and Coach Ratings Section.

Pass Catching Percentage Rating   Percentage of team passes caught by a particular RB, measured in comparison to the top rusher in this category

Passer Rating in Yards   A conversion of the NFL Passer Rating System (which see) into yards. This system is really a yards-per-attempt formula, with bonuses for completions and touchdown passes, and penalties for interceptions. The conversion formula is: NFL RATE = 100/24 × (Completions × 20 + Yards + Touchdowns × 80 − Interceptions × 100)/Attempts + 50/24. An expanded explanation of the steps leading to this formula is found in the authors' earlier *The Hidden Game of Football*.

Predicted Net Points   Calculated on the basis of yardage differential, the formula is: [(Net Yards Gained − Net Yards Allowed)/12] + 4 × (Turnovers Gained − Turnovers Allowed). The full explanation of this formula is found in *The Hidden Game of Football*.

Predicted Net Wins   Net Points divided by 40, the number that Pete Palmer's computer model of all NFL games has revealed to be the approximate requirement for one extra win over the course of a season; the method for the multivariate linear regression model is detailed in *The Hidden Game of Football*.

Rush Grade A measure of offensive line ability, expressed as: $[(\text{Rushing Attempts} - 3.5)/1.3] \times 30 + 70$.

Sack Average (or Sack Percentage) Sacks divided by Pass Attempts plus Sacks

Sack Grade A measure of offensive line ability, expressed as: $100 - [\text{Sack Average} - 2)/8 \times 30]$.

Spread The betting line established by the Las Vegas handicappers that is designed to create balance between two teams about to play each other: the spread indicates the anticipated margin of victory or defeat.

Standard Deviation A measure of predicted vs. actual values for events whose differences have normal distributions; calculated as the square root of the sum of the squares of the differences. For such events, two thirds (actually, 68.26 percent) of all differences will occur within one standard deviation from the norm and about 95 percent (actually, 95.46 percent) of all differences will occur within two standard deviations.

Touchdown Percentage Rating Percentage of team rushing (or receiving) touchdowns scored by a particular running back (or receiver), measured in comparison to the top rusher (or receiver) in this category

Win Probability Based upon Pete Palmer's computer model, the percentage of times a team in a given situation—encompassing score, time left, field position, down, and yardage to go—will win the game.

Win Probability Points Percentage points gained or lost in Win Probability by virtue of the outcome of a particular play; a team that, already leading in the game, completes a third-quarter pass may raise its chances of winning from 72.4 percent to 78.8 percent (6.4 percent, or 64 Win Probability Points).

Yardage Percentage Rating Percentage of team rushing (or receiving) yardage by a particular running back (or receiver), measured in comparison to the top rusher (or receiver) in this category.

ABBREVIATIONS

A Away
ATT Attempts
Att R Attempt Percentage Rating
ATT–YDS/PG Attempts and Yards Per Game
AVG Average
Avg G Average Gain
Avg R Average per Rush (or Reception) Percentage Rating
AY/S Average yards lost per sack
Blk Blocked
C Center
COM (or CO) Completions
Conf Conference
DE Defensive End
DG Defensive Guard
DLE Defensive Left End
DLG Defensive Left Guard

DLT Defensive Left Tackle
DRE Defensive Right End
DRG Defensive Right Guard
DRT Defensive Right Tackle
DT Defensive Tackle
DURA Durability Rating
FB Fullback
FC Fair Catches
FG Field Goal
FIN Finish
FS Free Safety
FUM/PLAY Opponent Total Plays divided by Opponent fumbles lost.
G Good, as in a field goal attempt indicated as 23G
GM Game
H Home
In 20 Punts out of bounds or downed inside the 20 yard line
IN Interception
L Loss
LBACK Linebackers
LCB Left Corner Back
LE Left End
LG Longest
LIB Left Inside Linebacker, in 3-4 defense
LLB Left Linebacker, in 4-3 defense
LOB Left Outside Linebacker, in 3-4 defense
LT Left Tackle
MLB Middle Linebacker, in 4-3 defense
N Not Good, as in a field goal attempt indicated as 23N
NEWS L NEWS Loss, or a rating of 5.10 or less in 1988 season
NEWS T NEWS Tie, or a rating from 5.11 to 6.47 in 1988 season
NEWS W NEWS Win, or a rating of 6.48 or more in 1988 season
NO Number
NOT RET Punts not returned
OG Offensive Guard
OLG Offensive Left Guard
OLT Offensive Left Tackle
OPP Opponent(s)
ORG Offensive Right Guard
ORT Offensive Right Tackle
OT Offensive Tackle
P Punter
PA Points Against
Pc R Pass Catching Percentage Rating
PC Passes caught
PCT Percentage
PEN Penalties
PF Points For
PK Place Kicker
POS Position
PRS NFL Passer Rating System
P/Gm Per Game
Q Quarter

QB   Quarterback
R   Result
RATE   NFL Passer Rating System
RB   Running Back
RCB   Right Corner Back
RE   Right End
RET YDS   Return Yards
RG   Right Guard
RIB   Right Inside Linebacker, in 3-4 defense
ROB   Right Outside Linebacker, in 3-4 defense
RT   Right Tackle
S   Safety
SAKS/YDS   Number of times Sacked and Yards Lost via Sack
SK   Sacks
SS   Strong Safety
SYDS   Sack yards, or yards lost to sacks
T   Tackle
T-F   Ties by Favorite team
T-U   Ties by Underdog team
TAK   Takeaways
TB   Total Blocked
TD   Touchdown
Td R   Touchdown Percentage Rating
TDP   Touchdowns by Passing

TDR   Touchdowns by Running
TDRt   Touchdowns by Returns of kicks, fumbles, or interceptions
Tm   Team
TOT   Total
TP   Total Points
TRN or TURN   Turnovers
Tu   Turf
Vs Lg   Versus League
W   Win
W-F   Wins by Favorite team
W-U   Wins by Underdog team
WGT   Weight
WK   Week
WP points   Win Probability points
WR   Wide Receiver
YDS   Yards
Yds R   Yardage Percentage Rating
YR   Year
%IN   Interception Percentage, or interceptions divided by passes plus sacks
%SAK   Sack Percentage, or sacks divided by pass attempts plus sacks
%TD   Touchdown Percentage, or touchdown passes divided by passes plus sacks